LESBIANS AND GAYS IN COUPLES AND FAMILIES

LESBIANS AND GAYS IN COUPLES AND FAMILIES

A Handbook for Therapists

Joan Laird and Robert-Jay Green,
Editors

Foreword by Monica McGoldrick

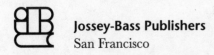

Jossey-Bass Publishers
San Francisco

Substantial discounts on bulk quantities of Jossey-Bass books are available to corporations, professional associations, and other organizations. For details and discount information, contact the
special sales department at Jossey-Bass Inc., Publishers (415) 433–1740; Fax (800) 605–2665.

For sales outside the United States, please contact your local Simon & Schuster International office.

TCF Manufactured in the United States of America on Lyons Falls Pathfinder Tradebook. This paper is
acid-free and 100 percent totally chlorine-free.

Library of Congress Cataloging-in-Publication Data
Lesbians and gays in couples and families : a handbook for therapists
  / Joan Laird and Robert-Jay Green, editors ; foreword by Monica
McGoldrick.
      p.   cm.
  Includes bibliographical references and index.
  ISBN 0-7879-0222-5
  1. Gays—United States—Family relationships.   2. Gay couples—
United States.   3. Gay parents—United States.   4. Family
psychotherapy—United States.   I. Laird, Joan.   II. Green, Robert-
Jay, date.
HQ76.3.U5L48   1996
305.9′0664—dc20

96-4534
CIP

FIRST EDITION
HB Printing   10 9 8 7 6 5 4 3 2 1

CONTENTS

PART TWO: FAMILIES OF ORIGIN   87

PART THREE: LESBIAN AND GAY COUPLES   183

PART FOUR: LESBIAN AND GAY PARENTS   341

To Our Life Partners
Ann Hartman and Carlos R. Chavez
and
In Memory of
John T. Patten, M.D.
Trailblazer, Family Therapist, and Gentle Soul

FOREWORD

MONICA MCGOLDRICK

This extraordinary book is a boon to our field—to all therapists, gay and straight, whether working in New York, Northampton, San Francisco, or Peoria. We all are connected to and work with lesbians and gays or with families with lesbian or gay members. Indeed, no less than 10 percent of the clientele of most family therapists consists of families with lesbian and gay members. Yet our homophobia or, as John Patten has described it, our "homoignorance," can be very costly to our lesbian and gay clients, to their partners, children, parents, families of origin, and families of choice, who have suffered much from our failure to acknowledge or understand their lives and relationships. *Lesbians and Gays in Couples and Families: A Handbook for Therapists* is a thoughtful, readable, and profound book, offering us an opportunity to expand our understanding and to explore our own prejudices.

As with so many issues that we as a nation do not want to face or take responsibility for, the straight world has left it to the gay, lesbian, and bisexual world to point out and deal with the prejudices, homophobia, and general cruelty and inhumanity to those whom heterosexuals label as "other" on the dimension of sexual orientation. The field of family therapy has assumed heterosexuality in its very definition of family and has been silent on the entire subject of homosexuality. Every topic in the field gets discussed from a heterosexual perspective, except in those few instances in which gays and lesbians themselves have spoken or written about issues that pertain to their experiences.

It is up to those of us who identify as heterosexual to expand our consciousness of the issues. The assumption of heterosexuality and the ignorance and prejudice that accompany that assumption create most of the problems gays and lesbians experience in this society. The family therapy field has left it up to women to speak out about sexism, which is primarily a male issue. Those of us who identify or are identified as White have left it to African Americans and others identified as "people of color" to confront the horrors of racism, which is a White construction and therefore a problem to be addressed by Whites. In this case, we have left it to lesbians and gays, White or of color, to discuss issues that pertain to homophobia, a problem of heterosexual society. Heterosexuals must begin to take responsibility for their own consciousness-raising, for overcoming the pervasive ignorance in the family therapy field. This book serves as an outstanding gift, presenting an opportunity for all of us to enhance our understanding of the experiences of lesbians and gays in the context of their couple and family relationships.

The best place to begin is probably with oneself. Only recently have I come to realize how much my own work, however unwittingly, has been part of the problem. I wrote about intergenerational themes in families, but rarely could gays or lesbians be found on my genograms. I wrote about the life cycle, couples, women, cultural diversity, but I meant the *heterosexual* life cycle, heterosexual couples, heterosexual women, and heterosexual cultural diversity, because my writings and my discussion rarely referred to the experiences of families of gays and lesbians. In this way, I rendered a significant population invisible and taught others to do so as well. Even when we depicted the bisexual relationships of Margaret Mead on the cover of our genogram book (McGoldrick & Gerson, 1985), we hardly referred to this dimension of her life in the text, again leaving gay and lesbian experience invisible.

Only very recently have I begun to notice the pain that the most ordinary everyday experiences may create for gays and lesbians, as I have become conscious of the insidious antigay jokes on television or that can be overheard in a restaurant or in a private living room. I have been thinking about how subtly we teach our prejudices to our children and how important it is for us to change these patterns.

Those who have been peripheralized in our society can perceive many things more clearly than can those at the center. Those of us at the center have more to learn from those who have been marginalized than the other way around, although traditional education works in the opposite direction. The assumption is that the privileged have all of the knowledge; their job is to bring it to those at the margins. Yet think about how much we have learned about manhood and about the lives of gay men as a result of the AIDS epidemic. The gay men who were so blamed, vilified, and isolated by the AIDS crisis pulled together in their traumatic situation. They questioned, and they moved themselves beyond the dominant society's rigid, stultifying, deadening roles for men. They have interrogated rigid definitions of manhood and masculinity and the dysfunctional boundaries between men that have for so long kept men in our society from developing intimate connections with each other. Gay men have helped to teach us what being a "real man"—husband, father, lover, brother, son—can be about. Likewise, lesbians are teaching the heterosexual world about developing true partnership in relationships, partnership that can help us move toward a new world order of equity in relationships—relationships in which a hierarchy of power is not the primary definer. Indeed, gays and lesbians have in numerous ways challenged this society's construction of gender roles that has crippled us for so long, offering us a wider glimpse of the possibilities for expanding our constricted definitions of gender roles, if only we can see them.

But the most important reason that our closed-mindedness about gays and lesbians has been so detrimental is that it has led us into a falsely closed, oversimplified life pattern and inhibited our human potential. We have drawn false maps of human psychology and of family connections. By remaining ignorant about gays and lesbians and their families, we have remained ignorant both about ourselves and those with whom we work, whether they are straight or gay.

This book is a wake-up call for the field of family therapy. It is time for family therapists to question their heterosexist assumptions and attitudes and to embrace more flexible definitions of family; it is time to take responsibility for our prejudices and to educate ourselves and each other. This book represents a major contribution toward shifting the kinds of discussions we have about families to include the experiences of gays, lesbians, and their families.

Joan Laird and Robert-Jay Green are two of the brightest luminaries in our field. They have a richness of knowledge about cultural anthropology, racism, sexism, research, and family experience that has enriched a whole generation coming along after them. In this book, they have brought together many of the most thoughtful and inspired explorers of lesbian and gay family life. This book should be required reading for all family therapists. We are in great need of the kind of careful, considered analysis and clinical intuition that these editors and their authors are bringing to us in this remarkable book. It is a volume that recognizes the enormous diversity *within* the lesbian and gay population, serving as a challenge both to heterosexuals and to lesbians and gays to question their assumptions and prejudices about race, gender, and class in the gay population. Included in this volume, for example, are chapters on African American lesbians—a footnote to a footnote in the annals of family therapy—and on the experiences of Hispanic American and Asian American lesbians and gays and their families. Several of the more general chapters also address themes of diversity.

We must repay these authors by hearing their message and joining them in our shared responsibility for educating ourselves, our trainees, and the field of family therapy in general.

Metuchen, New Jersey   Monica McGoldrick
April 1996   *Director, Family Institute of New Jersey*

Reference

McGoldrick, M., & Gerson, R. (1985). *Genograms in Family Assessment.* New York: Norton.

ACKNOWLEDGMENTS

JOAN LAIRD AND ROBERT-JAY GREEN

Several people have been instrumental in the preparation of this volume, and many more helped create the social climate from which it emerged. Janine Roberts, former editor of the *Journal of Feminist Family Therapy,* started the wheels turning by inviting Joan Laird to edit a special issue of that journal devoted to the topic of lesbian and gay families. The six papers published in that special issue formed the nucleus of this book. Joan then invited Robert-Jay Green to join in co-editing the journal issue.

As we began conceptualizing that project together, it quickly became apparent that an expanded, book-length treatment of the subject was warranted, and Alan Rinzler, acquiring editor at Jossey-Bass, welcomed our proposal for the present volume. He has offered many fine suggestions and has tenaciously countered our efforts to procrastinate.

Joan's life partner, Ann Hartman, contributed long hours to this project, carefully reading many of the first drafts of chapters. Her writing and editing wisdom provided a constant source of encouragement and counsel. The book might have been finished a bit earlier if Joan hadn't taken some time to enjoy the arrival of her first grandchild, a little girl, and to watch with delight as she began learning to explore her world with growing energy and confidence.

In California, Carlos R. Chavez gave endless support and good-natured humor, and his ideas and personal experience supplied a multicultural perspective that informs this book. Also important was the encouragement of many friends and close colleagues over the years, especially Lucy Rau Ferguson, Eliana Gil, Mary Herget, Richard Maisel, Karen Saeger, Paul Werner, and Victoria Zerbs. Further support came from the East Coast in the persons of Claudia Bepko, Jo-Ann Krestan, and Sallyann Roth. We would like to thank them for their encouragement and acknowledge them for their pioneering efforts in the field of lesbian family studies. Susan Donner and Carole Samworth also offered support and ideas.

Joan would like to thank the Smith College School for Social Work for helping to support her work with a grant from the Clinical Research Institute. This grant helped fund invaluable technical support from Marti Lawrence Hawley, whose patient and careful work is greatly appreciated.

The American Family Therapy Academy (AFTA), which is an interdisciplinary association of teachers and researchers in the field, has provided us an important forum for the exchange of ideas. AFTA has taken a leadership role by including lesbian and gay issues in the family therapy dialogue. It was through AFTA conferences that we first met each other, as well as members of AFTA's "Lesbian and Gay Families Interest Group," several of whom contributed chapters to this book. Froma Walsh, former president of AFTA, played a pivotal role in "opening up" the organization and the field by inviting Joan to participate in an AFTA plenary on gay and lesbian families and to contribute a chapter on the same topic to the second edition of her book, *Normal Family Processes* (1993). Joan also expresses her gratitude to Sallyann Roth for assuaging her anxiety and encouraging her to go forth.

During her tenure as president of AFTA, Froma invited Robert-Jay to present research on lesbian and gay couples in AFTA's "Normal Families Interest Group." We also are grateful to Monica McGoldrick, a close AFTA colleague, for writing the Foreword to this volume, advocating for the understanding of diverse family forms, and being a source of inspiration and deep personal friendship for each of us.

Finally, we are indebted to our colleagues who helped pave the way for this and other volumes on lesbian and gay family issues before their untimely deaths in recent years, among them Emery Hetrick, John Patten, Mario Ribas, and Alan Rockway. In this context, we are reminded of a passage written by Olive Schreiner (1900) about collective progress toward enlightenment:

And she listened intently, and she said, "I hear a sound of feet, a thousand times ten thousand and thousands of thousands, and they beat this way!"

He said, "They are the feet of those that shall follow you. Lead on! Make a track to the water's edge! Where you stand now, the ground will be beaten flat by ten thousand times ten thousand feet. . . . First one comes down to the water-edge, and is swept away, and then another comes and then another, and then another, and at last with their bodies piled up a bridge is built and the rest pass over."

She said, "And, of those that come first, some are swept away and are heard of no more; their bodies do not even build the bridge?. . . . And what of that?"

"They make a track to the water's edge."

"They make a track to the water's edge!" And she said, "Over that bridge which shall be built with our bodies, who will pass?"

He said, "The entire human race."

And the woman grasped her staff.

And I saw her turn down that dark path to the river.*

Although we have compiled this book, it is part of a much larger social narrative to which many pioneering professionals and untold generations of lesbian and gay families have contributed.

J. L.
R.G.

---

*Olive Schreiner, *Dreams* (Boston: Little, Brown, 1900). Quoted in S. G. Luthman, *Energy and personal power* (San Rafael, CA: Mehetabel, 1982), pp. 14–15.

INTRODUCTION

LESBIANS AND GAYS IN COUPLES AND FAMILIES

Central Issues

As this volume on lesbians and gay men in couples and families goes to press, what has been called the "last invisible minority" is occupying a central place in our nation's social and political discourse. Once again, political conservatives—mainly those in the right wing of the Republican party—are investing with new strength the "don't ask, don't tell" message and, more than that, seeking to further restrict lesbian and gay civil rights. We live in a society in which violence against lesbians and gays not only has increased in the last several years but often is sanctioned and sometimes goes unpunished.

The very definition of "family" is at stake again, as it is periodically in American politics. A war is being waged about who will gain control over the meaning of "family." On the one hand, lesbians and gays have received some favorable media coverage and are slowly but steadily becoming more visible in film and literature. We see increased pressure from lesbian and gay groups to win domestic partner benefits, and these groups have had surprising success. Some couples are "marrying," or otherwise declaring their life commitments, and celebrating their unions in public forums. An increasing number of lesbians are choosing to give

Expanded from an article previously published in the *Journal of Feminist Family Therapy*, Volume 7, #(3/4), 1995, pp. 3–13, and reprinted with the permission of The Haworth Press, Inc., Publisher, and the authors.

birth to or adopt children in the context of lesbian relationships. Gay men are choosing to build families through adoption or foster care or through the use of surrogate mothers. A growing body of research is documenting the fact that lesbian and gay couples seem to do as well on mental health and social functioning measures as other kinds of couples. Furthermore, there is growing evidence that their children, whether they are from prior marriages or are part of the "lesbian baby boom," are doing at least as well as children reared in other family forms. In fact, they may even develop special strengths.

On the other hand, in spite of these advances there are tremendous threats to the future of the lesbian and gay couple and the lesbian- or gay-parented family. Some communities and groups continue to launch anti–gay civil rights initiatives. In some jurisdictions, lesbian mothers and gay fathers continue to lose custody of their children in court for reasons of sexual orientation alone. The rights, and even the recognition, of coparents continue to be severely limited. Rates of depression and suicide among gay and lesbian youths remain high, as efforts to raise consciousness and develop educational programming in schools, as well as to foster recreational and other services in communities, face bitter attack from various organized groups and institutions. These last two years have seen the Republican Speaker of the House, Newt Gingrich, catapulted into a central position of power in which his anti–gay family rhetoric stimulates and supports further attack, while President Clinton's voice on this issue has all but faded away. It is clearly a crucial time for the future of the family with lesbian or gay members.

The Lesbian and Gay Family in the Family Therapy Field

Mirroring longstanding patterns in the larger sociopolitical context and in popular culture, until very recently the lesbian couple or lesbian-headed family has been virtually unheard of in the family therapy field and the gay family nonexistent. Furthermore, because mental health professionals, like everyone else, develop their professional stories out of those available in the larger social discourse, this field has a legacy of homophobia, heterosexism, silence, and a destructive mythology it must overcome.

This state of affairs parallels the fate of the gay and lesbian family in the larger field of family studies. Allen and Demo (1995), in a comprehensive review of the leading family research journals from 1980 to 1993, as well as a number of journals in related fields over the same period, found that lesbian and gay families were rarely studied. When they were included as part of larger studies, they were seen as problems and as basically alike; their diversity was ignored.

A similar picture would emerge if we were to do a statistical analysis of the mainstream family therapy literature. The first article on lesbian or gay families in the family therapy field appeared in *Family Process* in 1972; it was entitled "My Stepfather Is a She" and authored by Shelomo Osman. Interestingly, in this article, the therapeutic solution to a family crisis involving the behavior of a teenage boy was to place him out of the family, a solution seldom prescribed for other troubled families in the family therapy literature. Silence reigned for a few years, until the pioneering article by Krestan and Bepko in 1980, "The Problem of Fusion in the Lesbian Relationship," and another five years passed before Roth's (1985) article on psychotherapy with lesbian couples was published. This was followed with contributions from Roth and Murphy (1986), Krestan (1987), and Crawford (1988) but, until the 1990s, we needed fewer than ten fingers to total the journal contributions in the family field. Some clinical material on work with lesbian and gay families did appear in other professional journals (for example, Brown, 1989; DeVine, 1984) and in at least two books (Bozett, 1987; 1989), but the resources were scarce.

The American Family Therapy Academy (AFTA) and the American Association of Marriage and Family Therapy (AAMFT), the major professional organizations in the family therapy field, in recent years have increased their conference programming on lesbian and gay issues and have launched lesbian and gay interest groups and caucuses. Lesbian and gay family therapists are frequently invited to speak at conferences or to consult with agencies and training programs. They are becoming an increasingly visible presence in the family therapy field. There appears to be a rapidly increasing number of master's and doctoral students throughout the mental health professions who are pursuing research projects focusing on lesbian and gay couples and families.

Nevertheless, many family therapists are still not comfortable with or knowledgeable about lesbian and gay family life, prevailing social and legal trends, or the special therapeutic issues that arise. For those of us who have participated in the field of family therapy over the last twenty years and have experienced the brunt of its heterosexism, there still is much reason for concern. Only recently have family therapists approached lesbian and gay issues in a socially contextualized rather than pathologizing way, and our professional organizations still lag behind other mental health associations in this regard.

Myths and Misconceptions

A number of misconceptions about gays and lesbians continue to dominate thinking in the world of therapy. One common idea is that lesbians and gay men primarily seek out lesbian and gay therapists and, as a result, family therapists (the vast majority of whom are heterosexual) will encounter such cases only rarely in their practices. It has been estimated that one out of every four families in the United States has a gay or lesbian family member or, put another way, that some

50 million people are lesbian or gay themselves or are closely related to someone who is lesbian or gay (Patterson, 1995). If this is the case, it is clear that most family therapists do work with lesbian and gay individuals, couples, or most certainly with families with lesbian, gay, or bisexual members. In a recent randomized survey (457 responses), 72 percent of AAMFT clinical members reported that approximately one-tenth of their practices involved gays and/or lesbians (Green & Bobele, 1994). This figure implies that, in an average weekly caseload of twenty clients, these family therapists were seeing two cases each week that involved lesbian or gay members. One wonders, however, how prepared these professionals are—in terms of gay-sensitive attitudes, relevant knowledge, and specific skills—to work with lesbians and gay men. In light of other research showing that homophobia decreases with personal contact (Herek, 1994), an encouraging finding in the AAMFT study was that 70 percent of respondents said they had experienced a personal relationship with a lesbian or gay man for more than one year, such as a friendship or a relationship with a lesbian or gay family member.

Another set of myths concerns the relationship between gender and sexual orientation. Sexual orientation went relatively unnoticed during the rise of the feminist family therapy critique, partly because of the small number of out lesbians and gays identified with the family therapy movement. With the exception of a chapter in *Feminist Family Therapy: A Casebook* (Goodrich, Rampage, Ellman, & Halstead, 1988) and another by Sallyann Roth and Bianca Cody Murphy (1986), a variation of the 1985 Roth article in the McGoldrick, Anderson, and Walsh–edited volume (1989), and a few isolated case examples in works on more general topics (for example, Imber-Black, 1989; Laird, 1988, 1989), to our knowledge none of the major feminist family therapy volumes published in the second half of the 1980s addressed the particular interests of lesbians or the sexual orientation theme. Although gender was and remains a critically important issue in the family field, in retrospect, the omission of sexual orientation replicated some of the problems of patriarchy in the sense that the voice was largely White and middle-class and that heterosexuality was assumed.

The lesbian and gay family literature itself has largely reflected the White experience, while work by men and women of color in the family therapy field has largely assumed heterosexuality. By the mid 1990s, a few scholars were beginning to address the intersections of race, gender, social class, and sexual orientation (for example, Greene, 1995), recognizing that none of these social identities can be construed in isolation from any other.

Gender socialization, homophobia, and heterosexism have very close connections. One of the strongest and most consistent findings in research on attitudes toward homosexuals is that *homophobia* (irrational fear, prejudice, and willingness to discriminate against lesbians and gay men) is associated significantly with an individual's endorsement of traditional gender roles (Herek, 1994). Also, degree of homophobia is linked consistently to gender. For instance, heterosexual men are significantly more homophobic than heterosexual women in their attitudes toward both gay men and lesbians. Furthermore, heterosexuals of both sexes tend to be more homophobic toward homosexuals of their own sex than toward homosexuals of the opposite sex. The ranking (from most to least homophobic) is:

- Heterosexual men's attitudes toward gay men
- Heterosexual men's attitudes toward lesbians
- Heterosexual women's attitudes toward lesbians
- Heterosexual women's attitudes toward gay men

In short, sexism and traditional gender-role conformity go hand in hand with prejudice toward lesbians and gay men. Traditional, essentialist notions about "real" men and "real" women are used to cast gays and lesbians as "failed" men and "failed" women. Lesbian and gay gender nonconformity poses a grave threat to the maintenance of rigid gender dichotomies at the individual, family, and societal levels—a threat powerful enough to motivate some "real men" to use baseball bats in gay bashings, a threat powerful enough to nearly cripple Bill Clinton's presidency early in his tenure, when he proposed allowing open lesbians and gays to serve in the U.S. military. Viewing lesbians and gays as less than real women and men allows homophobic groups to dehumanize and demonize their targets, to take away basic human rights, to reframe civil rights efforts as demands for special rights, and to claim that lesbians and gays are trying to destroy their way of gendered family life. In fact, the converse is true. Homophobic individuals and institutions have severely damaged the careers and family lives of many lesbians and gays, past and present. The very moving memoir by Meme English that opens this volume testifies to the impact of that destructive context on one family's experience.

Because traditional gender-role conformity and homophobia covary, we can expect a reduction in homophobia to the extent that families and institutions in our society embrace the goals of feminism and adopt a social constructionist view of gender and sexuality as flexible, fluid, and multiple (rather than rigid, fixed, and dichotomous) (Goldner, 1991; Lorber, 1994; Stoltenberg, 1989). Given that sexism and heterosexism both are closely connected to traditional gender-role socialization, it is not surprising that lesbians (doubly oppressed by gender norms) often have been at the forefront of the feminist movement in the United States and that gay men are at the forefront of the profeminist men's movement.

Regarding the latter, for example, a survey of 126 men attending a profeminist men's gathering revealed that nearly half of the participants were gay men, and another 20 percent were bisexual men (Shiffman, 1987). In addition to their involvement in the profeminist men's movement, 39 percent of these respondents were dues-paying members of women's organizations, 48 percent did committee work for women's organizations, and 55 percent attended public demonstrations in support of the women's movement. There are, of course, important differences in the types of discrimination experienced by heterosexual women, lesbians, and gay men, many of them having to do with greater economic discrimination against women than against (closeted) gay men. That is, gay men who choose to hide their sexual orientation at work typically benefit from the same privileges conferred on heterosexual males in the workplace. Despite these differences among the three groups, the struggle for heterosexual women's rights, lesbians' rights, and gay men's rights are inextricably linked through their common source of oppression—sexism and pressures for gender-role conformity.

Other myths have been passed down unchanged from generation to generation of family therapists with little reference to any research on nonclinical populations. A common misconception among family therapists is that, in lesbian and gay couples, one partner assumes a traditional masculine-husband role, while the other assumes a traditional feminine-wife role (that is, "butch" and "femme" roles in lesbian and gay relationships). A colleague of the second editor (RJG) once explained his belief in this stereotype with reference to a supposedly "necessary polarity" or "role complementarity" in couple relationships, as if true equality or reciprocal androgyny were psychologically impossible in a couple. Again, the research literature refutes this stereotype and shows that rigid butch/femme roles and marked power differentials are not the norm in homosexual couples (Peplau, 1991). On the contrary, homosexual couples tend not to divide up roles along the lines of traditional gender dichotomies, and they tend to be substantially more egalitarian than heterosexual couples (Peplau, 1991; Zacks, Green, & Morrow, 1988). Generations of mental health professionals have been exquisitely attuned to analyzing butch/femme role-playing in lesbian and gay couples but oblivious and complacent about the much more pervasive butch/femme role-playing in heterosexual couples, as Green, Bettinger, and Zacks discuss in their chapter.

Another common misconception is that homosexuals fear or hate persons of the opposite sex or that homosexuality is caused by family of origin relationships. Although certainly, some lesbian and gay people have suffered emotional, physical, or sexual abuse in earlier family relationships, research on community (nonclinical) samples shows that, as individuals, their degree of traumatic experience is no greater than for matched samples of heterosexuals, an issue that Shoshana Kerewsky and Dusty Miller address in their presentation in this book. They discuss a model for working with lesbian couples in which one or both partners have experienced trauma. Moreover, although there is no formal research on this question, there is much obvious evidence of deep, long-lasting friendships between homosexuals and persons of the opposite sex, especially between lesbians and gay men, and between gay men and heterosexual women. A lack of emotionally close friendships between lesbians and heterosexual men, if such were the case, would not be remarkable in that most heterosexual men report that they have no close friends of either sex (Rubin, 1986). Interestingly, Kirkpatrick, Smith, and Roy (1981) found that lesbian mothers are more concerned than single heterosexual mothers that their children have male role models and good relationships with adult men. In their sample, lesbian mothers tended to have more adult, male family friends and included male relatives more often in their children's activities.

There is no clear evidence from studies of community samples that family of origin relationships contribute to the development of homosexuality (Bell, Weinberg, & Hammersmith, 1981). The causes of homosexuality still remain a mystery, although research is becoming centered increasingly on genetic factors and the prenatal-hormonal environment. In this emerging model, biological factors are viewed as predisposing conditions for subsequent internal and developmental-social processes that lead to self-labeling as lesbian or gay. Most likely, there are multiple routes to adoption of a homosexual identity, with biological predisposition playing a major role in some cases and no role whatsoever in others.

Purpose of This Book

These are just a few of the myths that dominate public conversation concerning lesbians, gays, and their families of origin, choice, and creation. In conceptualizing this volume, we set out to explore, comprehensively and in depth, what the couple and family relationships of lesbians and gays are like and what we might learn that could contribute to the field of family theory and practice. That means, on the one hand, deconstructing the many myths that dominate the conversation about lesbians and gays but, far more than that, attempting to better understand the complex linkages between the idea of *family* and the idea of *lesbian or gay*. These concepts are very rarely joined in common conversation in the larger community or in the family field. Some, in fact, consider the linkage an oxymoron. We believe that the two concepts need joining and that lesbians and gays are not only forming couple and family relationships that are viable and healthy but, in many ways, are pioneering couple and family relationship models that have much to offer all couples and families. To the best of our knowledge, this book on lesbian and gay couples and families is the first of its kind, that is, a book that links theory, research, and clinical practice on lesbians and gays in couple and family contexts.

We reached out in many directions to find authors who might bring different sets of ideas, who might offer multiple reflections and multiple points of view, who might represent the diversity in the lesbian and gay couple and family field itself. Many are academically based researchers, and some of those are also clinicians. Others are primarily clinicians, with research and scholarship interests. Some are firmly located in a modernist tradition; others stand on the boundary between modernist and postmodernist ideas; others are increasingly committed to post-modern thought. A strong feminist or gender consciousness is visible here, as is a recognition that sexual orientation must always be understood in the context of ethnicity, race, social class, and other powerful social mediators that shape individual and family narratives and experiences.

We recognize that, even though this volume is comprehensive, there are important issues left unaddressed. For example, while some authors include bisexuals in their discussions, most do not. Bisexuality in couple and family life is a very complex subject that deserves more attention. It is rarely addressed in the clinical literature and rarely in the family therapy field except, perhaps, for the occasional case vignette (see Nichols, 1994, for an exception). Transgendered persons, as they live in couple and family relationships, are invisible here; cross-dressing, which is more common in couples than many might think, is a fascinating topic that traverses sex, gender, and sexual orientation lines. Just as we could not represent all variations on the sexuality theme, so we were unable to represent all ethnic and racial groups. We hope the reader will keep in mind that lesbians and gays are as ethnically and racially diverse as heterosexuals.

Furthermore, the book is biased toward the younger ages of the life course. We regret that there are no chapters on aging gays and lesbians in families. We need to know much more about gays and lesbians in their roles as grandparents and as aunts and uncles in their families of origin, creation, and choice. We need to know about their relationships with each other and with their children as they grow old and face yet another source of oppression in this society. Aging, in fact, is a theme relatively neglected in the family field as a whole. There are other gaps as well. Clearly, we think of this book as a beginning. We hope that others will carry on the work.

It is impossible to even begin to understand the experiences of lesbians and gay men in couple and family relationships without close attention to the social and political contexts in which these relationships are embedded. In fact, social context issues demarcate the experiences of lesbians and gays from others most powerfully, and they account, in large measure, for differences of experience between heterosexual and gay couples and families. What does it mean to couple and to raise a family or to define adult relationships with one's family of origin when surrounded by homophobic and heterosexist assumptions, perhaps even emotional and physical threat? What does it mean to be both gay and a member of an oppressed ethnic or racial group?

While each author represented here confronts these issues in some fashion, Part One is devoted to an examination of some of these contextual themes. We begin with the personal, as Meme English offers a moving account of how homophobia helped to shape intergenerational relationships in her family. We then move on to the professional, with an intriguing dialogue between Stanley Siegel and Gillian Walker on the differing issues that come up in therapy for straight and gay therapists working with lesbian and gay couples and families. Ann Hartman then reviews some of the social and legal issues that serve as context and can limit the rights and opportunities for every lesbian and gay couple and family.

Not only have lesbians and gays, as individuals and in couple and family relationships, been invisible in the family therapy field until relatively recently, but lesbian and gay relationships with their families of origin are rarely discussed. In fact, one might be led to believe that lesbians and gays do not come from families or have any ongoing connections with families. Have you ever noticed that gay people seem to have no relatives? The family of origin, if mentioned at all, has often been portrayed solely as the entity one does or does not come out to. This is true, even in the lesbian and gay studies field. And here the prevailing picture is one of disappointment, rejection, compromise, loneliness, and physical or emotional cut-off. The family of origin, if it maintains contact with the younger generation at all, is seen as disrespectful of lesbian or gay couple and family boundaries.

But this is not the whole story. Family relationships are about more than coming out, and coming out also can result in very positive growth for both the individual and the family. It is this side we rarely hear about—the stories of the many families who are courageously supporting their lesbian and gay children. In Part Two, four authors demonstrate how complex family of origin issues—far beyond issues of disclosure or coming out—become relevant in clinical work. Joan Laird looks at the dominant narratives concerning the connections between lesbians and their families of origin in popular film and the professional literature, contrasting those narratives with what lesbians themselves have to say about their ongoing family connections. Suzanne Iasenza, Patricia Colucci, and Barbara Rothberg examine the mother-daughter bond in particular when lesbians come out; Peter Liu and Connie Chan discuss important themes in the family of origin relationships of lesbian, gay, and bisexual Asian Americans. Ritch Savin-Williams is particularly interested in how adolescents come to terms with a gay, lesbian, or bisexual identity and how they manage both disclosure and ongoing relationships with their families.

In Part Three, six authors explore various facets of gay and lesbian couple relationships. Robert-Jay Green, Michael Bettinger, and Ellie Zacks revisit the issues of fusion in lesbian couples and disengagement in gay male couples, in the process challenging many of our gender behavior assumptions about both heterosexual and gay men and women. Thomas Johnson and Michael Keren are also interested in couple boundary issues. In their chapter, they explore in some depth the rarely examined theme of boundary issues in gay male couples. Two of our authors enhance our understanding of the relationships among race, gender, and sexual orientation, a topic attracting increasing interest in the social sciences and mental health professions. Beverly Greene and Nancy Boyd-Franklin examine the special issues of African American lesbians in couples therapy. In the process, they provide a comprehensive overview of the intersections between race and sexual orientation and issues for interracial couples, while Eduardo Morales is particularly interested in the implications for family and couple relationships of Latino gay and bisexual men's conceptions of gender role. This section ends with two chapters that address special issues prevalent among lesbian couples. Shoshana Kerewsky and Dusty Miller investigate the effects of childhood trauma on lesbian couple relationships. Sandra Anderson then looks at how heterosexist bias enters into the treatment of lesbian couples who are chemically dependent.

In the concluding section of the book, Part Four, four contributors examine the special issues that arise for gay and lesbian parents. Valory Mitchell deconstructs gendered parenting, contrasting how heterosexual and lesbian women enact their coparenting roles. Her chapter, as does that of Cheryl Muzio, sheds light on how lesbians who choose to create families are changing both their self-narratives and the larger social narratives about parenting. Jerry Bigner is interested in the issues that gay fathers, who frequently are noncustodial parents, face as they come out, deal with divorce and its aftermath, and struggle to redefine themselves as gay and as fathers in varying contexts. Stacey Shuster also writes about gay fathers, in this case men with HIV disease. She explores clinical issues in working with both the fathers and their families. Finally, our fifth author in this section, Charlotte Patterson, presents her latest research on lesbian mothers and their children's functioning. In the process, she refutes many of the uninformed assumptions and biases about children raised in lesbian families that have led to termination of parental custody.

We are grateful to our pioneering authors and to those who have inspired them—their own families and friends, their clients, participants in their research studies, and many others whose stories might otherwise have remained untold—for their efforts in making this collection a reality. We hope their work will be as enlightening to readers as it has been to us, and that it will stimulate new efforts on all of our parts to bear witness to the stories of lesbian and gay families in our own work and family settings and in the larger professional and public worlds.

Finally, it has been a pleasure to work together on this project. We kept in weekly and sometimes daily contact by telephone, fax, e-mail, and various kinds of express mails. We shared ideas, enthusiasms, problems, puzzles, complaints, and much laughter—for the most part agreeing and for the rest of the time, cheerfully agreeing to disagree. All such partnerships should be as much fun and as rewarding!

April 1996

Joan Laird
Northampton, Massachusetts
Robert-Jay Green
San Francisco, California

References

Allen, K., & Demo, D. (1995). The families of lesbians and gay men: A new frontier in family research. *Journal of Marriage and the Family, 57,* 1–17.

Bell, A. P., Weinberg, M. S., & Hammersmith, S. K. (1981). *Sexual preference: Its development in men and women.* Bloomington: Indiana University Press.

Bozett, F. W. (1987). *Gay and lesbian parents.* New York: Praeger.

Bozett, F. W. (1989). *Homosexuality and the family.* Binghamton, NY: Harrington Park Press.

Brown, L. (1989). Lesbians, gay men, and their families: Common clinical issues. *Journal of Gay and Lesbian Psychotherapy, 1*(1), 65–77.

Crawford, S. (1988). Cultural context as a factor in the expansion of therapeutic conversation with lesbian families. *Journal of Strategic and Systemic Therapies, 7*(3), 2–10.

DeVine, J. L. (1984). A systemic inspection of affectional preference orientation and the family of origin. *Journal of Social Work and Human Sexuality, 2,* 9–17.

Goldner, V. (1991). Toward a critical relational theory of gender. *Psychoanalytic Dialogues, 1,* 249–272.

Goodrich, T. J., Rampage, C., Ellman, B., & Halstead, K. (1988). *Feminist family therapy: A casebook.* New York: Norton.

Green, S. K., & Bobele, M. (1994). Family therapists' response to AIDS: An examination of attitudes, knowledge, and contact. *Journal of Marital and Family Therapy, 20,* 349–367.

Greene, B. (1995). Lesbian women of color: Triple jeopardy. In L. Comas-Diaz & B. Greene (Eds.), *Women of color: Integrating ethnic and gender identities in psychotherapy* (pp. 389–427). New York: Guilford Press.

Herek, G. M. (1994). Assessing heterosexuals' attitudes toward lesbians and gay men. In B. Greene & G. M. Herek (Eds.), *Lesbian and gay psychology: Theory, research and clinical applications* (pp. 206–228). Newbury Park, CA: Sage.

Imber-Black, E. (1989). Rituals of stabilization and change in women's lives. In M. McGoldrick, C. M. Anderson, & F. Walsh (Eds.), *Women in families: A framework for family therapy* (pp. 451–469). New York: Norton.

Kirkpatrick, M., Smith, C., & Roy, R. (1981). Lesbian mothers and their children: A comparative survey. *American Journal of Orthopsychiatry, 5,* 545–551.

Krestan, J. (1987). Lesbian daughters and lesbian mothers: The crisis of disclosure from a family systems perspective. *Journal of Psychotherapy and the Family, 3*(4), 113–130.

Krestan, J., & Bepko, C. (1980). The problem of fusion in the lesbian relationship. *Family Process, 19*(3), 277–289.

Laird, J. (1988). Women and ritual. In E. Imber-Black, J. Roberts, & R. Whiting (Eds.), *Rituals in families and family therapy* (pp. 331–362). New York: Norton.

Laird, J. (1989). Women and story: Restorying women's self-constructions. In M. Mc-Goldrick, C. M. Anderson, & F. Walsh (Eds.), *Women in families: A framework for family therapy* (pp. 427–450). New York: Norton.

Lorber, J. (1994). *Paradoxes of gender.* New Haven, CT: Yale University Press.

Osman, S. (1972). My stepfather is a she. *Family Process, 11*, 209–218.

Nichols, M. (1994). Therapy with bisexual women: Working on the edge of emerging cultural and personal identities. In M. P. Mirkin (Ed.), *Women in context: Toward a feminist reconstruction of psychotherapy* (pp. 149–169). New York: Guilford Press.

Patterson, C. (1995). Sexual orientation and human development: An overview. *Developmental Psychology, 31*(1), 3–11.

Peplau, L. A. (1991). Lesbian and gay relationships. In J. C. Gonsiorek & J. D. Weinrich (Eds.), *Homosexuality: Research implications for public policy* (pp. 177–196). Newbury Park, CA: Sage.

Roth, S. (1985). Psychotherapy with lesbian couples: Individual issues, female socialization, and the social context. *Journal of Marital and Family Therapy, 11*(3), 273–286.

Roth, S. (1989). Psychotherapy with lesbian couples: Individual issues, female socialization, and the social context. In M. McGoldrick, C. M. Anderson, & F. Walsh (Eds.), *Women in families: A framework for family therapy* (pp. 286–307). New York: Norton.

Roth, S., & Murphy, B. C. (1986). Therapeutic work with lesbian clients: A systemic therapy view. In M. Ault-Riche & J. C. Hansen (Eds.), *Women and family therapy* (pp. 78–89). Gaithersburg, MD: Aspen.

Rubin, L. (1986). *Just friends.* New York: HarperCollins.

Shiffman, M. (1987). The men's movement: An exploratory empirical investigation. In M. S. Kimmel (Ed.), *Changing men: New directions in research on men and masculinity* (pp. 295–314). Newbury Park, CA: Sage.

Stoltenberg, J. (1989). *Refusing to be a man: Essays on sex and justice.* New York: Meridian.

Zacks, E., Green, R.-J., & Marrow, J. (1988). Comparing lesbian and heterosexual couples on the circumplex model: An initial investigation. *Family Process, 27,* 471–484.

PART ONE

PERSONAL, PROFESSIONAL, AND POLITICAL CONTEXTS

PART ONE

PERSONAL, PROFESSIONAL,
AND POLITICAL CONTEXTS

CHAPTER ONE

TRANSGENERATIONAL HOMOPHOBIA IN THE FAMILY

A Personal Narrative

Meme English

I remember when I was eight years old being brought to the Veterans of Foreign Wars building by my Uncle Ted and my father, along with my cousin and my younger sister. It was summertime, and the V.F.W. had swings and a slide in the back. In the bar were pinball machines and a jukebox. It was 1959. My sister Priscilla was five, and my cousin Beth was six. We liked to play pinball, and our fathers would continue to give us quarters as long as we wanted them. After a while, the quarters ran out, so we just sat around drinking Cokes with maraschino cherries in them and listening to the jukebox. I remember watching my father. He was tapping his ring on the table and his heel on the floor in time to the music. My father looked very neat to me. The son of a men's clothier, he always was smartly dressed—neat as a pin and very handsome. I imagined having a ring like my dad's to tap in time to the music, and I began tapping the heel of my sneaker on the floor. Men tapped their heels, I thought, and women tapped the toes of their pointy shoes. I didn't like those shoes, and I felt strange tapping my toe. I wanted loafers and polo shirts like my dad's and didn't have much use for dresses. My sister liked that stuff. I wanted a ring to tap like my dad's.

Previously published in the *Journal of Feminist Family Therapy*, Volume 7, #(3/4), pp. 15–28, 1995, and reprinted with the permission of The Haworth Press, Inc., Publisher, and the author.

My dad not only tapped his ring on the table in time to music, he also tapped it on the steering wheel as he sang along to the car radio. My dad wore a wedding ring, but the ring he tapped was a ruby ring, his college ring.

When we got back from the V.F.W., I started in on my mother the way any eight-year-old might. "Mom, I really want a ring. Do you think I can get a ring sometime soon?" Over the next several days, I expressed different variations on this theme a few hundred times. The part I couldn't figure out how to say was that I didn't want a girl ring—I wanted a boy ring, like my dad's.

Over the next several weeks, I got three rings. One my mother bought me, which was some kind of metal that turned my finger green and was definitely a girl ring. I didn't act rude about it or anything, but when it turned my finger green, I was glad because I had a good excuse not to wear it. The next ring I got was from the dentist. He didn't even have rings that were the kind I wanted. But my sister was there, and the choice was between girl rings and badges, like sheriff badges—plastic and very cool. I started to pick a badge, but my sister gave me a horrified look and I picked a ring. I gave it to her when we were in the car going home. She could have two girl rings—she loved them. Finally, the county fair was on, and there was a booth that had initial rings—they looked like boy rings. I got one and I became a ring-tapping maniac. I tapped my ring on my lunch box in the car on the way to day camp. I tapped my ring on the pew in church when I was a little bored, getting a glare from my grandmother. I tapped the ring on the handlebar of my bicycle. I tapped my ring on the table, even when the only music was in my head.

During those years, we spent a lot of time at our grandmother's house. My cousin Beth and I would play football in the long side yard, and my sister Priscilla would be the cheerleader.

I was a worried child. I remember the pediatrician telling my mom, "She's just a born worrier, Patty, you can't change her." I worried a lot, cried a lot, and was very serious about everything.

Also during those years, my father worked as a mutual funds salesman. He worked fourteen hours a day on commission, so often he would not be home when I went to bed. I would wake myself every night in the middle of the night and check my parents' bed to see if my father was home. Usually, he was there.

In the summer of 1962, when I was eleven years old, I checked to see if my father was there; he was not. I looked at my parents' alarm clock. It was 3:30 A.M. I woke my mother, asking "Where is Daddy?" She said, "Oh, he's downstairs filling the sugar bowl." Her answer seemed strange, and I decided to see for myself. I walked downstairs, checking the kitchen. He was not there. I looked in the living room, and in the spare room to see if he was sleeping somewhere else. He was not in the house, yet his car was in front of the house where it was always parked.

I woke my mother again. This time she really woke up, and I said that I had looked and that Daddy was not in the house and I wanted to know where he was. She told me that someone had beaten him up, that his jaw was broken, and that he was in the hospital. I couldn't understand why anyone would hurt my father. He was not a fighting type of person. He was not even very physical. He wore glasses, and he didn't like sports. He loved opera and singing and dancing and tapping his ring. He loved babies and dogs and cats and singing along with Mitch. Why would anyone punch my dad, and punch him hard enough to break his jaw?

I heard my mother on the phone. She was calling my father's parents. She said to them that they probably wouldn't put it in the *Daily News*, our local paper. She said that she thought someone was trying to rob my dad. That seemed weird to me. He didn't have a lot of money, and I had never seen him have a lot of cash. Then she said, "Oh no, I'm sure that will be all right. Certainly go ahead with your plans. I'll tell Don." My grandparents were leaving town to go visit my aunt in Philadelphia. It seemed strange to me that their son was hurt and in the hospital and they were leaving town. What I remember knowing was that they were very concerned about what people would think. Their leaving meant to me that there was some shame for my family in this incident. It would be years before I would understand this situation.

Soon the plan was made that I would be taken by my mother's parents to spend a week with my aunt in Pittsburgh, while Priscilla would stay with friends of my parents. I agreed to go because I knew my aunt would take me on the trolley to see the Pittsburgh Pirates play baseball. But I wanted to see my dad first. On our way out of town, my grandparents took me to the hospital. As we walked down the hall toward his room, two tall men came out wearing dark suits. My mother told me they were from the F.B.I. and that they were going to try to find the man who hurt my dad. They looked serious and intimidating.

My father's jaw was broken in seven places. My father, who usually looked so handsome, now looked like a monster. His swollen eyes were black and blue, his jaw wired shut. I felt sick and terrified. As we made the two-hour drive to Pittsburgh, nobody talked much. I remember my grandfather sang some songs, trying to keep some things normal.

The time with Aunt Jenny was fun. We ate TV dinners, which I thought of as a treat, played Monopoly, listened to the Pirates on the radio, and watched them on television, all at once. Aunt Jenny also knitted as she did all of these things. She bought me a whiffle ball and bat at Murphy's five and dime, and I stood in her kitchen in her upstairs apartment and pretended I was up to bat as we listened to the game on the radio. She didn't have a yard. We talked to my dad on the phone. His voice sounded strange because he couldn't open his mouth. On Saturday, my grandparents came back and took me home.

My father was out of the hospital. He looked thin, and his bruises were turning yellow. He had had one of his teeth pulled so that he could drink from a straw. My mother put everything in the blender for him to eat. On Monday, he had to go to see the doctor. I wanted to go everywhere with him, so I got to go along to the doctor. I didn't want to let him out of my sight. When we saw Dr. Smith, he told my father that the only thing to worry about was choking, because if he choked he could die. After I heard this, I would sit staring at my father with my chin in my hands while he drank his meals.

During the same summer, I was constantly in pursuit of two fourteen-year-old girls—Nancy and Cathy. They were beautiful. My mother didn't want me to spend time with them because that was the year "the pill" came out and, because they were Protestant, they might tell me about it. They never mentioned it, and I continued to disobey my mother, following these two very pretty blondes around. My mother was afraid I might learn about sex from them, or so she said. I *was* learning about sex from them, but what I was learning was not what she said she feared but rather what she couldn't say she feared—I liked girls.

My parents were split on the issue of my spending time with these two girls. My father one day told me I was allowed to have both of them spend the night. I asked the girls if we could pretend to be married as I slept between them on the double bed. I kissed them (not on the lips) and put my arms around them and held their hands. This was enough for me.

After my father had the wires removed from his jaw, he went back to work, and I resumed, with more dedication than before, my middle-of-the-night bed check. Sometimes as I got older, I would stay up waiting for his car to pull in, and if it was really late and he wasn't home, I would pray, "Hail Mary full of grace . . . please dear mother, let my father get home safe." I kept this vigil until I left home at nineteen.

I dated boys in high school. I didn't know how to "play the game," though. I liked to wear button-down collar Oxford shirts, crew-neck sweaters, wool skirts, knee socks, and penny loafers. If we could have worn pants, I would have. My hair was short—not like the flips set in orange juice cans that my sister and her friends wore.

In 1967, one of my sister's friends was spending the night at our house. It was Christmas night, and Susan and I stayed up talking to my dad. My sister and the rest of the family went to bed early. On our way up to bed, my sister's friend, who was fourteen, asked if she could sleep in my bed so that we could talk more. I was sixteen and I liked this girl, so I agreed. We scratched each other's backs and, after awhile, she turned me over and kissed me on the mouth. I was exhilarated. I couldn't believe what was happening. I was erotically just where I wanted to be. I remember thinking simultaneously two things: "I always wanted to kiss a girl" and "Oh my God. Am I homosexual?"

Susan and I both dated boys but continued to sleep together on the weekends. I guess I should say that she and I had a sexual relationship for the next year and a half. I spent many tortured hours trying to figure out if I was a lesbian and trying to get Susan to talk to me about what was going on. Mostly she would get reticent and scared and ask me not to talk to her about it. During these same years, we both lost our virginity to boys and had serious relationships with boys we thought we were in love with. We were still being sexual with each other and taking turns getting really jealous of each other's boyfriends. Meanwhile, my sister was completely in the dark about what was going on with us—she perceived that she had lost her best friend to her older sister and didn't learn the truth until much later.

In 1968, my father drove me to a job interview at a camp for handicapped children. I was interviewed by a large woman with very short cropped hair. As my father drove me away from this meeting, he explained that this woman was a lesbian and talked at length about rights for homosexuals. I loved it. But, I couldn't figure out where this conservative, White, Catholic, Republican had gotten such liberal views.

That summer, I met a young conscientious objector named Dan. He was sensitive, loved poetry and art, was very nonaggressive sexually, and I fell in love with him. He also reminded me a lot of my dad. We dated all that year and the next. I was still seeing Susan, who seemed more and more interested in men. I wanted to be more involved with Dan and less agonized by the possibility of thinking I was a lesbian.

In 1970, I moved with my family to Texas. I was a freshman at the University of Houston, and Dan was in college in Pennsylvania. At the end of the semester, Dan came to Texas. We made love for the first time. He cried and we broke up. It seemed to happen that fast. We had been dating for two years, considered ourselves engaged, and at the point we consummated our sexual relationship, he broke down. He said he was afraid of pregnancy, but I wondered if something else was going on. We hadn't seen each other for four months, and we each had changed. Dan returned to his family home in Colorado.

Three weeks later, I phoned him to say I was pregnant. He said, "Then we'll get married." I agreed. The marriage lasted two years, until December, 1972. By then our daughter, Joni, was almost two years old. Dan and I had been having sexual problems, and in August 1972, Dan told me that he was gay and had been having sex with men. He told me that the reason he had cried the first time we made love was that he had only been sexual with men before. At this point, I had not disclosed anything to him about Susan and myself. And I did not plan to. I went home to my parents and confided to my mother that Dan and I were getting a divorce because Dan wanted to come out as a gay man. He wanted my permission to go to the gay bars in Houston. I did not share my own gay feelings or experience—I was too frightened, given the political climate in Texas, that I would lose custody of my child.

My mother invited me to the club in Houston to have a drink with her. I was just twenty-one and had not had the opportunity to drink legally. It was odd that my mother would offer such an invitation, and I was curious about what it meant.

My mother knew that I had recently begun therapy. She began the conversation by saying that, since I was in therapy, there was something she felt she should tell me. She then told me that my father was gay and that she had known it for nineteen years, since my sister was a baby. The only other person she had told was the parish priest back in Pennsylvania. One of my father's lovers got drunk and was in a car accident. This man called in shock and panic in the middle of the night and told my mother that my father was his lover. My mother told me that she didn't really know what "homosexual" meant. She was raised Irish Catholic, had attended parochial school, and went to a Catholic hospital school for nurses' training. She said the only gay people she knew were "section eights" in her psychiatric nursing school rotation or people she worked with at the V.A. Hospital. And then she told me that, many years earlier, when my father's jaw had been broken, it was in a gay-bashing incident. Suddenly, a lot of things made sense. My mother then confided that her worst fear was that my father would get a sexually transmitted disease, and then the secret would be out. This was before AIDS.

I was overwhelmed with feeling. I wondered how to make sense of this new information in terms of its significance, considering my choice of Dan as a husband and my confusion about my own sexual orientation. Sworn to secrecy, I was told not to tell my sister or brother and to never tell my father that I knew. I kept the secret for four years. On my twenty-fifth birthday, in 1976, I told my father that I knew. He cried. He said that my mother had convinced him that we would all hate him if we knew. I reassured him that that was untrue and shared with him my own gayness. At the time I was trying to come out. My father and I began to have lunches together in the gay area of Houston. He began to confide in me—often in ways that were really inappropriate—ways that included explicit details of his sexual behavior and encounters. He seemed to forget that I was his daughter.

Terrified of my own homosexuality, I married again in 1976. I was frightened of being like my father. I didn't want to live a hidden life and had already experienced the impact of homophobia from my heterosexual women friends and even from other lesbians who reacted to my being a mother. Their feelings (and my own) of whether or not my being a mother *and* a lesbian would be healthy for my daughter confused me. Within the first six months of my marriage, I became infatuated with a woman. I thought being married would inoculate me against this confusion. Not true. And, once again, I was pregnant.

When my second daughter, Kate, was fifteen months old, my former husband Dan was killed in a car accident. My father was shaken by this loss and I, at twenty-six, began to feel that I might have less time than I thought to be honest about my life—to tell the truth about who I was. I noticed that I was listening a little more attentively to stories on National Public Radio about gay men or lesbians. Driving in the car with my dad about this time, I asked him, "How does it feel to live a double life?" He asked me what I meant. I said, "Well, you know, Dad, on the one hand it looks like you are the typical married heterosexual father and grandfather, and on the other hand, you spend hours a week at the gay baths." He told me he guessed he never thought about it. Not wanting any longer to lead a double life like my dad, I made a plan to leave my second husband. He was an alcoholic, whose dream was to have a bunch of kids and to live in the country, with an acre-long vegetable garden and chickens. The morning I was planning to leave, I discovered I was pregnant again.

When my son, Adam, was seven months old, the children and I left. In therapy again, I assured my therapist, after outlining my family history, that I had grappled with the gay question about myself and that I wasn't gay. Three months later I came out again—this time for good.

I did not want to live a gay lifestyle in the same city with my parents. I did not want to live in fear as a lesbian mother in Texas, and I did not want my mother to have to confront my gayness in the way she would have to if I were in the same city. It was clear to me that I was overinvolved in the day-to-day drama of my parents' relationship. In 1982, I made a decision to move with my three children to Massachusetts.

In 1986, just as I was graduating with my bachelor of arts degree, my father became ill and tested HIV-seropositive on the antibody test. He assured me that he was not HIV-positive. My mother contradicted him. I was in a long-term, committed relationship with a woman, Connie. We lived together with her daughter, Sarah, and my children. My parents, sister, and brother all came for my graduation, meeting Connie and Sarah for the first time. The focus of the visit might have been on my being out and in my first live-in relationship with a woman except for the anxiety generated by my father's illness. I don't remember much of my family's reaction to Connie and me, but I don't think it was on their minds.

When my father got sick, I may as well have been living next door to my parents—psychologically speaking. In March 1987, I traveled to Texas to see my family. My father met our plane. He had lost forty pounds since I had last seen him. When we arrived at my parents' house, my mother met us with a drink in her hand and whispered to me that I should come out onto the patio with her. I followed her. She said, "Your father has AIDS; he is taking an experimental drug from Mexico. Don't tell your sister, your brother, or your father that you know." I said, "No, Mom, we are not doing it this way again. I am here for ten days, and we are all going to talk about it."

When my father developed a rash on his back, I decided to drive him to the doctor's, since I wanted some time alone with him, and I wanted to speak with the doctor. My father asked her to look at his rash, and when they went into the examining room next door, I heard her say to him that the rash was often experienced by people with this virus. They came back into the other office and I asked her, even though I had overheard what she said to my father, what she thought about the rash. She said that it was often part of the virus. I asked, "What virus?" The doctor turned to my dad and asked him if it was okay to answer me. He nodded. She said, "The AIDS virus." I said, "So that means right now my father has the AIDS virus?" She said, "Yes." Since his hospitalization with pneumocystis carinii pneumonia the previous month, she had counted him as one of those who had moved from being HIV-positive to having AIDS.

As I drove us home, Dad looked out of the window at the Houston skyline. I do not believe he was listening. I asked, "So, Dad what are we going to tell everyone?" He said, "That's simple. I don't have AIDS." I explained to him that was not what the doctor said. He had stopped listening again.

I decided not to tell the children while we were in Texas about their grandfather's illness. I needed to get in a better place—a more supported place at home with Connie, before I could deal with their feelings along with my own. But even when I arrived home, I put off telling the children. I was much too upset myself and wanted a little more time to get comfort and consolation from my friends.

At one point during this period, I was driving with my son in the car. He said, "Mom, can I ask you something?" I said, "Sure, Adam, what is it?" "Did you have a baby that died before I was born or something like that kind of secret that I don't know about?" I took a deep breath and told him the one secret that I had been holding and that he somehow felt: that my father and his "Pappy" had AIDS. I then went home and told his sisters and Sarah, Connie's daughter.

In June, Connie and I were camping with the kids in Maine when my father entered the hospital again. I had been on the phone with my father's doctor, a lesbian, dozens of times, the campground managers had been alerted that I might receive an emergency phone call, and my mother and sister were given the number of our campsite. I called the hospital every evening. I wasn't a lot of fun.

I began to fall apart emotionally. I wasn't sleeping, and one night, in the Volkswagen bus where Connie and I were sleeping, I had a full-blown panic attack. My father was in intensive care in a Houston hospital with pneumocystis carinii again. He could not breathe. I felt as if I could not breathe—I didn't know if all panic attacks included this feeling of not being able to breathe or if I was having this particular symptom to somehow feel closer to my father. I could not figure out how I could know he was so sick and still be on vacation in Maine with my lesbian lover and our children. It seemed like what I had was what he would have wished for if he could have moved past the self-hate that was such a major ingredient in his coming-out attempts. How could I have this if he could not? How could I not feel guilty? I became unable to be sexual. I began to be obsessed with whether I would have enough time to get to Texas when my father was actively in his dying process. I drove the doctor crazy, calling her almost every day. My mother, sister, and brother, on the other hand, had never talked to or met the doctor. My mother had told no one about my father's illness except her friend, the gay pharmacist, at the hospital where she was a nurse. He would have known anyway because he filled my father's AZT prescriptions. I was beginning to experience my family's spill-over homophobia. When I suggested that my mother or sister call the AIDS service organizations in Houston, both my mother and sister said they could not call. They would feel strange talking to "those people." Once, when I suggested that someone in Houston call the doctor, my mother said that she didn't want to call the doctor because she was "one, too." It was as if they didn't know that these comments were insulting to me as a gay person. At the same time, they suggested that I continue making the calls because I wouldn't be as uncomfortable talking to other gay people. The doctor suggested that I come down to arrange AIDS support services for my father.

I flew to Houston in July, arriving in time for my father's birthday. We went to the AIDS clinic, early for the appointment. I reminded my father, who became irritable as we waited, that they were not late—we were early. He was not feeling well, and even at the best of times had become rude and belligerent. When the social worker, a woman, came to get him from the waiting room, my father was very anxious. He asked if I could come in with him. She said that would be okay. As a routine part of her history-taking, she asked, "Sexual preference?" My father, who had not had heterosexual sex in fifteen years, said, "Heterosexual." I didn't know what to do. I said, "Dad, you can tell the truth here." He looked at me with a face that had survived a gay-bashing twenty-five years before, a face that no longer knew the truth. He said, "Can my daughter answer these questions for me, my throat is hurting real bad." My heart was breaking, and I answered as best I could. It is impossible to ever tell anyone else's truth for them.

Given that we were both gay and the other family members were not, I had felt like my father's advocate since before the beginning of his illness—his ally in the family. I wanted to love him in the process, not blame him for having AIDS. My mother, who had been married to a gay man for forty years, was furious. This, after all, was her worst fear. My father was dying of a publicly acknowledged "gay disease." My sister allied herself with my mother. My brother, Matthew, was only twenty-two at the time, and he mostly stayed away from it all.

I was the prodigal daughter. I would swoop down from Massachusetts to be my father's champion. I talked to the doctor and to the people at the AIDS clinic. I told my father that if things became too conflicted between him and my mother, he could come and live with me, and I would take care of him. He and I both knew that he would never choose to leave my mother or his home. What did happen was that he would threaten my mother that he would come and live with me whenever he felt unloved or misunderstood by her. This hardened the straight-gay divisions developing in the family. My father was gay and sick—they couldn't be too mean to him. I, on the other hand, was gay and not sick. I was an easy target for my mother's and sister's overflowing homophobia and shame. Our family was like a microcosm of the larger society's struggle over homosexuality.

The "buddy" from the AIDS clinic came once to the house. My mother didn't like him—he seemed "too gay." My family's homophobic stance was painful for me. At one point, I invited my nephew, who was nine, for a visit, but my sister and brother-in-law didn't want him exposed to our lifestyle, to "sex," they said. They didn't know what to tell him about me and Connie, and they hadn't told him about my father's AIDS illness. He didn't visit.

In the grocery store a few days after I returned from my trip to Texas, a mother of one of the children's friends walked over to me in the produce section. She asked if I had had a good time in Texas. I didn't know this woman well, and I didn't know what to say. Finally, I said that it hadn't been a pleasure trip, that my father was quite ill, and that I had gone to see him. She said she was sorry, and she asked the question I had been dreading: "What is the matter with him?" A million thoughts flew through my head. I didn't want to answer. But I was aware of my ten-year-old daughter Kate's presence, immediately realizing that if I said "AIDS," this woman would think "gay," and I would have outed my father, myself, and Kate, who was and is a very private person. I was hit over the head with my own internalized homophobia and my community's homophobia. I took a deep breath and said, "He has AIDS." She burst into tears. I have no idea what was going on for her. I tried to comfort her and then after she apologized either for her tears or for her question or for my answer, Kate and I walked away.

Several weeks before my father died, he was in the hospital with pneumonia again and doing very poorly. Early one morning, before school had started, I received a call from my mother. I told the children that their Pappy was very sick and that this could be the beginning of his dying process.

An hour or so after school started, I received a call from the principal, saying that Adam was crying, very upset about his grandfather, and could I pick him up. She also said that Adam had some other ideas of what might be helpful that they would like to discuss with me. When I arrived at the school, the principal told me that Adam, who was in the fourth grade, had requested that a letter go home to the families of his classmates telling them that one of their classmates' grandfathers was dying of AIDS and asking that they talk to their children about AIDS. Adam also was remarking that there were jokes about AIDS going around school that he didn't like, jokes like, "Don't go to Provincetown, you'll get AIDS!" "If you step on the yellow squares, you'll get AIDS."

The difficult thing about this request was that Adam and Kate had different and, in fact, conflicting needs. Kate didn't want anyone to know, and Adam wanted to have a note go home to his classmates' parents. Kate finally agreed that she could sacrifice her privacy if it meant that Adam could feel more supported.

The families were not entirely appreciative, and some questioned why they needed to talk to their child about AIDS. One of the mothers came up to me at the holiday concert and told me that she disagreed with having to speak with her ten-year-old about AIDS. It is a complicated issue, and it was a difficult judgment call. It was, however, clear what Adam was needing and important to do what we could.

My father's condition worsened during January 1989. My mother was no longer able to care for him at home, and he was given a room at a hospice. The name of the facility was Casa de los Niños ("Home of the Children"). I had been calling every day, and had been able, starting in October 1988, to have my friend Gary, a gay man from Houston, meet and talk with my father regularly. It was critically important to me that someone meet with him who was gay and who did not hate himself or other gay people. I wanted positive gay energy to be some part of what my father received in his final days.

I was able to get some solace from the fact that Gary understood the family dynamics and would report to me with some accuracy the reality of my father's condition. Gary began to describe some incidents that sounded like my father's brain was beginning to be affected by the AIDS virus. He also reported that my mother looked more and more exhausted, and he agreed that the hospice placement was what needed to happen, given that my mother needed to continue to work every day and that my father was becoming weaker and in danger of falling or hurting himself in some other way. Dad didn't want to go to the hospice—he wanted to die at home. This was, unfortunately, impossible.

On January 25, I phoned my father at the hospice to see how he was doing. He was unable to speak loudly enough so that I could hear him on the phone. I told the nurse to tell him I loved him. She did and told me he said that he loved me, too.

I called Gary, who told me that he had visited my father that day and that my father had held onto his hand and talked for an hour. Gary said he really didn't understand a word my father said—it was like gibberish, but my father cried and held Gary's hand and seemed to be trying to communicate things that were very important for him.

My plane reservations were for February 3. I began to think I would need to go sooner. The next morning, there was a snowstorm. I settled in to drive to work late and began making pancakes for the children. The phone rang. It was my mother saying my father was in a coma. I asked her if I should come. She said she didn't know. I hung up and sat down at my kitchen table. I thought for a few minutes and then said to Connie that I felt like I needed to go that day.

I arrived in Houston at 10 P.M., my brother Matthew arriving from Dallas at around the same time. I had been afraid to phone from O'Hare to check on my father's condition. I was worried that if he had already died, I would have to be alone for the rest of the journey with the news. As it turned out, he was still hanging on and had been told by his doctor that Matt and I were on our way.

I arrived with my brother at the hospice, which seemed a lot like a little apartment. My mother and sister were keeping vigil there. My father woke up and spoke to my brother and me as we arrived. I had brought Joni's graduation pictures with me, which I showed him. He sat up in bed and said they were beautiful. I think those were the last words he spoke. I was impressed that he could rally.

He was very thin. He was wearing only a diaper, and he looked like the pictures of Christ as he was taken off the cross. He was emaciated, in pain, and struggling to breathe. He kept trying to get out of bed. It almost seemed like he thought he could escape death if he could just find the strength to get out of the bed.

My mother and sister were exhausted. They had been with Dad all day waiting for us. Matt and I were "wired" and not at all close to sleep. I had been worrying for months that I would not be there to love my father as he left this life. Having arrived, I was not going to miss one second. After a while, Matt fell asleep on the couch. My mother went to sleep in the living room. My sister and brother-in-law went to sleep on the floor in the other bedroom. It was the middle of the night. I cradled my father in my arms. I held him as if he were my child. I talked to him about not being afraid of death. I told him some people say that taking off life is like taking off a shoe that is too tight. I told him to look toward the light. I told him that I loved him very much and would never forget him. I was able to do everything I had worried about not being able to do.

My mother came back into the room and, noticing that my father's breathing was even more labored, called the nurse to medicate him again with morphine. She asked me to come into the other room with her while she smoked a cigarette. I said I didn't want to leave. She said that maybe my father was having trouble letting go because I was there. She said maybe he needed some privacy to die. I reluctantly went into the next room with her. It seemed like my father was sleeping. As we sat there, he tapped his ruby ring on the bedside rail—almost as if to signal us to come back in to be with him as he took his last breath. It was 6 A.M., January 27.

I had never been with a dying person before, and I didn't have any idea that dying was a lot like watching a laboring woman try to give birth. It moves in fits and starts and is not easy. The difference is, in the end, there is no baby, just the momentary deliverance of peace.

Six years have passed since then. Adam, my son, now wears my father's ruby ring. I was given my father's wedding ring. I turned it into a blue sapphire pinkie ring for myself.

CHAPTER TWO

CONNECTIONS

Conversations Between a Gay Therapist and a Straight Therapist

Stanley Siegel and Gillian Walker

Dolce guida è caro.

DANTE

In this chapter, we—Gillian Walker, a straight therapist, and Stanley Siegel, a gay therapist—join together in dialogue about the bicultural issues central to work with gay and lesbian clients. Gillian began seeing gay and lesbian clients several years ago through her work with people with AIDS. In those years, her practice mainly consisted of gay men for whom HIV was an issue for the individual, couple, or family. In order to be of help to gays, she believed she had to immerse herself in gay life. Work at the Gay Men's Health Crisis Center, an AIDS social service organization, was her point of entry.

Helpful in learning about the experience of being gay were conversations with gay friends; collaboration with the late John Patten, a distinguished gay therapist who was the codirector of the Ackerman Family Therapy Institute's AIDS Project; research for her book, *In the Midst of Winter* (1991, 1995); and her reading of gay literature. However, she believes now that the absence of ongoing di-

---

We dedicate this chapter to the memory of John Patten.
Note: In this chapter, the term *gay* is used to refer to both gay men and lesbians. The terms *he* and *she* are used randomly; one may be understood for the other in any context.

alogue with a gay consultant was impoverishing to her work and allowed her to fall back on psychologizing practices rather than investigating the cultural experience, particularly in relation to family of origin and couple issues. These conversations with Stanley Siegel have sharpened her understanding of her own responses to homosexuality, clarified the critical treatment issues that result from the experience of being gay in a straight culture, and illuminated critical differences in cultural values around sexual and relational issues.

Stanley Siegel has written about the experience of being gay from both personal and professional perspectives in his book, *Uncharted Lives: Understanding the Life Passages of Gay Men* (Siegel & Lowe, 1994). From his dual perspective—first as a married man living in a straight world and later as a gay man who came out in his mid thirties—he has explored the disjunctures between the two cultures. He believes that there is an absence of dialogue between gay and straight therapists about treating gay and lesbian clients and that there are far too few training opportunities for straight family therapists to work with an experienced gay or lesbian therapist on the issues particular to gay and lesbian individuals, couples, and families with gay or lesbian members. Gay therapists have felt the need for empowerment and mutual support through meeting and collaborating with each other and have not sought ongoing dialogue with straight therapists. Similarly, straight therapists have assumed that they can deal with the issues gay clients raise from the perspective of their generalist training without being in dialogue with gay therapists. However, understanding the psychology and the relational experiences of the gay or lesbian person requires understanding both the importance of what it means to negotiate an ever-present dominant, gay-oppressive culture from an outsider position and how this experience interfaces with childhood, adolescence, and adulthood.

Because the gay experience is so poorly represented in psychotherapy training programs, practitioners—in their language and treatment approaches—represent the heteronormative ideology of sexual practice and social convention. This representation can be experienced as homophobic by the gay client, since psychiatry and psychology share a history of equating homosexuality with arrested psychosexual development or constitutional inferiority, beliefs encoded in *DSM* until 1973 and still held by some mental health professionals. Even today, psychoanalytic institutes exclude homosexuals from training programs and practice "conversion" therapies. Even among enlightened professionals, where the discourse has shifted away from the mental illness equation, arguments continue over such topics as ego syntonic versus ego dystonic homosexuality—arguments that contain thinly veiled expressions of homophobia. The field of family therapy has its own prejudices, seen in its lack of appreciation of the legitimacy of "families of choice" and its privileging of families of origin. Until the mid 1980s, when

AIDS forced gay issues to the foreground, there were no openly gay groups or gay plenary speakers represented in the major family therapy organizations. One is reminded of the statement of a gay AIDS patient describing his stay at a Catholic Hospital: "They are very caring of us when they know we are dying."

The following conversations between Gillian and Stanley are an attempt to keep the cultural dialogue alive and, through the discussion both of case material and larger societal issues, to define those areas, common to gay and lesbian experience, which may not be evident to the straight therapist.

The First Conversation

On being a straight or gay therapist . . .

SS: What do you think are the differences in approaches to psychotherapy with gay and lesbian clients when practiced by gay and nongay therapists? Since most people assume that therapists, particularly family therapists, are heterosexual, I discuss my sexual orientation during the initial telephone contact. Whatever the client's orientation, I make sexuality an immediate part of the discourse. Disclosing my homosexuality frees me from worrying about if and when and how it will become an issue. This probably represents the first departure in approach, since most nongay therapists would not announce their heterosexuality to either their gay or nongay clients.

GW: I do say to gay or lesbian clients, "You've been referred to me. I am a heterosexual therapist. Would you prefer to see a gay therapist or do you want to come in and see how that goes for you? I can refer you to a gay or lesbian colleague if you think that would work better for you." And then they usually reassure me, "I've heard about you from other lesbians or gays whom you've treated and I would like to come see you." It strikes me that I do not make discussion of their choice to see a straight therapist a part of the therapy. If I asked questions such as, What went into your choice? Was there a discussion between the two of you about choosing a gay or lesbian or straight therapist? How do you think the therapist being either straight or gay or lesbian might influence the work?, the cultural context of the work might be more readily available for discussion. I can rationalize my decision not to explore this area as staying with the client's presenting difficulties, but I think it also represents my reluctance to explore the differences in our experience openly.

SS: Would you say to your nongay referrals, "I am a straight therapist"?

GW: No, I wouldn't . . . because I would assume the congruence of our sexual and cultural orientation. As I think about the issues you raise, I agree that the choice of a gay person to see a straight therapist should be carefully examined. Are there transferential issues related to the client's internalized homophobia? For example, is this choice influenced by an unconscious fantasy that a straight therapist, as representative of dominant U.S. culture, will provide a blessing that will dissipate gay self-hatred? Do clients come in expecting condemnation because part of themselves condemns what they are doing?

Of course, cultural insensitivity, contrasting value systems, and linguistic errors, among other things, will frequently trap straight therapists into inadvertently punishing behaviors. Perhaps in therapy with gay and lesbian clients, the normal transference in which the therapist is metamorphosized from the parent as enemy to the parent with whom the client ultimately must be reconciled, is intensified by cultural issues. For gay and lesbian clients, the expectation may be that the straight therapist—as a representative of the dominant culture and the family of origin—inevitably will prove to be the parent who ultimately condemns.

Does the client have a secret hope that the straight therapist will resolve his conflicts by curing him? One man chose me to help him reconcile his internal conflict between straight and gay mores by curing what, from the perspective of internalized homophobia, he saw as sexually addictive behavior. I saw his behavior as relatively gay normal, so he sought out an incest therapist who tried to "cure" him by dragging out traditional psychiatric formulations. For example, his gay activities were due to "the trauma" of an early sexual experience with an older boy (which, in fact, he had solicited and enjoyed), in combination with his mother's incestuous fantasies for him and his father's distance. He submitted to these powerful formulations, which were framed as "incest work," but he still wanted me to help him with his gay relationship. Ultimately, of course, the relationship failed—a victim of his homophobia, reinforced by the other therapy. I think he is still struggling with his feelings of self-hatred and shame as he pays straight therapists to reify them. He avoids gay therapists who might help him accept this "shameful part" of himself.

I do not think one can escape the issue of sexual orientation. Its meanings are always present, reemerging at various points in the work, as clients experience shame, outsiderness, or the fear that you will judge them negatively. With lesbians in particular, I have learned to be careful to scrutinize my interventions for their sensitivity to my client's vulnerability. A careless but well-intended remark can be experienced as a slight that can threaten to unravel the carefully constructed relationship and to rupture delicately given and taken trust. I remember, for example, being tired and taking a mother-daughter tangle too lightly in my attempt to bring perspective through humor to a tyrannized daughter's relationship with her (to my eyes) melodramatic parent. I almost lost the pair and was stunned at the depth of their hurt as well as my own hurt at their reaction. Perhaps because we were all women, there was a special care and feeling between us, so easily damaged, so subject to unseen dangers that could wound us. Although my remark was not about the daughter's lesbianism, my obliviousness to the depth of her feeling must have signified that central wound—the straight world's attempt to annihilate deep aspects of her being. I had become the representative of the outside world and the clients' internalized expectations of its cruelty. The therapy room had become the unsafe place that the world can be unless you are sheltered in the world of your lesbian group, your lesbian family. And I, as a therapist, was equally wounded because as a woman I experienced my clients as sisters who had mined women's experiences more deeply than most people. I was being pushed out of their family, and I felt great sorrow at losing this dialogue.

SS: The nongay therapist is more a part of the dominant culture, since nongay relationships are esteemed in the social hierarchy of sexual value and are rewarded with certified mental health and respectability. It is the exceptional nongay therapist who is willing or able to stand outside the dominant culture far enough to gain insight into what is heteronormative, what is heterosexist, and what is homophobic.

GW: Conceptualizing therapy as including ethnographic inquiry has helped me discover the unique meanings of a new culture and the values implicit in my own. For example, I ask questions such as, Does this behavior have a different meaning in your experience than it might have in mine? Most often, partners are at different levels of resolution about sexual orientation issues. If I can keep the discourse open to the idea that there could be an emergent, different culture from the heteronormative, both the partners and I become collaborative inquirers about these new territories of sexuality.

Ethnographic inquiry has also been a good corrective to family therapy's Pollyannaish attitude that all relationships are intrinsically similar and follow similar rules in that it explores culture and, for gays and lesbians, the ever-present conflict between dominant and nondominant cultures. I used to think the dynamics of gay and straight couples were very similar, but over time I have come to understand that gay core relationship issues are defined by the couple's bicultural experiences. For example, as a straight therapist I have to continue to remind myself to foreground the staging issues that you write about, that is, where a person is in the process of developing a gay identity. You write that major conflictual areas in the gay couple's life are often related to tensions that arise because partners are at different stages in the coming-out process. I might overlook this and solely attribute relationship problems to psychological processes, unresolved issues with family of origin, projections, and so on, or I might trivialize these issues by thinking of them as problem-saturated narratives in need of reframing.

But I believe that the therapy I am interested in doing moves back and forth from ethnographic narrative therapy to a more feminist and systems-informed psychodynamic inquiry. I think that adult patterns of emotion and behavior are constructed from internalized learning from childhood and adolescence, the witnessing of key relationships, the experience of the self in relationship, the effect of that self on the surrounding matrix of relationships, the ideas and premises to be accepted or rebelled against—the suitcase of childhood experience that always accompanies you.

SS: I think it's a question of when you do that. For someone beginning the process of coming out, it's much more meaningful and relevant to pay attention to the ways in which culture has influenced self-perception. Exploring the societal aspects of experience leads to the first steps of understanding and self-forgiveness, because gay people have been so punished. I know there are self-defeating behaviors that are separate from that but at that moment, it isn't useful to say that. You have to deal with the power of what is happening. Later, having gone through the process of unlearning and relearning, being farther along in the coming-out process, perhaps even many years later, the gay person is free to pull back a little and explore how his unique psychology plays a role in the way challenges are responded to. I think it is sometimes difficult for a nongay therapist to distinguish the uniqueness of the way in which a person negotiates a homophobic culture. For example, you referred Jason to me, whom you had in the initial stages of accepting his identity as a gay person. Jason now is in a relationship and ready to explore many of the issues you raised with him.

GW: He could not with me because he was so preoccupied with the turmoil of coming out. The stages of therapy, then, to some extent may parallel those of coming out, although throughout the process of therapy, therapist and client will intermittently focus on the effects of homophobia. It's so important to establish a bond with the person or couple by locating their experiences in the larger social context, that is, universalizing and normalizing rather than particularizing. Then, as people move along in the process of self-acceptance, therapy becomes an exploration of the "me." In work with a couple, it is often useful to explore childhood history to understand how each may be projecting transferential figures onto the other, the nature of their introjections, and so on. Therapy is also a constant exploration of how relationships are shaped by the unique ways each person digests and uses cultural-political experiences, integrates them into personal history, and brings them into the relationship.

SS: Exactly.

GW: Let's get back to what you were saying about the gay or straight therapist's presentation of sexual orientation in therapy. I'm curious. Do you ever ask your straight clients about their heterosexual orientation?

SS: At some point early in the therapy, probably in the first interview, I'll ask non-gay clients how long they have been heterosexual. This punctuation and resulting confusion creates an opportunity to enter into a dialogue about sexuality, gender, and sex, which is too often taken for granted by heterosexual therapists. As a gay man, sexuality is a primary part of my consciousness, and I am always seeking a way to utilize the benefits of that for both my gay and nongay clients. Would you, as a nongay therapist, introduce the question of sex so immediately?

On identity and sexuality . . .

GW: Probably not. Unless sexual problems were the presenting issue, I would deal with them later in the work. Sexual issues do come up more quickly in the therapy of gay men than they do in straight couples. I think this is probably because the open discourse of sexuality has such an important place in gay male life, whereas straight couples often live quietly dulled lives of sexual desperation. As a straight therapist, I have had to learn to view sex through the eyes of the gay community. In your book, you describe the major transition that many gay men go through as they reconceptualize the meaning of sex—from the predominant heterosexual idea of sex with relationship front-loaded and sex outside relationship as transgressive—to the gay male view of the multiple meanings of sexual experience. Sex may be viewed as relationship, self-discovery, or recreation. Male couples often present in therapy still operating from deeply embedded heterosexual definitions of the meaning of sexual experience, definitions that are in conflict with the mores of the gay male community. As a heterosexual therapist, I must guard against imposing heterocultural biases on clients who are struggling to create new relationship definitions.

Let me give you a clinical example of a gay male couple in which issues of different stages of identity development combine with differing views of normative sexuality and are at the heart of the conflict. Terry and Angelo came in because Terry is wildly jealous of Angelo's flirtations. Terry has been out to his family since he was fifteen. He had had his adolescence, slept around, and was ready to have a steady relationship. But the only model he knows for relationship is one like that of his parents—heteronormative. He admits that he identifies with his mother's possessiveness of his father and does not want Angelo to even flirt with anyone else. He knows that Angelo is impulsive, so he can never be sure that flirtation won't lead to a sexual encounter, as indeed it has in the past. And, of course, Terry's thinking can fit very neatly into my worldview as a straight therapist. "Terry is right to want this kind of relationship because that's the way relationships are made and, as a family therapist, I am trained to help them achieve a heteronormative relationship, get married, and live happily ever after à deux." Angelo, who is not out to his family, wants to go to gay bars, and says to Terry (because he doesn't want to lose him), "Well, look, I'm not going to sleep around, but I want to meet people and I want to be admired and I want to flirt." To which Terry answers, "I can't stand this." I think it threatens his heteronormative idea. He is afraid of losing Angelo to someone else because sleeping with someone else is regarded as the affair that jeopardizes the hetero-ideal.

SS: This raises another interesting point, which is about the meanings of sex to gay men and the way in which sexual experimentation operates in the process of the psychological and social construction of a gay identity. Most of the men I interviewed when researching *Uncharted Lives,* and others with whom I discussed sex in psychotherapy, reported having had many sexual encounters, and most regard their sexual histories positively. For the gay man, each sexual encounter offers the opportunity to claim what has been buried, hidden, denied, or repressed. He is free to explore every possible variation of himself. Over time, the gay man evolves sexually and realizes more clearly who he is. That helps him to re-create himself, socially and ethically, outside the heteronormative rules. Labeling this behavior as promiscuous is a heterosexist construct and a misunderstanding of the culture of male homosexuality.

GW: Or, rather, the "ideal" culture of homosexuality.

SS: The ideal culture. Sex has a variety of meanings and pleasures in gay male culture. It can be coupled with love, simply seen as recreational, or used as a vehicle for self-discovery. The experience of "cruising," or selecting a sexual partner, for instance, is deeper and more complex than it appears. It usually involves not only checking out the sexual readiness of total strangers but screening them carefully—if subconsciously—for particular aspects that might satisfy a cruiser's fantasy while actually blocking out distracting personal details. The process of claiming one's forbidden homosexuality involves getting to know many parts of the undiscovered self, through these temporary attractions to others. Acquiescing to the attraction allows the untried, unexplored traits to awaken, stretch, examine, and explore their own existence.

GW: I think that's a very important point. Gay men often come to me to deal with the issue of their puzzlement about how to manage conflicts between their primary relationship and their sexual lives outside the relationship. Cruising is an issue that your book helped me understand in a richer way. For many gay men seeking help, the issue of cruising is filled with shame. In fact some, understanding their behavior in the light of heteronorms, attend sexual addiction self-help groups to help them eliminate this behavior. Although in principle I oppose labeling and have rather broad views of morality and an interest in the richness of human experience, I have, with my most "liberal" colleagues, puzzled over the extent and range of practices involved in normal gay sexuality. At some level, despite my protests of neutrality, my uneasiness must have been conveyed to clients, although I think more to those clients who were equally disturbed by their own behavior. Your writing was liberating for me, as you conceptualized cruising within a framework of the self-exploration necessary to the consolidation and affirmation of gay identity, especially since gay identity is stigmatized, or constitutes, in Goffman's term, a "spoiled" identity. The man who flirts and is flirted with is playing out a foreshortened adolescence; each is exploring his sexual attractiveness and confirming his identity as a gay man who is attracted to and is attractive to other men. The shame that the client brings to cruising is no more, no less, than the shame attached to gayness itself. For the gay man asserting his sexuality is reclaiming a part of the self stolen by the heterosexual dominant society. The repeated acts of affirmation: I am gay; I am seen as gay and therefore I am gay; this is who I am sexually—these acts are critical reinforcing experiences that counter the enormous societal forces pulling against him.

SS: Even the most well-intentioned nongay therapist could miss or misread the subtlety and nuance that grows out of the experience of being gay or lesbian. I think what we are questioning is whether a nongay therapist can construct the kind of inquiry that would be relevant and meaningful to gay clients and remain judgment free. What is likely to be difficult for nongay therapists are questions about gay sex. If sex is used recreationally, for instance, how does that enter into the balance of a gay male relationship? Such questions are conceived from knowledge about the reasons why gays and lesbians couple, which may be very different from the reasons for heterosexual coupling. Let me ask you if you are personally able to decode the language and culture well enough to understand the choreography of gay relationships.

GW: Not without help from my clients and without reading gay literature, magazines, and novels and not without dialogues with gay therapists. No matter how much the straight therapist believes that he or she is open to gay experience and sympathetic with issues of difference and different identity formations, it's hard to keep clear that being gay is a different experience with its own set of rules that often stand in contrast to socially constructed heteronorms. You are inevitably pulled by straight culture, which surrounds you, which has shaped your views despite any attempt you may have made to rethink it. More than likely, the gay and lesbian client is also having difficulty defining and implementing separation from heteronorms.

SS: And the motivation for a gay or lesbian couple choosing a gay or lesbian therapist is equally significant. With some gay clients, I find myself in an ironic position. One gay man, for instance, who was just coming out, chose me as his therapist because I am known as an authority on gay issues. He then proceeded to dismiss my point of view because I am gay. He had, of course, internalized the dominant culture's view and rendered us both unworthy members of the same club.

On coming out to the family and to the gay community . . .

GW: Also, I was thinking about the advantages of being a heterosexual therapist with gay men who are in the early stages of sorting out gay issues. I've never been sought out by a lesbian who is in the process of beginning to deal with gay identity. Gay male clients often come to me in the first stages of coming out as gay men. I think that it's often too threatening at that point to go to a gay therapist.

SS: You and I, in fact, have exchanged cases at various points when you have worked with someone in those stages and referred them to me at a later stage.

GW: I have referred people to you whom I saw in the first stages of their beginning to come to terms with being gay. Jason, whom we mentioned earlier, was having tremendous difficulties even considering that he was gay, although, as I later found out, he had a much more extensive gay experience than he revealed. Although it was clear to me that his sexual orientation was toward men, his longing was to be in a straight relationship. He had a girlfriend whom he had loved and comforted after his mother's death, almost as an older sister. In the beginning of our work together he insisted that their sexual life was "good" but, at the same time, he carried on a series of simultaneous secret relationships with men who he said were exciting but not emotionally important to him. When his girlfriend came in for a session, she made it clear that, for Jason, sex with her seemed to be a chore, not something naturally erotic in him.

It was very hard for Jason to begin to deal with defining himself as a gay man. For many hours of our work, he was a client who could come in and put me to sleep. I liked him a lot, but it took a lot of coffee to stay awake and remain connected to him. Jason had a curious deadness due, I think, to this terrible suppression of who he was. But at a certain point in the treatment, I was able to suggest his having a consultation with a gay therapist. At first he was hesitant; he was very attached to me, a little like a child who found our sessions an area of safety, so I was very gentle and tentative about the transfer, leaving the door wide open for him to come back to me and knowing he never would. I think if I had suggested it toward the beginning of the therapy, he would have been too fearful to have accepted my suggestion. I saw Jason in a restaurant a few months ago after a year of work with you and he seemed more alive.

SS: When he first came to consult me, I felt enormously encouraged that he had already made the cognitive shift necessary to include himself in the category "homosexual," as a result of your having recast many of the negative connotations. He was just beginning to try on a homosexual identity but not quite ready to fully explore and experiment. I remember feeling excited by both his reluctance and anticipation.

GW: So, he can talk about the awakening part of himself, whereas with me he has to talk about the part of himself that is most dead and is not yet ready to acknowledge the birth of a new life in himself.

SS: Right. With my encouragement, he began to explore, sexually experiment, and then examine his emotional and sexual experience in a way that was unfamiliar to him. And he felt safe taking those risks, since he knew I had overcome them myself. I also connected him with people and places in the gay community that might have otherwise been unavailable to him. The combination of these social and sexual affiliations, with people for whom he had positive regard, served as a positive counterpoint to the stereotypical images he had internalized about gay men.

GW: When he came to me, he certainly said, "I don't want to live that life; I want to have a life with a family. I see older gay men, and I find it horrible. I'm perfectly capable of being with a woman."

SS: And that's the narrative that many gay men have accepted. Contact and association with the gay and lesbian subculture starts to heal some of the developing gay man's damaged self and provides him with positive images and role models. This helps him to see possibilities for a successful future. When I first met this young man, he was very conscious of the losses he might suffer, real or imagined. He understood that he would have to relinquish the safety of a heterosexual identity and consequently give up those guideposts that guaranteed a future as a successful member of the heterosexual community, including the respected role of husband and father. But if marriage and family were not in his future, then what was? What would give his life form and structure if he took a path contrary to his upbringing? I was able to offer my own experience, as a gay father, partner, and professional to help dispel the myths. Gradually, he defined new values and standards for himself along with a new sexual self and social identity.

On the strategies of silence and secrecy . . .

GW: The stasis that he was in about his own sexuality also was reflected in everything else in his life. He could not move out of a job that provided a kind of surrogate family, a job not commensurate with his intelligence or capacities. He could not move in any direction, leave his girlfriend, leave any of the three men he saw secretly, or confront his father. It was as though he was frozen. The deadness pervaded his life. A major issue—and maybe more for me as a heterosexual therapist than for you—is the issue of secrecy. Jason had four relationships going simultaneously, all of which were secret from each other. I sensed that the secrecy of these relationships and the secrecy of not coming out were similar.

SS: Absolutely.

GW: I've had two other clients for whom their secretiveness was the presenting problem for their partner in a relationship. Both men had neither come out to their families of origin nor were really out in the gay world. I don't think they were actually betraying their partner sexually, but they always acted as though the partner were the FBI, and they would hide the most innocent meetings with friends, which drove the partner to a frenzy of possessiveness. Possessiveness is of course the bedfellow of secrecy. For gay men, possessiveness can be heightened because gay relationships are so fragile and precarious in the face of societal sanctions against having an intimate relationship with another man. And the intensity of the need to possess and be possessed is also understandable in that, for the gay person, a sense of belonging has been so fragile since childhood.

SS: For a gay child, safety is an illusion. Most gay children learn to be secretive very early on, because it doesn't take long for them to know that acknowledging their differentness could bring great pain to themselves and their families. Alienation and rejection replace the sense of protection, comfort, and belonging to which childhood ought to entitle them. The gay child cannot rely on the protective context of "us" and "them." Instead of further alienating the heterosexual world, most gay children isolate themselves. They occupy themselves and find comfort in solo activities. They develop an apparatus for independence and a talent for secrecy, because they really cannot trust anybody. Secrecy, as an adaptive strategy, remains a part of most gay and lesbian repertoires. They learn to tiptoe with excruciating care through environments that could turn viciously hostile with one indiscreet gesture. The real losses and rejections that are the consequences of remaining out will continue to occur, and often that secret life is a highly creative experience. But it is an apparatus that I think continues long after men have come out and accepted themselves. It is in their repertoire to know how to do that.

GW: To be secretive even when you don't have to be secretive?

SS: Yes. Being secretive represents a sanctuary.

GW: You know, what you have said is very helpful. The very secrecy that affords sanctuary against homophobic punishment frequently permeates a gay relationship and is supported by the belief that authenticity *will* be greeted with punishment. Gay men grow up forced to keep everything that is precious about themselves secret, thus confusing what is valued with what is the subject of shame and disavowal. The effects of this growing-up experience are ingrained and long-lasting. One man said that, as he revealed something about himself, he would scan his partner for the effect of his revelation. The moment the other person was about to answer, he could feel himself withdrawing, every inch of his body filled with defensiveness and silence, expecting punishment for any act that revealed his authentic experience. It was reflexive—in his muscles. He longed for an authentically honest relationship, but of course his reflexive behavior was not conducive to trust and dialogue, nor was he in fact trained to be comfortable with intimacy.

SS: And that is not an easy thing to unlearn, even, as you're suggesting, when he has created a family and social circle that supports him. Secrecy has served him well, despite the fact that it has contributed to his sense of isolation and alienation and possibly caused him anxiety, depression, or the feeling of being an imposter. And even though he may be ready to confront and admit these costs, daily life regularly presents opportunities to choose to remain secretive. Work and personal situations still exist in which open homosexuality brings condemnation or legal consequences. Disclosure might cause the loss of a job, home, or even a child. Staying on the path of authenticity and honesty feels threatening in a society that has a national policy of "Don't ask, don't tell." So it's no surprise that secrecy would also appear as a central theme in gay relationships. Imagine the possible combinations of secrets and reactions among two people with such well-developed talents.

GW: It is very hard for a straight therapist who doesn't have that experience to not define secrecy in a relationship as a relationship issue. As a therapist, I think you can get past raw, brutal homophobia and be a sympathetic, caring, compassionate straight therapist who feels politically and personally that people have a right to love in whatever form it comes, in whatever form it takes for them. But I think these nuances that fly in the face of our learned hetero-family-therapy formulations (which lie less than innocently beneath even the most benign narrative questions—Foucault notwithstanding) are hard to grasp. We have learned to understand secrecy, for example, as a coalition, as a refusal to fully give yourself to this relationship, as family loyalty, or as difficulties with intimacy. It may have a totally different experiential origin and meaning for gay men; so it needs to be thought about in different terms—it's that minute by minute learning that's very hard. Even narrative inquiry can be stymied by the chance that one member of the couple will give it a heterosexual meaning, that is, secrecy in a relationship is a comment on the failure of the relationship, rather than a developmental stage, because that's what the heterosexual world will say about secrecy in a relationship. Straights are not confronted on a daily basis with what it means to be honest and what it means to lie, which is not to say that straight relationships are any more honest and open. It is just that we are less aware of honesty as a central issue.

Honesty seems less of an issue for lesbian couples. Unlike men, for whom connectedness and intimate relationships are discouraged in behalf of autonomy and performance, women develop a sense of self-in-connection and an ability to focus on deconstructing relationships. As a result, within the relationship world of women, in behalf of intimacy there is a sharing of secrets. In fact, often problems arise because partners become trapped in an obsessive deconstruction of the nuances of the meaning of relationship behaviors. Such deconstructions may have multiple meanings. They can be understood as an attempt to identify differences, a push to create space as selves merge and vanish into each other. When secrecy occurs, a partner may be attempting to institute boundaries, a move that is experienced by the other as a betrayal of the rules of intimacy. Deconstructing conversations may also be a defense against a feared rupture of connection because, when all is said and done, lesbian partnerships exist in a world hostile to their existence and one that constantly induces in the person a sense of "wrongness." Just as gay men feel that they are perceived as not being masculine, lesbian women feel that they are perceived as falling short of the feminine ideal of what a good girl should be and do. However, although there may be great intimacy in the relationship, many lesbians have to keep the relationship secret from the larger society or the family of origin; but this secrecy can rupture crucial relationships. As one woman said, "Being a lesbian has cost me the intimate relationship with my mother that was at the heart of my emotional life. Because I cannot tell her about my life and my partnership with Janet, our conversations are trivial. We no longer know each other." For this couple, the need to keep their relationship secret from the family of origin connotes shame and difference, which in turn infects central areas of their relationship with each other. When asked if either partner wanted to bear a child and have a family together, both said a passionate yes. Each had sensual fantasies of their partner pregnant. Both longed for children. Neither had shared these secrets with the other. The perceived need for public secrecy about a prohibited relationship prevented them not only from exploring this very natural desire but from sharing it with each other. Each partner said that she had silenced her longing out of pain and the internal shame that made her feel that childlessness was the price she must pay for transgressing heteronorms.

You speak of the need for straight therapists to keep open the discourse on homosexuality and the practices of homophobia as they operate on the relationship and being wary of not imposing heteronorms. Secrecy is a good example of an area that has specific resonances for gay people. Gay sexuality provides an even greater arena of experiences whose meanings can be misunderstood and subverted by heterotherapists, especially in this era of AIDS and its attendant fear that anal sex is dangerous and even evil.

SS: Exactly. There are many misinterpretations about gay sex. What does it mean, for instance, to a gay man to receive anal penetration?

GW: The culmination: "If I do this, this confirms my most secret and feared desire. If indeed I realize that desire, then I have given myself to this."

SS: And in terms of relationships—especially in familial relationships—that perhaps also is a complete disavowal of loyalty to heterosexual parents—fathers. The act of homosexuality is an act of disloyalty in most families. It is a mark of separation, of distinction, and gay sex is so fully loaded with these betrayals that I think it's hard for a nongay therapist to understand.

On sex and gender roles. Who's on top?

GW: Also, many cultures, like Latino culture, make definitions of gay and straight based on whether or not you are a recipient or a penetrating partner. If you are on this side of the fence, you are hetero, you are just enjoying sexually dominating a male. If you are on the "feminized," bad side of the fence . . .

SS: You betray masculinity, you betray maleness, you betray your father, you betray your culture.

GW: The mythology of the penetrated partner as the female partner. When I first started to see gay couples in the AIDS project, I think I was very concerned with roles. I saw them as quite fixed—who's the top, who's the bottom. I shared a hetero-distortion that gay people had to assume hetero roles in relationships—one of each—a husband and a wife. I remember my gay couples correcting me, "Well, sometimes I'm on the top; sometimes he's on the top." I always looked secretly for these arrangements as if I would have a better handle on the role structure of a relationship if I could figure it out. Most gay couples I see play multiple roles in their relationships.

SS: And I think that tends to be the more common pattern. Most of the men I've interviewed performed roles with flexibility and versatility during the course of their lifetimes. Few had committed to any one fixed position. It's interesting to examine the difference in how we might work with the concept of fixed roles as they appear in gay relationships. From my point of view, the fixing of either sexual or social roles represents a heteronormative limitation that is often the source of an individual or relational impasse, even when it achieves a working balance. I believe it's necessary for therapists to examine such impasses in light of the heterosexist constructs that maintain them.

GW: But some men do say that in a gay relationship, they are free to enact a more traditionally female role, which they find both reparative and comforting in that they have permission to be taken care of, as women do in traditional, patriarchal, heterosexual relationships. I wonder if role fluidity is necessary if you find a place where you are profoundly gratified and healed. Isn't it also possible that some gay relationships are influenced by the longing to reproduce the fixed roles inherent in traditional heterostructures?

SS: I think that's an interesting question. I believe that if there is a gay sensibility, it's one that encourages variety, versatility, and fluidity. Deprived of convention, we gays and lesbians create our own road maps to navigate the obstacles and challenges placed before us by a hostile society. In doing so, without encouragement from role models and families, we repeatedly invent original solutions to life's dilemmas. Becoming homosexual requires a good deal of unlearning of values, standards, and beliefs, and creativity is the currency for that survival.

On border crossings and bisexuality . . .

GW: I'd like to revisit with you the issue of bisexuality, because I think it is a sensitive and confusing area for both gay and straight therapists. Two former clients, who seemed to have successfully resolved their issues about sexual orientation, recently returned to treatment because heterosexual attractions had thrown their lives into confusion. I worked with Michael some years ago when he was coming out as a gay man. Now he returns to see me in the midst of a struggle to understand his new-found erotic attraction to women. Michael grew up in an ethnic, Catholic community in which—as the artistic, sensitive kid—he had always felt different, as gay kids feel different. As you might expect, he had a difficult relationship with his father, a traditional, sports-loving male who thought Michael a kind of sissy. Michael was a good runner, but his father wanted red meat sports, namely football, which Michael did not like. Until he went away to college and had his first gay experience, he hadn't allowed himself to know that he was attracted to men. He just felt ashamed and different. College was a time of tremendous pain and conflict about his emerging homosexuality and, shortly after college, he had his first serious relationship, in this case with an older man. He loved the feeling of being taken care of by a man who appreciated rather than scorned him, but after a while he wanted to move on. His lover took his revenge by calling Michael's parents to reveal their son's homosexuality. His parents reacted with less upset than Michael expected but assumed that this was a phase that would pass. Michael's traditional upbringing made him horrified that he was having a relationship with a man. Subsequently, he became involved in a series of platonic relationships with women and sought therapy. Through our work, he came to believe that authenticity was profoundly important to him and that somehow he must struggle to be honest with himself about his sexual orientation. He stopped dating women, although he kept women as intimate friends. He entered the gay world, built a gay friendship network, and explored his sexuality. He came back to me for couples therapy with a man his own age, a very needy, vulnerable man who adored him. It was a very difficult, turbulent relationship and they broke up, but he continued to pursue a rich life as a gay man and began to be more open with his family about his sexuality.

Four years later, he comes in to see me saying, "I have three relationships. The person I'm most erotically attracted to is a woman. I have another relationship with a man, which is emotionally important and one with a woman, which is not erotic but spiritual. But it is the erotic relationship with the woman that I want." And I'm sitting there stunned because he had been so clear about his gay sexual orientation.

SS: Did you ask what he meant by erotic attraction?

GW: He has terrific sex with her. It feels intense, passionate. He has never been able to do that with a woman before. That's what he has always wanted in his life. It should be added that, because she is a foreigner who only comes here for monthly business trips, they don't see each other all that much. Michael says that he wants a family and kids in the straight traditional sense, and he could have that with her.

Now, I think it is significant that his involvement in this relationship occurs simultaneously with his beginning a new relationship with a man, one he feels has depth and substance. In many ways, while it is not as hot as the last relationship, it is the healthy gay relationship he has dreamed of.

And then there is Pierre, whom I actually tried to send to you many years ago. He works with me in treatment, comes out to his family, joins a very, very gay community partly on Fire Island and partly here and has had many gay relationships. He grew up in a profoundly dysfunctional family in which he was verbally and physically abused. Rather expectedly, he has difficulty with relationships but not with gay sex. And he comes back to see me because he too has fallen in love with a woman, and his life has turned upside down. Like Michael, his heterosexual relationship is long distance but passionate.

And then that very day another gay man from Pierre's circle came in for a session and in passing said, "Did you hear that Pierre is being described as one of France's most eligible bachelors, and we all know what a joke it is because he's gay?" And I'm sitting there thinking, "But wait a minute, three hours ago Pierre told me his whole life has turned upside down again because he's fallen in love with this woman, so indeed he does qualify as one of France's most eligible bachelors!"

SS: So what do you make of it?

GW: This raises the whole issue of fluidity and performance of sexual roles. Both Michael and Pierre have fully accepted themselves as gay men, although both have areas of concealment as most gay people do—but not from friends or family. They had not previously been erotically attracted to women. I have had bisexual male clients who have talked about having passionate, hot, sexual relationships with women, having similar relationships with men, and then, for many reasons, self-identifying as gay. It's a community that they feel more comfortable in, an identity that feels more congruent, relationships that feel more loving and satisfying than heterosexual relationships. Sometimes, the gay relationship is not as erotic as the hetero relationship, but politically and personally, being gay is the self-identification they want. The two men I have described have always had their primary erotic relationships with men. Quite suddenly, they find that they are equally erotically attracted to women. Does the promise of heterocongruence or return to the familiar world inflame the promise of a straight relationship? Or do many of us have the capacity for fluid erotic attractions? Which, of course, brings into question the idea that one must find one's "essential" self. The social constructionists, by contrast, imply that sexual identity is fluid and is or can be constructed and reconstructed in varying contexts. For them, defining a sexual identity is a narrative choice, not a biological given.

As for my clients, do you see the desire to be straight as influencing these attractions? And, if so, is there a cost that will ultimately make the situation unbearable? Is this eroticized and powerful sexual relationship with a woman going to be durable? Can it last over time with no more or less discomfort than any long-term relationship? Or is the longing for that missing part of the self—the self in relation to men—going to reemerge and make the relationship unbearable?. They both feel that they can bring this puzzle to me, but I am more puzzled than they!

SS: Right. I've had a few cases of men and women who, after expressing their homosexuality through a series of sexual and affiliative experiences, show erotic interest in the opposite sex. In some cases, an interest in heterosexuality functioned as a temporary retreat from the difficulties of being an outsider. In others, the act of transgressing sexual boundaries—crossing from hetero to homo—has become part of the psychic repertoire. My approach is to encourage all erotic exploration as a method of self-discovery. I think one often understands the meaning of his desire after having expressed it.

GW: But it also speaks to the political issues. Once you cross the border, then you are in the other country and you can't go back. First you feel terrified because you have made this crossing, but then you begin to feel safe, guarded by the new community. If you recross the borders, the original land becomes dangerous because now you bear the secret of your defection.

SS: What are borders about? One thing borders are about is protecting people from danger.

GW: Going back to the joke on the other person who comes in and says, "Isn't it ironic that Pierre is considered such an eligible bachelor?" and I'm thinking, "You don't know how ironic it is. You think it's ironic because he's gay-identified, but I know that it's ironic because he is really trying to work out his erotic attraction to women." Now Pierre has another secret to keep, that of his emerging erotic attraction to women, just as he's had to keep the secret of his gayness for years (and probably still does from this female partner).

SS: This does raise the question of identity politics. The women's movement has set the example for the gay movement. Many gays and lesbians value the idea of gays identifying themselves, in the same way that it was important for women to identify as feminists. A lesbian or gay man who has sexual relations with the opposite sex may be viewed as someone who weakens the cause. But some leaders suggest that this form of identity politics is too limiting and are pressing to form coalitions that unite all "queer" groups—gays, lesbians, bisexuals, and transgendered and queer heterosexuals. The community is deeply divided over this.

GW: But can you allow an openness, if solidarity in a political community in a hostile external world is not necessary for survival? Both men are frightened of losing their hard-won gay families of friends, fearful that they will be thought of as defectors, people who didn't have the courage to stay the course and have capitulated to dominant social norms.

SS: They have attained exactly the same position they have always maintained by once again casting themselves in the role of the outsider. They protect their differentness.

GW: Both men came back to see me, having felt very good about our earlier work but now feeling very puzzled. They thought they had resolved their feelings about being gay, and now they experience this contradictory erotic urge. Is it longing to be included in the dominant society that still inflames this, or are they people for whom sexual orientation has a great degree of fluidity? But then neither man experienced earlier heterosexual erotic attraction—which is the more usual bisexual pattern.

SS: Or is it an attempt to re-create the position of outsider, which perpetuates a coherent and stable identity? In his case, what seems relevant is how he uses erotic desire to accomplish a continuous state of alienation and separation.

GW: Your take is different from mine, and I think this reflects our experience as gay and straight therapists. It is a dangerous journey for all concerned. There are political dangers for Michael and Pierre—the pain of losing their first experience of family, friendship, and community. A community endangered feels it can't afford defectors. My anxiety is that if these men choose straight relationships, I will be seen as encouraging heterosexuality. I have to be careful that I am not prematurely closed to their exploration of the heterosexual experience. If I get outside of the politics, I can explore your perception that Michael and Pierre need to maintain this fundamental identity as outsiders with secrets.

SS: Well, I would do what you and I are doing right now—initiate a dialogue about the importance of their remaining outsiders along with discussing the consequences of what too much connectedness to family, friends, or community might arouse. Would they feel trapped? Would they feel as if they could not live creatively? Do they fear losing their differentness? Their fear of losing friends or of being rejected by the gay community may be a real one. On the other hand, fearing loss and rejection and betrayal have been part of their psychological framework since childhood.

GW: I think those issues are very powerful.

SS: Loss, rejection, and betrayal are extremely provocative issues. Some gays and lesbians empower themselves by remaining outsiders. As a gay therapist, I might have an attraction to that idea that a heterosexual therapist might not.

GW: But the paradox of that, of course, is that if indeed either man marries a woman, he's back in the insider position, except that because he has lived a part of his life as a gay man, he will always know he is an outsider.

SS: And perhaps he will find yet another inventive way to enact or perform that.

GW: But he still will have to carry around the secrecy from everyone he speaks to out of his gay life.

SS: But that's what outsiders do to protect themselves. To survive they need to carry the secret.

GW: But the secret is very painful and burdensome. Let's assume for argument's sake that he decides to marry her and have a family with her. He's always carrying that secret, for the rest of his life. It's a shameful secret, so he is back where he started from. And yet the ambiguities are tremendous. Is he there because in the end he couldn't tolerate being an outsider, or is he there because he couldn't tolerate the insiderness of his gay life? He's an outsider with her because he carries the secret of his other life, and yet he's an outsider with gay friends because he has had to give up that life. Certainly, she would demand that he not have contact with that world. There's no solution. The moment he becomes a gay insider he seeks an opportunity to reexplore his heterosexuality.

SS: I wonder how he would respond to the idea of honoring his need to remain outside by shifting erotic attractions and creating secrets around them.

GW: As a gay man, he maintained his outsiderness by being extremely secretive in erotic relationships, but he is drawn to becoming heterosexual because he wants to have a family.

SS: He wants to have a heterosexual family.

GW: It is important to him to have biological children and raise them in a conventional way.

SS: Well, he can still do that as a gay man. But he wants, or you think he wants, a traditional, heterosexual family, because he could certainly find a lesbian with whom he could conceive and raise a child.

GW: Having a conventional family is a very strong pull. He wants to take his kid swimming, and he wants to be there at night when the child goes to bed.

SS: Well, he can do all that as a gay man, but what you mean is that he wants a wife with him to do that. Because he could certainly do that with a man.

GW: He could, but with some difficulty. And there are other stresses in gay life that he wants to be free of. Isn't there always a longing in gay young men not to have to deal with this world of political and health danger, and a world of tragedy and loss as well as of carnival and joy? We are living in a right-wing America, which is placing antigay statutes on the books, and there is the constant threat of violence. Eighty percent of gay men have experienced it.

SS: What are the implications of this for therapy? How do that secrecy and fear become part of each client's experience, and what are the manifestations of that in a relationship? Whereas the act of heterosexual coupling offers legally sanctioned support, gay coupling increases the opportunity for risk. Becoming a couple makes public what could have otherwise been kept private. This undeniable confirmation of one's identity arouses anxiety and fear for some. Some men in the early stages of identity formation reject attachments, fearing that a relationship will confirm their homosexuality and increase their visibility. While attachments offer refuge for some, they invite danger for others. Also important in the treatment of gay relationships is recognizing that unique conflicts arise when partners are in different stages of development. One may be celebrating his identity and be publicly out, while the other may be still struggling to define new values and standards.

GW: It's hard for both partners to be at the same stage. I know you haven't felt that emotionally you were in the same place as your lover.

On gay identity and couple relationships . . .

SS: Not in any way. My personal experience offers a good example. Five years into my partnership with Joey, the distance we had been experiencing began to express itself sexually, with his increasing lack of interest. I found myself at forty-four in a relationship in which sex was rapidly diminishing, after having spent enormous energy, struggle, and risk to claim my homosexuality after a lifetime of repression. For Joey, who had come out at fourteen, sex was much more matter-of-fact. He had already progressed sexually, which had given sex a less urgent perspective. I, having come out at thirty-eight, was not willing to settle for the remaining part of my life without frequent sex. The difference mattered a great deal.

GW: One of the things your work has clarified for me is this issue of stage difference. In one lesbian couple I treated, Mary had been out as a teenager, living through the pre-Stonewall years. She had created a gay family of choice, rich in friendships, and was passionately committed to gay rights. She was militantly out. I say this because this strong, gay persona is in such contrast to her wounded self, which still mourns for a place in a society that she knows will never accept her. Then she meets Jane, who has been married and now has adult children. Mary, like many lesbian women of her generation, never felt legitimatized to have the children she longed for, probably because of her own internalized homophobia magnified by society's censure. Ironically, her relationship with Jane intensified deep feelings that she was not entitled to her own world, her own existence. Because she is a good and just person, she struggles to overcome her resentment of Jane's attachment to her children. But that relationship represents Jane's entitlement to cross back and forth from that privileged world to her lesbian relationship, as well as being a constant reminder of the pain because she cannot. I think your idea that you can never really escape from that feeling, that society keeps hammering home, that there is something defective about you that makes you less than the person who has led more of an insider's life. This seems the case, even though you are into gay pride, you go to every march, you have a family of lesbian friends—you never escape from that internal feeling that there is something wrong. Mary told me, "You know, there's only one holiday in the year that is absolutely sacred to me and that is Gay Pride Day. If I didn't have that, I would be overrun by all these other holidays that become celebrations of the heterosexual experience." Jane, of course, says, "I have to spend holidays with biological family." Mary feels this terrible anxiety because she doesn't have any of that. And then she fights that feeling. And then that fight gets into the relationship. It's not about holidays at all; it's about what it's like to be a person who doesn't feel a part of holidays. There's no way of escaping the insidious feeling of being defective, no matter how strong your gay pride. The tension is always there.

SS: And you live with a sense of betrayal—betrayal to your own family, to those traditions.

GW: I was not the daughter who brought home the daughter or the son.

SS: And that's no easy thing to forget or work through. That takes a lifetime of experience—the betrayal is present. You are not what your parents are. You are not heterosexual. And your relationships in the community are a constant reminder of that. I think one of the unique things about being gay versus other belonging to ethnic or racial marginalized groups is that when you are Black or Latino, your family is too.

GW: You share your cultural experience with your biological family.

SS: And when you are gay, you are likely to be the only gay member of your family.

GW: Or else you've seen what happens with other gay members of your family. One man said, "How can I come out? I saw what happened to my cousin Eddie!" Why would he come out to that family? They've torn everyone else apart who is gay.

On families of origin and families of choice . . .

SS: This leads to another interesting point. For heterosexuals, generally speaking, a supportive family is a given, a comforting and comfortable condition of life. Gays either cannot depend on their blood ties or legitimately fear losing them. In the absence of such assurances, the gay man or lesbian seeks and selects a new family, new concentric circles of family. They organize and establish their families through love, choice, and creativity. Familial ties emanate from trust rather than forced exclusivity. These families serve as more than partial substitutes for the family of origin. Psychological support and assistance play a big part in their existence. It's difficult for nongay therapists to appreciate the importance and strength of these bonds, since their own experience with friends tends to be peripheral to their nuclear families. For gay men or lesbians, the family of friends tends to be the nuclear family.

GW: I was thinking about that with Mary and Jane, both savvy, political, knowledgeable women. But Mary privileges Jane's family of origin and her children over her relationship with Jane, just as Jane had a more hetero attitude toward the boundaries of the couple and the definition of family. That is, grandparents and kin are family—the partner's lesbian family takes second place. Old lovers must be discarded according to hetero custom rather than included in the extended family network. When I asked Mary, "As a committed couple, why doesn't your lesbian family have the same weight as Jane's family when you plan holidays?" she seemed startled by the equivalence I had underlined. She said, "When I think of spending a holiday alone with Jane or asking her to share it with my lesbian friends, I immediately begin to think, "Being away from her children and family will be too painful for Jane. It's too important, too powerful. I have to defer to it." Of course one cannot separate cultural experience from psychological history. Mary was raised by a single mother who never validated any of her desires and to whom, in order to keep the peace and obtain a modicum of love, Mary always had to defer. This psychological history dovetailed with her feelings that, as a lesbian woman, she had less standing as a person than her partner, who had been married and had borne a child. Despite goodwill and political sophistication, holidays are nonnegotiable, because neither woman can escape the deeply ingrained heterobias. And, in addition, as a straight therapist it was hard for me to truly honor the equivalence of these two families.

SS: Nongay therapists would not necessarily see that equivalence. You're probably the exception. Routinely, I invite to therapy the members that gays and lesbians consider their family, in the way I would include a nongay person's family of origin. This circle constitutes the more significant family—men and women with whom they share dinners, celebrate holidays, lean on for support and nurturing, and with whom they may exchange financial support.

GW: I have to say with some shame that I have never extended that invitation unless the person was ill with AIDS—that was the family of necessity. Working in vivo with the family of choice is something I have not done.

SS: I'm curious about why you wouldn't, since you are so oriented that way. You don't give it the same value and meaning.

GW: I don't give it the same value and meaning. When she says, "I want to spend Thanksgiving with my lesbian friends," I don't say, "Who's in your family? Tell me about them. What are these relationships like?" It would be a statement of respect to have the same interest in learning about the lesbian family as I have in the family of origin. I think it's a habit—thinking about friendships as less important than family of origin. I believe in the importance of family of choice intellectually. I understand the intensity of Mary's feelings, but I don't take the next step. As a straight therapist working with gay and lesbian clients, you need to ask at every point, "Am I honoring that experience of the other person? Am I really understanding it? Am I really questioning it? Am I looking at it from inside my own lens? Are my behaviors congruent with my ideas?" It's hard to get outside of the heterosexist norms to really understand and learn from a community that has created customs and mores of great inventiveness and that really challenge stereotypical norms. For example, this discussion generates the questions, What is family? Why do we privilege blood ties over those who know us more deeply and have seen us through with greater compassion and understanding? Thinking about gay issues certainly has made me question the received values in which one is imprisoned, and I like to think I am freer because of that. But I also see that, despite my best intentions, therapy gets slanted toward the more heterosexually oriented partners, because their experience fits with mine. I see why Christmas is so important for Jane's lonely mother and father, but I don't fully recognize Mary's loneliness for her lesbian family.

SS: I think developmentally, though, based on my interviews, that the process of accepting one's homosexuality involves a stage of ghettoizing one's experience, drawing affirmation, building a sense of community, and moving from a feeling of acceptance to a feeling of pride. Most people whom I talked with expressed an experience like that, however short or long it was, and then talked about reconnecting to the heterosexual world from a position of power, entitlement, and strength. Most move beyond the ghetto. Some remain for a variety of reasons that have to do with survival and comfort and security.

And back to secrecy and the problem of authenticity . . .

SS: Some do not remain in a gay ghetto but still lead very secret lives. They may be out to gay men and their families but not out to the straight world. And almost every gay client speaks with pain and confusion of the areas of his life where it would be economically dangerous to be out. Ironically, entering a stable gay relationship forces all these painful issues to the surface. I remember one client who, earlier in life, had sexual relationships with women, telling me that at times he would experience overwhelming hatred for his gay lover because he loved him so much. Strategies of provoking fights and withholding affection failed to scare his lover away. As a result, he had to unequivocally accept the pain of acknowledging that there was no escape from his predominant sexual orientation and no choice about facing a series of decisions about how to accept and manage this socially stigmatized new identity in a homophobic world where his professional life depended on appearing to be straight. Could you talk about the impact of being forced or choosing to lead two totally different lives? You are out as a therapist, to the straight world. You have published books; you are known; nobody thinks of you as heterosexual any more.

SS: Even though I am out, there are many times during the course of every day when I must consciously choose how to disclose myself. Such constant honesty requires vigilance, but if I want to maintain a sense of authenticity and integrity, I cannot choose to masquerade. Heterosexuals never have to think about disclosing themselves in quite the same way. For gay men and lesbians, their survival in any given situation often depends on what choices they make around this secret. And I think that, unless you are gay, it's hard to appreciate that.

GW: For the gay person, secrecy becomes an adaptive defense against physical, legal, and psychological threats, which arise from the terror of gayness that permeates the heterosexual community.

SS: If, as an adaptive strategy, one has developed a facility for secrecy, it's often accompanied by an ability for detecting these strategies in others. A gay therapist is likely to be expert at reading such subtexts of secrecy, that is, those moments when the client is hiding or dissimulating.

GW: Do you mean that, as a gay therapist, you can be more probing about a client's statements?

SS: Potentially, there's a secret in every statement.

GW: It's important for heterosexual therapists to recognize that, for gay people, secrecy has deeply protective aspects and that it is omnipresent and may characterize the early phases of therapy. Jason's "deadness" really was associated with secrets he could neither tell himself fully nor me partially. I think I have learned from that. I am not sure I would be more probing, but I would be more patient with his need to disclose slowly. Therapists generally believe that secrets are very bad, but here they may be held on to as life-saving.

SS: I appreciate that as a gay therapist. I am both curious and want to know what the secret is, but I also respect it.

GW: Another issue I would like to speak about is the immense appeal, for the heterosexual therapist, of being gay and perhaps the danger of romanticizing gay experience. In some sense, the heterosexual may feel very constrained by the limits of heterosexual life. Both the terror and the appeal of the gay world is that it is so subversive. It turns everything upside down. Every erotic and gender performance fantasy that you've ever had and you haven't acted upon is being acted upon. I think the terror of gayness is that internally, all of us struggle to contain anarchic feelings. Gay sexual experience often pieces together elements of a person's being that have been disowned in behalf of societal mandates. Every heterosexual therapist has to acknowledge the anxiety that gay liberation from the constraining norms arouses. It's easy to relate to the pain of gay life, but I think it's harder and more frightening to look at its appeal. It's easy to be compassionate with the gay struggle, with the pain of a man's life in coming out. But I think the part that may be hardest for the heterosexual therapist is acknowledging that we'd really like to do that too, that is, explore our gay or lesbian feelings in their broadest definition. As heterosexuals, we are constrained by our willingness to settle for a life that provides a cocoon of acceptance, safety, and privilege. I, as a heterosexual, have not been as courageous as the gay client who is seeking my advice. I have not had to summon the courage to struggle to define who I am, to cross borders in behalf of authenticity, to examine and honor my erotic and loving feelings. And I think it's very easy to pity the other as a defense against the recognition that in some sense, what they are doing is much braver than what most therapists do. Or to put the other into a kind of heterosexual category of understanding, which obviates the need to look at the daring behind the breaking of taboos. No wonder so many artists are gay. They have the daring and fluidity to create outrageous new visions of what we can be. When I look at your book, it is an immensely brave, courageous journey. I think that the courage of being gay is often ignored.

The Second Conversation

GW: These conversations are enormously useful to me as a straight-identified therapist working with gay and lesbian couples. For example, our last talk helped me be more sensitive to pressures on relationships when partners are at different phases of exploration of their gayness or of coming out. Had you and I not talked, I would not have returned to a deeper exploration of Mary's feelings of illegitimacy or been as sensitive to the inequity of their arrangement. I doubt if I would have charted Mary's lesbian family of choice, because Mary herself downplayed the importance of those relationships—they weren't stuck together by platelets, if you like. In a subtle sense, I might not have helped Mary claim her right to a gay life but rather privileged the homophobic story.

On coming out to the family of origin . . .

SS: And that's supported by societal mandates and reinforced by injunctions against giving meaning and value to the creation of a family of choice.

GW: Jane told Mary, "I have always felt that what I was giving to you was a family. For instance, when you came to Thanksgiving, I was so moved by the fact that my father came up to you and said, "Mary, I missed you." At that point, Mary was able to say, "Yeah, but if I were a heterosexual partner, it wouldn't be that you were moved by the fact that your father said, 'I missed you.' Don't you understand that makes me feel even less legitimate, because it's as if he makes a concession to me and then I feel much more my outsiderness." These seemingly kind words, "I have to accept you and I've even come to like you," are deeply wounding to someone as vulnerable as Mary. I think she was more able to articulate her pain, because you and I had spoken, and I was sensitized to the nuances of hurt that I might have overlooked in a sentimental wish not to see the pain that I, as representative of a straight world, inflict.

SS: For heterosexuals, generally speaking, a supportive family is a given—at least on the basis of their assumed heterosexuality. Gays and lesbians either cannot depend on their blood ties or legitimately fear they cannot depend on them. Even in an ideal situation—if one exists—in families in which a gay member is completely and lovingly accepted, where his sexuality is no more an issue than his height or his hair color, he is still alone among family members with his feelings about who he is and where he fits into the larger society. He has no one in his family who feels quite the way he feels, and the knowledge sometimes makes him feel like a living paradox, desperately alone among people who love him. He cannot help but know that the members of his family felt a profound sense of loss upon their discovery of his being gay. His being—who he is—saddens his family. Even when a family evolves through a process of acceptance of a gay or lesbian member, they work themselves through the stages of loss and grief, as does the gay family member.

GW: I would like your ideas on how straight therapists could be sensitive and helpful to the gay person coming out to the straight family. While I have learned what the experience means from the descriptions of clients, I think it's hard for me to be fully sensitive to the nuances of pain.

SS: Over the years, I have become increasingly cautious about encouraging gays and lesbians to come out publicly. Too often, I have observed occasions in which the initial excitement of self-discovery has led to a premature disclosure in which the gay man or lesbian was not prepared for their family's reactions. The process of coming out starts with a self-awareness from which the person begins to tell a few people privately. As he progresses through developmental stages toward accepting his homosexuality, he accumulates the confidence and support necessary to present himself publicly. A premature public announcement, which is to say, a pseudo coming out, can easily lead to further humiliation. In most cases, gays and lesbians are dealing with so much negativity from the outside world that some amount of shame exists as part of their experience. Managing both their personal and public responses to feeling or being shamed should be part of the therapeutic preparation for coming out to family and friends. Coming out publicly should represent the culmination of dealing successfully with developmental issues.

GW: When one partner is out to her or his family and the partner is not, there often is a tremendous pressure for the other person to come out. John, for example, came out to his family when he was very young. In family sessions with me, he and his family of origin worked through many feelings about his being gay. Now he's in a relationship with Patrick, who is not out. John resents the fact that he cannot spend holidays with Patrick, who has to carry on this straight charade for fear that the family will find out. Patrick is openly gay with his friends, but his unreadiness to come out to his family creates tremendous tension in an otherwise loving relationship. As a result, John constantly pressures Patrick to reveal his gayness to at least one family member. I think what you're saying is that while Patrick may be clear about being gay, and he may be in an important gay relationship, he may not feel intact enough to go back into this most powerful arena—his family of origin.

SS: He can't go back and deal with his own and others' reactions. Although my parents knew the reasons for the break-up of my marriage, it took me a number of years to speak honestly and frankly with them about my homosexuality. Their first reaction to learning that I was gay was to distance themselves, though they had generally supported my decisions in most other situations. It wasn't until three years after my marriage had ended and I had gone through my first love affair that I developed the confidence to have a frank discussion with my parents. One morning, I sat down with them at their kitchen table and asked, "Why have you been so remote?" My mother took her time in responding. Finally, she said, "I guess we haven't been able to bear the guilt." So simple, and I had not focused on it. Like so many people, my parents not only saw my homosexuality in its worst light, as they had been taught, but they had also swallowed the popular psychological view of its origins, and now they were blaming themselves for having failed, for having been bad parents, fervently believing that if they had done something differently, I would have been heterosexual. I remember taking a deep breath and saying to them, "Mom and Dad, you did not do this. My homosexuality has nothing to do with the way you behaved toward me, although I must admit there was a time when I thought that myself." Then I added with pride, "But more important—you can't take the credit for it." They looked up and, after a brief pause, they laughed. After that moment, the mood in our lives seemed to begin to change.

GW: But you were in a place where you could do that and you had worked out all those issues.

SS: That's right. I could speak so confidently at that time only because I had moved beyond my own shame and guilt and was beginning to feel a sense of pride in the gay community.

GW: When we were working in the AIDS project, people with AIDS urgently wanted to reconcile with their families before they died. Frequently, our experience was that, when they went back home, even if we had worked hard on preparation, contacted gay-friendly family members who would support them, and so on, they got sicker. And that was true, even if the family had been reasonably accepting, because of the stress of dealing with the pain and the issues that were involved with coming out both as gay and as having AIDS. For me, that experience is always a reminder of the potential impact of such a painful experience on people who are already enormously vulnerable. But it's hard to resist the individual, relational, and community push to come out. In deference to the longing to reveal, which counterbalances the longing to conceal, I have experimented with identifying one family member who might be a transitional support. But there are dangers in the sense that any information in a family can spread like wildfire.

SS: There are always real and imagined dangers in dealing with homosexuality and coming out always has profound consequences.

GW: I think the things that might elude me are the more nuanced responses. I can anticipate the negative ones. I'm not sure that I can anticipate how a positive response can inflict subtle pain.

SS: Right. When a family member or friend says to a gay person upon disclosing his homosexuality, "I still love you," it generally means I love you despite your homosexuality.

GW: I think that what you are saying is that you have to be comfortable enough in yourself to be able to deal with the pain of that. Yet I don't know at what point a person is strong enough to challenge the implications of "I still love you."

SS: That point comes when one understands the experience of one's own shame and no longer surrenders to it, though one knows, at some level, that it will always exist with a certain amount of autonomy. That knowledge empowers the gay man or lesbian to consciously organize a response that is meaningful and relevant to any situation—whether to take a political position or to follow a calculated personal agenda.

GW: You have to have done a lot of work on yourself to get to a point at which you can both anticipate those responses and manage the responses that you have to them. You have to have found an internal acceptance that what you are doing is on balance more important for you than the pain you will have to endure— because you are not going to go through this without pain. I think heterosexual therapists often cast themselves in the role of the fellow-traveling, gay-friendly brother or sister and hope that the client's experience in talking to a sibling will be soothing. If one does work with gay or lesbian clients, I think one has some guilt for the pain that gay people experience at the hands of straight society, which results in denying that pain in any aspect of coming out is inevitable.

SS: Every time a gay person conceals his sexuality, he makes the choice to live inauthentically. Until he has consolidated his private and public selves which, for most, develop in increments, he lives the irony of publicly disavowing who he is, while simultaneously struggling to be himself.

GW: That inauthenticity isn't limited to your relationship with your family but becomes a pervasive practice of secretiveness that infects all intimate relationships. The habit of lying because truth is associated with pain and punishment isn't limited to truth-telling in relationship to the heterosexual world but becomes part of the expectation in any relationship, including your gay relationships. John's pressuring Patrick to come out to his family follows from his instinct that greater authenticity in the relationship with his family of origin would make a difference in their relationship as a couple. So, these are very difficult junctures that you have to live with.

SS: What matters most may not be that one partner has achieved greater authenticity but that each may be at different stages of acceptance, struggling with different developmental issues. It's generally this imbalance that creates misunderstandings.

Achieving greater authenticity may not be as essential to improving a couple's relationships as is an understanding of these developmental differences. On the other hand, handling the issue of my homosexuality with my daughter Alyssa, for example, set the pattern for extraordinary openness, but ours was a different kind of coupling. The marriage had ended two years earlier, and Alyssa, then eleven, had moved with her mother to San Francisco. On one of my early visits, I told her I had something important to tell her. I took a deep breath, and before I could exhale she said, "You're gay." "I'm gay," I said. "Do you know what that means?" I hadn't finished enunciating my words when I saw that she began to sob. "I knew somehow that you were," she said. "And yes, I know what it means. But putting it into words makes it, like, very real." I learned many years later when Alyssa was interviewed by a magazine on the subject of having a gay father that she felt glad that my being gay had taught her that she could be whoever she was. It had set an example for her. But she wished I had told her from the start. She said her father had made a decision to live his life honestly, and yet he did not express the decision honestly to her, and she was most angry at that. There would be no more secrets between us.

Heterosexual couple endings and gay beginnings . . .

GW: A conflict that often arises in therapy between the parent who comes out as a gay person and the heterosexual parent who has been left is over the gay parent's wish to disclose his gayness to the children in the interest of having an authentic relationship. Diana refused to allow her ex-husband Greg to inform their children of his homosexuality. Certainly, she is reacting to the pain, humiliation, and betrayal of her own experience as well as to her anxiety about how the children will be able to deal with secrecy or the stigma of revelation that a parent is gay. It is natural that parents should want to protect their children from pain, but the importance of the gay parent being able to form an authentic relationship with the child seems to me to override those concerns. I also believe that children deal much better with truth than with half-imagined truths. Even though it changed everything for your daughter, it meant that she could begin to come to terms with your experience, as well as hers of you as her father, and have an authentic understanding of why her family broke up. While the moment was extraordinarily painful, she had permission to put words to it, to talk with you about it, if she wanted to or not, to think about it, to deal with it, to work through the pain. I used to think that, as a straight therapist I would be persuasive in helping the straight partner work through these issues. Now, I think if I am sensitive to the gay partner's position, I am often categorized as gay-identified. Perhaps I am experienced by the straight partner as more abandoning, because the partner who has been left feels shaken in her sense of efficacy and identity and seeks confirmation when defensively demonizing her ex-partner and gayness. One woman whom I saw managed to drum up a great deal of literature that said that telling a child before they asked questions was destructive. Of course, children know what can be asked and what cannot, so they will almost never be the initiators.

SS: When homosexuality becomes the reason a marriage ends, the decision to move out and establish a gay identity tends not to be a straightforward negotiation but an involved process that sometimes requires moving back and forth, in and out of the marriage, reaching different levels of pain, dissatisfaction, and despondency on the one hand and desire and hope on the other. Each level seems to be achieved through a painful searching process, wherein the individual struggles to negotiate the larger world in his different and seemingly mutually exclusive roles as spouse, parent, and gay person. Complicating this process is the extent to which each spouse loved and protected the other. No doubt, the nongay partner will suffer feelings of anger and betrayal. She must contend with the possibility of years of duplicity and questions of her own complicity, while the gay partner wrestles with both the other's pain and the guilt and shame he feels for fooling or having tried to fool both of them. When a frank and open dialogue about the marital issues is absent, children may be encouraged to mediate the struggle; what and how to tell the children may become part of the conflict.

GW: Diana and Greg are at different stages in their preparedness for disclosure. Diana is still deeply wounded by the marriage and by the failure of her expectations, despite the fact that she was never passionately in love with Greg, and as a couple they had a limited sexual life. She wants to bury the issue of Greg's homosexuality for now. Greg's wish to reopen this issue in behalf of his relationship with his kids forces her to review her life choices. Her displaced rage at herself becomes transformed into a contempt for him and a refusal to allow him an honest relationship with his children.

SS: That's possible, but if she discloses her husband's homosexuality to their children, it also forces the question of who she is and why she was complicit so long. Fear and shame may be part of what restrains her.

GW: Are you implying that he has to tolerate the time it takes for her to work through her own feelings about him? And that as her therapist, my task is to help her understand that, since at some point the children are going to learn about this? And that it would be better if she were in a place where she could make some peace with what has happened to her?

SS: Yes, and that requires that she understand the complex nature of their marriage, her own sexuality, and the reason for her complicity. Most often, the gay partner does not create a perfect charade, and the women who marry them contribute to the conspiracy.

GW: His belief that he must reveal his homosexuality to the children was intensified by the fact that his teenage daughter was becoming symptomatic and had begun to make suicidal gestures. Since the break-up of the family, she had identified herself as his only protector, which created conflict with her mother at a point when she desperately needed both parents. Greg had become seriously ill as the family broke up. It was as though the stress of beginning to admit his sexual orientation was so great that it created a sort of autoimmune depletion, a weakening but nonspecific illness. In fact, only when he began to come out to friends did he begin to improve. His illness must have been terrifying for his daughter. There were signs that she guessed her Dad was gay and secretly worried that he had AIDS, but the parents' pact of secrecy prevented her from openly discussing her fears. Her suicide gestures were, in fact, the only language available to symbolically convey her fear and her helplessness regarding her father's potential death.

SS: And it may be as much about her mother's inauthenticity as it is about her father's.

GW: The mother's inauthenticity in not being able to deal with this issue, you mean. I haven't paid enough attention to how critical this issue is. The mother wants to escape and focuses on the ongoing crisis with the children, which buries the overarching issue that her husband's being gay caused the dissolution of the marriage. As I, too, focus on the moment-to-moment crises, which are much easier to deal with, I collaborate with her on "disappearing" the issue.

SS: That's probably how the family has been dealing with issues all along—they allow one family matter after another to distract them so that discussions of painful marital issues never take place. This family has years of experience concealing issues and emotions, and focusing on the moment-to-moment crisis may serve as an elaborate device for maintaining that pattern. My experience suggests that women married to gay men ignore the signals about their spouses' homosexuality as a way of staying in a relationship that meets their needs.

GW: I think she always knew, because there had been rumors that he was gay. Diane probably stayed in this relationship because she was terrified of being alone.

SS: And the decision to end the marriage did not begin as her choice. By coming to terms with his homosexuality, he violated their agreement to protect one another. In most cases, the other partner feels angry and betrayed, not only by the truth but also because the gay spouse made the decision to deal with it.

GW: As a straight therapist, I need to recognize that it must elicit countertransference anxiety in me, which keeps my focus away from this profound and central issue. It takes effort to look for the openings to keep it alive and on the table.

SS: In this case, it's important to respect the position of the wife and discourage the husband from telling the children until these other issues are more fully understood. Although it may postpone a more genuine relationship between the father and his children, the decision to come out to them for the wife must re-stimulate a feeling of losing control that she first experienced when her husband announced his homosexuality. Ironically, a nongay therapist might be more sympathetic with the husband's desire for authenticity and miss the importance of the wife's desire to maintain some control of a life that is slipping away. She may also worry about the questions the children might raise about who she is.

GW: I think you are right. He can be authentic with the children in other areas. As a straight therapist, I feel the unfairness of his not being able to speak, but if he could accept the need for silence until she works it through, it would strengthen their future relationship. He is entitled, however, to know that she is intent on working it through.

SS: And he should be able to respect the fact that his wife is entitled to the same period of self-exploration that he has given himself, if you remind him.

GW: I think she's far from doing that. For her, because she's heterosexual, that kind of self-discovery doesn't seem to have that urgency. In her mind, she fits the norm, she knows who she is, she's a heterosexual woman who got mixed up in this marriage with this man who is a little bit weird and they didn't have a good sex life. But she sees it as a flaw in him, not something that's a difficulty in her. The way she defends herself is to see him as wounded and damaged and she sees her role as to protect the children from his damagedness. Society agrees with her, so it is hard to keep the subject of her own identity open. Her defense system is hard to budge, since people experience her as the robust and righteous one. For her to look at her own woundedness would be turning upside down the dominant story of this family. Furthermore, her ex-husband sees her as powerful, angry, and bigger than life. In a way, he constructs her as heterosexual, oppressive America.

She is so big for him that he can't hold his own in a room with her. His only way of being able to deal with her is not to deal with her. He has really known that he was gay all his life but buried the knowledge in a fundamentalist Christian sect that arranged his marriage to her. So for him, she embodies many symbolic meanings—his capitulation to the oppressor, the wrath of homophobic America that he has spent a lifetime placating, a salvation that failed . . .

SS: When a marriage ends for reasons of homosexuality, there may come a time when the gay partner begins to perceive the marriage—which once functioned as a refuge—as an institution of oppression, and the ex-partner may been seen as the oppressor. In these situations, I offer an elaborate explanation of the ex-partner's woundedness, which generally facilitates compassion.

GW: It's important to rehumanize her for him, to make her smaller. Her anger has become the anger of the whole world, including his parents' anger if they had learned his true nature. His whole life has been running away from that anger and suddenly it's there.

SS: Like other oppressed groups, gays and lesbians have been demonized and some, consequently, become facile at demonizing others. Do unto others as others do unto you.

GW: You are right. He is demonizing her, and I need to discuss that with him. For this family, dealing with the fundamental issue of Greg's being gay has also been delayed by Diane's brief and destructive marriage with a macho, sexual, but wounded and disturbed man who expressed all the anger and hostility that Greg repressed. In retrospect, that relationship was a first attempt at repairing the damage to her self-concept that resulted from her marriage to Greg and his coming out to her. But because I allow the crises with the kids and those in the new relationship to dominate the therapy, we delay dealing with the core issue of Greg's sexual orientation and its effect on her. I can now see that, because I sense her pain, I collude with her in not dealing with it. I am interested in why it's so hard for me.

SS: For exactly the reasons you stated earlier. As a heterosexual person, society does not force you to ask the question, Who am I? A gay person has to justify his existence to himself and to the world every day.

GW: So, as non-gay-identified, I am not comfortable dealing with the questions his "homo" sexuality raises about her or my "hetero" sexuality? Transgressive border crossings make us realize the vulnerability of our own borders. In a sense, I am more at ease with the activity of "protecting" him against the pain of her anger and profoundly uneasy dealing with the underlying pain and confusion that her choice of a spouse arouses in both her and me.

SS: You identify with her as a heterosexual woman and therefore don't challenge her to consider who she was in this marriage and where she stands with her own life.

GW: I had an interesting case of a woman who consulted me about a marriage because her husband was involved in a serious relationship with a man. She did not know what to do. He did not want to leave the marriage and, furthermore, his practice as a prominent lawyer depended on his respectability. She married him knowing he was bisexual and had only a moderate sexual interest in her. She said that for both of them the need for an affiliative relationship in which each felt deeply understood was initially more important than the sexuality. They had lived with this, and she was content. Unfortunately for their marriage, his casual gay relationship turned to a passionate love that he wants to pursue. Although she still hoped he would stay, it was clear he was in the process of leaving. As they grappled with his wish to leave her for a man, her life of secrecy struck me as even more painful than his. At least he is in dialogue with other gays, many of whom have been through the same experience and who belong to the community he is entering. He has a gay friend who acts as a mentor to help him through the process. She can speak to no one because of shame and a wish to protect both of them from exposure in the straight world. She cannot acknowledge that she knew he had gay relationships before marriage, because people will never understand that her love for him made her disregard that. If he leaves, she probably will cover by saying that he is having an affair with another woman. But what remains for both of them, in a way that it usually does not for a straight couple who are separating, is their affection for each other. For at least the protagonist in a straight couple, having an affair that represents the end of the marriage also represents the end of attachment and love. In this experience, a fated difference in sexual orientation has intervened to end their marriage, but their affiliative love remains to haunt both of them.

SS: I think that in these marriages, because a couple protects each other so much, much is forgiven in the service of this protection. Fundamental issues of difference are not noticed.

The Third Conversation

On insiders and outsiders . . .

SS: Since we last talked, my thoughts have wandered back to Michael, the case you described earlier in which, despite his desire to belong, his behavior may have been driven by an opposing desire to maintain his position as an outsider—an experience that preserves the continuity of his history. It occurs to me that, for many gay men, the experience of becoming the outsider is intimately linked with a childhood experience of feeling different. Researchers have found that in childhood, whenever memories of homosexual proclivities reach back that far, there exists evidence of a preconscious awareness of a different sexual orientation, though no language yet exists for the child to describe it. The child himself feels different. It doesn't take long for him to begin to feel alienated or alone. His alienation from within then precipitates behavior on his part that may encourage alienation from without. The gay child may then separate himself or be isolated by his peers. Because he really can't count on anyone, he develops an apparatus for independence—he learns to occupy himself and find comfort in his differentness. This adaptive strategy, which served him so well during his childhood and youth, may later prevent him from belonging to a community that welcomes his membership. The desire to belong is opposed by an equal desire to preserve his separateness, which originated as a defense to manage the social consequences of his differentness. It might prove worthwhile to explore this question with Michael. How can he belong and simultaneously preserve his differentness?

GW: Inclusion is a major issue here. Although Michael has rich networks of gay friends, he still has difficulty feeling at home in an explicitly gay-identified community. Michael's dilemma of finding himself attracted to women as well as to a male lover raises a number of questions. Does Michael's recent attraction to women represent a fluidity of sexual orientation, which some people do experience? Is his questioning of his sexual orientation about maintaining his outsiderness? Does it represent a longing to be included in a straight world that would obviate the profound struggle he experiences over values? Michael feels a profound need to remain connected to meaningful aspects of his past and has joined a church, where a few confidantes know his sexual ambivalence but where he still has to hide any gay inclinations from the larger congregation. Of course, organized religions by and large reject homosexuality—especially the orthodox churches of most people's childhoods. So, at the heart of deeply spiritual gay people remains this painful empty space—a religious homelessness. Teasing out the answers to these questions involves patiently peeling layer upon layer of complexly nested feelings. I agree that outsiderness, a feeling of difference, is at the heart of Michael's identity, and yet he would describe his life search as one for inclusion, a search to become emotionally connected. But I think you're right, that the piece I haven't explored with him is his need to preserve difference.

SS: Speaking personally, when a situation arises in which a commitment to belong is required, my first instinct is to refuse. My reaction seems more a move to preserve my independence than a reaction to a fear of intimacy. As painful as not belonging can be, being an outsider allows differentness to go unchallenged.

GW: You are predicting that, as he experiences intimacy, he also will experience a longing to disrupt the connection in order to preserve outsiderness, or a sense of difference. For example, an experience of connecting to his gay lover might be followed by an attempt to reconnect to a woman. Exploring his need to preserve that sense of differentness, the outsider in him, may be helpful in deciphering these sexual oscillations. Certainly in his vague memories of himself as a child and adolescent, the sense of being different was the dominant and almost wordless experience. Other than that, he has almost no memory of any kind of dating experience from the age of twelve to college, when he first had an affair with a man. As a result, there is a part of him that hasn't really ever been young . . .

[*Editor's Note:* The conversation continued, revisiting developmental issues, exploring biological and constructionist views of homosexuality, and moving to larger political issues of sexuality and reproduction, now and in the future. Sadly, because of space limitations, we cannot include it here.]

Epilogue

Stanley, I want to share with you an epiphany that our work together helped Michael experience. In the spirit of our conversations, Michael's resolution is not meant to be normative, but it represents one man's courage to confront his life and the healing that followed. You remember that when I was puzzling, as Michael was, about the meaning of his bisexuality, you suggested that I ask him about his need to preserve his sense of outsiderness, which was such an essential part of his history and personality. Following your advice, I asked him to think about that over the holidays, which he was going to spend with his family of origin. In our first session after the New Year, he told me that he had decided to talk to his siblings about his homosexuality. He spoke to them of his experience of being gay and its meaning for over an hour. His parents were sitting on the other side of the room, in the shadows, so that he could not tell if they were listening or not. Quite suddenly, as he finished speaking, his mother came over to him, put her arms around him, and weeping said, "Whatever you do with your life, I only want you to do what will make you happy. That is all I have ever wanted for you." He was crying as he told me that he and his Mom had always had this silent river of connection, but she had never before come out of the shadows to speak to him of her feelings, most certainly because of her deference to her husband's values. Even in this small moment, one sees how Michael's courage to be honest about his sexuality gave his mother the courage to make a break with the indwelling laws of patriarchy that had defined and constrained her life. All Michael's life, he had longed for his mother to speak, but he too dared not break their silence. Instead, he searched vainly for other mothers who could give him what he longed for from her. Of course, he never really found them. "After she had done that," he said, "I felt somehow liberated in my relationships with women. I was strong enough to call the woman I had been seeing and tell her that I did not think I could be honestly as committed to a relationship with her as she deserved. Then I had the most profound experience of connection with the man I love. I knew in that moment with my family that I no longer could live a fragmented life."

As I think about what needs to be done, it is exactly that—the creation of connections through dialogue. Michael did not need any loan of courage to take the profoundly brave step of disclosing himself to his family. But I think it was the questions that you helped me ask that illuminated for him his deep training in being an outsider, disconnected from his family, his lover, and, in the end, from himself. As I write this to you, I have some more questions to ask, some thoughts to share with you. When can we get together to talk?

References

Siegel, S., & Lowe, E., Jr. (1994). *Uncharted lives: Understanding the life passages of gay men.* New York: Dutton.

Walker, G. (1991). *In the midst of winter: Systemic therapy with families, couples, and individuals with AIDS infection.* New York: Norton.

Walker, G. (1995). *In the midst of winter: Systemic therapy with individuals, couples, and families with AIDS infection,* rev. ed. New York: Norton.

CHAPTER THREE

SOCIAL POLICY AS A CONTEXT FOR LESBIAN AND GAY FAMILIES

The Political Is Personal

Ann Hartman

All Americans live within the context of social policies that shape their lives, define opportunities and limitations, establish rights and protections, and set out the rules and mutual responsibilities included in the social contract between citizens and the state.

Lesbians and gay men, as individuals or living as couples or in families, have a particularly complex and difficult relationship with the state and its various rules and procedures, a relationship that influences their experience on a daily basis. The years since the riot at the Stonewall bar in New York City have brought major changes in attitudes toward gay men and lesbians, and some important changes have taken place in the social policy arena. These changing attitudes and policy shifts, as well as the growing activism and visibility of some gays and lesbians, can lead those not immediately involved to think that the battle for equal rights and protection for gay men and lesbians is nearly won.

Unfortunately, although gains have been made, much remains to be accomplished. Lesbians and gay men continue to be marginalized, discriminated against, unprotected, and even punished in our society. They continue to be excluded from a variety of benefits and subjected to dramatic and subtle discriminatory policies and practices with very little opportunity for redress. Anyone who works with gay men and lesbians in clinical practice must be informed about the social policy context faced by their clients and be aware of its impact. Too often, "liberal" straight therapists underestimate the dangers and rejection faced by gay men and lesbians, pushing them to come out and characterizing their reluctance to do so as problematic, as internalized homophobia, as pathological.

In this chapter, I will explore the relationship between gay men and lesbians and social policy, with special attention to family policy issues. First, I will define family and social policy and show how family, social, and public policies interrelate, with particular attention to the civil rights of gay men and lesbians, the couple relationship, parenting and coparenting, and separation.

What Is Family Policy?

Family policy is a part of social policy, and social policy is in turn a part of public policy, which consists of the body of laws, regulations, statutes, executive orders, and programs that emanate from the various branches and levels of government. Public policy includes economic, military, social, and myriad other areas of policy about which the government takes collective action. The sources of public policy are many, including the Constitution and the Supreme Court, as well as all the other federal, state, and local courts, the various lawmaking bodies on every level, and the executive and administrative offices of federal, state, and local government. Public policy intentions and values are not only expressed in legislative enactments but also through the extent to, and manner in which, laws and regulations are actually implemented.

Social polices pertain particularly to the ordering of social relations, including the protection of civil rights, the distribution of social benefits, and the meeting of social need. Clearly, all areas of governmental action have some direct or indirect impact on social well-being, social structures, and the quality of life.

Included in social policies are those sometimes described as family policies, that is, policies explicitly or implicitly affecting or pertaining to some aspect of family life. Some policies can be clearly identified as family policies, such as the Family Leave Act; others include the various decisions and enactments around reproduction. Other policies affecting families may be embedded in education, military, labor, or other areas of policy and not recognized specifically as family policies. For example, the recent effort in Congress to enact a rider to the education bill disallowing funds to any school system that includes positive material about gay men and lesbians in its curricula would have created new family policy embedded in educational policy if it had succeeded. The "don't ask, don't tell" policy concerning gay men and lesbians in the military is another example of family policy that is not labeled as such. Obviously, in casting the net so widely, almost every government policy can be considered family policy. In this chapter, I will focus on policies, no matter where they are located, that have a crucial impact on gay and lesbian families.

Social policy also goes beyond the enactments at the various levels of government to include procedures and policies established in the private sector by businesses, educational institutions, and other private associations that have crucial social implications and may or may not be monitored and shaped by governmental force. The government's role in this situation is to prohibit discriminatory actions in the private sector and to protect the civil rights of individuals and groups. For example, civil rights, affirmative action, and fair employment practices legislation, as well as antidiscrimination legislation, establish how nongovernmental organizations may operate in some social realms and give legal recourse to those who have experienced injustice.

The Civil Rights of Gay Men and Lesbians

As I mentioned, the years since the Stonewall uprising have brought major changes in attitudes toward gay men and lesbians; these attitude changes have led to mixed results in the policy arena. Through arduous, lengthy, and expensive tests in the courts, discrimination has been challenged, and the civil rights of gay men and lesbians have been both supported and curtailed. The struggle for equal rights under the law has been at times encouraging and at other times fraught with failure and disappointment.

There has been an effort by gay rights advocates at both state and federal levels to include gay men and lesbians in antidiscrimination legislation to assure them redress when they meet with discrimination. Such legislation has been passed in eight states and over one hundred municipalities. A backlash against this effort is also mounting, as evidenced by the growing number of propositions prohibiting such protection that have been placed on the ballots or that are being developed in several states and communities. The infamous Proposition 2, passed by Colorado voters in 1992, is a case in point. This wide-sweeping amendment would prevent the state or any of its political subdivisions from adopting or enforcing laws or policies protecting lesbians, gay men, or bisexuals from public or private sector discrimination. Described by its supporters as an effort to make sure that gays and lesbians get no "special treatment," Proposition 2 makes it illegal to legislate against discrimination on the basis of sexual orientation. A permanent injunction against the enforcement of this proposition is currently in force. The Colorado courts found it to be in violation of the Constitution in that it denies these groups the fundamental right of political participation guaranteed by the First and the Fourteenth Amendments. The governor and attorney general announced their intention to appeal this decision before the United States Supreme Court. The Court heard the case in October 1995, and the decision is pending.

The history of a similar proposition in Cincinnati is particularly instructive, as it demonstrates how tortuous is the legal struggle for the protection of the civil rights of gay men and lesbians. The Cincinnati "Issue 3," an amendment to the city charter very similar to Colorado's Proposition 2, was passed by the voters of that city in 1993. An immediate temporary injunction against the enforcement of the proposition on the grounds that it violates the Constitution was made permanent following a trial in June 1994. The far-reaching opinion by U.S. District Court Judge Arthur Spiegel was hailed by gay rights advocates. The judge found Issue 3 to be unconstitutional because it denied gay men and lesbians the fundamental rights of equal access to the political process, free speech, freedom of association, and the right to petition the government. Judge Spiegel took the position that the Cincinnati amendment "does not demonstrate devotion to democracy . . . but rather makes a mockery of it" (Logue, 1994, p. 29).

Of even greater significance was the judge's opinion that sexual orientation is a "quasi-suspect classification," an issue that has provoked much of the conflict surrounding civil rights for gay men and lesbians. If a classification is defined as "suspect," any action that might be considered to discriminate against or unfairly limit the rights of the group included under that classification is subject to heightened scrutiny. In other words, discrimination is suspected, and an action or enactment will be very carefully evaluated on that basis. Under this classification, important and compelling governmental interests must be identified, or a law can be declared unconstitutional. Gay rights advocates have sought to have sexual orientation defined as a suspect classification, generally without success.

A suspect class must meet the following criteria:

1. Subjection to a long history of persecution for irrational reasons
2. Inability to obtain redress from the nonjudicial branches of the government
3. Immutability of the trait that characterizes the classification, which in turn makes it impossible or highly unlikely for its members to escape from the class

Race, for example, is a suspect classification. Thus, any action that uses race as a basis for treating members of that race differently from others is presumed to be invidious, discriminatory, and constitutionally prohibited, in violation of "equal treatment under the law." The criterion upon which the efforts to assign suspect classification to sexual orientation has foundered has been the requirement of immutability. If it becomes widely accepted, the increasingly popular claim that homosexuality is biologically or genetically based could strengthen the case for making sexual orientation a suspect classification.

Judge Spiegel, dealing very carefully with this sensitive issue, disagreed with jurists who had previously rejected other efforts to make sexual orientation a suspect classification on the basis that homosexuality is defined by conduct. He held that

> sexual orientation is set in place at a very early age and is involuntary and un-amenable to change. It is a deeply rooted complex of factors including predis-position toward affiliation or bonding with the opposite and/or the same sex. It is distinct from conduct. (Logue, 1994, p. 29)

Thus, Judge Spiegel held that sexual orientation is a quasi-suspect classifica-tion and rarely an appropriate basis for unequal legal treatment. This stunning victory, however, stimulated even more concerted efforts from the conservative far right, as a legal team headed by former Supreme Court nominee Robert Bork led the appeal of Spiegel's decisions, and Edwin Meese, former attorney general, spearheaded extensive fund-raising efforts. The higher court reversed every one of Judge Spiegel's rulings and upheld the constitutionality of Issue 3. The panel of judges denied that gay men and lesbians could be a class subject to discrimi-nation on the grounds that they could successfully conceal their orientation. Further, not only did the court strike down the lower court's finding that Issue 3 violated the First Amendment rights of gays and lesbians, but they added that the amendment was valid because it enhanced the freedom from association of those who do not want to associate with gay people. The inconsistency between the view that homosexuals can hide their orientation and that the amendment protects those who do not want to associate with gay men and lesbians seems not to have occurred to the court. It is similar to the military's view that heterosexual men will be more comfortable in the shower room if they do not know who in the room may be gay.

Gay rights advocates are now preparing to appeal the Cincinnati decision, which I have reported in some detail. I did so not only because the civil rights issue is critical to all lesbians and gay men and their families but because it demonstrates the arduous, expensive, unpredictable, and frequently heartbreaking task of at-tempting to change public policy—state by state and community by community.

As the 1996 elections approach, it is clear that antigay propositions will ap-pear on several ballots—propositions that have been carefully worded to avoid the language that made the earlier propositions vulnerable to constitutional challenge.

Criminalization of Same-Sex Sexual Contact

The other crucial and influential policy area that defines and threatens gay and les-bian individuals and families are laws criminalizing sexual contact between people of the same sex. This criminalization was supported and reinforced in the devastating Supreme Court decision in *Bowers v. Hardwick* (1986). This decision upheld the constitutionality of a Georgia antisodomy statute. The challenge to this statute was brought on the basis of the right to privacy, the same right protected in *Griswold v. State of Connecticut* (1965), which found a fundamental right to privacy in a married sexual union, and *Eisenstadt v. Baird* (1972), which extended that right to the individual in terms of procreative or nonprocreative sexual contact. The Supreme Court determined that the right to privacy did not extend to include individuals in same-sex sexual relationships.

Sodomy laws currently exist in over twenty states; their existence and the current refusal to strike them down leaves the door open for selective prosecution and encourages homophobic interest groups to pursue further discriminatory actions. Although state sodomy laws are rarely enforced, destructive use has been made of *Bowers v. Hardwick*. For example, its implied assumption of criminality has been cited to support discriminatory decisions in other venues, for instance in discrimination in the workplace and in denying gay and lesbian parents custody of their children. And, of course, the acceptance by courts of the criminalization of same-sex sexual contact defeats any effort to protect gay men and lesbians from discriminatory behavior. Clearly, people defined by criminal behavior will not be considered a suspect class.

Definition of the Family

A third central issue of particular concern to lesbian and gay families is the definition of the family embedded in policy. Among the broadest definitions is that of the Bureau of the Census, which defines the family as two or more people living together and related by blood, marriage, or adoption (Poverny & Finch, 1988). Even this fairly broad definition excludes gay and lesbian couples. The definition of the family is a crucial policy issue, as it defines which relationships are eligible for certain entitlements on the basis of being a family and which are excluded from certain advantages such as tax breaks, family leave, Social Security benefits, and myriad other public and private benefits. The lack of validation for and protection of gay and lesbian family relationships affects these families on a daily basis in ways that cannot be anticipated. This is true from the cradle to the grave—from custody issues for the coparent when a lesbian couple has a child, to artificial insemination, to issues around burial. For example, the town of Hempstead, New York, refused to allow two gay men who had shared their lives for more than twenty years to buy a cemetery plot with a shared headstone because the men were not related. After considerable advocacy by gay rights groups, the town has relented, but not without considerable pain and stress for the couple (Marks, 1994).

The extent to which our public policies and an endless range of entitlements and protections are family-based on every level of government is dramatically evidenced by the fact that in the *United States Code,* the term *family* appears no less than 2,086 times and appears in every area of governmental functioning. In the New York state statutes, the word *family* appears 2,149 times, and in California, 4,149 times (Robson, 1994). The definition of the family, as it appears in these public policies and rulings, is critical.

The tragic and widely publicized case of Sharon Kowalski and Karen Thompson dramatically demonstrates the lack of protection available to the lesbian or gay family relationship. In 1983, Sharon Kowalski, age twenty-seven, who had lived in a committed relationship with thirty-six-year-old Karen Thompson for almost four years, was in a head-on car collision with a drunk driver. Sharon suffered severe brain stem injury, losing both her mobility and her ability to speak. Karen worked very successfully with Sharon in her rehabilitation program but was forbidden any further contact with her by Sharon's parents, who were awarded sole custody of their daughter. The parents placed Sharon in a minimum care facility, where she was isolated from Karen and her friends. Her condition deteriorated markedly. Karen fought in the Minnesota courts to gain the right to visit Sharon, to intervene in her medical situation, and to bring her home, as Sharon repeatedly requested. After almost ten years, the family finally withdrew from the situation, and Sharon was able to return home, but not before she had suffered irreversible damage from years of isolation, neglect, and depression (Griscom, 1992). The issue was the definition of the family and the protection of family rights and authority. Finally, after ten years of litigation, the judge who allowed Sharon to return home stated that Karen and Sharon were a family of affinity that ought to be accorded respect (Benkov, 1994).

The Kowalski case underlines the importance of the recognition and support of gay and lesbian family relationships when a couple is faced with illness. Gay and lesbian couples have found little help through public policy or policy in the world of work. Health insurance, for example, is rarely available to same-sex domestic partners through employee benefit programs, and gay and lesbian partners are not eligible for family leave under the Family Leave Act. The devastating demands and effects of AIDS on couples have most dramatically demonstrated the precarious situations of gay couples in dealing with an overwhelming health crisis.

In the past few years, there has been some movement toward broadening the definition of the family. Perhaps most important has been the groundbreaking decision in *Braschi v. Stahl* in New York state's highest court. The court found in favor of the longtime partner of a man who had died; the partner wished to retain a lease on the rent-controlled apartment they had shared. As leases are only transferable to cohabiting family members, the court, in making this historic decision, stated that the government's proper definition of "family" should not "rest on fictitious legal distinctions or genetic history, but instead should find its foundation in the reality of family life" (LAMBDA, 1992, p. 5). The opinion in this case set forth the following criteria for determining family status: (1) degree of emotional commitment and interdependence (which includes such notions as that of an interwoven social life, holding yourself as a couple or family, thinking of yourself as a couple or family, and visiting each other's families of origin), (2) financial interdependence, (3) cohabitation, (4) longevity, and (5) exclusivity (*Braschi v. Stahl,* 1989).

The importance of this decision cannot be overestimated, but it must be noted that in this situation, the judge was validating the relationship in which one of the partners was safely dead. This is reminiscent of the editorial policy of the *New York Times.* I know from my own experience that the *Times* recognizes the existence of the life partner of the deceased in an obituary but recently refused, on the basis that "only family members may be included," to acknowledge the existence of the coparent in a wedding announcement—a coparent who had fully participated in the groom's rearing and support for almost thirty years. What is the subtext of this contradictory policy?

The *Times* society page editor aside, progress is being made in the establishment of a more inclusive family definition in the policy arena and in making some of the benefits previously limited to heterosexual couples available to same-sex partners. Several communities have instituted the opportunity for domestic partners to register as such. Many universities and colleges and several businesses and communities have made same-sex partners of employees eligible for spousal benefits. In Hawaii, although the matter is still in the courts, it appears possible that marriage between same-sex partners will eventually become legal. Gay rights advocates are now preparing to fight for the recognition of such marriages in the other forty-nine states.

While progress is being made, a powerful backlash from the political far right is being generated to support a 1950s definition of the family. These people seem to believe that they have special ownership of "family values." In the current political climate, this backlash is likely to continue and to receive considerable support nationally. For example, in the consideration of the Hate Crimes Statistics Act of 1990, there was a struggle over whether sexual orientation should be included with race, religion, and ethnicity so that violent crimes against gays and lesbians on the basis of prejudice could even be counted or included in hate crime statistics. Sexual orientation was left in only after a vigorous debate and a compromise providing that a statement be added proclaiming that the American family is the foundation of American society and that nothing in the act should be construed to promote or encourage homosexuality (Pub. L. No. 101–275).

Some have taken the position that instead of trying to be included within the definition of the family, gays and lesbians should advocate that the family not be used as an organizing category and that benefits should not be based on family status (Robson, 1994). This is similar to the position against family-based policy taken by Barbaro (1979) many years ago when he warned that a national family policy would inevitably violate civil liberties and discriminate against "nonconventional families." Although there is considerable merit in this argument, when one considers the extent to which the word *family* is woven into the fabric of our laws and policies, the expansion of the definition, as difficult as it is, may be easier than attempting to reframe those thousands of laws, statutes, and regulations.

There is no way to anticipate, identify, and seek protection from every encounter with heterosexual privilege. However, in the absence of the kind of advantages and legal protection heterosexuals take for granted, it is essential that gay men and lesbians, and the clinicians who work with them, be aware of heterosexual privilege and of a couple's vulnerability and find ways of building in protection. The cautionary tale of Alice B. Toklas, Gertrude Stein's life companion for forty years, is instructive. Toklas, who survived Stein for almost twenty years, spent her old age in grave financial straights because Stein, who owned a fortune in paintings, died without a will; her siblings claimed their legal if not their moral due, leaving Toklas without an inheritance from Stein's estate.

For their legal and financial protection, gay and lesbian couples should be encouraged to meet with attorneys and financial planners who are sensitive to and knowledgeable about legal vulnerabilities. Couples can thus better protect themselves and assure their futures through wills, living wills, health care powers of attorney, and the deliberate, careful management of property, investments, retirement accounts, and other resources. Not only is this essential for the protection of a couple, but uncertainty and lack of clarity is these areas can lead to tension in the couple's relationship.

Finally—and perhaps most important—it is essential for therapists to become aware of the extent to which heterosexual privilege and the denial of civil rights protections and equal treatment under the law for lesbian and gay citizens limits options, curtails freedom, reduces benefits, and denies the existence of or invalidates the experience of gay and lesbian couples and families.

Lesbians and Gay Men as Parents

Although for many years it has been assumed that lesbians and gay men are childless, the contrary is true. Many couples raise children born to one or both of them through previous relationships, and a growing number of couples are choosing to become parents through adoption or birth (see Chapter 15). Because lesbian and gay families are invalidated and repudiated, and their rights are unprotected, parenthood for gays and lesbians entails a number of risks.

Stepfamilies

Gay men and lesbians who are parenting children from previous relationships face at least two areas of uncertainty and insecurity. The first is that of custody. Until quite recently, lesbians and gay men frequently lost custody of their children to their former spouses on the grounds that their sexual orientation made them unfit parents. Any former spouse of a gay man or lesbian could use these grounds to obtain custody of minor children and even to prevent visitation. Gay and lesbian parents still cannot feel safe from court action, as was recently demonstrated by the ruling of the Virginia Supreme Court in the widely publicized case of Sharon Bottoms. In September 1993, Judge Buford Parsons Jr. awarded custody of Sharon's son Tyler to Sharon's mother, Kay Bottoms, on the grounds that Sharon had violated the state's sodomy law. That ruling was overturned by the Virginia Court of Appeals in June 1994, and Tyler was returned to his mother. This outcome was then reversed in a sharply divided 4–3 decision by the state supreme court with the following justification:

> We have previously stated that living daily under the conditions stemming from active lesbianism practiced in the home may impose a burden on the child by reason of the "social condemnation" attached to such an arrangement, which will inevitably affect the child's relationship with its peers and with the community. (Bull, 1995)

The position is thus taken that parents shall be deprived of their children, and children shall be deprived of their parents, because the world is discriminatory and homophobic. This is in direct conflict with the principle established in *Palmore v. Sidoti* (1984), the custody case involving a White child whose divorced mother married an African American man. The biological father claimed that it was not in the best interest of the child to grow up in a racially mixed household because of prejudice and stigmatization. The case was finally heard by the U.S. Supreme Court, which ruled for the mother on the grounds that she should not be deprived of the custody of her child because of the racist views of the community. Justice Berger wrote in his opinion:

> The question, however, is whether the reality of the private biases and the injury they might inflict are permissible considerations for removal of an infant

child from the custody of its natural mother. We have little difficulty concluding that they are not. The constitution cannot control such prejudices, but neither can it tolerate them. Private biases may be outside the reach of the law, but the law cannot, directly or indirectly, give them effect. (*Palmore v. Sidoti*, 1984)

Although other courts have found Palmore relevant in gay and lesbian child custody suits (*S.N.E. v. R.L.B.*, 1985; *M.P. v. S.P.*, 1979), in awarding the custody of Tyler to his grandmother, the Virginia court took the position that, in the case of lesbianism, private biases are given powerful effect and can justify the removal of a child from his or her mother, regardless of the politically negative effects of removing the child from a primary attachment figure and regardless of the parental level of functioning in the child-rearing role.

Although cases such as the one cited here are less common than they once were, such an outcome is a vivid reminder that as long as the parental rights of lesbians and gay men are not guaranteed through legislation and case law, these parents and their children will continue to be vulnerable to the homophobic views of the particular judges in particular courts and particular states and communities. Especially vulnerable have been gay fathers whose HIV status has been used in custody disputes, at times successfully, to deprive them of their rights.

The position of the "stepparent" or the coparent of a child born to his or her partner is generally undefined and unprotected. In almost all situations, the coparent may claim no rights in relation to the child. Repeatedly, coparents have lost when they have approached the courts for the establishment or protection of their rights. Typical was a recent Wisconsin Supreme Court decision in which custody, visitation, and enforcement of a coparent contract were denied a lesbian coparent on the basis that if the court were to allow custody to persons who stood in the place of parents, the door would be open for multiple parties to claim custody of children based on that status (LAMBDA, 1991). Similarly, the effort of a coparent to gain visitation rights to a child she had nurtured and supported for many years was defeated when the judge ruled that the lesbian nonbiological parent was outside the definition of parent and thus had no standing to bring a petition for visitation against the child's biological mother (Matter of Alison D., 1991).

A coparent's connection to a child born to and raised by a lesbian couple can also be jeopardized by the child's biological grandparents if the biological mother should die, as was demonstrated in a well-publicized Florida case. After the death of the biological mother of Kristen, the five-year-old daughter that two women had jointly planned for and raised, custody was awarded to the birth mother's parents. The grandparents adopted the child and forbade any contact with Janine, the coparent. Janine fought for five years for custody and finally, when the child was ten and old enough to tell the court her wish (which was and always had been to be with Janine), the custody decision was reversed, and the child went home to her other parent (Benkov, 1994).

In an attempt to legitimate coparents' rights, efforts have been made to enable a coparent to adopt a child when the biological mother has sole permanent custody, such as when the father is dead, has relinquished parental rights, or when the child was conceived through artificial insemination by an unmarried lesbian. This effort has been successful in New York, California, Oregon, Massachusetts, Washington, Alaska, Vermont, and the District of Columbia. Illinois and Wisconsin have refused adoptions by same-sex coparents.

Foster Parenting and Adoption

Gay men and lesbians have long been fostering children in need of parents. Agency policies and attitudes toward gay and lesbian foster parents vary, and often these parents are closeted, or the agency adopts a "don't ask, don't tell" stance. The great need for good foster homes tends to reduce agencies' concerns about placing foster children with gay men or lesbians. Again, however, the situation is not secure. For example, in 1985, in the socially progressive state of Massachusetts, neighbors complained that two openly gay men were foster parents for two little boys, and there was a violent homophobic public outcry. This reaction, which was precipitated by the press, led to a law forbidding any foster placement of children in the homes of gay men or lesbians. This law was on the books for five years, disrupting many families, causing a great deal of pain, and depriving children of needed homes. Fortunately, the only state that followed suit was New Hampshire, where state agencies are still forbidden to place children with gay or lesbian foster parents. In fact, the application form to be completed by potential foster parents includes a question asking whether anyone in the family is homosexual.

Gay men and lesbians are also becoming parents—with difficulty—through adoption. Although only two states (Florida and New Hampshire) have passed legislation prohibiting adoption by gay men or lesbians (and the prohibition is now being tested in Florida), most adoption agencies will not knowingly approve gay men or lesbians as adoptive parents. Couples may evade this restriction by hiding their sexual orientation and having one of them adopt as a single parent. Sometimes, a sympathetic adoption worker in an agency will look the other way, and agencies tend to be more open about the adoption of older children and children with special needs. Couples who find themselves unable to adopt in their communities may approach the international adoption market, which is not only very expensive but also increasingly troublesome, as information surfaces about the widespread abuse and exploitation of poor Third World women and children in the international adoption market (Herrman & Kasper, 1992).

In almost all situations like the one just described, only one parent can adopt legally as a single parent. This means that although the couple may have agreed upon, planned, and financed the adoption, and may have supported and reared the child together, only one is the legal parent; the other has neither legitimate rights nor clear responsibilities. This establishes an asymmetrical relationship between the two parents and the child, an asymmetry that the parents face on a regular basis as they deal with everything from school visits and medical permission forms, to requirements for support in the case of a separation, to eligibility for Social Security survivors' benefits in the case of the death of a coparent. This asymmetry may well have long-term consequences for family relationships as well. Clinicians working with gay and lesbian families in this situation must be sensitive to these issues and be ready to explore the impact of social policies that affirm the existence of only one of the two coparents.

Social Policy Issues and the Baby Boom

As reproductive technology and changing social norms make what was unthinkable a generation ago now an option, thousands of lesbians and some gay men are choosing to become birth parents. The complexities and the risks in these choices are many, as social policy lags far behind human inventiveness in providing a protective and enabling social and policy structure for these new families.

One way lesbians can become parents is through alternative insemination, that is, insemination by an anonymous donor. A physician usually performs the procedure. Making this choice brings lesbian couples, as it does heterosexual couples who take this route to parenthood, into a situation that is largely ungoverned by standards and procedures (Annas, 1981). Bioethical issues abound, such as multiple uses of the same donor and the inadequate investigation of donors' health histories. Lack of information about donors leaves children and families to face many mysteries; the total anonymity and unavailability of the biological father may raise problematic identity issues for the child. Another deterrent to anonymous-donor insemination is its enormous expense. Because the sperm have been frozen, conception is less likely to occur, and each attempt to conceive is costly.

Lesbian couples who wish to become parents must also go through the often demeaning experience of finding a physician who is willing to work with them. In many areas, there is no such physician available, and lesbians are denied the right to parenthood on the basis of private opinion and bias on the part of powerful professionals.

Some lesbian couples choose to select a known, willing donor—a friend, a gay man who wants to become a father, or a relative of the coparent. Although there are many good reasons for choosing this option, because of the lack of policy and law in this area, the mother, the coparent, and the donor are embarking on a journey through a legal minefield. Agreements worked out between the involved parties do not necessarily stand up when tested in the courts. Mothers are not necessarily protected from unwanted intrusions and demands by the father, and donors may well find themselves facing unanticipated requirements for financial support of the child.

In working with gay men and lesbians who wish to become parents, clinicians should understand the different options, along with the risks and advantages of each, and then refer couples to an attorney with expertise in this area, since laws and policies differ sharply from state to state.

Breaking Up

As there is no marriage for lesbian and gay families, so is there no divorce, no body of laws that governs separation and offers requirements and guidelines for custody, visitation, or support of coparented children, or for the division of property. These issues are rarely settled with ease in the case of heterosexual divorce, even with the existence of some social policies and precedents. In the case of lesbian and gay couples separating in a policy vacuum, the possibility of a fair and equitable separation depends on "goodwill." However, when a relationship terminates, there is often bitterness, recrimination, and vengefulness—rarely goodwill. Although some couples do work out separation collaboratively or with the help of mediation, there are many stories of couples translating their bitterness and anger into punitive actions around separation. A key area of struggle concerns custody and visitation. As discussed above, the nonbiological parent has no rights, and coparents have generally been unable to gain visiting rights through the courts. No matter how much they have invested—emotionally, financially, and in time—in the rearing of a child, the biological mother has the power to sever contact between the child and coparent after a separation. Of course, this impasse may be avoided and coparents' rights may be protected through the adoption of a partner's biological child in the few states where this is possible and when this is the mother's wish.

Horror stories abound of people who have been ruined financially or unjustly treated through the separation process. For example, a woman who has put her career aside and invested in and supported the career of her partner for many years may find herself, as many wives have in the past, without a career, money, or any portion of her more affluent partner's savings or retirement accounts. "Palimony" suits have rectified this situation in the cases of some celebrities who have the resources to pursue legal action, but most lesbians and gay men have neither the resources nor the will to invest in this kind of struggle.

In working with gay and lesbian couples, it is essential to explore with them how they are handling money and community property. It is appropriate to ask questions such as, What would happen to each of you if you lost the other? What would happen if you were to separate? It is important for couples to think these issues through when there is goodwill, as this will stand them in good stead should their relationship founder. In fact, in the absence of the protection provided by divorce and support laws, a couple's willingness to think through financial arrangements in which each would be protected in the case of death or separation is often a bellwether of the nature and extent of mutual trust and commitment. As one woman commented, "We couldn't get married formally and officially, but when we began to feel married was the day that we decided to pool our resources."

In the absence of goodwill and a previously arranged financial plan that protects both partners, the best solution is to encourage the couple to seek mediation, although even agreeing to mediation is a sign of some willingness to collaborate.

The Future

Social policy in all its forms is an expression of the values, the culturally based preferences, and the worldviews of those in power. It is a translation into action of the dominant discourses. Today, the future for gay and lesbian families hangs in the balance between those progressive forces that would continue the slow and uneven progress toward the recognition and validation of gay and lesbian families and the establishment of equal treatment under the law, and the forces of backlash and oppression that support the criminalization of homosexuality as well as continued discrimination and subjugation. The antigay plank in the platform of the far right is very clear and, if the United States continues to move in that direction, even the gains that have been made are in jeopardy. As one lesbian commented with ironic humor, "Maybe they let up on us so we would all come out . . . and now that we are out, they know who we are and can come after us."

The ambivalence toward homosexuality runs deeply through the American population and includes a widespread antipathy countered by a sense of fairness. One of the solutions to this ambivalence has been the "don't ask, don't tell" public policy, which extends far beyond the armed forces. It enacts the idea that homosexuals can be tolerated, overlooked, and ignored if they remain invisible. This paradoxical "solution" has been translated into public policy and has been considered by some to be benign. Living a secret life, being invisible, being denied community recognition and support, is never benign. Not only is the policy demeaning, disempowering, and overwhelmingly silencing, it also excludes gay men and lesbians and their families from the many benefits and supports available in heterosexual unions.

The U.S. Supreme Court, after agreeing to rule on the constitutionality of Colorado's Amendment 2, recently heard competing arguments, with the State of Colorado and its many allies on one side and gay, lesbian, and civil liberties advocates on the other. This is an enormously important case for the future of lesbian and gay civil rights. The Court will be the final arbiter in this era of whether gay men and lesbians can be excluded from the political process and excluded from the rights guaranteed to all citizens by the Constitution. The Court's decision may well mean for gay men and lesbians what the 1954 Supreme Court decision against racial separation in *Brown v. Board of Education* meant for African Americans. Will the highest court in the land uphold a state's right to prohibit the passage of laws and ordinances that would protect lesbians and gays against discrimination? We await the results with hope and anxiety.

References

Annas, G. J. (1981). Fathers anonymous: Beyond the best interests of the sperm donor. *Child Welfare, 60*(3), 161–170.

Barbaro, F. (1979). The case against family policy. *Social Work, 24,* 455–457.

Benkov, L. (1994). *Reinventing the family.* New York: Crown.

Bowers v. Hardwick, 478 U.S. 186 (1986).

Braschi v. Stahl, 74 NY 2d 201, 543 N.E. 49, 211–213 (1989).

Bull, C. (1995, May 30). Losing the war: The courts disregard evidence in denying lesbian mother custody of her son. *The Advocate,* p. 33.

Eisenstadt v. Baird, 405 U.S. 438 (1972).

Griscom, J. L. (1992). The case of Sharon Kowalski and Karen Thompson: Ableism, heterosexism, and sexism. In P. S. Rothenberg (Ed.), *Race, class, and gender in the United States,* 2nd ed. (pp. 215–225). New York: St. Martin's Press.

Griswold v. State of Connecticut, 381 U.S. 479 (1965).

Herrman, K. J., & Kasper, B. (1992). International adoption: The exploitation of women and children. *Affilia, 7*(1), 45–58.

LAMBDA. (1991). *LAMBDA Update, 8*(1).

LAMBDA. (1992). *Domestic partnership: Issues and legislation.* New York: LAMBDA Legal Defense and Education Fund.

Logue, P. (1994). Cincinnati: The anatomy of a victory. *LAMBDA Update, 11*(3), 1, 29–30.

Marks, P. (1994, April 17). Shared lives won't accept eternity apart. *New York Times,* p. A14.

Matter of Alison D., Court of Appeals, New York State, May 2, 1991.

M.P. v. S.P., 169 N.J. Super. 425, 404A, 2d 1256 (App. Div. 1979).

Palmore v. Sidoti, 104 SCt. P1879 (1984).

Poverny, L. M., & Finch, W. A. (1988). Gay and lesbian partners: Expanding the definition of the family. *Social Casework, 69*(2), 116–121.

Pub. L. No. 101–275, 104 Stat. 140 Amending 28 U.S.C. 534.

Robson, R. (1994). Resisting the family: Repositioning lesbians in legal theory. *Signs, 19*(4), 975–996.

S.N.E. v. R.L.B., 699P.2d876 (Alaska Sup. Ct., 1985).

PART TWO

FAMILIES OF ORIGIN

FAMILIES OF ORIGIN

CHAPTER FOUR

INVISIBLE TIES

Lesbians and Their Families of Origin

Joan Laird

My life partner, Ann, and I recently celebrated the thirtieth anniversary of our lives together. My son, Duncan, born during my eight-year marriage to his father, was sixteen months old when Ann came into our lives. He called her "Baboo" and loved her very much, while she returned that love and showed it by fully sharing the child care, the responsibilities, the joys, and the pains of parenthood. It took many years (indeed, decades) for us and the world to change enough for her to claim parental legitimacy, but she now calls him "my son," experimenting somewhat hesitantly but proudly with a language long disallowed by the social world around us.

Two years ago, Duncan, now a social worker, married Meg, herself a social worker from a family with a strong social work tradition. Although the *New York Times* would not allow Ann's name to be included in the engagement announcement, Ann's and my names were on the wedding invitation, along with the names of our daughter-in-law's father and stepmother. The wedding ritual was wonderfully expressive of the cultures of both families, blending the traditional, the innovative, and the young couple's hopes for the future, all witnessed by a larger kinship network that included Ann's and my families, as well as our old and newer friendship families. The fact that both Ann and I walked Duncan down the aisle, wished him well, and danced together at his wedding modeled—for younger lesbians and for the straight world—one way that lesbian relationships can be enacted in the larger family context and how central rituals can be adapted to express particular definitions of kinship.

A few months ago, Meg and Duncan had their first child and Ann and I our first grandchild, a beautiful, sturdy little girl, Hannah. I bought them a baby book and one day, when I was visiting, began to look through the first entries. Meg had drawn in new branches on the published version of the family tree—an illustration on which there was no room for nonbiological or nonheterosexual kin—branches for Ann and her roots. Several pages later, inserted in the illustrated pages for intergenerational information on parents and grandparents, was a beautifully drawn and painted page for Ann's biography.

I begin with this very personal story to illustrate the central point in this chapter, a point that would seem simple and obvious but has been all but neglected in both popular culture and in the professional literature and research on lesbians and gays. Ours is not an unusual story. Lesbians and gays come from families and are connected to these original families. Many of us live in families of choice as well. (*Family of choice* is a political and ideological term used by gays and lesbians to describe the families they have created outside of legal marriage that may include a partner, adopted or biological children, and/or an extended network of friends, usually but not exclusively lesbian and gay, who perform functions similar to those of close, extended biological families.) Most of us are *not* cut off from our families—not forever rejected, isolated, disinherited. We are daughters and sons, siblings, aunts and uncles, parents and grandparents. Like everyone else, most of us have continuing, complicated relationships with our families. We participate in negotiating the changing meanings, rituals, values, and connections that define kinship. Lesbians and gays *do* have role models (and those role models may be straight, gay, or bisexual) and themselves serve as role models for others in their families. Lesbians and gays are *not* bereft of ritual lives, of culture, of histories. Like everyone else, they have parts of themselves they openly share and parts they keep silent about—choosing between what will be said and what will be unsaid as they move from one context to another in their daily lives.

This chapter is about intergenerational family relationships, primarily about lesbians' relationships with their families of origin. Two themes seem to dominate in common impressions and assumptions about lesbians and their families. First, since the family relationships of lesbians are so invisible and knowledge about them so unavailable, the first theme is a nonimpression, a theme of invisibility. We might be led to believe that lesbians do not have family connections, since these connections are so rarely portrayed or discussed. Secondly, when they are acknowledged, the relationships are usually viewed as tortured. Families of origin are portrayed as hurt, dismayed, and confused at best when they learn a child of theirs is lesbian or gay; they are shown as angry, hostile, and utterly rejecting—even violent—at worst. The major metaphor is one of loss, of mourning all that has gone wrong and all that might have been.

Generally viewed as a source of rejection and homophobia and as negatively affecting the psychological and social life of the lesbian, the family of origin also is seen to lack relevance to the here-and-now life of the adult gay or lesbian with or without a family of creation. How often have we heard or read that gays and lesbians have had no role models, no family experiences that prepare them for coupling, for role division, for parenting? But a family is about far more than sexual orientation—it is about values, morality, human connectedness and relationship, legacy and generativity, and much, much more. As lesbians and gays, we would not wish to promote the idea that we are incapable of providing role models for our own (usually heterosexual) children, for passing on family and cultural values, ethics, and skills for living to our heterosexual children and grandchildren. Lesbians, in fact, are pioneering both coupling and family ideas that may be useful to our heterosexual siblings and that may gain the admiration and respect of our heterosexual parents. Similarly, we are very much psychologically and culturally part of our (probably heterosexual) families and they part of us. Our (probably heterosexual) parents and grandparents have taught us who to be and how to be, who not to be and how not to be, through both positive and negative example.

My effort here is to look more closely at the narrative of family invisibility, rejection, and alienation that prevails in popular culture and in the professional literature, contrasting this narrative with what lesbians themselves say about their relationships with their families. In this work, I focus primarily on adult lesbian daughters' relationships with their parents. Since these relationships are virtually unexplored in any systematic way in the professional literature, my sources of information are eclectic.

First, since our personal stories are shaped, influenced, and to a great extent limited by the repertoire of available narratives and the dominant social discourses in the larger surround, I briefly explore popular film for its portrayals of gay and lesbian family of origin connections. This is one way of trying to expose the dominant narrative, in this case how family relationships are viewed in the larger culture. A tiny effort here, it nevertheless suggests how lesbians are reminded every day of their invisibility and the invisibility of their family relationships—or worse yet, if they do not deconstruct the homophobic dominant discourse, how they may come to believe themselves that such relationships do not exist, that is, that lesbianism means disconnection from family. Second, I examine the professional literature, which is primarily a literature from psychology, for insight into these relationships. Third, I comment on some of the popular lesbian literature for the same purposes. Finally, I turn to nineteen transcribed interviews with lesbians that I have completed over the last three years. I am interested in what lesbian intergenerational relationships (particularly with parents) look like and how they seem to work, in their complexity and their quality. I end with some thoughts about the implications of this work for clinical practice.

Gays, Lesbians, and Families in Popular Film

In an exploration of lesbians and lesbian images in popular film that began with Marlene Dietrich's cross-dressing adventures in the 1930 film *Morocco*, I failed to find a single instance of lesbians portrayed in the context of their families until this year, 1995. Lesbians have been depicted as self-loathing, doomed creatures whose ultimate solution was death, a fate that Shirley MacLaine suffered in the 1961 film *The Children's Hour*. Sandy Dennis, in *The Fox* (1967), a homophobic, ironic, and phallocentric film suggesting that all a lesbian really needs is a man, is crushed to death when a giant tree falls between her legs. To be sure, one of the two women in the sexually ambiguous French film *Entre Nous* (1983) returns to family, broken and in despair, but we learn nothing of her family relationships. She and her woman friend (lover?) both have children from their heterosexual marriages but are portrayed as neglecting them, as their intense friendship consumes them. Lianna, the heroine of John Sayles's 1982 Canadian film of the same name, forfeits her children to her cruel and philandering husband after she tells him of her affair with a female college teacher. She is subsequently alienated from her best friend and, indeed, from everyone around her. In one scene, Lianna is heard talking to her mother on the telephone, a perfunctory conversation in which she shares nothing of her troubles. Until very recently, the future for the lesbian couple or parent in film was indeed grim.

Gay men have suffered similar fates in popular film over the decades. They have been portrayed not at all or as sick, exotic creatures, as drag queens, but never as men in stable couple relationships or as men connected to their families. Nevertheless, gay men have fared better than lesbians in the family department. They began to be awarded families beginning with the 1978 French farce *La Cage aux Folles*. Readers may remember that Renato has an-about-to-be-married son, a rite of passage that serves as the centerpiece for this marvelous romp. Renato's lover, Alban, has helped raised the young man. Who can forget Alban's booming "Here's Mother!" as he appears in drag at the first meeting with the prospective daughter-in-law's parents? We learn nothing of the two men's parents, however. *La Cage* was followed in 1988 by an American film, *Torch Song Trilogy*, a partly autobiographical story that originated in the theater. Harvey Fierstein's powerful portrayal of a gay man's attempts to build a family and to stay connected with and demand respect from his critical and guilt-making but ultimately caring mother represents a breakthrough in American film. Arnold, a female impersonator by profession, and his lover are in a committed relationship. In a commentary on the extreme homophobia in our society, the young lover is brutally murdered on the street below by a gang of gay haters. Arnold later takes in a foster child, a fifteen-year-old gay boy—a move that is beyond his mother's comprehension—and continues his struggles to forge a connection with his mother that is authentic and that recognizes his right to mourn the loss of his lover and to form a family of his own.

Philadelphia, to my knowledge, was the first film to give a gay person, in this case a son living with and then dying of AIDS, a loving and supportive family that welcomes and includes his partner. Some gay people themselves were critical of this film, for they found it difficult to believe such families exist. Most recently, a 1995 Australian film, *The Sum of Us*, pivots around a loving relationship between a gay man and his straight father, who is worried that the young man isn't settled down with a life partner and keeps trying to fix him up.

These few films have represented breakthroughs in locating gay males in the contexts of their families in popular culture. What the films proclaim is that gay men come from families, and, through thick and thin—homophobia, nonaffirmation, and even vicious attack from Arnold's mother in *Torch Song Trilogy* and lawsuits and AIDS in *Philadelphia*, and the debilitating stroke suffered by the father in *The Sum of Us*—families seem to stick together. However imperfect, these films are pioneering efforts to shift one of the most powerful narratives in American culture, a narrative that says that the concept of gay male and the concept of family may not be linked in common discourse.

As Tom Johnson and Michael Keren point out in their chapter on gay male couples in this volume, in recent years there also have been some excellent popular and documentary films portraying gay men in the context of their families of choice—films such as *Parting Glances* and *Longtime Companion*. But what about gay women? In keeping with the combined forces of homophobia, heterosexism, and sexism that plague gay women, it is even rarer for the lesbian to be granted a family of origin, choice, or creation in popular culture. The first film to show in some depth the relationships between a lesbian, her children, *and* her family of origin, in this case her father, was the award-winning made-for-television biographical account *Serving in Silence: The Marguerite Cammermeyer Story*. This is the story of a courageous woman who successfully defies the military's injunction of "don't ask, don't tell," with the support of her children and, finally, her usually critical father as well.

Not only are gays and lesbians themselves largely invisible in popular film and rarely envisioned in the context of intergenerational relationships with parents or children, but lesbians and gays of color were virtually beyond the collective imagination as represented in popular film—until *The Wedding Banquet*. In this 1993 Taiwanese-Chinese-U.S. comedy, we see contrasted the lavish cultural celebration of the (false) heterosexual wedding and the (true) silent, secret love between two young men—Simon, an American, and Wai Tung, a Taiwanese American. The film represents a fascinating juxtaposition of the meanings of filial piety, kinship norms, and the values of the traditional Chinese family and the new cultural ingredients of Wai Tung's couple relationship with a White American gay man. It is a rare and wonderful moment when Wai Tung's traditional Chinese father, in spite of his powerful cultural values that prescribe traditional marriage, figures out how to have his kinship cake and eat it too, in this case his son, his son's lover, his new daughter-in-law, and the grandchild on the way.

During the writing of this chapter, the first American film portraying lesbians in the contexts of their families made its debut. Again, the film centered around an interracial relationship. A low-budget, art theater delight, *The Incredibly True Adventures of Two Girls in Love* (1995) is about a White working-class teenager who knows she is lesbian and dresses the part—wrinkled man's shirt, vest, and baggy jeans—who is ready for love. She is a loner—isolated, marginalized, and seen as a weirdo by her peers. This young woman lives with her aunt, a leather-jacketed lesbian, and her aunt's partner. The boundaries of this family are quite permeable, as various assorted other characters from time to time join this caring, flamboyant, and slightly chaotic family of choice; it is a household in which everyone contributes to the politically correct vegetarian stew and everyone has advice for the teenage heroine. The young lesbian begins to pursue a friendship with an African American girl in her school, a girl from an upper-middle-class professional family. This girl is popular, beautiful, and immaculately dressed in preppie style. She goes home to a loving, divorced mother, a successful professional woman who runs a well-organized, well-decorated home where nothing is out of place, life is highly ritualized, and meals are quiet, orderly affairs. Differences in race, social class, and lifestyle fade away as these two young women tentatively begin to explore their feelings for each other, upending their families and the entire community in the process.

These few films penetrate the wall of invisibility and the myth of isolation from family that has characterized the portrayal of lesbians and gays in popular film. It is a beginning. Other hopeful signs that the discourse is changing concern the recent occasional spot for the lesbian or gay character on television, such as Sandra Bernhardt's role on *Roseanne,* and the increasingly "daring" traditions of writing gay and lesbian lives on and off Broadway and in other theaters, such as in Tony Kushner's two-part play, *Angels in America.* Nevertheless, there still are almost no openly lesbian or gay performers in the media, short of those tragically exposed by AIDS. There are, of course, rumors.

Lesbians and Family in the Professional Literature

The ideas of "lesbian" and "family," then, have rarely been joined in popular film. In the professional literature, the dominant theme in work on lesbian relationships with family focuses on disclosure or coming out (for example, Berzon, 1979; Brown, 1989; Kleinberg, 1986; Krestan, 1988; Strommen, 1989; and Zitter, 1987). There is virtually no exploration of lesbian relationships with families of origin over time other than in the isolated clinical vignette, although DeVine (1984) and others comment on the developmental stages a family must go through to move toward acceptance of their child's homosexuality. Slater's (1995) comprehensive and otherwise excellent work on the lesbian family life cycle, except for the isolated comment, virtually ignores the family of origin, as does Benkov's (1994) fine account of lesbians with children. An exception is to be found in Walker's (1991) pioneering work with families of gay men with AIDS.

There is, in fact, a small but growing collection of research on lesbians with children, both children from heterosexual marriage and children born to or adopted by lesbians as single parents and in same-sex couple relationships, as well as a modest body of clinical literature that weaves together theory and example (see Chapter Eighteen of this book for a review). There also have been numerous studies of lesbian and gay couple relationships, a few of which include some data on family of origin connections (for example, Kurdek & Schmitt, 1987; Levy, 1989; and Murphy, 1989).

Nevertheless, if the lesbian's family of origin has been largely invisible in the media of popular culture, it is also ignored in the professional research and clinical literature as well. Five probable reasons for this state of affairs are as follows:

First, as scholars and practitioners, lesbian researchers and clinicians are not immune from the knowledge and power arrangements, the larger social stories, that form the cultural depository from which we can select our own personal and professional narratives. In those social stories, lesbians and gay men are assumed to have few if any meaningful connections to their families.

Second, in the early days of the women's movement, more radical feminists and lesbian feminists declared the family the seat of patriarchy. In some lesbian circles, politically correct lesbian politics substituted the lesbian community for family and frowned on long-term coupling and monogamy. Choosing children through birth or adoption, although not storied in social discourse, was rare but did occur. Lesbians with children, and particularly lesbians who felt their ex-husbands and families should play a meaningful role in their children's lives, were often treated as "politically incorrect" by the lesbian community and isolated from their peers. Family, including the so-called rejecting family of origin, belonged to the hated and feared heterosexual culture and supposedly had little to offer.

Third, our individualistic society, with its emphasis on the inner life and self-fulfillment, drew attention away from an emphasis on community, family, and kinship.

Fourth, psychoanalytic and psychodynamic psychologies, with their focus on the therapist-client relationship and the phenomenon of transference, paired with the virtual ignoring of the client's lived experiences in the real world where the self is constructed intersubjectively, fostered inattention to current family relationships, focusing, rather, on childhood family experiences.

Finally, in the family field, the traditional family, in spite of its growing obsolescence, remained the central metaphor for "family" in the development of family therapy models.

Even as various other kinds of diversity gradually became recognized—diversity in ethnic or racial heritage and identity, in social class, in family structure—heterosexuality was assumed for all families. Through the 1980s, the gay- or lesbian-headed family was surely beyond the pale during an era when we had barely begun to notice how important gender was in constituting family relationships. Even when feminist family therapists began to critique the lack of attention to gender and the patriarchal features of systemic models, lesbians and their families of origin and creation, with a few notable exceptions, remained invisible.

In fact, the entire field of "family," both in family studies and in the application of family theory to the clinical professions, has ignored and neglected the lesbian and gay family. Allen and Demo (1995), in a comprehensive review of the leading family research journals from 1980 to 1993, as well as a number of journals in related fields over the same period, found that lesbian and gay families were virtually invisible, rarely studied. And when they were included as part of larger studies, they were regarded as problematic or deviant, and their diversity was ignored. Allen and Demo conclude, among other things, that "lesbian and gay kin relations offer new conceptual inroads into older concepts in the family literature" (p. 14) and believe that investigations of intergenerational and extended family relations beyond the procreative family life cycle should become a priority.

A similar picture would emerge from a statistical analysis of the mainstream family therapy literature. The first article I know of appeared in 1972 in *Family Process*, the flagship clinical journal, and was titled "My Stepfather Is a She" (Osman, 1972). The clinical solution to a problem with an adolescent boy being raised in a lesbian household was to place him elsewhere, a solution we seldom see in the family therapy literature. The pioneering article by Krestan and Bepko (1980), "The Problem of Fusion in the Lesbian Relationship," which drew from Bowen's family of origin theory, appeared in *Family Process* a few years later. Several years passed before Roth's (1984) chapter was published. Both quickly became classics and have been reprinted in several collections. In 1988, Krestan published a second article, this time on lesbian mothers and daughters; Roth teamed with Murphy (1986) for further exploration of family system issues. Until very recently, we would not need all ten fingers to count the journal contributions in the family therapy field. Occasionally, writers in the more generic journals in social work, psychology, psychiatry, and other counseling professions addressed family themes, but the list is short (see Laird, 1993a).

When the family of origin is mentioned in what might be called the heterosexual clinical literature, which of course is always sensitive to problem and pathology, and in the psychological literature on gay and lesbian identity-making, it is often portrayed solely as the thing that one does or does not "come out to." The prevailing picture that emerges is often one of disappointment, rejection, compromise, loneliness, and physical and/or emotional cut-off. It is, of course, often the nightmarish family that attracts attention in the press, as in the case of the Sharon Kowalski story, in which a homophobic and neglecting family reclaims custody of Sharon after she sustained a head injury in an automobile accident (Griscom, 1992). More recently, lesbian mother Sharon Bottoms was sued for custody of her son by her own mother in a case heard eventually in the Virginia Supreme Court (see Hartman's account, Chapter Three). The presiding judge concluded that Sharon's lesbianism and the fact that she had had oral sex—a felony in Virginia—contributed to making her an unfit mother.

These kinds of stories captivate the press. We are less likely to hear stories like that of the Filipino American mother who made a beautiful, traditional Filipino wedding gown and prepared the wedding party dinner for her lesbian daughter Trinity's marriage to Desirée, a woman of Japanese, Chinese, native Hawaiian, and German ancestry (Ordoña & Thompson, 1990). Nor do we hear stories like that of Kathy, one of the women I interviewed, now in her late forties, who came out to herself and to her family of origin just a few years ago. Not long after, her Mormon father said to her life partner, as the two women visited him in his hospital room during the last days of his life, "Dorothy, I am so happy for the two of you and so grateful that Kathy has you to take care of her and to love her."

Brown (1989), highlighting clinical issues in coming out to family, describes common patterns for juggling the closet and the family. In the first scenario, the person may maintain rigid geographical and emotional distance from the family of origin, the lesbian feeling more or less estranged and the family often hurt and puzzled. In a second adaptation, which she calls the "I know you know" pattern, there is a conspiracy of silence. No one will ask about the gay person's personal life, and he or she is afraid to tell. In this situation, the gay or lesbian individual is usually treated as single and available to the family of origin for holidays, extra help, and so on. In yet a third situation, the "don't tell your father, it would kill him" story, the secrecy supports various family coalitions and keeps the lesbian daughter's life hostage to the family. In all of these adaptations, as Murphy (1989) pointed out in her study of the effects of perceived parental attitudes on the lesbian couple, the couple relationship may be rendered more vulnerable, as one individual may blame her partner for all she has lost and for all their togetherness is costing. Brown (1989), Murphy (1989), Krestan (1988), and others have helped to articulate the possible effects of disclosure to families on the lesbian daughter and lesbian couple relations, offering useful implications for clinical practice. But the initial disclosure—coming out—while certainly an important event and an important part of the evolving self and family narrative, is far from the whole story. Family relationships are about much more than coming out, and coming out, although it can be a painful and debilitating process for some, for others is a most self-authenticating and differentiating process that can result in very positive growth for both the individual and the family. We rarely hear about that side of family life.

We need to know more about the everyday lives, the stories, the kinship and community connections, the special rituals, of lesbians and gays, in their families of choice and in connections with their wider kinship networks. What is missing from the professional clinical literature and the social science literature (with a few notable exceptions) is the ethnographic study of lesbian and gay life in the United States and, more particularly, the ethnographic study of the cultural life of the lesbian and gay family. It is in "culture" that, in recursive fashion, we both learn who we are and continually construct and reconstruct ourselves. In a sense, we construct our psychology, our "selves," as we participate in larger cultural surrounds, from family to society. And relationships with the family of origin, family of choice, and extended kin networks are an essential part of the cultural.

Anthropologist Gilbert Herdt has led the way in calling our attention to the "cultural" in gay studies. His stunning book, *Gay Culture in America* (1992), although not particularly about families or lesbians, demonstrates how the use of cultural and constructionist metaphors can open up new dimensions for understanding gay life. It moves us away from an exclusive focus on the psychological and away from deficit perspectives. Although this kind of research effort in gay and lesbian studies is in its infancy, in the last few years there have been at least three major ethnographic studies of lesbian culture that shed new light on lesbians and their family relationships.

First, Weston's (1991) study of the kinship relationships of eighty lesbians in the Bay Area explores what "family" means to lesbians. She became convinced, as she pursued her research, "that gay families could not be understood apart from the families in which lesbians and gay men had grown up" (p. 3). Her work represents a tremendous breakthrough in examining the complexity of kinship meanings and arrangements in lesbian lives, as she captures the creativity. Second, Kennedy and Davis (1993) conducted a fascinating ethnographic/historical study of lesbian bar culture in Buffalo, New York, from the late 1930s to the early 1960s. These scholars go beyond conversations with the White, middle-class, well-educated, and often professional lesbians overrepresented in the research in order to capture the richness of and the contributions to lesbian culture of the lives of women of color and working-class and poor women as well.

A third work of import is Ellen Lewin's (1993) study of lesbian mothers, again an ethnographic adventure that explores the everyday lives, experiences, meanings, and relationships of lesbians. These three works combine to give us an emergent portrait of lesbians in family relationships that takes us beyond the trauma of disclosure, beyond hostility and emotional distance to redefinition and recreation, to a much more complex view of how lesbians define and construct kinship networks.

Interestingly, and supportive of a point I made earlier, it becomes clear in these studies of nonclinical populations that the physical and emotional cut-off of the lesbian from her family is much rarer than commonly assumed. (In fact, that may be true among clinical populations as well). Davis and Kennedy, for example, in their study based on the oral histories of forty-five working-class lesbians, found that there were various degrees and forms of family disapproval that ranged from avoidance to, in one case, severe beatings. None were warmly accepted, yet none were completely rejected by their families. In fact, within several years of coming out, each woman had established a truce and was maintaining contact with her family—this in an era when out lesbianism was far more dangerous and largely confined to bar culture and when no woman was expected to move from home until she married. Many of these women fought to maintain connections *and* to protect their families from the social stigma and ridicule they knew were inevitable were it to become known that a daughter had become lesbian. Some families were openly supportive. For instance, one conservative Italian Catholic mother insisted that her daughter bring her friends home for Sunday dinner and invited her daughter's friends who were visiting from out of town to stay with the family.

Lewin (1993), in her study of lesbian mothers, found that mothers regarded family members, especially their parents, as the most reliable sources of support when times were bad. Even when cut-offs occurred, neither the lesbian daughter nor her parents could endure permanent ruptures—family ties were too profound, she believes. Becoming a mother oneself seems to enhance the need for stronger kinship ties for both the new mother and her parents, and the sense of commonality and identification of the younger woman with her own mother. Lewin's findings fly in the face of the lesbian literature, which tends to support the idea that families of lesbians will not be helpful and that they have little to offer these newly created families.

These lesbian mothers also tended to identify and spend time with other young mothers—heterosexual mothers—more than they did with single lesbians, contradicting the notion that only other lesbians, peers, or parents may serve as role models for daily living. Clearly, her work points to the need to know more about how lesbian mothers and their children construct kinship and community relationships with both heterosexuals and gays and lesbians and, similarly, how lesbian mothers and grandmothers are connected to their children and grandchildren as well as to the wider kinship network.

Lesbians, Gays, and Family in Popular Literature

It is often the nonprofessional, nonacademic person who carves out new paths, raising consciousness and pointing the way for new professional learning and practice. Clinical practice and research have been influenced, for example, by the various self-help movements in the fields of sexual abuse, alcoholism, and adoption. Ordinary people tell their stories, breaking longstanding silences and questioning long-held "truths" in what Foucault (1980) has called the insurrection of subjugated knowledge, and we "experts" finally listen, inventing new professional languages and models of practice and investing them with expertise.

One rich source to be mined in exploring the ethnography of lesbian and gay life is the personal narrative, as it is told in biography, autobiography, novels, poems, and other fiction, in memoir and oral history, and in the self-help literature. Again, much of the trade literature on lesbians' relationships with their families of origin focuses on coming out. But there are also a number of works demonstrating that lesbians and gays do indeed come from families and that they are connected, sometimes ambivalently or painfully, with families in the present and haunted by ghosts from the past (for example, Hall Carpenter Archives, 1989a, 1989b). The popular and self-help literatures attest in a way the professional literature does not to both the importance of families of origin and their presence in the lives of gay sons and lesbian daughters. For example, Bernstein (1995), in his account of the parents in Parents, Families, and Friends of Lesbians and Gays (P-FLAG), begins in true journalistic style with horror stories of violence against gays, high rates of adolescent suicide among lesbians and gays, family rejection and isolation, all by way of prelude to the stories of family courage and, indeed, heroism, of parents in P-FLAG who have come to join the marches and to lead in fighting the new initiatives against gay civil rights, often at great personal risk and cost. This is a side of families we rarely see in the professional literature. Other parents have shared their joys and heartaches in living with and loving gay and lesbian sons and daughters (for example, Dew, 1994; Griffin, Wirth, & Wirth, 1986). Butler's (1990) anthology of lesbian commitment ceremonies recounts many stories of how families of widely varying ethnic and social class backgrounds participated in their children's weddings and other unions. Martin, in her *Lesbian and Gay Parenting Handbook* (1993), translates the expertise of the psychologist into highly readable language available to all gay and lesbian families and includes attention to families of origin in many places throughout her work. And stories of coming to terms with family, sometimes precipitated by impending death from AIDS, often lie at the heart of biography and anthology—witness the works of Monette (1991, 1992, 1994) or Preston (1992).

Here I can suggest only some of the themes appearing in the popular literature. But this literature offers us one way to listen to the narratives of the "subjugated" themselves, to listen and to move beyond the biases built into the heterosexist and homophobic social discourses in which professional assumptions are shaped. Those assumptions, in turn, can shape our pre-understandings in such a way that we cannot listen to and do not hear the "family" stories in the life of the lesbian or gay client, or the gay and lesbian stories in families. How many of us, for example, find the lesbian or gay couples on family genograms or explore further the stories of the "maiden aunt" or the "confirmed bachelor"? How many of us, as therapists, have dared to say the unsaid or ask the unasked?

Lesbian Family of Origin Narratives

My own observations about ongoing family of origin connections in the lives of lesbians come from my personal experience, from the experiences of others in my social network, from some twenty-five years of clinical experience as a family therapist working with both straight and lesbian individuals, couples, and families, and from a series of research interviews conducted with lesbians and lesbian couples. It is the latter source of data that I report on in the following pages. These observations in sum contradict the impression generated in popular culture and in the professional literature of the isolated, rejected lesbian, disconnected from family and from her roots, adrift without models for living or sources of support.

The purpose of my study was to explore the uses of the language of lesbianism in varying contexts, with a view toward better understanding the impact of secrecy, the unsaid, the unspoken, on lesbian lives (Laird, in press). I wanted to know how these women storied their lives in exchanges with family, work, community, and so on. For one thing, I had become impressed over the years with how, in spite of the secrecy, silence, and homophobia that seemed to characterize their lives, so many of the lesbians I had come to know through clinical work and through friendship had such clear strengths and were leading such productive lives. In the field interview process, I learned a good deal about their relationships with their families, the norms for language use, the rewards, as well as the accommodations and compromises made.

My sample, which was one of convenience, consisted of nineteen lesbians. Eight of the women were interviewed in couple format, although each woman had the opportunity to tell her own story. Six were living alone and were not in committed relationships at the time of the interview. All of the women were White, and all had completed high school. All but two had completed college, and most had advanced degrees. Contrasted with these commonalities, there was wide variation in ethnic, religious, and social class backgrounds. Two women had grown up on public assistance and one of them, whose family had been on public assistance for two or three generations, was receiving assistance herself. At the other end of the economic continuum, one of my informants was reared in a very privileged, wealthy family in Great Britain in which her father was a diplomat and her mother a champion amateur athlete. Raised primarily by nannies and governesses, she was shipped off to boarding school at an early age. The women ranged in age from twenty-six to sixty-eight, their stories reflective of very different eras and different social contexts.

The audiotaped interviews averaged two hours each; they were subsequently transcribed, and a copy was sent to each informant for comments and editing. One woman called me and asked me to come back, because she felt she had left out some important information. I hope to continue similar interviews with a more varied sample and to return to all of their homes, to pursue some of the many new questions generated from their narratives and particularly to study intergenerational family connections in more depth. But certainly, some family information can be reported at this stage. The following major themes have emerged from these conversations.

Separations and Connections

First, my research supports the conclusions of research cited earlier: Kennedy and Davis (1993), Kurdek and Schmitt (1987), Levy (1989), Lewin (1993), Murphy (1989), and Weston (1991) —namely that lesbians typically are not cut off from their families. Every woman in my sample remains very much in complex connection with her family of origin, although certainly the nature and quality of those connections vary a great deal, as they do in all families. For some of the women, there were periods of conflict and distancing from their families of ori-

gin after coming out or during periods of trying to come out, particularly during
late adolescence and early adulthood. For some, there were brief periods of alienation and emotional cut-off. Sometimes parents made rather extreme moves to
erase the homosexual possibility. Two of the women I interviewed, Lila and
Cheryl, in a practice that was not and may still not be uncommon, were ejected
from their families in late adolescence by being committed to mental hospitals.
Both believe that their personal stress during that period, as well as the solutions
of their families and mental health professionals, resulted from larger social forces
that defined homosexuality as a sickness or mental illness.

A third woman, Deborah, of Jewish origin and now in her sixties, reminisced:

> I think they never wanted me to be at college in the first place . . . [and then] I
> came back with a degree . . . and with this woman and on top of everything
> else she was Japanese, and we took an apartment in New York, and so my
> mother's way of breaking this up . . . [was] my father had a cold, which she de-
> cided was pneumonia, and so they had to move back to the city and into my
> apartment. I asked, "What do you expect me to do with Gail? It's her apart-
> ment too." My mother said, "You can send her to the Y." My grandfather sent
> me a telegram . . . saying that my parents were dying of heart attacks and were
> mailing themselves to me in separate coffins. Well, when they moved into the
> apartment and discovered we were gone, that's when my mother had hysterics
> and I was out of touch with my family for two years.

Deborah's mother is still going strong at ninety-eight, living independently
and financially supported by Deborah, who takes her someplace very special every
year on her birthday and keeps in close contact.

Robin, forty-three, a woman who so far has survived leukemia and lives in a small
house in the woods built by herself and a community of women, cleans houses and
sells her weaving to make a living. This former hippie and political radical reports a
difficult childhood and a long period of cut-off from a family that neglected her during her years of severe medical crisis. When she was about thirty-five and about the
time she came out to herself and others, she reconnected with her mother and brother
(her father had died ten years earlier) and, like Beth, Lila, and Deborah, Robin has
become a most dutiful daughter during her mother's later years. Robin's mother, who
now has Alzheimer's disease, easily accepted and in fact expected Robin's lesbianism,
seeing that as perhaps just one more aspect of her earlier "sixties" rebellion against
her family's values. Robin feels that during the last few years, even with her mother's
illness, she and her mother have become meaningfully close for perhaps the first time.

Although the stories of Beth, Lila, Deborah, and Robin are more dramatic
than some, the pattern of leaving and returning is typical—leaving physically

for a period of time or emotionally distancing in order to come to terms with independence and choices for living that are troubling for the family, later returning to renegotiate the terms of the relationship when the women themselves feel more secure in their choices. This is a common phenomenon in the lives of young heterosexual women as well.

In Robin's case, the lesbian theme mirrors an earlier struggle for independence and individuation, probably ancillary to other, even more powerful family themes that may or may not have been resolved. Janet, now fifty-six, was raised in a Southern Baptist farm family in which overt racist language and practice was the norm. Family loyalty, family pride, and family values were very clear, and the ties very strong, but Janet became an early, active participant in the civil rights movement. She made it clear then that she loved her family and would maintain close connections but would march to a different drummer. And sometimes the lyrics to her music would be her own, unspoken but enacted.

Early on, she wrote to her parents from college, "Even though our *definition* of what's right and what's wrong may differ, I appreciate that you taught me that there *is* a right and a wrong." Racist beliefs and practices were part of family culture, but at some point, during a family conversation, Janet said, "We have very different beliefs, a different position on these things, but I'm not going to argue with anybody, I'm not going to fight with you about it, but I just want you to know that I'm here and you're there. And, said Janet, "I never discussed it again."

She recounted an exchange with her father, when some of her sisters were visiting:

> And he started one of his tirades about niggers. And I just sat opposite him at the table, and I just looked at him. And he stopped. And later, I don't remember how I heard this story, he was sitting around the store with the boys, and someone was ranting and raving—as they were playing checkers—about this nigger-lovin' guy who's running for governor, and my father said, "Aster, now we had our day, and we did it our way. Now it's time for somebody else to do it their way. . . ." And that was a big change.

Janet handled her positioning as a lesbian in much the same way; she is much respected in the family and maintains close ties with her mother, siblings, their children, and the extended family.

One of the things Janet's story, and the stories of most of the women I interviewed, suggests is that these are women individuating-in-connection, questioning some of the politics, gender prescriptions, values, and lifestyles of their families of origin. The "lesbian" theme is an important one, and it can become for a time the pole around which the daughter's struggles for self-definition pivot. But here it is not an issue powerful enough, over the long haul, to supersede the importance of family connection.

In fact, for many of the women I interviewed, whatever else the lesbian choice may imply about one's fundamental sexual orientation, it has also meant a way to escape this society's constraining gender expectations for women. Many of these women talked of how important the women's movement and feminist thinking has been in their lives, allowing them freedom to construct a story for their lives that is different from those prescribed for their female predecessors—a story that opened up many options, including the possibility that one could choose a woman rather than a man for a life partner.

Folk wisdom suggests that it is even more difficult for men or women from certain ethnic or racial groups to choose a gay or lesbian identity, particularly gays and lesbians from families with old-world values or from families of color. Certainly, definitions of family and what it means to be in a family vary among groups, and the issues for the lesbian daughter can vary as well. Although all of the women I interviewed were White, several chapters in this book (Chapters Six, Ten, and Eleven) describe how cultural and racial themes and meanings intersect with the meanings of gay or lesbian choices (Greene & Boyd-Franklin, Liu & Chan, Morales). Different cultural values about such issues as gender, sexuality, individuation, the meanings of "family," and loyalty to family will have an impact on the son's or daughter's choices and subsequent relationship with the family. Furthermore, lesbians and gays of color can find themselves abandoned or neglected by both the family and community of origin and the gay community, making it more difficult to build new families of friendship.

Nevertheless, Tremble, Schneider, and Appathurai (1989), in a study of the influence of ethnicity on the relationships of gay and lesbian young people and their families, found that "when apparently intractable cultural strictures collide with the facts of life, the parents' response was more flexible, complex, and subtle than we had expected" (p. 256). Interestingly, one would think that more traditional values and expectations for traditional marriage and family would predict a more negative family response to the lesbian or gay child. As these researchers point out, these same values point to the importance of family, to maintaining ties, and to reconciliation. They found that both parents and children developed various strategies of accommodation that might not be optimal but prevented cut-off. For example, families storied the lesbian and gay behavior as a bad habit, an addiction, or a seduction, externalizing the blame and removing responsibility from themselves or the child, while their children kept their gay friends and lives separate from their families and ethnic communities, sometimes feeling lonely and isolated.

Lesbianism as the Family "Red Herring"

Relationships in all families must be continually renegotiated, family values embraced or discarded, stands taken, and compromises made or refused on all sides. The lesbian daughter's attempts to become more the author of her own life are no different from any other daughter's, except that she chooses an identity and a course for her life that may be painful or initially unacceptable for her family, an identity that is socially stigmatized. Not unlike the daughter who chooses to marry someone from a different and presumably less socially valued racial, ethnic, social class, or religious grouping or the daughter who rejects her family's politics, the lesbian daughter challenges the family's closely held expectations for its children. Some families, like Janet's or Kathy's, although concerned and worried about what the future may hold—for their children and for themselves—are accepting and supportive from the beginning. Most families, although there may be some initial conflict and separation, at the very least accommodate over time, gradually absorbing and at least tolerating their daughter's choices. A few, like that of Louise, dig in and use the lesbian narrative for other purposes.

> Louise, twenty-eight, the youngest of eight siblings from a working-class Irish Catholic family, at age eighteen became aware of her attraction to Gerry, her longtime best girlfriend in high school. When the two began to spend more and more time together and Louise began to think about moving in with Gerry, Louise's mother became frantic. She intercepted phone calls and letters, screaming that Gerry was a "devil" and the relationship the "work of the Devil, an attack on God." One of Louise's brothers, twenty-two, living at home and drunk at the time, told her it was a stage she was going through. "If you weren't my sister," he said, "I would take you upstairs and fuck you and then you'd get over this lesbian thing."

> Her siblings sided with Mom, while her Dad was silent. Louise left home rejected, sad, and angry—at once uncertain about what being with another woman might mean for her self-definition and her future but fiercely determined to make her own choices.

> Louise believes that her choice to self-identify as a lesbian, to leave home, and to move in with Gerry allowed her to escape what were extremely limiting constraints for the females in her family. In this family, gender roles were highly traditional and the family boundaries extremely rigid. Girls were to marry and to have children but to maintain primary loyalty to their parents; spouses were included but never really welcomed. College for girls would not be supported or

even discussed. Louise believes that it was her lesbian choice and the support of her partner, Gerry, that allowed her to differentiate enough from her family to move beyond the limited possibilities for the females in her family. After working for a few years, she attended a prestigious college on the West Coast (where she won many awards for her scholarship) and has launched a promising professional career. It has taken ten years for Louise—who maintained rather superficial and rigidly ritualized contact with her family during this period, compromising as necessary to maintain the connection—to take a stand with them on defining her as part of a lesbian couple and including Gerry as part of the family. Her parents had not allowed Gerry in their home, had forbidden her contact with any of the many children of Louise's siblings, and had never visited Louise and Gerry in their home. Nevertheless, this family has reluctantly accepted Louise's recent pronouncement that Gerry will be accompanying her on visits to her family, if they wish to see Louise at all. It is a significant move for a family that, at Louise's college graduation, was utterly bewildered by the unknown educational and professional worlds their daughter had entered, changes that threatened the family's coherence as much if not more than the lesbian connection.

This is a family in which it was and is extraordinarily difficult for any of the children to break a rule, a home that was extraordinarily difficult to leave. Louise's lesbianism afforded a convenient target for warding off any challenges to the parents' grip on their children's lives or any threats to the only story they could recognize, as well as a way to escape the constraints of traditional marriage and roles for women as conceptualized in her family. Her marginal choice has allowed her to question the center in ways that seem to have been healthy and growth-producing for her. In other families of some of the women I interviewed or have known in other contexts, parents, with more or less subtlety, use the daughter's own anxieties and sensitivity about her lesbianism, what has been termed "internalized homophobia" in the professional literature, her fears of losing her ties to her family, to bind her loyalties. In these situations, it may be difficult for the lesbian daughter to form other central attachments or, when she does, it introduces tension and conflict in the lesbian couple relationships, as it would if she were to "leave home" in the context of a heterosexual relationship. But in the case of lesbianism, the homophobia in the larger community, like racism or sexism, can support the family's efforts to thwart any innovative choices.

One couple, when I began to see them clinically several years ago, had lived together for thirty-five years and had yet to spend a major holiday together. Neither was invited, on these occasions, to the home of the other's parents, and each felt she must spend the holiday with her family of origin. These women had not openly defined their coupleness in their families of origin, and their families had never asked about it. These were women who, when the family of origin made demands, made serious compromises and repeatedly jeopardized their own relationship to retain family approval. It is difficult to know whether either woman, if she had not somehow found the other, might ever have been able to marry and leave home. I wondered whether husbands would have been included within the family of origin emotional system; in the context of the unrecognized lesbian relationship, everyone concerned could define each of them as "single" when necessary.

Voicing the "L" Word

Some narrative and constructionist theorists believe that, until something is "languaged," it does not exist. One of the themes I explored at some length in these interviews was how, in what ways and in what contexts, women differentially languaged—gave words to—their lesbianism and the nature of their love relationships. This is a theme I report on in another work (Laird, in process). "Outness" has typically been defined in the literature as verbal disclosure and is seen as vital to the development of a healthy gay or lesbian identity. Nondisclosure, secrecy, and silence are seen as problematic, as signs of unresolved developmental issues and internalized homophobia, a risk to mental health. Using verbal criteria, several studies indicate that self-disclosure rates are very low and that gays and lesbians are "invisible."

But meanings are communicated in many powerful ways, through ritual, story, metaphor, and through everyday action. As Healy (1993) points out, behavior can and does often speak louder than words. The language of action can conceal or reveal lesbian identity, affirm or invalidate relationships, recognize or disqualify commitments. It is during ritual times that families most vividly define themselves, through words but also through actions and symbols, constructing and shaping their definitions. All of the lesbians in my research were out to their families of origin nonverbally or behaviorally, that is, in the ways they wore their lives for family to clearly interpret the signals and to make whatever meanings of their situations they chose. Some, however, rarely use the "L" word, so associated with sexuality in public discourse, much as most heterosexual couples do not go around using sexual language or highlighting the sexual parts of their relationship for their parents. But lesbians may clearly occupy one bedroom, co-own a home and a car with another woman, spend their major rituals as a couple with their respective extended families, and in most actions make clear they are partnered and committed.

And though some of their families might wince at the word "lesbian," sending powerful "don't use that awful language" messages, most of these same families show through their actions that they care deeply about and remain tied to their daughters. When the daughter is partnered, they acknowledge and validate the lesbian relationship to the extent that they open up their family boundaries to include the partner and to define her as "family member" in various ways. If there are children, there is even more reason in both generations to remain solidly connected.

All but one of the women I spoke with felt she was out to her family, but this sense of outness had different meanings. Maureen, at sixty-eight the oldest women with whom I spoke, said that she had been lesbian all of her life and thought her parents and siblings probably had known, but she had used the "L" word for the first time in our conversation. Since that opportunity to review her life and to think about her family relationships, she has come out to her brother, who in turn shared some of his own secrets and life disappointments with her. Maureen told me in a later conversation that she has become much closer to her brother, as they seem now to be able to talk more openly about many things. Most women reported that they rarely used the "L" word in their families or in work contexts. For most, it was part of a special language used with lesbian and gay friends and in gay culture contexts.

Most of these women had at some point verbally disclosed to their parents and siblings and saw themselves as out to their families. That is, they had made it clear that they loved women and continued to demonstrate that implicitly in their life choices and actions. For those who were partnered, for the most part their partners were defined as "family" and included in nuclear and extended family gatherings and important family rituals. Most women indicated that their partners had gradually become included in gift-giving and card exchanges with their families of origin. This is even the case for Marilyn, the one woman I interviewed who has not come out to her family verbally. Marilyn was raised in a poor family, and she spent several years on public assistance after her husband abandoned her and her three children. She has now completed a master's degree, and she and her children live with Judy. She has come out verbally to her three children, a process that was extraordinarily difficult and painful and she is, tentatively and gradually, enacting her new coupleness in contacts with her family of origin, inviting them to her home on special occasions. She is gradually introducing them to her new world but does not feel they could accept or even tolerate an overt "lesbian" definition.

Most of the women who came out verbally to their families have learned, in the years following initial disclosure, to screen their language. Using the "lesbian" descriptor generated tension and sometimes a visible shrinking back or flinching on the part of a parent or sibling, even after many years of knowing the daughter's lesbian identity. Often an awkward silence would follow, or the subject would be changed.

Of course the daughter's not languaging her lesbianism allows families to story her and her relationships in whatever ways they choose. Although this situation is often represented as deplorable and asks for too many compromises on the part of the lesbian daughter, it also seems to allow for family connections, however precarious, to be maintained. And this is a compromise all seem willing to make or at least resigned to making for the sake of maintaining peace and family connectedness.

> Deborah has never minced words with her now ninety-eight-year-old mother, but her mother has ingenious strategies for transforming lesbian language. A few years ago, Deborah and her mother were visiting a lesbian couple, long-time friends of Deborah's, for the weekend. Deborah had explained to her mother that the women were lesbians and had lived together for forty years. As she was taking her mother home after the visit, Deborah asked whether her mother had enjoyed the visit. She said, "Yes, dear, but you are mistaken about them. I'm sure they are sisters, they look so much alike." "Yes, Mother," sighed Deborah, "they are indeed Sisters."

In one of my efforts to language my own relationship, some years ago I ventured to say to my mother over the telephone, "Ann and I will be celebrating our twenty-fifth anniversary together next week." A long and uncomfortable silence ensued. Not to be quite so easily discouraged, the next week I described to my mother the beautiful ring Ann had given me. Again, there was a long pause and my mother finally said, with some asperity, "Don't you have enough jewelry?"

My mother, myself, and all but the youngest of the women I interviewed, and their families, have grown up in a world that has forbidden the naming of the lesbian relationship, as Oscar Wilde called it, "the love that dares not speak its name" (Sanders, 1993). "Lesbian," for most of us, conjured up deep, dark, dirty, and forbidden part-images or resided even beyond the imagination. Several of the women with whom I spoke, even at very young ages when they suspected they might be different, knew enough not to tell anyone or to use the forbidden word, even to themselves. It was common to go the library and to subversively try to find some book or article on homosexuality that might tell them about themselves. That, too, was a painful experience, since what little they could find was full of dismal forebodings for their futures. Most of us growing up never met anyone who was a lesbian, or we noticed, in our families, some woman or couple pointed at or whispered about. I went to a women's college reputed to be a hotbed of lesbianism but never knowingly met a lesbian.

Priscilla, the daughter of rather socially liberal, highly educated parents, reported that her parents "accept" her partner, welcome her into the family, but maintain silence about the relationship outside of the family. She wishes, for example, that her parents could be joyful for her, would show her family pictures to friends and neighbors, could brag about her publicly the way they do about their other children and grandchildren. The lesbian relationship, accepted and sometimes even languaged inside the family, is rarely spoken of beyond the family borders.

Although naming the relationship seems to raise the tension level in most of these families even when, in general, the communication patterns seem relatively comfortable and open, sometimes the lesbian language theme fits into a larger pattern of constrained or problematic family communication. Several of the women reported, for example, that no conflictual or negative conversation was allowed in their families. In other families, such as Gerry's, which has been relatively accepting and inclusive of Louise, there is a concern that younger children not be exposed to lesbian language or openly expressed affection, as if lesbianism were like a virus and might be catching.

Sometimes parents seem to understand about their daughter's sexual orientation even before their daughters have any language. In two situations, when the daughter finally disclosed to her mother, each mother said something like, "I wondered how long it would take you to find out. I've known for years."

Certainly, the experience of self-disclosing, of coming out in contexts in which one previously has been censored or has censored oneself, can be enormously self-empowering—and the terror of being discovered can be debilitating. Certainly, there can be serious costs to silencing and censoring oneself and being silenced by others. But all of us make choices about what we will share or not share about ourselves every day. In every sentence, we select what we wish to bring into the conversation—in our body language, through dress, in the ways we organize our homes, and in other uses of the said and the unsaid. Most of us wish to present ourselves well, to construct stories of self that are marketable and communicate a coherent sort of self to the other. There are always rules and strategies for conversation in any family; the things we talk about and do not talk about with varying people; even the genres for speech are prescribed, differing by gender, age, ethnicity, social class, education, family and community culture, and so on.

We have tended to assume that silence and secrecy are problematic for individual identity development, but every human being manipulates language. We all use it strategically and intersubjectively, constructing with our families and others how we will talk together and be together, editing and reediting our personal narratives for ourselves and for those around us (Laird, 1993b).

The lesbian literature, I believe, often exaggerates the differences between lesbians and other human beings and overlooks the tremendous diversity within lesbian culture. These narratives demonstrate both the commonalities these women share with all women defining connections with their families, as well as considerable diversity in the forms these connections take. One can speculate that these women are as close to or as distant from, as involved or uninvolved, as one might find in any sample of nineteen heterosexual women.

Strength and Resilience

One reason I undertook this study was that I perceived an enormous gap between the people I knew and the generally dismal impression many people have of the gay and lesbian individual and the ravages of heterosexism and homophobia. Gays and lesbians I was meeting in my own life were some of the most interesting, talented, strongest people I had ever had the privilege to know. Who was writing about them, about their strengths and their creativity? What gave them such resilience in a world that finds homosexuality deviant and even disgusting?

Many of the lesbians I know seem to be the strongest and most differentiated members of their nuclear families. I have been interested in the fact that there is so little writing on the tremendous strength and resilience exhibited by gays and lesbians, *in spite of* experiences of oppression and having to negotiate one's life in negatively defining, homophobic environments. My own impressions and personal experiences seemed to belie the dismal portrayals of pathology in the clinical literature and popular media. The women I interviewed, regardless of social class, seemed to support my impression. For example, Cheryl, twenty-six, whose family is characterized by generations of alcoholism, unemployment and underemployment, and welfare, is the first person in her twelve-member family to get dry and the first to attend college. She takes one or two courses at a time at a community college and is hoping to get her associate's degree next year. Louise, described earlier, defied her family's gender prescriptions and with the support of her partner, Gerry, graduated Phi Beta Kappa from a top college, winning five major awards. Grace, who grew up in a rejecting and critical family with two seriously dysfunctional alcoholic parents, has gone on to become a well-known writer and expert on work with alcoholic families.

The lesbian issue affords not simply conflict but also possibility and opportunity. It is often the pivot around which the tasks of individuation or differentiation occur and continue to occur throughout life, not in some neat and tidy arrangement of stages. We never, in my view, "resolve" our lesbian identities; it is a narrative without end, always being edited and reshaped as we and our contexts change.

Judy, forty-six, a graduate school professor and clinician herself, was on a car trip with her mother. Her mother was talking about one of Judy's sisters, who had been going through a very difficult phase in which she was expressing a great deal of anger at their mother and had recently said some things the mother found very hurtful.

> And so my mother said, "Well, do you feel that way [about me]?" And I thought, well, I don't want to just dismiss this, to leave my sister looking like she owns this whole problem. But neither did I have the same degree of feeling about it as my sister. Anyway, I said, "You know, Mom, sometimes I think that all of us in the family suffer from a great amount of judgmentalness. And that you have it too, and that sometimes when I talk to you I feel the first place you're coming from is some sense of moral judgement about things . . . and that can really make it hard to want to talk to you sometimes."

Judy went on, in this conversation with her mother, to use the example of how her mother, when talking about lesbian or gay issues, always begins with something like, "Well, of course I don't really quite understand, uh, what it's like." This really bothered her, she told me, her mother always acting as if a gay relationship is some "*totally* foreign animal!" So she said to her mother:

> I feel like when you say that, you've been married to my father for fifty-two years, you know something about loving somebody, and when you say that, you're totally distancing yourself from something that you *do* know about and putting me in this category that's . . . totally foreign, and it isn't. And I went on to say, "And, I think you can do better than that."

Said Judy to me:

> I'm not sure she completely got it, but I knew she was going to go home and think about it. . . . And I felt like at that point, I had a right to expect more from her in terms of understanding my relationship. Even if she wouldn't choose it for me, even if she didn't think it was great—she did have some human experience to connect with me about it. And she wants to connect with me about it, that's really the whole context of what the discussion was about. *It wasn't about being gay; it was about how she connected with her children* (emphasis added).

In another example, Janet, from the rural Southern Baptist family described earlier, has not hidden her lesbian orientation, but as in matters of race, she does not attempt to convince others—her style is not to argue or to provoke rupture. Her family is too important to her, but she does not compromise her own convictions—about race or about sexual orientation. Her partner and she frequently travel to Tennessee to spend time with her mother (her father is now deceased), and her mother and adult siblings often visit her. *Family* is more important here than politics or sexuality, and she manages well what we might think of as biculturality. One senses that she has taught her family a great deal as she has, in her actions, steadfastly made clear who she is and what she believes—in relation to, not separate from, family.

The daughter's lesbianism, then, can be used by the family as a rationalization for binding her loyalties and preventing her from authoring a life too different from that of the family, or it can be used by the daughter herself as a marker of angry rebellion and demands for quick and complete acceptance of difference. But in most cases, as Judy's and Janet's narratives both illustrate, the lesbian theme is just one facet of the ongoing complex task of working on family relationships. With another son or daughter, a different theme may emerge as pivotal.

Certainly, many of the women I interviewed wish for more. They wish their families could more openly admire and affirm them and could brag about *their* families as well as their individual accomplishments to their neighbors and friends. They wish they could do more than often reluctantly accept the inevitable. But they understand how both history and social context continue to make this leap into affirmation and voice extraordinarily difficult, and they forgive their families for their failures to stand up against social homophobia because they know how hard it was for them, and they know their families do not have the same supports they have, that is, another context in which they can use the language of lesbianism.

Families of Choice

Although this chapter is about families of origin, I do not believe that lesbians *need* their original families to forge meaningful, rich, and full family lives—I do believe we can also choose and build new families that may work better for us. But it may mean tremendous costs which, if we worked harder at it, we might not have to suffer (Bowen, 1978; Hartman & Laird, 1983). In Butler's (1990) work on commitment ceremonies, if families did not attend, the couple often lamented the fact that they were not or could not be there; it was often a great sadness that their special commitment could not be shared. The costs to Louise of maintaining her lesbian position and maintaining a distanced and ritualized relationship with her family may be greater than the costs of the compromises she has had to make to stay in connection. We don't have to like our relatives or agree with them or even spend much time with them, but, if Bowen (1978) is correct, we do have to come to terms with our own emotional reactivity in the family of origin system and to differentiate sufficiently for our new relationships to be free of what he has termed the "emotional baggage" of the past.

Family therapists, however, tend to overemphasize the dire consequences of cut-off from families of origin and at the same time to minimize the richness and importance of families of choice. Most of the women I interviewed both maintain connections with blood families *and* have forged new and meaningful extended networks of friends that come to behave like close extended families. Priscilla, Sheila, and Robin, for example, live in a small, rural, politically radical enclave in which a community of women serve as extended family for each other. This family seems to be forged around similar political beliefs, such as nonmaterialism, and shared activities such as exchanges of labor and extensive recycling of material goods. Deborah, who finds little in common with most of her blood relatives, has constructed an extended family pieced together from the families of former lovers and connections with other lesbians from all over the country.

The area in which this study was conducted and fourteen of the women live, particularly the small city of Northampton and environs, is known as a lesbian-friendly and lesbian-affirmative community. This means that most of the women have formed extensive lesbian (although not exclusively lesbian) friendship networks which, at least some of the time, serve similar functions as those served by extended families—participating in "family" rituals, helping out at times of illness or other crisis, lending money or sharing other resources, and so on. We know too little about how such networks operate, and it is clear that we rarely ask about them in our clinical work, a point made by Gillian Walker in her dialogue with Stanley Siegel in Chapter Two.

Implications for Clinical Practice

In this chapter, I have visited the prevailing narrative of family of origin invisibility in the life of the lesbian, examining popular film, family studies, and family therapy literature, as well as the popular or "trade" literature concerning their portrayals of these ties (or lack of ties). The picture that emerges—largely one of invisibility, rejection, loss, and cut-off—is contrasted with what lesbians themselves have told me in a series of interviews. I find that lesbians are not usually cut off from their families and that their patterns of separating and connecting seem similar to those of daughters in general. Furthermore, the issue of the daughter's lesbianism becomes just one of the salient issues in her individuation-in-relation process and, as was the case with some of the women I talked with, can sometimes actually be very helpful in that process, offering both opportunity and new possibilities for self-definition and for couple and family life.

It is also clear that coming out is not simply a matter of verbal disclosure. Commitment to a lesbian relationship may be demonstrated in many ways, behaviorally and verbally, in the family of origin and in other contexts. Lesbians, like everyone else, make careful judgments about how and in what contexts they will communicate, about what they will say, and about what they will leave unsaid, to themselves and to others.

The family's response to the daughter's lesbianism reflects its more enduring patterns of organization and the extent to which the autobiographical family narrative is available for rewriting. Families who tend to be inflexible concerning rules for behavior and visions for their children are often inflexible about many things. Families that have difficulty talking about sensitive or controversial issues of any kind will have more trouble talking about this one. Families that have difficulty allowing their children to leave or to grow up, for whatever reasons, can use the convenient "red herring" of lesbianism to stall their child's leaving or to insist on loyalty to traditional social, religious, or political ideas.

To the extent that relationships with families of origin are important or relevant to clinical work with any client, so are they in work with the lesbian. Family of origin relationships may become part of the therapeutic conversation in any clinical modality—in individual, couple, child, family of origin, family of choice, and group interviews.

What the narratives of lesbians themselves most clearly reveal is (1) that these family connections are important and ongoing, and (2) that the "lesbian" theme is very much intertwined with and expressive of other relational issues. How well the lesbian daughter and family together are able to integrate the lesbian story into their lives and to embrace new definitions for couple and family life is expressive of how well parents are able to come to terms with their daughters becoming the authors of their own lives as independent women.

Certainly, "lesbianism" adds an important ingredient to the family stew. These women have experienced some of the pain, rejection, isolation, and anger from families we commonly hear about, and their families have undergone periods of anger, confusion, anxiety, concern, and loss over the daughter's lesbian identity. But it is clear that these women and their families travel beyond the rocky road of initial disclosure and forge more or less satisfying ongoing relationships, maintaining connections and continuing to negotiate how familiness will be defined. These are tasks in all families.

The lesbian daughter must deal with her family's heterosexist assumptions and their homophobia, as well as her own; and all concerned must face how they will support each other in a more or less homophobic context, one that does not ordinarily allow for the sharing of either joy or pain outside the family. The family must learn to live with and perhaps to fight against a sense of marginality they never expected they would have.

Most of the family of origin issues lesbians bring into therapy are, as White and Epston (1990) would frame it, "problems with problems," and they look like the problems anyone might bring—everything from how to hold one's own with a critical mother, how to set limits with an interfering father, how to cope with a parent's failing health, to how to recover from a childhood of abuse and despair or how, as a couple, to deal with different family of origin cultural styles and levels of acceptance or how to define grandparent relationships.

It is crucial that the therapist be able to bracket and to move beyond his or her own prior understandings and assumptions that probably have been shaped in a heterosexist and homophobic context. These understandings and assumptions, or "maps," can not only keep us from hearing what the lesbian client is saying but can mean that we fail to ask the good questions. For instance, we may fail to fully explore the meanings of "family" for the lesbian and lesbian couple. On the one hand, we may ignore family of choice relationships, colluding with feelings of hurt and rejection, or on the other hand, we may too easily fail to question and more deeply explore cut-offs from families of origin.

We may make either the alpha error of exaggerating the differences between lesbians and heterosexual women or the beta error of minimizing the differences (Hare-Mustin, 1987), leading us to behave clinically with lesbians in ways we would never otherwise consider. The alpha error can happen in the case of therapists who, for example, may have stereotypical assumptions about lesbian culture and how lesbians are "different" from other women, failing to explore themes or appreciate relationships in ways that they ordinarily would with women clients. Clinicians who make the beta error may underestimate the power of homophobia, thus perhaps prematurely urging lesbians to come out to their families and in other contexts and underestimating the potential negative reactions of others. Both groups may fail to note the tremendous diversity of lesbian experience among lesbian clients, by virtue of social class, race or ethnicity, age, geography, and other social markers, or simply because of profoundly different life experiences and life contexts.

In general, lesbian women seem to be more like heterosexual women, for example, than they are like gay men. Gender, seemingly, is a more powerful determinant of certain kinds of values and behaviors than sexual orientation (Blumstein & Schwartz, 1983). If Gilligan (1982), the Wellesley College Stone Center researchers (see, for example, Jordan & Surrey, 1986), and other women scholars are correct, women more than men, for whatever reasons, nature or nurture, tend to forge relationships in connection. In this regard, it would be very interesting to know whether the relationships of gay men with their families of origin follow different patterns than those of women. Since the literature and research on homosexuality, as well as popular cultural narratives, have centered around the lives of gay men, it is possible that the portrayal of gays and lesbians as separate and isolated from family better reflects gay male than lesbian experience.

In sum, as clinicians we need to be as knowledgeable as possible about lesbian culture and lesbian experience, not so as to lead from our own knowledge or theory in a way that makes prior assumptions, but so as to be able to fully listen—to ask the questions and listen to the answers in a way that lack of knowledge or fixed ideas can prevent us from doing. Only then will we be able to help lesbians, in the context of their families of origin, creation, and choice, move ahead in ways that recognize their strength and resilience and that make the most of their potential for positive connection and mutual support. There are, of course, many sources for this "knowledge," but none better than the narratives of those who have lived the experience, from the "native's point of view," if you will. We need to listen to the stories of lesbians themselves and to the stories of their families, who have been neglected by heterosexually and homosexually oriented scholars. As one mother of a lesbian daughter said recently in the question period after a series of presentations of therapists on lesbian families, "We're out here, we want to support you, and you need to listen to us." At another conference in which I presented, a Mennonite couple with a lesbian daughter described how they had formed a church group to support parents of gay and lesbian children and to educate fellow church members and how this idea had spread to several congregations. They *are* out there, and they are willing to bear witness to their experiences in a way that can be helpful to clinicians and to the larger community.

I want to end this chapter with another moment from my own experience—a moment that attests to the richness and complexity of life in the lesbian family. This moment is part of a family transition, an intergenerational and kinship ritual centered around a child's bat mitzvah, a time in most families when individual and family narratives are edited to rewrite the old and to incorporate the new. In this case, we as therapists can learn a great deal about how we might help lesbian daughters and families with lesbian members to express their connectedness through narrative and ritual.

Lila, whom I interviewed, is also a longtime friend and the first lesbian I knew to choose to become a mother through donor insemination. I regard her as a courageous pioneer. Lila gave birth to her daughter, Edith, in the context of what she thought at the time was a lifetime partnership with Elaine, a formerly married lesbian with a son of her own. The two later separated and, again, were pioneers in figuring out, in spite of the hurts and disappointments, how to coparent in the best way possible the children they had shared and how to maintain ties with their own and their partners' families of origin and their own extended family of choice.

Now it was time for Edith, the daughter of Lila and Elaine, to enter young womanhood through the ritual of the bat mitzvah. The congregation was filled with family and friends—lesbian couples and their children, straight couples and their children, and family members. Although Lila's parents are now deceased, her sisters and their families came, an aged friend of her father's from New York arrived to represent the grandparent generation, and Elaine's father and stepmother came from three thousand miles away to be present.

Edith moved through her parts of the bat mitzvah perfectly, singing and speaking the traditional Hebrew words in a clear and beautiful way. Toward the end, when it came time for her own reflections, she spoke of the meaning her participation in the Jewish faith has had for her and the questions she continues to probe. She ended by speaking of her family:

> Through the years, when describing my *different* family situation, I have gotten a wide variety of responses, some consisting of disbelief, some of total amazement, and an occasional few of disgust. One thing that I have come to understand is that it makes no difference *what* the family consists of, as long as there is love, honesty, and humor. . . .
>
> My family consists of my biological mother, Lila, my other parent, Elaine, my stepmother, Helen, and my nonbiological brother, Doug. I have no shame that my parents are [and here there was a smile and a twinkle in her thirteen-year-old dark, bright eyes, as she said, loudly and crystally clear], well, shall I say it? Lesbians! The only problem I have with it is that they are sometimes discriminated against. Just for loving who they want to love. It bothers me that in this day you are discriminated against just for being who you are.
>
> Having my parents be lesbians makes *me* stronger. Now when I see someone being discriminated against for who they are and not hiding it, I make sure that the discriminator knows that they are the wrong one. Denying someone the right to be who they are is like telling someone that they cannot have water.
>
> Discrimination is dependent upon fear. . . . I believe that if you do not agree with someone's sexual preference, race, class, gender, size, age, or looks you should still respect them for who they are. As many people say, don't judge a person by who they are on the outside, but instead who they are on the inside.

Her mother, Lila, in her talk, remarked on the load that Edith carried—in her backpack and on her shoulders—her talents, her grace, her marvelous sense of humor, her generosity, her rage, and her forgiving spirit, and Elaine spoke of the unusual challenges Edith has been presented with in her thirteen years and how courageously she has met them.

What courtroom judge, given half the chance, wouldn't have awarded custody of this wonderful young woman to some challenger of her mothers' sexual orientation? But what is "family," if not the strength and beauty that flourishes in this kind of social arrangement?

References

Allen, K. R., & Demo, D. H. (1995). The families of lesbians and gay men: A new frontier in family research. *Journal of Marriage and the Family, 57,* 1–17.

Benkov, L. (1994). *Reinventing the family: The emerging story of lesbian and gay parents.* New York: Crown.

Bernstein, R. (1995). *Straight parents gay children: Keeping families together.* New York: Thunder's Mouth Press.

Berzon, B. (1979). Telling your family you're gay. In B. Berzon & R. Leighton (Eds.), *Positively gay* (pp. 88–100). Milbrae, CA: Celestial Arts.

Blumstein, P., & Schwartz, P. (1983). *American couples: Money, work, sex.* New York: Morrow.

Bowen, M. (1978). *Family therapy in clinical practice.* Northvale, NJ: Aronson.

Brown, L. (1989). Lesbians, gay men, and their families: Common clinical issues. *Journal of Gay and Lesbian Psychotherapy, 1*(1), 65–77.

Butler, B. (Ed.). (1990). *Ceremonies of the heart: Celebrating lesbian unions.* Seattle, WA: Seal Press.

DeVine, J. L. (1984). A systemic inspection of affectional preference orientation and the family of origin. *Journal of Social Work and Human Sexuality, 2,* 9–17.

Dew, R. F. (1994). *The family heart: A memoir of when our son came out.* New York: Ballantine Books.

Foucault, M. (1980). *Power/knowledge: Selected interviews and other writings.* New York: Pantheon.

Gilligan, C. (1982). *In a different voice.* Cambridge, MA: Harvard University Press.

Griffin, C. W., Wirth, M. J., & Wirth, A. G. (1986). *Beyond acceptance: Lesbians and gays talk about their experiences.* New York: St. Martin's Press.

Griscom, J. (1992). The case of Sharon Kowalski and Karen Thompson: Ableism, heterosexism, and sexism. In P. R. Rothenberg (Ed.), *Race, class, and gender in the United States: An integrated study.* New York: St. Martin's Press.

Hall Carpenter Archives. Gay Men's Oral History Group (1989a). *Walking after midnight: Gay men's life stories.* London: Routledge.

Hall Carpenter Archives. Lesbian Oral History Group. (1989b). *Inventing ourselves: Lesbian life stories.* London: Routledge.

Hare-Mustin, R. (1987). The problem of gender in family therapy theory. *Family Process, 26,* 15–27.

Hartman, A., & Laird, J. (1983). *Family-centered social work practice.* New York: Free Press.

Healy, T. (1993). A struggle for language: Patterns of self-disclosure in lesbian couples. *Smith College Studies in Social Work, 63*(3), 247–264.

Herdt, G. (Ed.). (1992). *Gay culture in America: Essays from the field.* Boston: Beacon Press.

Jordan, J. V., & Surrey, J. L. (1986). The self-in-relation: Empathy and the mother-daughter relationship. In *The psychology of today's woman: New psychoanalytic visions.* Hillsdale, NJ: Analytic Press.

Kennedy, E. L., & Davis, M. D. (1993). *Boots of leather, slippers of gold: The history of a lesbian community.* New York: Routledge.

Kleinberg, L. (1986). *Coming home to self, going home to parents: Lesbian identity disclosure.* Work in Progress Series No. 24. Wellesley, MA: Wellesley College, Stone Center for Women's Development.

Krestan, J. (1988). Lesbian daughters and lesbian mothers: The crisis of disclosure from a family systems perspective. In L. Braverman (Ed.), *Women, feminism, and family therapy* (pp. 113–130). New York: Haworth Press.

Krestan, J., & Bepko, C. (1980). The problem of fusion in the lesbian relationship. *Family Process, 19*(3), 277–289.

Kurdek, L., & Schmitt, J. P. (1987). Perceived emotional support from family and friends in members of homosexual, married, and heterosexual cohabiting couples. *Journal of Homosexuality, 12*(2), 85–99.

Laird, J. (1993a). Lesbian and gay families. In F. Walsh (Ed.), *Normal family processes* (4th ed., pp. 282–328). New York: Guilford Press.

Laird J. (1993b). Women's secrets—women's silences. In E. Imber-Black (Ed.), *Secrets in families and family therapy* (pp. 243–267). New York: Norton.

Laird, J. (in press). Silence, secrecy, and strategy in lesbian language. In J. Laird (Ed.), *Lesbians and lesbian families: Multiple reflections.* New York: Columbia University Press.

Levy, E. (1989). Lesbian motherhood: Identity and social support. *Affilia, 4*(4), 40–53.

Lewin, E. (1993). *Lesbian mothers: Accounts of gender in American culture.* Ithaca, NY: Cornell University Press.

Martin, A. (1993). *Lesbian and gay parenting handbook: Creating and raising our families.* New York: HarperPerennial, 1993.

Monette, P. (1991). *Halfway home.* New York: Avon.

Monette, P. (1992). *Becoming a man: Half a life story.* New York: HarperCollins.

Monette, P. (1994). *Last watch of the night.* San Diego, CA: Harcourt Brace.

Murphy, B. C. (1989). Lesbians and their parents: The effects of perceived paternal attitudes on the couple. *Journal of Counseling and Development, 68*(1), 46–51.

Ordoña, T., & Thompson, D. (1990). A thousand cranes. In B. Butler (Ed.), *Ceremonies of the heart: Celebrating lesbian unions* (pp. 81–90). Seattle, WA: Seal Press.

Osman, S. (1972). My stepfather is a she. *Family Process, 11,* 209–218.

Preston, J. (1992). *A member of the family: Gay men write about their families.* New York: Dutton.

Roth, S. (1984). Psychotherapy with lesbian couples: The interrelationships of individual issues, female socialization, and the social context. In E. Hetrick & T. Stein (Eds.), *Innovations in psychotherapy with homosexuals.* Washington, DC: American Psychiatric Press.

Roth, S., & Murphy, B. C. (1986). Therapeutic work with lesbian clients; A systemic therapy view. In M. Ault-Riche & J. C. Hansen (Eds.), *Women and family therapy.* Gaithersburg, MD: Aspen Press.

Sanders, G. (1993). The love that dares to speak its name: From secrecy to openness—gay and lesbian affiliations. In E. Imber- Black (Ed.), *Secrets in families and family therapy.* New York: Norton.

Slater, S. (1995). *The lesbian family life cycle.* New York: Free Press.

Strommen, E. F. (1989). "You're a what?" Family members' reactions to the disclosure of homosexuality. *Journal of Homosexuality, 18*(1/2), 58.

Tremble, B., Schneider, M., & Appathurai, C. (1989). Growing up gay or lesbian in a multicultural context. In G. Herdt (Ed.), *Gay and lesbian youth* (pp. 253–264). New York: Haworth Press.

Walker, G. (1991). *In the midst of winter: Systemic therapy with families, couples, and individuals with AIDS infection.* New York: Norton.

Weston, K. (1991). *Families we choose: Lesbians, gays, kinship.* New York: Columbia University Press.

White, M., & Epston, D. (1990). *Narrative ends to therapeutic means.* New York: Norton.

Zitter, S. (1987). Coming out to Mom: Theoretical aspects of the mother-daughter process. In Boston Lesbian Psychologies Collective (Ed.), *Lesbian psychologies: Explorations and challenges* (pp. 177–194). Urbana: University of Illinois Press.

CHAPTER FIVE

COMING OUT AND THE MOTHER-DAUGHTER BOND

Two Case Examples

Suzanne Iasenza, Patricia L. Colucci, and Barbara Rothberg

The mother-daughter bond represents one of the most powerful, complicated, and emotionally charged relationships in the family. When a daughter discloses a lesbian identity to her mother, the personal, familial, and cultural threads that bind mother to daughter are stretched. Some bonds resist the stretch; some become more flexible; some break. Our purpose in this chapter is to discuss the complex issues involved in the mother-daughter relationship when a daughter has or is planning to disclose a lesbian identity to her mother. We will identify the cultural and familial themes that serve as the context for disclosure and will demonstrate the use of a Bowenian family of origin approach to working with lesbian daughters. Most important, we wish to illustrate, through two case examples, the *long-term processes* of coming out and family reconciliation, as most accounts of the coming-out process tend to focus only on the initial disclosure and immediate family response.

The Mother-Daughter Bond and the Effects of Disclosure

For many families, the disclosure of a daughter's lesbian identity disturbs the entire family equilibrium. Family positions and roles may shift, as some members move in, and others are distanced or distance themselves. For example, a daughter who held the position of favorite child may lose it after revealing a lesbian identity. Her "troublemaking" brother may experience an increase in status merely because he is heterosexually married. The mother-daughter relationship is central to family process in these instances because mothers are usually the emotional gatekeepers for the family. Mothers often act as the transmitters of disclosure to other family members in the system, such as fathers, aunts and uncles, and grandparents. In our clinical practices, we have noticed several patterns of behavior after a daughter discloses to a mother, ranging from acceptance to cut-off. Some mothers are hostile, some deny the information, and some display a pseudoacceptance, placing conditions on whether, how, and when the daughter's lesbianism will be integrated into the family system.

Surprisingly few therapists have offered guidelines for working with lesbian clients and their families. Roth and Murphy (1986) discuss how to develop hypotheses for different life contexts—the individual context, the lesbian couple context, the family of origin context, the therapy context, and the lesbian and heterosexual community context. Krestan (1987) describes coaching techniques that support the disclosure of a lesbian's identity to her family of origin. These and other works on the subject explore what we believe to be two central relationships: the relationship between disclosure and differentiation from the family of origin and the relationship between disclosure and authenticity in family relationships. We borrow the definition of authenticity from Surrey (1985) as the "ongoing challenge to feel emotionally real, connected, vital, clear and purposeful in relationship" (p. 6), as well as Bowen's definition of differentiation, which is described below.

In the following two cases, we demonstrate the use of a Bowenian family of origin approach to working with lesbian daughters. This approach provides a multigenerational perspective on the family system that helps a lesbian daughter to explore and interpret family patterns as they relate to her disclosure of her sexual identity, allowing her to rewrite her own story in the process. Bowen family systems theory contains four major interlocking concepts: the emotional system, multigenerational transmission process, differentiation, and the emotional triangle (Friedman, 1991; see also Chapter Eight of this book). In this theory, the family is defined as an emotional system operating across generations. In other words, our families serve as our emotional blueprints in life, setting the stage for the ways in which we relate and connect emotionally to others (Carter & Orfanidis, 1976).

Differentiation is defined by Bowen as being able to take "I" positions in one's family of origin, that is, being able to define one's own position in an autonomous, goal-directed way. A critical point in Bowenian theory is that one does not achieve differentiation through cut-off—quite the contrary. A cut-off implies reactivity and fusion—the opposite of differentiation. The goal is to achieve differentiation while remaining connected. This is a particularly important point for lesbian daughters who, in their anger, fear, or despair about being rejected by their families may resort to cut-offs.

Bowen cited the homosexual as one example of a type of person who is poorly differentiated (lower-functioning), linking homosexuality to intergenerational family patterns when he stated that "the most extreme forms of manic-depression, alcoholism, obsessive compulsive neurosis, and homosexuality develop over the course of at least several generations" (Kerr & Bowen, 1988, p. 241). He further believed that the family members of a homosexual person, just by virtue of being in the same family system, would be functioning at the same low level of differentiation as the identified homosexual member.

Although Bowen's model continues to be the cornerstone of multigenerational theory and practice and has very useful applications in work with lesbians and gays, clearly it has ethnocentric, androcentric, and heterosexist biases that need to be modified in such work. Carter and McGoldrick (1988) have stressed the need to integrate race, gender, ethnicity, and social class into a multicontextual model. Others have critiqued Bowenian theory for not taking into consideration that women are socialized to take primary emotional responsibility in the family, a role that may appear to be overly involved (Ault-Riche, 1986; Luepnitz, 1988).

Unlike Bowen, we believe that a lesbian self-definition may coexist with a high level of differentiation. In fact, we believe that disclosing and integrating one's lesbian identity into one's family of origin is necessary for an individual to develop authentic, differentiated relationships with family members. There are different ways of achieving such differentiation. Lesbian daughters who are not out might be coached to cultivate authentic relationships with family members before disclosing, while others may have already disclosed and need to integrate sexual identity issues into their family relationships.

In the examples that follow, the first case highlights the interactive nature of the mother-daughter bond. As the daughter becomes more secure about her sexual identity, taking "I" positions with her mother that affirm her lesbianism, her mother responds with greater acceptance. The second case emphasizes the importance of assessing the family system before disclosure in order to identify and track the way the system generally responds to difference and to try to predict what intergenerational patterns may interfere with disclosure.

CASE 1: STACEY

Stacey is a thirty-six-year-old Jewish woman who is the only surviving child of Holocaust survivor parents. Her parents were in different concentration camps when they were young; both were liberated at the end of the war, having lost their families in the camps. The two young people later met in Europe, and a strong bond developed between them, in part because of the tremendous losses each had endured. The re-creation of "family" was vitally important to both of them. Five years earlier, Stacey's brother, then thirty-seven, had died of cancer, leaving a wife and three children. In the same year, her father died of an aneurysm. Two years later, Stacey's mother married again. She married a man who was himself a Holocaust survivor and whose wife had died.

Stacey identifies as a lesbian. She came out fifteen years ago when she was living in Israel on a kibbutz. Although this was not an accepted lifestyle in this environment, it was not unknown for young women to experiment sexually. Because she was living so far away from home during that period, she felt it was unnecessary to tell her parents about her lifestyle, particularly because she was unsure of what she would feel when she returned home to the States.

Upon her return, Stacey felt compelled to reveal her sexual orientation because she wanted to continue to live a gay lifestyle. She became involved with a woman and decided to break the news to her parents. Her mother, the main communicator in the family, had a dramatic response, not unanticipated by Stacey: "I'm going to kill myself!" This dramatic statement was followed by her angry insistence that she would never accept such a thing and that no girlfriend of Stacey's would be welcome in her home. Stacey was quite upset and hurt but not at all surprised. Her mother, also hurt, grieved over the fact that Stacey would never get married and have children. (Today, of course, many lesbians are "getting married," if not legally, at least in the sense of making lifetime commitments that are often marked by commitment ceremonies, and many lesbians are having children through alternative insemination or adopting children.)

Stacey's reaction to her mother's pain was also quite predictable. She felt extremely guilty, having always carried a heavy burden of guilt because her parents had had such terrible losses. Somehow, it was her job to make up for their tragic past, to make her parents' lives easier. How could she add more pain to lives already burdened with such trouble? She was not at all connected to her own anger and sense of rejection over her lifestyle being unacceptable in their eyes. Stacey continued to maintain the same basic relationship with her parents, visiting frequently, joining them for dinner, participating in family events, and rarely mentioning her sexual identity, for she knew it would only cause upset and pain. Thus, for all intents and purposes, she stayed in the closet. After four years, her love relationship ended. Stacey never integrated her lover into her family and never dealt with the situation.

Seven months later, Stacey became involved with Ellen. She also began treatment at this time. She was encouraged by her therapist to discuss her life more honestly with her family. She told her mother of her new involvement, trying to share her excitement and testing out whether time had helped her mother accept her sexual identity. Her mother was no more accepting than she had previously been. Although Stacey was disappointed, she did not push the issue, still feeling that she was ruining her mother's life by living her own life in a manner that was unacceptable to her family. Her therapist helped her to deal with this by coaching her to gradually share more of her relationship experiences with her family while not insisting that they wholeheartedly accept her lifestyle.

During this period, her brother became ill with cancer and died, a tragic occurrence that revived all of the earlier losses. In the year following his death, life was extremely stressful for Stacey as she dealt with her brother's loss, a process that necessitated considerable family involvement. Ellen, Stacey's lover, was also very involved in the family during this period; gradually they accepted her as Stacey's friend. When there is a major illness in a family, priorities shift. The nature of Stacey's relationship with Ellen faded into the background as the family struggled with her brother's illness and death. Shortly thereafter, Stacey's father died. Again, Ellen was very supportive to Stacey's mother through this crisis as well; her help and caring were much appreciated. These experiences seemed to open the family boundaries so that a space could be made for Stacey's partner to become more accepted and integrated.

A crisis is often a catalyst for change, as was true in this situation. Stacey's mother accepted Ellen as her daughter's best friend and loved her for being so helpful and supportive to the family. Ellen participated in family gatherings, was present at shiva (a Jewish mourning ritual), and seemed to be accepted as a family member. The fact that she was Stacey's lover, however, was not discussed or acknowledged verbally, although the definition of the relationship was clear. Stacey's mother came to know and care for Ellen as a person and as a friend of her daughter's whom she grew to love and appreciate.

During the family crisis, it started to become evident that Stacey and Ellen were having some problems in their relationship; however, they chose not to deal with the issues until life was a bit calmer. After the storm, the problems in their relationship became clearer and, with the help of Stacey's therapist, the couple decided to separate. Stacey again became depressed as she suffered yet another very painful loss. It took several years before she was able to find a new meaningful relationship.

When Stacey became single, she spent considerable time with her mother as they mutually grieved and shared the losses they had endured. They became quite close and once again the subject of Stacey's lesbianism arose. As they began to talk about the issues, it became quite clear that her mother had moved considerably in her position; she was no longer threatening to kill herself over Stacey's sexual identity and, in fact, she had accepted Stacey's lover Ellen in her home, something she had said she would never do. Ellen had been invited to family events and dinners because she had been so helpful during the crisis periods. Stacey came to believe that her future lovers probably would be more welcomed into the family from the beginning and that she could maintain both her lesbian identity and her close connection with her mother.

Therapy was extremely important for Stacey during this time. Her therapist helped her explore her feelings of rejection and anger about her mother's initial lack of acceptance of her lifestyle. She also was able to appreciate her mother's experiences of loss and the binding effects the legacy of the Holocaust had in determining family expectations for the next generation of Jewish children.

Stacey was now the only surviving child, and her mother was mourning the fact that she would never marry and produce grandchildren. Stacey introduced the idea that even though she was a lesbian, she could bear children through the process of alternative insemination. At first, her mother was horrified at the prospect and said she would never accept that kind of child as a grandchild. Stacey felt that she could not disturb her mother any further with this issue, at least for the time being, and tabled the idea of having children. At that time, she was in her early thirties, and the idea of having children was not yet urgent for her. Besides, she felt she only would want to have a child within the context of a relationship, and she was not involved with anyone at that point in her life.

After several years passed, Stacey met Maggie, with whom she now has been involved for two years. She believes that this is a long-term, committed relationship. From the beginning of this union with Maggie, Stacey decided to take a stand with her mother. She wanted Maggie introduced into her family and accepted. Initially, when she shared her joyful news with her mother, she was greeted with something less than excitement.

At the first occasion for a family dinner, Stacey was expected to attend, as always, and she asked if she could bring Maggie. She was told emphatically no, which left her feeling that she was right back where she had been before Ellen was accepted into the family. But this time Stacey responded differently. She made it clear that she would not attend if she could not bring her lover. This was a marked difference in her behavior from earlier times when she attended dinners and family events alone, even though she was in a relationship. Now Stacey refused several family invitations because she decided she would not attend solo. She felt quite unhappy about not being part of family gatherings, but it was clear that her priorities had shifted. Her mother also was unhappy about not having her daughter participate in family affairs.

For a few months, they spoke little to one another. Stacey was overwhelmed by her feelings of loss and lack of connection to her mother. Her therapist coached her to open communication, and they discussed how to approach her mother. Her mother was receptive and they began spending time together again. Stacey's stepfather was more receptive to her lesbian identity than was her mother, which in turn helped her mother become more accepting. Stacey began going to her parents' home for dinner, bringing Maggie with her and, as her parents got to know Maggie, they began to genuinely like her. They could see that their daughter was happy with this woman and that they needed to be more open and accepting. Maggie soon became a regular at family dinners, and everyone seemed to enjoy these occasions.

Problems arose, however, when there was an extended family function. Stacey's sister-in-law was planning to remarry and did not invite Maggie to the wedding because she felt it would be embarrassing and inappropriate. Stacey was furious and decided she would not attend the wedding either. Her mother was very distressed, as she wanted Stacey's loyalty and support during this important family occasion. Even though Stacey would have liked to have been helpful to her mother, with her therapist's help she chose to support her own position and her increasingly public definition of herself and Maggie as family. She refused the invitation. Growth in the relationship with her mother was quite evident, as the bond between them remained intact during this differentiating move on Stacey's part. They were able to commiserate together over the sister-in-law's rigid position on this issue and, in the months that followed, Stacey's mother became more open to Maggie. She now was able to embrace her as one of the family, hugging and kissing her as she came and went, as she did with her own daughter.

Now that Stacey and Maggie are feeling more secure about their commitment to the relationship, they have begun to discuss insemination. Stacey has always wanted a child, and it is important to her that she have her mother's blessing and that a child be welcomed into her family. Stacey has introduced the idea to her mother once again and her mother, though she is less than enthusiastic, has not flatly rejected the idea. She is worried that it will be very difficult for a baby to grow up with two mothers and no father and thinks it might be unfair to bring up a baby in a lesbian relationship. As with other issues surrounding her lesbian daughter that have emerged over the years, Stacey's mother needs time, and Stacey needs to be patient in allowing her mother time to adjust to this idea, to accept this new child and love him or her as she does her other grandchildren.

This case clearly demonstrates coevolving changes in Stacey, in her mother, and in their relationship with each other. They grieved together over family losses and experienced changes in self-narratives as the meanings of lesbian identity and families with lesbian daughters shifted through therapy. The stronger Stacey became in shaping her own self-definition as a lesbian and in standing up for her own choices, the more her mother began to accept these choices. Stacey's developing a positive identity as a lesbian was the most significant factor leading toward change. In earlier years, Stacey had accommodated to being in the closet. However, as she became more clear about how she wanted to live her life, she became less able or willing to make compromises. As the two definitions of family and two differing sets of loyalties competed, Stacey gave priority to her family of choice, making it clear that she was no longer willing to compromise that commitment in favor of her original family's demands. She also felt more willing to take risks and more able to weather potential rifts in her family. As her positive feelings about her lesbian identity continued to solidify, her growing self-acceptance helped her differentiate from her family of origin.

Stacey's feelings about her lesbian identity developed within the many overlapping contexts that Roth and Murphy (1986) identify—the individual context, the couple context, the family of origin context, the therapy context, and the lesbian community context. In addition, she traversed the predictable life-cycle transitions, resolving loyalty issues and prioritizing her couple relationship over time (Carter & McGoldrick, 1988; Slater, 1995). As she gained more experience in lesbian relationships, she began to feel more comfortable with her sexual identity. She began meeting more lesbians, developing friendships, and becoming part of a lesbian network. Coming out to families is always a popular topic of conversation in lesbian groups; such groups can offer information, share experiences, and offer considerable support. Therapy helped Stacey feel she had chosen a normal, if unpopular, path and helped her gain the courage to speak up to her mother and to define her own needs as valid. As she worked to understand her legacy of guilt, she began to realize that even though her mother had suffered many traumatic losses, the compromises that she was being asked to make were not reasonable and would not be helpful to her mother. Both must live their own lives in their own ways, hopefully retaining their strong connections to one another.

For Stacey's mother, change came slowly and is continuing. It is difficult to know how much of her resistance to Stacey's choices represented her internalization of society's homophobic and heterosexist assumptions and her genuine fears for her daughter's future and how much represented her difficulties letting her daughter become autonomous under any circumstances. Her flexibility is apparent, however, as over time she has allowed herself to embrace new and, for her, painful ideas. Meeting the particular women involved in her daughter's life and getting to know and care for them as individuals has helped enormously. The most significant changes, however, came about as a result of changes in Stacey's sense of herself and her growing courage in taking a stand. As Stacey became clearer about her own needs and her own self-definition, she no longer was as dependent on her mother's approval.

CASE 2: ANN AND SUSAN

Ann and Susan were referred to a family therapist by Ann's individual therapist. Ann had been in individual treatment for one year. The original therapist felt that Ann and her partner needed to be in couples therapy because of Ann's uncertainty about whether she wanted to be in a same-sex relationship. Ann and Susan met in the winter of 1991 at a mutual friend's holiday party and had dated exclusively from that point on.

Ann complained that Susan was adding confusion to her life, reporting that in spite of how much she loved Susan, she was unsure if the relationship would work because she (Ann) was so uncomfortable about being in a same-sex relationship. She repeatedly said that she did not know whether she was straight or gay and felt as though she needed time to explore her options. Susan, on the other hand, was ready to live with Ann and plan their future together. Ann, because of her ambivalence, could not commit to the relationship the way Susan wanted her to. In addition, Ann had recently begun dating a man in an attempt to try to figure things out. In spite of how painful this was for Susan, she felt that Ann needed to get this out of her system in order for the two of them to move on as a couple. Ann acknowledged how hard this was for Susan and repeatedly assured Susan that she was very much in love with her and had never had such a fulfilling relationship with anyone. Susan was committed to waiting for Ann to come to terms with her confusion and to make a choice.

Both Ann and Susan grew up in socially prescribed heterosexist households in which a woman was expected to take care of her man. Both of their mothers had always put their own emotional needs after those of their spouses. Ann had difficulty living up to this expectation in her own previous heterosexual marriage and had concluded that she had a commitment problem. Susan, on the other hand, reported that she had always had difficulty taking a position for herself. Sacrifice for others was a major theme in Susan's life.

Ann is the elder of two children; her brother is three years younger and married with two children. Her mother works full-time as a receptionist, and her father is a physician. Ann was in a heterosexual marriage from 1980 to 1987, a relationship she describes as distant and unfulfilling, the same way she describes her parents' relationship. She has not come out to her parents. Although she describes her relationship with her brother as close, she believes that he knows nothing about her romantic relationship with Susan.

Ann reports that because of her father's busy schedule, her mother always relied on the kids to keep her busy when they were younger and to serve as confidantes and companions when they got older. The burden of this fell more on Ann than on her brother. She attributes this to her parents' belief that a man is a man until he takes a wife, but a daughter is a daughter for the rest of her life. Ann's father has always placed himself on the outside, a position he still occupies. Ann describes her father as very critical, especially of his wife. Her maternal grandfather was also quite critical, and Ann feels that her mother has gone to great lengths to maintain an outwardly calm household.

Ann has received powerful messages from her parents, reinforced by larger social notions that assume heterosexuality and include rather rigid definitions for gender-appropriate roles and that prescribe how she should be living her life. She often feels torn between her parents' agenda for her future and her own. This feeling of being torn is also how she describes the struggle with her sexual identity. "I'm happy with Susan. . . . There's no one else that I'd rather spend the rest of my life with. . . . It's my parents and the rest of the world that will never accept this relationship."

Susan is the youngest of three children. She has two brothers, both of whom are married with children and live out of state. Susan's father is an architect, and her mother is an interior decorator. Her parents divorced when she was ten years old, an event that was devastating for Susan, who was extremely close to her father. Even though her father provided child support, Susan's mother had to increase her work hours from part-time to full-time in order to support the family. Her mother placed a great deal of responsibility on Susan, as the only female child, to take care of the household.

In spite of Susan's father's efforts to help her understand and to maintain his relationship with her, it took Susan many years to forgive him and accept him back into her life. At this point, however, she has come out to him as well as to her brothers. They are all accepting of Susan and welcome Ann into the family. She has not yet come out to her mother. Susan's explanation for this is that her mother has been hurt enough in her life. It is not necessary that she know. Her father and brothers agree that Susan's mother needs to be protected from further emotional distress.

Susan describes her relationship with her mother as close; however, in the same breath she indicates that her mother knows little about her and she, in turn, knows little about what her mother really thinks and feels. Since the time of the divorce, Susan reports being protective of her mother.

Ann's continuous questioning as to whether she is gay or straight was not simply a homophobic response. There were quite a few circles of friends in which she felt free and comfortable in defining herself as a lesbian and revealing her relationship with Susan. One major problem, according to Ann, was that her family was not aware of her sexual identity, especially her mother. The dilemma was that she felt unable to proceed in the relationship with Susan without her mother's knowledge. However, she was not willing to come out to her mother. Her anxiety even in thinking about taking a step in either direction left her feeling paralyzed.

As Ann shared her story, it became clear that her family prescribed that she was to marry well, have children, and remain loyal to her family. Ann's parents, particularly her mother, were devastated when Ann divorced. They urged her endlessly to try to work things out. Ann reports that the divorce was amicable, but most devastating to Ann was her mother's disappointment. In an effort to make it up to her, Ann spent more time with her parents, especially her mother. She felt that her mother needed to see that she was doing all right and that she needed to convince both of her parents that she was still a good daughter.

In order for Ann to understand her present dilemma, the therapist felt that it was important for her to understand her past. For example, for years she had resented her position as the family caretaker. It was critical for her to understand how this set of responsibilities had taken shape and become rigid, as well as what her contribution as an adult might be in perpetuating this role.

As a means of accomplishing this task, she was coached to begin to get to know her parents as individuals rather than as who they were in their roles as mom and dad. She was encouraged to have individual conversations with each parent about their own childhoods, their dreams, expectations, and disappointments. The therapist helped Ann prepare for these conversations by having her research her parents' backgrounds. As Ann visited and wrote to various family members, gathering information and different points of view about the family, the therapist and she jointly constructed a genogram, working to understand the themes, patterns, stories, myths, losses, and other experiences that together constituted her family legacy. As Ann began to better understand the contexts and patterns that had helped to shape the interactions in her own immediate family, she began to make plans concerning what steps she wanted to take in changing her relationships with each of her parents and how she could alter her own typical behaviors. Together, she and her therapist discussed how her parents, separately and together, might react.

What eventually became clear to Ann was that the way in which her parents interacted with one another was related to their own respective family scripts. Her mother came from an alcoholic family system. Her maternal grandfather was an alcoholic, and her maternal grandmother a social drinker. As she reconstructed family scenes, Ann remembered that the more her grandfather drank, the more he angrily berated both his wife and daughter, the entire atmosphere becoming tense and unpleasant.

Ann's mother, an only child, learned quickly in life that the way to avoid her father's attacks and to help maintain equilibrium in the household was to be as perfect as possible. This also is the way Ann's mother dealt with her husband. Ann said repeatedly that her mother walks on eggshells to avoid her father's criticism. Ann's father, on the other hand, had been cut off from his parents for years, reconciling with his mother only after his father's death. His mother died a few years later, and he had little contact with his two siblings. Her father had never shared the story behind these cut-offs with Ann. She, in turn, had never asked about it.

As Ann grew to understand her parents' stories, especially her mother's, she began to think that she was now carrying the torch in her family that her mother had carried in hers—both were good girls, always afraid to make any waves. Ann was unable to pursue her own ideas for self-definition or her own life choices as she helped her parents avoid dealing with themselves and their relationship. Ann realized that she had not truly ever emotionally left home, and that in fact she was contributing to the pattern. She grew to believe that the way in which her parents interacted with one another was not her responsibility and that these patterns had been in motion long before she was born. Ann's tentativeness regarding commitment was a result of her not feeling emotionally free to move on and make her own life. She was too triangulated into her parents' relationship. The goal, as defined by Ann, was to take more of a differentiated position with both her mother and father while remaining connected to them. This included coming out to her parents, beginning with her mother.

Ann was coached to begin to take small steps toward achieving her goal. For example, she typically had been having dinner with her mother at least three times during the week and once when Susan joined them over the weekend. Although she enjoyed these visits, there were many times when she had been either exhausted or had wanted to make other plans but felt both sorry for and obligated to her mother because her mother was alone. Ann began to strategize with her therapist about how to cut down the number of visits while at the same time making each one more meaningful. Together, she and her therapist discussed what she anticipated her mother's response might be and prepared for how she would handle her own anxiety.

She also began to work toward building a better relationship with her father, beginning by inviting him to have lunch with her alone. Even though both of these beginning steps proved to be very uncomfortable for Ann, she persevered. Ann's fear of abandoning her mother was eventually replaced by the enjoyment she was experiencing at having a more adult mother-daughter relationship, one that could be more mutual, open, and honest. She saw that she was able to take a stand for herself without sacrificing the mother-daughter bond.

While Ann was busy reconstructing her relationship with her family, Susan was doing work of her own. She also familiarized herself with her family script, including her own role and contribution to the couple's problems. In contrast to Ann's complete emotional paralysis, Susan had come close to coming out to her mother for several years but didn't know how to approach her. When Susan began to see her mother as the competent, resourceful woman she was, instead of the woman who needed to be sheltered and taken care of, she was much less reluctant to come out to her.

Eventually both women felt emotionally ready to come out to their respective mothers. Ann approached her mother first. Her mother, while not surprised to hear the news, said that she was upset not for herself but about Ann's future. She was worried that Ann would not have anyone to take care of her as she got older. Rather than becoming reactive, Ann realized that this was one of her mother's own fears. She gently let her mother know that she was quite capable of taking care of herself. She also reminded her mother that her relationship with Susan was one of mutual love and support.

When the day came for Susan to disclose to her mother, her mother beat her to it. Before the words came out of her mouth, her mother said that she knew what Susan wanted to tell her. Susan, convinced that her mother did not know, went on to tell her that she was a lesbian and in a committed relationship with Ann. Her mother said that she had known this for quite a while and felt that when Susan was ready to tell her she would. Susan's mother let her know that she loved her for who she was, and that she loved Ann as well.

Within three months of Ann's disclosing to her mother, the couple began planning to move in together. Ann was now emotionally free to be in a committed relationship with Susan. After disclosing to her mother, Susan became less conciliatory and more able to take "I" positions with Ann. One way this emerged was in the gentle but firm way Susan insisted that Ann negotiate plans to commit herself more to the relationship.

Both Ann and Susan's processes of disclosure were enhanced by first assessing their family systems and developing authentic, differentiated relationships with members of their families of origin. This built foundations within their family systems to support the process of disclosure. The preparation for disclosure—

including understanding the family's multigenerational history, each person's current role, and taking small differentiating steps leading up to disclosure—increased the likelihood that Ann and Susan would remain firm in their commitments to their individual lesbian identities. This more solid grounding in self and the disclosures paved the way for their commitment to their couple relationship.

Conclusion

These cases illustrate the complex processes by which the mother-daughter bond influences and is affected by the disclosure of a daughter's lesbian identity. Disclosure accompanied by "differentiation in connection" often increases the authenticity of the mother-daughter relationship. Disclosure and differentiation are intertwined processes, each contributing to the other.

As therapists working with lesbian clients, it is important to appreciate the complexities of the mother-daughter bond, including the cultural context in which it exists. One needs to assess the family system, tracking the way difference is handled within the family, identifying intergenerational patterns that may influence differentiation and disclosure, and reconstructing family relationships to support and integrate the process of disclosure.

We believe that the use of a Bowenian family of origin approach is particularly useful in working with lesbian daughters, although it may also be used with mother-daughter pairs, as well as with the entire family. The approach helps daughters to understand multigenerational patterns and utilizes coaching, sometimes intermittently over many years, to support the development of authentic and differentiated family relationships. Most important, this approach focuses our attention on coming out as a long-term process extending well beyond the initial disclosure and its immediate aftermath. If we can help clients and therapists develop this long-term view of the process, their efforts to come out will be less vulnerable to short-term setbacks, and their persistence will lead eventually to successful outcomes in the majority of cases.

References

Ault-Riche, M. (1986). A feminist critique of five schools of family therapy. In M. Ault-Riche & J. C. Hansen (Eds.), *Women and family therapy* (pp. 1–15). Gaithersburg, MD: Aspen.

Carter, E., & McGoldrick, M. (1988). *The changing family life cycle.* New York: Gardner.

Carter, E., & Orfanidis, M. (1976). Family therapy with one person and the family therapist's own family. In P. Guerin (Ed.)., *Family therapy: Theory and practice* (pp. 193–219). New York: Gardner.

Friedman, E. (1991). Bowen theory and therapy. In A. Gurman & D. Kniskern (Eds.), *The handbook of family therapy* (vol. 2, pp. 143–170). New York: Brunner/Mazel.

Kerr, M., & Bowen, M. (1988). *Family evaluation.* New York: Norton.

Krestan, J. (1987). Lesbian daughters and lesbian mothers: The crisis of disclosure from a family systems perspective. *Journal of Psychotherapy and the Family, 3*(4), 113–130.

Luepnitz, D. (1988). *The family interpreted.* New York: Basic Books.

Roth, S., & Murphy, B. C. (1986). Therapeutic work with lesbian clients: A systemic therapy view. In M. Ault-Riche & J. C. Hansen (Eds.), *Women and family therapy* (pp. 78–89). Gaithersburg, MD: Aspen.

Slater, S. (1995). *The lesbian family life cycle.* New York: Free Press.

Surrey, J. (1985). *Self-in-relation: A theory of women's development.* Work in Progress No. 13. Wellesley, MA: Wellesley College, Stone Center for Developmental Services and Studies.

CHAPTER SIX

LESBIAN, GAY, AND BISEXUAL ASIAN AMERICANS AND THEIR FAMILIES

Peter Liu and Connie S. Chan

The issues for lesbian, gay male, and bisexual Asian Americans (LGBAAs) are both diverse and complex, as cultural, racial, religious, social, and psychological themes intersect. In this chapter, we integrate information from psychological, sociological, and historical sources in an examination of LGBAAs and their relationships with their families. Despite the scant literature and the lack of empirical studies, a theoretical framework for understanding the LGBAA experience can be established. Since the Asian American population is highly diverse and includes many ethnic groups, for the purpose of this discussion we will focus on East Asians, namely Chinese, Japanese, and Koreans. This subgroup was selected for their shared Confucian and Buddhist influences, similar sociocultural dynamics, historical connections, and comparable conditions for lesbian, gay, and bisexual (LGB) individuals and their families. However, there are important cultural distinctions between and within each of these ethnicities, including racial diversity, religious affiliation, socioeconomic status, education, and level of acculturation.

Exploring sexuality in relation to LGBAAs can be a challenge, since a cultural prohibition surrounds the entire topic. Same-sex sexual behavior, awareness, and identification are shrouded in secrecy, stigma, and the sometimes overwhelming power of cultural expectations. In East Asia, homosexual activity is almost universally "underground" and is rarely disclosed to society at large. The topic of sexuality itself, including heterosexuality, is traditionally considered taboo, and socially visible attempts to pursue sexual desires are strongly discouraged.

Women who express sexual desire are often labeled "dirty" or "lacking principles," while male expression of sexual desire is also discouraged (although less so) and perceived as improper or vulgar. There is little sanction for sexual expression beyond the familial expectation of procreation. Moreover, topics of sexuality and erotic desire are rarely discussed directly, even within the context of a physically intimate relationship.

Influences on the East Asian Family

The family is the most basic unit in East Asian societies, where ties of blood have particularly strong meaning. Obedience to parents, deference to elders, and loyalty to the family are enforced cultural rules. East Asians value collectivism and interdependence among family members, whereas Americans value individualism and increasing independence from the family. Although there is variability among families, familial and gender roles are very well defined for East Asian women and men. In the family, women are expected to be domestic and family-centered, nurturing, and submissive to males; men are expected to be stoic, strong, and dominant. The ideal is a very tightly knit extended family, with two parents who are both morally principled and dedicated to their families, are not openly affectionate, and are clear about communicating rules and enforcing discipline among children. Parents expect obedience, an awareness of responsibilities, and a sense of honor and duty to the family.

The hegemonic American ideal, on the other hand, includes a somewhat loose extended family, with two parents who are in love with each other, family members who are openly affectionate and emotionally expressive, and parents who support their children's growth and increasing independence. Essentially, the American family is based on romantic love, emotional communication, and intimacy, whereas the East Asian family is based on respect, order, and duty (Dion & Dion, 1993). Although these qualities are not mutually exclusive, the divergence in values in the two prototypes of family systems is pronounced. The expectations and demands on sons and daughters and their responsibilities to the family can differ greatly. As a result, the choices available to East Asian individuals may be limited.

The East Asian family has been heavily influenced by Confucianism, Taoism, and Buddhism. Confucius, who lived from 551 to 479 B.C., may be seen as the greatest single influence on East Asian philosophy and society. The Confucian tradition involves a highly detailed and orderly system of moral philosophy that emphasizes ordered relationships and roles (Ruan, 1991). Although first established in China, the influence of Confucianist ideals spread throughout Asia and permeates all Asian societies, particularly in East Asia. The profound influence of Confucianism can be seen in the highly structured gender and generational roles seen within the East Asian family, in which parent-child, father-mother, and older sibling–younger sibling roles are well defined. For example, the child must do what the parents dictate, the wife must obey and support the husband, and the older sibling has more authority and responsibility than the younger sibling. Homosexual relationships are problematic because they do not fit into the Confucian order. There are simply no rules that dictate the hierarchical roles for two men or two women who are romantically or sexually involved. For society at large, such a relationship is often unfathomable and certainly not officially recognized. For the same-sex couple, relationships can be particularly difficult to negotiate unless they follow preexisting roles, such as that of father-son (Chan, 1995).

Taoism, a philosophy and religion developed in the fifth century B.C., focuses on the individual's experience of life and supports tranquility and practicality as personal ideals (Ruan, 1991). This influence can be seen in the East Asian family, where strife and conflict among family members is strongly discouraged, and peacefulness in the household is of great importance. The heart of Taoist religion, which sprung out of philosophy, utilizes the ancient principles of *yin* and *yang*, in which all things are made of yin (the weak, passive, and negative force) and yang (the strong, active, and positive force). Harmony of yin and yang is believed to be the key to happiness and the rightful order. This concept is well-known even in the West and has become a central philosophical theme across all Asia.

The harmonious union of yin and yang is symbolized by the marriage of female and male as the pinnacle of human fulfillment; females are associated with yin, and males are associated with yang. Thus, same-sex relationships may disrupt not only the Confucianist order of the family but also are viewed as violating the natural balance of yin and yang. The expectation of heterosexual marriage and the powerful association of yin-yang in female-male relationships both serve to obscure and trivialize same-sex relationships. For example, the fact that a thirty-five-year-old daughter is unmarried may be of much greater concern to her parents than if she engages in same-sex relationships. The focus is thus not on her sexuality but on how her behavior may disrupt the "natural order" of heterosexual marriage and family and the potential for yin-yang fulfillment.

The final major traditional influence on East Asian religion and philosophy is Buddhism, which was first introduced to China from India in the first century A.D. The central premise of Buddhism is that emptying oneself of one's desires is a key to personal salvation (Ruan, 1991). This emptying involves the voiding of one's personal will, lusts, and demands as a way of channeling the divine and accepting one's fate. Over lifetimes of reincarnation, this path leads eventually to the spiritual heaven, nirvana. The impact of Buddhism on the East Asian family and East Asian psychology is unmistakable in the cultural value of subordination of individual will. Thus, whereas the hegemonic American has a strong will and aims to achieve self-actualization, the traditional East Asian accepts his or her role in society and is emptied of selfish personal desires. For example, parents refrain from being indulgent and from engaging in too much play with their children, since this may encourage personal willfulness.

The emptying of desire in Buddhist thought includes sexuality, and following one's sexual desires is discouraged. At the very least, pursuit of sexual fulfillment is traditionally viewed as vulgar and vain and, at the most, it may disrupt not only Confucian and Taoist order but also will slow one's path to salvation. Any sexual activity outside the context of marriage is seen in this light, but this is particularly true in the case of homosexuality, because same-sex activity is not visible in society or even discussed. Homosexual behavior thus can only be a result of pursuing one's sexual lust. It must be noted, however, that although homosexual behavior is a reflection of impurity according to Buddhism, there is no concept of homosexuality itself as a sin or reflective of other internal flaws, and engaging in homosexual activity will not directly result in divine punishment (Ruan, 1991).

These three forces—Confucianism, Taoism, and Buddhism—coexist in a curious mixture in East Asian societies and very much shape the nature of relationships within the family. Western psychological theories of family systems and interpersonal relationships often fall short in understanding the East Asian family because familial relationships are so strongly defined by centuries of religious, philosophical, and cultural tradition. Only in the context of this tradition can East Asian family dynamics be adequately examined, which may help explain some of the complex issues and conflicts that many LGBAAs face.

In both the United States and Asia, Christianity has become a large part of the lives of a sizeable number of East Asian families, particularly in Korean and Chinese communities. Asian American churches and informal Bible study groups are commonplace, serving both religious and social functions. Often, these organizations also include ethnic language schooling, and social and sport activities for children to involve the entire family in the group. Participation in a church with other East Asian families of the same background can help provide a sense of community and an opportunity to meaningfully incorporate one's ethnic identity and traditional values into life in America. The influences of Confucianism, Buddhism, Taoism, and family tradition are retained and reinterpreted through a Christian lens.

One of the implications of the influence of Christianity on LGBAAs is the concept of sin and the internal stigmatization of homosexuality—ideas that did not exist in traditional Asian religions (Chan, 1995). This stigmatization is particularly problematic for LGBAA Christians, who may experience not only inner turmoil and confusion regarding their sexual orientation or behavior but also traditional and intense pressure from their families to marry, have children, and fulfill their gender and filial roles. With the added parental enforcement of strict obedience and discipline and with the discouragement of sexual exploration, the challenge of psychological incorporation of one's homosexual behavior and LGB identity can be particularly difficult and painful.

Traditional Family Dynamics

According to Morales (1990), "An individual's value system is shaped and reinforced within the family context which usually reflects the broader community norms" (p. 218). Because the East Asian traditional family unit is especially cohesive and restrictive, self-concept and identity revolve primarily around the family and the values it holds. The child's behavior is carefully scrutinized by the parents over the life span. Some aspects of the child's life may be harshly criticized and other areas heavily encouraged and reinforced. Parents are actively involved in shaping their children's lives as part of their duty and also to prepare them for the scrutiny of the extended family and the community at large.

Stemming from Confucian influences is the concept of "face," a combination of honor, dignity, and persona, whereby the individual correctly fulfills prescribed roles in the family and in society. An individual's face is intertwined with that of the family, so a deviation from expected behavior reflects not only upon the individual but also upon all of the relatives. Homosexuality will be tolerated by the family only to the extent that it does not interfere with the individual's family duties and eventual marriage. Furthermore, both the individual's and the family's face must remain intact in the context of the larger community (Chan, 1995).

Both the language and the behavior of sexuality, whether homosexual or heterosexual, are unseen and unheard in Asian American families. Children are discouraged from sexual and romantic exploration and often are not allowed to date until young adulthood. Overt sexual behavior may be seen as shameful, distracting to academics or to work, vulgar, or disruptive to the family. For young LGBAAs beginning to be aware of same-sex attractions, the aura of silence and restriction from exploration can make their sexuality unusually difficult to understand and integrate within a cohesive self-image (Chan, 1994).

One of the features of East Asian families that contrasts greatly with American families is the hierarchy of loyalties. In East Asian families, the traditional primary loyalty is to one's parents, the next to one's siblings, and the next to one's spouse—a hierarchy of loyalty that is reversed for most Americans. Thus, the LGBAA may be especially reluctant to risk losing closeness with his or her family by coming out and may be resistant to forming a primary relationship with a same-sex partner. The tight bond of family and the instillment of traditional values for Asian Americans on the one hand can be harsh and oppressive for LGB individuals but, on the other hand, can give support. Because Asian Americans' individual identities are so tied to family identity, even if sexuality is not disclosed or openly discussed, the adult daughter or son may still feel very secure and cared for and may not be willing to risk jeopardizing this relationship by coming out. As Tremble, Schneider, and Appathurai (1989) concluded, "When the love of children and the value of family ties is strong, nothing, including homosexuality, will permanently split the family. Ultimately, when the family system is bound by love and respect, a way is found to embrace the homosexual member" (p. 257). However, the threat of rejection and stigmatization by the family, particularly by one's parents, remains one of the primary concerns for LGBAAs.

In Chan's 1989 study of Asian American lesbians and gay men, the majority (77 percent, or twenty-seven of the thirty-five participants) had come out to a family member. A sibling, usually a sister, was the first person in the family to whom this group disclosed their lesbian or gay identity. However, only nine respondents (27 percent) had come out to their parents, in spite of the fact that the individuals in this study had been out for a mean of 6.2 years and most reported that they were out to most of their friends (Chan, 1989). Specific cultural values probably define their expected roles within their family, which may help explain the reluctance of LGBAAs to come out to their families, especially their parents.

In addition to traditional family expectations, overt acknowledgment of an LGB identity may be even more restricted by Asian American cultural norms than it is in hegemonic U.S. society. In Chan's (1989) study, when respondents were asked to describe the Asian American community's perception of lesbian and gay Asian Americans, more than half of the sample replied that there was a denial of the existence of Asian American lesbians and gay men. This supports the idea that homosexuality is commonly perceived by ethnic minority groups as a White, Western phenomenon. Chan's results were similar to those noted by Espin (1987), who found that Latina lesbians were reluctant to be out in the Latino community because of the importance placed on family and community by most Hispanics. The threat of possible rejection and stigmatization by the Latino community becomes more of a psychological burden for the Hispanic lesbian, while rejection from mainstream society does not carry the same weight. Assuming a similar importance of family and community relationships in East Asian American cultures, it is likely that LGBAAs have not come out to their parents because of the overwhelming fear of rejection and stigmatization. As one respondent in Chan's study reported, "I wish I could tell my parents—they are the only ones who do not know about my gay identity, but I am sure that they would reject me. There is no frame of reference to understand homosexuality in Asian-American culture" (p. 19).

The fear of rejection and stigmatization by the family may have several sources. First, when an individual's self-concept is strongly associated with the family, loss of the family may be devastating to self-esteem. Second, when the concept of face is deeply rooted, and maintaining a public appearance that fulfills gender-role expectations is demanded by the family, the psychological experience can be a perception of constant scrutiny by others, leading to vigilance in maintaining the proper image in the eyes of one's family and community. Third, as the East Asian family is often defined by and immersed in traditional culture, rejection by one's family can be experienced as a totalizing disconnection from one's ethnic identity and entire community. Finally, alternative, nonfamily resources for LGBAAs may be limited because of social, cognitive, and emotional isolation, as well as racial discrimination in the predominantly Euro-American LGB community at large (Chan 1994; Greene, 1994).

The negotiation of one's sexual identity within the family for LGB East Asian Americans can be particularly complex then, given the powerful proscriptions against the discussion of sexuality. For East Asian Americans coming out to family, the pressure of family hopes and expectations of heterosexual marriage can be extremely difficult to manage, let alone challenge. Cultural, religious, and generational differences can also remain daunting obstacles. Communication in the East Asian family, as defined by Confucian philosophy, traditionally occurs in one direction, from parent to child and from elder to younger. East Asian parents often choose not to discuss or accept their adult child's sexuality, for it is the child's duty to accept the parents' rules and demands. For some East Asian parents, it may be completely unacceptable to validate their daughter or son's homosexual identity. Avenues of help, such as family therapy or some other form of counseling, may also be limited because mental health treatment is not only a foreign concept to many East Asians but it also may be perceived as a potential loss of face for the family to discuss its problems and conflicts in front of a stranger (Sue & Sue, 1990).

For many LGBAAs, one way to incorporate their sexual identity and same-sex partners into their lives is through invisibility and silence. In other cases, when LGB identity is disclosed, the family may continue to pressure the individual with traditional expectations and refuse to discuss her or his identity or lifestyle, which in turn may lead to isolation from the family. For other LGBAAs, the only acceptable alternative is to be open about one's sexual orientation and to deal with parental expectations over time while maintaining close contact. Often, this may elicit initial rejection, but with continued contact, the opposition from parents may lessen. Some LGBAAs do establish new and more open relationships with their parents. In any case, traditional East Asian family dynamics and values play a central role in the experience for many East Asian American lesbians, gay men, and bisexuals.

Acculturation and Multiple Identities

There is great diversity both among and within East Asian families, as well as different degrees of acculturation. Previously, our discussion focused primarily on issues for East Asian Americans who are immigrants or first generation, a population in which parents and families tend to be more traditional. With each succeeding generation, East Asian cultural influences and values may have less impact on the family's reaction to the lesbian, gay, or bisexual identity of a family member. It is also important to note, however, that level of acculturation cannot be assumed by the interval of time a family has been in the United States. Some East Asian American families that are third or fourth generation may still hold very traditional East Asian values. Likewise, new East Asian immigrant families may already be quite acculturated to Western values and styles or may quite quickly become so. It is important to assess both the specific level of acculturation and specific attitudes toward sexuality held by different family members to help determine the extent to which traditional East Asian culture shapes the personal and familial experiences of lesbians, gays, and bisexuals.

East Asian Americans who come from more traditional families may often feel caught between East Asian and Western influences and may have difficulty integrating their LGB identities with their ethnic identities. Those who openly identify as being LGB in some contexts are more likely to be acculturated and to have been more influenced by American or Western culture. Nevertheless, they still may keep their LGB social, romantic, and sexual world completely secret and separate from their families and their East Asian community. Some may predict that their parents will not be able to understand them because of both cultural and generational gaps. The pressure of family and cultural expectations may conflict greatly with American values, leading to internalized stress, isolation, and sometimes conflict within the family. More acculturated East Asian Americans may seek out other communities in which their sexual identity will be more accepted than within their families or ethnic communities. Many of these individuals, however, also experience being stereotyped and unacknowledged in the larger gay, lesbian, and bisexual community. LGBAAs, like LGB members of other ethnic minority groups, may be considered to have a double minority status. They face the challenge of negotiating their personal identity issues in a context of not feeling totally comfortable in either community; each community—the family and the LGB community—may fail to acknowledge a significant part of their identity (Chan, 1995). This may contribute to a sense of social invisibility in both communities, contributing to feelings of isolation, marginalization, and rejection (Chan, 1992).

Multiple roles and multiple communities can present challenges to LGB East Asian Americans but can also be sources of strength and resilience. These individuals essentially have two cultural and ethnic identities to draw upon to varying degrees, which may offer a depth and breadth of perspective on their families and in their life experiences outside the family. It may be easier to shift one's cultural lens when one has been exposed to both East Asian and Western views, allowing for more flexibility and adaptability in interpreting and responding to life events. In Chan's 1989 study, LGBAA research participants (who tended to be more acculturated) were asked which terms they used to identify themselves and with which part they more strongly identified. The results suggested that an individual may choose to identify and ally more closely with being LGB or Asian American at different times—depending on need, situational factors, and self-concept. Although LGBAAs may have particular difficulties in overtly acknowledging their lesbian, gay, or bisexual identities, they may also have some flexibility and freedom in integrating their sexuality and sexual behavior, which may differ substantially from more rigid Eastern or Western models for integration.

For LGBAAs, there are both culture-specific and gender-specific psychological and social issues in accepting and affirming a sexual identity. As therapists, we need to be careful not to stereotype behaviors based on our own limited generalizations of Asian cultural values and customs. At the same time, we must be careful not to assume that the sexual identity of LGBAAs follows Western prototypes. Clinicians must affirm their clients' understanding of their ethnic and sexual identities, as well as help them explore the ways in which these identities may be problematic or limiting for them (Chan, 1992).

In addition to a more general understanding of cultural themes and a theoretical framework for working with LGBAAs, clinicians also need to be alert to the more specific situational factors that may be relevant for particular clients. The following questions are important to keep in mind when working with individuals, couples, or families in family therapy:

1. Are the client and his or her family members immigrants or American-born?
2. What ethnic group does the family belong to?
3. What are the specific cultural values of this ethnic group, of the client's family members, of the client?
4. How strongly do the client and other family members follow traditional customs?
5. What is the socioeconomic status of the client and family?
6. What is the level of bilingualism for the client? For the family?

7. What religion or philosophy do the client and family members embrace, and how orthodox are their views?
8. What are the client's and family's educational levels?
9. What are the client's and family members' views regarding gender roles, sexuality, and homosexuality?

The concepts we have discussed may be illustrated best by case examples in which family dynamics and East Asian American culture interact to form a backdrop for the more unique aspects of each situation. The first case, from Connie Chan's clinical practice, is that of a Korean American client in psychotherapy, who is struggling with her cultural and sexual identity. The second case, from Peter Liu's clinical practice, describes two men—a male Chinese American who incorporates his homosexual behavior into a more traditional framework, and a Euro-American male who wishes more commitment to the couple relationship.

CASE 1: CATHY

A native of Seoul, Korea, Cathy moved to New York City with her family when she was twelve. Hardworking, serious, and academically successful in her high school, she spent most of her time throughout her high school years at the family restaurant, working or studying when business was slow. When Cathy came to the Boston area to attend college, it was her first experience having independence and free time that was not tied up with work or family responsibilities. Shy and reserved as a high school student, Cathy established her first close relationships with individuals other than family members while she was in college, and she began to socialize more.

During her junior year of college, Cathy spent a great deal of time with Darlene, a close Caucasian woman friend. She began to feel very attracted to her. Eventually, they began to spend nights together and, after their first night of sexual intimacy, Cathy felt both frightened and excited by her feelings. This experience led her to seek psychotherapy. She phrased the presenting issue as, "I think I'm in love with a woman and I don't know what to do. I want to spend all my time with her, but if my family found out, they would disown me." Initial therapy sessions focused on Cathy's understanding of herself and how she felt she could not be an independent person, even at twenty-one years of age, because she was expected to behave in ways that her family would approve. Her new relationship and behavior with her female lover were the first actions in Cathy's life that did not meet her family's expectations, and she felt great cognitive dissonance at experiencing so much pleasure from something her parents would condemn. Although she was able to tolerate this dissonance for a short time, Cathy began to feel more and more disloyal and torn as a dutiful daughter in not telling her family about her relationship and her activities. She felt that her only options were to discontinue the relationship in order to be honest with her family about her life, or to continue the relationship but lie to her family about her activities. Neither seemed to be viable alternatives to Cathy, and she felt stuck.

The work of the psychotherapy sessions was to explore the unique familial and cultural issues in Cathy's life and to help her find an option that would not require that she give up either of her "primary" relationships—the relationship with her lover or with her family. While Cathy felt certain that her Korean and family cultures would not approve of a lesbian relationship, she also felt that she would not be true to herself if she denied herself a supportive, loving relationship. In balancing the needs of the family against her own personal needs, much of Cathy's work was to define for herself what was most important to her in life. At this developmental stage, Cathy did understand that she was in the process of separating and individuating from her family—a process that had begun even before she fell in love with Darlene—and that this process would continue throughout her life. The form that the individuation was taking was different from what many Korean women her age would experience (through marriage), but Cathy realized that she could no longer turn back what she had begun when she went to college and established her own sense of independence. Our goal in therapy then focused on how she could integrate this independence with her family's expectations of marriage and what they considered acceptable behavior for a Korean American daughter.

During our sessions, Cathy began to see how she was caught in a situation where she could not please her parents and follow her own desires. While she was frightened of her parents' anger and rejection, Cathy believed that she was raised in American culture, which encouraged her to be her own person and independent of her family. Cathy also felt supported by her lover, Darlene, who felt strongly that Cathy should pursue her own identity and self. Cathy then set a goal of being more open with her parents and other relatives about her sexuality, her activities, her relationship with Darlene, and her desires. In therapy, Cathy role-played with me discussions with her parents in which she would share more information, rehearsing how she would react and how she would continue to move the conversation a little further each time. As she was quite fearful of her parents' disapproval, Cathy made slow progress in being more open. As a result, she sometimes disappointed Darlene, who was far more impatient and more direct in her manner than Cathy was.

Although she was afraid of her family's disapproval, Cathy decided that she wanted to be open about her relationship with Darlene. In the context of a discussion about an upcoming family gathering, Cathy announced that she wanted to bring Darlene. When her family expressed surprise, Cathy told them that she considered Darlene her partner and that Darlene was part of their family now. Cathy's decision to come out to her family in this manner developed after several therapy discussions, during which she explored several options, including not disclosing her relationship. She decided to come out by using the language of family inclusion rather than that of individual identity because she thought it was the context to which they might be able to relate. As it turned out, Cathy's family was stunned, as it had never occurred to them that their daughter and Darlene were a couple. Cathy's parents were angry and initially refused to recognize the relationship, but they did maintain their connection with Cathy. As Cathy persisted in bringing Darlene's name up in conversation and in inviting her family over when Darlene was present, they slowly became more accustomed to her. Over a long period of time, Cathy's parents gradually began to acknowledge the relationship and its importance to their daughter.

As her therapist, I tried to allow her to take the pace she found tolerable and continued to work with her sense of loss at not being the dutiful, marriageable Korean daughter her parents desired. It was important to acknowledge the loss she was experiencing, as well as the many positive aspects of finding her independence and a loving relationship. Over time, Cathy learned to negotiate the tightrope between meeting her own personal needs and meeting her family's demands that she be a proper Korean woman. At times, she did not fulfill their expectations, and at other times she gave up personal desires, both of which caused some distress, but she worked consistently to develop a sense of self that allowed her to adapt and adjust to both sets of often-conflicting demands.

CASE 2: CHUNG-LO

Chung-Lo was born in Brooklyn, New York, to parents who emigrated from southern China. Chung-Lo has one older brother, Chung-An. The extended family members are all currently in either Hong Kong or China. Chung-Lo's parents were very traditional, with strong Confucian and Buddhist values, and were strict and restrictive with the two boys through childhood and adolescence. The only language permitted in the house was Cantonese. Both Chung-Lo and Chung-An were socially isolated from other students and had little opportunity to spend time with peers outside of school. Chung-Lo was particularly introverted and had few friends.

Chung-Lo entered a city technical college and pursued a bachelor's degree in electrical engineering. Both brothers continued to live at home, commuting to classes. The routine of the home remained intact over the years. Meals were always eaten together; chores were regular; schedules were consistent. During his second year in college, Chung-Lo met a Chinese classmate who introduced him to a local Chinese evangelical church, where many young people were members. Although Chung-Lo was introverted and reserved, he was interested in this group and began regularly attending meetings. This became his only social network aside from his family, though Chung-Lo was acquainted with his classmates. Up until then, Chung-Lo had had no social relationships or sexual involvement with either men or women.

At age twenty-eight, Chung-Lo was approached by Steven, a twenty-eight-year-old Caucasian male who worked in close proximity to his own firm and whom he had seen many times walking down the street; Chung-Lo was surprised and intrigued by the attention. They began to meet for lunch, and over the next month, Chung-Lo became sexually involved with Steven. Typically, they would meet after work at Steven's apartment. However, Chung-Lo would not stay long and refused to stay overnight, which he was afraid would disrupt the order in his family's house. He was aware that his behavior would not be acceptable to his parents, but as long as he continued to be consistent in his family duties, dating Steven would not raise any questions. Chung-Lo was also resistant to spending much time with Steven, as his religion condemned homosexuality. He was fond of Steven and liked regular contact with him, but placing limits on his time with Steven and his availability to him made the conflict he was feeling more tolerable.

Chung-Lo and Steven began couples therapy at Steven's insistence, as Steven became unsatisfied with his relationship with Chung-Lo over time. Chung-Lo was initially reluctant to participate because he was uncomfortable with the idea of entering therapy. He eventually agreed. The initial sessions involved a careful assessment of the couple's presenting difficulties, relationship history, and cultural attitudes. Chung-Lo spoke very little in the early sessions and was somewhat defensive with me, initially viewing the process as alien to him and as a hostile attempt to change his beliefs and values. But he gradually warmed up as it became clear to him that I was interested in exploring his perspectives, as well as his cultural and family background. The process of therapy focused on helping both men communicate with each other more effectively and on increasing their mutual understanding of each other's cultural perspectives and emotional needs.

Chung-Lo incorporated his homosexual behavior into his life by carefully compartmentalizing his involvement with Steven, viewing him as a secret sexual partner and companion and limiting the romantic or love attachment. His primary attachments remained only with his family. He experienced only minor distress regarding his relationship with Steven, given that it had little impact on his family life or family priorities. After the problem was defined and the individual and couple histories were explored, Chung-Lo and Steven were asked to verbalize to each other what their hopes, needs, and disappointments were. Initially, this was difficult for both partners, since Steven tended to talk for Chung-Lo, who was generally very quiet. However, as I opened up space for Chung-Lo to talk, he began to be more expressive of his own feelings and beliefs. Steven was encouraged to try asking questions instead of demanding or complaining, and Chung-Lo was encouraged to express more of his feelings and thoughts about the relationship. Over time, Steven began asking Chung-Lo to express more affection and commitment, without demanding. This request, however, was confusing and sometimes irritating for Chung-Lo, because he felt that his affection and commitment did not need to be verbalized in order to be felt, a style consistent with his family's and culture's ways. Steven had difficulty accepting this style, because he perceived that a mutually satisfying relationship must be based on verbal communication and expression of love and affection, a distinctly Western and particularly American ethos.

Another point of conflict between the couple involved Chung-Lo's time with his family. Steven often felt excluded and frustrated that Chung-Lo spent more time with his family than with him. Steven also felt hurt that Chung-Lo seemed always to place his family responsibilities and plans above their relationship. Consistent with traditional East Asian family dynamics, Chung-Lo expressed that his family would always come first. Although he was able to recognize and verbalize that he valued Steven and sometimes felt guilty that he could not meet Steven's expectations, he felt that he could not change his family loyalties and values. Steven had a difficult time accepting this. Although he loved his own family, Steven considered intimate relationships to be of primary importance in his life. Again, the cultural discrepancies between their expectations was paramount.

Over the last sessions with me, both partners came to understand more about their relationship expectations in cultural context and were better able to articulate their needs and feelings about the relationship. Chung-Lo was satisfied with the level of intimacy and contact but wanted Steven to respect and accept that their relationship would always be secondary to his family. Steven felt very strongly about Chung-Lo but felt that the intimacy in the relationship was not sufficient and that spending more time together was necessary. Eventually, both Chung-Lo and Steven decided to end their relationship amicably because their individual needs were not being adequately met. The final session focused on the couple's sharing what they had learned about each other and themselves. Both partners appreciated having achieved greater clarity about their attitudes toward relationships and families and what they would look for in future partners.

Although such an ending lacks the happily-ever-after expectation usually fulfilled in stories of couples therapy, the mutual respect and self-understanding that accompanied their separation rendered this therapy a qualified success. Furthermore, the positive therapeutic alliance with each client makes it more likely that each partner will be more open to therapeutic professional help in the future as needed. Clearly, Chung-Lo's resolve to relinquish his relationship with Steven to preserve family harmony cannot be easy to maintain, and perhaps he will go on to seek other partners and find other resolutions. Or perhaps he will find other partners whose relationship expectations and priorities match his own.

Conclusion

Family, couple, and individual psychotherapy with LGB East Asian Americans requires the awareness of cultural and family values for each client. Therapists are most helpful when their work with clients is based on a foundation of cultural understanding and when it incorporates the unique perspectives, needs, and vocabularies of both the client and the client's family. With the growing population of Asian Americans in the United States, the issues for Asian Americans and their families become increasingly important and relevant for all therapists. Research on LGBAAs and their families is minimal at this stage, and study of this population is complicated for a number of reasons. These include cultural inhibitions regarding discussion of sexuality, lack of visibility, difficulty in obtaining research participants, and a wide diversity in levels of acculturation and experience. As some of these barriers are overcome, learning more about the lives and experiences of LGB East Asian Americans and their couple and family relationships can only be helpful to mental health professionals working with this population in clinical, educational, and prevention programs and in providing consultation to institutions and agencies.

This chapter is a first attempt at bringing together ideas about East Asian families with lesbian and gay members and principles of gay-affirmative therapy. We hope the material presented here will serve as a stimulus to further theory, research, and practice development in the coming years.

References

Chan, C. S. (1989). Issues of identity development among Asian-American lesbians and gay men. *Journal of Counseling and Development, 68*, 16–20.

Chan, C. S. (1992). Cultural considerations in counseling Asian-American lesbians and gay men. In S. Dworkin & F. Guttierez (Eds.), *Counseling gay men and lesbians: Journey to the end of the rainbow* (pp. 115–124). Alexandria, VA: American Association for Counseling and Development.

Chan, C. S. (1994). Asian-American adolescents: Issues in the expression of sexuality. In J. M. Irvine (Ed.), *Sexual cultures and the construction of adolescent identities* (pp. 88–99). Philadelphia: Temple University Press.

Chan, C. S. (1995). Issues of sexual identity in an ethnic minority: The case of Chinese American lesbians, gay men, and bisexual people. In A. D'Augelli & C. Patterson (Eds.), *Lesbian, gay, and bisexual identities over the lifespan* (pp. 87–101). New York: Oxford University Press.

Dion, K. K., & Dion, K. L. (1993). Individualistic and collectivistic perspectives on gender and the cultural context of love and intimacy. *Journal of Social Issues, 49*(3), 53–69.

Espin, O. (1987). Issues of identity in the psychology of Latina lesbians: Explorations and challenges. In Boston Lesbian Psychologies Collective (Ed.), *Lesbian psychologies: Explorations and challenges* (pp. 35–55). Urbana: University of Illinois Press.

Greene, B. (1994). Ethnic-minority lesbians and gay men: Mental health and treatment issues. *Journal of Consulting and Clinical Psychology, 62*(2), 243–251.

Morales, E. (1990). Ethnic minority families and minority gays and lesbians. In F. W. Bozett & M. B. Sussman (Eds.), *Homosexuality and family relations* (pp. 217–239). New York: Haworth Press.

Ruan, F. F. (1991). *Sex in China.* New York: Plenum Press.

Sue, D. W., & Sue, D. (1990). *Counseling the culturally different.* New York: Wiley.

Tremble, B., Schneider, M., & Appathurai, C. (1989). Growing up gay or lesbian in a multicultural context. In G. Herdt (Ed.), *Gay and lesbian youth* (pp. 253–267). New York: Haworth Press.

CHAPTER SEVEN

SELF-LABELING AND DISCLOSURE AMONG GAY, LESBIAN, AND BISEXUAL YOUTHS

Ritch C. Savin-Williams

Lesbian, gay, and bisexual (LGB) youths face two distinct, though related, developmental tasks. The first, *self-labeling*, is a series of internal processes by which individuals become aware, recognize, and then define their sexuality as lesbian, gay, or bisexual. Self-labeling usually begins with an early awareness of being different from others, followed after the onset of puberty by a recognition that this differentness has a sexual component, and completed with the acceptance that the implication of same-sex desires is membership in a socially defined sexual identity category, such as lesbian, gay, or bisexual. The self-labeling process may begin during early childhood and is usually resolved during adolescence or young adulthood. In some cases, however, completion is postponed several years, decades, or a lifetime, especially if negative cultural values and beliefs regarding homosexuality are internalized. (Note that self-labeling tends to be more fluid and more subject to revision over the life course in women than in men; see Golden, 1996.)

A second developmental task for LGB youths is the *disclosure* of their homoerotic desires, sexual experiences, or sexual identity to others. First told is usually

Some ideas in this chapter are drawn from Cohen and Savin-Williams (1996) and Savin-Williams (1990, 1996). I am deeply indebted for the editorial assistance and ideas of Kenneth M. Cohen and for the excellent suggestions made on an earlier draft by Robert-Jay Green and Joan Laird.

a best friend. Family members, a particular concern in this chapter, often are told thereafter—sometimes years later or never. Final or ultimate disclosure is achieved when individuals no longer care who knows and are thus out to society at large.

Although the internal processes that result in self-labeling begin from the point of earliest memories, and the external processes of disclosure ultimately conclude at one's deathbed, the critical developmental "crises" of self-labeling and first disclosure frequently occur in today's cohort of youths during the adolescent and young adult years. The description and significance of the developmental processes by which a youth comes to recognize his or her homoerotic affections and discloses these sexual feelings to others are reviewed in this chapter. Although most LGB youths successfully navigate these terrains to become healthy, well-functioning adults, it is not always an easy journey. Some do not survive, and others are left with permanent physical, emotional, cognitive, and social scars (Savin-Williams, 1994).

In this chapter, I examine the psychological and social repercussions of self-labeling as a gay, bisexual, or lesbian person and the public expressions of those same-sex attractions. Because the family is often the most important, yet frightening, context for the evolution of these processes, special attention is given to psychological issues that separate LGB youths from their families. The unique stresses faced by ethnic minority youths as they reconcile family and community loyalties require independent consideration in this chapter as well. Clinical interventions that can help LGB youths overcome their fears and anxieties are briefly outlined. The chapter concludes with suggestions for helping families when a youth discloses to them a gay, lesbian, or bisexual identity.

Overview of Sexual Identity Development

Coming-out models have been proposed to describe the movement from first awareness to full disclosure. In most cases, these models have been cast as an orderly or linear series of stages based on a particular theoretical perspective (see Cohen & Savin-Williams, 1996). Sophie (1985–1986) delineates four essential stages of identity development that characterize most coming-out models:

1. First awareness
   - An initial cognitive and emotional realization that one is "different" and a feeling of alienation from oneself and others
   - No disclosure to others
   - Some awareness that homosexuality may be the relevant issue

2. Test and exploration
   - Feelings of ambivalence that precede acceptance of homosexuality
   - Initial but limited contact with gay and lesbian individuals or communities
   - Alienation from heterosexuality
3. Identity acceptance
   - Preference for social interactions with other gays and lesbians
   - Evolution from negative identity to positive identity
   - Initial disclosure to heterosexuals
4. Identity integration
   - View of self as gay or lesbian with accompanying anger at society's prejudice
   - Publicly coming out to many others
   - Identity stability: unwillingness to change and pride in oneself and one's group

Coming-out models have been useful for understanding the processes by which individuals evolve from an assumed heterosexual to an LGB identity. However, many pathways exist to allow individuals to achieve final self-labeling and full disclosure. For example, many lesbians, gays, and bisexuals report that the coming-out process is not a series of discrete stages in which gestalt shifts occur. Rather, coming out appears as a gradual, continuous endeavor laden with setbacks, changes, and surprises—"a series of realignments in perception, evaluation, and commitment, driven by the affirmation 'I am gay'" (Davies, 1992, p. 75). This protracted operation occurs before an ever-expanding audience—first the self and then a best friend, other gay people, family members, and "anyone who cares to know" (Ponse, 1980). Coming out also has been construed as a personal transformation, a rite of passage, and a declaration of social rights (Herdt & Boxer, 1993).

The developmental processes described in this chapter have been most clearly articulated and documented for gay and bisexual males. There is a growing recognition, however, that not all individuals who temporarily or ultimately identify as LGB experience either the process, sequence, or timing that have been proposed by developmental theorists. In regard to women, Golden (1996) argued:

> Much of this research is based on male subjects and, as with most areas of psychological research and theorizing, may not be generalizable to women . . . [A] woman's sexual orientation, as determined by attraction and arousal, may not always be consistent with her sexual behavior or the sexual identity she adopts. Similarly, the claim that sexual orientation is clearly established by adolescence and stable across the life course may not be applicable to women. (p. 243)

Thus caution is advised in any attempt to apply the general conclusions of this chapter to a particular individual.

In this chapter, the term "coming out" is avoided because it blurs the distinction felt by many LGB youths between self-labeling and disclosure of sexual identity. "Individuation" (whereby an individual arrives at the conclusion he or she is gay, lesbian, or bisexual) is thus differentiated from "disclosure" (the process by which others learn about an individual's homoerotic attractions). The two are not orthogonal or antithetical but "exist in a dialectic relationship: coming out to others constantly redefines one's notion of self and the development of a self-identity drives the process of disclosure" (Davies, 1992, p. 76). Kahn (1991) supports this position when she notes that lesbians who expect a positive and supportive response to their disclosure are more likely to disclose to others.

It is possible, however, to disclose to self and not others and to disclose to others and not to self. For example, some individuals recognize their homoerotic desires during adolescence but never disclose this information to anyone during their lifetime. This is most likely to occur during repressive times, such as the formative years of our parents' or grandparents' generations, and in some social institutions such as convents and seminaries. Some, perhaps many, adolescents resolve to conceal their homoerotic affections as the final solution to their "homosexual crisis." This may be a short-term resolution, "until I get to college," or a lifelong pattern.

The reverse, disclosure to others but not to self, is exemplified by adolescents who are known or highly suspected of being gay before they arrive at that same realization. Such adolescents may deny that they are lesbian or gay but engage in same-sex encounters with others, thus disclosing by implication to sexual partners their sexual orientation. A particular case of this can be ethnic minority youths, many of whom, for cultural reasons, do not construe their same-sex behavior as part of a more global gay or lesbian self-identification (Manalansan, 1996; Savin-Williams, 1996). Thus youths may indirectly or nonverbally disclose their homosexuality or bisexuality to others before they have arrived at that same conclusion.

Regardless of the sequence of events, the outcome of self-labeling and disclosure has significant ramifications for all aspects of development. McDonald (1982) notes that the process of revelation to self and others is

a developmental process through which gay persons become aware of their affectional and sexual preferences and choose to integrate this knowledge into their personal and social lives, [thus] coming out involves adopting a nontraditional identity, restructuring one's self-concept, reorganizing one's personal sense of history, and altering one's relations with others and with society . . . all of which reflects a complex series of cognitive and affective transformations as well as changes in behavior. (p. 47)

To help readers fully appreciate these developmental processes, I describe them below in a more or less chronological order. First, before self-definition, is the often-experienced childhood feeling of being different.

Feeling Different

Long before many youths with homoerotic attractions identify themselves as gay, lesbian, or bisexual, they experience vague but distinct feelings of being different (Newman & Muzzonigro, 1993; Savin-Williams, 1995; Telljohann & Price, 1993). Perhaps the first manifestation of sexual orientation is the undeniable but equivocal sense of being different from others. This is present in some rudimentary form before the ability to reflect and label sexual feelings and attractions emerges after pubertal onset. These feelings, which are not solely the domain of sexual minority youths, are often recalled as having existed from as young as four or five years of age (Herdt & Boxer, 1993; Savin-Williams, 1990) and characterize the childhood of over 70 percent of lesbians and gays (Bell, Weinberg, & Hammersmith, 1981). They are not likely to be perceived initially as sexual but rather as a strongly experienced sense of not having the same interests as other members of their sex.

This was humorously illustrated by Idgie in the movie *Fried Green Tomatoes*. Idgie was more comfortable in a tree house than at a wedding and more comfortable wearing shorts and t-shirts than laces and dresses. What marks these behaviors and interests as particularly suggestive of her sexual orientation is her question to her older brother, "What if God made a mistake?" Her later attachment to Ruth represents a prototypical lesbian relationship of her era and geography.

Isay (1989) describes this sense of differentness in boys: "They saw themselves as more sensitive than other boys; they cried more easily, had their feelings more readily hurt, had more aesthetic interests, enjoyed nature, art, and music, and were drawn to other 'sensitive' boys, girls, and adults" (p. 23).

The source of these feelings is difficult to discern, because "pre-gay" children are seldom asked if and why they feel different from other children. Thus researchers must rely on retrospective data from adolescents and young adults. These later recollections, however, may be distorted by the awareness of current sexual identity. Reasons given in retrospect for feeling different include an early and pervasive captivation with members of one's own sex that feels passionate, intimate, exciting, and mysterious (especially characteristic of "pre-lesbian" girls; see Golden,

1996); a desire to engage in play activities and to possess traits not typical of their sex; and a disinterest in, or sometimes an aversion toward, the activities socially prescribed for their own sex (Bailey & Zucker, 1995). Not uncommonly, intrapsychic tensions increase for such youths when they doubt their ability to meet the heterosexual obligations that are promulgated by their peers and family members.

Some youths report an especially early, prepubertal awareness of same-sex attractions and disinterest in sexual relations with the other sex. They may act on these erotic attractions at an early age and engage in childhood same-sex activities. These "sex play" encounters evoke little awareness or meaning regarding the label that the participants eventually will attach to the behavior or to a future sexual identity. For these youths, early same-sex "experimentation" is not incidental, as it may be for heterosexual youths who engage in sex play due to curiosity or for sexual release. Some pre-gay youths know that they are uninterested in romantic relationships with, and do not fantasize about, opposite sex members, "although they cannot indicate exactly what it is that they *do* want" (Sanders, 1980, p. 282).

A feeling of being alone, deserted, or in a vacuum characterizes the childhood of many youths who eventually will identify as bisexual, gay, or lesbian. Such youths feel that they belong nowhere and that they have no base of support. As noted later, these experiences have profound repercussions for self-acceptance and self-rejection, which evolve during later adolescence.

Self-Labeling

The growing realization that a sense of being different may mean being homosexual usually appears with the onset of puberty and thereafter increases exponentially (Coleman, 1981–1982; Remafedi, 1987; Robertson, 1981; Troiden, 1979). For some youths, it is as if puberty *stamps in* homosexuality, providing clarity and a label to heretofore poorly understood feelings. Little consensus exists regarding what it is about puberty that renders it such a convincing context for labeling and understanding. Perhaps it is the dramatic increase in hormone production that sexualizes the physical appearance of the body and the youth's cognitions, affects, and behaviors. In addition, because a youth now looks, acts, thinks, and emotes sexuality, others understand and interact with her or him in a sexual manner. This interplay between biology and the environment is consistent with a developmental perspective of sexuality during adolescence. The new sexual universe open to the pubescent girl and boy provides the context for self-reflection and interpretation.

A sixteen-year-old boy recalled his reaction four years earlier when he learned the meaning of his sexual interests: "It was a shock to discover that my impassioned, if unarticulated, love affairs with fellow schoolboys which had held so much poignant beauty carried that weighty word *homosexual*" (Heron, 1983, p. 104). Eighteen-year-old Joanne remembered when she first realized that she was a lesbian:

> Like a bolt of lightning . . . all the feelings of attraction I had been having for women, and the isolated feelings about myself due to my lack of "femininity" came together and pointed to the label, *Lesbian*. As a result, I walked around like a shell shock victim for days. (Heron, 1983, pp. 9–10)

The application of a sexual identity label provides not only an explanation for formerly vague and misunderstood feelings, but it affords a context in which future thoughts and emotions can be understood.

Of course, not all youths allow these processes to enter into their awareness. Although defenses against self-recognition are discussed later, it is apparent that many LGB youths are self-defining their sexual identity at increasingly younger ages, largely because of the recent visibility of homosexuality in the media and the social reality of homosexuality presented by gay and lesbian culture to adolescents. Defenses are shattered or rendered unnecessary because homoerotically inclined adolescents now have available to them a construct and role models of homosexuality, making it less frightening to recognize and honestly label their same-sex attraction.

Disclosure to Others

Although the process of disclosing to others can be arduous and protracted—requiring continual decisions about when and where to disclose and to whom—many clinicians believe it is crucial for mental health. Even though disclosure may invite negative reactions that compromise one's physical safety and psychological security, there are many advantages to publicly proclaiming one's sexuality. Disclosure to others leads to decreased feelings of loneliness and guilt (Dank, 1973); identity synthesis, integration, and commitment (Cass, 1979; Coleman, 1981–1982; Troiden, 1989); healthy psychological adjustment and positive self-esteem (Gonsiorek & Rudolph, 1991; Savin-Williams, 1990); and a positive gay identity (McDonald, 1982). Fitzpatrick (1983) found that those who disclosed their sexual identity had a greater sense of freedom, of being oneself, of not living a lie, and of experiencing genuine acceptance.

Many youths nonetheless choose to conceal their same-sex attractions from others because they more strongly fear negative reprisals than believe in the long-term positive consequences of disclosure to others. Many who recognize their same-sex attractions remain closeted because they fear the unknown, wish not to hurt or disappoint a loved one, and want to avoid being rejected, harassed, or physically abused by parents and peers (Carrier, Nguyen, & Su, 1992; Rector, 1982; Savin-Williams, 1994). Davies (1992) notes that some choose to compartmentalize their lives by developing two distinct groups of friends: those who know (mainly other gay people) and those who do not know (mainly heterosexuals).

When inquiring about disclosure, it is critical to distinguish among who is told earliest, who is most important for the youth to tell, and to whom it is most difficult to disclose. For example, although many youths report that it feels most difficult and yet is most important to disclose to family members, they usually reveal their sexual orientation first to close friends who will be supportive and understanding (Herdt & Boxer, 1993; Savin-Williams, 1990). Typically, the nuclear family is told sometime thereafter, although this is likely to vary depending on such characteristics as sex, social class, ethnicity, temperament, family dynamics, and religious values.

Sex differences may be particularly influential. For example, studies have consistently reported that lesbians disclose their sexual identity at a slightly older age. Reasons given include that women take longer to connect feeling different to their same-sex erotic feelings and behaviors; bisexuality and a sense of fluidity in constructing sexuality may be more prevalent options for women than for men (Golden, 1996), thus prolonging the disclosure process; and it is easier for women to publicly express affection toward other women without arousing suspicion—thus there is less need for women to disclose their lesbianism (Gagnon & Simon, 1973).

Another sex difference is that disclosure among lesbian youths may be contingent upon first feeling comfortable internally with private aspects of their sexual identity (Dubé, Giovanni, & Willemsen, 1995). They tend to integrate their sexual identity with other aspects of personal identity before disclosing this very intimate part of self to others. Thus for lesbian youths, an *internal* working-through process may precede outward disclosure. Consistent with this view, lesbians are more likely than gay men to self-label and disclose within an affectionate, emotional relationship with another woman (Schafer, 1976). By contrast, gay male youths are more likely to disclose earlier in the sexual identity formation process and to use outward social and sexual activity in order to develop self-acceptance as a gay person—an *external* working-through process.

Empirical support for such an internalizing/externalizing sex difference in identity formation comes from a large study of LBG youths (Savin-Williams, 1990). Compared to gay and bisexual male youths, lesbian and bisexual female youths were more likely to believe that they had a choice in their sexual orientation, and those who were most fully disclosed felt most comfortable with their sexual identity. They were more discriminating in their disclosures, divulging first to close friends before family and the general public. On the other hand, gay and bisexual male youths felt that their sexual orientation was beyond their control (that is, inborn or ingrained and not a matter of personal volition). Once the male youths began disclosing their sexuality, they essentially told "everyone."

Despite the recent publicity and visibility of LGB issues in newspapers, television shows, movies, and on-line computer networks, many youths remain fearful of disclosing their sexuality at home. Perhaps no single event evokes more fear and anxiety from LGB youths than disclosure to parents (D'Augelli, 1991). Notwithstanding, many report never feeling completely comfortable or "gay" until they disclosed their sexual orientation to their parents. Youths' disclosure to parents may feel like their final step out of the closet.

Disclosure to the Family

Many youths feel that they have few options other than to conceal their same-sex attractions from the family. In most homes, the prevailing unexamined expectation is that all children inevitably turn out to be heterosexual. Any deviance from this prescription implicitly or explicitly separates youths psychologically from their family of origin. Disclosure frequently interferes with the ability of heterosexual parents to identify with their child and vice versa. Thus for many youths, the most difficult decision is whether to reveal to their parents that they will not be carrying the parents' heterosexual expectations and dreams to fruition. In some families, this intergenerational discontinuity in sexual orientation intensifies an already wide emotional chasm and lack of identification between parents and youth.

The psychological toll that this state of affairs takes on sexual minority youths can be devastating. They can become

> half-members of the family unit, afraid and alienated, unable ever to be totally open and spontaneous, to trust or be trusted, to develop a fully socialized sense of self-affirmation. This sad stunting of human potential breeds stress for gay people and their families alike—stress characterized by secrecy, ignorance, helplessness, and distance. (MacDonald, 1983, p. 1)

The process of deciding to tell parents is poorly understood. Relatively little empirical research exists on factors that determine whether adolescents will reveal their sexual identity to parents, the effects that such disclosure have on youths' self-esteem and psychological health, and typical parental reactions to the disclosure.

In general, youths are more likely to disclose to mother than to father and other family members (Cramer & Roach, 1988; D'Augelli, 1991; Herdt & Boxer,

1993; Remafedi, 1987; Savin-Williams, 1990). Perhaps because children tend to have more distant relationships with their fathers, more mothers than fathers are told directly rather than indirectly, and nondisclosers more often fear the reactions of their fathers than mothers (Cramer & Roach, 1988). This may be explained in part by the finding that adult males in general are more homophobic than adult females (Herek, 1994). D'Augelli (1991) reported that mothers were more likely to respond in an affirming manner; less than 10 percent of mothers were rejecting compared to almost one-quarter of fathers.

The most accurate generalization that can be made regarding the reaction of parents to the news is that it will be unpredictable, although a positive prior relationship with the parents is a good omen for a healthy resolution. Even well-educated, liberal parents, however, often react somewhat negatively when initially informed about their child's same-sex attractions (Robinson, Walters, & Skeen, 1989). Perhaps more important than the initial response is the aftermath. Is the topic discussed again, or is it avoided by the parents and youth? Is the youth's sexuality used by the parents as a "weapon" to berate the youth? After disclosure or being discovered as lesbian, bisexual, or gay, is the youth psychologically mistreated, physically abused, or ostracized by family members in the years following?

Many youths never disclose to their parents because they do not want to disappoint or hurt their parents, do not want to place the parents in an awkward position with relatives and neighbors, and fear the long-term effects that such disclosure would have on their relationships and status within the family. Martin and Hetrick (1988) found that family problems were a common presenting complaint of the New York City sexual minority youths they interviewed, ranging "from feelings of isolation and alienation that result from fear that the family will discover the adolescent's homosexuality, to actual violence and expulsion from the home" (p. 174). Nearly one-half who had suffered violence because of their homosexuality reported that it was enacted by someone in their family, usually the father. In a study by Herdt and Boxer (1993), one in ten youths who disclosed being homosexual to his or her father was expelled from the home.

Harassment from parents may include physical assault. The majority of violent physical attacks experienced by 500 primarily Black or Latino sexual minority youths occurred in the family and were gay-related (Hunter, 1990). Data from studies of male prostitutes, runaways, and homeless youths confirm this home-based violence, most often from fathers, father-substitutes, and older brothers (see Savin-Williams, 1994, for a comprehensive review). Unwanted and physically abused in their families, these LGB runaways have been aptly termed "throwaways" in the recent social science literature.

Violence in the home also may include sexual abuse. One in five sexual minority youths reported being the victim of sexual abuse (Martin & Hetrick, 1988).

Sexual abuse occurred primarily in the home—perpetrated by fathers, uncles, grandfathers, or older brothers. Not infrequently, youths blamed themselves for the sexual abuse because they felt that they must have seduced the adult or did not say "no" convincingly enough.

Despite these risks, most youths want to reveal their sexual orientation to parents because it is such a profound and central aspect of the self. The initiative usually is taken by youths who would like a closer, more authentic relationship with their parents. Cramer and Roach (1988) report that the reasons most often cited for disclosing to parents are "a desire to share one's personal life, being tired of concealing one's sexuality, a desire for more freedom, and a desire for more intimacy with one's parents" (p. 87).

Youths report that their relationship with parents usually deteriorated immediately after disclosure but improved considerably thereafter—sometimes to a level more positive than prior to disclosure. For fathers, a sex effect has been observed—more daughters than sons report negative changes in their relationship with their father. However, this finding may be because the father and gay son relationship was so impaired prior to the revelation that any minor improvement in honesty, communication, and trust would be considered a positive development for their relationship (Cramer & Roach, 1988; Herdt & Boxer, 1993). Gay and bisexual males interviewed by Savin-Williams (1995) reported that they never felt particularly close to their fathers because they did not enjoy the activities that their fathers wanted to do, such as playing sports, doing farm chores, and fixing cars. To them, their fathers appeared embarrassed or disappointed in the sons' sex-atypical behaviors and interests; the gay and bisexual sons more typically enjoyed reading, artistic efforts, housework, and quiet games. Once a son disclosed to his father, the relationship improved, perhaps (some youths speculated) because the father felt absolved of any blame for his son's less "masculine" and more "feminine" interests and behaviors. These sex-atypical characteristics of the son now had an explanation and were recognized as permanent by the father.

Factors that predict how the family will react once the child has disclosed to the family are poorly understood. Several studies suggest that adherence to "traditional family values" may be an important variable. Newman and Muzzonigro (1993) report that adolescents who grow up in families that embrace the values of traditional religion, marriage, children, and retaining a non-English primary language are most likely to perceive that their parents are disappointed with their homosexuality. These youths are not, however, less likely to disclose to their parents or to do so at a later age. Cramer and Roach (1988) found that gay sons who reported that their mothers had traditional sex-role attitudes and that their fathers were high on religious orthodoxy perceived that their parents were accepting of them. The authors speculate that the parents' greater emphasis on family unity, rather than traditionalism or conservatism per se, resulted in their enhanced ability to come to terms with the family crisis.

The effects that disclosure to parents has on the self-evaluations of sexual minority youths have not been systematically explored. It has been suggested that if the consequences are affirming and supportive, disclosure to parents enhances the youth's self-esteem (Borhek, 1993). However, positive self-esteem could just as easily be a precursor to, and thus a cause of, youths disclosing to parents. It is unclear whether a satisfying relationship with parents encourages youths to disclose to them or whether their relationship is satisfying because youths have disclosed to them. Perhaps both are true. In most cases, parents are a significant factor in their child's developing sense of self-worth and sexual identity, especially in terms of youths feeling comfortable with their sexuality and disclosing that information to others (Savin-Williams, 1990).

This was the conclusion reached in a survey of 317 lesbian, bisexual, and gay youths between the ages of fourteen and twenty-three years (Savin-Williams, 1990). Lesbian or bisexual female youths were most likely to feel comfortable with their sexual orientation when they believed that their parents accepted or would accept their sexual orientation. A lesbian who reported an overall satisfying relationship with her parents and who had relatively young parents was most likely to be out to them (see also Kahn, 1991). Among gay and bisexual male youths, parental acceptance was related to feeling comfortable being gay *only if the youth also reported that his parents were important for his sense of self-worth.* Gay and bisexual male youths who were out to their mother and had a satisfying but infrequent relationship with their father were likely to report high self-esteem.

Some parents experience a period of subliminal awareness or suspect consciously for many years that their child is other than heterosexual. This may be based on their perception of the child's sex-atypical behavior, the emotional attachments that the child develops, or other factors. By contrast, some parents appear to have no idea and, for some time after the revelation, feel as if their child is a stranger in their midst.

Robinson, Walters, and Skeen (1989) report that some parents, after learning of their child's homosexuality, progress through stages similar to those Kübler-Ross (1969) described regarding a death: shock, denial, guilt, anger, and acceptance. Most parents eventually arrive at tolerance or acceptance, although some remain at early stages or occasionally regress temporarily to previous phases.

The process of "slowly conceding" to a sexual minority identity entails weighing the costs to one's psychic self and one's relationship with others (Coleman, 1981–1982; MacDonald, 1983). A youth must decide whether to remain a part of the heterosexual community and perhaps feel estranged and confused or move into a lesbian or gay community and risk conflicts with parents and friends. When a youth decides to *disclose* to the family or is discovered as bisexual, lesbian, or gay, a family crisis may ensue.

As a result of these factors, many adolescents strategically conceal their sexuality until late adolescence or early adulthood, when they are less emotionally and financially dependent on their parents or are living away from home. For many youths, parents are among the last to learn about their homoerotic attractions. Although the decision to delay initially protects youths from feared parental reactions, it may create a fissure in the parent-child relationship. In addition, some youths feel that hiding their sexual orientation is more stressful than disclosing their identity to parents (Rotheram-Borus, Rosario, & Koopman, 1991). The closer an LGB youth is to the parent receiving the disclosure, the more the parent's reaction will affect the youth, for better or worse.

Ethnic Sexual Minority Youths and Their Families

Ethnic minority LGB youths share with majority youths many of the same difficulties in disclosing their sexual orientation to their families. However, disclosure may be even harder for ethnic minority youths, who depend on their family as the primary support system during "the arduous times of experiencing discrimination, slander and inferior treatment" (Morales, 1983, p. 9). Because ethnic minority nuclear families tend to be embedded deeply in their extended families and ethnic communities, alienation from the nuclear family may simultaneously jeopardize a youth's associations with other members of the ethnic group. Such alienation may delay the youth's integration of ethnic and sexual components of the self into a unified, esteemed whole (Morales, 1983; Savin-Williams, 1996).

The ethnic family support system more resembles a tribe with multiple family groups than a nuclear family structure consisting solely of parents and children. For ethnic persons, the family constitutes a symbol of their basic roots and the focal point of their ethnic identity (Morales, 1983 p. 9).

Ethnic minority youths may feel that they can never publicly disclose their same-sex attractions for fear of humiliating and bringing community shame to their close-knit, multigenerational extended families. Chicana poet Torres (1980) expressed this sentiment in response to pressure she received from other lesbians to disclose to her parents:

> Somehow it would be disrespectful to say to them, "Look, I'm a lesbian, and you're going to have to deal with it." I don't have the right to do that. They've been through so much in their lives about being Chicanos and living in this

society. They've just taken so much shit that I won't do that to them until I feel like it can be said. (p. 244)

If Asian American youths disgrace themselves, shame is brought not only to the immediate family but to all past generations, living and dead (Carrier et al., 1992; Chan, 1989, 1995; Pamela H., 1989; Tsui, 1985). The family's honor is tarnished; it is not the children who have failed but the parents. For example, one interviewee noted, "Japanese are taught humility and being gay is often associated with shame. You tend to keep it quiet so you don't bring shame to your family" (Wooden, Kawasaki, & Mayeda, 1983, p. 241).

Parents who suspect that their child is lesbian or gay may be hesitant to publicly acknowledge the issue for fear of embarrassing relatives and their community. Thus a wall of silence is likely to form around a family with a lesbian daughter, gay son, or bisexual child. Even if a youth progresses to the point of self-recognition of her or his sexual status, the cultural proscriptions against stating this publicly may block further self-development.

In fact, many ethnic minority youths never directly, verbally disclose to their parents, or they delay such self-disclosure until well into adulthood. Siblings, usually sisters, are told before, and perhaps in lieu of, parents. For example, Chan's (1989) study of Chinese, Japanese, and Korean young adults found that almost 80 percent had disclosed to a family member, usually a sister; only one-quarter had disclosed to parents. A primary reason for disclosing to nonparent family members was to gain confidantes and invaluable sources of support.

Given the importance and centrality of the extended family, some youths feel that they are forced to choose between their ethnic affiliations and their sexual identity. Tremble, Schneider, and Appathurai (1989) note that minority youths often "excluded themselves from cultural activities in order to avoid shaming the family in front of friends" (p. 261). Youths may have greater fear of homophobia in their ethnic communities than of racism in the predominantly White LGB community and so may decide to participate in the activities of that community. However, they may feel as if they do not fit well anywhere because in either community, some valued parts of the self remain unrecognized, unappreciated, inexpressible, or intentionally hidden.

It is important to understand these youths' subjective experiences of stress in managing their dual identities, incompatible roles, loyalty conflicts, and endless psychological adjustments in switching codes of behavior across disparate contexts. Whereas in most of the United States, White heterosexual high school students can surround themselves with many friends like themselves and hence can avoid feeling isolated, LGB ethnic minority high school students endure two stigmas, being an ethnic and a sexual minority. They are continually vulnerable to prejudice and ostracism from all sides—from their heterosexual family and ethnic community, the LGB White community, and the heterosexual White community. On the most central mirroring dimensions of race and sexual orientation, they often cannot find *anyone* like themselves in their high schools.

Even after high school, they are perpetually susceptible to—and all of them sometimes encounter—racism in the predominantly White LGB community, as well as homophobia in their ethnic communities. Especially in smaller cities and towns, there may be few or no interpersonal contexts in which they can feel safe from potential prejudice. To achieve a sense of personal coherence and continuity through time, they must try to maintain their ethnic group ties as well as develop ties to the open LGB community, which in most locales is predominantly older, White, and middle-class. Furthermore, most of these youths are attempting to achieve this sense of personal coherence without a reference group of persons similar to themselves in ethnicity, sexual orientation, and age who could provide support and validation along the way (Morales, 1983; see also Chapter Eleven of this book).

Forming an integrated multiple self-identification that includes ethnic and sexual identities is likely to be a protracted developmental process. However, it is possible that learning the skills to manage one minority status, ethnicity, may facilitate at least some individuals' later handling of a second minority status, such as a gay, lesbian, or bisexual orientation. Having successfully contended with the difficulties of being a member of a marginalized ethnic group, such youths may utilize similar cognitive and interpersonal skills in coping with being sexually different. They already know what it is like to be vulnerable to discrimination. They also have learned how to marshall righteous anger, self-validation, and action-oriented solutions in response to society's prejudice rather than internalizing that prejudice. Future researchers should examine how minority youths' ethnic socialization in their families of origin (including ethnic knowledge, pride, and preparation for handling discrimination) influences their subsequent coping with LGB identity development.

Clinical Concerns

While growing up, youths of all ethnicities internalize, to some extent, society's condemnation of same-sex behavior. As a result, "most teenagers describe themselves as heterosexual unless there is compelling evidence to the contrary; and predominantly homosexual adolescents often waffle between heterosexual, homosexual, and bisexual labels" (Coleman & Remafedi, 1989, p. 37). Attempts to reconcile the cultural homophobia that has been internalized with homoerotic attractions pose a formidable developmental task.

Social Isolation, Defense Mechanisms, and Psychiatric Problems

For those who feel they must hide their sexual orientation, interactions with friends, parents, teachers, and others are often based on lies and half-truths. As a result, growing up as a sexual minority can be an exceedingly isolating experience (Hetrick & Martin, 1987; Martin & Hetrick, 1988; Sears, 1991). Nineteen-year-old Aaron Fricke recalled this isolation:

> I became withdrawn. I had no means of expression. My school grades dropped and I retreated into a life of non-stop eating and listening to the radio. In seventh grade I weighed 140 pounds; by eleventh grade, I weighed 217 pounds and spent eleven hours a day listening to the radio. I had trouble dealing with the outside world. And every day I lived in fear that there was nothing else, that I would never know anyone who could understand me and my feelings. (Heron, 1983, p. 39)

Feelings of isolation and loneliness are particularly problematic for youths raised in small, rural towns in which exposure to and acceptance of diversity are limited (Sears, 1991). Brown (1976) notes that small towns offer little hope that homoerotic needs or social acceptance will be fulfilled. Youths who attempt to establish a same-sex relationship in a small town may fear detection, blackmail, and verbal or physical assault. In some cases, these fears are not groundless because discovery frequently begets a hostile response.

Youths who acknowledge their socially unacceptable desires to themselves may have severe doubts about their normality, thereby lowering their self-esteem. How can a youth consider himself or herself respectable when society maintains that a central aspect of self is bad? Brandon, a seventeen-year-old teenager recalled, "When I realized I was homosexual, the first thing I did was sit down and cry. I wept for myself, but mostly I cried because I didn't conform. I couldn't be this way, because it 'just wasn't right' " (Heron, 1983, p. 15).

A self-depreciating or negative identity may be adopted at a time when most other youths are gradually building self-esteem and establishing a positive identity. Those who fear the "pathology" of their desires may attempt to alter their sexual orientation by praying for God's intervention, dating the other sex, or denying altogether their sexuality. These defenses constitute a futile effort doomed to fail, thus undermining or delaying the development of a positive self-image.

Although psychological defense mechanisms often are used by youths whose same-sex attractions are surfacing, the impulses tend to emerge into full consciousness eventually, creating panic or causing a major disruption of coping strategies that have been established. To ward off anxiety and conflict, an individual may try to *pass* as heterosexual. This common adolescent response to the fear of disclosure and its attendant feelings of guilt and anxiety (Dank, 1971; Martin, 1982; Sears, 1991) is illustrated by two youths trying to cope with their homoerotic desires (Savin-Williams, 1995):

> I feared not being liked and being alienated. I was president of various school clubs and once I beat up a guy for being a faggot. I was adamant that fags should be booted out of the Boy Scouts. Other kids asked me why I was so rough on them. I did not say. No one suspected me because I did sports and had several girlfriends.

> Still, I try, even now, to cover up myself. I'm very conscious of my masculine appearance. I won't cross my legs or limp my wrists in public. I'm always monitoring myself, my clothing, and jewelry. I'd like not to let others know I'm gay unless I decide it. I want control.

Sears (1991) reports that few in his sample of lesbian and gay Southern youths publicly objected to gay-related jokes made by peers, and most dated other-sex peers. In another study, 85 percent of lesbian and gay adolescents pretended to be heterosexual some of the time (Newman & Muzzonigro, 1993). To facilitate passing, pronouns of dating partners are changed, partners or lovers are introduced as "friends," and discussion of their personal lives is avoided (D'Augelli, 1991).

Passing, however, may lead to feelings of depression, awkwardness, and shame in interpersonal relations. Several humanistic psychologists (Jourard, 1971; Maslow, 1954) have proposed that healthy personality development requires significant and substantial self-disclosure to others. Personal authenticity brings self-validation as a person of self-worth. To forego this, as in passing, engenders feelings of hypocrisy and self-alienation (Lee, 1977; Martin, 1982). Thus closeted LGB youths have little opportunity to integrate same-sex desires into their dawning identity. If this integration does not occur, a temporary developmental moratorium takes place in which identity formation is truncated and problems of underachievement in school, unhappy heterosexual relations, and chronic psychological disequilibrium are common (Malyon, 1981).

Other psychologically problematic defensive strategies used by youths to forestall acceptance of homoerotic feelings include

- Rationalization: "It's something I'll outgrow," "I did it because I was lonely," "It's just a means to earn money," "I was drunk/high."

- Relegation to insignificance: "It's just sexual experimentation or curiosity that is natural at my age," "I did it only as a favor for a friend."
- Compartmentalization of sexual desire: "I mess around with other boys/girls, but that does not make me a faggot/dyke," "I just love this person, not all men/women."
- Withdrawal from provocative situations to remain celibate or asexual: "I'm saving myself for the right girl/boy."
- Denial, frequently engaging in heterosexual dating or sexual behavior: "I can't be gay—I've had a girlfriend/boyfriend for years."
- Sublimation, redirection of energies to other efforts, such as intellectual or work pursuits.

Martin (1982) suggests that sexual promiscuity may be a defense for some male adolescents who resort to casual, one-time sexual encounters. Although this may satisfy sexual needs, allowing youths to drop their facade for a short time, it also compartmentalizes this aspect of themselves from the rest of their lives. Because such sex is anonymous, an emotional connection does not develop. The young men may rationalize that they engaged in the act solely for sexual gratification, rather than out of a "love" of other males. This allows them to maintain, "I may have homosexual sex, but I'm not a homosexual." Male youths also may avoid specific activities during sexual encounters, such as kissing, giving oral sex, and receiving anal sex, that symbolize to them "real homosexuality" as opposed to mutual masturbation, receiving oral sex, and being the inserter in anal sex, which may be framed as experimentation or for the purpose of mechanical release only.

These defensive strategies for avoiding or forestalling the recognition of one's sexual orientation never succeed completely. When they fail and a youth is subjected to intense harassment from peers and lack of family support, emotional or behavioral problems may also emerge: inexplicable phobias, generalized anxiety, school problems (underachievement, truancy, dropping out), running away, prostitution, homelessness, substance abuse, depression, suicidality, and other forms of self-destructive behavior (Savin-Williams, 1994). In particular, several studies report that a very large proportion of lesbian and gay youths (20 to 40 percent) have made suicide attempts, half of these youths have made multiple attempts, and LGB youths are two to three times more likely to commit suicide than heterosexual youths are. These and other data suggest that a substantial percentage of LGB youths are socially isolated, clinically depressed, and potentially suicidal.

Most LGB youths, particularly in high school, remain closeted, and if they seek or are referred for psychotherapy, it will most likely be for one or more of the psychiatric disorders just listed, school problems, running away, or substance abuse. They typically will not bring up the topic of their sexual orientation in therapy, either because they are experiencing sexual identity confusion or nonacceptance or because they fear public disclosure and discrimination. They may lie to the therapist if asked directly before sufficient trust has developed. Therapists who use nonheterosexist language with their clients (rather than, for example, using language that presumes that girl clients have boyfriends or that boy clients have girlfriends) provide a context in which youths may feel most comfortable raising the topic of sexual orientation later.

Family Problems Following Disclosure or Discovery

Although many more parents today respond in an overall supportive manner after learning that their adolescent is bisexual, lesbian, or gay, the revelation of a youth's sexual orientation frequently produces a family crisis. In the worst-case family responses, the youth is physically abused by parents or siblings, thrown out of the house, subjected to religious rites and exorcisms, harassed to the point of decompensation or running away, or hospitalized involuntarily to be "cured" of homosexuality. More commonly, parents subject a youth to verbal castigations, anguished warnings, and denials and invalidations of the youth's feelings, or they attempt to find religious counseling or outpatient psychotherapy that will "cure" (eliminate) the homoerotic desires.

In response to these family efforts, if the youth's self-esteem and sexual identity are still tenuous, she or he may become withdrawn, depressed, or suicidal. On the other hand, if the youth's self-esteem is high and sexual identity is fairly well consolidated, the youth may become hostile toward the parents for their failure to understand and embrace this basic aspect of identity.

To illustrate common reactions of parents following the revelation, a vignette of a mother's attempt to understand her bisexual son's sexual orientation follows. This excerpt is from a conversation that took place in the winter of 1992. A mother and son were invited to discuss the son's recent disclosure to his mother of his sexuality. Although the mother was eventually supportive of her son, the shock of the disclosure initially sent her into a tailspin of denial, projection, and rationalization. First, she attributed her son's bisexuality to an "excessive" need for love:

> I think that you are bisexual because you have a strong need for love and affection. You've always been that way and therefore you need so much [love and affection] that you believe that you need it from both sexes.

The mother then tried to persuade her son that he could easily choose to lead a heterosexual life—if only he tried hard enough.

> If you are bisexual, then you can avoid the abnormal and lead a normal, satisfying life. If you can be bi, then you can be normal. Why confuse your life? Concentrate on the norm. You *must* follow the normal path. . . . Program your mind, and then the emotions and physical attractions will follow.

When the son explained that his feelings and attractions went beyond mere choice and were deeply rooted in his personality, the mother asserted:

> You can never be happy [living a gay lifestyle] so just accept this as a momentary thing. . . . It is of this world, this physicality, and don't make a big issue out of [your bisexuality]. . . . Just put the other [same-sex attractions] out of your head. Maybe you just have not had the kind of relationship with a girl that would be a real test. . . . You have not sampled the real thing. . . . Don't allow yourself to become preoccupied with this garbage. It doesn't allow you to find a girl. You are not allowing yourself the choice and to know how good it can be.

The mother continued:

> It is sex, pure and simple, just physical. . . . Don't allow yourself to get involved. It's sick. You'll die [from AIDS]. We did not raise you to see you die, to come to this [homosexuality].

These words reflect the mother's anguish about losing her hopes and aspirations for her son. Her refusal to accept her son's homoerotic attractions and her insistence that it is a passing phase—the result of previously unsatisfactory heterosexual relationships, or a desire for sex, pure and simple—invalidate the son's subjective experience and expressed feelings. She implies that she knows her son's real feelings, needs, and motives better than does he—a form of mystification that risks undermining his confidence in his own internal perceptions.

Moreover, she communicates the message that gay is bad—it is garbage, not normal, sick. Such parental reactions usually alienate the youth, contributing to the youth's depression or suicidality and blocking further communications in the family. If a youth's self-esteem remains intact during such an onslaught, the youth may lose respect for the parent because of the latter's apparent ignorance, become inpatient with the parent's lack of understanding, or become angry and rejecting in return, thus starting a vicious cycle of reciprocal recriminations followed by reciprocal withdrawal.

For example, following the above interchange, the son reported to the interviewer that the conversation left him feeling rejected and abandoned by his mother's conditional love; misunderstood, frustrated, angry, and hurt by her blatant disregard for his feelings; uncertain about her ability to meet his future emotional needs; scolded for having "chosen" to love members of the same sex; insulted by her simplistic recommendations for changing and by her implication that he did not really know his own feelings; and frightened by her assertion that he would never live a happy life.

In this regard, it is useful to think in terms of *mutually* rejecting versus empathic interactions between parents and young people. Youths sometimes become extremely inpatient with their parents, hoping for or demanding immediate parental acceptance and understanding of their sexual orientation, even though it may have taken the youths themselves many years to accept and understand their homosexuality. There is, of course, no reason to expect parents to reach the same level of acceptance more easily, especially given that they usually have less exposure than their child to people and information that would refute their negative stereotypes about homosexuality. Thus, whereas a youth likely has spent many months or years coming to terms with same-sex attractions and with the loss of a socially prescribed heterosexual future, parents are usually caught off-guard by the suddenness of the revelation, even if they previously had suspicions.

Extending the analogy to the work of Kübler-Ross (1969) on grieving, some children and parents—in separately coming to terms with the youth's sexual orientation—experience a sequence of adaptational phases, including (1) *denial* ("No, not me/my child"), (2) *anger or guilt* ("Why me/my child?" "Who is to blame for this outcome?"), (3) *bargaining* ("Yes me/my child, but maybe it can be changed"), (4) *depression* ("Yes, me/my child, and it will be very difficult"), and (5) *acceptance* ("Yes me/my child, and it's all right"). However, at the point of initial disclosure, most youths and their parents will be somewhat or dramatically out of step in this sequence, making it difficult for them to empathize with one another's dilemma. So while the parents may be in denial at the time of the revelation, the youth may be at any of the other phases, producing combinations that reciprocally forestall or advance the youth's and family's ultimate acceptance of the youth's sexual orientation.

For example, the parents may completely deny the validity of the youth's assertion of a lesbian, gay, or bisexual identity, while the youth—a little farther along in the process—may be "bargaining" on a conversion to heterosexuality through psychoanalysis. Or the parents may engage in protracted self-recriminations, blaming themselves or each other for the child's homosexuality, whereas the youth has reached a high level of self-acceptance in which causality is not even a relevant question. Furthermore, the parents may seek family therapy with the intention of eliminating the youth's homosexuality, whereas the youth views therapy as a vehicle to greater self-acceptance and celebration of her or his sexual identity. Thus phase differences in youths' and parents' acceptance levels largely determine the focus and course of family-oriented treatment.

Family Systems Interventions

As the above illustrations make clear, large discrepancies in parents' and youths' acceptance levels and extreme differences in their goals for therapy may greatly complicate the therapist's role. Conflicting family members may, for example, pressure the therapist to take sides for or against trying to eliminate the youth's homosexuality, sometimes rendering conjoint family sessions untenable while making individual therapy for the youth and separate therapy for the parents a better alternative, at least initially.

As a general rule of thumb, if the youth or the parents express confusion, doubts, or disdain about the youth's sexual orientation, therapists should take the following stances: (1) sexual *orientation* is nonvolitional; (2) neither therapists nor parents nor the youths themselves nor anyone else can engineer a person's sexual orientation; (3) the youth may be helped in therapy to discover her or his own sexual orientation if the youth is confused about this question; and (4) as a separate individual, the youth will discover over time how to live with her or his sexual orientation in ways that will bring the most fulfillment.

A second rule of thumb is that a youth should not be prematurely encouraged to disclose to parents or to participate in conjoint family sessions until the youth has attained a fair measure of sexual identity consolidation and self-acceptance or unless the parents are very accepting of homosexuality. A young person who is confused about sexual orientation or lacking in sexual identity self-esteem should not be subjected in therapy sessions to parental attempts to refute her or his same-sex attractions. Parents may say things that can never be withdrawn or ameliorated ("You can't do this to me! You are killing us, ruining our lives! I can never show myself again in the neighborhood! I'd rather you were dead!"). Until the youth is more secure in her or his sexual identity, such parental statements in family sessions are likely to inflict deep wounds. Progress can be delayed if the youth feels that the therapist is unable to provide adequate support and protection in the family sessions or that the therapist subtly colludes with or submits to the parents' negative view of homosexuality.

If parents are continually plagued by guilt, anger, depression, or grief and if the youth is still tentative in self-acceptance, then separate sessions with the parents and with the youth should be held. It is probably best that parents' pain not be shared, except in a general manner, with the disclosing youth. That is, the parents should not make a futile attempt to hide their distress, but neither should they encumber the youth in family sessions or at home with excessive expressions of their feelings of guilt, remorse, sadness, or fear. It is highly likely that the youth is heavily burdened with her or his own issues and may be overwhelmed with guilt or shame for "causing" the pain and suffering that the parents are experiencing. The therapist should encourage the parents to channel their expressions of pain into separate meetings with the therapist or parent support groups, and frequent sessions should be scheduled to help the parents contain their intense negative feelings until the immediate crisis passes.

On the other hand, if and when the youth (through individual therapy, group therapy, or otherwise) has attained a stronger sense of sexual identity, can understand the parental criticism or pain as an irrational homophobic response, and can empathize with the parents' need for time and patience to cope with the youth's disclosure, conjoint family sessions can be highly productive. Ideally, the youth would be able to take a position such as the following in family sessions:

> My sexual orientation has not been caused by you, nor is it designed to hurt you, nor should you or I do anything to try to change it. What is hurting you is the misinformation about homosexuality that you have been taught by society. I know that it will take you a long time to understand this, just as it has taken me a long time. I am willing to give you lots of time to learn about this. I'll answer serious questions, provide you with information, tell you about my recognition and acceptance of my sexual orientation, tell you about my life and my friends' lives as lesbians or gay people, tell you about my own fears and expectations, and discuss with you how you might handle the news with your friends and our relatives.

Obviously, few youths of high school age or younger can maintain such a differentiated, nonreactive position in the face of heated parental criticism or expressions of pain, especially when the youths' support systems outside the family tend to be weak. However, some late adolescents and young adults approximate this level of individuation, and conjoint family sessions may then be useful for all concerned.

Parents who adjust best to their offspring's homosexuality prioritize and reinterpret their values, maintaining, "You are my child and I love you no matter what" (Tremble et al., 1989, p. 259). Preserving family unity is given first priority. Parents who accept their gay or lesbian child find precedents for homosexuality among lesbian and gay friends and family members. Conjoint family therapy sessions are indicated in those circumstances in which the parents are as, or even more, accepting of homosexuality than is the youth, as the following examples demonstrate:

> I was very close to my mother. . . . I went home [at the age of twelve] and told my mother, and my mother treated it moderately lightly—that is, she said that since I was very young, that I was much too young for such an announcement, that I should probably wait a few months at least before deciding that this was an absolute fact. But if it turned out, indeed, that I was a Lesbian, then that was fine. . . . [It was expected of me that] I was to be an honorable person in every way all of my life, and if I were honorable all of my life, nothing but good would come to me. (Grier, 1980, p. 236)

> When I wrote and told my mother I was bisexual, she replied: "Yes, we all are, aren't we?" That blew me away—she was taking it much more calmly than I was! My transition to Lesbianism did not surprise or unduly bother her. . . . Of course she has had to do some fast growing and information-gathering on the subject, but she has never hesitated in her support and love for me. . . . [My father] too was very accepting. (Anonymous, 1980, p. 77)

> I think my mother knew [I was gay as a young boy], certainly she was aware of the grief I got at school. We talked but never said the word *gay*. She wanted me to be in therapy since seven or eight, not to change me but so that I could be happy and sure of my homosexuality. (Savin-Williams, 1995)

Despite the youth's possible discomfort with the topic, parents who are (or who become through therapy) reasonably comfortable with homosexuality should encourage their child to discuss the history of her or his same-sex attractions, who else knows and how they have reacted, and future concerns and expectations. Once is not enough. This discussion should be the first of an ongoing series of conversations about the youth's feelings and concerns. If the young person does not initiate the topic, parents should probe, in as unobtrusive a manner as possible, to normalize the youth's sexuality, dating relationships, and the parent-child partnership. Parents should be encouraged to continue educating themselves about gay, lesbian, and bisexual communities, lifestyles, and culture. Subscription to the local gay, lesbian, and bisexual newspaper or newsletter is helpful in this regard.

Finally, in families in which parents are deeply homophobic, such as when parents are embedded in fundamentalist religious communities and are unwilling to participate in therapy or other activities that counter homophobia, the therapist should encourage the youth to intentionally develop a significant ongoing support system with responsible adults and youths outside of the family—a so-called family of choice. In these instances, the youth may need to suspend efforts and expectations for fuller parental acceptance. The parents' rigidity can best be interpreted as a function of their socialization in a generally homophobic society and in their specifically homophobic social institutions, past and present. That is, in the final analysis, the family's enemy is homophobia, with its viselike grip on the parents' minds.

Self-Help Books and Organizations for Parents

In addition to therapy, self-help books and support groups for parents can be extremely valuable. Fairchild and Hayward's (1989) classic book, *Now That You Know: What Every Parent Should Know About Homosexuality,* and others (Borhek, 1993; Clark, 1987; Griffin, Wirth, & Wirth, 1986; Woodman & Lenna, 1980) suggest strategies for parents who need help coping with the news of their child's homosexuality. Further support and information can be obtained from local chapters of Parents, Families, and Friends of Lesbians and Gays (P-FLAG) or through the national P-FLAG office (postal address: 1012 Fourteenth Street N.W., Suite 700, Washington, DC 20005; telephone: 202–638–4200; Internet address: PFLAGTL@aol.com).

P-FLAG offers self-help meetings for parents and other family members, basic education, and ongoing parent and family support groups. P-FLAG also provides public speakers to community groups and does other organizing work on behalf of LGB civil rights. Information about P-FLAG should be offered at some point to every family that seeks to cope with an LGB youth's orientation.

The self-help books and P-FLAG offer similar advice for the most frequently asked question by parents: What did I do wrong? After the youth's initial disclosure, parents who view homosexuality negatively tend to blame themselves in the following ways:

"I did not pay enough/paid too much attention to you. Perhaps I favored your brother/sister too much."

"Our marriage set a bad example."

"Your mother/father provided a bad model."

"You played with the wrong children in the neighborhood."

"I didn't make you masculine/feminine enough."

To address these concerns, P-FLAG (1988) offers three "facts" that all parents of an LGB son or daughter could benefit from recognizing and ultimately accepting as truth:

Same-sex attractions are as natural as heterosexuality.

Sexual orientation is not a matter of choice.

There is *no* pattern in the kinds of families who produce a lesbian, gay, or bisexual child.

The self-help literature, P-FLAG, and gay-affirmative family therapy or parent counseling all encourage parents to reject the notion that homosexuality is a disease or a sin, or that parents are the cause of the child's sexual orientation. Parents ideally should accept the view that homosexuality is a healthy, natural fact of life. Their child's sexual orientation cannot be changed, and any attempt at conversion is made at a high cost—the youth's alienation and dispiritedness. The basic message to parents is that they are not to blame for their offspring's homoerotic desires. Of course, this information should be baseline knowledge for *all* parents, regardless of the sexual orientation of their children. In reality, however, parents only feel a need for such information after their own LGB child has disclosed to them.

Conclusion

Although all families are different, and each situation is unique—with its own history, moderating circumstances, and likely outcome—the ultimate goal of family intervention is to provide acceptance and ongoing support for the youth's individuated fulfillment of an LBG orientation. By the end of therapy, the youth should receive the consistent message from the parents that without a trace of doubt, she or he belongs as a whole person in the family. At termination, parents should have come to the understanding that their child has not changed. Rather, the parents and the youth both know the child better and more completely than they did previously. The youth's emergence from the closet should be perceived as a victory over homophobia for everyone in the family, not a disgrace. It began as a gift of disclosure from child to parent because of the parents' importance in the child's life. Also, at the conclusion of a successful therapy, the son or daughter should feel confident that the family will be a strong support through the uncertainties of the future. The message from the family should be this: We will help you cope with whatever you face in the future.

Once comfortable with the issue of homosexuality, parents can become agents of social change as a way of indirectly helping improve the life of their child. In small, personal ways, they can help other parents who are struggling with a bisexual, gay, or lesbian child. Parents also can provide accurate information to other uninformed individuals among their friends and neighbors. On a larger scale, parents can speak publicly in the community and distribute accurate information on homosexuality; march in gay pride parades; and advocate for fair local, state, and national ordinances, laws, and policies. Lesbian, gay, and bisexual youths tend to feel most completely affirmed by parents who will join with them in actively countering homophobia through social activism in their schools and communities.

References

Anonymous (1980). My coming out herstory. In J. P. Stanley & S. J. Wolfe (Eds.), *The coming out stories* (pp. 70–78). Watertown, MA: Persephone Press.

Bailey, J. M., & Zucker, K. J. (1995). Childhood sex-typed behavior and sexual orientation: A conceptual analysis and quantitative review. *Developmental Psychology, 31,* 43–55.

Bell, A. P., Weinberg, M. S., & Hammersmith, S. K. (1981). *Sexual preference: Its development in men and women.* Bloomington: Indiana University Press.

Borhek, M. V. (1993). *Coming out to parents: A two-way survival guide for lesbians and gay men and their parents* (2nd ed.). Cleveland, OH: Pilgrim.

Brown, H. (1976). *Familiar faces, hidden lives: The story of homosexual men in America today.* San Diego, CA: Harcourt Brace.

Carrier, J., Nguyen, B., & Su, S. (1992). Vietnamese-American sexual behaviors and HIV infection. *Journal of Sex Research, 29,* 547–560.

Cass, V. (1979). Homosexual identity formation: A theoretical model. *Journal of Homosexuality, 4,* 219–235.

Chan, C. S. (1989). Issues of identity development among Asian-American lesbians and gay men. *Journal of Counseling and Development, 68,* 16–20.

Chan, C. S. (1995). Issues of sexual identity in an ethnic minority: The case of Chinese-American lesbians, gay men, and bisexual people. In A. R. D'Augelli & C. J. Patterson (Eds.), *Lesbian, gay, and bisexual identities over the lifespan: Psychological perspectives* (pp. 87–101). New York: Oxford University Press.

Clark, D. K. (1987). *The new loving someone gay.* Berkeley, CA: Celestial Arts.

Cohen, K. M., & Savin-Williams, R. C. (1996). Developmental perspectives on coming out to self and others. In R. C. Savin-Williams & K. M. Cohen (Eds.), *The lives of lesbians, gays, and bisexuals: Children to adults* (pp. 113–151). Fort Worth, TX: Harcourt Brace.

Coleman, E. (1981–1982). Developmental stages of the coming out process. *Journal of Homosexuality, 7,* 31–43.

Coleman, E., & Remafedi, G. (1989). Gay, lesbian, and bisexual adolescents: A critical challenge to counselors. *Journal of Counseling and Development, 68,* 36–40.

Cramer, D. W., & Roach, A. J. (1988). Coming out to Mom and Dad: A study of gay males and their relationships with their parents. *Journal of Homosexuality, 15,* 79–91.

Dank, B. M. (1971). Coming out in the gay world. *Psychiatry, 34,* 180–197.

Dank, B. M. (1973). The homosexual. In D. Spiegel & P. Keith-Spiegel (Eds.), *Outsiders USA* (pp. 269–297). San Francisco: Rinehart.

D'Augelli, A. R. (1991). Gay men in college: Identity processes and adaptations. *Journal of College Student Development, 32,* 140–146.

Davies, P. (1992). The role of disclosure in coming out among gay men. In K. Plummer (Ed.), *Modern homosexualities: Fragments of lesbian and gay experience* (pp. 75–83). London: Routledge.

Dubé, E., Giovanni, C., & Willemsen, E. (1995). *"Coming out": Social influences and self-perceptions.* Paper presented at the Western Psychological Association Annual Meetings, Los Angeles.

Fairchild, B., & Hayward, N. (1989). *Now that you know: What every parent should know about homosexuality* (updated ed.). San Diego, CA: Harcourt Brace.

Fitzpatrick, G. (1983). Self-disclosure of lesbianism as related to self-actualization and self-stigmatization. *Dissertation Abstracts International, 43,* 4143B.

Gagnon, J. H., & Simon, S. (1973). *Sexual conduct: The social sources of human sexuality.* Hawthorne, NY: Aldine de Gruyter.

Golden, C. (1996). What's in a name? Sexual self-identification among women. In R. C. Savin-Williams & K. M. Cohen (Eds.), *The lives of lesbians, gays, and bisexuals: Children to adults* (pp. 229–249). Fort Worth, TX: Harcourt Brace.

Gonsiorek, J. C., & Rudolph, J. R. (1991). Homosexual identity: Coming out and other developmental events. In J. C. Gonsiorek & J. D. Weinrich (Eds.), *Homosexuality: Research implications for public policy* (pp. 161–176). Newbury Park, CA: Sage.

Grier, B. (1980). The garden variety lesbian. In J. P. Stanley & S. J. Wolfe (Eds.), *The coming out stories* (pp. 235–240). Watertown, MA: Persephone Press.

Griffin, C. W., Wirth, M. J., & Wirth, A. G. (1986). *Beyond acceptance: Parents of lesbians and gays talk about their experiences.* New York: St. Martin's Press.

Herdt, G., & Boxer, A. M. (1993). *Children of Horizons: How gay and lesbian teens are leading a new way out of the closet.* Boston: Beacon Press.

Herek, G. M. (1994). Assessing heterosexuals' attitudes toward lesbians and gay men: A review of empirical research with the ATLG Scale. In B. Greene & G. M. Herek (Eds.), *Lesbian and gay psychology: Theory, research, and clinical applications* (pp. 206–228). Newbury Park, CA: Sage.

Heron, A. (Ed.). (1983). *One teenager in ten.* Boston: Alyson.

Hetrick, E. S., & Martin, A. D. (1987). Developmental issues and their resolution for gay and lesbian adolescents. *Journal of Homosexuality, 14,* 25–44.

Hunter, J. (1990). Violence against lesbian and gay male youths. *Journal of Interpersonal Violence, 5,* 295–300.

Isay, R. A. (1989). *Being homosexual: Gay men and their development.* New York: Farrar, Straus & Giroux.

Jourard, S. M. (1971). *The transparent self* (2nd ed.). New York: Van Nostrand.

Kahn, M. J. (1991). Factors affecting the coming out process for lesbians. *Journal of Homosexuality, 21,* 47–70.

Kübler-Ross, E. (1969). *On death and dying.* New York: Macmillan.

Lee, J. A. (1977). Going public: A study in the sociology of homosexual liberation. *Journal of Homosexuality, 3,* 47–78.

MacDonald, G. B. (1983, December). Exploring sexual identity: Gay people and their families. *Sex Education Coalition News,* pp. 1, 4.

Malyon, A. K. (1981). The homosexual adolescent: Developmental issues and social bias. *Child Welfare, 60,* 321–330.

Manalansan, M. F., IV. (1996). Double minorities: Latino, Black, and Asian men who have sex with men. In R. C. Savin-Williams & K. M. Cohen (Eds.), *The lives of lesbians, gays, and bisexuals: Children to adults* (pp. 393–415). Fort Worth, TX: Harcourt Brace.

Martin, A. D. (1982). Learning to hide: The socialization of the gay adolescent. *Adolescent Psychiatry, 10,* 52–65.

Martin, A. D., & Hetrick, E. S. (1988). The stigmatization of the gay and lesbian adolescent. *Journal of Homosexuality, 15,* 163–183.

Maslow, A. H. (1954). *Motivation and personality.* New York: HarperCollins.

McDonald, G. J. (1982). Individual differences in the coming out process for gay men: Implications for theoretical models. *Journal of Homosexuality, 8,* 47–60.

Morales, E. S. (1983, August). *Third World gays and lesbians: A process of multiple identities.* Paper presented at the 91st Annual Convention of the American Psychological Association, Anaheim, CA.

Newman, B. S., & Muzzonigro, P. G. (1993). The effects of traditional family values on the coming out process of gay male adolescents. *Adolescence, 28,* 213–226.

Pamela H. (1989). Asian American lesbians: An emerging voice in the Asian American community. In Asian Women United of California (Eds.), *Making waves: An anthology of writing by and about Asian American women* (pp. 282–290). Boston: Beacon Press.

Parents, Families, and Friends of Lesbians and Gays. (1988). *About our children.* Los Angeles: Author.

Ponse, B. (1980). Lesbians and their worlds. In J. Marmor (Ed.), *Homosexual behavior: A modern reappraisal* (pp. 157–175). New York: Basic Books.

Rector, P. K. (1982). The acceptance of a homosexual identity in adolescence: A phenomenological study. *Dissertation Abstracts International, 43,* 883B.

Remafedi, G. (1987). Male homosexuality: The adolescent's perspective. *Pediatrics, 79,* 326–330.

Robertson, R. (1981). Young gays. In J. Hart & D. Richardson (Eds.), *The theory and practice of homosexuality* (pp. 170–176). London: Routledge.

Robinson, B. E., Walters, L. H., & Skeen, P. (1989). Response of parents to learning that their child is homosexual and concern over AIDS: A national study. *Journal of Homosexuality, 18,* 59–80.

Rotheram-Borus, M. J., Rosario, M., & Koopman, C. (1991). Minority youths at high risk: Gay males and runaways. In M. E. Colten & S. Gore (Eds.), *Adolescent stress: Causes and consequences* (pp. 181–200). Hawthorne, NY: Aldine de Gruyter.

Sanders, G. (1980). Homosexualities in the Netherlands. *Alternative Lifestyles, 3,* 278–311.

Savin-Williams, R. C. (1990). *Gay and lesbian youth: Expressions of identity.* Washington, DC: Hemisphere.

Savin-Williams, R. C. (1994). Verbal and physical abuse as stressors in the lives of sexual minority youth: Associations with school problems, running away, substance abuse, prostitution, and suicide. *Journal of Counseling and Clinical Psychology, 62,* 261–264.

Savin-Williams, R. C. (1995). *Sex and sexual identity among gay and bisexual males.* Unpublished manuscript, Cornell University, Ithaca, NY.

Savin-Williams, R. C. (1996). Ethnic- and sexual-minority youth. In R. C. Savin-Williams & K. M. Cohen (Eds.), *The lives of lesbians, gays, and bisexuals: Children to adults* (pp. 152–165). Fort Worth, TX: Harcourt Brace.

Schafer, S. (1976). Sexual and social problems of lesbians. *Journal of Sex Research, 12,* 50–69.

Sears, J. T. (1991). *Growing up gay in the South: Race, gender, and journeys of the spirit.* Binghamton, NY: Harrington Park Press.

Sophie, J. (1985–1986). A critical examination of stage theories of lesbian identity development. *Journal of Homosexuality, 12,* 39–51.

Telljohann, S. K., & Price, J. P. (1993). A qualitative examination of adolescent homosexuals' life experiences: Ramifications for secondary school personnel. *Journal of Homosexuality, 26,* 41–56.

Torres, A. (1980). Ana Torres. In R. Baetz (Ed.), *Lesbian crossroads* (pp. 240–244). New York: Morrow.

Tremble, B., Schneider, M., & Appathurai, C. (1989). Growing up gay or lesbian in a multicultural context. *Journal of Homosexuality, 17,* 253–267.

Troiden, R. R. (1979). Becoming homosexual: A model of gay identity acquisition. *Psychiatry, 42,* 362–373.

Troiden, R. R. (1989). The formation of homosexual identities. *Journal of Homosexuality, 17,* 43–73.

Tsui, A. M. (1985). Psychotherapeutic considerations in sexual counseling for Asian immigrants. *Psychotherapy, 22,* 357–362.

Wooden, W. S., Kawasaki, H., & Mayeda, R. (1983). Lifestyles and identity maintenance among gay Japanese-American males. *Alternative Lifestyles. 5,* 236–243.

Woodman, N. J., & Lenna, H. R. (1980). *Counseling with gay men and women.* San Francisco: Jossey-Bass.

PART THREE

LESBIAN AND GAY COUPLES

CHAPTER EIGHT

ARE LESBIAN COUPLES FUSED AND GAY MALE COUPLES DISENGAGED?

Questioning Gender Straightjackets

Robert-Jay Green, Michael Bettinger, and Ellie Zacks

The lives of lesbian and gay male couples contradict some of family therapists' most cherished notions and offer fresh insights about the link between gender and intimacy for all couples. In this chapter, we examine three assumptions that mental health professionals—including lesbian and gay therapists—commonly hold about same-sex couples:

Assumption 1: As a consequence of female gender-role socialization, lesbian couples have a tendency to be emotionally fused.

Assumption 2: As a consequence of male gender-role socialization, gay male couples have a tendency to be emotionally disengaged.

Assumption 3: It is essential for the well-being of lesbian and gay male couples that the partners come out to their families of origin.

We will explore these notions from both theoretical and research standpoints. First, we review the family systems concepts of fusion and disengagement, which have contributed to the three assumptions listed above. Next, we present some research findings that call into question the validity of these common beliefs about lesbian and gay couples. The results of these studies are interpreted in light of the California Inventory model of family connectedness and recent findings about gender-role nonconformity among lesbians and gay men. We conclude by offering some new "lenses" for therapists to use when working with same-sex couples.

Fusion, Disengagement, and Related Family Systems Ideas

Concepts of fusion and disengagement have been central in the major systems theories of couple and family dysfunction. A basic premise in these theories is that relationships contribute to the development of psychiatric symptoms when family members' individuality is stifled or when their separate functioning is restricted (Green & Framo, 1981). Among the concepts that family therapists have proposed to describe these phenomena, Bowen's (1966) notions of emotional fusion and differentiation of self and Minuchin's (1974) concepts of enmeshment and disengagement have captured the imagination of the field most strongly. More recently, some aspects of these concepts have been incorporated into the Circumplex Model of marital and family functioning and the Family Adaptability and Cohesion Evaluation Scales (FACES), which we used in the studies reported later in this chapter (Olson, 1993).

In the last fifteen years, the concepts of fusion and disengagement also have filtered into the literature on same-sex couples, as reflected in the three assumptions stated at the outset of this chapter. Therefore, we will outline in detail the original meanings of the terms *fusion* and *disengagement* and then look at how these ideas have been applied to lesbian and gay couples in the family therapy literature.

Bowenian Theory: "Emotional Fusion" and "Differentiation of Self"

Bowen originally defined *fusion* as a state of excessive emotional reactivity in which family members' responses to one another have a reflexive, predetermined quality, unmediated by higher-order intellectual processes such as anticipating, reflecting, deciding, or planning (Bowen, 1966, 1978; Guerin, Fay, Burden, & Kautto, 1987; Kerr, 1981). Prototypes of such emotional reactivity include sudden explosive violence toward a partner, or mindless, submissive obedience and appeasement based on fears of rejection or disapproval from the partner. Such reactivity entails responding automatically out of anxiety, without being able to consider the consequences for self and partner, or whether one's responses fit with one's inner feelings, needs, values, opinions, or long-term interests. Over time, reactivity serves to maintain the couple's interactional status quo, preventing a fuller articulation of separate selves (differentiation) that could improve the relationship and lead to genuine mutuality and individual need fulfillment.

As depicted in Bowenian theory, emotional reactivity often takes an avoidant form, involving a submergence of self in order to maintain a relationship—an automatic deference to a dominant partner's wishes or to the rules of the relationship in order to avert conflict. One partner may be in an overfunctioning, overly responsible, caregiving position, neglecting and denying self in order to focus exclusively on the needs of the other who, complementarily, is in an underfunctioning and weak position in the relationship. Whether one is in a dominant and overfunctioning position or a submissive and underfunctioning position, having "no self" or being a "false self" or a "partial self" ultimately preserves only the semblance, the shell, of a relationship and precludes the experience of being an authentic self-in-relation.

Bowen (1966) coined the phrase *differentiation of self* to describe the process of individuating (becoming an authentic self-in-relation). Such differentiation requires both an awareness of self (knowing one's own beliefs, opinions, values, needs) and a declaration of self in relationships. The latter consists of communicating self in nonreactive but assertive ways, taking appropriately flexible "I" positions, and being able to stick to them when necessary. Differentiation also requires accepting the other's self, respecting the other's individuality, and distinguishing one's own wishes, feelings, needs, motives, perceptions, values, and opinions from those of the partner (not projecting onto the partner).

According to Bowenian theory, there are four common outcomes of fusion in a couple relationship: (1) emotional distance between the partners, (2) unresolved couple conflict, (3) dysfunction (mental or physical) in one partner, or (4) triangulation (involvement of third parties to deflect anxiety away from the original couple dyad).

Triangles involve two "insiders" and one "outsider," the insiders becoming fused in a coalition against the outsider who, in turn, becomes excluded and isolated. Typically, triangulation involves a coalition between one member of the couple and (1) a child (usually resulting in the child's psychological distress); (2) a sexual or romantic partner outside of the couple relationship (an affair); (3) a member of the extended family; (4) a friend or work associate; or (5) a therapist, physician, or other professional in the community. Ultimately, the four typical adaptations to fusion (distance, unresolved conflict, individual dysfunction, or triangulation) serve only to exacerbate the partners' inability to differentiate selves and achieve genuine mutuality.

A further axiom in Bowenian theory is that levels of fusion and differentiation are transmitted intergenerationally, from the family of origin to the family of procreation over successive generations. Bowen believed that a particularly problematic way of coping with fusion in the family of origin was the *emotional cut-off* of an adult from her or his family of origin. Cutting off from family of origin could take the form of geographical distance with no contact, or keeping contacts brief and infrequent, or overall avoidance of important, anxiety-provoking topics when with family of origin members. According to Bowenian theory, an emotional cut-off from the family of origin renders the individual prone to developing intense fusions and emotional cut-offs in subsequent relationships. The underlying problem of fusion in the family of origin is not solved by cut-off; rather, it is transferred to the next interpersonal context such as an intimate relationship or a parent-child relationship.

Because of the prolonged dependency of childhood and the regressive pull of parent-child relationships, Bowen believed that if an individual could differentiate a self in the family of origin, she or he also would be able to do so in a couple relationship, in parenting children, or in any other interpersonal context. Conversely, Bowen believed that an adult's continued avoidance or inability to differentiate a self in the family of origin would make it difficult or impossible for that person to develop a successful couple relationship. Based on these ideas, Bowen (1978) developed a therapy procedure he eventually named *coaching*. This method involves helping an adult take differentiating steps in relation to family of origin as a way to improve current couple and parenting relationships. These differentiating steps include taking nonreactive "I" positions in the family of origin, detriangulating self from conflicts between other family members, and developing authentic person-to-person (dyadic) relationships with each family of origin member (Guerin et al., 1987; Kerr, 1981; McGoldrick, 1995).

Structural Family Therapy: "Enmeshment" and "Disengagement"

In the period 1974–1978, Minuchin synthesized many of the earlier concepts about family functioning and called his theory "Structural Family Therapy" (Minuchin, 1974; Minuchin, Rosman, & Baker, 1978). Minuchin's model favors an architectural metaphor—a family structure composed of interrelated subsystems—the spouse subsystem (the marriage relationship), the parental subsystem (parent-child relationships), and the sibling subsystem (sibling relationships). Family structure is defined as "the invisible set of functional demands that organizes the ways in which family members interact" (Minuchin, 1974, p. 51). Boundaries are characterized as "the rules defining who participates and how," especially in terms of each family member's inclusion or exclusion from various subsystems' operations (p. 53). For example, in well-functioning families, children typically are excluded from participation in major decisions about family finances and from involvement in their parents' marital conflicts, which remain the exclusive preserve of the spouse subsystem. Parents are expected to maintain a strong alliance with one another, maintaining united leadership of the children (a strong "generational hierarchy").

Structural family therapists conceive of interpersonal and subsystem boundaries as existing on a continuum ranging from diffuse boundaries (enmeshed), to clear boundaries (normal range), to inappropriately rigid boundaries (disengaged). Clear boundaries promote successful adaptation to changing intrafamilial and extrafamilial demands and are associated with family and individual well-being. Diffuse boundaries (enmeshment) or rigid boundaries (disengagement) are opposite extremes on the boundary clarity continuum, and both are considered generally dysfunctional, contributing to family distress and individual symptoms.

From the structural family therapy perspective, enmeshment involves excessively rapid and intense emotional reactivity, too much closeness, and too much dependency, thus blocking individual family members' autonomy. Disengagement entails delayed and insufficient emotional reactivity, too much autonomy and separateness, lack of feelings of loyalty and belonging, and loss of the capacity for interdependence. Minuchin seldom applied the labels "enmeshed" or "disengaged" to whole family systems; he stressed instead that some subsystems in a family may be disengaged while other subsystems may be enmeshed.

Applications of Bowenian and Structural Family Theories to Same-Sex Couples

In 1980, the family therapy field's leading scholarly journal, *Family Process*, published what has become the classic family systems statement on same-sex couples—"The Problem of Fusion in the Lesbian Relationship" by Krestan and Bepko. Much of what has been written subsequently on this topic by other clinical authors has echoed similar themes of fusion, enmeshment, and merger in lesbian couples (see, for example, Burch, 1982, 1986; Elise, 1986; Kaufman, Harrison, & Hyde, 1984; McCandlish, 1982; Mencher, 1990; Roth, 1989; and Slater & Mencher, 1991). Furthermore, most of these authors imply or explicitly state that whereas lesbian couples are prone to fusion, gay male couples are prone to disengagement. Next, we review this classic argument. However, we wish to acknowledge that Krestan and Bepko have discarded some of their earlier ideas about fusion being pathological in lesbian relationships (personal communication, June 1994), even though these ideas seem to survive as clinical lore passed down through generations by other therapists and authors.

Articles on fusion in the lesbian relationship typically begin by noting the differences between female and male socialization:

In our society, in which men and women are groomed for gender-specific social roles, women have learned (a) to define themselves in relation to others (Chodorow, 1978); (b) to define morality in terms of responsibility and care

(Gilligan, 1982); (c) to develop exceptional sensitivity in noticing the needs of others and to demonstrate empathy even by experiencing the needs of others as their own (Chodorow, 1978); and (d) to suppress aggressive and competitive desires in order to avoid hurting others and to prevent the feared result of such self-expression, social isolation (Miller, 1976). [Roth, 1989, p. 288]

In particular, Chodorow's (1978) frequently cited theory proposes that boys and girls have different experiences in regard to separation from their mothers, and these early experiences set the stage for later patterns of female versus male intimacy. Girls, being the same sex as their mothers, are able to maintain a primary attachment and identification with their mothers throughout childhood, thereby remaining more comfortable and more concerned with connection, empathy, and merger. Boys, being of a different sex from their mothers and having to shift toward identifying with their fathers, must detach and defend against their dependency and identification with their mothers, thereby becoming more concerned with achieving interpersonal separation, distance, and autonomy. Following Chodorow's thesis, authors writing about same-sex couples postulate that lesbian couples are likely to suffer from fusion because they are composed of two women, both of whom have been socialized to seek connection. As a corollary, gay male couples are thought to suffer from disengagement because they are composed of two men, both of whom have been socialized to seek separation (Rubin, 1983).

The second theme appearing in articles about lesbian fusion pertains to the impact of homophobia on the couple's functioning. In particular, clinical authors suggest that same-sex couples tend to "turn inward upon themselves" in the face of oppression from the larger heterosexual community, lack of acknowledgment and support from their families of origin, and lack of legal validation through marriage, tax laws, insurance benefits, inheritance laws, and so on. Thus for lesbian couples, the normative tendency toward merger arising from female gender socialization is intensified by the lack of external social support and validation for the couple. These processes are presumed to be amplified even further because both partners in the couple are women. That is, unlike the male partners in heterosexual or gay male couples, neither partner in a lesbian couple has been socialized to seek and maintain autonomy and relational distance. As Krestan and Bepko (1980) originally stated of lesbian couples:

> Their tendency is to rigidify those boundaries further and to turn in on themselves, adopting what has been described as a "two against a threatening world" posture. The rigid definition makes for an increasingly closed system, with the lesbians often cutting themselves off from others. As a result, the in-

tensity of the fusion between the partners increases. Individual boundaries become blurred. Next, typical responses to fusion such as distancing, open conflict, or overt symptomatology occur to an intense degree in the relationship. (p. 278)

Also, based on gender-role socialization theory, authors hypothesize that gay male couples have problems opposite to those experienced by lesbians (Elise, 1986; Krestan & Bepko, 1980; Rubin, 1983). Gay men are assumed to have stereotypical male difficulties with connection, intimacy, closeness, dependency, expressiveness, and commitment, and to use sex outside the relationship as a distancing maneuver:

It is interesting to note that in dysfunctional relationships between gay males, a common response to systemic pressures is reactive distance rather than fusion. The gay male who is troubled by conflict in a relationship is more likely to triangle in a third party, separate himself by forming a separate household, or engage in "tricking" [brief sexual liaisons with outsiders] rather than attempt to maintain a monogamous relationship at all. In general terms, these two different responses to relationship pressures seem to reflect the differences in socialization between men and women: women cling, men distance. (Krestan & Bepko, 1980, p. 284)

In keeping with Bowenian theory, many authors writing about lesbian couples state explicitly that such couples suffer greater fusion and its negative consequences (emotional distance, conflict, individual dysfunction, or triangulation) if either partner remains emotionally cut off from her family of origin:

Cutoff results in the rigidly closed system that promotes fusion. A model of functional relatedness for the committed lesbian couple involves the formation by both the couple and the larger [family] system of boundaries that are clear and respected, although not rigid, with a minimum of cutoff or entanglement. (Krestan & Bepko, 1980, p. 279)

As in traditional Bowenian conceptions, cutting off from family of origin can take the form of geographical distance with infrequent contact or overall avoidance of anxiety-provoking topics when with family of origin members. An especially salient form of cut-off for lesbians and gay men is to remain closeted in their families of origin, that is, not disclosing their sexual orientation to family members, which necessitates hiding and lying. Lesser forms of cut-off include such behaviors as leaving a partner out of family holidays and events, rarely mentioning a partner in the presence of family of origin members, or concealing the extent of involvement with a partner (Krestan & Bepko, 1980; Slater & Mencher, 1991; see also Chapter Five in this book).

Overall, the images of lesbian and gay male couples that emerge in these writings skew toward the negative and pathological—lesbian couples tend to be portrayed as fused; gay male couples tend to be characterized as disengaged; both types of couples are believed to be prone to cut-offs from family of origin, which purportedly hinder the couple relationship. However, it is possible that this negative portrayal reflects the special preoccupations and tasks of therapists and the dysfunctional qualities of lesbian and gay couples who are in psychotherapeutic treatment, as compared to lesbian and gay couples who are not in treatment.

Typically, clinical authors do not address the potential lack of representativeness of their clinical (patient) samples and seldom qualify their theories as applying solely to distressed couples in therapy. However, there is an inherent danger in generalizing from clinical samples to nonclinical populations, especially when depicting minority populations. For example, compared to same-sex couples in treatment, distressed heterosexual couples in treatment may show equivalent degrees of fusion, disengagement, and family of origin cut-off; but clinical authors would not generalize such problems to all heterosexual couples, nor would they attribute these problems to heterosexuality or the heterosexual lifestyle.

Therefore, in order to understand whether fusion, disengagement, and emotional cut-off are more typical and problematic for same-sex couples as compared to heterosexual couples, it is necessary to investigate two major questions: (1) Do community samples of heterosexual, lesbian, and gay male couples who are *not in therapy* show differential rates of fusion, disengagement, or family emotional cut-off? and (2) Do distressed samples of heterosexual, lesbian, and gay male couples who are *in therapy* show differential rates of fusion, disengagement, or family emotional cut-off?

As an essential counterpoint to the clinical literature, we will describe our own initial studies that pertained to the first question (Bettinger, 1986; Zacks, Green, & Marrow, 1988). These studies compared lesbian, gay, and heterosexual couples recruited from the community rather than from the caseloads of mental health professionals. To our knowledge, the second question (comparing clinical samples of same-sex and heterosexual couples) has never been explored through formal research, and such studies should be a high priority for the future.

A Research Odyssey

In this section, we summarize a series of studies on community samples of lesbian and gay male couples in Sacramento and San Francisco, California. It is important to note that these studies were carried out during the early 1980s, before the AIDS epidemic had taken a major toll on the lives of gay men.[1] In this sense, the findings may not be entirely applicable to gay couples now living with knowledge of HIV infection. On the other hand, this sample does allow us to understand gay couples in more ordinary circumstances, when they are not living through a community health crisis. In the next sections, we describe the participants, procedures, and results of these studies. Then we discuss the implications of these findings for the three assumptions highlighted at the outset of this chapter.

Because this chapter is written primarily for a clinical readership, only descriptive results are presented in the text. The most important findings are summarized at the end of this discussion. For more research-oriented readers, details of methodology and tests of statistical significance can be found in the Notes section at the end of the chapter.

Participants

The participants in these studies included fifty-two lesbian couples (104 individuals) living in the Sacramento area and fifty gay male couples (100 individuals) living in the San Francisco Bay area. Participants were obtained through advertisements in the local gay newspapers and flyers distributed at the local lesbian and gay bars, bookstores, social events, and community groups.

Originally, the information from the gay male and lesbian couples was collected for separate doctoral dissertation projects by the second and third authors of this chapter (Bettinger, 1986; Zacks, 1986). Subsequently, Zacks and Green conducted a two-year follow-up of the lesbian couples. Because one of the same questionnaires was used in the two original studies, we were able to compare lesbian and gay male couples for the present chapter. In addition, using published norms for various questionnaires, we were able to compare our same-sex couples to a group of 1,140 heterosexual married couples from a national study (see Olson et al., 1983) and a group of 218 married couples from another study (see Spanier, 1976).

All couples had been living with their partners for a minimum period of six months, and both partners were asked to complete their questionnaires independently. Eighty-four percent of the lesbians and 88 percent of the gay men were Caucasian. These participants were mainly college-educated, and most of them worked in business or professional positions.

In each of the groups, participants ranged in age from their early twenties to their seventies or eighties (average ages were lesbians, thirty-six years; gay men, thirty-seven years; wives, forty-three years; and husbands, forty-six years). The lesbian couples had lived together for a median 3.5 years (ranging from one to thirty-four years), and the gay male couples had lived together for a median 4.0 years (ranging from six months to forty-seven years). The heterosexual couples in the 1983 study by Olson and colleagues had been married for a median eighteen years (ranging from six months to sixty-seven years).

In this and previous studies, lesbians and gay men report couple relationships that are significantly shorter than those of married heterosexual couples, and they show higher yearly rates of breaking up in the first ten years (Blumstein & Schwartz, 1983; Kurdek, 1995). Elsewhere (Zacks et al., 1988), we have speculated that these different relationship lengths may stem from the following factors:

1. Married couples may receive greater social validation and support, and greater family and peer pressure, to stay together.
2. Married couples are more likely to be raising children together, which provides shared goals and a strong incentive for them to stay together even if they are dissatisfied otherwise at various points in the marriage.
3. Married couples may have greater tendencies toward social conformity and more traditional, conservative, or religious value systems that keep them together despite unhappiness.
4. Married couples may perceive fewer relationship alternatives to their current marriage (for example, wives may anticipate less likelihood of remarriage, especially if they are older or have primary custody of children).
5. Married couples face greater legal and economic barriers to getting divorced (especially when children are involved or when wives are dependent on their husbands financially).
6. The greater flexibility of lesbians and gay men makes them more able and likely to leave relationships that are unsatisfying.

The relationship lengths of the same-sex couples in our study are similar to those reported by other investigators using much larger national samples or various samples in other parts of the country (Bell & Weinberg, 1978; Blumstein & Schwartz, 1983; Bryant & Demian, 1994; Kurdek & Schmitt, 1986; Peplau, Cochran, Rook, & Padesky, 1982). Thus we believe that our same-sex couples are reasonably representative of such couples in the United States in terms of relationship longevity.[2] Also, we wish to stress that because all of our findings are based on community samples of predominantly White, middle-class lesbians and gay men from large metropolitan areas in Northern California, we advise caution in generalizing these findings to other kinds of lesbian and gay male couples, particularly couples from other ethnic or racial groups or other social classes, or to those who live in small towns (see Chapters Six, Ten, and Eleven).

Questionnaires and Procedures

Here we describe each of the questionnaires given to participants and the overall design of the study.

Demographic Information All partners independently completed a background information questionnaire, which asked for age, ethnicity, length of relationship, education, occupation, and (for the lesbian sample only) whether they had been in therapy during the past year.

Family Adaptability and Cohesion Evaluation Scales (FACES III) Partners independently completed the FACES III—Couples Form, which is a twenty-item questionnaire for assessing Cohesion and Flexibility in couples (Olson, Portner, & Lavee, 1985). *Cohesion* is a measure of overall relationship closeness—"the emotional bonding that family members have toward one another" (Olson, Russell, & Sprenkle, 1983, p. 70). *Flexibility*, which was formerly called "adaptability" (Olson, 1993), is defined as "the ability of a marital or family system to change its power structure, role relationships and relationship rules in response to situational and developmental stress" (Olson et al., 1983, p. 70).

We interpret very low scores on Cohesion as indicating "disengagement" and very low scores on Flexibility as indicating "rigidity"—both being signs of problematic functioning. Conversely, based on new information about FACES III, we interpret very high scores on Cohesion and Flexibility as signs of extremely positive functioning (Cluff, Hicks, & Madsen, 1994; Green & Werner, 1996; Olson, 1993). We categorized each couple's Cohesion and Flexibility scores as being either "very low," "moderately low," "moderately high," or "very high" using procedures based on national norms (Olson et al., 1985).[3] This categorization allowed us to compare the percentages of lesbian, gay male, and heterosexual couples at the four levels of Cohesion and four levels of Flexibility.

Overall Relationship Quality/Satisfaction To obtain a measure of overall relationship quality (ranging from distressed/dissatisfied to well-functioning/satisfied), lesbian partners were asked to complete the Family Satisfaction Scale (Olson et al., 1982), and gay male partners were asked to complete the Dyadic Adjustment Scale (Spanier, 1976). For these questionnaires, the lesbian and gay couples' responses were compared to the published norms for married heterosexual couples. Scores on the Family Satisfaction Scale and the Dyadic Adjustment Scale will both be referred to as "Couple Satisfaction" scores in the discussion that follows.

Outness to Family of Origin For the lesbian sample only, we asked each partner if she was out (had disclosed her sexual orientation) to her mother, father, and one or more siblings; and we added up the total number of family members to whom she had come out (scores ranging from 0 to 3 family members). This "outness to family" information was then examined in relation to Couple Satisfaction.

Predicting Which Couples Will Break Up over a Two-Year Period For the lesbian sample only, we recontacted participants two years later by mail to ask if they were still together as a couple or whether they had broken up (ended their couple relationship). For couples who had broken up, we asked an open-ended question about reasons for the separation. For couples who were still together, we asked respondents to rate their current level of Global Couple Satisfaction on a 7-point scale (ranging from "Extremely Dissatisfied" to "Extremely Satisfied").

From the original sample of fifty-two lesbian couples, we were able to recontact at least one of the partners for forty-eight couples. Out of these forty-eight couples, 71 percent (thirty-four couples) were still together, whereas 29 percent (fourteen couples) had separated. For couples that were still together, we examined whether their initial Satisfaction and follow-up Global Satisfaction were related. Most importantly, we looked at whether a couple's breaking up during the two-year period could be predicted by the partners' earlier Cohesion, Flexibility, Satisfaction, and Outness to family of origin members (mother, father, siblings, and total family outness).

Findings

The results of the studies are organized below in terms of the major questions they answered. The questions and the most important results for each question are emphasized in italics.

Question 1 *Do lesbian, gay male, and heterosexual couples differ in terms of relationship Cohesion?* Based on the family systems and gender socialization theories reviewed earlier, one would expect lesbian couples, because they are composed of two women, to have more Cohesion (closeness) than heterosexual couples and gay male couples. In addition, heterosexual couples, because they contain a female partner, would be expected to have more Cohesion than gay male couples, because the latter are composed of two men, neither of whom would have been socialized as strongly as a woman partner to seek closeness in relationships.

We discovered, in line with family systems and gender socialization theories, that lesbian couples show higher levels of Cohesion than gay male and heterosexual married couples. Lesbian couples are the most cohesive of the three couple types. However, opposite to the theories' predictions, gay male couples show higher Cohesion than heterosexual couples. Heterosexual partners are the least cohesive of the three groups.[4]

Thus overall, *lesbian couples reported more Cohesion than gay male couples, who in turn reported more Cohesion than heterosexual married couples.* Look at the top half of Table 8.1 for the percentages of lesbian, gay male, and heterosexual couples reporting various levels of Cohesion. Most notably, 46.2 percent of lesbian couples, 26 percent of gay male couples, but only 13.6 percent of heterosexual couples report the highest level of Cohesion.

In addition to confirming that lesbian couples are more cohesive than the other groups, *these findings challenge the family systems and gender theory notion that gay male couples are disengaged compared to heterosexual couples. In fact, the opposite seems true.* Husbands and wives appear more likely to be disengaged (very low scores on Cohesion in Table 8.1) and less likely to be extremely close (very high scores on Cohesion in Table 8.1).

Question 2 *Do lesbian, gay male, and heterosexual married couples differ in terms of relationship Flexibility?* In contrast to stereotypes about partners in same-sex couples assuming fixed masculine/feminine ("butch/femme") roles (as in the film *La Cage aux Folles*), past research has shown that lesbian and gay male partners overwhelmingly tend to show much greater equality and gender-role flexibility than heterosexual couples do (Bell & Weinberg, 1978; Blumstein & Schwartz, 1983; Peplau, 1991; Kurdek, 1995). Being of the same sex, two women or two men together cannot fall back on traditional gender-role divisions to structure their reciprocal behaviors in areas such as leadership, instrumental and expressive functions, and rules for who does what in the household. Therefore, we expected same-sex couples to establish egalitarian, highly flexible decision-making and household arrangements, scoring significantly higher on Flexibility than heterosexual married couples.

The results are in line with our predictions. Both lesbian and gay male couples show dramatically higher levels of Flexibility than heterosexual married couples. In addition, lesbian couples show more Flexibility than gay male couples.[5] Thus overall, *lesbian couples report more Flexibility than gay male couples, and both groups of same-sex couples report strikingly more Flexibility than heterosexual married couples.* Look in the bottom half of Table 8.1 for the percentages of lesbian, gay male, and heterosexual couples reporting various levels of Flexibility. Over 80 percent of both lesbian and gay male couples show very high Flexibility compared to only 16 percent of heterosexual couples. Conversely, only 2 percent of lesbian couples and 6 percent of gay male couples fall into the lower two levels of Flexibility that typify over half of the heterosexual couples (55 percent).

We also looked at the combination of levels of Cohesion and Flexibility within each couple. For example, a particular couple could be very high on Cohesion but very low on Flexibility, which would indicate that the couple was very close but

TABLE 8.1. PERCENTAGES OF LESBIAN, GAY, AND HETEROSEXUAL COUPLES AT FOUR LEVELS OF COHESION AND FOUR LEVELS OF FLEXIBILITY.

	Cohesion			
	Very low	Moderately low	Moderately high	Very high
Lesbian[a]	1.9%	15.4%	36.5%	46.2%
Gay Male[b]	6.0%	34.0%	34.0%	26.0%
Hetereosexual[c]	16.3%	35.8%	36.3%	13.6%

	Flexibility			
	Very low	Moderately low	Moderately high	Very high
Lesbian[a]	0.0%	1.9%	13.5%	84.6%
Gay Male[b]	0.0%	6.0%	12.0%	82.0%
Hetereosexual[c]	16.3%	38.3%	29.4%	16.0%

Note: Results of statistical tests for significance between the groups' Cohesion and Flexibility scores can be found in notes 4 and 5 at the end of this chapter.

[a]*n* = 52 lesbian couples.

[b]*n* = 50 gay male couples.

[c]*n* = 1,140 heterosexual married couples.

also very rigid. The percentages of lesbian, gay male, and heterosexual couples showing various combinations of Cohesion and Flexibility are displayed in Table 8.2. There are sixteen possible combinations of Cohesion and Flexibility.

Most remarkable is the concentration of lesbian and gay male couples in the upper right-hand section of Table 8.2, which denotes a combination of very high Flexibility with either moderately high or very high Cohesion. *Overall, 79 percent of lesbian couples and 56 percent of gay male couples exhibit these combinations of higher Flexibility and Cohesion, whereas only 8 percent of heterosexual couples do.*

Question 3 Does couple Satisfaction differ between lesbian and heterosexual couples or between gay male and heterosexual couples? Based on the family systems literature's depictions of lesbian couples as fused and gay male couples as disengaged, one would expect same-sex couples to show less satisfaction (more distress) than heterosexual married couples.

Contrary to the clinical literature's emphasis on the distress of lesbian couples, *the lesbian sample reports significantly more Satisfaction than the heterosexual sample* on Olson and colleagues' (1982) Family Satisfaction Scale.[6]

TABLE 8.2. PERCENTAGES OF LESBIAN, GAY MALE, AND HETEROSEXUAL COUPLES REPORTING VARIOUS COMBINATIONS OF COHESION AND FLEXIBILITY IN THEIR RELATIONSHIPS.

Flexibility		Very low	Moderately low	Moderately high	Very high
			Cohesion		
Very high	L[a]	0.0%	5.8%	32.7%	46.2%
	G[b]	4.0%	22.0%	28.0%	28.0%
	H[c]	3.0%	4.7%	5.4%	2.9%
Moderately high	L	0.0%	9.6%	3.8%	0.0%
	G	2.0%	4.0%	6.0%	0.0%
	H	4.7%	10.0%	11.3%	3.5%
Moderately low	L	1.9%	0.0%	0.0%	0.0%
	G	0.0%	6.0%	0.0%	0.0%
	H	5.8%	13.3%	14.1%	5.0%
Very low	L	0.0%	0.0%	0.0%	0.0%
	G	0.0%	0.0%	0.0%	0.0%
	H	2.9%	5.7%	5.7%	2.1%

[a]Lesbian; $n = 52$ couples.

[b]Gay male; $n = 50$ couples.

[c]Heterosexual; $n = 1,140$ married couples.

The gay male sample reports slightly less couple Satisfaction than the heterosexual married sample on Spanier's (1976) Dyadic Adjustment Scale, although it should be stressed that the gap between the two groups' average Satisfaction is not very large (only 5 points on a 151-point scale). Overall, the results indicate that gay male couples as a group are about as well functioning and satisfied as Spanier's married sample and dramatically more satisfied than Spanier's divorce sample (which scored 39 points lower than the gay male sample).[7]

Question 4 *Is there a significant link between lesbian partners' Outness to family of origin members and the couple's relationship Satisfaction?* Based on Bowenian theory's dire predictions about the effects of family of origin emotional cut-off on adults' couple relationships, one would expect that lesbian partners who are not out to their family of origin members would have poorer couple relationship quality (greater distress and dissatisfaction) than out lesbian partners. Look in Table 8.3 for the percentages of lesbian participants' who are out to their mothers, fathers, siblings, and combined totals of each group. These results on outness to family are consistent with very recent findings from the National Lesbian Health Care Survey of 1,925 lesbians located in fifty states (Bradford, Ryan, & Rothblum, 1994). For example, 19 percent of lesbians in the National Survey report being out to no family members; 45 percent fall into the middle range of being out to between 11 and 75 percent of their family members; only 27 percent are out to all family members. Also similar to our results, other studies show that lesbian and gay youths are more likely to disclose their sexual orientation to their mothers than to their fathers (see Chapter Seven).

Contrary to predictions based on Bowen systems theory and much clinical lore about lesbian couples, we discovered that *Satisfaction of the lesbian couples in our study is entirely unrelated to whether partners are out to their mothers, fathers, siblings, or a combination of the three.* Apparently, this form of emotional cut-off from family of origin does not have a negative effect on a lesbian couple's well-being.

Question 5 *What factors predict lesbian couples' breaking up over a two-year period?* Of the initial fifty-two lesbian couples in our study, we were able to collect follow-up information after two years from at least one of the members of forty-eight couples. Out of these forty-eight couples, fourteen of them (29 percent) had separated. This rate of separation seems analogous to the rate in Blumstein and Schwartz's (1983) large national study, in which 19.4 percent of lesbian couples separated over a shorter follow-up period of eighteen months.

Looking at our lesbian participants' reasons for breaking up (they could give more than one reason), we informally categorized their responses and tallied them as follows: conflictual communication—eight couples; sex outside the relationship—five couples; financial, value, lifestyle differences—five couples; lack of sexual desire—four couples; and drug or alcohol problems—four couples.

From our follow-up study, the most important discovery was this: *Couples that separated had reported lower Cohesion and Flexibility at initial testing two years earlier. None of the family of origin Outness categories (to mother, father, siblings, or combined) was related to whether the couple stayed together or separated.*[8] Based on the lesbian sample's comparatively high Cohesion and Flexibility initially, these results suggest that lesbians may be especially unwilling to stay in relationships that are less than very close and less than very flexible (for example, to stay in the kind of less cohesive and less flexible relationships that are normative for many heterosexual married couples).

Also, *for the thirty-four lesbian couples that had stayed together, we found that higher Cohesion, Flexibility, and Satisfaction at the start of the study were associated with higher Global Satisfaction two years later, showing relative stability over time. None of the Outness categories was related to these couples' Global Satisfaction two years later.*[9]

TABLE 8.3. LESBIAN PARTICIPANTS' OUTNESS TO FAMILY OF ORIGIN.

	Percent of sample	Number of participants*
Out to whom?		
Mother	61.5%	64
Father	38.5%	40
One or more siblings	72.1%	75
Totals		
Out to *no* family member	15.4%	16
Out to *one* family member	25.0%	26
Out to *two* family members	31.7%	33
Out to *three or more* members	27.9%	29

*Total participants: n = 104 individuals.

Additional Findings All of the questionnaires that were originally designed for use with heterosexual couples proved to be reliable with lesbian and gay male couples. Also, there is evidence that the lesbian and gay male participants' questionnaire responses were valid. For example, lesbian couples who had been in individual or couples therapy during the past year reported significantly lower levels of Satisfaction with their relationships than lesbian couples not in therapy. This result suggests that lesbian couple Satisfaction scores are pragmatically relevant and realistic, with less satisfied couples being more likely to actually seek treatment.

Second, within lesbian and gay male couples, there was a significant positive correlation between the two partners' independent evaluations of their Cohesion and Flexibility.[10] This finding shows that a participant's answers to the questionnaires were meaningfully associated with his or her partner's separate answers, which indicates a significant degree of validity in their responses.

For both lesbian and gay male couples, higher Cohesion and Flexibility are associated with more relationship Satisfaction.[11] Given that the original notion of fusion connoted intense emotional turmoil, distress, and suffering, it seems unlikely that the higher Cohesion and Flexibility scores of the lesbian and gay male couples in this study represent the kind of pathological fusion, merger, enmeshment, or relational chaos so often reported in the clinical literature on lesbian couples.

Summary of Results Taken together, the outcomes of our research converge on five main conclusions:

1. Compared to heterosexual married couples, both lesbian and gay male couples are more cohesive and much more flexible. Higher cohesion and flexibility are distinctive characteristics of same-sex couples.
2. Lesbian couples are even more cohesive and flexible than gay male couples.
3. Same-sex couples that are more cohesive and flexible report greater satisfaction with their relationships.
4. Lesbian couples that are less cohesive and less flexible are more likely to break up within a two-year period.
5. Outness to family of origin members bears no relationship to lesbian couples' satisfaction, relationship durability over a two-year period, or the level of follow-up satisfaction among couples that stay together.

Our results dispute the three assumptions about same-sex couples put forth by various family systems and gender theorists. Lesbian couples appear to be close and satisfied, not negatively fused. Gay male couples appear to be more cohesive than heterosexual married couples, not more disengaged. Being out to family of origin members is unrelated to lesbian couple satisfaction or continuity over a two-year interval.

Our findings concur with a substantial amount of related research showing that lesbian and gay male couples generally function as well as (and lesbians sometimes better than) heterosexual couples (Kurdek, 1988b, 1995). Moreover, there now is considerable evidence from other studies that the same set of factors tends to predict relationship quality across all types of couples, regardless of sexual orientation: (1) partners' placing more value on security, permanence, shared activities, and togetherness; (2) partners' placing lower value on having separate activities and on personal autonomy; (3) higher expressiveness; (4) more perceived intrinsic rewards for being in the relationship; (5) fewer perceived attractive alternatives to the relationship; (6) more perceived barriers to ending the relationship; (7) less belief that disagreement is destructive; (8) higher trust in partner—viewing partner as dependable; (9) better problem-solving and conflict-negotiation skills; (10) higher shared or egalitarian decision making; and (11) perceived social support from sources outside the relationship (Peplau, 1991; Kurdek, 1995).

What Do the Findings Mean?

In what follows, we will reconsider the three assumptions listed at the start of this chapter, with a view toward developing a new framework for understanding lesbian and gay male couples' functioning. In particular, we believe that prior thinking about same-sex couples has been constrained by three factors:

1. Family systems theory's lack of clarity about the specific components of positive closeness versus pathological fusion
2. Traditional gender socialization theory, which generally assumes dichotomous gender-role development and gender-role conformity for all biological males and females—"straightjackets" that do not fit the modal lesbian and gay experience
3. A tendency in the larger society and within the field of family therapy to give unquestioned primacy to intergenerational, biological, and matrimonial family relations while devaluing voluntary relations that lack legal ties (such as close friendship networks or "families of choice")

Distinguishing Between Pathological Fusion and Positive Forms of Couple Connectedness

In a 1993 group discussion at the American Family Therapy Academy meeting, Jo Ann Krestan, one of the authors of "The Problem of Fusion in the Lesbian Relationship" (Krestan & Bepko, 1980), quipped that they should have titled their article "The *Joy* of Fusion in the Lesbian Relationship"! This humorous remark engages what seems to be a recurring paradox about the lives of lesbian couples, and it mirrors thoughtful attempts by various authors to reformulate the terms *fusion* and *merger* to fit women's unique psychosocial development.

Mencher (1990) asserts that the high connectedness of lesbian partners, which had been described as "fusion" in the prior literature, might be functional rather than pathogenic. Based on qualitative interviews with six lesbian partners who were in stable relationships, she found that

> these satisfying, enduring lesbian relationships were characterized by fusion—but that these patterns did not cause the couples particular disturbance. In fact, the women interviewed accounted for the success of their relationships by naming as relational advantages the very same traits which often are labeled fusion. The intense closeness of the partners and the placement of the relationship as an axis around which their lives turned were cited as significant advantages of these relationships. Contrary to the idea that fusion limits the growth of individual identity, these women conveyed that the intense intimacy creates the trust and safety which foster self-actualization and risk taking. For these women, the intimacy patterns that some would call fusion promoted a sense of security and faith in the relationship, and assurance that the women would be accompanied along life's journeys. (p. 4)

Mencher later suggests that many of the processes that have been labeled "fusion" actually may be signs of women's relational strengths—the capacity for mutual engagement, mutual empathy, mutual empowerment, and relational authenticity. Her paper was followed by a spate of similar articles describing the potential benefits, as well as the pitfalls, of women's alleged tendency toward "merger" or "fusion" (for example, Burch, 1986).

However, in efforts to reformulate these concepts, we believe authors conflate concepts of fusion and concepts of intimacy in a manner that blurs important distinctions. It would be simpler and clearer to select a label with a genuinely positive valence (Zacks et al., 1988). As Mencher also comments: "In the state of distortion and bias which surrounds fusion in the literature, it may be impossible to de-toxify the term and to relieve it of malignant connotations" (1990, p. 9). We couldn't agree more.

Fusion, as Bowen (1966) defined it, carried a singularly negative meaning and referred to a deeply destructive, pathogenic interpersonal process, linked originally with the development of schizophrenia over three generations in families. Given its widely understood negative meaning in the mental health fields, the term *fusion* seems antithetical to the positive processes Mencher uncovered in her interviews and to the high cohesion and satisfaction of lesbian couples in our sample.

Our findings indicate that lesbian couples are exceptionally close and more satisfied with their relationships than gay male and heterosexual couples. These results seem inconsistent with the idea that lesbian couples are pathologically fused in the original sense of this term. However, because FACES Cohesion only seems to measure global "closeness versus distance," we cannot claim to have fully tested lesbian couples' levels of fusion. Keeping in mind that "emotional distance between the partners" is just one of the possible manifestations of fusion according to Bowenian theory, our study revealed only that lesbian couples are not fused in this particular way. There remains the possibility that lesbian relationships are fused in the second major way proposed by Bowen—unresolved couple conflict— which could show up either as partners' intense emotional reactivity (constant anger, criticism, overinvolvement that carries a negative affective charge) or as marked avoidance of conflict and a false presentation of self. Nevertheless, it seems to us that "intense emotional reactivity" or "submergence of self in order to avoid conflict" are incompatible with the high relationship satisfaction shown by lesbian couples in our community (nonclinical) sample.

Citing the persistent confusion in the literature over whether lesbian couples are functionally close or pathologically fused, Green and Werner (1996) contend that therapists must discriminate more clearly between the positive and negative components of interpersonal connectedness. They offer a new model based on the *California Inventory for Family Assessment* (Werner & Green, 1989), which calls for conceptualizing family interaction in three separate domains:

- *Closeness-Caregiving* (defined as higher warmth, time together, nurturance, physical intimacy, and consistency)
- *Openness of Communication* (defined as higher self-disclosure and lower conflict-avoidance)
- *Intrusiveness* (defined as higher separation anxiety, possessiveness/jealousy, emotional interreactivity, projection/mystification, anger/aggression, and dominance)

When working with a couple in treatment, therapists should use their observations and inquiries about each partner's functioning in the three domains to form a coherent portrait of the couple's fusion and differentiation of self. In relation to the different ways of manifesting fusion, low Closeness-Caregiving is equivalent to Bowen's (1978) concept of emotional distance (or what the structural family therapists call disengagement). Low Openness of Communication captures Bowen's concept of being a false, adaptive self in order to avoid conflict. High Intrusiveness fits Bowen's concepts of intense emotional reactivity and lack of self/other differentiation.

Conversely, Bowen's concept of differentiation of self seems equivalent to a combination of high Closeness-Caregiving, high Openness of Communication, and low Intrusiveness. In Exhibit 8.1, readers will find definitions of thirteen key constructs from the California Inventory for Family Assessment (Green & Werner, 1996; Werner & Green, 1989, 1993).

In view of our research findings about high cohesion in well-functioning lesbian and gay couples—as well as the likelihood that fusion and disengagement may characterize distressed couples of all kinds—we invite therapists to use the definitions in Exhibit 8.1 to conceptualize client dynamics in treatment. Given the field's confusion over whether lesbian couples are positively close or pathologically fused, it seems particularly important for all of us who are working with same-sex couples to distinguish more carefully between positive and negative forms of couple connection. As an aid in the evaluation of fusion versus differentiation, the California Inventory model gives behaviorally specific anchors for pinpointing couples' interactional problems, recognizing their strengths, setting focused treatment goals, and planning interventions in brief or longer-term therapy.

Gender Straightjackets

We are witnessing now a resurgence of interest in how lesbians' and gay men's lives might be fundamentally different from each other's and from heterosexuals' lives

EXHIBIT 8.1. THE CALIFORNIA INVENTORY FOR FAMILY ASSESSMENT: DEFINITIONS OF CONSTRUCTS AND THEIR PRIMARY GROUPING INTO THREE DOMAINS.

CLOSENESS-CAREGIVING

1. *Warmth:* The degree to which Person A shows warmth, kindness, acceptance, caring, friendliness, love, and positive regard toward Person B.
2. *Time Together:* The degree to which Person A seems to enjoy, puts a high priority on, seeks to spend time with, and gives attention to Person B.
3. *Nurturance:* The degree to which Person A extends emotional comfort, help, caretaking, and emotional support to Person B.
4. *Physical Intimacy:* The degree to which Person A hugs, holds hands, cuddles with, kisses, seeks physical closeness to, and enjoys touching and being affectionate with Person B.
5. *Consistency:* The degree to which Person A's behavior toward Person B is consistent, clear, predictable, and emotionally constant from day to day (as opposed to emotionally labile, inconsistent, confusing, unpredictable, changeable, ambivalent).

OPENNESS OF COMMUNICATION

6. *Openness/Self-Disclosure:* The degree to which Person A is open, self-revealing, honest, direct, and forthright with Person B (as opposed to keeping self hidden, guarded, closed, or secretive).
7. *Conflict Avoidance:* The degree to which Person A tries to avoid facing conflict, denies that there are differences of opinion or needs, evades discussing sources of tension (for example, by changing the topic), pretends to agree or pretends that everything is harmonious, and generally tries to "sweep difficulties under the rug" in their relationship.

INTRUSIVENESS

8. *Separation Anxiety:* The degree to which Person A acts uncomfortable, upset, anxious, worried, hurt, or left out when Person B wants to spend time alone, have privacy, or spend time doing things independently.
9. *Possessiveness/Jealousy:* The degree to which Person A acts possessive, insecure, neglected, threatened, jealous, or afraid of losing to others Person B's attention.
10. *Emotional Interreactivity:* The degree to which Person A acts overidentified with and overreacts emotionally to, problems in Person B's life (for example, Person A may worry excessively or become more upset than Person B when B is sad, anxious about something, going through a hard time, etc.).
11. *Projective Mystification:* The degree to which Person A erroneously assumes that he or she knows what is on Person B's mind without checking it out first ("mindreading," projection of feelings or motives), especially the degree to which Person A presumes that he/she knows better and interprets what B *really* needs, thinks, or feels and why B acts in various ways.
12. *Anger/Aggression:* The degree to which Person A gets angry, is critical, gets annoyed, uses harsh words, says hurtful things, raises his/her voice, and acts in an aggressive/hurtful way toward Person B.
13. *Authority/Dominance:* The degree to which Person A is dominant and more in charge of the relationship in terms of having final say over how things are done, taking the lead, getting his/her own way when disagreements arise, setting the rules for Person B's behavior, taking the initiative, and making decisions for Person B or for what they will do together.

Source: Werner & Green, 1993, tab. 4. Reprinted by permission of the authors.

on dimensions other than sexual attraction and sexual behavior. Especially since the publications of Bell, Weinberg, and Hammersmith's (1981) *Sexual Preference: Its Development in Men and Women* and Williams's (1986/1992) *The Spirit and the Flesh: Sexual Diversity in American Indian Culture,* questions about lesbians' and gay men's gender-role conformity and about biological predispositions for homosexuality have occupied a newly respectable place in research after years of being cast aside as irrelevant or vilified as homophobic. In analogous developments on the political front, one aspect of the movement toward "queer consciousness" is an attempt by the community to proclaim broader legitimacy, not just of its sexuality but of its greater nonconformity to traditional gender roles, embracing the special androgynous qualities of gay men and lesbians.

Related to these issues, the assumptions that lesbian couple fusion and gay male couple disengagement would be the natural outgrowth of female and male gender-role socialization seem to be predicated on a deeper, underlying premise, which might be called the *premise of homosexual/heterosexual gender-role equivalence.* This proposition holds that in terms of gender-role socialization and gender-role conformity, lesbians and heterosexual women are similar to one another, and gay men and heterosexual men are similar to one another. This notion of homosexual/heterosexual gender equivalence, along with the idea that females are socialized toward seeking closeness, naturally leads to the prediction that relationships with more women in them will be more cohesive.

However, our results show that gay male couples are more cohesive than heterosexual married couples. Traditional gender theory also predicted that lesbian couples would be more cohesive and more fused than the other groups. Although our results are consistent with the prediction of greater cohesion for lesbians, their high satisfaction provides indirect, tentative evidence that fusion may not be characteristic of lesbian couples. These two results, especially the finding for gay male couples, appear to refute some of the central assumptions in traditional gender theory. The most direct explanations for this failure of gender theory are either (1) that traditional gender theory is incorrect for all women and men or (2) that traditional gender theory is correct for heterosexual women and men but neglects to consider the gender uniqueness of lesbians and gay men.

To presume that gender-role conformity is identical for all heterosexual and lesbian women and for all heterosexual and gay men is a bit like claiming that all women, or all men, are alike. We view this particular application of male/female stereotypes to the lives of lesbians and gay men as a kind of "gender straightjacketing" that unwittingly superimposes on lesbian and gay men an ill-fitting set of gender assumptions that are based on the experiences of straight people. Thus gender straightjacketing is a form of heterosexism that involves presumptive generalizing from heterosexuals' gender roles and identity to lesbians' and gay males' gender roles and identity.

These gender straightjackets are based on what has been called biological-sociocultural essentialism, that is, the notion that gender is shaped primarily by biological factors in concert with invariant socialization processes in the family and society (Hare-Mustin & Marecek, 1988). In such an essentialist view, the gender of the psyche inevitably does, or at least invariably should, match the sex characteristics of the body in a traditional, dichotomous way (exclusively male or female, which are construed as opposites) (Bem, 1993). Genetic males and females are expected to follow divergent developmental paths, with the unfolding of traditional gender-role behavior being the inevitable outcome. Chodorow's (1978) developmental theory, upon which so much theorizing about lesbian and gay male gender seems to have been based, is a feminist version of essentialism. Even though it honors women's relational capacities more than earlier psychoanalytic thought did, it still presumes that an invariant set of developmental processes rooted in family experience inevitably shapes children with male bodies into masculine personalities and children with female bodies into feminine personalities.

However, as Goldner (1991) argues, such essentialist thinking ignores the possibility that too much "gender coherence, consistency, and conformity . . . create a universal pathogenic situation, insofar as the attempt to conform to their dictates requires the activation of a false-self system" (p. 249). The logic of such essentialism also leads to the unwarranted conclusion that the gender-role conformity of lesbians and gay men (being genetically male or female) must be exactly like heterosexuals' except in one delimited area, that is, choosing same-sex partners for sexual activity. However, it does not leave space for the alternative possibility that homosexual behavior may reflect being differently gendered than heterosexual males or females, perhaps even biologically different than heterosexual males or females before socialization in the family starts. Regardless of causality, if lesbians and gay men are different for whatever reasons in gender-role conformity and gender self-images, then choice of partner for sexual activity may be only one factor in a much larger complex of meaningful gender-role differences between heterosexuals, lesbians, and gay men. For example, *one might conceptualize heterosexual women, heterosexual men, lesbian women, and gay men as representing four distinct gender-role categories, with the specific sexual behavior of the latter two groups not even being their primary defining gender-role characteristic.*

Elements of gender role such as sexual orientation (attractions), sexual behavior (acts), sexual orientation identity (self-labeling), and gender-role conformity (the fit and compliance of behavior with traditional gender-role norms) need not go hand in hand (as in the case of heterosexual men who have sex with men in prison). However, when these elements do appear together as a well-defined constellation of personality attributes, interpersonal behaviors, and overall lifestyle, then we might best conceptualize such a constellation as a coherent gender role fitting known groups of persons in the culture, instead of categorizing such persons solely on the criteria of their outward bodies and their sexual behavior (see Williams, 1992; see also Chapter Eleven of this book).

If we begin to understand lesbians and gay men as enacting unique gender roles within a distinct subculture, then our predictions about their couple relationships might be very different from predictions based on the premise of homosexual/heterosexual gender-role equivalence. Our findings point to the need for what might be called a "Multiplex Gender Theory" to encompass the unique gender paths of lesbians and gay men, as well as those of women and men of different social classes, races, and ethnicities. Such a multiplex gender theory should replace the kind of uniform theories that have led to gender straightjacketing of lesbians and gay men and to other forms of imposing gender stereotypes on groups that are not part of the White, heterosexual middle class (Brown, 1994; Clatterbaugh, 1990; Magraw, Stearns, & Green, in preparation; see also Chapters Six, Ten, and Eleven of this book).

In the next sections, we review research related to lesbians' nonconformity to the traditional female gender role, which could help explain why lesbian couples may be close but not necessarily fused. Second, we review research related to gay men's nonconformity to the traditional male gender role, which may help explain why gay male couples may be cohesive rather than disengaged. Overall, we cite evidence that lesbians and gay males from childhood onward do not conform as strongly as heterosexuals to traditional gender-role norms, and this lack of traditional gender-role conformity is one possible explanation for our research results.

Lesbians' Nonconformity to the Traditional Female Gender Role and Implications for Couple Fusion

If, as we suspect, lesbian couples are simply very close rather than fused, we must question whether the idea of a greater tendency toward fusion among women in general is correct. Does female gender-role socialization—which emphasizes closeness, caregiving, emotional responsivity, expressiveness, and empathy—render women more predisposed to fusion in relationships? And if such a gender-linked propensity toward fusion exists, is it equally as strong for lesbians as for heterosexual women?

Although there is much in the research literature on female socialization to warrant the conclusion that women are more oriented toward achieving closeness and giving nurture, we find no concrete evidence for the notion that women as a group are destined for pathological fusion as a result of normative female socialization. Rather, we think it more likely that family therapists and some gender theorists—adopting a male-centered conception of mental health—have misconstrued women's positive capacity for closeness, functional interdependence, and caregiving by interpreting them as signs of undifferentiation, merger, or fusion (Green & Werner, 1996). We believe, for example, that it is possible for lesbian partners to be both extremely close and highly differentiated—"individuation-in- relation," as the Stone Center theorists might phrase it (Surrey, 1985).

Of perhaps great significance for understanding and comparing couple relationships, lesbians differ in key respects from heterosexual women in terms of conformity to the traditional female gender role. For example, a large amount of research has revealed consistently that lesbians are substantially less conforming to the female gender role in childhood (see Bailey & Zucker's 1995 meta-analytic review of forty-one previous studies). Lesbians recall engaging in more rough play and having greater interest in boys' competitive sports; more enjoyment of boys' play materials; being more likely to have a social reputation as a tomboy; and generally showing more behavior traditionally associated with boys' gender role. *Fully 81 percent of lesbians report rates of cross-gender behavior in childhood that are above the median rate reported by heterosexual women.*

As a second illustration, a study of women who were part of lesbian or heterosexual couples revealed that the self-schemas of lesbians incorporated more instrumentality and masculinity than heterosexual women's but equal amounts of expressiveness (Kurdek, 1987). *Instrumentality* consists of traits such as "acts as a leader," "assertive," "has leadership abilities," "strong personality," and "forceful," whereas *expressiveness* involves traits such as "tender," "compassionate," "warm," "sympathetic," and "understanding." Lesbians were found to be significantly more androgynous than heterosexual women, reporting a balance of instrumentality and expressiveness in their self-schemas.

We wish to emphasize here that studies like those reviewed above do not mean that lesbians are more similar to heterosexual men than to heterosexual women. Rather, they show that lesbians are simply more androgynous when compared to heterosexual women. They display more cross-gender role behavior, interests, and personality characteristics than heterosexual women do. One possible implication of lesbians' lower conformity to the traditional female gender role is that they may be less susceptible to fusion in relationships than heterosexual women are. If Krestan and Bepko's (1980) aphorism "women cling, men distance" (p. 284) is correct, then the greater instrumentality of lesbians may be a sign that they are less likely than heterosexual women to engage in clinging behavior in relationships and are more likely to be assertive. In this regard, we think future research should explore three questions: (1) Are women in general more fusion-prone than men? (2) Are heterosexual women more fusion-prone than lesbians? (3) Are lesbians who are more conforming to the traditional female gender role also more prone to fusion than lesbians who are less conforming to the traditional female gender role?

Gay Men's Nonconformity to the Traditional Male Gender Role and Implications for Couple Closeness Versus Disengagement

Contrary to predictions based on traditional gender theory and the related straightjacketing of lesbian and gay gender experience, our research reveals that gay male couples are more cohesive than heterosexual couples. In fact, heterosexual couples as a group appear to be the most disengaged. On the other hand, everyone looks disengaged in comparison to lesbian couples!

Thus the answer to our question, Are gay male couples emotionally disengaged? hinges on the reference group (heterosexual or lesbian) used as a standard of comparison. If we designate "all couples in the United States" as the normative standard (as most family theorists implicitly would do), then we can conclude that gay male couples appear to be significantly more cohesive than the modal type of couple in our society—married heterosexuals. This finding directly challenges the predictions about male couples' disengagement, which were based on traditional gender theories.

It seems the notion that gay male couples would be disengaged stems from a cultural stereotype about gay men that, at root, reflects a cultural stereotype about all men. That is, when left to their own devices (which is to say, not restrained by women's and children's needs for commitment), men are alleged to be mainly sexually driven and instinctively sexually promiscuous (nonmonogamous). Such nonmonogamy is supposed to be incompatible with wanting, or being capable of sustaining, intimate couple relationships. Therefore, two gay men are presumed not to want or to be capable of sustaining a committed couple relationship. This generalization of the "sexually driven man," even if it were true of both heterosexual and gay men, still ignores the many ways heterosexual and gay men may differ in gender-role behavior other than in terms of the biological sex of their partners.

For example, if we consider each of the various norms that make up the traditional male gender role in the United States, it appears that gay and heterosexual men's gender-role behavior may be alike in a few respects but dissimilar in most others. Based on writings in the field of men's studies (Green & Korin, in press; Kimmel & Messner, 1992; Levant & Pollack, 1995; Pleck, 1981; Thompson & Pleck, 1995), the norms of the traditional male gender role seem to include toughness, aggression, leadership and dominance, giving primacy to work and achievement, providing for and protecting family, self-reliance, suppression of emotional vulnerability, sexual prowess and separation of sex from commitment, avoiding femininity and behaviors traditionally associated with women's role, and homophobia or avoidance of closeness with other men.

Based on what we know of gay men's sexual behavior, we might conclude that they are hyperconforming to one traditional norm of the male gender role—"sexual prowess and separation of sex and commitment." Also, they may be average compared with heterosexual men in "giving primacy to the work role" and "self-reliance." On the other hand, gay men may diverge from virtually all of the other traditional norms of the male gender role. Such nonconformity raises the possibility that *gay men in general—and especially gay men who create and sustain couple relationships—have been socialized differently than other men and therefore have distinctive relational styles, abilities, and values that differ from those of heterosexual men.*

We turn now to a perusal of some research that bears on three questions related to the issues raised above: Do gay men differ from heterosexual men on conformity to the traditional male gender role? Do gay men want committed couple relationships? Are gay men sexually not monogamous and, if so, how can such nonmonogamy be compatible with forming close and committed couple relationships? The answers to these questions may help explain the greater cohesiveness of gay male couples in comparison to heterosexual couples.

Question 1 *Do gay men differ from heterosexual men on conformity to the traditional male gender role?* The failure of traditional gender theory to predict the levels of cohesion in gay male couples follows from its neglect of the research on gay males' gender nonconformity. A large amount of research (some of it self-report and retrospective and some of it observational, prospective, and longitudinal) has revealed consistently that gay men, as compared to heterosexual men, are substantially less conforming to the traditional male gender role in childhood (see Bailey & Zucker's, 1995, meta-analysis of forty-one previous studies). For example, as compared to heterosexual boys, gay men when they are children: engage in less rough play; have less interest in competitive sports; display more enjoyment of girls' play activities (playing house); spend more time in solitary and artistic activities (drawing, music, reading); are more likely to have a social reputation for cross-gender behavior (more likely to be called a "sissy"); and generally show more behavior traditionally associated with girls' gender role. *Fully 89 percent of gay men display rates of cross-gender behavior in childhood that are above the median rate for heterosexual men.*

In a study of men who were part of gay or heterosexual couples, Kurdek (1987) found that the self-schemas of gay men incorporated more expressiveness and femininity but equal amounts of instrumentality in comparison to heterosexual married men's self-schemas.[12] Gay men were significantly more androgynous than heterosexual men, reporting more of a balance of instrumentality and expressiveness in their self-schemas. Again, we wish to emphasize that findings such as the above do not mean that gay men are more similar to heterosexual women than to heterosexual men. Rather, gay men are simply *more androgynous when compared to heterosexual men*—displaying more cross-gender role behavior, interests, and personality traits than heterosexual men do.

Along these lines, Devoss (1991) investigated heterosexual and gay men's *gender-role ideals,* that is, their definitions of the "ideal man." Heterosexual males defined the ideal man as having an external moral system, seeing women as ineffective, being violent and competitive, and being family-oriented. Gay males defined the ideal man as putting a higher value on interpersonal development and spiritual development, being both internally and externally oriented in his moral system, asserting strength and dominance, being feminist, and having freedom of sexual expression. No differences emerged between the groups' views of the ideal man's sexual monogamy or his being self-serving, materialistic, altruistic, responsible, flexible, in control, or protective of loved ones.

In light of this research, one implication of gay men's nonconformity to the traditional male gender role is that they seem to be more oriented toward close connection (expressiveness and emphasis on interpersonal development) than heterosexual men are. Again, if Krestan & Bepko's (1980) aphorism "women cling, men distance" (p. 284) is correct, then the greater expressiveness and interpersonal orientation of gay men may be a sign that they are less likely than heterosexual men to distance emotionally in relationships. This difference may account for our finding of greater cohesiveness in gay male couples as compared with heterosexual married couples. The greater emotional distance of husbands may render heterosexual couples less cohesive overall. In this regard, we think future research should explore two questions: Are heterosexual men more distance-prone in couple relationships than gay men? Are gay men who are more conforming to the traditional male gender role also more likely to distance in couple relationships than gay men who are less conforming to the traditional male gender role?

Question 2 *Do gay men want committed couple relationships?* In contrast to some portrayals of gay men as purely sex-driven singles destined for a life of random promiscuity and noncommitment, surveys consistently show that 40 to 60 percent of gay men are currently in steady dating or more committed relationships (Peplau, 1991). These figures actually may underestimate the proportion of gay men involved in couple relationships because most research participants have been recruited through singles-oriented settings such as gay bars.

Another national survey conducted by Teichner Associates in 1989 indicated that 97 percent of gay men (average age 33.6) had been involved in at least one ongoing couple relationship in the past ten years; the average number of such relationships was 2.5; and 60 percent of the respondents were currently in a couple relationship. Similarly, based on a survey of five hundred gay men in San Francisco, Parker (1995) reported that 86 percent had tried to meet a partner for a monogamous relationship; 79 percent had succeeded in doing so in the past or present; and 48 percent of respondents who were currently in a relationship reported being monogamous. These results show that large proportions of gay men want, have previously been in, and are currently in ongoing relationships. The idea that most gay men prefer being unattached is simply a myth.

Question 3 *Are gay men sexually nonmonogamous, and is monogamy essential for couple cohesion?* Over the years, substantial data have accumulated suggesting that gay male couples are dramatically less monogamous than heterosexual and lesbian couples. These findings have contributed to the perception that gay male couples must be disengaged. How can they be cohesive if the partners are "constantly" having sex with outsiders? For example, in a large national survey conducted in the mid to late 1970s, Blumstein and Schwartz (1983) reported that 82 percent of gay male partners, 28 percent of lesbian partners, 26 percent of husbands, and 21 percent of wives had been nonmonogamous at some point during the relationship. Furthermore, fully 72 percent of gay male partners had been nonmonogamous in the previous year.

However, in another large national survey conducted during 1988, Bryant and Demian (1994) found that 63 percent of gay male partners reported being monogamous. Also, in a 1995 survey in San Francisco, 48 percent of gay men reported being monogamous in their current relationships (Parker, 1995). Perhaps the large increases in rates of monogamy between the mid 1970s (18 percent monogamous) and the more recent studies (63 percent monogamous in 1988; 48 percent monogamous in 1995) reflect the influence of the AIDS epidemic and changing norms in the gay male community as a result. Even so, the rates of sex with persons outside the couple relationship still seem significantly higher for individuals in gay male couples as compared to individuals (male or female) in other types of couples.

Does this nonmonogamy reflect or cause emotional disengagement? Other findings are relevant here. Several studies show that the greater overall nonmonogamy of gay male couples does not necessarily indicate frequent sex outside the primary relationship or emotional involvement with outside sexual partners. For instance, one sample of gay male couples that had sexually open relationship agreements reported that, in practice, they had sex outside the relationship never (9 percent) or only rarely (80 percent) (Kurdek, 1988b). Blumstein and Schwartz (1983) found that of the 82 percent of gay male partners that had sex outside the relationship at least once, only 15 percent had ever had a meaningful affair. These results reveal that gay men's sex outside the primary relationship may be less frequent than many mental health professionals imagine, and it is rarely emotionally involving. Many of these sexual encounters may not even be as involving as a one-night stand.

Moreover, there is substantial research suggesting that sex outside the primary relationship for gay male couples does not typically have the same meaning and negative charge ("lack of commitment," "disloyalty," "lack of love," "triangulation") as such behavior often has for lesbian and heterosexual couples. As Blumstein and Schwartz (1983) and McWhirter and Mattison (1984) confirm, gay men traditionally have viewed sex from a "trick mentality," meaning they regard sexual activity as "recreational"—much like going to a movie with a friend or finding a stranger to play pool, tennis, or cards with at a club. Such recreational sex, lacking in sustained emotional attachment, gratifies a different set of needs than the primary couple relationship does, and the partners do not necessarily perceive it as threatening or even related to their primary commitment. Given that both partners in a male couple are likely to have had substantial experience with recreational sex before becoming a couple and that they have in common a similar sexual responsivity to other males, there seems to be a greater mutual understanding and shared frame of reference regarding outside sex than is the case for most heterosexual married partners.

Although sustained "love affairs" or compulsively driven sex with outsiders seem more likely to reflect on, or to create, distance in the primary relationship, we believe that most of the recreational nonmonogamy of gay male couples should not be interpreted as a sign either of disengagement or triangulation. In support of this view, Blasband and Peplau (1985), Blumstein and Schwartz (1983), and Kurdek (1988b) all found that relationship quality of sexually monogamous and nonmonogamous gay couples was equivalent. Blumstein and Schwartz found essentially no relationship between nonmonogamy and gay male couples' breaking up over an eighteen-month period.

In regard to commitment and monogamy, the essayist Edmund White (1994) described the modal long-term gay couple as follows:

If it all goes well, two gay men will meet through sex, become lovers, weather the storms of jealousy and the diminution of lust, develop shared interests (a hobby, a business, a house, a circle), and end up with a long-term . . . camaraderie that is not as disinterested as friendship or as seismic as passion or as charged with contradiction as fraternity. Younger couples feel that this sort of relationship, when it happens to them, is incomplete, a compromise, and they break up in order to find total fulfillment (i.e., tireless passion) elsewhere. But older gay couples stay together, cultivate their mild, reasonable love, and defend it against the ever-present danger of the sexual allure exercised by a newcomer. . . . They may have . . . regular extracurricular sex partners or even beaux, but . . . with an eye attuned to nuance . . . at a certain point will intervene to banish a potential rival. (p. 164)

Although tending toward caricature, this excerpt illustrates some of the qualities of cohesion, commitment, and high flexibility (including sexual nonmonogamy) that make the lives of well-functioning gay male couples unique in some respects but ordinary in many others. The notion that nonmonogamy among gay male couples is a sign of emotional disengagement seems based on a heterocentric frame of reference. Except in unusual instances, sex outside the primary relationship does not have the same meaning or impact for gay male partners as it ordinarily does for heterosexual married partners.

Gendered Couple Systems

Thus far, we have been speaking of gender mostly as if it were a trait of individuals. However, partners' gender-role behaviors are not a simple sum of their invariant, preexisting "gendered personalities." Rather, gender roles in couples also involve reciprocal shaping of one another's behavior in the evolving couple relationship itself. Furthermore, gender roles are subject to influence from the partners' current families of origin, children, work settings, and peers.

To illustrate, all of us have some culturally encoded mental pictures of the different roles for wife and husband in marriage or the different roles for father and mother in parenting, whether we endorse those roles or not. The behavior of wife and husband may conform or not conform to traditional roles, but in either case, the meaning of their behaviors is contextualized in light of the culturally prescribed divisions. Spouses know when they are choosing not to comply with the gender dichotomy. Married partners who want to create less traditional marital and parenting roles must make conscious, vigilant, joint efforts to avoid falling into the traditional pattern that they have been socialized throughout their lives to enact. In addition, heterosexuals face considerable direct and subtle social pressure from the surrounding community not to deviate too greatly from the traditional norms. This is not so for same-sex couples.

There are no culturally prescribed differences in the roles of lesbian Partner A versus lesbian Partner B in their couple or parenting relationship. Each same-sex couple must invent anew some reciprocity of instrumentality and expressiveness, some sharing or fair division of household labor, some balance of power in decision making. Not having been socialized since birth to enact a particular gender-role division in a lesbian or gay male relationship, and not facing social pressure from others to fulfill preordained roles, the participants in same-sex couples appear much more likely to achieve equality.

Substantial research evidence documents that same-sex couples (especially lesbian couples) have more egalitarian relationships than heterosexual couples (Blumstein & Schwartz, 1983; Peplau, 1991). Although a very small minority of lesbian and gay male partners divide tasks up along traditional male/female, husband/wife, butch/femme gender-role lines (apparently about 7 percent did so in the early 1970s), for most same-sex couples, such a division of labor would require an intolerable level of pretense and constraint (Bell & Weinberg, 1978).

In contrast to the findings of greater equality in same-sex couples, there is considerable evidence that most heterosexual couples, even when both parties work full-time, do not entirely succeed in casting off the traditional roles, especially when it comes to housework, child care, care of aging parents, and decision-making processes (Hochschild, 1989). In addition, it seems that heterosexual partners tend to become more gender-role conforming after getting married and again after the birth of children (Cunningham & Antill, 1984; Feldman, Biringen, & Nash, 1981). Normative divisions of labor in marriage and coparenting, as well as income differentials between spouses, tend to maintain or amplify gender-role conformity of wives and husbands over time. However, such divisions of labor are not the case for lesbian coparents, who assume much more equal child-care responsibilities (see Chapter Fourteen).

In the area of couples' conflict negotiation, unequal power between the partners is linked to sex of partner only in heterosexual, not lesbian or gay male, couples. For example, in a study of partners' attempts to influence one another, heterosexual men were more likely to use "strong" tactics (direct bargaining or reasoning); heterosexual women were more likely to use "weak" tactics (negative emotional expression or withdrawal—becoming silent, cold, distant). However, gay male couples and lesbian couples did not show the same gender linkage, that is, with men using strong tactics and women using weak tactics (Falbo & Peplau, 1980). In all types of couples, the partner who perceives self as more powerful (usually the partner who has a higher income or less emotional investment in the relationship) is likely to use strong tactics, and the partner with less power (usually the one with lower income or more investment in the relationship) is likely to use weak strategies (Blumstein & Schwartz, 1983). However, only in the heterosexual couples are strong and weak power tactics linked to sex of partner, and this may be partly because wives are likely to have lower incomes (facing greater barriers to divorce) and are likely to be more emotionally invested in their relationships than husbands are.

The implications are clear that the gender and economic differences between partners in heterosexual couples tend to create an enduring inequality of power, whereas such is not the case in lesbian and gay male couples. Thus our own finding of lower flexibility in heterosexual couples may be a sign of their gender-linked rigidities in instrumental or expressive roles, the division of household labor, and decision making between spouses. To the extent that such inequality produces tension and negative affect, heterosexual spouses may also end up being less cohesive in their relationships.

Overall, then, the higher levels of cohesion we found in same-sex couples may be a function of three facets of gender: (1) the differently gendered personalities of the lesbian and gay participants to begin with (more androgyny, greater similarities between partners' instrumental or expressive behavior, higher total amounts of expressiveness by both partners); (2) more equal power in the relationship; and (3) fewer social pressures from the surrounding social network to conform to traditional gender roles. In this sense, lesbian and gay male couple relationships—by virtue of their greater androgyny and the gender similarity of partners—are based on what has been described as an egalitarian "best friend model" (rather than a traditional husband/wife model). Such egalitarianism implies greater flexibility and may foster greater cohesion between same-sex partners than between heterosexual partners (Peplau, 1991).

Despite such findings of high gender-role flexibility and equality in same-sex couples, one of the great paradoxes of heterosexism is that the general public still seems quite convinced of, and scandalized by, what it imagines is the widespread playing of artificial butch/femme roles by partners in same-sex relationships. Yet this same public remains largely unconscious about its own problematic conformity to the socially constructed butch/femme roles in heterosexual relationships.

Family Values

Our study revealed that outness to mother, father, siblings or a combination of these family members bears no relationship to lesbian couples' satisfaction, to whether the couple stays together or breaks up over a two-year period, or to the level of follow-up satisfaction among couples that stay together. These findings run counter to predictions based on Bowen's (1978) idea that emotional cut-off—including avoidance of discussing important, anxiety-provoking topics with family of origin members—is a manifestation of fusion and will have profound negative consequences for the couple relationship. Because hiding and lying to cover one's sexual orientation from family members seems like such a prime illustration of what is meant by "emotional cut-off," we can only conclude that Bowenian theory appears to be wrong on this account.

We believe that the most appropriate message for therapists to take from these findings on outness is *a caution against universally implying to lesbian couples that being out to their family of origin members will somehow positively influence the functioning of their couple relationships.* Our findings show that being out to family of origin members did not affect this lesbian sample's couple relationships for good or ill.

To guard against the possibility that readers may overinterpret these results, we wish to point out what they do *not* mean. These findings provide no information about whether a lesbian's disclosing her sexual orientation to her family of origin members would improve or worsen her relations with those family of origin members. Nor do these findings mean that such disclosure would have either negative or positive effects for her psychological well-being as an individual. Our study did not examine links between *coming out* to family members and couple satisfaction but rather the connection between *being out* with family members and couple satisfaction. That is to say, the process of coming out to family of origin members may be more stressful and more disruptive to the couple relationship than the fact of already being out. In this context, it seems likely that lesbians who already have come out to their family members may have had more positive family relations prior to the disclosure, whereas those who are not out may have had more conflictual family relations all along. Thus for lesbians who wait longer to do so, the process of coming out to family may be more stressful than for those who come out earlier.

From a clinical point of view, therapists must exercise judgment about whether, in an individual case, the results from our study are applicable. It is important to keep in mind that conclusions derived from research projects consist of inferences about groups of people and can be used only as tentative, working hypotheses (educated guesses) when approaching a given case. There may be individual circumstances in which being out to family of origin would improve the couple relationship. For example, if a couple spends a great deal of time with the family, believes the family would respond positively over the long run, but finds maintaining the secret unbearable and stressful for their relationship, then it would seem that disclosure might be beneficial for their couple relationship. Conversely, if a couple spends little or no time with the family, has clear evidence suggesting that the family would respond negatively over the long run, finds minimal relations with the family comfortable, and believes that disclosure would add significant stress to an already fragile couple relationship, then there may be good reason to think disclosure might negatively affect the couple relationship. Again, these couple-oriented considerations imply nothing whatsoever about whether disclosure might be beneficial or harmful for the individual or for her relations with family of origin members. In general, unless the stress of maintaining the secret is having a clear and direct negative effect on the couple, we would assume that being out to family would make little difference for the well-being of the couple relationship per se.

Consistent with our results on outness, substantial research (Kurdek, 1988a; Kurdek & Schmitt, 1987) shows that support from family members makes no difference to the psychological adjustment or relationship quality of lesbian or gay male partners. Lesbian, gay male, and heterosexual partners receive equal amounts of social support from outside the couple, but the sources differ. The same-sex couples get significantly more of their support from friends; greater support from friends is associated with better psychological adjustment and relationship quality.

The heterosexual couples receive more social support from family sources than the same-sex couples do. With reference to Bowenian theory, these results imply that supportive family of origin relationships are indeed important for the well-being of heterosexual couples but not for lesbian and gay male couples.

In a large-scale national survey, the sources of social support for lesbian and gay male couples included (from most to least support): lesbian/gay friends, various lesbian/gay organizations and groups, heterosexual friends, co-workers, siblings, boss, mother, other relatives, father, and mainstream church (Bryant & Demian, 1994). In this ranking, it is noteworthy that co-workers are ranked higher as a source of support than any family members and that parents are ranked lower than bosses. Moreover, it seems that well-functioning lesbian and gay male couples are making up for the lower amounts of social support they receive from family members by getting such support from friends.

Recent thinking about social support for lesbians and gay men has centered on the notion of "families of choice" (Weston, 1991). Such families might consist of a life partner, children from a former marriage or through alternative insemination, friends, partners of friends, ex-partners and their new partners, and relatives, all providing emotional support, material help, conflict resolution for disputes in relationships, and a shared history. One can think of these families as networks of what anthropologists used to call "fictive kin," although the word *fictive* implies that they are somehow less than real and therefore marginal.

In terms of evaluating the quality of social support available to lesbian and gay couples, we suggest using the criteria listed here, derived mainly from network theory and therapy (see Kliman & Trimble, 1983):

1. *Network size*—the number of people in the couple's friendship and acquaintance network
2. *Frequencies and lengths of contact with network members*
3. *Mode of contact with network members* (for example, in person, by phone)
4. *Types of activities with network members*
5. *Participation in holiday and other rituals* including birthdays, anniversaries, Thanksgiving, weekly dinners, yearly trips, and the like (Imber-Black, Roberts, & Whiting, 1988; see also Chapter Nine in this book).
6. *Network density*—the extent to which individuals in the network know each other and provide support to one another, including the extent to which close subgroups within the network have overlapping memberships
7. *Multisetting versus single-setting ties with network members* (for example, friends who are also co-workers, co-workers who are also cousins, cousins who are also neighbors)
8. *Types of support* (emotional support, material or financial assistance, practical help such as child care, moving, health care, and so on)

9. *Reciprocity of support*—bilateral versus unilateral
10. *Families of choice*—defined here as the index couple plus two or more network members, all of whom are part of each other's regular emotional support system

A major difference between many friendship networks and biological families is the degree of density, meaning the extent to which members of the collection know one another and are engaged in mutual support. To the extent that the couple's closest friends are also close friends with one another, the support system begins to take on the characteristics of a family of choice. In our experience, network density is often a neglected factor in theories of social support but an extremely important one from the standpoint of couple stability and a feeling of secure embeddedness. We expect that a well-functioning family of choice also would show high closeness-caregiving, high openness of communication, and low intrusiveness (see Exhibit 8.1).

The findings on outness to family and the importance of social support from friends stand in stark contrast to ideas of intergenerational family therapists, particularly Bowen (1978). Bowenian theory seems to have missed the mark in the assumption of a one-to-one concordance between relations in family of origin and relations in the couple, as if the two systems were inevitably deeply connected either in practice or symbolically. When it comes to lesbians and gay men in couple relationships, such cross-system effects may exist more in the minds of therapists than in actuality. As illustrated in Chapter Four and several other chapters in this book, many lesbian and gay individuals and couples seem to carry on their lives quite well despite minimal or conflictual relations with family of origin members.

In light of our data on outness to family of origin members, it seems the field of family systems therapy has participated in a grand confusion between family form and family substance. We must distinguish more clearly between the traditional family as a "value" and the "family values" inherent in many other kinds of close relationships. The old adage, "Blood is thicker than water"—implying that relationships with biological kin are intrinsically more substantive, more dependable, more nurturing, and more meaningful than nonbiological ties with friends— is turning out to be one among many assumptions that the lives of lesbian and gay couples invite us to rethink.

Clinical Implications: Looking for Fusion in All the Wrong Places

In this chapter, we presented information that challenges some common misconceptions about lesbian and gay couples. These earlier assumptions painted a rather negative portrait of lesbian and gay male relationships. However, our studies and other investigations converge on an image of same-sex couples being cohesive, highly flexible, and receiving meaningful support from friends. In addition, the lesbian couples as a group seem to be functioning exceptionally well, with or without family knowledge of the partners' sexual orientation.

We believe that earlier theorists misunderstood lesbian and gay male couples, partly because they started out with an ambiguous definition of fusion, no clear concept of positive closeness, and a dichotomous rather than multiplex theory of gender roles. It also seems that these theorists overgeneralized from couples in treatment to same-sex couples as a whole. Moreover, because of their professional training, therapists are oriented toward perceiving and unearthing pathology—assessing for fusion, enmeshment, disengagement, and the like (Green & Werner, 1996).

In a chapter on self-fulfilling prophecies, Watzlawick (1984) quotes Einstein as saying, "It is the theory that determines what we can observe" (p. 101), and then Watzlawick goes on to say:

> The chronic problem that still plagues modern psychiatry is that we have only the vaguest and most general concepts for the definition of mental health, while for the diagnosis of abnormal behavior there exist catalogs perfected to the last detail. (p. 105)

Brown (1994), a prominent feminist author, put this idea more plainly: "If you call it a skunk, you will assume that it smells" (p. 131).

Is it fusion or cohesion? Disengagement or differentiation? Therapists, like scientists, need theories in order to see. It is impossible not to have one. One's theory and its underlying assumptions can be unconscious, implicit, ineffable or can be made conscious, explicit, and intelligible.

Future progress toward understanding lesbian and gay male couples, whether that understanding occurs in therapy or as part of formal research, rests on our ability to formulate explicit, practical theories of their functioning. In this chapter, we have suggested three central frameworks for thinking about lesbian and gay male couples: (1) the California Inventory domains of closeness-caregiving, openness of communication, and intrusiveness; (2) the idea of unique lesbian and gay male gender roles versus conformity to traditional gender-role norms; and (3) the notion of families of choice.

Each of these frameworks provides a way of seeing, that is, of magnifying certain processes and leaving others unaddressed. No theory can be so comprehensive as to bring everything into view at once. We must filter, decide what is relevant or irrelevant, and focus toward some goal in therapy sessions.

Although every couple has strengths, mental health professionals have only *DSM-IV.* We have no catalogue of strengths "perfected to the last detail." Will there ever be a *Diagnostic and Statistical Manual of Psychiatric Competencies*? If we can name only one way of being psychologically healthy and that way is stated in the negative—"health is the absence of illness"—what are we likely to see in our clients? The theory determines what we can observe.

If you only have dark lenses, you will have a dim view, and the mental health professions have historically promoted a dim view of lesbians and gay men. We are not suggesting rose-colored glasses as an antidote, but if we are bound to have theories with conjectures about lesbian and gay male couples, let them be grounded in some systematic attempts to gather information. We would suggest the following hypotheses as a basis to guide future clinical work and research:

Hypothesis 1: As a function of their unique gender-role development and greater androgyny, lesbian couples have a tendency to be exceptionally flexible, close, and satisfied with their relationships as compared with other couples.

Hypothesis 2: As a function of their unique gender-role development and greater androgyny, gay male couples have a tendency to be exceptionally flexible, somewhat closer than most heterosexual couples, and about equally satisfied with their relationships.

Hypothesis 3: The well-being of lesbian and gay male couples is enhanced if the partners create a support system of close friends that has the qualities of a family of choice.

Hypothesis 4: Compared to well-functioning couples, distressed-symptomatic couples such as those in therapy show higher intrusiveness, lower closeness-caregiving, lower openness of communication, less social support from outsiders, and greater gender-role conflict—attempts to conform and force one's partner to conform to traditional gender-role norms (O'Neil, Good, & Holmes, 1995).

In reference to this last hypothesis, because our research only involved community (nonclinical) samples, the question still remains unanswered as to whether lesbian and gay male couples who are in therapy might be more fused and disengaged, respectively, than heterosexual couples who also are in therapy. However, we see no basis for predicting that lesbian, gay male, and heterosexual couples in therapy will show differential patterns of functioning on these dimensions. Using the California Inventory model and its associated questionnaire (Werner & Green, 1989), two doctoral students at the California School of Professional Psychology (Kristi Roper and Kevin Campbell) will be testing some aspects of these hypotheses with community samples in the near future. Eventually, we also hope to study couples in therapy and couples from more diverse racial and socioeconomic backgrounds.

Until then, therapists would do well to consider that lesbian and gay male couples in the community appear to be functioning at least as well as married couples. Same-sex couples' high egalitarianism, flexibility, and cohesion seem to be real assets. The goals of therapy should include building on such strengths, and in order to do so, therapists must be able to distinguish clearly between positive and negative forms of couple connectedness. We hope the three frameworks presented in this chapter will enhance therapists' abilities to draw such distinctions in future work with lesbian and gay male couples.

Notes

1. Of the one hundred gay men (fifty couples) participating in this study, only three of the respondents indicated that they had been diagnosed with AIDS. To examine the impact of the AIDS epidemic on all gay male participants, an open-ended question was asked concerning the impact of the AIDS epidemic on their couple relationship. Responses to this question were coded into four categories: changes in sexual relations both in and outside of the relationship; relationship is closer; no change; no agreement between partners as to the effect of the epidemic. Scores on these four codes were examined statistically for their associations with couple Cohesion, Flexibility, overall relationship quality (Satisfaction), and discrepancy in Satisfaction scores. These analyses failed to uncover any significant associations among these variables, suggesting that the advent of AIDS was not exerting a marked effect on these couples' relationships at the time of the study.

2. *Regarding representativeness and matching of samples for length of relationship:* Given the differences in relationship lengths between our same-sex and married heterosexual samples, it can be argued that the ideal demographically matched heterosexual comparison group would consist of couples that were cohabiting (rather than married) for a median 3.5 to 4.0 years (matching the relationship longevity of the same-sex couples). However, such cohabiting heterosexual couples would not be representative of heterosexual couples in the United States (most of whom are legally married). Furthermore, the general population of cohabiting heterosexual couples is much younger than the population of cohabiting lesbian and gay male couples; and an older cohort of cohabiting heterosexual couples would be likely to have yet other idiosyncratic characteristics. To isolate the impact of the single variable, "sexual orientation of couple," it may be ideal to use a four-group design, comparing heterosexual cohabiting, heterosexual married, lesbian, and gay male couples matched for age and length of relationship, but this might necessitate using younger groups of couples that are not representative of most couples in the United States (see Blumstein & Schwartz, 1983, and Kurdek & Schmitt, 1986, for examples of this four-group research design). For our purposes, we believe that *a married heterosexual normative comparison group better*

enables us to understand and contrast lesbian, gay male, and heterosexual couples as they ordinarily exist in the United States.

Also regarding matching of groups for length of relationship, it is important to note that Zacks (1986) found no significant correlations between the major study variables (Cohesion, Flexibility, and Satisfaction) and lesbian partners' ages or length of current relationship. These results imply that the higher scores of lesbian couples on these variables are not a function of relationship length or stage of relationship (such as a "honeymoon" phase in the first few years). Hence, matching for length of relationship between the same-sex and heterosexual couple samples may not be as important as one might think, provided couples have been living together for some minimum time.

Lastly, our lesbian sample was recruited in the large Sacramento metropolitan area, whereas the gay male sample was recruited in the even larger San Francisco Bay area. Whether relationship differences exist between lesbian and gay couples purely as a function of living in these two different geographical communities is simply unknown. However, in terms of relationship length, both of our samples were quite similar to larger samples recruited by other investigators around the United States between 1978 and 1994 (Bell & Weinberg, 1978; Blumstein & Schwartz, 1983; Bryant & Demian, 1994; Kurdek & Schmitt, 1986; Peplau et al., 1982).

3. Olson and colleagues (1983) originally characterized the four levels of Cohesion (from very low to very high scores) as "disengaged, separated, connected, and enmeshed" and the four levels of Flexibility as "rigid, structured, flexible, and chaotic." However, based on consistent findings by many researchers and theoretical considerations, it now seems that high scores on Cohesion and Flexibility are most accurately viewed as extremely positive (rather than as signs of "enmeshed" and "chaotic" interactions). Hence, for the present chapter, we will refer to the four levels without using most of Olson and others' original quadrant labels. See Cluff and colleagues (1994), Green & Werner (1996), and Olson (1993) for more complete discussions of interpreting FACES scores.

4. *Statistical comparisons among lesbian, gay male, and heterosexual married couples' Cohesion.* Lesbian couples' Cohesion: $M = 44.5$, $SD = 4.1$; gay male couples' Cohesion: $M = 41.9$, $SD = 4.9$; heterosexual couples' Cohesion: $M = 38.5$, $SD = 4.7$. Lesbian couples scored significantly higher on Cohesion than both gay male couples ($t = 2.90$, $p < .01$) and heterosexual couples ($t = 10.17$, $p < .001$). Gay male couples scored significantly higher on Cohesion than heterosexual couples ($t = 4.81$, $p < .001$).

5. *Statistical comparisons among lesbian, gay male, and heterosexual married couples' Flexibility.* Lesbian couples' Flexibility: $M = 35.2$, $SD = 5.0$; gay male couples' Flexibility: $M = 33.1$, $SD = 5.7$; heterosexual couples' Flexibility: $M = 24.1$, $SD = 3.6$. Lesbian couples scored significantly higher on Flexibility than both gay male couples ($t = 1.98$, $p < .05$) and heterosexual couples ($t = 15.63$, $p < .001$). Gay male couples scored significantly higher on Flexibility than heterosexual couples ($t = 11.07$, $p < .001$).

6. *Tests for differences between lesbian and heterosexual couples' relationship satisfaction (using Olson, McCubbin, and colleagues' 1982 Family Satisfaction Scale).* Chi-square $= 30.62$, $df = 4$, $p < .001$ (performed on frequencies of couples at five levels of satisfaction for heterosexual and lesbian couples). Median lesbian couple satisfaction level was "High Satisfaction." Median heterosexual couple satisfaction level was "Medium Satisfaction."

7. *Tests for differences between gay male and heterosexual couples' relationship satisfaction (using Spanier's 1976 Dyadic Adjustment Scale).* Heterosexual married couples' Satisfaction: $M = 114.8$, SD

= 17.8; gay male couples' Satisfaction: $M = 109.5$, $SD = 12.2$; $t = 2.52$, $p < .01$. In interpreting this significant difference, it is important to note that the variability (standard deviation) of Satisfaction scores is larger for the married than for the gay male sample. Thus one standard deviation below each group's mean is an identical score of 97 for both groups, whereas one standard deviation above each group's mean is a score of 133 for the married couples and 122 for the gay male couples. In other words, the gay male sample's scores cluster densely near the means of both groups—a smaller proportion of them reaching into the higher levels of Satisfaction reported by some married couples but most of them still falling within one standard deviation of the married sample's scores. The married and gay male couples' means and standard deviations also can be contrasted with Spanier's (1976) norms for divorced heterosexual couples, whose average score was 70.7 ($SD = 23.8$). Thus despite the significant difference in the married versus gay male samples' means for Satisfaction, the gay couples were still scoring at a functional, nondistressed level, similar to Spanier's married sample rather than his divorced sample. It also is worth noting that Kurdek (1995) discovered, using the satisfaction subscale of Spanier's test, that although gay male couples reported slightly but significantly lower satisfaction than heterosexual couples did, comparisons between gay men's scores and heterosexual husbands' scores showed no significant difference. This implies that men in general (gay and heterosexual) tend to report lower satisfaction than women on the Dyadic Adjustment Scale.

8. *Significant comparisons between means of the still together and separated groups of lesbian couples on initial Cohesion, Flexibility, and Satisfaction.* Cohesion: together $M = 45.6$, $SD = 3.5$; separated $M = 42.2$, $SD = 4.9$; $t = 3.79$, $p < .01$. Flexibility: together $M = 36.2$, $SD = 5.6$; separated $M = 33.7$, $SD = 5.4$; $t = 2.08$, $p < .05$. Satisfaction: together $M = 53.8$, $SD = 10.4$; separated $M = 50$, $SD = 10$; $t = 1.66$, $p < .10$.

9. *Significant correlations between lesbian couples' initial Cohesion, Flexibility, and Satisfaction scores and their Global Satisfaction scores at follow-up (for the thirty-four lesbian couples that were still together).* Initial Cohesion and Follow-up Global Satisfaction: $r = .32$, $p < .01$. Initial Flexibility and Follow-up Global Satisfaction: $r = .26$, $p < .05$. Initial Satisfaction and Follow-up Global Satisfaction: $r = .43$, $p < .01$.

10. *Correlations between the two partners' independent responses to questionnaires.* Between lesbian partners' Cohesion responses: $r = .62$, $p < .01$. Between lesbian partners' Flexibility responses: $r = .40$, $p < .01$. Between gay male partners' Cohesion responses: $r = .39$, $p < .01$. Between gay male partners' Flexibility responses: $r = .69$, $p < .01$.

11. *Correlations between Satisfaction, Cohesion, and Flexibility.* Between lesbian couple's Satisfaction and Cohesion: $r = .77$, $p < .01$. Between lesbian couple's Satisfaction and Flexibility: $r = .62$, $p < .01$. Between gay male couple's Satisfaction and Cohesion: $r = .77$, $p < .01$. Between gay male couple's Satisfaction and Flexibility: $r = .52$, $p < .01$.

12. Despite the intriguing findings reviewed here, the only existing attempts to investigate the link between gender conformity and same-sex couples' interaction patterns have relied exclusively on the Bem Sex Role Inventory—a measure of gender-role self-schema (self-perceptions of personality traits) (see, for example, Kurdek, 1987). The Bem measure is disadvantaged by not being behaviorally specific and by leaving the respondent free to select an internal normative standard against which to compare the self. We suggest that to examine these questions more fully, researchers need to use observational measures of gender-role conformity or behaviorally specific self-report questionnaires tapping gender-role ideology (ideals) and gender-role conflict (comfort with deviance from prescribed gender roles). See, for example, the measures reviewed in O'Neil, Good, and Holmes (1995) and Thompson and Pleck (1995).

References

Bailey, J. M., & Zucker, K. J. (1995). Childhood sex-typed behavior and sexual orientation: A conceptual analysis and quantitative review. *Developmental Psychology, 31,* 43–55.

Bell, A. P., & Weinberg, M. S. (1978) *Homosexualities: A study of diversity among men and women.* New York: Simon & Schuster.

Bell, A. P., Weinberg, M. S., & Hammersmith, S. K. (1981). *Sexual preference: Its development in men and women.* Bloomington: Indiana University Press.

Bem, S. L. (1993). *The lenses of gender: Transforming the debate on sexual inequality.* New Haven, CT: Yale University Press.

Bettinger, M. (1986). *Relationship satisfaction, cohesion, and adaptability: A study of gay male couples.* Unpublished doctoral dissertation, California Graduate School of Marital and Family Therapy, San Rafael, CA.

Blasband, D., & Peplau, L. A. (1985). Sexual exclusivity versus openness in gay couples. *Archives of Sexual Behavior, 14,* 395–412.

Blumstein, P., & Schwartz, P. (1983). *American couples: Money, work and sex.* New York: Morrow.

Bowen, M. (1966). The use of family theory in clinical practice. *Comprehensive Psychiatry, 7,* 345–374.

Bowen, M. (1978). *Family therapy in clinical practice.* Northvale, NJ: Aronson.

Bradford, J., Ryan, C., & Rothblum, E. D. (1994). National lesbian health survey: Implications for mental health care. *Journal of Consulting and Clinical Psychology, 62,* 228–242.

Brown, L. S. (1994). *Subversive dialogues: Theory in feminist therapy.* New York: Basic Books.

Bryant, A. S., & Demian. (1994). Relationship characteristics of American gay and lesbian couples: Findings from a national survey. In L. A. Kurdek (Ed.), *Social services for gay and lesbian couples* (pp. 101–117). Binghamton, NY: Harrington Park Press.

Burch, B. (1982). Psychological merger in lesbian couples: A joint ego psychological and systems approach. *Family Therapy, 9,* 201–208.

Burch, B. (1986). Psychotherapy and the dynamics of merger in lesbian couples. In T. S. Stein & C. J. Cohen (Eds.), *Contemporary perspectives on psychotherapy with lesbians and gay men* (pp. 57–71). New York: Plenum.

Chodorow, N. (1978). *The reproduction of mothering: Psychoanalysis and the sociology of gender.* Berkeley: University of California Press.

Clatterbaugh, K. (1990). *Contemporary perspectives on masculinity: Men, women, and politics in modern society.* Boulder, CO: Westview Press.

Cluff, R. B., Hicks, M. W., & Madsen, C. H. (1994). Beyond the circumplex model: I. A moratorium on curvilinearity. *Family Process, 33,* 455–470.

Cunningham, J. D., & Antill, J. K. (1984). Changes in masculinity and femininity across the family life cycle: A re-examination. *Developmental Psychology, 20,* 1135–1141.

Devoss, L. L. (1991). *Masculine gender ideals of heterosexual and homosexual males.* Unpublished doctoral dissertation, California School of Professional Psychology, Alameda.

Elise, D. (1986). Lesbian couples: The implication of sex differences in separation-individuation. *Psychotherapy, 23,* 305–310.

Falbo, T., & Peplau, L. A. (1980). Power strategies in intimate relationship. *Journal of Personality and Social Psychology, 38,* 618–628.

Feldman, S. S., Biringen, Z. C., & Nash, S. C. (1981). Fluctuations of sex-related self-attributions as a function of stage of family life cycle. *Developmental Psychology, 17,* 24–35.

Gilligan, C. (1982). *In a different voice: Psychological theory and women's development.* Cambridge, MA: Harvard University Press.

Goldner, V. (1991). Toward a critical relational theory of gender. *Psychoanalytic Dialogues, 1,* 249–272.

Green, R.-J., & Framo, J. L. (Eds.). (1981). *Family therapy: Major contributions.* New York: International Universities Press.

Green, R.-J., & Korin, D. (in press). Boys will be men: Male gender role socialization and the family life cycle. In E. Carter & M. McGoldrick (Eds.), *The changing family life cycle* (3rd ed.). Needham Heights, MA: Allyn & Bacon.

Green, R.-J., & Werner, P. D. (1996). Intrusiveness and closeness-caregiving: Rethinking the concept of family "enmeshment." *Family Process, 35,* (2).

Guerin, P. J., Fay, L. F., Burden, S. L., & Kautto, J. G. (1987). *The evaluation and treatment of marital conflict: A four-stage approach.* New York: Basic Books.

Hare-Mustin, R. T., & Marecek, J. (1988). The meaning of difference: Gender theory, postmodernism, and psychology. *American Psychologist, 43,* 455–464.

Hochschild, A. (1989). *The second shift: Working parents and the revolution at home.* New York: Viking Penguin.

Imber-Black, E., Roberts, J., & Whiting, R. (Eds.). (1988). *Rituals in families and family therapy.* New York: Norton.

Kaufman, P. A., Harrison, E., & Hyde, M. L. (1984). Distancing for intimacy in lesbian relationships. *American Journal of Psychiatry, 141,* 530–533.

Kerr, M. E. (1981). Family systems theory and therapy. In A. S. Gurman & D. P. Kniskern (Eds.), *Handbook of family therapy* (vol. 1, pp. 226–264). New York: Brunner/Mazel.

Kimmel, M. S., & Messner, M. A. (1992). *Men's lives* (2nd ed.). New York: Macmillan.

Kliman, J., & Trimble, D. W. (1983). Network therapy. In B. Wolman & G. Stricker (Eds.), *Handbook of family and marital therapy* (pp. 277–314). New York: Plenum.

Krestan, J. A., & Bepko, C. S. (1980). The problem of fusion in the lesbian relationship. *Family Process, 19,* 277–289.

Kurdek, L. A. (1987). Sex-role self-schema and psychological adjustment in coupled homosexual and heterosexual men and women. *Sex Roles, 17,* 549–562.

Kurdek, L. A. (1988a). Perceived social support in gays and lesbians in cohabiting relationships. *Journal of Personality and Social Psychology, 54,* 504–509.

Kurdek, L. A. (1988b). Relationship quality of gay and lesbian cohabiting couples. *Journal of Homosexuality, 15,* 93–118.

Kurdek, L. A. (1995). Lesbian and gay couples. In A. R. D'Augelli & C. J. Patterson (Eds.), *Lesbian, gay, and bisexual identities over the lifespan: Psychological perspectives* (pp. 243–261). New York: Oxford University Press.

Kurdek, L. A., & Schmitt, J. P. (1986). Relationship quality of partners in heterosexual married, heterosexual cohabiting, and gay and lesbian relationships. *Journal of Personality and Social Psychology, 51,* 711–720.

Kurdek, L. A., & Schmitt, J. P. (1987). Perceived emotional support from family and friends in members of homosexual, married, and heterosexual cohabiting couples. *Journal of Homosexuality, 14,* 57–68.

Levant, R. F., & Pollack, W. S. (Eds.). (1995). *A new psychology of men.* New York: Basic Books.

Magraw, S., Stearns, S., & Green, R.-J. (in preparation). *Voices of women family therapists: Feminist thinking and multiculturalism.* New York: Guilford Press.

McCandlish, B. M. (1982). Therapeutic issues with lesbian couples. In J. C. Gonsiorek (Ed.), *Homosexuality and psychotherapy* (pp. 71–78). Binghamton, NY: Haworth Press.

McGoldrick, M. (1995). *You can go home again: Reconnecting with your family.* New York: Norton.

McWhirter, D. P., & Mattison, A. M. (1984). *The male couple: How relationships develop.* Upper Saddle River, NJ: Prentice Hall.

Mencher, J. (1990). *Intimacy in lesbian relationships: A critical re-examination of fusion.* Work in Progress No. 42. Wellesley, MA: Wellesley College, Stone Center for Women's Development.

Miller, J. B. (1976). *Toward a new psychology of women.* Boston: Beacon Press.

Minuchin, S. (1974). *Families and family therapy.* Cambridge, MA: Harvard University Press.

Minuchin, S., Rosman, B. L., & Baker, L. (1978). *Psychosomatic families: Anorexia nervosa in context.* Cambridge, MA: Harvard University Press.

Olson, D. H. (1993). Circumplex model of marital and family systems: Assessing family functioning. In F. Walsh (Ed.), *Normal family processes* (2nd ed., pp. 104–137). New York: Guilford Press.

Olson, D. H., McCubbin, H. I., Barnes, H. L., Larsen, A., Muxen, M. J., & Wilson, M. A. (1982). *Family inventories.* St. Paul: University of Minnesota, Department of Family Social Science.

Olson, D. H., McCubbin, H. I., Barnes, H. L., Larsen, A., Muxen, M. J., & Wilson, M. A. (1983). *Families: What makes them work.* Newbury Park, CA: Sage.

Olson, D. H., Portner, J., & Lavee, Y. (1985). *FACES III.* St. Paul: University of Minnesota, Department of Family Social Science.

Olson, D. H., Russell, C., & Sprenkle, D. (1980). Circumplex model of marital and family systems: II. Empirical studies and clinical intervention. In *Advances in family intervention, assessment and theory* (vol. 1, pp. 129–179). Greenwich, CT: JAI Press.

Olson, D. H., Russell, C., & Sprenkle, D., (1983). Circumplex model of marital and family systems: VI. Theoretical update. *Family Process, 22,* 69–83.

O'Neil, J. M., Good, G. E., & Holmes, S. (1995). Fifteen years of theory and research on men's gender role conflict: New paradigms for empirical research. In R. F. Levant & W. S. Pollack (Eds.), *A new psychology of men* (pp. 164–206). New York: Basic Books.

Parker, D. A. (1995). *The cruising project report.* Unpublished manuscript, Center for Education and Research in Sexuality, San Francisco State University.

Peplau, L. A. (1991). Lesbian and gay relationships. In J. C. Gonsiorek & J. D. Weinrich (Eds.), *Homosexuality: Research implications for public policy* (pp. 177–196). Newbury Park, CA: Sage.

Peplau, L. A., Cochran, S., Rook, K., & Padesky, M. (1982). Loving women: Attachment and autonomy in lesbian relationships. *Journal of Social Issues, 34,* 7–27.

Pleck, J. H. (1981). *The myth of masculinity.* Cambridge, MA: MIT Press.

Roth, S. (1989). Psychotherapy with lesbian couples: Individual issues, female socialization, and the social context. In M. McGoldrick, C. M. Anderson, & F. Walsh (Eds.), *Women in families: A framework for family therapy* (pp. 286–307). New York: Norton.

Rubin, L. B. (1983). *Intimate strangers: Men and women together.* New York: HarperCollins.

Slater, S., & Mencher, J. (1991). The lesbian family life cycle: A contextual approach. *American Journal of Orthopsychiatry, 61,* 372–382.

Spanier, G. (1976). Measuring dyadic adjustment: New scales for assessing the quality of marriage and other similar dyads. *Journal of Marriage and the Family, 38,* 15–28.

Surrey, J. (1985). *Self-in-relation: A theory of women's development.* Work in Progress No. 13. Wellesley, MA: Wellesley College, Stone Center for Women's Development.

Teichner Associates. (1989, June 6). Gay in America: A special report. *San Francisco Chronicle,* p. A-19.

Thompson, E. H., Jr., & Pleck, J. H. (1995). Masculine ideologies: A review of research instrumentation on men and masculinities. In R. F. Levant & W. S. Pollack (Eds.), *A new psychology of men* (pp. 129–163). New York: Basic Books.

Watzlawick, P. (1984). Self-fulfilling prophecies. In P. Watzlawick (Ed.), *The invented reality* (pp. 95–116). New York: Norton.

Werner, P. D., & Green, R.-J. (1989). *California Inventory for Family Assessment (CIFA)*. Unpublished questionnaire, California School of Professional Psychology, Alameda.

Werner, P. D., & Green, R.-J. (1993). *Preliminary manual: California Inventory for Family Assessment (CIFA)*. Unpublished manuscript, California School of Professional Psychology, Alameda.

Weston, K. (1991). *Families we choose: Lesbians, gays, kinship.* New York: Columbia University Press.

White, E. (1994). Sexual culture. In D. Bergman (Ed.), *The burning library: Essays by Edmund White* (pp. 157–167). New York: Knopf.

Williams, W. L. (1992). *The spirit and the flesh: Sexual diversity in American Indian culture.* Boston: Beacon Press. (Originally published 1986)

Zacks, E. (1986). *Relationship cohesion, adaptability, and satisfaction: A comparison between lesbian and heterosexual couples.* Unpublished doctoral dissertation, California Graduate School of Marital and Family Therapy, San Rafael.

Zacks, E., Green, R.-J., & Marrow, J. (1988). Comparing lesbian and heterosexual couples on the circumplex model: An initial investigation. *Family Process, 27,* 471–484.

CHAPTER NINE

CREATING AND MAINTAINING BOUNDARIES IN MALE COUPLES

Thomas W. Johnson and Michael S. Keren

Historically, the concept of boundaries has been a key concern in clinical and theoretical family systems literature. The concept has become so ubiquitous that it even has entered into mainstream cultural discourse about relationships. Much has been written about boundaries in (presumably) heterosexual couples and families, beginning with Minuchin's germinal work, *Families and Family Therapy* (1974). A body of literature has emerged about boundaries in lesbian systems, beginning with Krestan and Bepko's (1980) groundbreaking article. However, no literature examining boundary creation and maintenance in the male couple has surfaced to date.

The definition of boundaries offered by Minuchin in 1974—"the rules defining who participates and how" (p. 53)—has endured over the past twenty years and continues to be used in training and practice. Krestan and Bepko (1980) further specified the concept as "the rules and structured interactions" that "differentiate [a system] *from* the larger system and define its relationship *to* that system" (1980, p. 278). Minuchin claims that the function of boundaries is a protective one—the protection of the system's unique identity and viability. He further as-

The cases presented in this article are hypothetical composites based on actual cases.
Previously published in the *Journal of Feminist Family Therapy*, Volume 7, #(3/4), pp. 65–86, 1995, and reprinted with the permission of The Haworth Press, Inc., Publisher, and the authors.

serts that clarity of boundaries in a system is an indicator of its functional effectiveness. In this theoretical perspective, then, boundaries are crucial in helping a system define and maintain its unique identity and in modulating the effects of the external, larger system. However, it is also important to remember that boundaries are defined in a sociocultural context. Thus, no concept of boundary has universal meaning nor does it represent an intrinsic property of all systems. It is crucial to recognize that fundamental concepts of boundaries used in prevailing family theories are derived from a cultural context that privileges White, middle-class, heterosexual, male, Judeo-Christian perspectives.

Boundary creation and maintenance are extremely complicated processes for male couples. Given homophobic and heterosexist biases, these couple relationships are not recognized in the cultural mainstream. The bonds are given no legitimacy and, in many instances, the couple's very existence is under attack. In addition, because there are no readily available models of how to form and maintain such relationships, the procedures to follow in living as a male couple are trial-and-error, experimental, and tentative. Some examples from the authors' clinical practices will illustrate this complexity.

CASE 1: MAX

Max came into therapy two years after separating from his wife of ten years. Shortly after the separation, he developed his first relationship with a man and moved in with him after six months. Max's separation was amicable, and his wife accepted the revelation of his homosexuality after a relatively brief period of anger and sadness. A joint custody arrangement was developed easily for Max's five- and six-year-old sons. Max's wife and his lover developed a friendship, and all three adults spent many weekend outings together with the two children. Max wanted help answering several questions: What do I want from my relationship with my lover? What kind of relationship do I want with my wife? Can three adults form a family of sorts with my sons?

CASE 2: PAT

Pat presented for help after his lover died from AIDS, explaining that the two had lived together for seven years with another man as a committed threesome and that this third man also had died from AIDS. Pat was overwhelmed with a double load of loss and bereavement. Little support was forthcoming from his family, who had had enough difficulty recognizing a gay couple relationship, much less a triadic one. Indeed, many of his friends, both gay and straight, struggled to understand his relationship system, given the dominance of dyadic models of intimate relationships in this society.

CASE 3: ALEX

Alex remarked one session that he was dreading the upcoming Christmas season, especially Christmas Day with his large extended family. After describing his various concerns about the holiday, he remembered that he had seen a list his mother had drawn up of the names of family members who would be entered into a gift-giving selection pool. The name of his lover of three years was not included, even though the lover was a regular participant in family events as Alex's partner.

These examples show how boundary creation and maintenance are made complicated for male couples by the lack of rules, models, and cultural legitimacy. However, the absence of these resources also can be a blessing. When the rules are up for grabs, the couple's unique needs and values can shape the relational process.

Boundary-making for male couples, as for all couples, involves two important tasks: (1) developing intracouple boundaries, including the establishment of patterns of closeness and distance, and (2) developing boundaries between the couple and the outside world. The boundaries establish an identity for the couple, norms for their dyadic process, affirmation of the couple's existence, and norms for their interaction with the external world.

Krestan and Bepko (1980) were the first to explore the variables that color boundary formation and maintenance in the lesbian couple. They highlighted the interaction of the lesbian couple at the boundaries between them and the larger heterosexual culture, as well as between the couple and the family of origin. In addition, they examined intracouple boundaries, raising the question of whether the double dose of female gender socialization in the lesbian couple created significant risk factors for couple dysfunction. Krestan and Bepko (1980) and their critics (for example, Mencher, 1990) have highlighted gender as a key variable in the discussion of same-sex relationships. These writers argue that the same stimuli that encourage women to fuse also push men to distance. They suggest that male couples have a repertoire of relational moves that supports the maintenance of distance; furthermore, the fact that many male couples allow sex outside the relationship is believed to demonstrate a preference for emotional distance. We believe, from our own clinical experiences, that these common premises about male couples, endorsed by many therapists, demand further investigation.

Mediating Variables in Boundary Negotiation

The following questions guide our exploration of the variables that seem to influence how the male couple negotiates boundaries:

1. How does *male gender-role socialization* affect the couple's boundaries?
2. How do relationships with the *family of creation* and the *gay and lesbian community* affect couple boundaries?
3. How do gay cultural *norms regarding sexuality* affect a couple's boundaries?
4. How do relationships with the *family of origin* influence the nature of the couple's boundaries?
5. What role do *ethnicity and culture* play in shaping the couple's boundaries?
6. What is the impact of *homophobia*—internal and external—on the male couple's boundaries?

The resources we draw from in exploring these issues include a review of relevant literature, clinical work, and our own experiences as a gay couple. We bring to bear our own experiences with each other, with our respective families, and with gay colleagues and friends who are also in the process of developing and maintaining couple boundaries.

Here, it is important to note a bias in clinical writings on men and their relationships, namely that men are intrinsically deficient when it comes to relationship abilities. This position implies that gay male couples are doubly deficient. We refer to this as the "deficit-bias model" of male relationships, a model we do not believe is supported by empirical research on male couples. For instance, Kurdek and Schmitt (1986) found that gay men do not differ from lesbians or heterosexuals in measures of perceived relationship quality and dyadic adjustment. In fact, Kurdek and Schmitt conclude that gay men form relationships that are intimate, satisfying, and committed. However, male-male intimacy may differ from male-female or female-female intimacy, both in style and in relational aesthetics.

Male Gender-Role Socialization

It is commonly assumed in the dominant culture that men are, at their core, thoroughly different human beings from women. This essentialist position also implies that all men—heterosexual or gay, White or of color, working-class or professional—are alike. Men are seen as deficient in relationship skills and in the ability to be intimate with others, a widespread assumption that permeates cultural images of men. For example, this notion surfaces repeatedly in television situation comedies like *Married . . . with Children.* (Sometimes, of course, the humor emerges from a legitimate critique of male oppression and privilege in family and couple relationships.) However, one possible pernicious outcome of the relational deficiency assumption is further entrenchment of the idea that men cannot relate in a close, intimate, and nurturing manner, a reductionist notion that fails to credit the tremendous variability in both male and female gendered functioning. Weingarten (1991) makes the case that, if one believes that men fear intimacy and women yearn for it,

> this belief may then discourage one from believing that the man can modify his behavior and requesting that he do so. If on the other hand, one has a point of view that is less saturated with the biases of the individual capacity discourse, one can imagine that men and women are equally capable—though perhaps not equally desirous—of behaving intimately and restraining from non-intimate interactions. (p. 290)

This male deficit bias can have a deleterious impact on the male couple, as men internalize these common cultural assumptions, most acutely on the intra-couple boundary of closeness and distance. Comments made in our clinical and friendship contexts by gay men illustrate the point: "Gay relationships never last— men can't commit" or "I can't tell my lover how bad I feel—guys just don't do that" or "If we keep getting close like this, people will think we're really lesbians." Mainstream cultural images of male couples depict relationships marked by betrayal, competition, vicious and "bitchy" repartee, and sexual jealousy. There are few images of love, affection, commitment, and care.

Such deficit notions of relatedness can complicate the male couple's life by engendering a sense of inadequacy, incapability, and increased anxiety about trust and exposure of vulnerability. Male couples indeed may have a style of relatedness that is, given their gender socialization, qualitatively different from a so-called female style, but it is no less intimate and connected.

Research on male couples calls into question the ubiquity of the male deficit premise, at least in a gay context. For example, it is questioned in popular culture whether gay men even want relationships. However, Bell and Weinberg (1978) found that two-thirds of their large sample of gay men wanted an enduring, close relationship and that 40 to 60 percent were involved in steady, ongoing relationships. As for the fundamental issue of whether gay men are capable of establishing mutually satisfying couple relationships, two different sets of researchers (Kurdek & Schmitt, 1986; Peplau & Cochran, 1981) found that male couples were not significantly different from lesbian or heterosexual couples in measures of relationship satisfaction and of love for one's partner. And, as noted earlier, Kurdek and Schmitt (1986) also found that male couples were not significantly different from female couples in measures of dyadic attachment.

Even though male couples suffer as a result of the dominant culture's gender narrative, it also is important to note the power and privilege accorded to men that undergirds the social construction of the male role. Male couples also must address this issue in their couple relationships. For example, Blumstein and Schwartz (1983) report that money has a privileging effect in male couples and that work assumes an important role in the relationship. As with heterosexual males in relationships, gay men struggle with the intrusion of the workplace and with anxiety about earning enough money. Blumstein and Schwartz also note that, in relation to work achievement, a power hierarchy develops in male couples that is based on income production.

In addition, the dominant culture's male script has some relational requirements that affect the emotional functioning and relational aesthetics of male couples. David and Brannon (1976) claim that there are four of these requirements: (1) be the "big wheel" and strive to be respected for success and achievement; (2) be the "sturdy oak" and never show weakness and dependence; (3) "give 'em hell" and seek adventure, daring, risk, and aggression; and (4) show "no sissy stuff," which translates into avoiding anything stereotypically feminine. In our experience, even though gay men frequently report a history of gender nonconformity (Bell, Weinberg, & Hammersmith, 1981) and demonstrate care, connection, and nurturance in their relationships, a struggle often exists around adherence to the male gender script. Clinical explication of this dilemma occurs in the work both of us are engaged in at the Gay and Lesbian Family Project at the Ackerman Institute for Family Therapy in New York City. The project entails clinical consultation, research, and training about the norms and clinical issues of gay and lesbian families. From our observations of male and female couples in clinical consultation at the Project, it seemed that male couples displayed a relational style in therapy marked by (1) a more limited investment in discussion of relational process and emotional responsivity than lesbian couples; (2) easier access to anger than sadness, vulnerability, or dependence; and (3) more urgency about problem resolution and termination. The four requirements delineated by David and Brannon (1976) are clearly in evidence here. However, it is important to recognize that this relational style is socially constructed and thus more amenable to deconstruction and readaptation than is commonly assumed.

Larry and James have been a couple for eight years. Larry is a businessman who earns four times James's salary as a schoolteacher. They presented with heated battles over James's persisting unhappiness with the relationship and Larry's fury over James's frequent criticism of him in front of friends. Eventually, in treatment, the couple saw the privileging effect of Larry's income and James's experience of disempowerment. A pooling of finances and a weekly ritual of negotiation of financial decisions seemed to reduce the couple's tension.

The Gay Community and the Family of Creation

The gay community has two important historical markers, the Stonewall Riots of 1969 and the HIV epidemic. The riots gave birth to a visible gay culture (at least to a White, urban, middle-class gay culture) and an open and large-scale activism. Gay men at this time reveled in their sexual liberation and glorified nonmonogamy. Coupling often was viewed as an oppressive cultural institution of the heterosexual establishment, not applicable in the gay world. Often boundaries were not respected, and sexual intrusions on the couple's space were frequent.

However, gay politics notwithstanding, couples did find each other in this era, as documented by Bell and Weinberg (1978) and McWhirter and Mattison (1984). Despite popular beliefs that gay coupling was not an important institution and that gay male relationships were transient, these studies documented relationships that lasted ten years or more during this era. Yet, in this period, gay couples were rendered invisible by the gay community in much the same way gays were rendered invisible by the dominant culture.

With the emergence of the HIV epidemic in the gay community in 1983, coupling became more desirable, and male couples became much more visible. Boundaries were more respected and legitimized by the community. Support groups for couples and dating services for gay men proliferated throughout the gay community. More and more male couples were seeking couples therapy rather than dissolving their relationships.

These events and shifts over twenty-five years are reflected in changes in popular culture, particularly in film. In the early 1970s, *The Boys in the Band* was hailed as a revolutionary film because it brought gay men to the screen in an unhidden and unapologetic manner. However, they were portrayed as lonely, bitter "flames" incapable of intimacy and commitment. Compare this with the 1993 film *The Wedding Banquet,* with its humorous look at a male couple's attempts to preserve its existence in the wake of a visit by one the men's traditional Chinese family of origin. Or consider the 1994 film *The Adventures of Priscilla, Queen of the Desert,* in which a gay man's family of creation gathers together to help him heal the wounds of the death of a lover. Here the happy ending includes a coupling, supported and envied by all. (The last two films were produced outside the United States but were released in U.S. cities and extolled by gay audiences. Examples of U.S.-made films that support the authors' position include *Longtime Companion, Parting Glances,* and *Philadelphia.*)

Both of the latter films demonstrate the power of the family of creation. Ethnographic research by anthropologist Kath Weston (1991) confirms that gay men and lesbians define family in a number of ways that extend beyond families of blood and include close friends who are vital supports in their lives and relationships. These families of creation are capable of validating, marking, and celebrating the boundaries of the gay couple.

The following example demonstrates the important supportive function of a family of creation.

Dan is a nineteen-year-old gay male who has been in and out of treatment since he came out at age fourteen. He recently met Josh, who is thirty-two, HIV-positive, and a successful salesman. He lives a somewhat closeted life in a rural area. Dan often spends long evenings without Josh at Josh's home because Josh has social commitments in his heterosexual world. Dan is kept company, however, by Josh's large circle of gay friends, a group that includes Josh's roommate, next-door neighbor, and friends from gay clubs. Josh and Dan are struggling with the boundary issues created by Josh's double life. However, Dan is supported by this family of creation to stay with Josh and to deal with Josh's struggle about coming out. They believe that Dan is good for Josh, and they provide both instrumental and emotional support to the couple. For example, this family of creation nurtures Dan by taking him out in the community and "showing him the ropes" of life in the gay world.

Sexual Norms in the Gay Male Community

In discussions of homosexuality, nothing arouses as much controversy as the topic of gay male sexuality. The gay community's normative acceptance of casual sex, anonymous sex, and nonmonogamy in couple relationships represents a dramatic departure from heterocentric norms and values.

Family therapists tend to invoke such clinical terms as "triangulation," "difficulty with intimacy," and "male objectification" in trying to make sense of the presence of nonmonogamy in male couples, while psychoanalytic theorists (Socarides, 1978) have struggled to understand the phenomenon in terms of narcissism and pre-Oedipal relatedness. It is difficult for many clinicians to understand why nonmonogamy might not disturb the boundaries in the relationship.

These sexual norms need to be understood in a nonheterocentric, nondeficit context. There is considerable diversity in sexual norms among gay couples, but most have had experience with nonmonogamy (Bell & Weinberg, 1978; Blasband & Peplau, 1985; Blumstein & Schwartz, 1983; McWhirter & Mattison, 1984). Earlier researchers posited that most male couples move from a "honeymoon" phase of initial sexual exclusivity to nonmonogamy later (for example, McWhirter & Mattison, 1984); but later researchers found that this developmental premise did not hold up empirically (Blasband & Peplau, 1985). Male couples report a wide array of contracts around monogamy: long-term sexual exclusivity, initial open-

ness moving toward monogamy, initial monogamy moving toward openness, varying contracts to suit the shifting psychosocial circumstance of the couple's life, and
long-term openness. The crucial point is that the issue of sexual exclusivity exists on a continuum for male couples. There is no dichotomous either-or pattern
(Blasband & Peplau, 1985). Variability exists also in how the couples handle nonmonogamy. Some couples set down rules such as no affairs, only one-night stands
or tricking, no disclosure about the outside sex, full disclosure about outside sex,
or mutual participation in the outside sex as a threesome or foursome.

Monogamy seems to be hardwired into spoken and culturally sanctioned
norms for heterosexual relationships. However, one wonders if it is so hardwired
at the level of actual lived experience, given the statistics on the frequency of ex-
tramarital affairs in heterosexual relationships (Meth & Pasick, 1990). It is commonly assumed, by both professionals and the public, that nonmonogamy
implies dysfunction or that it engenders dysfunction. Empirical research on male
couples contradicts this notion, at least in a gay context. Research comparing
open and closed couples indicates that the two types of couples are more similar than different in terms of psychological adjustment and relationship quality
(Blasband & Peplau, 1985; Kurdek & Schmitt, 1985–86). Blumstein and
Schwartz (1983), working with a large sample of gay male couples, found that
the nonmonogamy was not harmful to the relationships and that the "outside
sex" was reported to be just that—impersonal or casual sex that had little significance in terms of intimacy and posed little threat to the primary relationship. In essence, the integrity of the boundaries around the male couples in their
sample was not threatened by the outside sex, which was viewed as a kind of
recreational activity.

Blumstein and Schwartz (1983) also suggest that the experience of gay men
illustrates the premise that men, as constructed by our culture, are able to enjoy
sex that is primarily recreational, even when some of the properties of intimacy
are missing. However, gay couples, like most men, also have a need for intimate
connectedness, and primary couple relationships are maintained for this reason,
even though monogamy may wax and wane over time. It also is interesting to note
that, according to the Blumstein and Schwartz study, gay men report no loss of
satisfaction with the primary relationship if sexual interest in their partner de-
clines. General sexual interest remains high, but outside sexual encounters satisfy these needs. In fact, in the sample, gay couples were much less likely to view
infrequent sex with a partner as a signal of relationship conflict than heterosexual partners. Nonmonogamy thus does not have the same meaning and valence
for male couples or within the gay subculture, as it does in the dominant heterosexual culture. However, this does not mean that nonmonogamy "works" for all
couples or that it works all the time for any one male couple. For some male

couples, and at varying times over the course of the relationship in other couples, nonmonogamy can threaten the integrity of the couple boundary.

Families of Origin

Male couples, like lesbian couples, tend to encounter two kinds of boundary problems in their relationships with families of origin: (1) lack of visibility and invalidation of the couple relationship in the family of origin; and (2) intrusions and disrespect in terms of how the family of origin relates to the couple. The case of Paul illustrates both themes.

Paul was the middle of five sons. He had always been the son most emotionally responsible for his parents. When his elderly mother suffered a stroke, it was assumed that Paul would stay with his parents in their home during the recovery period. He was given the explanation that his married brothers weren't available—that their wives would resent the intrusion. However, Paul was involved in a ten-year relationship with his lover Sean, and it was assumed by the family that no conflict would ensue if Paul moved in with his parents for a month. Part of the issue revolved around Paul's longstanding overresponsibility and overfunctioning in his family. However, his parents also viewed his couple relationship as having less claim upon him than their other sons' marriages. Paul was coached to discuss with his parents the importance of his relationship with Sean and to negotiate dividing up caregiving responsibilities with his brothers.

Family of origin relationships also can have an impact on the boundaries of intimacy within the couple. Partner differences in terms of openness with extended family and the issue of competing loyalties both affect the couple's emotional process. For example, when a family refuses to invite a son's lover to a family event, the son is left with the untenable choice of lover versus family. These kinds of dilemmas exert a pressure on the couple no matter what stand they take with their families.

Tim was a forty-five-year-old Irish Catholic man who had always been the good, adaptable child in his family. His homosexuality was never openly discussed in his family, but his parents knew. His lover of two years, Jack, was a Jewish man, the family provocateur who had always been out to every member of his family. Terrible conflict surfaced every time Tim was invited to an event in his family. Jack pushed Tim to include him in an upcoming celebration and felt betrayed by Tim's resistance. Tim felt Jack just didn't understand how reactive his elderly parents would get if the couple attended, for example, a cousin's upcoming wedding. Jack felt marginalized by his lover and spoke of leaving the relationship.

Many gay men minimize the impact of the family of origin on their lives, as do many men in general, at the outset of therapy. Perhaps this pattern relates to the dominant culture's male gender narrative in which autonomy, independence, and self-sufficiency, even in the context of one's family, are prized. Unfortunately, this stance may evolve into a cut-off with various members of the extended family system and, according to Bowen (1978), leave these men with distance regulation problems in their couple relationships. However, Bowen's premise has not been tested empirically, and some authors contend that family of origin relationships marked by distance and denial may not necessarily have a deleterious effect on the relational functioning of gay and lesbian adults (Laird, 1993).

We have observed considerable diversity in the impact of family cut-offs on gay men, individually and in their couple relationships. Some men have responded to the cut-off by "putting all their eggs in one basket" in their couple relationship, which can provoke conflicts around autonomy and dependence. Other men tend to employ this same cut-off response defensively when conflict emerges in their couple relationship or their work systems. Still others invest more deeply in the couple relationship and in a chosen family of friends, with little observed dysfunction resulting from the cut-off. No one pattern stands out. However, this is a topic that bears further investigation.

The Impact of Culture

Race, social class, and culture affect male couple boundaries as they do for all couples. However, when one or both members of the couple belong to a disenfranchised racial, ethnic, or class minority, the process of boundary formation may become even more complicated.

Controversy exists as to whether there is such a thing as gay culture. Some writers maintain that there is a dominant ethos in the community with norms and standards and that the architects of these norms are White, middle-class, privileged men (Champagne, 1993). The dominant gay cultural script maintains that gay men should be visible in terms of their sexual orientation in most, if not all, contexts of their life—in other words, that it is healthier to be out. However, this aspiration seems absurd to many gay men in differing ethnic, racial, and class contexts. Risks and losses exist that may have different meanings for gay men of color, for example, than for their White counterparts.

A number of authors have discussed the complexity of being both gay and a member of an ethnic or racial minority group in relation to the family of origin, the gay and lesbian community, and the dominant culture (Chan, 1989; Espin, 1987; Morales, 1990; Tremble, Schneider, & Appathurai, 1989). Certain group norms prohibit homosexuality altogether, while others explain it as a White phenomenon totally inconsistent with valid minority culture, and still others prohibit open discussion about sexuality. For example, Chan (1992) notes that in Asian families, sexuality exists in the domain of the private self. Public discussion of one's sexuality—as occurs in a gay son's coming out—would constitute a grievous offense against the cultural code and bring shame upon the family. Chan suggests that in various Asian cultural scripts, private homosexuality might be acceptable as long as it is not publicly discussed. Certainly, a Chinese gay son's decision to conceal his sexuality from his family could not be easily dismissed as simply a personal or political decision to remain in the closet or as a failure to differentiate. Morales (1990) makes a cogent point in explaining that the risks of alienation from the family and from the ethnic community by coming out pose different strains for nondominant culture gays and lesbians. The family and the ethnic community are havens in a hostile dominant culture, and the White gay and lesbian community often can be as racist and discriminatory as the White heterosexual community. In addition, for many minority gays or lesbians, culture is as crucial to personal identity as is gay or lesbian sexuality.

In the context of the couple relationship, the minority gay man may not directly speak of a lover's existence to his family, or he may present the lover as his friend or roommate. The family may know indirectly and may or may not respect the couple's boundaries. One of us worked with an African American–Jewish interracial couple in which the African American man's family treated the two men as a couple without ever having a direct discussion of their son's homosexuality. Racism and class prejudice also can affect the interracial couple's relationship with the gay and lesbian community to the extent that the couple may choose not to affiliate. The couple will be fortunate if their community consists of other ethnic or racial minority gays. Otherwise, isolation may ensue, and the couple relationship may be threatened by the absence of external supports. As Bowen (1978) contends, distance regulation issues may surface if the boundary around the couple is not open to external support and validation.

Intracouple boundaries also are very complex when two men of disenfranchised minority groups couple (Almaguer, Busto, Dixon, & Lu, 1992; Almeida, Woods, Messineo, Font, & Heer, 1994). Minority men "colonized" by the aesthetic standards for physical beauty and desirability of the White dominant culture may bring negative expectations and cultural narratives into the relationship that affect intimacy and threaten couple boundaries. Noted African American filmmaker Marlon Riggs, in his documentary about African American gay men, *Tongues Untied*, addresses this issue and, in an incantatory way, repeats during the film the statement, "Black men loving Black men is the revolutionary act." Similarly, in an article by Almaguer, Busto, Dixon, and Lu (1992), a gay Asian man remarks, "Loving another Asian becomes a deeply liberating and affirming event, both personally and politically" (p. 32).

When men of differing races and cultures couple, they must negotiate differing notions of power and privilege, expectations around visibility, and expectations of where and how support for the couple will be sought. This complexity is illustrated in the case of an interracial couple seen by one of us:

Leo was a thirty-six-year-old Jewish man who came into therapy with dissatisfaction in his one-year relationship with a twenty-eight-year-old Cuban man named Marcos. The tension revolved around Leo's frustration with Marcos's absence most weekends because of family obligations. Leo had been out to his family for many years. Nevertheless, family members subtly rejected Leo's relationship with Marcos because of ethnic and religious differences. Leo's response was to cut them off and focus on the relationship. Marcos refused to come out to his family, who assumed Leo was a roommate. In addition, the two men were in conflict over Marcos's discomfort with Leo's largely White circle of gay friends. Marcos felt marginalized and dismissed. He also began to express feelings that Leo only wanted him for sexual reasons—that Leo was attracted to him because he was "exotic" and "other." Leo, on the other hand, felt very threatened by discussions of culture and privilege. He protested that, as a Jew, he knew what it was to be "other" in the dominant culture.

Interventions included normalizing the cultural differences, underscoring the strengths of the relationship that held the couple together despite the differences, punctuating their existence as a couple no matter how visible or invisible they were, and pushing the couple to give voice to their differing vantage points. Considerable attention had to be paid to supporting Leo in his ability to listen to and absorb Marcos's "story" about the effects of marginalization and disempowerment on his life. Similarly, Leo has needed time to discuss his "story" as a Jewish man without it being dismissed by Marcos. Both men were encouraged to join support groups germane to their cultures. For example, Leo was referred to a social and support program for Jewish gays and lesbians, while Marcos was referred to a similar group for Latinos. They were also encouraged to bring each other to social events run by each of the groups. In addition, an important part of the therapy included work on family of origin issues that were affecting their couple relationship. For example, Leo needed to address the impact on his life of his cut-off from his family, while Marcos had to struggle with the tension between family norms and maintaining his relationship with Leo.

Internal and External Homophobia

Krestan and Bepko (1980) note the central place homophobia occupies in boundary formation and maintenance in lesbian couples. No lesbian couple is immune to its influence, and the way it is managed is a powerful force in shaping the couple's relationship. For example, the authors suggest that homophobia precipitates a "two of us against the world" frame for the lesbian couple's experience. Homophobia is also a key dynamic in male couples. It is not clear yet whether the tendency, for most male couples, is to draw closer together or to distance in response to external or internalized homophobia. We have seen both inclinations in the male couples we know and treat.

Clearly, one way homophobia exerts its influence on the male couple is the stress it imposes. Male couples contend with a broad range of assaults. Antigay violence, real or feared, can limit the couple's ability to be open and to feel safe. The couple relationship is largely unprotected by legal sanctions. Numerous anecdotes exist of gay men who have lost homes, possessions, and privileges upon the death of a partner because of the legally sanctioned rights and power accorded to blood relations over same-sex partners. On a more day-to-day level, gay couples face the denial of couple boundaries afforded to straight couples by employment policies, tax and other laws, employee benefits, and civil rights protections. All of this can create heightened tension and vigilance in a male couple in that they are forced to take a position about their identity as a couple on a regular basis and to deal with the fallout from their visibility in the community.

For example, some gay men may endorse the conventional wisdom that their relationships do not work and fail to protect their relationship. They will not take risks to get closer to partners or to publicly affirm their couplehood. Most men, straight or gay, are raised in a social context that dictates emotional distance between men. Closeness between men suggests the worst possibility—homosexuality. Gay men who have not freed themselves of this script will keep extreme emotional distance in their relationships or vacillate between closeness and distance. Intimacy with another man can provoke a man to feel unmasculine and worthless, whereas distance may render him lonely and depressed. For such men, sexual orientation is experienced as a perpetual double bind, permitting no comfortable solution and causing havoc in their couple relationships.

Clinical Interventions to Aid Boundary Creation and Maintenance

In our practices, we integrate a Bowen family systems model with a sociocultural perspective that addresses race, culture, gender, and class. We also take great pains to underscore individual and couple strengths and competencies and to help couples develop alternative narratives about their lives that are more useful (White & Epston, 1990). In the following section, we delineate those clinical practices that we feel are particularly helpful in boundary creation and maintenance.

Therapeutic Use of Rituals

Societal homophobia, invisibility, and gay men's frequent rejection of family and dominant culture loyalties often serve to deny male couples access to rituals that could help define and affirm their boundaries. As the most glaring example, society denies the male couple the institution of marriage. Without a marriage date, nodal events in the couple's life are obscured.

According to recent theories, rituals serve five different functions in people's lives: relating, changing, healing, believing, and celebrating (Imber-Black & Roberts, 1992). Rituals facilitate people's functioning in these arenas, and without them, personal development can be stunted. Rituals are particularly powerful in the development of couple relationships because they mark boundaries and validate couplehood.

Gay male couples must work on their own and outside the dominant culture to establish definitional rituals. As men, this may be complicated by a lack of experience in creating and recreating rituals because, in our culture, such activities traditionally have been women's domain. Certainly, many gay male couples have developed new and creative rituals, but for others, help in creating rituals is a fundamental therapeutic task.

Many gay couples are choosing to reclaim old rituals and to redesign them to match a gay life more clearly. For example, gay men are marrying or are having union or commitment ceremonies in growing numbers (Imber-Black & Roberts, 1992; Marcus, 1988). In relation to the family of origin, because family holidays can constitute times of exclusion and resentment for gay men, male couples need to create their own holiday rituals. These rituals can serve to heal cut-offs, help members reconnect to their pasts, cement couple togetherness, and point toward a positive future. In our own relationship, we take responsibility for designing major religious holiday rituals in our own home. By including both family and friends in our Christmas dinners and Passover seders, we have accomplished many things. First, each of us prevents the exclusion of the other from family of origin rituals, which had been an issue early in our relationship. Second, the rituals gradually have become more personally relevant, as we have added pieces such as readings and music that are important to us. This helps both to mark us as a unique couple and to bring us closer as we explore what is meaningful to us. In addition, the rituals serve to keep alive our familial and cultural connections. Finally, and perhaps most important, ritual creation helps us clarify our couple boundaries. For example, our intracouple boundaries repeatedly are challenged and clarified as we divide the labor of preparation. By hosting in our home, we are saying to others: "We are a couple, and we welcome you to join us," thereby strengthening the boundaries between us as a couple and the external world. By including both families, we are acknowledging their importance to us and stating that they have a relation to each other (Jews refer to this as *machatenim*). Finally, by bringing our families and our friends together, we make a statement that both are important to us in defining who we are.

Although this ritual-making has worked for us, it will not necessarily work well or may not be important for everyone. Imber-Black and Roberts (1992) emphasize that, for rituals to work, they must be personally relevant.

Systems Coaching

As far as we know, Krestan and Bepko (1980) were the first clinicians to delineate the suitability of a Bowen (1978) coaching approach for same-sex couples. They focused on the lesbian couple, but the approach clearly applies to male couples as well. Because the lives of gay men are complicated by the negative social construction of a gay sexual orientation, and because gay men are likely to encounter considerable homophobic emotional reactivity from the many systems in which they are embedded, special care is needed in navigating their way through the extended family system, the family of creation, the work setting, the gay and lesbian community, the dominant culture, and—no less important—the couple relationship. Thus, a coaching approach seems ideal. The case of Max, which was mentioned earlier, illustrates the application of such an approach.

Max presented for therapy with anxiety and multiple stress-related medical problems. Six months earlier, he had come out to his parents, who were not talking to him. He had maintained a close relationship with his ex-wife, Laura, and had handled the disclosure of his sexuality with minimal conflict but had not yet revealed to her his relationship with his lover, Timothy, explaining that they were just good friends and roommates. As noted earlier, Max and Timothy spent weekends together with Laura, as well as with Max's five- and six-year-old sons, Billy and Sam. Timothy denied having any difficulty with dissembling, although he had recently become depressed, withdrawn, and demanding. Max initially indicated that the family arrangements were working well for everyone. His sons were especially happy about having the attention of three loving adults.

However, as treatment progressed, Max began to realize he was not unequivocally happy. Through genogram work and coaching prescriptions geared to helping him bridge the cut-off with his parents, he began to recognize how much of a good, adaptable, and overly responsible child he had been in his family and what an anxiety-ridden position this created for him. He began to understand that his parents were particularly reactive because their "good son" had ended up being "tainted." With coaching, Max began to reach out to his siblings for support, trying to temper his role as the good, wise, older brother. He talked to his parents and wrote them letters about loving them, needing them, and feeling hurt by their silence, instead of trying to patch over their pain or relieving it. He also began to speak directly to his family about the presence of Timothy in his life.

In time, Max began to recognize his overfunctioning with Laura and how confusing his significant relationships were for him. After considerable discussion and planning in therapy, he eventually told Laura about the exact nature of his relationship with Timothy and sat through her anger without running in to fix things. He and Laura began to talk about negotiating a divorce agreement in order to get on with their lives.

Examination of the Male Gender Role

Given the importance of male gender constructions in the intimate lives of all men, discussion of the influence of this variable on the boundary-creation and boundary-maintenance functions of the male couple becomes a crucial component of treatment. Groans about political correctness may emerge from the couple, and the therapist may have some ambivalence about the application of the political in the clinical context, but this topic is key in helping male couples.

Direct conversations about these issues are often helpful and can move back and forth from the personal to the sociocultural levels of experience. For example, each member may look at the gender narrative he has constructed about intimacy or vulnerability, based on experiences in the family of origin. Genograms are often a helpful map in this tracking process. In addition, the impact of race, class, and culture on the construction of the gender narrative for both the family and the individual couple member is a critical component of the conversation. Within this process, couples often increase their empathic understanding of each other, and the issue of culture becomes more visible and less toxic in discussions of couple functioning. Conversations may also move to the level of the larger cultural context. For example, when male couples are struggling with the issue of power in making boundary decisions, it may be helpful for the couple to look at the issue in terms of larger culture scripts about the expression of power in male functioning.

Helping the couple search for exceptions to traditional gender practices may enhance their couple development. It is helpful at the outset of this process to identify ways that traditional gender scripts constrain role flexibility as well as the couple's relationships with others, including their families of origin. It also may be helpful to construct a supportive context for gender flexibility by asking each member circular questions such as, Who in your life would have accepted your being a different kind of man?

Legal Intervention and Social Activism

Denied the recognition provided by marriage, gay male couples have no legal validation of their boundaries. Marcus (1988) addresses the importance of a "living-together contract" which, when drawn up with a lawyer, can help protect property rights in the event of the dissolution of the relationship or the death of one partner. These documents also, however, serve to mark a relationship. In addition, Marcus stresses the importance of gay couples having legal documents such as durable powers of attorney, wills, and living wills in order to empower the partner in the case of an emergency in which he would normally have no rights or voice. A therapist can facilitate the process by helping a couple deal with the discomfort or the remnants of internalized homophobia that may stand in the way of drawing up such contracts. The very act of a therapist inquiring about a couple's legal vulnerability is therapeutic in its support of the couple's boundaries.

Conclusion

In the homophobic, heterosexist dominant culture in which we live, the gay couple makes a political as well as a relational statement with every public identification as a couple. Sometimes, however, a couple may intentionally self-identify publicly through social activism and protest. These experiences should be seen as acts of courage, for the couple is risking reprisal in order to say, "We are a couple! We love, we live, and we will not be denied or rendered invisible." Such messages can have reverberations in the couple's relationships with family of origin and other systems, such as the workplace. In 1987, when we traveled to the second March on Washington, our parents questioned our wisdom and begged us to stay out of the papers. Five years later, as we were leaving for the third March on Washington, they called to let us know how proud they were of us and to let us know they admired our efforts to dignify our lives separately and together. This was one outcome of a long and ongoing process of establishing our identity as a couple to ourselves and our families.

It is important that family therapists, gay or straight, take a stand for gay and lesbian couples' rights. Therapists have a body of knowledge and experience that needs to be voiced in multiple contexts in order to effect change. We can have a powerful influence in convincing legislators and the population at large—through publications, presentations, and expert witness testimony—that homophobia is destructive to all families, that heterosexism is discriminatory, and that the relationships of gay men and lesbians deserve recognition, acknowledgment, validation and, most importantly, celebration.

We can also have an effect on both the dominant culture and the community of mental health professionals and researchers by undertaking rigorous examination of some of our most cherished truths about families and couples, using large and diverse samples. Some of the assumptions that bear further empirical investigation are mentioned throughout this chapter. And finally, we can have a dramatic effect on the lives of the gay couples we treat by ensuring that our premises are valid and that we offer places of safety, respect, and affirmation in our offices.

References

Almaguer, T., Busto, R., Dixon, K., & Lu, M. (1992). Sleeping with the enemy? Talking about men, race and relationships. *Outlook, 4*(3), 30–38.

Almeida, R., Woods, R., Messineo, T., Font, R. J., & Heer, C. (1994). Violence in the lives of the racially and sexually different: A public and private dilemma. *Journal of Feminist Family Therapy, 5*(34), 99–126.

Bell, A. P., & Weinberg, M. S. (1978). *Homosexualities: A study of diversity among men and women.* New York: Simon & Schuster.

Bell, A. P., Weinberg, M. S., & Hammersmith, S. K. (1981). *Sexual preference: Its development in men and women.* Bloomington: Indiana University Press.

Blasband, D., & Peplau, L. A. (1985). Sexual exclusivity versus openness in gay male couples. *Archives of Sexual Behavior, 14,* 395–412.

Blumstein, P., & Schwartz, P. (1983). *American couples: Money, work and sex.* New York: Morrow.

Bowen, M. (1978). *Family therapy in clinical practice.* Northvale, NJ: Aronson.

Champagne, J. (1993). Seven speculations on queers and class. *Journal of Homosexuality, 26,* 159–174.

Chan, C. S. (1989). Issues of identity development among Asian-American lesbians and gay men. *Journal of Counseling and Development, 68,* 16–20.

Chan, C. S. (1992). What's love got to do with it? Sexual/gender identities. *Division 44 Newsletter, 8*(3), 8–18.

David, D. S., & Brannon, R. (1976). The male sex role: Our culture's blueprint of manhood and what it's done for us lately. In D. S. David & R. Brannon (Eds.), *The forty-nine percent majority: The male sex role* (pp. 1–45). Reading, MA: Addison-Wesley.

Espin, O. (1987). Issues of identity in the psychology of Latina lesbians. In Boston Lesbian Psychologies Collective (Ed.), *Lesbian psychologies: Explorations and challenges* (pp. 35–55). Urbana: University of Illinois Press.

Imber-Black, E., & Roberts, J. (1992). *Rituals for our times: Celebrating, healing, and changing our lives and our relationships.* New York: HarperCollins.

Krestan, J. A., & Bepko, C. S. (1980). The problem of fusion in the lesbian relationship. *Family Process, 19,* 277–289.

Kurdek, L. A., & Schmitt, J. P. (1985–86). Relationship quality of gay men in closed or open relationships. *Journal of Homosexuality, 12,* 85–99.

Kurdek, L. A., & Schmitt, J. P. (1986). Relationship quality of partners in heterosexual married, heterosexual cohabiting, and gay and lesbian relationships. *Journal of Personality and Social Psychology, 51,* 711–720.

Laird, J. (1993). Lesbian and gay families. In F. Walsh (Ed.), *Normal family processes* (2nd ed., pp. 282–328). New York: Guilford Press.

Marcus, E. (1988). *The male couple's guide to living together: What gay men should know about living together and coping in a straight world.* New York: HarperCollins.

McWhirter, D. P., & Mattison, A. M. (1984). *The male couple: How relationships develop.* Upper Saddle River, NJ: Prentice Hall.

Mencher, J. (1990). *Intimacy in lesbian relationships: A critical examination of fusion.* Works in Progress No. 42. Wellesley, MA: Wellesley College, Stone Center for Developmental Services and Studies.

Meth, R. L., & Pasick, R. S. (1990). *Men in therapy: The challenge of change.* New York: Guilford Press.

Minuchin, S. (1974). *Families and family therapy.* Cambridge, MA: Harvard University Press.

Morales, E. (1990). Ethnic minority gays and lesbians. In F. W. Bozett & M. B. Sussman (Eds.), *Homosexuality and family relations* (pp. 217–239). Binghamton, NY: Harrington Park Press.

Peplau, L. A., & Cochran, S. (1981). Value orientations in the intimate relationships of gay men. *Journal of Homosexuality, 6,* 1–19.

Socarides, C. W. (1978). *Homosexuality.* Northvale, NJ: Aronson.

Tremble, B., Schneider, M., & Appathurai, C. (1989). Growing up gay or lesbian in a multicultural context. *Journal of Homosexuality, 17,* 253–267.

Weingarten, K. (1991). The discourses of intimacy: Adding a social constructionist and feminist view. *Family Process, 30,* 285–305.

Weston, K. (1991). *Families we choose: Lesbians, gays, kinship.* New York: Columbia University Press.

White, M., & Epston, D. (1990). *Narrative means to therapeutic ends.* New York: Norton.

CHAPTER TEN

AFRICAN AMERICAN LESBIANS

Issues in Couples Therapy

Beverly Greene and Nancy Boyd-Franklin

African Americans as a group are marginalized in the United States. This marginalization is even more stark for African American lesbians. Until recently, ideas pertaining to African Americans and lesbians have been treated as mere footnotes in the annals of family therapy. African American lesbians have been like the footnote to a footnote that never appeared. The position of African American lesbians in the mainstream family therapy literature has been one of complete invisibility.

In this chapter, we open the doors of family therapy to the world of African American lesbians' relationships. We begin with an exploration of the psychohistorical context of African American lesbians' lives. Then, families of origin, couple relationships, and couples therapy—with both African American and interracial lesbian couples—will be discussed.

African American Lesbians and the Mental Health Professions

The vast majority of clinical and empirical research on lesbians has focused overwhelmingly on White, middle-class respondents (Amaro, 1978; Chan, 1989, 1992; Garnets & Kimmel, 1991; Greene, 1994a, 1994b, 1996; Gock, 1992; Mays & Cochran, 1988; Mays, Cochran, & Rhue, 1993; Morales, 1989; Roberts, 1981;

Tremble, Schneider, & Appathurai, 1989; Wooden, Kawasaki, & Mayeda, 1983). To the extent that research has been conducted with African American women at all, this scant literature rarely acknowledges a diversity of sexual orientations, which leaves unexplored the complex interactions between sexual orientation and ethnic and gender-identity development. Research on African American women rarely states that its generalizability is limited to heterosexual African American women, any more than typical research on lesbians stresses its limited applicability to lesbians who are White.

Such narrow clinical and research perspectives omit the realistic psychosocial tasks and stressors that are a component of lesbian identity formation for African American women. They also ignore an exploration of how the vicissitudes of racism, sexism, homophobia, and gender socialization affect the couple relationships of African American lesbians. Practitioners are left with a limited understanding of the diversity among African American women and within lesbians as a group, which impairs professional competence to address the clinical needs of African American lesbians in culturally sensitive and literate ways.

The reports by Bell and Weinberg (1978), Bass-Hass (1968), Croom (1993), Mays and Cochran (1988), and Mays, Cochran, and Rhue (1993) are among the few published empirical studies that include all or significant numbers of African American lesbian respondents. Among their findings, African American lesbians tended to have more contact with men and heterosexual peers than their White counterparts, suggesting that they are more involved with the heterosexual social community and its norms regarding gender roles and homosexuality. Compared to their White counterparts, *African American lesbians were more likely to have children, maintain close relationships with their families, and depend more on family members or other African American lesbians for support.* These results attest to the prominence of ongoing family of origin relationships in the lives of adult African American lesbians.

Also in contrast to White lesbians, African American lesbians reported greater tension and loneliness. However, they were less likely to seek professional help. This reluctance to come for therapy may leave them more vulnerable to negative psychological outcomes by the time they seek treatment (Greene, 1994a, 1994c).

Triple Jeopardy: Racism, Sexism, Homophobia

African American lesbians live in triple jeopardy, that is, they are vulnerable to the social discrimination and internalization of all the negative stereotypes traditionally aimed at African Americans, women, and lesbians. Living in triple jeopardy has implications for African American lesbians' family, couple, and therapy relationships, which are embedded in larger sociocultural systems that have traditions of prejudice. For example, the underpinnings of traditional approaches to mental health are replete with androcentric, heterocentric, and ethnocentric biases that often reinforce the triple discrimination that lesbians of color face (Garnets & Kimmel, 1991; Glassgold, 1992; Greene, 1994a, 1994c).

A therapist's understanding of what it means to be an African American lesbian requires careful examination of race, gender, and sexual orientation issues at multiple systems levels including (1) *American Society:* racism, sexism, and homophobia in the society as a whole; (2) *African American Culture:* racial identity, gender roles, and homophobia within the African American community; (3) *Couples/Families:* the interactions among partners' and family members' racial identities, gender-role attitudes, and attitudes toward lesbianism; and (4) *Individuals:* the dynamic interactions within the individual of racial, gender, and sexual orientation components of identity. Most important is to grasp how ethnosexual myths, superimposed by the larger society, have affected African American cultural views of women and lesbianism which, in turn, have affected the particular family relationships of African American lesbians. Thus before we examine therapy, the psychohistorical context of African American lesbians' lives must be understood.

Gender Roles and Ethnosexual Myths

From a historical perspective, African Americans are a diverse group, with cultural origins primarily in the tribes of West Africa, who were brought to the United States as slaves. The tribal legacy includes strong family ties encompassing nuclear and extended family members in complex networks of mutual obligation and support (Boyd-Franklin, 1989; Greene, 1986, 1994a, 1994c, 1996; Icard, 1986). Traditional African culture involves more flexible gender roles than European and other ethnic groups, due in part to values stressing interdependence and a greater egalitarianism in precolonial Africa.

In African American culture, flexible family structures and lack of rigid gender-role stratification were also responses to racism in the United States. Lack of employment opportunities made it difficult for African American men to conform to the Western ideal of male-as-provider and required women to work full-time outside the home. Notwithstanding this greater gender-role flexibility in African American culture, sexism continues to exist in African American communities (Greene, 1994a, 1994c).

In addition, historically oppressed groups that have faced racist genocidal practices, specifically African Americans and Native Americans, have accorded reproductive sexuality greater importance than other groups in order to continue their presence in the world. Thus African Americans sometimes look upon nonreproductive sexual practices as another threat to group survival, a view Kanuha (1990) terms "fears of extinction" (p. 176). Although a lesbian sexual orientation does not preclude having children, particularly among lesbians of color, the internalization of this view may make it harder for a lesbian of color and her family to accept affirmatively her sexual orientation.

Because they arrived in America as objects of the United States slave trade, African American women were considered to be property, and forced sexual relationships with African males and White slavemasters were the norm. Afro-Caribbean women, who are not of Latin descent, often possess cultural values and practices reflective of the colonization of their islands, particularly by Great Britain or France. The sexual objectification of African Americans during slavery was reinforced by the public images propagated about this population, feeding stereotypes of sexual promiscuity and moral looseness (Clarke, 1983; Collins, 1990; Greene, 1986, 1990a, 1990b, 1990c; Icard, 1986; Loiacano, 1989). Such ethnosexual myths are relevant in terms of self-image and how the larger family and African American community view gay or lesbian members.

It is useful to explore the relationship of such ethnosexual beliefs to an African American's attitudes about lesbian sexual orientation. These myths, perpetrated by the dominant culture, often represent a complex combination of racial and sexual stereotypes designed to objectify women of color, isolate them from their idealized White counterparts, and promote their sexual exploitation and control (Collins, 1990; Greene, 1994a, 1994c; hooks, 1981). The symbolism of these racial and sexual stereotypes and their interactions with other stereotypes held about lesbians can be central areas of clinical inquiry in family therapy.

Ethnosexual stereotypes about African American women have their roots in images created by White society. African American and Caribbean women clearly did not fit the traditional stereotypes of women as fragile, weak, and dependent, as they were never allowed to be this way. The "Mammy" figure is the historical antecedent to the stereotype of African American women as assertive, domineering, and strong. Such traits were applauded in a woman as long as those qualities were put to the caregiving service of her master and mistress.

Popular images of African American women as castrating were created in the interest of maintaining the social power hierarchy in which African American men and women were subordinate to Whites and women were subordinate to men. These images of the so-called "castrating woman" were used to stigmatize any woman who wanted to work outside the home or cross the gender-role stereotypes of a patriarchal culture (hooks, 1981). Today's stereotypes are a product of those myths and depict African American women as not sufficiently subordinate to African American men, inherently sexually promiscuous, morally loose, assertive, matriarchal, and as castrating or masculinized females when compared to their

White counterparts (Christian, 1985; Clarke, 1983; Collins, 1990; Greene, 1986, 1990b, 1990c, 1994a, 1994c; hooks, 1981; Icard, 1986; Silvera, 1991). Stereotypes of lesbians as masculinized females coincide with racial stereotypes of African American and Afro-Caribbean women. Both are depicted as defective females who want to be or act like men and are sexually promiscuous.

Institutional racism plays a prominent role in the development of myths and distortions regarding the sexuality of African American and Afro-Caribbean lesbians. Males in the culture are encouraged to believe that strong women, rather than racist institutions, are responsible for their oppression. Racism, sexism, and heterosexism combine to cast the onus upon African American women for family problems in the African American population. The ideas that African American women are at fault for the problems of African American families and men's oppression imply that the remedy for liberating people of African descent is to reinforce male dominance and female subordination.

Many African American and Afro-Caribbean women, including lesbians, have internalized these myths about strong, independent women, which compromises their ability to obtain support from the larger African American and Caribbean communities (Collins, 1990; Greene, 1994a, 1994c). Thus the legacy of gendered racism plays a role in the response of many African Americans to lesbians in their families or as visible members of their communities. African American men and women who have internalized the racism and sexism inherent in the patriarchal values of Western culture may scapegoat any strong, independent woman. Lesbians are easy targets for such scapegoating.

Thus false stereotypes include the notions that lesbians typically are: wishing to be men; mannish in appearance (Taylor, 1983); unattractive or less attractive than heterosexual women (Dew, 1985); less extroverted (Kite, 1994); unable to get a man; victims of traumatic relationships with men that presumably turned them against men; or defective females (Christian, 1985; Collins, 1990; Greene, 1994a, 1994c; Kite, 1994). In African American communities, the assumption that sexual attraction to men is intrinsic to being a normal woman often leads to a range of equally inaccurate conclusions, such as the notion that reproductive sexuality is the only normal and morally correct form of sexual expression (Garnets & Kimmel, 1991; Glassgold, 1992), or the myth that there is a direct relationship between sexual orientation and conformity to traditional gender roles within the culture (Kite & Deaux, 1987; Newman, 1989; Whitley, 1987).

The latter idea presumes that women who do not conform to traditional gender-role stereotypes must be lesbian, whereas women who do conform must be heterosexual. These assumptions are used to threaten women with the stigma of being labeled "lesbian" if they do not adhere to traditional gender-role stereotypes about males being dominant and females being submissive (Collins, 1990;

Gomez & Smith, 1990; Smith, 1982). This pressure to conform occurs in African American communities despite their history and traditions of greater flexibility for women in family decision making and work roles.

Being labeled a lesbian can prevent women, whether they are lesbian or not, from seeking nontraditional roles or engaging in nontraditional behaviors. Some scholars who are women of color may feel that simply writing about or acknowledging lesbian themes will raise questions about their own sexual orientation and that they will be viewed negatively as a result (Clarke, 1991). Such an atmosphere leads many scholars to refrain from focusing on lesbian themes, further contributing to the invisibility of African American lesbians. In a society wherein male dominance and female subordination have been viewed as normative, the fears of being labeled lesbian, with its negative consequences, may serve to further perpetuate patriarchy.

Homophobia

It is important to explore how sexuality and gender interrelate with culture. Espin (1984) suggests that in most cultures, a *range* of sexual behaviors is tolerated. The clinician needs to determine where the client's behavior fits within the spectrum for her particular culture (Espin, 1984). In exploring the range of sexuality tolerated by the woman's culture, it is helpful to know whether *formally* forbidden practices are tolerated, as long as they are not discussed or labeled. As with their ethnic-majority counterparts, the strength of African American family ties often mitigates against outright rejection of gay and lesbian family members.

Nevertheless, the African American community is viewed by gay and lesbian members as extremely homophobic, generating the pressure to remain closeted (Clarke, 1983; Croom, 1993; Gomez & Smith, 1990; Greene, 1990c, 1994a, 1994c, 1996; Icard, 1986; Loiacano, 1989; Mays & Cochran, 1988; Poussaint, 1990; Smith, 1982). Homophobia among African Americans and Afro-Caribbeans is multiply determined. These cultures often have a strong religious and spiritual orientation. For adherents to Western Christianity, selective interpretations of Biblical scripture may be used to reinforce homophobic attitudes (Claybourne, 1978; Greene, 1994a, 1994c, 1996; Icard, 1986; Moses & Hawkins, 1982). Silvera (1991) writes that when her grandmother discovered that she was a lesbian, she took out her Bible and explained: "This was a 'ting only people of mixed blood was involved in" (p. 16). Certain non-Christian African American sects view homosexuality as a decadent Western practice.

Clarke (1983), Silvera (1991), and Smith (1982) cite heterosexual privilege as another factor in the homophobia of African American and Afro-Caribbean women. Because of sexism in both dominant and African American cultures and racism in the dominant culture, *African American women may find heterosexuality the only privileged status they can possess* (Greene, 1994a, 1994c). As such, they may be reluctant to jeopardize the privileges associated with this status by explicitly coming out.

Internalized racism is another determinant of homophobia among African Americans and Afro-Caribbeans. For those who have internalized the negative stereotypes about African Americans constructed by the dominant culture, sexual behavior outside societal norms may be viewed as a negative reflection on all African Americans (Greene, 1996; Poussaint, 1990). Lesbianism may be experienced as a particular embarrassment to African Americans who most strongly identify with the dominant culture. Hence, there may be an exaggerated desire among some African Americans to model normalcy to the dominant culture and a related antipathy toward lesbians and gay men (Clarke, 1983; Monteflores, 1986; Gomez, 1983; Greene, 1986, 1994a, 1994c, 1996; Wyatt, Strayer, & Lobitz, 1976).

Indeed, the only colloquial names for lesbians in the African American community—"funny women" or "bulldagger women"—are derogatory (Jeffries, 1992, p. 44; Omosupe, 1991). Silvera (1991) writes of her childhood in Jamaica:

> The words used to describe many of these women would be "Man royal" and/or "Sodomite." Dread words. So dread that women dare not use these words to name themselves. The act of loving someone from the same sex was sinful, abnormal—something to hide. (pp. 15–16)

She explains that the word *sodomite,* derived from the Old Testament, is used in Jamaica to brand any strong, independent woman: "Now all you have to do is not respond to a man's call to you and dem call you sodomite or lesbian" (p. 17).

Clarke (1983) and Jeffries (1992) observe that there was a greater tolerance for gay men and lesbians in some poor African American communities in the 1940s through 1950s, which Clarke explains as "seizing the opportunity to spite the white man," and Jeffries attributes to the empathy African Americans felt, as oppressed people, toward members of another oppressed group. However, a strong component of this tolerance may have been the relative invisibility of homosexuals within the African American community and the dominant culture. The recent heightened visibility of lesbians may challenge the denial that permitted this tolerance in earlier times. Lesbians may not be tolerated as easily in the African American community to the extent that they no longer are viewed as helpless and silent victims of oppression who exist only in small numbers.

Despite the homophobia in the African American community, African American lesbians claim a strong attachment to their cultural heritage and cite their identity as African Americans as *primary,* compared to their identity as lesbians (Acosta, 1979; Croom, 1993; Mays et al., 1993). Therefore, they often experience a sense of conflicting loyalties between the African American community and the mainstream lesbian community. Most are unwilling to jeopardize their ties to the African American community, despite realistic concerns about rejection or ridicule if they openly disclose their lesbian sexual orientation (Dyne, 1980; Greene, 1990a, 1990c, 1994a, 1994c, 1996; Icard, 1986; Mays & Cochran, 1988; Mays et al., 1993). Another factor adding to the sense of conflicting loyalties is the racial discrimination African American lesbians face in the broader, predominantly White, lesbian community, including discrimination in admission to lesbian bars, employment, and advertising (Greene, 1994a, 1994c, 1996; Gutierrez & Dworkin, 1992; Mays & Cochran, 1988).

In analyzing the history of discrimination of an ethnic group, the group members' own understandings of their oppression and coping strategies must be incorporated. Accepting the dominant culture's perspectives on such groups may only reinforce ethnocentric, heterocentric, and androcentric biases. Thus rather than making assumptions, it is important to explore with each couple in therapy how the partners perceive the constraints they and their family members are under from the larger culture and from their specific communities and neighborhoods.

Family of Origin

In therapy with African American, lesbian clients, many questions about the family of origin need to be explored, especially (1) How much do parents or other family of origin members continue to control or influence adult children and grandchildren? and (2) How important is the extended family as a source of economic, emotional, and practical support (Mays & Cochran, 1988)? Other factors to be explored include (1) the degree to which procreation and continuation of the family line are valued; (2) closeness of ties to the ethnic community; (3) the degree of acculturation or assimilation of the client and whether it is significantly different from that of other family members; (4) the family's religious beliefs; and (5) the oppression the family group has faced and continues to face within the dominant culture.

Historically, the African American family has functioned as a refuge to protect group members from the racism of the dominant culture. Villarosa (interviewed in Brownworth, 1993) observes that the importance of African American family and community as a survival tool makes the coming-out process for African American lesbians much different from that of their White counterparts:

It is harder for us to consider being rejected by our families. . . . All we have is our families, our community. When the whole world is racist and against you, your family and your community are the only people who accept you and love you even though you are black. So you don't know what will happen if you lose them . . . and many black lesbians (and gay men) are afraid that's what will happen. (p. 18)

Because of the strength of family ties, there is a reluctance to expel a lesbian from the family despite an undisputed rejection of a lesbian sexual orientation. This may result from varying levels of tolerance for nonconformity, denial of the person's sexual orientation, or even culturally distinct ways of conveying negative attitudes about a family member's sexual orientation. In African American families, lesbians are not "disowned," as Villarosa observes, because of the importance of family members to one another; rather, they "keep you around to talk you out of it" (Brownworth, 1993, p. 18).

The clinician should not interpret apparent tolerance as approval (Acosta, 1979), as the family's tolerance is usually contingent on a lesbian's silence. Serious conflicts *may* occur once a family member openly discloses, labels herself, or discusses being a lesbian. For example, a lesbian family member's lover may have been treated well until the relationship is labeled openly as "lesbian" or until the lesbian family member seeks her family's support or direct acknowledgment of her lesbian sexual orientation, relationship, or partner. Even when family members are accepting and supportive, the broader African American or Caribbean community may not be.

Couples Issues and Therapy

There is great diversity among couples within the African American lesbian community, which we will illustrate with clinical case examples. It is crucial for the reader to first understand that the race or ethnicity of the partner of an African American lesbian can greatly affect the dynamics of the relationship, as well as its degree of visibility and therefore how it is perceived and received by the African American family and community.

Many African American lesbians' relationships are largely unsupported outside the lesbian community. These women encounter unique challenges in relationships, given that their partners have the same gender socialization in a culture that conspicuously devalues their person and devalues their relationships on many levels. Moreover, the culture provides few open, healthy models of such relationships. Those in lesbian relationships may find tacit support for their relationship within the African

American community; however, this support is often marked by a collusion of silence, ambivalence, and denial. African American lesbians who have received family support for their struggles with racism, and perhaps sexism, cannot presume that this support will extend to their romantic relationships or that their families will empathize with their distress if the relationship is troubled. This lack of understanding is compounded upon seeking professional assistance, only to find few, if any, therapists of color who have training in addressing issues in lesbian relationships (Greene, 1994a, 1994b, 1994c).

Interracial Lesbian Couples

Compared with White lesbians, African American lesbians and lesbians of color in general have a higher proportion of relationships with women who are not members of their same ethnic group (Croom, 1993; Greene, 1995; Mays & Cochran, 1988; Tafoya & Rowell, 1988). This has been attributed in part to the larger numbers of White lesbians in the United States (Tafoya & Rowell, 1988). While heterosexual interracial relationships often lack the support of each member's family and community, lesbian interracial relationships face even greater challenges to a situation already fraught with difficulty.

An interracial lesbian couple may be more publicly visible and thus more readily identifiable as a couple than two women of the same ethnic group, which may exacerbate homophobic reactions from the outside world. In addition, the White partner may be forced to experience the realities of racism for the first time in her life. Clunis and Green (1988) observe that racism does not disappear from relationships because women have "worked on" the issue. Because racism is an ever-present reality and stressor for lesbians of color, they often wear a protective psychological armor (Sears, 1987) and usually have developed a variety of coping strategies using it. A White partner who has never confronted racism may be unprepared to deal with it (Clunis & Green, 1988). For example, a White partner may be oblivious to slights that are racist in origin and experience her partner's anger as inappropriate; she may overreact and criticize her partner for complacency; or she may even take on the protective role of "rescuer," which her partner may find presumptuous, unwanted, unneeded, and even patronizing (Greene, 1994a, 1994c).

A White partner may also feel guilty about racism. Unable to distinguish between her personal behavior in the relationship and the racism in the outside world, a White partner may attempt to compensate her African American partner for the racism the partner faces in the world—a task the White partner cannot do successfully and that will ultimately leave her feeling angry and frustrated.

Neither partner in such relationships should rely on the White person's politics or intentions as a realistic predictor that she is free of racism (Clunis & Green, 1988; Garcia, Kennedy, Pearlman, & Perez, 1987). Also, the African American lesbian partner may need to be alert to her own jealousy or resentment of her lover's privileged status in the dominant culture and in the lesbian community. Both partners may be perceived by others as lacking loyalty to their own ethnic or racial group and may even feel ashamed of their involvement with a person of a different group (Clunis & Green, 1988; Falco, 1991; Greene, 1994c, 1995, 1996). This both complicates the resolution of issues within the relationship and intensifies the complex web of loyalties and estrangements for lesbian women of color.

While interracial issues and cultural differences offer realistic challenges to lesbian relationships, they are not the source of every problem within them. However, couples sometimes overinterpret these highly visible differences as causal explanations for their problems. Attributing the source of difficulties to racial differences may allow the couple to avoid looking at more complex, often painful personal issues in their relationship (Greene, 1994c, 1995). Therapists should be aware that although racial differences are often the cause of significant difficulties, other problems arising out of conflicts over intimacy, internalized homophobia, or character issues and symptoms may be "racialized," that is, experienced as if they are about the couple's racial or ethnic differences.

Choices of partners and feelings about those choices may, but do not automatically, reflect an individual's personal conflicts about racial and ethnic identity. Such conflicts may be enacted by African American lesbian women who choose or are attracted to White women exclusively or who devalue African American or lesbians of color, viewing them as unsuitable partners. African American lesbians who experience themselves as racially or culturally deficient or ambiguous may seek a partner from their own ethnic group to compensate for their perceived deficiency or demonstrate their cultural loyalty. An African American lesbian in an interracial relationship with a non–African American lesbian of color may tend to presume a greater level of similarity of experiences or worldviews than is realistically warranted. While their common oppression as women of color and as lesbians may be similar and important in the early development of their relationship, their views on their respective roles in a relationship, maintaining a household, and the role of other family members in their lives may be very different (Greene, 1994c, 1995).

African American lesbians may be appropriately sensitive to what Sears (personal communication, 1992) refers to as "pony stealing" and to what Clunis and Green (1988, p. 140) describe as "ethnic chasing." These terms are used to describe White women who seek out lesbians of color as partners to assuage their own guilt about being White, their lack of a strong ethnic identity, or as proof of their liberal attitudes. In addition, the belief in ethnosexual stereotypes of African

American lesbians as less sexually inhibited than their White counterparts may serve to motivate this behavior (Greene, 1994c). An ethnic chaser may seek, usually unconsciously, to gain from an African American lesbian whatever they perceive to be lacking in themselves. This attempt at self-repair is doomed to fail, and the White partner may respond by feeling angry, resentful, and somehow betrayed by her partner. In treatment, it is helpful to clarify such women's expectations about being in *any* relationship. Beyond this general assessment, the kinds of assumptions held about ethnic or White women within an intimate relationship should be explored (Greene, 1994a, 1994c).

Exclusive choices in this realm may also reflect a woman's tendency to idealize people who are like her and devalue those who are not, or vice versa. When this is the case, the reality often does not live up to the fantasy, resulting in disappointment and self-denigration. It is important to remember that such decisions and preferences have many different determinants and that these are often made outside her conscious awareness.

A therapist should not presume that participation in an interracial lesbian relationship is an expression of cultural or racial self-hate in the African American lesbian. Similarly, the therapist cannot accurately presume that her presence in a relationship with another African American woman is anchored in either loyalty or respect for that culture. The aforementioned problematic premises may not be present at all. Therapists simply need to be aware of a wide range of clinical possibilities and be prepared to explore them accordingly.

A case example of an interracial lesbian relationship is presented below, followed by discussion of the therapeutic issues involved.

CASE 1: INTERRACIAL COUPLE

JoAnn is a thirty-eight-year-old White lesbian from a Midwestern Presbyterian background who has lived for the last five years in the urban Northeast. At the age of twenty, she came out to her parents during a visit home from college. Both rejected and essentially disowned her. She has had no meaningful contact with them for the past ten years or with her only sibling, an older sister who is married and has two children. Her partner, Marion, whom she met in graduate school, is a thirty-five-year-old African American lesbian who is part of a large, enmeshed African American extended family, most of whom live in the same urban Northeastern city in which she was born and raised and currently resides.

Marion has never told any member of her family of her sexual orientation but assumes that they know. The couple has entered treatment because of the exclusion JoAnn experiences from Marion's intense involvement with her family. It became apparent as therapy progressed that there was not only a sense of lack of family in JoAnn's life but an absence of ethnic identity as well. JoAnn used the term *vanilla* when asked to describe her ethnic identity, as this word clearly evoked the White homogeneity of her Midwestern upbringing.

Marion grew up as the oldest and parental child of four siblings in a large, extremely close African American extended family. She has a very intense relationship with her maternal grandmother, who is unambivalently nurturing. Her relationship with her mother, while intense, can be both loving and painfully critical. Her parents divorced after a brief marriage, and Marion has had no contact with her father since early childhood.

In the first session, the partners explained that they had been a couple for four years, although they lived in separate apartments. The discussion of moving in together precipitated a crisis in the relationship. In subsequent sessions, the therapist helped both members of the couple to express their conflicts and concerns about the move and the escalation of their involvement.

For JoAnn, the most painful issue is her perception of Marion's exclusion of her from her "other life." Marion sees, interacts with, or speaks by telephone to members of her extended family several times a week; JoAnn has only been included in family gatherings on two occasions. As JoAnn angrily describes this experience of being left out, Marion for the first time in their relationship begins to explain her fears about her family's response to disclosure of her sexual orientation.

The therapist explored Marion's assumption that some members knew she was a lesbian, despite the fact that she has never actually told anyone. The therapist also explored Marion's fears about disclosure. Marion's response, which is not unusual, was that she anticipated total rejection from her family. The therapist helped Marion construct a genogram and inquired about the responses of specific family members. During this process, Marion expressed her desire to stop leading a double life. The therapist then explored whether or not JoAnn was willing to support Marion in what might be a slow and difficult process of disclosure. JoAnn agreed. The couple decided it would be easier for JoAnn to enter the family system by attending holiday celebrations. Over a period of the next few months, Marion included JoAnn at Thanksgiving dinner, the exchange of presents on Christmas morning, and finally and most significantly, Mother's Day. The couple discussed each occasion with the therapist and the feelings that were aroused. In the final phases of therapy, the therapist helped Marion decide who would be the safest members of her family to come out to. It was important to include JoAnn in supporting Marion's process.

Marion identified her grandmother, whom she felt would love her no matter what, and her next oldest sister, whom she described as "pretty hip." The grandmother's response, "Honey, I've known for some time," was particularly gratifying. Disclosure was more difficult with her sister, Velma, who was very concerned about their mother's reaction and thus was less supportive than Marion had anticipated. In addition, Velma's concerns emphasized the interracial aspect of the relationship by characterizing JoAnn as "that White woman who made you this way." Marion was unprepared for this reaction, which created a crisis in the couple relationship.

Marion withdrew somewhat from JoAnn and became more silent in treatment sessions, while JoAnn became increasingly angry. The therapist apologized to both for not raising the possibility of this response sooner and explored the concept of ambivalence. The therapist also noted the importance of assisting the couple in identifying possible allies within the family before disclosing to family members who are less likely to be allies. The therapist had to work with the couple on giving up their fantasy of the happy ending outcome in which everyone is satisfied, instead emphasizing the importance of JoAnn and Marion nurturing their own relationship, particularly on developing gay-affirmative networks of friends and ultimately developing a family of choice. Marion expressed her preference that this be extended to include lesbians of color, because their current circle of friends consisted primarily of White lesbians.

Over the next year, Marion continued the process of gradual disclosure to specific members of her extended family, and JoAnn continued to attend an increasing number of family gatherings. Finally, at Christmastime, Marion came out to her mother. As anticipated in the therapeutic role play, her mother was initially rejecting and used her fundamentalist religious beliefs to tell Marion that homosexuality in their religion was a sin. She chastised Marion for not fulfilling her role as a Black woman by having children. As Velma had done, Marion's mother disparaged the interracial aspect of Marion's relationship by referring to JoAnn as "that White woman." "She put you up to this," Marion's mother said. "She is coming between you and your family and your people."

Although Marion was hurt and angry during and after this discussion, the therapeutic rehearsal had precluded the emotional devastation that may have otherwise resulted. Initially, Marion's mother banned both JoAnn and Marion from family gatherings. The therapist offered to meet with Marion and her family during this period, but the family rejected the therapist's suggestion. Marion's mother relented somewhat and allowed Marion to come to her family's home alone. Many months later, she took the chance of bringing JoAnn again.

Approximately one year later, Marion and JoAnn moved in together, having strengthened their relationship by the therapeutic process. Marion remained engaged with her extended family; JoAnn participated on certain occasions. They had learned as a couple how to anticipate some of the responses they would receive and how to compromise on their fantasy of perfect acceptance. Marion was out to all of her significant family members, and JoAnn was included in important family gatherings, albeit grudgingly, and the issue of their lesbian relationship was never discussed openly in Marion's family, despite a great deal of therapeutic work and discussion of this issue.

It is not unusual for a member of a couple who is essentially cut off from her own family to be attracted to a partner who is intensely involved with her own family of origin. This can be problematic in the couple relationship in that it often conceals an unexpressed fantasy of being included in the partner's close involvement with her family. When this fantasy is not realized, feelings of exclusion and rejection can result. The exclusion by the partner's family reactivated preexisting feelings of loss, abandonment, envy, and jealousy in JoAnn.

When discussing disclosure issues, it is important that therapists explore the responses of specific individuals and not accept the expectation of blanket rejection or acceptance from everyone in the client's family. Often family members in large African American extended families are overwhelmed by the prospect of coming out to the whole family all at once.

It is important for the therapist to anticipate possible negative reactions to disclosure, especially in interracial lesbian relationships in which the other partner's race may become a more comfortable focus of the anger in the family. Therapists also should be aware that, despite their best efforts, the outcome may not be as ideal for all parties as they might wish. As this case illustrates, although the couple grew closer and Marion was out to all of her family members, her family still avoided open discussion of the lesbian relationship.

An educational strategy is important here. Both members of the couple need to be warned not to overreact to the initial response of family members, which may be negative. The person who is coming out is usually at a very different developmental stage of accepting lesbianism than is the person to whom they come out. Their acceptance of their own lesbian orientation has taken time and did not take place overnight. An affirmative understanding or acceptance will not take place immediately for the family member either. Its absence at this juncture does not mean that it can never take place but that it may require time to develop. Furthermore, all of this may be compounded if the partner is White. The therapist must assist the couple in anticipating best and worst scenarios. At the end of each scenario they should be helped to problem solve about different outcomes. Both members of the couple will require assistance in learning how to be supportive of each other during this difficult period.

African American Lesbian Couples

Because of the extended nature of African American families, strong friendship ties between two African American adult women are very common. There is a culturally defined role within the African American community for the nonrelated adult girlfriend who has an often very intense nonsexual, spiritual, and emotionally connected relationship with an African American woman friend and her family. This is reflected in the greetings "girlfriend" or "sister," which acknowledge and confer kinshiplike status on a close adult female friend who is not blood-related but is experienced as intensely as "family." These women are often informally adopted by the family and are referred to by children and younger family members with terms such as *aunt, play aunt, play mama,* and *sister.* Sometimes there is a formal religious aspect to this relationship when this person is a godparent to a child in the family. Given the existence of this role in African American culture, the importance accorded to fictive kin, and because of the proclivity for African American families to deny the existence of lesbian relationships within their midst, it can be easy for African American families to avoid acknowledging the lesbian nature of a relationship between two adult women.

African American lesbian couples can sometimes collude in this denial by keeping their sexual orientation a secret. Others may not keep the information a secret but still never fully come out to their family members. Other couples may come out to their families without the families' dealing with the issue of the lesbian relationship and lifestyle but, rather, pretending that the lesbian relationship does not exist and accepting the lover in the culturally accepted role of "girlfriend" or "sister." Some African American families have evolved to the point that a lesbian couple is accepted and their relationship acknowledged by the extended family. It is important for clinicians to keep in mind the tremendous diversity of reactions. Different adaptations may exist among the various family members.

This diversity can also extend to the degree of involvement or participation that the lesbian couple has in the Black community and in the community's response as well. African American lesbian women often have children in their relationships. Because of the tradition of "multiple mothering" and grandmother involvement, it is likely that women in the extended family have been more involved in child rearing than their White counterparts (Boyd-Franklin, 1989; Greene, 1990b, 1994c).

Sometimes the question of who is raising the child or who is the ultimate authority in the child's life can be an issue or a problem in African American families. This is further complicated in the context of a lesbian family in which the generational boundaries are unclear. There are, for example, a number of dilemmas for the lesbian couple who are raising children within an extended family context (many of which are also common to heterosexual relationships). Therapists often view lesbian couples and families through the eyes of the couple. When children are involved, it is easy to feel as if one is treating only a "nuclear" lesbian family. In many African American couples, this assumption is often incorrect. The following case, involving two African American women who are raising a child with extended family involvement, illustrates the therapeutic importance of a multisystems, intergenerational view.

CASE 2: AFRICAN AMERICAN COUPLE

Kadija, a twenty-nine-year-old African American lesbian woman, and Aisha, her thirty-five-year-old African American lover of seven years, presented for couples and family therapy. They were raising Kadija's twelve-year-old son, Jamal, who was acting out at home and in school. They reported that they were intensely involved in each other's extended families. Within the last two years, they had been experiencing more conflict in their relationship. Both women dated the beginning of that conflict to their move from a separate apartment in Kadija's mother's house to a place of their own. Prior to the move, Kadija's mother had been Jamal's primary caretaker, as Kadija had been seventeen at the time of his birth.

Aisha, who had been a friend of the family before becoming Kadija's lover, was ambivalently accepted by both Kadija's mother and Jamal. While their lesbian relationship was never openly discussed, Kadija reported that she had come out to her mother and that her family knew about her involvement with Aisha. It was striking, however, that the couple reported that Jamal did not know the true nature of their relationship. As treatment progressed, it became apparent that prior to the move, Kadija's mother had served as a buffer between the couple and Jamal. Once the move occurred, they were unprepared for the full responsibility for raising a preadolescent child.

The therapist explored their denial of Jamal's knowledge of the true nature of their lesbian relationship. In a session alone with Jamal, the therapist discovered that Jamal was well aware of his mother's relationship with Aisha, and he resented it—first, because he thought they were lying to him and second, because he was being teased by his friends. Finally, it became clear that Jamal had a very close relationship with his grandmother and had discussed his mother's lesbian relationship with her. Ironically, they both participated in the ruse of the denial. In addition, Jamal had been able to camouflage his mother's lesbian relationship from his peers as long as they all lived in his grandmother's house. The move had, in his words, "blown my cover."

The therapist facilitated a number of meetings in which she helped Jamal, Kadija, and Aisha talk more openly about the lesbian relationship. Both members of the couple were surprised at his anger and his embarrassment. As they began to talk about these issues, the tensions in the couple and the acting-out on Jamal's part began to ease. At the therapist's suggestion, Kadija's mother also was invited to participate in a few sessions in order to help all parties negotiate a new way of relating. It became apparent that Jamal and his grandmother often engaged in special alliances and that some of her directives to him were often different from those of Kadija and Aisha.

In the final phase of therapy, additional work was done with Kadija and Aisha to help them make separate time in their lives to nurture their relationship as a couple separate from other family members.

This case illustrates the complexity of extended family relationships within African American families. Therapists working with lesbian couples within this culture should be aware that although the couple may present for treatment, there are often many other family members involved. The collusion and denial evident in this family is not unusual in the African American community.

Therapy often serves the role of helping to open up discussion among family members on the taboo subject of the couple's lesbianism. Jamal's response as a preadolescent is also a common one. Boyd-Franklin (1989), in her book on Black families in therapy, discusses the impact of "toxic secrets." For Jamal, his mother's lesbianism is a toxic secret that is known on some level but denied and never fully discussed. Therapists working with African American lesbian couples with children must be sensitive to these issues and help the couple facilitate discussion with the young person involved. Timing is crucial, and therapists may have to work with each family member individually first in order to hear and understand their concerns before bringing the whole family together.

Finally, one of the most important aspects of this treatment is helping the couple to nurture each other and their relationship while these complex family dynamics are being explored in therapy. All of this work takes place in an environment that is antagonistic to African American lesbians and that contains little support for their relationships. Developing supportive social networks becomes another important aspect of this challenging work.

References

Acosta, E. (1979, October 11). Affinity for Black heritage: Seeking lifestyle within a community. *Washington Blade,* pp. A-1, A-25.

Amaro, H. (1978). *Coming out: Hispanic lesbians, their families and communities.* Paper presented at the National Coalition of Hispanic Mental Health and Human Services Organization, Austin, TX.

Bass-Hass, R. (1968). The lesbian dyad: Basic issues and value systems. *Journal of Sex Research, 4,* 126.

Bell, A., & Weinberg, M. (1978). *Homosexualities: A study of human diversity among men and women.* New York: Simon & Schuster.

Boyd-Franklin, N. (1989). *Black families: A multisystems approach to family therapy.* New York: Guilford Press.

Brownworth, V. A. (1993, June). Linda Villarosa speaks out. *Deneuve, 3,* 16–19, 56.

Chan, C. S. (1989). Issues of identity development among Asian American lesbians and gay men. *Journal of Counseling and Development, 68,* 16–20.

Chan, C. S. (1992). Cultural considerations in counseling Asian American lesbians and gay men. In S. Dworkin & F. Gutierrez (Eds.), *Counseling gay men and lesbians: Journey to the end of the rainbow* (pp. 115–124). Alexandria, VA: American Association for Counseling and Development.

Christian, B. (1985). *Black feminist criticism: Perspectives on Black women writers.* New York: Pergamon.

Clarke, C. (1983). The failure to transform: Homophobia in the Black community. In B. Smith (Ed.), *Home girls: A Black feminist anthology* (pp. 197–208). New York: Kitchen Table-Women of Color Press.

Clarke, C. (1991). Saying the least said, telling the least told: The voices of Black lesbian writers. In M. Silvera (Ed.), *Piece of my heart: A lesbian of color anthology* (pp. 171–179). Toronto: Sister Vision Press.

Claybourne, J. (1978). Blacks and gay liberation. In K. Jay & A. Young (Eds.), *Lavender culture* (pp. 458–465). San Diego, CA: Harcourt Brace.

Clunis, M., & Green, G. D. (1988). *Lesbian couples.* Seattle, WA: Seal Press.

Collins, P. H. (1990). Homophobia and Black lesbians. In *Black feminist thought: Knowledge, consciousness, and the politics of empowerment* (pp. 192–196). Boston: Unwin Hyman.

Croom, G. (1993). *The effects of a consolidated versus nonconsolidated identity on expectations of African American lesbians selecting mates: A pilot study.* Unpublished doctoral dissertation, Illinois School of Professional Psychology, Chicago.

Dew, M. A. (1985). The effects of attitudes on inferences of homosexuality and perceived physical attractiveness in women. *Sex Roles, 12,* 143–155.

Dyne, L. (1980, September). Is D.C. becoming the gay capital of America? *Washingtonian,* pp. 96–101, 133–141.

Espin, O. (1984). Cultural and historical influences on sexuality in Hispanic/Latina women: Implications for psychotherapy. In C. Vance (Ed.), *Pleasure and danger: Exploring female sexuality* (pp. 149–163). London: Routledge.

Falco, K. L. (1991). *Psychotherapy with lesbian clients.* New York: Brunner/Mazel.

Garcia, N., Kennedy, C., Pearlman, S. F., & Perez, J. (1987). The impact of race and culture differences: Challenges to intimacy in lesbian relationships. In Boston Lesbian Psychologies Collective (Ed.), *Lesbian psychologies: Explorations and challenges* (pp. 142–160). Urbana: University of Illinois Press.

Garnets, L., & Kimmel, D. (1991). Lesbian and gay male dimensions in the psychological study of human diversity. In J. Goodchilds (Ed.), *Psychological perspectives on human diversity in America* (pp. 137–192). Washington, DC: American Psychological Association.

Glassgold, J. (1992). New directions in dynamic theories of lesbianism: From psychoanalysis to social constructionism. In J. Chrisler & D. Howard (Eds.), *New directions in feminist psychology: Practice, theory and research* (pp. 154–163). New York: Springer.

Gock, T. S. (1992). Asian-Pacific islander issues: Identity integration and pride. In B. Berzon (Ed.), *Positively gay* (pp. 247–252). Berkeley, CA: Celestial Arts.

Gomez, J. (1983). A cultural legacy denied and discovered: Black lesbians in fiction by women. In B. Smith (Ed.), *Home girls: A Black feminist anthology* (pp. 120–121). New York: Kitchen Table-Women of Color Press.

Gomez, J., & Smith, B. (1990). Taking the home out of homophobia: Black lesbian health. In E. C. White (Ed.), *The Black women's health book: Speaking for ourselves* (pp. 198–213). Seattle, WA: Seal Press.

Greene, B. (1986). When the therapist is White and the patient Black: Considerations for psychotherapy in the feminist heterosexual and lesbian communities. *Women and Therapy, 5,* 41–66.

Greene, B. (1990a). African American lesbians: The role of family, culture and racism. *BG Magazine,* December, pp. 6, 26.

Greene, B. (1990b). Stereotypes of African American sexuality: A commentary. In S. Rathus, J. Nevid, & L. Fichner-Rathus (Eds.), *Human sexuality in a world of diversity* (p. 257). Boston: Allyn & Bacon.

Greene, B. (1990c). Sturdy bridges: The role of African American mothers in the socialization of African American children. *Women and Therapy, 10,* 205–225.

Greene, B. (1994a). Ethnic-minority lesbians and gay men: Mental health and treatment issues. *Journal of Consulting and Clinical Psychology, 62,* 243–251.

Greene, B. (1994b). Lesbian and gay sexual orientations: Implications for clinical training, practice and research. In B. Greene & G. Herek (Eds.), *Psychological perspectives on lesbian and gay issues: Vol. 1. Lesbian and gay psychology: Theory, research, and clinical applications* (pp. 1–24). Newbury Park, CA: Sage.

Greene, B. (1994c). Lesbian women of color: Triple jeopardy. In L. Comas-Diaz & B. Greene (Eds.), *Women of color: Integrating ethnic and gender identities in psychotherapy* (pp. 389–427). New York: Guilford Press.

Greene, B. (1995). Lesbian couples. In K. Jay (Ed.), *Dyke life: From growing up to growing old—a celebration of the lesbian experience* (pp. 97–106). New York: Basic Books.

Greene, B. (1996). African American lesbians: Triple jeopardy. In A. Brown-Collins (Ed.), *The psychology of African American women.* New York: Guilford Press.

Gutierrez, F., & Dworkin, S. (1992). Gay, lesbian, and African American: Managing the integration of identities. In S. Dworkin & F. Gutierrez (Eds.), *Counseling gay men and lesbians: Journey to the end of the rainbow.* (pp. 141–156). Alexandria, VA: American Association for Counseling and Development.

hooks, b. (1981). *Ain't I a woman? Black women and feminism.* Boston: South End Press.

Icard, L. (1986). Black gay men and conflicting social identities: Sexual orientation versus racial identity. *Journal of Social Work and Human Sexuality, 4,* 83–93.

Jeffries, I. (1992, February 23). Strange fruits at the purple manor: Looking back on "the life" in Harlem. *NYQ, 17,* 40–45.

Kanuha, V. (1990). Compounding the triple jeopardy: Battering in lesbian of color relationships. *Women and Therapy, 9,* 169–183.

Kite, M. (1994). When perceptions meet reality: Individual differences in reactions to lesbians and gay men. In B. Greene & G. Herek (Eds.), *Lesbian and gay psychology: Theory, research and clinical applications* (pp. 25–53). Newbury Park, CA: Sage.

Kite, M., & Deaux, K. (1987). Gender belief systems: Homosexuality and the implicit inversion theory. *Psychology of Women Quarterly, 11,* 83–96.

Loiacano, D. (1989). Gay identity issues among Black Americans: Racism, homophobia and the need for validation. *Journal of Counseling and Development, 68,* 21–25.

Mays, V., & Cochran, S. (1988). The Black women's relationship project: A national survey of Black lesbians. In M. Shernoff & W. Scott (Eds.), *The sourcebook on lesbian/gay health care* (2nd ed., pp. 54–62). Washington, DC: National Lesbian and Gay Health Foundation.

Mays, V., Cochran, S., & Rhue, S. (1993). The impact of perceived discrimination on the intimate relationships of Black lesbians. *Journal of Homosexuality, 25,* 1–14.

Monteflores, C. de. (1986). Notes on the management of difference. In T. Stein & C. Cohen (Eds.), *Contemporary perspectives on psychotherapy with lesbians and gay men* (pp. 73–101). New York: Plenum.

Morales, E. (1989). Ethnic minority families and minority gays and lesbians. *Marriage and Family Review, 14,* 217–239.

Moses, A. E., & Hawkins, R. (1982). *Counseling lesbian women and gay men: A life issues approach.* St. Louis, MO: Mosby–Year Book.

Newman, B. S. (1989). The relative importance of gender role attitudes toward lesbians. *Sex Roles, 21,* 451–465.

Omosupe, K. (1991). Black/lesbian/bulldagger. *Differences: A Journal of Feminist and Cultural Studies, 2,* 101–111.

Poussaint, A. (1990, September). An honest look at Black gays and lesbians. *Ebony,* pp. 124–131.

Roberts, J. R. (1981). *Black lesbians: An annotated bibliography.* Tallahassee, FL: Naiad Press.

Sears, V. L. (1987). *Cross-cultural ethnic relationships.* Unpublished manuscript.

Silvera, M. (1991). Man royals and sodomites: Some thoughts on the invisibility of Afro-Caribbean lesbians. In M. Silvera (Ed.), *Piece of my heart: A lesbian of color anthology* (pp. 14–26). Toronto: Sister Vision Press.

Smith, B. (1982). Toward a Black feminist criticism. In G. Hull, P. Scott, & B. Smith (Eds.), *All the women are White, all the Blacks are men, but some of us are brave* (pp. 157–175). Old Westbury, NY: Feminist Press.

Tafoya, T., & Rowell, R. (1988). Counseling Native American lesbians and gays. In M. Shernoff & W. A. Scott (Eds.), *The sourcebook on lesbian/gay health care* (pp. 63–67). Washington, DC: National Lesbian and Gay Health Foundation.

Taylor, A. T. (1983). Conceptions of masculinity and femininity as a basis for stereotypes of male and female homosexuals. *Journal of Homosexuality, 9,* 37–53.

Tremble, B., Schneider, M., & Appathurai, C. (1989). Growing up gay or lesbian in a multicultural context. *Journal of Homosexuality, 17,* 253–267.

Whitley, E. B., Jr. (1987). The relation of sex role orientation to heterosexual attitudes toward homosexuality. *Sex Roles, 17,* 103–113.

Wooden, W. S., Kawasaki, H., & Mayeda, R. (1983). Lifestyles and identity maintenance among gay Japanese-American males. *Alternative Lifestyles, 5,* 236–243.

Wyatt, G., Strayer, R., & Lobitz, W. C. (1976). Issues in the treatment of sexually dysfunctioning couples of African American descent. *Psychotherapy, 13,* 44–50.

CHAPTER ELEVEN

GENDER ROLES AMONG LATINO GAY AND BISEXUAL MEN

Implications for Family and Couple Relationships

Eduardo Morales

The ability to recognize, label, accept, and disclose a homosexual orientation to significant others is largely determined by the beliefs about gender and homosexuality that the person involved holds. The reactions of significant others are also largely determined by such beliefs. As is true in many cultural groups, Latinos and Latinas generally rely on gender-role stereotypes in their understanding of homosexuality. They tend to believe that all gay males are feminine (effeminate) and therefore are not complete, or "real," men. Heterosexual males, however, are believed to be masculine and are therefore real men. These assumptions play a central role in the intrapsychic, familial, and community relationships of Latino gay men. Such stereotypes, acquired during socialization and maintained by the family's cultural milieu, often affect the way these men view themselves and each other and how well they cope with a stigmatized sexual identity and with discrimination.

In addition, for Latinos as a cultural group, gender-role identity is part of an overall philosophy of life that is defined by secular society and religion. An exceptionally strong emphasis on gender dichotomy is evident throughout Latino societies and belief systems. Most emphatically, it is central to the Spanish language. Gender is assigned not only to living beings but to inanimate objects in the world, so everything in the world is essentially either male or female. Hence, *one's whole universe is partitioned into the masculine or the feminine, and correct classification is important. This is a gendered way of perceiving and thinking that is internalized by individuals growing up in the culture.*

Although some authors (for example, Carrier, 1976, 1977, 1989) have pointed to strong gender-role strain experienced by Latino gay men as individuals, there has been little discussion of its interpersonal effects. In this chapter, I examine notions about gender roles and male homosexuality in Latino culture and explore the implications of these beliefs for family and couple relationships among gay and bisexual Latino men. I begin with an overview of Latino culture and the position of Latinos historically within the gay civil rights movement. I then turn to a discussion of Latino gay identity development and conventional Latino attitudes toward homosexuality. Lastly, I consider the effects of these cultural factors on family and couple relationships of Latino gay men, concluding the chapter with two brief case examples.

Latino Cultures: An Overview

The term *Latino* refers to cultural groups from Central America, South America, and the Caribbean whose primary language is Spanish. Although the term *Hispanic* is sometimes used to describe this population (the U.S. Census Bureau uses the term), many members of these cultures feel that *Hispanic* refers to being conquered by Spain and implies a current identification with Spain; hence, many prefer the term *Latino*.

Differences Across Latino Cultures

Latinos represent a wide variety of nations and races, rendering the group multicultural and multiracial. Although Latinos may share the same language, all types of races are found among the different Latino nations, including Black, Asian, Native American (American Indian), and Caucasian. Multiple combinations are also possible, including mulatto (mixed African Black and Euro-Caucasian heritage) and mestizo (mixed American Indian and Euro-Caucasian heritage). Consequently, one must bear in mind that differences in Latino groups should be taken into account in tailoring clinical services for them. The clients' countries of origin, socioeconomic positions, and race relations within their original countries should all be considered. For example, because of significant historical and cultural differences, a Puerto Rican therapist working with a Mexican client should be viewed as doing cross-cultural therapy, even though both participants may speak Spanish and are considered to be Latinos. Furthermore, Latino therapist-client dyads can vary by race, with the therapist being of one race (for example, Black or mulatto) and the client being of another (for example, South American Indian or mestizo).

Therefore, cross-cultural and interracial aspects of Latino couple, family, and therapy relationships must be incorporated into any concept of the dynamics of these relationships. Character attributes stereotypically ascribed to one race by Puerto Ricans can be radically different or even opposite to those ascribed to the same race by Mexicans or Argentineans. Furthermore, for mulatto or mestizo persons, skin color and other physical criteria used to differentiate membership in a given race are not the same in all Latino nations. For example, the same individual might be considered a Black person in some countries, such as Argentina, but a White person in other countries, such as Panama. Or a person viewed and treated as a White or mulatto in his or her country of origin may be viewed and treated as a Black person in the United States.

Some Traditional Commonalities Across Latino Cultures

Despite some large cultural differences among various Latino countries, commonalities pertaining to language and traditional value systems also exist. These normative cultural values have been termed *familismo, machismo, marianismo, simpatía, personalismo, respeto,* and *saludos* (Bernal, 1982; Falicov, 1982; Garcia-Preto, 1982).

Familismo refers to the importance of the family as the primary social unit and entails the very active involvement of the extended family as a source of instrumental support (for example, help with finances or child care), social support (guidance, camaraderie, and emotional nurture), and social identity in the community. Godparents of the children tend to function as coparents *(compadre, comadre)* and are considered central to the family, like brothers or sisters of the parents. Although some Euro-Caucasian families also show strong intergenerational involvement over time, Latino extended family members tend to be more closely entwined, elders hold more enduring authority, and one's membership in the family group and carrying the family's name are major parts of one's social identity in the community.

Machismo refers to a man's responsibility to provide for, protect, and defend his family. His loyalty and sense of responsibility to family, friends, and community make him a good man. The Anglo-American definition of *macho* that describes sexist, male-chauvinist behavior is radically different from the original Latino meaning of *machismo,* which conveyed the notion of "an honorable and responsible man."

Marianismo refers to the responsibility of a woman to provide for, protect, and nurture her family and to value motherhood strongly. Her self-sacrificing dedication to the family and motherhood is viewed with great esteem and is expected of Latinas. The term comes from the biblical Virgin Mary (María) and refers to her purity and sanctity in relation to the family and her influence in maintaining high moral and ethical standards.

Simpatía refers to the sense of empathy and to the importance of smooth relations and social politeness; confrontation and persistence are viewed as offensive. Commonly, in order to avoid disagreement and confrontation, a Latino listener may appear to agree with the speaker in a conversation. A Latino may be particularly agreeable with authority figures, as a sign of respect and politeness.

Personalismo refers to a preference by Latinos for forming personal relationships with others based on a strong sense of trust, cooperation, mutual help-giving, and inclusion rather than exclusion. For health care workers who have established rapport, it is quite common for Latinos to relate to the health care provider as if he or she were a member of their family.

Respeto refers to the need for respect, especially for authority figures, and the need for persons to be treated with dignity. This is especially true for honoring the dignity of older citizens, for example, by using the title *Don* or *Doña* before their names.

Saludos refers to the importance of greeting others, touching, and expressing affection and to the proper ways of addressing others. Introducing people to each other and using correct social protocol when meeting others are important ways of displaying *simpatía* and *respeto*.

With reference to the traditional values of machismo and marianismo, many contemporary Latinos and Latinas object to the sex-role stereotyping that these traditional constructs represent. For example, many Latinos and Latinas now view *marianismo* as an oppressive syndrome that makes women subservient and sacrificial and gives them no right to fulfill their own needs and desires. Specifically, in the author's discussion groups with Latino gays and Latina lesbians in North American urban settings, participants' reactions to the practices of *machismo* and *marianismo* were generally very negative. They viewed these practices as oppressive both in Latino society and in their own lives, and they had difficulty understanding how these traditional roles might have been adaptive and might have served a positive function under other circumstances.

For them, the positive connotations that originally accompanied the ideas of *machismo* and *marianismo* are overshadowed by the negative connotations. Their reactions reflect their changing values and heightened awareness of the oppressive aspects of traditional sex roles in Latino society and other cultures. Furthermore, among the various subgroups within Latino cultures, lesbians and gays may be the most victimized by Latino gender-role norms and by sanctions for not conforming to those norms.

Becoming Biculturally Competent

The issues of acculturation and assimilation have been discussed extensively in the literature on Latinos in the United States, and these terms sometimes have been confused with one another. *Acculturation* refers to a person learning and adopting the characteristics, language, mannerisms, norms, and style of another culture. *Assimilation* refers to the person's blending into the other culture until cultural differences are minimized. By contrast, *biculturalism* and *multiculturalism* refer to a person's ability to know and use the characteristics, language, mannerisms, norms, and styles of two or more cultures and to understand the differences between them and know how to apply that knowledge effectively in the appropriate contexts.

Recent thinking about immigration and acculturation has centered mainly on these notions of developing a bicultural identity and bicultural social competence. In empirical studies, Latino individuals with greater *bicultural competence* have shown more resiliency and less likelihood of using risky coping mechanisms related to stress, such as substance abuse. By contrast, high- and low-acculturated individuals have been at greater risk for developing mental health problems (Santisteban & Szapocznik, 1982; Marshall, 1993). Thus, for their psychological well-being and physical health, Latino persons living in the United States should be supported by their therapists in achieving bicultural involvement and competence rather than unilateral assimilation into the new society.

Overall, the notion of biculturalism provides a general conceptual framework and some common ground between client and therapist. Becoming more biculturally competent (and ultimately multiculturally competent) is a task for both therapist and client in their work together and in adapting to ethnic changes in their communities.

Latino Gay and Bisexual Men: Invisible in History

For Latino American gays and bisexuals, cultural considerations like the ones described set the tone for socialization and bonding with family, friends, and community. Given that they live in the United States as a minority within a minority, the way Latino gay and bisexual men incorporate their sexuality intrapsychically and in the family must be conceptualized with reference to *multiple social networks* (extended family, friends, schools, work settings) embedded within at least *two evolving ethnic cultures* (Latino American, European American, and, in some cases, African American or Asian American) and within *two sexual orientation cultures* (heterosexual, homosexual). Thus, to maintain their personal equilibrium, integrity, and safety over time and across contexts, most Latino gay and bisexual men learn to perform very complicated balancing acts. They must manage their social identities and self-presentations in these multiple contexts carefully, or they risk rejection and discrimination.

Many Latino gay and bisexual men keep their homosexuality hidden from the heterosexual community, and this invisibility perpetuates stereotypes about homosexuals within the Latino population. Also, most accounts of gay history written by Euro-Caucasian American authors ignore the contributions of Latinos. Resource guides such as *The Big Gay Book* by John Preston (1991) do not even mention Latinos, nor is the word indexed, although African American, Asian American, and American Indian gay organizations and resources are listed and indexed. The absence of Latinos in gay literature reinforces a sense of their marginality in society at large, in the Latino community, and in the gay community.

For example, many heterosexual Latinos, especially outside the major urban areas, seem to believe that homosexuality is a phenomenon only in the Euro-Caucasian culture because they seldom, if ever, have met an openly gay Latino man in their social circle, nor have they heard or seen one depicted in the media. In contrast to many Euro-Caucasian gay youths today, Latino gay youths often feel as if they are the only one of their kind. They cannot find examples of Latino gay men in their local communities, in the general communications media, or even in the gay media.

Ironically, despite this invisibility in both the heterosexual and Euro-Caucasian gay communities, professional historians agree that gay Latinos played the major role in the single most important turning point in the gay liberation movement—the Stonewall riots in June 1969 (which took place in Greenwich Village, New York City). The Stonewall riots were primarily a series of confrontations between the New York City police and Puerto Rican and African American transvestites and gays. When police raided the Stonewall Bar and harassed its largely Puerto Rican and African American gay clientele, these gay men bravely fought back, resisting arrest and risking their physical safety. This event sparked several days of uprisings by gays in the streets of Greenwich Village, catching the police by surprise because they viewed homosexuals as weak—easy targets for persecution.

Since then, the annual Gay Freedom Day parades held during June in major cities throughout the United States commemorate the Stonewall riots and symbolize the struggle for gay civil rights throughout the world. However, the cultural symbol of Stonewall has been taken over by middle-class Euro-Caucasian gays, and most mainstream journalists neglect to explain that Latinos played a pivotal role in the Stonewall protest. This invisibility reinforces the public's misperception that Latino gays are extremely rare or nonexistent, and it contributes to many Latino gays' feeling that they do not quite belong anywhere, especially when they first recognize their sexual orientation.

More recently, several writers have begun to document the life experiences of Latino gays, and several films have been produced about the lives of Latino gay men in the United States and in Latino countries. Local, state, and national Latino gay and Latina lesbian organizations have emerged, with ever-expanding memberships. In San Francisco alone, there are four major gay and lesbian Latino organizations, with many active dues-paying members. These groups have sponsored large conferences that have provided a way for Latino gays and Latina lesbians to discuss their shared concerns, as well as to develop their social networks and organize politically.

Latino Gay Identity: Developmental States and a Typology

Latino gays and bisexuals in the United States lead their lives within three communities: the gay and lesbian community (which is predominantly Euro-Caucasian), the Latino heterosexual community, and the predominantly Euro-Caucasian heterosexual mainstream society. Each of these social contexts has its unique set of norms, values, and lifestyles, some of which are fundamentally in opposition to each other. Therefore, some Latino gays and bisexuals keep each community separate. For example, they may never bring their families and their gay friends together; others vary the way they integrate their communities. Each community offers a different kind of support for their lifestyles and identities. The gay and lesbian community supports the full expression of sexual orientation identity; the Latino community supports family attachments and the maintenance of a positive ethnic identity; the mainstream Euro-Caucasian heterosexual society provides a national and international social identity and controls most of the institutions and opportunities for employment, education, social services, and health care in the United States.

Psychosocial Tasks in the Development of a Positive Latino Gay Identity

Morales (1983, 1990, 1992) proposed an identity model of five psychosocial states of identity integration for ethnic-minority gays and lesbians. This model focuses on how minority gay individuals manage their dual minority status, including how Latinos (1) put together their ethnic identity, Latino, with their sexual identity, gay, in a way that leads to a positive self-image and (2) how they integrate or keep separate their relationships in the heterosexual Latino and gay communities. The resolution of each state is accompanied by decreasing anxiety and tension through the successful management of the psychosocial task involved. As cognitive and lifestyle changes occur over time, an individual's conflicting identifications are integrated into a positive whole, leading toward greater self-understanding, a better sense of personal coherence, and the development of a multicultural perspective and competence. The proposed psychosocial states related to identity integration for Latino gays in the United States are as follows.

State 1: Denial of Conflicts. In this state of psychosocial consciousness, individuals tend to minimize the reality of discrimination they may experience as a gay Latino in the United States and believe they are being treated the same as others. They also deny the extent to which they may have to hide their authentic selves and present a false self to the world, for example, by acting straight or acting White, in order to avoid discrimination in various social contexts. Their sexual orientation may be repressed or suppressed, or may not be clearly defined at all. Thus, they may engage in extensive homosexual behavior but not connect this behavior to a congruent self-image of being gay, believing that they are still heterosexual or refusing to consider the question. They talk as if their personal lifestyle and sexual activities have limited consequences for their self-definition or their interpersonal lives, but their presenting symptoms suggest that they are avoiding thinking about and dealing with many aspects of their situations.

The focus of therapy with clients in this psychosocial state centers around developing a more accurate picture of the conflicting environmental stresses that affect their self-definitions and relationships. They need to consider what it would mean in their lives for them to identify with being a Latino and what it would mean to identify with being gay, with the eventual goal of embracing these two identities as a step toward greater self-fulfillment and personal growth.

State 2: Bisexual versus Gay. Some Latino gays prefer to think of and identify themselves as bisexual rather than gay. Upon examining their sexual and affectional lifestyles, however, there may be no difference between those who identify themselves as gay and those who identify as bisexual.

The focus of therapy for individuals in this state of consciousness is to explore the sense of hopelessness and depression that can result from continued conflict over whether they are bisexual or gay. The difficulties they have with self-labeling are considered in the context of the cultural messages they receive about what it means to be a heterosexual, bisexual, or gay Latino man. Although some persons in this state of awareness may be genuinely bisexual in orientation, a great many others are predominantly gay and are having difficulty bringing their self-definitions in line with their feelings and behavior.

State 3: Conflicts in Allegiances. The simultaneous awareness of being both Latino and gay triggers anxiety about maintaining relationships in the two communities and about whether to keep relationships in the two communities separate.

The possibility of betraying or losing either one's Latino or one's gay or lesbian relationships becomes a major concern. The problem becomes how to maintain relations and be loyal to family members as well as to dating partners.

The need to prioritize allegiances to, and time spent in, various relationships in order to reduce the conflicts becomes the focus in therapy. Individuals in this state need help in selecting from each community the beliefs that sustain a positive self-image, and they need to internally reject from each community the beliefs that contribute to a negative self-image. The main goal of therapy here is to help clients manage the feelings of disjointedness that arise from participating in heterosexual Latino rather than gay social situations, and to reduce guilt they may experience about betraying significant others or moral values in one or both cultural contexts. Drawing from both communities, the individual must discover his own blend of values and relationships that support a sense of personal worth and ethics.

State 4: Claiming a Latino Gay Identity.

State 4: Claiming a Latino Gay Identity. Feelings of resentment concerning the lack of acceptance among the communities are central in this state. Persons in State 4 identify as being gay and Latino, and they have feelings of anger stemming from experiences of rejection by the predominantly Euro-Caucasian gay community because of their ethnicity or rejection by the predominantly heterosexual Latino community. The need to validate and explore angry feelings becomes a central focus in therapy. Experiences of prejudice and discrimination must be looked at in detail, with an eye toward helping the individual protect his sense of self and helping him take appropriate actions to stop such discrimination in the future. Encouraging the client to make connections with other gay Latino men and support groups (where available) and to begin working politically against ethnic discrimination in the gay community are important parts of therapy for such clients.

State 5: Integrating the Various Communities.

State 5: Integrating the Various Communities. For Latino gay men, the need to more fully integrate various aspects of their lives and develop a multicultural perspective becomes a major concern. Adjusting to the reality of the limited social options currently available for many gay and lesbian people of color becomes a source of anxiety and feelings of isolation and alienation. In many communities, it is difficult to find social groups for Latino gays and lesbians, and such clients are deprived of needed social opportunities because they have few personal contacts with others like themselves.

The focus of therapy for persons in this state centers around validating the client's personal experience and putting it in a multicultural perspective. Referral to gay Latino support groups and political organizations (if available in their cities) is useful, and some clients can take the initiative to start such groups. Mainly, these clients need reassurance that, indeed, their life does and will require a constantly evolving balancing act, as they attempt to maintain a coherent and authentic identity across two divergent social contexts, each of which is important to their sense of belonging. Also, they can, over time, learn to better predict the outcomes of their attempts to integrate members of the two communities. In this state, the person is conscious of his situation and has developed a multicultural perspective that enables him to maneuver successfully in many different sociocultural contexts, without experiencing damage to self-esteem or unnecessary ruptures in significant relationships with Latinos or non-Latinos, straight or gay. Many, but not all, gay Latinos in this state may choose to come out explicitly to their family members, heterosexual friends, and selected co-workers. They may also take steps to bring members of the different groups together at social events (for example, bringing gay partners to family events or inviting family members to come along on social activities with gay friends). Persons in State 5 tend to benefit rapidly from brief therapy or support groups during the process of integrating their communities.

The model proposes relatively fluid states rather than rigidly sequential stages, implying that individuals may find themselves dealing with issues at more than one state or moving to earlier states in response to specific events in their lives. For example, a person may identify as being bisexual, yet lead an exclusively gay life in terms of behavior (State 2). This same person may have a strong identification with the Latino gay community and be concerned with discrimination from the predominantly Euro-Caucasian gay community (State 4). Moreover, in this model, a person's state is determined not only by his evolving ego identity but also by changes in the social contexts that shape his self-perception. Such changes might take place when a person takes a new job, moves to another part of the country, or starts or ends couple relationships with other Latinos or with persons of other ethnic groups. The ever-shifting sociopolitical situation for Latinos and gays in a given locale over time is another example of how context can change.

A Typology of Latino Men Who Have Sex with Men

Based on a recent study of 182 Puerto Rican men in New York who have sex with other men, Carballo-Diéguez (1995) developed a typology of sexual identities based on participants' behaviors, sexual histories, and perceptions of their own sexual identities. Through interviews, observations, and focus groups using quantitative and qualitative data-gathering procedures, Carballo-Diéguez distinguished four major identity types of Puerto Rican men who have sex with men: (1) straight-identified men, (2) bisexual-identified men, (3) gay-identified men, and (4) drag queens.

Straight-identified men see themselves as heterosexual and do not consider that having sex with men makes them any different from men who only have heterosexual sex, even though one-third of the straight-identified group had sex only with men in the preceding year. In order to maintain this straight identity, they control the conditions under which they will have sex with other men. They take only the active (inserter) role in anal sex and do not kiss the other man or touch his penis. Often, straight-identified men state that their homosexual encounters are caused by extenuating circumstances such as the need for money or shelter, or to a lack of self-control due to substance use or incarceration. They prefer to have sex with men who tend to be effeminate, play the passive role in sex (insertee), and essentially enact the traditional role of a woman. These straight-identified men tend to be of lower socioeconomic status, to have traditional sex-role values, to be the most homophobic of all groups, and to see themselves as always playing the male role in a hypermasculine way. Some of these men refer to themselves as *bugarrón, macho, varón, chillo,* or simply *hombre.*

Bisexual-identified men, or *hombres modernos* ("modern men"), are those who could be in love with a man or with a woman. They see themselves as being involved with both sexes and feel comfortable with the term *bisexual.* However, they scored high on the homophobic scale compared to gay-identified men and drag queens. They can have a primary relationship with a woman and a relationship with a man on the side. Compared to the straight-identified men, the bisexual-identified men engage in more versatile sex with other men, which could include kissing, being penetrated, fellatio, and fondling the other man's genitals. Interestingly, their proclaimed identity as bisexual remains intact, even when they have had sex exclusively with men for a year or more (as was true for 20 percent of the bisexual-identified men in the research study). Also, some men are in a transient state. They are sometimes teasingly referred to in the Latino gay community as *confundido* ("confused") because they feel more strongly for one sex than the other but cannot make up their minds about their sexual identity. The researchers viewed the *confundido* as a subtype within the identity dimensions of bisexual and gay—caught between being bisexual and being gay—although they may label themselves as bisexual.

Gay-identified men, or *entendidos* ("those who understand"), primarily choose men as sexual partners, feel more attracted to men, and express their liking and affection for men. They were, by far, the most numerous—out of 182 men who had sex with men in the entire sample, 119 were *entendidos* (gay-identified). *Gente del ambiente* ("people of ambiance") is another phrase commonly used by Latinos to refer to gays and lesbians. For this group, sex with other gay men is usually versatile and more so than for any of the other groups. The socioeconomic status of the *entendidos* was higher than that of the other three groups, and they were the least homophobic of all the groups. Various members of this group reported different definitions of being a gay person—from viewing gay as simply engaging in homosexual behavior to having emotions and affection for someone of the same sex to being a homosexual with a consciousness about the gay community and politics.

Drag queens identify, act, and live in a traditionally feminine way and refer to themselves as women. Members of this group are commonly referred to as "transgendered." They tend to adopt a stereotypically feminine, traditional woman's image, appearing to be submissive, naive, delicate, or sexually provocative. Their physical look is extremely important, and they endure much pain and sacrifice in order to look more feminine. Their efforts to do so include using electrolysis to banish unwanted hair, hormones to develop their breasts, creams to make their skin smoother, and hairstyles to impart a feminine look. Plastic surgery and implants may be used to reshape parts of the body. Sex change is not the goal. The development of the most believable female image is paramount. Being both a man and a woman—a "she-male," having the body of a woman but the mind of a man—is the desired state and is believed to be an object of desire for certain masculine men. In this study, drag queens tended to be of lower socioeconomic status (similar to the straight-identified men) and to endorse traditional gender-role value systems.

Also in this study, Carballo-Diéguez (1995) identified three subtypes, which included the *confundido* (the confused bisexual noted earlier), the *poncas* (an effeminate male who dresses like a man but acts like a woman), and *Joseador* (one who adopts a tough macho appearance but is more versatile in sexual practices and engages in sex as a business). Although the numbers of persons in these subtypes were small in this study, the researchers thought that those in the subtypes were in some transitional state or were placed along the dimension of two of the major types noted above. The *confundido* falls somewhere between bisexual and gay, the *ponca* is between gay and drag queen, and the *Joseador* is between straight and bisexual.

For all types and subtypes within the larger sample, the issue of masculinity and femininity played an important role in how they defined their sexual orientation identities and how they viewed each other:

> Participants' responses to the questions about sexual identity showed that, although they were quite familiar with a classification system based on sexual behavior, they applied to themselves another classification system based on gender role. (Carballo-Diéguez, 1995, p. 108)

In another study, Carballo-Diéguez and Dolezal (1995) also examined the relationship between sexual abuse prior to the age of thirteen and the prevalence of high-risk behaviors for HIV infection. Unprotected, receptive anal intercourse was significantly related to having a history of childhood sexual abuse. Also, those who had been sexually abused by force were most likely to have unprotected anal intercourse as adults. Men of Latin American origin were twice as likely as Blacks or White men to engage in receptive anal intercourse with sexual partners (Bartholow et al., 1994). These data support the notion that sexual history, gender roles, and sexual orientation identity among Latino men who have sex with men is an important factor in their HIV-risk behaviors. Efforts to prevent HIV infection, if they are to succeed, must take into account the unique sexual orientation identities of subgroups within the Latino gay community.

Homophobia and Gender Dichotomy

As I mentioned at the outset of this chapter, gender polarity is embedded strongly in the Spanish language and the metaphysical belief systems of Latinos. Masculinity and femininity are contained in every thought and phrase. Hence, the psychological concept of androgyny remains somewhat foreign to Latinos. Similarly, the notion of being a gay man (which connotes to many heterosexual Latinos something akin to "being a female male") is self-contradictory and nearly inconceivable, given that men are, by definition, masculine. Thus, for Latinos, gay men are a striking and puzzling exception to the rules, and their existence conflicts with the culture's perception of the natural order.

Homophobia in Latino Culture

This deviance of gays from the expected order of things contributes to Latinos' generally negative views of gay persons, which can be categorized into the three types of reactions described next.

The first reaction is that *gays are alien*. Because the culture's frame does not logically incorporate the notion of relationships other than heterosexual ones, men who have intimate and sexual relationships with other men are viewed by Latinos as alien. Labels and phrases commonly used are *raro* ("odd"), *del otro lado* ("of another way"), or *quebrado* ("broken, genetically flawed"). These labels connote alienation and foster ostracism of the referent group.

A second reaction is that *gays are feminine*. A common perception is that gay men are feminine beings, which is contrary to manhood and *machismo*. Because a man cannot be feminine and maintain respect as a man, many Latinos use negative and antifeminine references about gay men. Words that suggest effeminate mannerisms include the names of certain animals that are considered feminine in their characteristics. Such feminine animals' names used to describe gays in a derogatory manner include *pajaro* ("bird"), *mariposa* ("butterfly"), and *pato* ("duck," referring to its funny walk). Reference to birds and to feather boas, which are worn by Las Vegas–type showgirls and in drag queen shows, are also incorporated into such sarcastic remarks as *hay mucha pluma aquí* ("lots of feathers here"), *que plumero* ("what feathers!"), or *hechando pluma* ("displaying feathers"), suggesting that many of the men present are gay and effeminate. These references in Spanish are frequently used in a contemptuous manner, indicating an antifeminine sentiment whenever femininity and attraction to men are displayed by men. It is interesting that birds' names are used to refer to gays. One reason seems to be that birds have their sexual organs in the same opening as the anus. Because Latinos view gay men as feminine and as being only the insertee or passive recipient in sexual encounters, the anus (as with birds) is perceived as their primary sex organ.

In many Latino countries, gays and bisexuals themselves refer to the gay man's anus as a vagina (for example, Dominicans refer to it as *la tota*). Other Latinos may refer to gays as *culera,* derived from *culo* ("anus" or "behind"). As an insult to gay men, who are presumed to be effeminate, words with extreme negative connotations for femininity are used, such as *maricón* ("sissy, faggot") or its slang version *marica, loca* ("crazy woman"), or *partida* ("damaged or genetically flawed woman").

The third reaction is that *gays are inferior.* Other negative references to gays involve more extreme depersonalization and hatred toward gender nonconformity. Thus, some of the words that refer to being gay are also used as general insults to seriously defame a person's character. In combination with the terms already mentioned above, these homophobic epithets are used to ostracize Latino gays from society and place them in a subhuman, degraded position. Such labels include referring to a gay person as *puto* ("prostitute"), *joto* ("person of insignificance and no worth"), *hueco* ("vain, hollow, affected"), or *cochón* ("filthy, dirty person").

Religious Influences

The Latino cultural concepts of gender have been strongly reinforced by Christian religions such as Catholicism and by European cultural influences. Such imported belief structures have strong, rigid guidelines for gender assignments based on the biological sexes and strongly sex-negative value systems. Upon discovery of the Americas, Christianity and European cultural customs were imposed by the conquerors, forcing practitioners of indigenous religions to go underground or mask their beliefs. For example, in Santeria, an African-based religion in many Caribbean nations, certain saints of the Catholic religion were used in tandem with the different gods and demigods of the indigenous religions, based on the similarity in their function and symbol. Catholicism became the predominant religion among Latinos. Thus, traditional gender roles were reinforced by a set of religious beliefs that complemented cultural beliefs about gender and the Spanish language's bipolar gender references.

Interestingly, an examination of some of the indigenous religions reveals more of a trend toward androgyny and variability in sexual expression than in the Catholicism of the conquerors. In the Afro-Caribbean religions such as Santeria, masculinity and femininity are seen as forces within each person. Spiritual evolution requires the recognition and development of these gender forces within oneself. The ability to fully recognize each gender within the self is a sign of great spirituality. Thus, some indigenous religions view gays and lesbians as having *greater* potential than other persons for spiritual development because of their unique androgynous natures and because gays and lesbians must develop their masculine and feminine sides in order to truly love a person of the same sex.

Furthermore, some of the indigenous religions incorporated gays and lesbians as a special part of humanity, with special protectors represented as either saints or goddesses. Among gays and lesbians who practice Santeria, Santa Barbara is viewed as their patron saint, guide, and protector. In some of the Mexican indigenous religions, there is reference to the goddess Inez, a goddess who makes love to women. Xochiquetzal is the goddess of nonproductive sexuality and of carnal desire.

The existence of these concepts of androgyny in some of the indigenous, precolonial religions—and their decline after colonization by Spain and the ascendance of Catholicism—shows that the social construction of gender and sexual orientation can evolve dramatically over time and depends on who holds the power to define moral and religious beliefs. Clinicians should be aware that some Latino families from the Caribbean and from Brazil (which is Portuguese-speaking) may have retained aspects of precolonial religious beliefs and indigenous African religions. Some of these families may have more flexible attitudes about gender than is the norm among Latino Catholics.

Gay Men: A Third Gender

The varieties of Latino men who have sex with men illustrate that *biological sex* (genetic maleness or femaleness), *gender identity constancy* (the enduring perception of oneself as a male or female), *gender-role behavior* (conformity to culturally defined norms of masculinity or femininity), *sexual behavior* (heterosexual, homosexual, or both), *sexual orientation* (feelings of attraction to males, females, or both), and *sexual orientation identity* (self-recognition as straight, gay, or bisexual) do not always fit together in expected ways. These discrepancies challenge simplistic notions of a "natural" gender dichotomy in which genetic males and females are destined to become stereotypically masculine and feminine, respectively, and heterosexual.

Yet the notion of a clear, universal, natural, and desirable gender polarity persists in most cultures and is embedded firmly in most languages. Neither in English nor in Spanish do we have clear terms to describe a gender other than male or female, masculine or feminine. Even definitions of androgyny denote a combination of female and male characteristics, requiring reference to the original gender dichotomy to achieve definition.

Thus emerges the question: Is an androgynous person simply one who demonstrates a balance of both traditional masculine and feminine characteristics, or is an androgynous person one who shows something that is not just masculine plus feminine but rather something altogether different—a new, third gender that is not linked to genetic maleness or femaleness? Is the whole gender gestalt of an androgynous person greater than the sum of his or her supposedly constituent masculine and feminine parts? And if such biopsychosocially androgynous persons exist—regardless of whether they are male or female, heterosexual or homosexual in orientation—might societies be better off constructing a legitimate gender-role category for them rather than trying to fit them into the existing gender-role dichotomy?

Once cultures accept the existence of gender-nonconforming persons into their collective consciousness—rather than keeping them invisible or outside consciousness—the question arises as to how to define their unique gender-role behavior as part of the natural or expected order of things rather than as pathological or, in some other way, undesirable. What nonpejorative gender-role labels exist for the large number of persons who occupy positions "in-between" traditional genders—effeminate heterosexual men, masculine heterosexual women, masculine homosexual men, feminine homosexual women, effeminate homosexual men, and masculine homosexual women—who do not conform to the traditional gender-role dichotomies? It is as if our society is dumbstruck and silent when gender roles and sexual orientation do not conform to traditional notions based on genetic sex. Without suitable language to describe what cannot be denied, the society then invents terms of derogation and depersonalization—as if such persons should not or cannot exist as human beings.

Perhaps it would be useful for mental health professionals and our society to think of lesbians and gay men as embodiments of new gender categories rather than as mere deviations from society's two gender categories—femininity and masculinity (and their companion, compulsory heterosexuality). In some American Indian cultures, for example, certain men (the *berdaches*) are viewed as a third sex, different from male or female. The berdaches hold respected roles and a unique status in the community, which encompasses their generosity, spirituality, androgyny, preference for doing woman's work, and preference for having sex with men (Williams, 1992). Such individuals usually are recognized by the family and the tribe as being special during childhood because their interests and talents are atypical for male children, and preparation for their special position in society begins at an early age, usually not later than age twelve.

Moreover, the tribe knows that there always have been and always will be such individuals, and the appearance of such a child is viewed as perfectly natural by the family and the community. The child, also aware of his difference from other males, believes it is his natural destiny to fulfill this social role because it already fits with his different way of being. A child is not coerced into or prevented from becoming a berdache but rather voluntarily moves into the role with the assent of his family members and community, who have seen other tribal members assume that status.

Although berdaches are seen as different or unusual, they are viewed as part of the natural order of things—a natural variation, not a surprise to the community, not a disgrace to the family. As adults, they often serve functions akin to shamanistic healers, indigenous therapists, educators, spiritual advisers, go-betweens, and foster parents. According to Native American religious teachings, berdaches play an important role in the evolution of the human race and have double vision—the gift of prophecy:

> The berdache receives respect partly as a result of being a mediator. Somewhere between the status of women and men, berdaches not only mediate between the sexes but between the psychic and the physical—between the spirit and the flesh. Since they mix the characteristics of both men and women, they possess the vision of both. They have double vision, with the ability to see more clearly than a single gender perspective can provide. This is why they are often referred to as "seer," one whose eyes can see beyond the blinders that restrict the average person. Viewing things from outside the usual perspective, they are able to achieve a creative and objective viewpoint that is seldom available to ordinary people. By the Indian view, someone who is different offers advantages to society precisely because she or he is freed from the restrictions of the usual. (Williams, 1992, pp. 41–42)

Especially striking is the Native American idea that the homosexuality of a berdache is simply a manifestation of his broader essential nature, which encompasses spirituality, generosity, and androgyny as central components. Homosexuality is not the primary defining characteristic. Thus, whereas men in the tribe may engage in incidental or repeated homosexual behavior with a berdache, the former are simply men, not berdaches.

By contrast, Latino and Euro-Caucasian societies have not considered or adopted this perspective, and there are no formal, acceptable roles for gays in these societies. Instead, these cultures elect to ostracize individuals for their perceived nonconforming gender behaviors and homosexuality. Although it is not likely or even desirable that Latino or Euro-Caucasian cultures will create highly specific social and occupational roles for gays equivalent to the berdache tradition, a principle struggle in our cultural evolution is to create nonpejorative categories for gays and lesbians and others who do not conform to traditional gender roles. These new gender categories must legitimize normally occurring human variations in gendered behavior and pave the way for institutional validation of the special position of gays and lesbians in society (such as marriage laws, health care coverage, adoption, and the like). When the category "gay" can hold gender uniqueness, homosexuality, and a positive valence for society at large, it will constitute something like a third gender role, much as the berdache role does in many American Indian tribes. Until then, Latino and other American gay men and their families will struggle with the kind of gender-dichotomous thinking that typically permits only the partial reconciliation of self, family, and society.

Coming Out in the Latino Family of Origin

As I have noted, the centrality of the family is emphasized among Latinos, with an expectation of loyalty, respect, and responsibility. Families are the primary support network consisting of many generations, roles, and relationships. The extended family tends to be in close communication with the nuclear family members, and godparents are expected to play an active role, functioning as co-parents (*compadre* and *comadre*). Coming out to the family tends to be a source of high stress and anxiety, as the gay person fears personal rejection and family ostracism. For Latino gays, family acceptance varies, and it is not clear whether Latinos have more or less difficulty in coming out to their families than other ethnic groups. A unique challenge for Latino parents is the intense conflict they experience between valuing the son as a family member and having negative attitudes about his being gay. For some families, it is easier to cope if a woman is still in their son's life, through dating, being married, or being recently divorced. If the family believes the son is still or was recently involved with women romantically, they may dismiss the son's conflict of identity as a capricious act rather than a way of life.

For many Latino gay men, disclosure to family members creates anxiety for reasons related to Latino cultural values. Disclosing one's sexual orientation may be perceived as causing harm and pain to parents and relatives. This goes against the cultural expectation of machismo in that Latinos are expected to protect the family from harm. In a study of culturally sanctioned secrets, Latinos, as compared to their Euro-Caucasian counterparts, tended to withhold their HIV-positive status from parents to keep the parents from worrying rather than to avoid personal rejection (Mason, Marks, Simoni, Ruiz, & Richardson, 1995). Acculturation also played an important role in disclosure. Among the Latino gay and bisexual men in this study, Spanish-speaking, as compared to English-speaking Latinos were more likely to withhold their HIV-positive status and sexual orientation from family members. This implies that Latino gays who are more acculturated are more likely to disclose their sexual orientation to their families.

The awareness of sexuality among family members varies by generations, values, and beliefs. Understanding someone being gay is different for different members of the family, such as children, parents, adolescents, young adults, grandparents, uncles and aunts, sisters and brothers, *padrinos* (godfathers) and *madrinas* (godmothers). It is likely that some family members will harbor negative perceptions about gayness due to the linguistic and cultural influences of Latino experience. This disjunction of family members' attitudes and the Latino gay person's actual life will be a major source of conflict within the family. If the family member holds the culturally defined, stereotyped, public view of a gay person, that is, that gays are alien, feminine, or inferior, then the perceptions of that family member will conflict with the actual identity and self-perception of the Latino gay person.

For instance, a gay person may see himself as an androgynous, gay-identified male, whereas a family member may think all gays are feminine-identified drag queens. When the gay person discloses his sexual orientation to this family member, the latter is likely to superimpose a drag-queen frame of reference onto the gay person's disclosure. The family member may thus hear the disclosure as if it were an announcement of being something akin to a transvestite prostitute. This two-person dynamic can be compounded further by other family members' misconceptions, which may include viewing him as living contrary to God's wishes and therefore being a sinner, or viewing him as a confused bisexual man who will eventually change and get married, or seeing him as someone who has been corrupted by White society and is abandoning his own people and Latino customs.

Learning how to cope with these potentially conflicting perceptions is critical for the Latino gay. Before coming out to the family, he should consider the advantages and consequences of doing so, including the likelihood that other family members will filter his disclosure through radically different interpretive frameworks than the one he has in mind.

Coming out to family members inevitably changes one's relationships with them. One should ask, Why do I want to come out to my family, and am I likely to achieve my purpose? What frames of reference will they use to understand my disclosure? Will I be able to manage the emotional fallout in each relationship in the family? Unlike other family issues, coming out to one's parents invariably changes the relationship dynamic from a parent-son paradigm to an adult-adult paradigm. Revealing the affectional and emotional parts of one's adult life as an equal with parents sets up the possibility that they will be expected to do the same in return. To what extent will parents be able to adapt to this new adult-to-adult reciprocity? Will the disclosure bring up questions about other family members' sexual behavior? How will that information be managed? Preparing for such scenarios is very important in the decision-making process of coming out to family. Most important, the gay person should prepare himself for the possibility that the family's accurate understanding of his life may take many, many years or may never happen to his satisfaction.

As changes occur within the family following disclosure, the family may need assistance in coping. The main focus of family intervention at this point is to clarify the differences in perceptions about what it means to be a gay person and how there are different types of Latino gay people with different sexual identities and lifestyles. Helping family members become aware of how the broader society influences their attitudes should be a central theme of the intervention. The Latino value placed on respecting the family and all of its members should be emphasized. Accepting the gay person as a family member and emphasizing the family's responsibility to be loyal to him, as he would be loyal to them, should be a primary goal. Once the gay person's continuing membership in the family is affirmed, the nature of the family's loyalty and support can be discussed.

Subsequently, the family's development of a realistic understanding of what it means to be gay can begin in earnest. Under most circumstances, this process will take at least several years. There will be many ups and downs; tolerance and comfort will grow over time. The success of the process will depend partly on the gay person's own commitment, persistence, happiness, and self-confidence in his sexual orientation identity, as well as the strength of his social support network outside the family. If the gay person starts out this process but lapses into a state of confusion, self-hate, depression, loneliness, or unassertiveness, his disclosure is more likely to be met with extreme and continuing ambivalence and resistance by the family. Hence, the timing of the initial disclosure and other steps in integrating his two communities should be determined by the gay person's own self-acceptance and ability to anticipate and cope with whatever the family's reaction may be.

Latino Gay Couples

The five states of Latino gay identity integration and the four-category typology of Latino men who have sex with men describe factors that influence the way these men view and interact with one another. By integrating gender-specific characteristics in their sexual orientation identities, they incorporate the broader societal notions of how two adult persons should relate to each other romantically and sexually. Heterosexual couples are the all-pervasive and visible models in Latino families and communities. The lack of acceptable models for gay couple relationships and the strong Latino emphasis on a masculine-feminine gender dichotomy predisposes many Latino gay men to use heterosexual relationships as templates for their own relationships. This use of heterosexual models may contribute to the gender-role assignments some Latino gays and bisexuals believe they must follow in order to be coupled. For example, straight-identified Latino men who have sex with men may seek drag queens as partners, and vice versa, because their gender roles are (at least on the surface) complementary and reflective of society's ubiquitous heterosexual arrangements.

Hence, combinations of partners' different identity states tend to be accompanied by particular dynamics in the relationships, which in turn affect the shape of the interaction patterns and the partners' general relationship satisfaction. Masculinity, femininity, androgyny, states of identity integration, stages of coming out, socioeconomic status, being monocultural versus bicultural, spirituality, religiosity, and family relationships—combined with each partner's personal history and life experience as a Latino gay man—together constitute a myriad of factors that come into play when Latino gay men have relationships.

Interracial and cross-cultural relationships involving Latinos present additional dynamics so complex as to warrant an entire additional chapter in the future. However, one can readily imagine how differences between partners with regard to racial and cultural perceptions, combined with personal histories, can set up power dynamics based on cultural heritage, race relations in the society, and gender-role characterizations of power. Discrepancies in values, sexual identity, culture, gender role, skin color, and socioeconomic status between partners can be sources of conflict and stress. The stories of Miguel and Juan, and of José and Luis, illustrate some of these couple dynamics.

CASE 1: MIGUEL AND JUAN

Miguel, a soft-spoken, polite man with a gentle smile walked into my office and quietly sat down. I noticed he was wearing some women's accessories and perfume. Speaking English with a strong Spanish accent, he told me that he had been depressed for the past several months. He had not been able to sleep, and he felt very anxious. Miguel was born and raised in Mexico and had lived in the United States for the past ten years. His family still resided in Mexico. He explained that he was in a relationship with another man, Juan, who identifies as bisexual and also was born and raised in Mexico. They have been together for three years, seeing each other daily.

Miguel feels a lack of reciprocity in the relationship. Juan is married and has a family, including two children. In addition, Juan is very jealous and controlling, wanting to know at all times where Miguel is and whom he has been with each day. Miguel reports that he does a lot of work in the house, taking care of and cleaning the home, whereas Juan contributes little in this effort. Miguel also helps Juan by sometimes providing financial assistance for Juan's family. Miguel believes that things would go better if Juan would spend more time with him and talk through their problems rather than provoking the kind of arguments that have led to physical confrontations in the past.

In addition, Miguel feels his friends are tired of hearing his story, and he has no one to talk to about his situation. He does not want to give up the relationship and feels that Juan loves him. He describes how Juan shows his love in several ways, such as being gentle, warm, caring, and romantic. In addition, he states that Juan is *un hombre devera* ("a real man"), which is important to Miguel, as he is attracted only to men who enact a very masculine gender role. He believes that Juan will not come to therapy.

It is clear that the gender-role identity issues play a central part in this scenario. Miguel appears to be somewhere between being gay-identified and a drag queen or perhaps a *ponca,* while Juan is bisexual- to straight-identified. Consequently, Miguel enacts a more feminine role (*marianismo*); he feels responsible for the care of the household and Juan's family. For his complementary part (*machismo*), Juan feels pulled between taking care of his family members and of Miguel, all of whom depend on him to be strong emotionally and decisive. As for identity formation, since both partners were born and raised in Mexico, Miguel did not experience conflicts pertaining to differences over their allegiances to a Mexican identity.

For Juan, State 2 (bisexual versus gay) appears to have some relevance because he identifies himself as bisexual, he has been in a primary love and sexual relationship with Miguel for three years, but he still maintains a strong familial attachment to his wife and children. Juan may be in a process of coming out and eventually identifying as gay, but he has not been able to rethink or prioritize the nature of his commitments to his family and to Juan.

For Miguel, his different circles of friends seem frustrated over his unresolved conflict with Juan, and their frustrations mirror his own internal conflicts in allegiances (State 3 in sexual identity integration). Miguel's gay-identified Euro-Caucasian and Latino friends see the couple's problem as reflecting both partners' internalized homophobia. By contrast, his Latino friends who identify as poncas or drag queens see his behavior as part of the negative aspects of marianismo, and they tease and confront him for acting like "María de la Pendeja" (Maria, the suffering fool).

If Miguel favored the ideology of his gay-identified friends, he would view himself as suffering from internalized homophobia, a lessening of which might lead to his rejecting Juan in favor of finding a gay-affirmative future partner who could commit to gay couplehood and a more symmetrical relationship. If he favored the ideology of his friends who are drag queens or poncas, Miguel would view himself as a self-sacrificing, foolish girlfriend, and the solution might be to insist that Juan show more respect, give more comfort, spend more time together, be more willing to listen to Miguel's feelings, provide more financially, and perhaps eventually leave his wife in order to be Miguel's "husband." Finally, if Miguel viewed the relationship from the perspective of heterosexual Latino culture and gender roles (marianismo), he might view himself as not being self-sacrificing enough, and the solution might be to put more of his own needs aside, lovingly support the man's (Juan's) wishes, and honor and protect the intactness of Juan's heterosexual family of procreation.

Miguel is thus caught among three discrepant cultural frameworks for evaluating the relationship (reflective of State 3, conflicts of allegiance), and his own feelings oscillate among these three positions. In this "couples therapy through one person," helping Miguel clarify the nature of his internal conflict (and the three social reference groups that contribute to it) may enable him to take consistent actions in relation to Juan. In turn, such a stance by Miguel will eventually trigger changes in the relationship that will determine its future. For example, in response to more consistent requests from Miguel, Juan may rework his sexual orientation identity and make a stronger commitment, as a primarily gay rather than bisexual man, to Miguel. If Juan does not change, Miguel eventually may seek a more gay-identified partner who is prepared for a primary commitment.

CASE 2: LUIS AND JOSÉ

I received a call from Luis requesting couples therapy. In the first session, Luis and his partner, José, entered the room and sat close to each other, a sign of committed couplehood and the comfortable gay identification of both partners. Luis is a Black Cuban, thirty-eight years of age, who now identifies himself as gay although he was married in the past. He was born and raised in Cuba and came to the United States about fifteen years ago. His primary language is Spanish, and he speaks English with a Cuban accent. Luis was able to complete his high school education in Cuba and took some courses at a community college in the States. Now he works for the U.S. Postal Service.

José is of Puerto Rican descent and was born and raised in a large metropolitan area in the United States. He is very light skinned. José has a master's degree and is working for a large company directing a department. He identifies himself as gay. He has never married and speaks mostly English, although he understands some Spanish. José is actively involved in different gay-identified organizations, whereas Luis tends to be more of a homebody, preferring to center his activities around family and home life.

José has been feeling lonely and isolated in the relationship, stating that Luis does not understand why he is involved in different activities. When José brings up this problem for discussion, Luis tends to shut down and seems lost in the conversation. Luis accuses José of being too White and gay-identified in his organizational activities and feels that José is bringing these problems on himself. Luis also states that he does not like the social affairs he attends with José because he feels out of place being around what he calls high-class gays, who tend to avoid him because he is Black.

Conversely, José also expresses difficulty going to places that Luis likes because he, too, feels out of place. All of the people are straight, they speak Spanish, and he feels that they are critical of his Spanish because they constantly correct his word choice and grammar. Also, he questions their real acceptance of his being gay and the couple relationship. Both Luis and José still believe in the viability of their relationship but feel that their differences have put them at an impasse.

A variety of issues put stress on this couple. The matter of race affects them in terms of how others, who are not Latino, view them. Although José would like both partners to be active together in community affairs involving the broader gay and lesbian community, subtle and not-so-subtle racism during these events negatively affects Luis's participation and contributes to his nonattendance. So José goes to these meetings alone, and Luis feels alienated and abandoned. On the other hand, José's limited proficiency in Spanish and embarrassment about this limitation make him feel inadequate about his own ethnic identity, raising the question in his mind about whether he is "Puerto Rican enough" or whether he is sacrificing his ethnic identity to conform to the White gay community. Inevitably, this dynamic places both Luis and José in State 4 of the identity formation model (claiming a Latino gay identity).

The lack of integration between these different communities drives a wedge in the couple's relationship, and the partners tend to personalize this division, feeling hurt by each other's disappointment and the separateness of their social activities. Among other therapeutic tasks, the therapist can help them to externalize their conflicts— attributing the causes to the very real racial, ethnic, and homophobic prejudices that exist in their various social groups. This externalization of the conflict will unite the partners in a shared understanding of the discrimination they both experience and their determination to fight it. In addition, the couple can be helped to deal with such discrimination when it occurs, preventing the exclusions or corrections of one partner during social interactions with outsiders. Finally, the couple may be encouraged to become active in local, state, and national organizations whose agendas include the elimination of prejudice in the gay and heterosexual communities.

Conclusion

For family therapists who are new to the topic of Latino gay and bisexual men, the concepts presented in this chapter may seem extremely complicated or exotic. However, as I and other community psychologists have learned, Latino gay and bisexual men spontaneously confirm the relevance of these ideas through stories told to us every day. When these concepts have been offered to focus groups for their feedback, Latino gay participants easily recognize their lives in these descriptions. The opportunities that have been created over the years for these men to discuss their lives with one another is the most rewarding aspect of this work.

For the researcher, the challenge is to truly discover naturalistic, culturally at-tuned paradigms that fit the experiences of Latino gays and bisexuals without imposing theories and constructs developed in other cultures. Qualitative research methods, clinical and community experience, and observations in natural social settings have been essential in developing an understanding. The analogous tasks for therapists are twofold: (1) to develop specific bicultural competence in work-ing with this population so that the relevant questions are raised, and (2) to use the most basic reflective listening skills of therapy to guard against making hasty, pre-sumptuous, or ethnocentric interventions. Therapists should listen intently to clients' subjective narratives and continually check to make sure their understanding of clients' experiences is full and fitting—from *the clients'* frame of reference.

This chapter is a first effort to integrate thinking about gender roles, family re-lationships, and couple functioning among Latino gay and bisexual men. As such, it opens some new vistas but cannot provide a comprehensive map of the territory that ultimately needs to be explored, especially in terms of applying these concepts in conjoint couples and family therapy sessions. Many of the traditional approaches to family therapy—Bowenian, structural, narrative, solution-focused, and cognitive-behavioral—are useful in helping Latino gay and bisexual clients resolve some of the difficulties traditionally presented for therapy. However, I believe that *when it comes to the cultural dimensions of family problems that are highlighted in this chapter, it is most valuable clinically to provide an opportunity for these men to talk to each other in groups and to gen-erate solutions to the couple and family difficulties they commonly face.* Such groups help fos-ter participants' clearer awareness of the constraints and advantages in their Latino, gay, and mainstream contexts. The chance to describe and compare their unique couple and family experiences contributes to a sense of community, of fully be-longing, and of understanding themselves on their own terms.

References

Bartholow, B. N., Doll, L. S., Joy, D., Douglas, J. M., Bolan, G., Harrison, J., Moss, P. M., & McKirnan, D. (1994). Emotional, behavioral and HIV risk associated with sexual abuse among adult homosexual and bisexual men. *Child Abuse and Neglect, 18,* 747–761.

Bernal, G. (1982). Cuban families. In M. McGoldrick, J. K. Pearce, & J. Giordano (Eds.), *Eth-nicity and family therapy* (pp. 187–207). New York: Guilford Press.

Carballo-Diéguez, A. (1995). The sexual identity and behavior of Puerto Rican men who have sex with men. In G. M. Herek & B. Greene (Eds.), *AIDS, identity, and community: The HIV epidemic and lesbians and gay men: Psychological perspectives on lesbian and gay issues* (vol. 2, pp. 105–114). Newbury Park, CA: Sage.

Carballo-Diéguez, A., & Dolezal, C. (1995). Association between history of childhood sexual abuse and adult HIV-risk sexual behavior in Puerto Rican men who have sex with men. *Child Abuse and Neglect, 19,* 595–605.

Carrier, J. (1976). Family attitudes and Mexican male homosexuality. *Urban Life, 5,* 359–375.

Carrier, J. (1977). "Sex-role preference" as an explanatory variable in homosexual behavior. *Archives of Sexual Behavior, 6,* 53–65.

Carrier, J. (1989). Sexual behavior and spread of AIDS in Mexico. *Medical Anthropology, 10,* 129–142.

Falicov, C. J. (1982). Mexican families. In M. McGoldrick, J. K. Pearce, & J. Giordano (Eds.), *Ethnicity and family therapy* (pp. 134–163). New York: Guilford Press.

Garcia-Preto, N. (1982). Puerto Rican families. In M. McGoldrick, J. K. Pearce, & J. Giordano (Eds.), *Ethnicity and family therapy* (pp. 164–186). New York: Guilford Press.

Marshall, S. C. (1993). *Psychosocial correlates of substance abuse among Latino adolescents.* Unpublished doctoral dissertation, California School of Professional Psychology, Alameda.

Mason, H.R.C., Marks, G., Simoni, J. M., Ruiz, M. S., & Richardson, J. L. (1995). Culturally sanctioned secrets? Latino men's nondisclosure of HIV infection to family, friends and lovers. *Health Psychology, 14,* 6–12.

Morales, E. (1983). *Third World gays and lesbians: A process of multiple identities.* Paper presented at the 91st National Convention of the American Psychological Association, Anaheim, CA.

Morales, E. (1990). Ethnic minority families and minority gays and lesbians. In F. Bozett & M. Sussman (Eds.), *Homosexuality and family relations* (pp. 217–239). Binghamton, NY: Haworth Press.

Morales, E. (1992) Counseling Latino gays and Latina lesbians. In F. Gutierrez & S. Dworkin (Eds.), *Counseling gay men and lesbians: Journey to the end of the rainbow* (pp. 125–139). Alexandria, VA: American Association for Counseling and Development.

Preston, J. (1991). *The big gay book.* New York: Viking Penguin.

Santisteban, D., & Szapocznik, J. (1982). Substance abuse disorders among Hispanics: A focus on prevention. In R. M. Becerra (Ed.), *Mental health and Hispanic Americans: Clinical perspectives* (pp. 83–100). Philadelphia: Grune & Stratton.

Williams, W. L. (1992). *The spirit and the flesh: Sexual diversity in American Indian culture.* Boston: Beacon Press.

CHAPTER TWELVE

LESBIAN COUPLES AND CHILDHOOD TRAUMA

Guidelines for Therapists

Shoshana D. Kerewsky and Dusty Miller

It is not known how many women in the United States have been victims of childhood trauma and sexual abuse. Regardless of the actual numbers, it is more likely that issues related to sexual abuse will be present in a lesbian couple simply because it consists of two women. Although some of the challenges raised by childhood trauma may be shared by any couple, some may be unique to the dynamics of lesbian relationships. The secrecy and isolation common to many lesbians and to many trauma survivors may present obstacles to integrating, making sense of, and moving beyond these experiences.

In preparing this article, we utilized a narrative approach (Polkinghorne, 1988), gathering ideas by interviewing therapists whose practices include lesbian couples with trauma and related dynamics. These therapists' reflections are intertwined with theoretical formulations that help typify both the difficulties and benefits that lesbian couples may experience as they work through their trauma-related issues. We then suggest a treatment approach that combines strate-

The authors wish to thank Elaine Campbell, Yvonne Lutter, Caryn Markson, and Robin Moulds for their participation in these interviews.
Previously published in the *Journal of Feminist Family Therapy*, Volume 7, #(3/4), pp. 115–133, 1995 as "Lesbian Couples and Childhood Trauma," and reprinted with the permission of The Haworth Press, Inc., Publisher, and the authors.

gies from both authors' work with other populations. By making lesbian and other culturally marginal experiences "core and central" (Brown, 1989), we may illuminate unexamined assumptions in the majority culture. Even as we try to demarginalize lesbians, we are aware that our chapter does not necessarily represent the experience of many nondominant subgroups, for example, lesbians who are physically challenged or ethnically diverse or lesbians of color. Although this study is just a beginning, the paucity of research on lesbian health issues demands that more research be undertaken.

Locating the Problem

Estimates of child abuse have ranged from 25 percent of all women in the United States (Nichols, 1987) to as high as 70 percent of psychiatric emergency room patients of both genders (Briere & Zaidi, 1989, as cited in Herman, 1992). Determining the rate is complicated by different researchers' definitions of what constitutes trauma and abuse. In the examples and discussion that follow, we use the complex Post-traumatic Stress Disorder (PTSD) model (Herman, 1992), which can be summarized as trauma such as child sexual abuse that is sustained over a prolonged period, is perpetrated by someone in a caretaker role in the child's life, and tends to be more damaging than a single traumatic incident. The nature of the abuse is less important than the fact that it is sustained abuse in the context of an ongoing relationship.

The relationship between traumatic experiences in childhood and adult sexual orientation is poorly understood and by no means simple. Though some theorists have held that traumatic experiences with men cause women to become lesbian, little empirical research was conducted until recently (Bradford, Ryan, & Rothblum, 1994; Brannock & Chapman, 1990; Peters & Cantrell, 1991). Some researchers are reluctant to undertake studies that may contribute to a vision of lesbianism as originating in pathology (Rothblum, 1994). However, in recent studies, Brannock and Chapman (1990) found *no significant difference between matched samples of lesbian and heterosexual women's reports of number of negative sexual experiences with men*. Peters and Cantrell (1991) report similar findings. In an attempt to reconcile their findings with previous research, they speculate that "lesbians from *clinical* samples [appear to] have experienced more negative heterosexual experiences with men than have heterosexual women from similar settings" (p. 13, emphasis added) but that non-clinical samples show no difference. Loulan (1987) found a reported history of sexual abuse in 38 percent of the lesbians in her sample; this is comparable to the percentage of both lesbian and heterosexual women in Brannock and Chapman's (1990) and in Peters and Cantrell's (1991) samples. The ambitious National Lesbian Health Care Survey found that of 1,925 lesbians surveyed, 24 percent reported physical abuse while growing up; 21 percent reported rape or sexual attack; and 19 percent reported incest (Bradford et al., 1994).

Regardless of the findings of empirical research, some women with histories of childhood abuse may themselves attribute their lesbian identity to these experiences (see Browning, Reynolds, & Dworkin, 1991), while others do not. Learning how the client understands her lesbian identity and the relationship she perceives between childhood events and adult identity may provide the therapist with important information about the client's worldview and self-narratives.

For some women, there does indeed appear to be a causal link between abuse and identity but in the reverse direction. Recent studies on gay, lesbian, and bisexual youth report that early lesbian identity or activities can in fact lead to various forms of sexual, physical, verbal, and emotional abuse by relatives, peers, and strangers, who respond to the disclosure with anger and violence (Governor's Commission on Gay and Lesbian Youth, 1993; Hetrick & Martin, 1987; Martin & Hetrick, 1988; Savin-Williams, 1994).

The fact that a lesbian couple consists of two women means that the chance is greater than in a heterosexual couple that a history of trauma will be present (Clunis & Green, 1993; Loulan, 1987). However, some of the challenges and concerns raised by childhood trauma may be shared by any couple. Meiselman (1990) reviewed studies of women in psychotherapy and found "many more sexual problems in incest survivors than in other women from the same clinical population" (p. 56). Typical relationship areas of concern for many trauma survivors include sexual intimacy, trust and protection, gender identification, social isolation, shame and secrecy, self-injury, and caretaking dynamics.

In a lesbian relationship, some of these issues may be avoided at least partially, while others are heightened. For example, the problems a heterosexual survivor may experience with her male partner, especially in power-based interactions or during sexual intimacy, are potentially less likely to occur with a female partner, simply because the female partner does not so literally represent male power dynamics or male anatomy. On the other hand, issues of shame, secrecy, and isolation may be amplified and compounded for survivors in lesbian relationships by factors such as outward and internalized homophobia and lack of social, family, and peer supports. We have found it useful to understand a traumatic history as forming the third point of a triangle for the couple, a metaphor we now discuss in some detail.

Major Themes in Couples Treatment

In order to enrich our understanding of prominent areas in which trauma may be profitably viewed as being triangulated in the lesbian couple, we relied not only on the authors' clinical experience and the literature reviewed above but also on interviews with four experienced therapists who work extensively with Caucasian lesbian clients and trauma survivors. The second author used an unstructured interview to avoid imposing her preconceptions on the conversation (Polkinghorne, 1988) and to invite the respondents' reflections on major themes that emerge in their work with lesbian couples. Following the authors' treatment perspectives (Kerewsky, 1995b; Miller, 1990, 1994) and the narrative approach (Laird, 1994; Polkinghorne, 1988; White & Epston, 1990), we understand these interviews as information or stories about the couple and their relationship.

Triangulation

In the family therapy literature, many writers, notably Bowen (1978) and Minuchin (1974), have proposed models of systemic function characterized by triangular functioning. When we use the term *triangulation,* we refer not to a third person but to the sustained presence of a third, metaphorical entity utilized by the couple to perpetuate their static modes of interaction. Often, triangulation is viewed as a problem for couples and an issue for their therapists' consideration. Many clinicians think of triangulation as something undesirable, demanding inspection and then elimination. From our perspective, triangulation more neutrally describes a third presence in the couple. It can be a helpful presence or an unwelcome one, depending on what the couple and the therapist decide to do with it. Understanding an issue as creating triangulation in the couple is one way to *externalize the problem,* a perspective central to the work of the narrative-focused therapists (O'Hanlon, 1994; White & Epston, 1990). Instead of seeing the couple as "conflictual" or "splitting," we can use the concept of triangulation to place the problem outside the couple and make it into a third presence. If, for example, conflict is the third point of the triangle, we might see the couple as being dominated or hypnotized by Conflict, which in this way is framed as an entity existing outside the couple. When problems are externalized, they become available for scrutiny and treatment. We follow White and Epston (1990) in capitalizing the externalized problem (for example, Conflict or Trauma). This usage has the effect of highlighting the problem by treating it anthropomorphically as an entity rather than as an attribute of the client herself. However, we do not reify the problem or suggest that it is a permanent and immutable member of the partnership. Rather, presenting the problem anthropomorphically allows clients to see it as bounded and external to themselves.

Externalizing the problem provides clients with a new way to understand and retell their experiences. This demonstrates that the client's world has the potential to be reunderstood in a different light, thus modeling the process of therapeutic change and suggesting an avenue for introducing new narratives. As clients gain experience and skill at restorying their experience, they are encouraged to keep their metaphors lively and descriptive of their concurrent circumstances.

We next turn to a brief description of areas where triangulation may occur.

Sexual Intimacy

It would seem that the lesbian couple might have an easier time avoiding what we have termed *perpetrator projection,* in which the trauma survivor projects the internalized image of the abuser onto her partner and therefore experiences the partner as dangerous, violating, or repulsive. Because the majority of child sexual abuse is perpetrated by males, certainly the actual anatomy of the partner will be different from that of an abuser (except in the less common instance of female-perpetrated child abuse). In addition, dominance-submission dynamics of sexual intimacy are generally less overt in lesbian sexual activity.

Yet it is as if lesbian couples have a silent, symbolic bed partner triangulated regularly in the form of one or both women's trauma history. Sexual activity may be used as a way to try to address or compensate for the trauma. One therapist described a cycle she sees in many of her client couples: "They want to feel safety, they retreat into homogeneity, and moving forward stops—and sex stops." Clients had problems with sexual addictions, while some had illicit, secretive sex through affairs, seemingly as a way of repeating the trauma of childhood sexual abuse. "Some couples with a trauma history come to therapy around being overly attached to sexuality as the only means of expressing connection," said one therapist. "Or else they come in because they don't want to have sex at all."

For many survivors of childhood abuse, adult sexual activity can stimulate flashbacks and very specific, localized sexual aversions. Lesbian couples may not readily talk about their sexual life together. Avoidance of talking about sex (or of sexual activity altogether) may seem appealing to partners both socialized to avoid making sexual demands or socialized to believe that sex isn't really that important.

All of the therapists interviewed concurred that there are heightened issues of sexual jealousy for their "survivor" couples. "At any moment, ex-lovers or friends can be viewed as dangerous," explained one therapist, "because family closeness in childhood also could turn suddenly into sexual betrayal. I have to work with the couple in this situation to make Trauma, not a third person, the third member of the couple so we can deal with it."

Trust and Protection Issues

Most survivors of childhood trauma have compelling concerns connected to their experience of not feeling protected in childhood (Miller, 1994). Their childhood trust in adult caretakers was doubly betrayed by both the acts of violation they experienced and by the horror of not being shielded, rescued, or comforted by the parent who "should" have been there. Issues of trust and protection most often raise unhealed ambivalence toward mothers, an especially complex issue for lesbians in relationship.

The therapists we talked to often focused heavily on "the mother issue" in talking about lesbian couples and triangulation. "The neglectful, nonprotective, abandoning mother projection is *always* there with survivor lesbian couples," one therapist commented. "The partner can look like the enemy. The hope to be understood is disappointed—it's like the original betrayal all over again." Another therapist talked about the problem the couple may have "locating responsibility for protection . . . so that the survivor can collapse her need for mothering in the arms of the other. [The survivor] can hold the other responsible for her own self-care. She may have to learn not to hand over her [Inner] Child to her partner for care."

Another form of triangulation may occur when one woman brings her partner's family into their relationship symbolically or metaphorically. The nontraumatized partner may triangle in the abusing family at times of stress or disjunction in the couple's relationship. Similarly, the traumatized partner may be painfully envious of a nontraumatized partner's imagined better-functioning family.

Gender Identity

The trauma survivor's ambivalence toward her mother also may surface in complications of gender identification. Although this is also true for heterosexuals, for the lesbian it may have special relevance for her couple relationship. Being female may represent being weak, vulnerable, and powerless because she, as a female child, was vulnerable to the male abuser and because her female parent was powerless to protect her. If her abuser was female, the survivor may have additional reasons to avoid identifying with the "bad" female.

This has obvious implications for the lesbian couple. When gender identification plays a negative role in the couple's attitudes about femaleness, several different situations may occur. If the couple is made up of one survivor and one nonsurvivor, the survivor may express both covert and openly misogynist prejudices. She may devalue herself or may choose to take on a more androgynous or masculine style to avoid the vulnerability she associates with being female. She may additionally (or alternately) devalue her partner's femaleness, fearing that her partner may replicate the female position of vulnerability or betrayal she experienced in childhood. She also may worry about taking on a reciprocal, abusive role in her partnership.

In sexual interactions, these dynamics may be played out in various ways. For example, "A lesbian survivor may, as a reaction to her childhood experience of trauma, insist on being instrumental rather than receptive in order to protect against vulnerability," explained one therapist. "The partner can feel very constricted and frustrated by this, wishing to have some opportunities to also feel more assertive or instrumental in sexual activities." This may lead to a silent impasse in which sexual activity decreases or ceases altogether.

Social Isolation, Shame, and Secrecy

Family-situated violations such as incest, physical abuse, and psychological terrorism create chronic conditions of isolation, shame, and secrecy for all family members, especially the victims. This pattern often continues into adult life (Miller, 1993, 1994) and is replicated in the adult survivor's relationships and general life functioning. Unfortunately, it also is true that many gays and lesbians are forced into patterns of secrecy and isolation. External homophobia may generate internalized homophobia, characterized by a general feeling of shame. It is not surprising, then, that lesbian couples in which one or both partners have a history of trauma often experience a double level of secrecy, isolation, and shame in daily life. One therapist described this as "creating a false self, a lack of authenticity in [the survivor's] self-narrative. This can lead to her identity in the couple being clouded . . . and it can keep the lesbian couple from being able to take their partnership out into the world for fear of how the world will receive them."

A related observation was expressed by one of the therapists, who noted that both lesbians and trauma survivors are sexually delineated: "Lesbians are identified in the heterosexual world by the choice of who they're sexually intimate with, and sexual trauma survivors are also identified by a history of stigmatized sexual activity." The lesbian couple may feel an intensified sense of being sexualized by the outside world and thus stigmatized and shamed.

Another form of isolation develops when the couple fears sexual betrayal by women close to them. Thus, the experience of isolation in one's family of origin and the isolation of the entire family may be unwittingly replicated by the social isolation of the lesbian couple, who may feel unsafe both within the predominantly heterosexual community and within the lesbian community as well. When isolation, shame, and secrecy are repeated, the metaphorical presence of Trauma may play a decidedly malevolent role.

Where there is a strong sense of lesbian community, however, there may be more overt and well-organized support for trauma survivors than in more heterogeneous communities and therefore for the couple struggling with trauma-related issues. In many communities, lesbians have well-established support groups dealing with both lesbian identity and trauma issues. Community support can help lesbian couples be less isolated and more able to find helpful ways to connect with others around the challenges of the trauma influence in the couple relationship.

Self-Injury

"Some couples seem to triangulate trauma-related addictions as if the addiction is a third person in the triangle," said one therapist. "They seem to reenact the childhood abuse through the use of alcohol or drugs or sexual addiction, so the third party in the system is the alcohol or the sexual acting out."

Many female survivors of childhood trauma suffer a variety of self-harmful behavior patterns in adult life (Miller, 1994). Lesbian trauma survivors are, of course, no exception. When one or both members have self-injury problems such as substance abuse, eating disorders, or self-mutilation, the couple may be affected in a variety of ways. The addictive behavior may force the partner into a codependent role or may create conflict and mistrust. If the trauma survivor is heavily dependent on her addiction as a means of coping with the aftereffects of the trauma or uses her trauma history to excuse her addictive activities, the nonsurvivor partner may feel silenced, resentful, and hopeless.

More positively, being lesbian may help the couple cope more effectively with a trauma-based addiction. In highly organized lesbian communities, there are many resources for those with addiction issues and their partners. Instead of cloaking the addictive behavior in secrecy and shame, the survivor is encouraged to be open and to seek support, which of course benefits her partner as well. The support that the couple receives in combating the addiction may provide them with a model to use in organizing themselves against the triangulated presence of trauma.

Caretaking Dynamics

In discussing generalized power and control issues related to lesbian couples' trauma histories, one therapist commented that the tendency among some lesbian couples to merge or fuse was often counteracted in the Couple-Trauma triangle. "It could feel unsafe for the survivor to allow merging. Survivors have individuation issues in their couple." This dynamic also may be more positively understood as, or bear the seeds of, the capacity to maintain a successful sense of individual identity as well as of connection.

Another therapist took a somewhat different view, describing the problem of the nonsurvivor partner being put in the caretaker position. "Because of how all-consuming the survivor's recovery work gets, the caretaker's needs get swallowed up in the relationship. Often the caretaking partner ends up feeling betrayed because her needs are being ignored and she leaves. Then the survivor feels abandoned."

Several therapists identified challenges for the couple when both are trauma survivors. In the best circumstances, the couple has a mutually heightened capacity to understand and support each other, but too frequently, the needs of both are overwhelming, and they can easily trigger each other. This led one therapist to comment on the importance of helping lesbian trauma survivors to move beyond the identity of being wounded and stigmatized.

The therapist went on to explain:

> The lesbian trauma survivor can feel three times stigmatized: She's part of three stigmatized groups because she's a woman, a lesbian, and a trauma victim. And she can be made to feel that her choice to be a lesbian is stigmatized if it's seen as a negative choice—if she had a bad experience with a man [i.e. her perpetrator], then that's why she's a lesbian. So she can get into believing herself [to be] wounded even if that view of her is coming from within.

Summary and Caveats

Trauma can function as an externalized presence that may either dominate and intimidate or work to the benefit of the lesbian couple. Trauma is then a powerful third member of the system, which the couple can view as either unwelcome and distracting or as a source of strengthening, resilience, or enhancement. It is important to bear in mind that some survivors respond to their experience of childhood trauma by demonstrating unusual qualities of resilience (Baures, 1994; Herman, 1992; McCann & Pearlman, 1990). For example, the experience of trauma may lead to a capacity for heightened empathic attunement (Miller, 1994), which may benefit both the couple and others in their community network. Lesbian couples' positive solutions to, and outcomes of, childhood trauma may serve to guide not only lesbians, but all survivors.

Suggestions for Therapists

In developing the treatment strategy that follows, we have integrated aspects of our previous work. Our therapeutic frame is the second author's three-stage treatment model for working with families and adults affected by trauma (Miller, 1994). The first author has worked extensively with the uses of writing and expressive art objects in clinical and nonclinical contexts (Kerewsky, 1995a, 1995b). Her workbook for lesbian and bisexual women serves as our guide for exploratory and follow-up writing assignments. These exercises help the couple externalize the issues triangulated in their relationship, manage thoughts and feelings aroused by engagement with the trauma, and make their therapeutic gains tangible.

Suggested Treatment Model

Miller (1990) has summarized her treatment model as follows:

> [The model] integrates . . . the systemic and the intrapsychic, and moves through three major stages, the Outer, Middle, and Inner "Circles" of conversation. Moving from the outer, or systemic, circle, the therapist gathers information about family rules, myths, beliefs, and sequences which provide information necessary to construct a new, more trust-based relationship with the client.

> In the Middle Circle, the problematic behaviors are addressed directly. The clients are helped to connect with relevant peer support resources, like 12-step recovery groups and other professional systems such as hospitals, legal systems, or school personnel. Then, within the inner, or intrapsychic, circle, the therapist can work with the client on reconfiguring the internalized schema. The use of sequential circles also allows the client time to observe the therapist and engage at her own pace. (pp. 18–19)

This general model (elaborated in Miller, 1994) has fruitful applications to work with lesbian couples who are struggling with triangulated complex PTSD. We now turn to the role that writing may play in the resolution of trauma in general, then in the more specific context of this population and treatment model.

As Harber and Pennebaker (1992) remark, trauma survivors "struggle . . . tenaciously to find meaning in their ordeals" (p. 374). They suggest that writing helps trauma survivors regain their emotional and physical equilibrium, in part "by giving their traumas clear beginnings, middles and ends" (p. 376). As we are concerned that our therapeutic interventions not distress or disorganize our clients, we match assignments to the therapeutic foci and tasks of the three circles.

Writing assignments may help bridge therapeutic sessions for disorganized or dissociated clients, serving to hold and consolidate therapeutic gains. Writing may help the client to externalize Trauma and restory her experience. As Lax (1996) comments, "Stories are not . . . neutral, as they always come from some social or political context" (p. 8); these stories may contain factors that discourage the client's sense of personal agency (Anderson & Goolishian, 1992). Identification of the sources and assumptions that inform the client's story may assist her in creating a new understanding of her experiences. Penn and Frankfurt (1994) suggest the production of what they call "participant texts" by clients, in which "monological experience becomes an internal dialogical experience" (p. 218) through the discovery of different internal voices through guided writing, reading aloud, and revising of texts by the client, including "journals, letters to persons living and dead . . . 'notes' between sessions, personal biographies, dreams, poetry, and dialogues" (p. 219). The articulation of voices other than the dominant voice or perspective with which the client enters therapy parallels the externalization of the problem described above. In an example given by Penn and Frankfurt, "As mother's silent voice inside . . . [became] audible, [the client] could reply to it at last" (p. 227).

The multiple narratives of the participant text may help the client hold those events, feelings, and meanings that do not fit her self-narratives or schemas and which therefore provoke distress. By making room for the discrepant and discontinuous as well as the narrative and linear, the multiple text may provide the client with relief from the urgent press to create a unified story of her experience. Similarly, the partners of survivors also create narratives that must be externalized and examined.

In the discussions of writing that follow, several examples are given to suggest the direction that writing exercises might take within each of Miller's circles. In addition, popular sources of writing exercises abound (for example, Adams, 1990; Cameron, 1992; Goldberg, 1986, 1990; Kano, 1989), and many clients need little or no encouragement to define their own writing assignments. Posing questions the client herself has asked is another avenue for generating assignments.

We now turn to a more detailed exploration of our treatment suggestions.

The Outer Circle

Learning about the client's world and worldview provides the therapist with important insights into the client's understanding of her trauma history, her approach to therapy, and her understanding of her lesbian identity and lesbian relationships. The therapist's respectful information-gathering is nonintrusive, nonjudgmental, and curious and thus models a form of relational connectedness that may be very different from the traumatized client's previous experiences.

This first stage in the treatment is important for several reasons. First, the therapist has the opportunity to correct assumptions she or he may have about the lesbian couple. Some couples may begin talking with the therapist about the influence of the trauma and their beliefs about their lesbian couple identity as if there were a universal set of correct answers held by all trauma experts, survivors, and lesbians. Conversely, the partners may not have discussed these issues with each other enough to have established any degree of collective clarity. Attention to the dynamics between the couple as well as to the content of their stories may help the therapist gain a broader understanding of the couple's particular concerns.

In the early stages of working with the lesbian couple, the therapist may create opportunities for the couple to understand Trauma in a very different way. Instead of digging into the painful details of trauma history, the couple can instead experience new ways of relating to the trauma as a presence to be explored. They can learn to externalize and examine the trauma rather than see it as part of their essential couple identity.

Through explorations of the couple's often previously unspoken premises about power, control, secrets, gender privilege, and being different from others (in the family or in the world), the couple and the therapist can create a map for their therapeutic journey. Instead of going directly to the past and its nightmares of trauma, disappointment, betrayal, and fear, the therapist moves into the third place in the triangle usually occupied by Trauma and offers herself as a curious and respectful guide. Most clinicians and writers suggest that safety needs to be established prior to working on the trauma material (Herman, 1992; Miller, 1994). Lesbian clients who are well educated about PTSD may need to be persuaded that there are compelling reasons to explore, for example, *the meaning of telling secrets* before actually telling the secret itself. By avoiding the temptation to move quickly toward the potentially shameful and secret material, the couple and therapist work together to avoid reactivating old feelings of terror, victimization, and aloneness.

We ask early in treatment whether the client writes letters, poetry, or stories or keeps a journal (or has ever contemplated or tried keeping a journal). If the client has found writing useful, the invitation to write as part of the therapy is often eagerly accepted. If she has not written, a discussion of all the ways to write in a journal (for example, tracking emotions, logging behaviors, quoting songs, or writing imagistic associations to dreams) can liberate an astonishing outpouring of material. Clients are reassured that their writing is good enough by seeing examples of others' writing or writing exercises that invite deliberately "bad" writing (messy, ungrammatical, repetitious, boring, and so on), such as Goldberg's (1990) helpful statement that "you are free to write the worst junk in America" (p. 4).

Clients who are considering writing need to have a safe place to keep their work and must also have agreements with others about the privacy of their writing. Clients may be tempted to write about emotion-laden topics and then hand their writing to the therapist. Initial emphasis on establishing and maintaining safety may prevent this from happening. Clients may be redirected to write not about the trauma story but about what it would be like to tell that story. They also may list, using brief notations, topics that they may want to write about later in the therapy. Clients who hand their writing to the therapist may be asked to discuss what thoughts and feelings underlie their urge to give their writing away, asked to look it over and decide what they can read aloud of it, and invited to read sections aloud in the therapy. This prevents secret communications between one partner and the therapist and helps ensure that clients do not rashly reveal material they are ambivalent about revealing or give away something they cannot spare emotionally.

Clients in the Outer Circle should focus on information gathering, including preparing genograms, describing family members, and articulating unspoken rules and assumptions. They also may write about questions that arise in the therapy, the history of the couple, their relationship to their own lesbian identity, thoughts about therapy, ideas for treatment directions, or dialogues of true and false selves. Clients may externalize Trauma by engaging it imaginatively and dialogically, or through poems, drawings, and articulation of the meaning of Trauma in the couple's relationship. Cognitive-behavioral assignments adapted from the many mainstream self-help resources available (for example, Burns, 1980) may be useful for clients who are overwhelmed by old feelings. Indeed, at this initial stage of treatment, cognitive-behavioral exercises (which may involve putting names to emotions, counting occurrences of a behavior, practicing positive affirmations, and so on) may give clients practice at discrete, bounded writing tasks.

Some clients simply do not wish to write or do not have sufficient privacy to do so without experiencing fear of violation. Rather than seeing this as resistance, the therapist may regard the choice not to write as the client's decision about the parameters of her therapy.

The Middle Circle

In the second or Middle Circle stage of therapy, the problems brought by the couple are addressed more directly. This is also a time to reactivate and develop more support resources for both members of the couple. If there are troubling sexual issues, self-harmful behaviors, jealousies, or any other distressing current problems, this is the stage in which alternatives are explored.

What would happen, for example, if the couple could look at the dominant presence of drugs or eating disorders or Jane Doe and understand them as masking the "face of Trauma," the powerful third member of the couple? Once exploration begins, the couple can find and activate sources of support for both the couple itself and for each partner.

Caretaking that has exceeded its usefulness and become crippling is also addressed in the Middle Circle stage. The over-caretaker is helped to pull back gradually and allow room for more resources to be used, such as twelve-step recovery groups, friendship networks, new activity groups, or political groups. Where excessive dependence on such groups has become a problem for one or both members of the couple, this stage of therapy can be used to help move the more dependent person into new experiences of connection that do not focus primarily on deficits but instead help to expand the repertoire of competencies and interests of those involved. For couples who are isolated from other gay and lesbian people, Middle Circle therapy can help connect them with others; network options can be explored, depending on geographical, social, and belief system constraints.

In this circle, clients may begin to engage with contents from the list of topics generated in their Outer Circle writing, revisiting earlier writings, elaborating on, or changing them. Clients also may give voice to their triangulated problems. Dialogues or letters to and from the externalized issues expand an understanding of and appreciation for not only the aspects of this triangulated relationship that are painful or result in paralysis but also the function it serves in perpetuating a static set of relationships and dynamics. For example, a client who writes letters to Bulimia and from Bulimia to herself may discover that Bulimia is not just "a hungry, evil beast who makes me break the rules" but also "your only constant companion" who "gives you good excuses not to be intimate with anyone." When both partners in a couple write, they may be startled to discover that their visions of the same phenomenon, constellation of activities, or externalized problem are quite discrepant. This may help them examine assumptions and dynamics in their relationship that were previously unarticulated and inaccessible.

Writing in the Middle Circle also has a pragmatic component. Isolated couples may brainstorm, research, and identify what their community has to offer. Many good-sized cities and towns boast a variety of social, athletic, artistic, political, and psychological resources for lesbians. Clients may be asked to discover what their community offers, list the possibilities, and log their progress in choosing and contacting organizations and attending activities. Clients who live in rural areas may not be aware of national gay and lesbian help lines, magazines, and mail-order bookstores and may need the therapist's assistance in finding them.

Couples who tend to do all of their activities together may be encouraged to try one separate activity, then write about that experience. For couples engaged in over-caretaking, such an activity may arouse a flurry of anxiety that may be given voice in the follow-up writing.

The Inner Circle

In the Inner Circle, the client learns to understand trauma as both a form of disconnection and as a presence in her relationships. This last stage of treatment allows for remembering the trauma and exploring the many meanings it holds, both for the survivor and for her partner. The survivor is helped to understand how early trauma creates a fragmentation of self, a dissociative process in which the victim tends to split off the roles of the punitive Abuser and the helpless Nonprotecting Bystander, and incorporates these presences within herself (Miller, 1993, 1994).

We begin by exploring the roles each partner plays in reenacting the trauma. For some lesbian couples, one or both is suffering the effects of what Miller (1993, 1994) calls "Trauma Reenactment Syndrome," a condition that causes the survivor to reenact all roles of the original trauma by replicating the abusive behavior, the Nonprotecting Bystander role, and the victim position. She may infuse the couple's relationship dynamics with this "triadic self" repetition by introducing injurious interpersonal behaviors (for example, by having an affair).

The first task in the Inner Circle is to help the couple tell the stories of each person's experiences of trauma and to understand how these histories create repetitions of trauma dynamics. Often identifying these parts of the self—the Abuser, Victim, and Nonprotecting Bystander—and externalizing Trauma helps each member of the couple identify the ways in which Trauma has developed a large and intrusive place in the relationship. Not only can each person see what she has been doing to repeat dynamics from a traumatic childhood but each can see how the nontraumatized parts of the self have been drawn into this Trauma Reenactment Syndrome.

The couple's relationship with the therapist is critically important to the process of healing. The therapist has become empathically attuned to these unique clients and the nuances of their relationship through curiosity and careful attention during the Outer and Middle Circle stages. Whether just one or both of the women have survived childhood trauma, both are able to feel a new level of understanding and support from the therapist. Various transference-rich connections can be explored, both as practice in nonpathological ways of relating and as valuable material for therapeutic examination. The therapist is able to help the couple revise the old abuse story by deconstructing confusing meanings that have clustered around it over the years. The stories become manifest through the process of remembering and retelling and also through understanding the roles, distortions, and longings each partner projects onto the therapist and her partner.

In the Inner Circle, writing may engage directly with the trauma story, telling and retelling it from a variety of perspectives or in different moods, readdressing an earlier text by writing commentaries as new insights unfold, or transforming the story symbolically into a fairy tale or teaching story. The client's stories may include facts, emotions, and the details that make them particularly hers. Couples may wish to coauthor a dialogical story that represents their accomplishments and efforts, as well as the work still to be done. Clients may acknowledge the powerful role that Trauma has played in their lives and explore scenarios in which past Trauma has a new, different role in the present moment. These stories might propose multiple answers to questions such as "If Trauma were not so central in our life together, what would our relationship be like?" Clients may restory themselves as successful and possessing personal agency rather than as helpless or passive.

Clients at this stage in their therapy may be able to tolerate, and indeed enjoy, a playful pushing at the boundaries of their writing. A client who enjoys the writing for itself, not just as a therapeutic modality, may find in writing a model for developing new interests and means of self-expression, grounded in a more integrated, healthy vision of herself.

If the Outer Circle work has adequately explored the various meanings that the clients have attributed to engaging in therapy and if appropriate support systems and resources have evolved in the Middle Circle, then the Inner Circle work should be freeing and healing. If the trauma is revisited and restoried without the necessary Outer and Middle Circle work, however, the Inner Circle work can push the couple into another round of triangulation with the presence of unresolved Trauma. Thus, it is important that the work proceed with careful monitoring and thoughtful discussion.

Conclusion

Therapists and their lesbian clients may work with intrusive trauma sequelae through the externalization of Trauma within the triadic model. Writing exercises provide an important vehicle for resolving problems associated with their trauma history.

Therapists who work with lesbian couples should consider what may be unique to their experience as well as what may be shared by all trauma survivors. Researchers similarly should not rely on assumptions about lesbians based on anecdotal and pathologizing inquiries but should continue to interview lesbian clients and therapists to learn more about their concerns, needs, and strengths.

We are concerned about other populations for whom issues of isolation, stigmatization, and marginalization may be doubled in the context of trauma histories. Assumptions about such nondominant groups as men and women of color and physically challenged people may be reevaluated through the principles and treatment models addressed in this chapter.

References

Adams, K. (1990). *Journal to the self: 22 paths to personal growth.* New York: Warner Books.

Anderson, H., & Goolishian, H. (1992). The client is the expert: A not-knowing approach to therapy. In S. McNamee & K. J. Gergen (Eds.), *Therapy as social construction* (pp. 25–39). Newbury Park, CA: Sage.

Baures, M. (1994). *Undaunted spirits: Portraits of recovery from trauma.* Philadelphia: Charles Press.

Bowen, M. (1978). *Family therapy in clinical practice.* Northvale, NJ: Aronson.

Bradford, J., Ryan, C., & Rothblum, E. D. (1994). National lesbian health care survey: Implications for mental health care. *Journal of Consulting and Clinical Psychology, 62,* 228–242.

Brannock, J. C., & Chapman, B. E. (1990). Negative sexual experiences with men among heterosexual women and lesbians. *Journal of Homosexuality, 19,* 105–110.

Brown, L. S. (1989). New voices, new visions: Toward a lesbian/gay paradigm for psychology. *Psychology of Women Quarterly, 13,* 445–458.

Browning, C., Reynolds, A. L., & Dworkin, S. H. (1991). Affirmative psychotherapy for lesbian women. *Counseling Psychologist, 19,* 177–196.

Burns, D. D. (1980). *Feeling good: The new mood therapy.* New York: Signet Books.

Cameron, J. (1992). *The artist's way: A spiritual path to higher creativity.* Los Angeles: Tarcher.

Clunis, D. M., & Green, G. D. (1993). *Lesbian couples: Creating healthy relationships for the '90s.* Seattle, WA: Seal Press.

Goldberg, N. (1986). *Writing down the bones: Freeing the writer within.* Boston: Shambhala.

Goldberg, N. (1990). *Wild mind: Living the writer's life.* New York: Bantam Books.

Governor's Commission on Gay and Lesbian Youth. (1993). *Making schools safe for gay and lesbian youth: Breaking the silence in schools and in families* (Publication No. 17296–60–500²/₉₃— C.R.). Boston: Author.

Harber, K. D., & Pennebaker, J. W. (1992). Overcoming traumatic memories. In S.-A. Christianson (Ed.), *The handbook of emotion and memory: Research and theory* (pp. 359–388). Hillsdale, NJ: Erlbaum.

Herman, J. L. (1992). *Trauma and recovery.* New York: Basic Books.

Hetrick, E. S., & Martin, A. D. (1987). Developmental issues and their resolution for gay and lesbian adolescents. *Journal of Homosexuality, 14,* 25–43.

Kano, S. (1989). *Making peace with food: Freeing yourself from the diet/weight obsession* (Rev. ed.). New York: HarperCollins.

Kerewsky, S. D. (1995a, February). *The AIDS memorial quilt: Personal and therapeutic uses.* Paper presented at Affirming Every Person: The New England Conference About Lesbians and Gay Men, Keene, NH.

Kerewsky, S. D. (1995b). *A coming-out workbook for women.* Unpublished manuscript, Antioch New England Graduate School.

Laird, J. (1994). Lesbian families: A cultural perspective. In M. P. Mirkin (Ed.), *Women in context: Toward a feminist reconstruction of psychotherapy* (pp. 118–148). New York: Guilford Press.

Lax, W. D. (1996). Guidelines for reflections. In S. Freidman (Ed.), *The reflecting process.* New York: Guilford Press.

Loulan, J. (1987). *Lesbian passion: Loving ourselves and each other.* Minneapolis, MN: Spinsters Ink.

Martin, A. D., & Hetrick, E. S. (1988). The stigmatization of the gay and lesbian adolescent. *Journal of Homosexuality, 15,* 163–183.

McCann, L., & Pearlman, L. (1990). *Psychological trauma and the adult survivor: Theory, therapy, and transformation.* New York: Brunner/Mazel.

Meiselman, K. C. (1990). *Resolving the trauma of incest: Reintegration therapy with survivors.* San Francisco: Jossey-Bass.

Miller, D. (1990). The trauma of interpersonal violence. *Smith College Studies in Social Work, 61,* 6–26.

Miller, D. (1993). Incest: The heart of darkness. In E. Imber-Black (Ed.), *Secrets in families and family therapy* (pp. 181–195). New York: Norton.

Miller, D. (1994). *Women who hurt themselves: A book of hope and understanding.* New York: Basic Books.

Minuchin, S. (1974). *Families and family therapy.* Cambridge, MA: Harvard University Press.

Nichols, M. (1987). Lesbian sexuality: Issues and developing theory. In Boston Lesbian Psychologies Collective (Ed.), *Lesbian psychologies: Explorations and challenges* (pp. 97–125). Urbana: University of Illinois Press.

O'Hanlon, B. (1994). The third wave. *Family Therapy Networker, 18,* 19–29.

Penn, P., & Frankfurt, M. (1994). Creating a participant text: Writing, multiple voices, narrative multiplicity. *Family Process, 33,* 217–231.

Peters, D. K., & Cantrell, P. J. (1991). Factors distinguishing samples of lesbian and heterosexual women. *Journal of Homosexuality, 21,* 1–15.

Polkinghorne, D. E. (1988). *Narrative knowing and the human sciences.* Albany: State University of New York.

Rothblum, E. D. (1994). "I only read about myself on bathroom walls": The need for research on the mental health of lesbians and gay men. *Journal of Consulting and Clinical Psychology, 62,* 213–220.

Savin-Williams, R. C. (1994). Verbal and physical abuse as stressors in the lives of lesbian, gay male, and bisexual youths: Associations with school problems, running away, substance abuse, prostitution, and suicide. *Journal of Consulting and Clinical Psychology, 62,* 261–269.

White, M., & Epston, D. (1990). *Narrative means to therapeutic ends.* New York: Norton.

CHAPTER THIRTEEN

ADDRESSING HETEROSEXIST BIAS IN THE TREATMENT OF LESBIAN COUPLES WITH CHEMICAL DEPENDENCY

Sandra C. Anderson

People who are chemically dependent and those who are lesbian share a history of social oppression and neglect. When lesbian clients have substance abuse problems, heterosexist bias may occur in both their assessment and treatment (Rabin, Keefe, & Burton, 1986). A recent study of treatment providers revealed that most had limited knowledge about how to evaluate and treat lesbian alcoholics and rarely discussed sexual orientation with their clients even though they considered it important. Their training and supervision related to lesbian issues were described as substandard or nonexistent (Hellman, Stanton, Lee, Tytun, & Vachon, 1989). There is homophobia throughout much of the mental health profession (De Crescenzo, 1984) and bias against research on lesbian issues (Gagnon et al., 1982). This has resulted in relatively little sound research on alcoholism in this population and even less on other drug use (Israelstam & Lambert, 1989). For this reason, most articles discussed in this paper refer to alcohol.

I would like to thank Barbara Friesen for her insightful comments on an earlier version of this chapter and David Freeman for his creative thinking on working with couples.
Previously published in the *Journal of Feminist Family Therapy*, Volume 7, #(3/4), pp. 87–113, 1995 as "Addressing Heterosexist Bias in the Treatment of Lesbian Couples with Chemical Dependency," and reprinted with the permission of The Haworth Press, Inc., Publisher, and the authors.

The inadequate treatment resulting from heterosexist bias can be compounded by the existence of negative attitudes toward female clients who are chemically dependent (Corrigan & Anderson, 1985; Kagle, 1987; Wilsnack, 1991). Even if therapists lack homophobic and negative attitudes, they may not be competent to treat lesbian couples for problems related to alcoholism. Therapists also need knowledge and expertise about the nature of lesbian relationships, substance abuse and dependence in women, lesbian-affirming practice and, in my view, family of origin theory and practice. My assumption here is that, given existing bias and lack of knowledge, the percentage of therapists who can competently treat lesbian couples with an alcohol problem is probably quite small (Corrigan & Anderson, 1985).

In this chapter, I address the heterosexist and sexist biases that permeate some approaches to working with lesbian couples with alcohol problems and propose a model that is strengths-based and assumes that clients have or can develop competence in dealing with substance abuse, relationship, and family of origin issues. The new psychology of women, the concepts of fusion and codependency, and the myth of therapist neutrality are discussed as they apply to the assessment and treatment of lesbian couples. The proposed model integrates traditional alcoholism treatment with family-centered therapy and focuses on both family of origin and family of creation issues.

Lesbians and Alcoholism

Estimates of alcoholism among lesbians have been based primarily on three early studies (Fifield, 1975; Lohrenz, Connelly, Coyne, & Spare, 1978; Saghir & Robins, 1973) and have clustered around a prevalence rate of 30 percent. It should be noted that these studies have serious methodological limitations that include an oversampling of bar patrons who are predominantly White, middle-class, and more likely to be heavy drinkers than individuals in the general population (Clark, 1981).

More recent studies have avoided some of these methodological problems and have included drugs other than alcohol. McKirnan and Peterson (1989) conclude that, when compared to those in the general population, lesbians were much more similar to gay men in their use of alcohol and other drugs, and both lesbians and gay men showed far less decline in use with age. They did *not* find the very heavy alcohol and other drug use often ascribed to this population. With heavy drinking defined as more than sixty drinks per month, there were similar rates of heavy drinking in the gay and lesbian and the general populations (15 percent and 14 percent, respectively). If patterns of substance use are changing in the lesbian community, it may be due to greater awareness of the relationship between alcohol and HIV infection and to the women's and gay rights movements, which have encouraged greater openness about lesbian identity and created more opportunities for socialization away from bars.

Even if substance use is declining in lesbian communities, a substantial number of these individuals drink problematically. McKirnan and Peterson (1989) found that, although lesbians reported rates of heavy consumption similar to those of general population women (9 percent and 7 percent, respectively), they reported higher rates of alcohol problems. With "problem" defined as at least two alcohol-related symptoms over the previous year, 23 percent of lesbians reported problems, compared to 8 percent of women in the general population. McKirnan and Peterson point out, however, that the existence of at least two symptoms does not necessarily reflect a diagnosis of alcoholism.

To date, no evidence exists that lesbians have biological differences that would inordinately predispose them to develop a physical dependence on alcohol. However, experiences of oppression, unresolved coming-out issues, or other special stresses could produce higher rates of alcoholism than those found among heterosexual women. If you are interested in a discussion of alcoholism in lesbian clients that addresses theories of etiology, prevention issues, individual and group treatment approaches, self-help groups, and treatment settings, see Anderson (in press) and Anderson and Henderson (1985).

To work effectively with lesbian substance abusers, we must examine our stereotypes about chemical dependency and work through our own homophobia. Homophobia has been found to be positively related to sexist attitudes and inversely related to positive self-concept (Cummerton, 1982). Morales and Graves (as cited in Paul, Stall, & Bloomfield, 1991) studied substance abuse treatment providers and found that 9 percent scored "homophobic" and 17 percent scored "marginally homophobic" in attitudes toward homosexuality. This is very likely to be an underestimate of homophobia, since some providers declined to participate and expressed the opinion that their attitudes toward homosexuals were irrelevant to their quality of care. Garnets, Hancock, Cochran, Goodchilds, and Peplau (1991) found that 58 percent of the psychologists they surveyed knew of incidents of bias in treating gay and lesbian clients. Therapists' reactivity to lesbians can be subtle and very damaging to them and their families (Bushway, 1991). Clearly, many lesbian substance abusers continue to receive biased, inadequate, and inappropriate treatment.

Characteristics of Lesbian Couples

Lesbian couples have been virtually ignored by the family therapy field. While they are, in many respects, like all couples, they differ in several significant ways. Because they are stigmatized, they may rely more heavily on one another for social support. Because they may have to remain silent about life experiences taken for granted by heterosexual couples, their self-esteem may be negatively affected (Sussal, 1993). Because there are no legal supports or socially sanctioned rituals to honor their significant events, their relationships do not receive ongoing validation; as a consequence, many couples view their own relationships as temporary or unimportant. When relationships end, there are no socially acceptable mechanisms for mourning, so it is not unusual to see unresolved loss carried into the next relationship (Decker, 1984). In most instances, these differences between lesbian and heterosexual couples are painfully obvious to the lesbian couple and to their families of origin. I am currently seeing a family struggling with the recent coming out of the twenty-five-year-old daughter. The parents are open about their heterosexism and feel stigmatized by their daughter's lesbianism. They are both only children; their parents are deceased; they feel angry, disappointed, and abandoned by their daughter. The mother, in particular, is experiencing profound loss, as she assumes that there will be no wedding ceremony or grandchildren. The daughter, feeling quite rejected by her parents, is distancing from them and turning to her partner and friends for support. She has always felt very close to her mother, always believed that she could tell her anything, and is extremely hurt and disappointed about her mother's reaction to her disclosure. When the family was first seen, the daughter was experiencing considerable loss of self-esteem and having doubts about the importance and permanence of her relationship with her partner.

Given these distinct cultural disadvantages, it is interesting that lesbian couples report significantly higher levels of cohesion, adaptability, and satisfaction than do heterosexual couples (Zacks, Green, & Marrow, 1988). Lesbian couples want more time with their partners and place more value on equality, independence, and equitable distribution of household duties (Blumstein & Schwartz, 1983). Overall, studies indicate that the majority of lesbian couples view their relationship as extremely close, personally satisfying, and egalitarian (Peplau, Cochran, Rook, & Padesky, 1978). In an attempt to explain the "superior functioning" of lesbian couples, Zacks and colleagues (1988) note that lesbians have fewer sanctions against ending unhappy relationships, the egalitarian nature of lesbian relationships enhances the competencies of both partners, and "the superior relational skills of two women enable them to form better-functioning relationships" (p. 480).

Krestan and Bepko (1980) note that the presenting problem of most lesbian couples is anxiety related to too much closeness or too much distance. Couples also may be concerned about their sexual relationship, unequal access to resources, coming-out issues, and issues around ending the relationship (Roth, 1989). One or more of these issues may be related to alcohol abuse or dependence. Wilke

(1994) notes that male alcoholic behavior is assumed to be the standard for both males and females. The unique treatment needs of women, and the ways in which these needs differ from those of men are often either ignored or defined as deviant. This results in alcoholic women being judged sicker and harder to treat than alcoholic men. I recently received a referral from a treatment program of an alcoholic woman described as "severely impaired, but in denial, unmotivated, and resistant to appropriate treatment." During our first session, it became clear that the program was ignoring significant imbalances in power and social roles between men and women. Because of her profound guilt and low self-esteem (the hand that rocks the cradle must never be a shaky one), she did most of her heavy drinking alone, a pattern viewed as more pathological than bar drinking. She had refused to attend mixed Alcoholics Anonymous meetings, because the group advocated powerlessness and self-sacrifice, and she had left the program prematurely because she was unable to afford adequate child care. As is clear from this case example, our work with lesbian couples with an alcohol problem must be sensitive to both sexist and heterosexist bias.

Heterosexism

Heterosexist bias is a belief system in which heterosexuality is seen as superior to and/or more "natural" than homosexuality (Morin, 1977). As stated by Brown (1989):

> North American psychology, besides being biased by sexism, racism, and other exclusionary modal perspectives, views human behavior through the lens of heterosexist experience and is thus inherently heterosexist. . . . Our knowledge base is heterosexist. . . . More precisely, white, middle class, North American, married, Christian, able-bodied heterosexuality is defined as the norm. All other forms of experience are viewed in contrast to the norm. (p. 447)

Heterosexist bias is pervasive in our language, theories, and interventions. It can be a significant problem for therapists working with lesbian clients, manifesting itself in both blatant and subtle forms.

Although some issues are common to all couples, those presented by lesbian couples need to be viewed in the context of same-sex socialization, internalized homophobia, and societal oppression (Buhrke & Douce, 1991). When heterosexual norms are applied to lesbian couples, their behavior can become defined as abnormal. For example, it is not at all unusual for lesbian couples to discuss breaking up while continuing to live together and to remain close friends after the break-up (Becker, 1988). This is not typical of break-ups of heterosexual couples and is frequently labeled by therapists as pathological.

When a lesbian in a couple relationship presents herself for treatment, couple therapy may not even be considered, although it is usually the therapy of choice. This is because lesbian clients are typically viewed as single and their relationships considered transient and insignificant.

Once a lesbian is in treatment, heterosexism can impede change in a number of ways. Therapists may assume that all presenting problems were created by the client's sexual orientation, with little recognition of the role of societal homophobia or sexism. They may encourage lesbians to move toward heterosexuality or may perceive lesbianism as a symptom of an underlying psychiatric problem. They may be preoccupied with the causes of lesbianism (Riddle & Sang, 1978). Clients' self-denigrating comments about lesbians may go unchallenged. The therapist may collude with the client to "make the best of it," accept certain limitations without question, and treat relationships as if they could never be as valid or healthy as heterosexual ones (Cabaj, 1988). Therapists who are uncomfortable with a couple's closeness may label it as immature and pathological (McCandlish, 1982). Therapists needing to establish themselves as liberal may divert attention from clients' treatment needs by assuring them repeatedly of their positive views about lesbianism. Others may point out all the supposed lost opportunities being lesbian carries, emphasize the positive aspects of clients' heterosexual relationships and the negative aspects of their lesbian relationships, and discourage coming out to family and friends (De Crescenzo, 1984). Lesbians may be expected to have high self-esteem in spite of societal attitudes (Riddle & Sang, 1978). One of my clients, a young physician who had been an active lesbian since her teens, was told by her previous therapist that her depression was a direct result of her sexual orientation, which probably resulted from her fixation at an immature developmental stage. She was encouraged to date men and delay further coming out until she was absolutely sure that she was a lesbian.

The attitude that sexual orientation makes no difference ignores the significance of a rejecting society (Tievsky, 1988), and being too accepting may lead to missing important issues and romanticizing the couple's out relationship. McCandlish (1982) points out that lesbian therapists are particularly prone to "idealizing the relationship, overidentifying with the couple, and becoming invested in the therapy outcome" (p. 74). The lesbian therapist may attribute all problems to societal and internalized homophobia, losing sight of important family of origin and relational issues. It is critical to recognize that age, social class, ethnicity, and race make every relationship unique.

Morin and Charles (1983) note that some theories are inherently heterosexually biased, some are value-free but generally applied in a heterosexually biased manner, and some are neither biased nor applied in a biased manner. They point out that heterosexist bias is reflected in language by connotation, inference, contiguity, and omission. For example, the term *homosexual* has acquired a negative connotation, whereas *lesbian* connotes a proud identity. The phrase "with homosexual tendencies" may lead to negative inferences based on stereotypes. Discussing lesbianism in the same context as "sexual deviations" demonstrates heterosexual bias through contiguity. And finally, omission may be the most pervasive form of heterosexual bias in language. *Spouse* is used instead of *partner,* and heterosexual assumption is pervasive on insurance and medical history forms.

Goodrich, Rampage, Ellman, and Halstead (1988) point out that several core concepts in family therapy (triangle, fusion, and boundary) contain heterosexist bias and can result in a pathologized description when applied to lesbian couples. Drawing in a third person (triangulation) may make conflict resolution possible for women, both lesbian and nonlesbian, and is not always dysfunctional. The concept of fusion is heavily gendered and will be discussed in depth later in this chapter. Boundaries often are prescribed to protect hierarchies and the patriarchy, and lesbian couples can be labeled as sick when their boundaries are less rigid than those of heterosexual couples. For example, many of my lesbian clients successfully use former partners for support when experiencing conflict with their current partner. This situation is highly unlikely to occur in heterosexual relationships.

When lesbian couples enter treatment for problems related to alcoholism in one or both partners, they are likely to encounter sexism, heterosexism, and a treatment field that has been very slow to recognize difference. As noted by Schaefer, Evans, and Coleman (1987), chemical dependency counselors often assume the male is the alcoholic and the female the codependent. Women clients are frequently held to a more rigid set of sex-role expectations than are men clients (Sandmaier, 1980), and women alcoholics often are viewed as unfeminine or seductive. Lesbian partners typically are not included as significant others in alcohol treatment programs (Nicoloff & Stiglitz, 1987), and the treatment relationship may be sexualized through intrusive questions about lesbians' sexual experiences (Stevens & Hall, 1988).

Assessment

The new psychology of women and the concepts of fusion and codependency are assessment issues that are particularly vulnerable to heterosexist bias.

The New Psychology of Women

In the past twenty years, research and theory development has departed from traditional psychological thought about women, resulting in what is frequently called a new psychology of women. It is now hypothesized that socialization greatly affects the formation of female identity and that women experience themselves as selves-in-relationships throughout their lives (Berzoff, 1989; Chodorow, 1978; Gilligan, 1982; Miller, 1976, 1984). Serious questions have been raised about male-biased frameworks that emphasize separation and autonomy as the goals of healthy human development. From this new perspective, women's problems do not result from a failure to separate but rather from trying to maintain connections while maintaining their own sense of self (Collins, 1993). Vargo (1987) attempted to apply these ideas to lesbian couples seen in treatment and concluded that fusion or blurring of individual boundaries is more likely the result of successful socialization than of ego weaknesses or poor communication patterns. Women who are lesbian need to balance their needs for autonomy (self-actualization) and intimacy (attachment) in the context of a homophobic society.

Fusion in Lesbian Couples

Much of the clinical literature on lesbian couples focuses on the concepts of fusion, merging, or enmeshment (Burch, 1982, 1986, 1987; Decker, 1984; Krestan & Bepko, 1980). Mencher (1990) notes how patterns of intimacy in lesbian couples have been pathologized as fusion and reviews theories about the sources of these dynamics. (For more information, see Berg-Cross, 1988; Bograd, 1988; Elise, 1986; Goodrich et al., 1988; Green, 1990; Laird, 1993; Lindenbaum, 1985; McKenzie, 1992; Pearlman, 1989; Roth, 1989; Slater & Mencher, 1991; and Zacks et al., 1988.)

Mencher concludes that the relationship characteristics most valued by lesbian couples are those that would be labeled as "fusion" and that enduring lesbian relationships are characterized by fusion. She quotes Benjamin (1988) on how psychoanalytic thought may have distorted our understanding of intimacy:

> The classic psychoanalytic viewpoint did not see differentiation as a balance, but a process of disentanglement. Thus it cast experiences of union, merger, and self-other harmony as regressive opposites to differentiation and self-other distinction. Merging was a dangerous form of undifferentiation. (pp. 46–47)

Bowen (1978) has been unfairly criticized for devaluing the "feminine" relationship orientation and overvaluing separateness and autonomy. In fact, he repeatedly emphasized the importance of balance, viewing a fused and reactive emotional position, not a relationship orientation, as problematic. As Walsh and Scheinkman (1989) point out, poorly differentiated people are dominated by their emotions and are overdependent on others, either too closely fused, reactively distanced, or cut off from their families. Differentiation always involves the maintenance of self *in relation to* one's family, being *both* separate and connected. Autonomy and intimacy are equally valued and not mutually exclusive (Nelson, 1989).

Pearlman (1989) believes that intense emotional bonding occurs in most relationships to varying degrees. In some, it is present mainly during sexual or emotional closeness. In others, "it is a normative preference for intense connection which can include some loss of individuality" (p. 78). In still others, it is more permanent and includes excessive dependency and loss of self. Intense bonding may appear more easily in lesbian relationships because of similar socialization, joining forces against a hostile world, or many other reasons. When it is excessive, couples complain of feeling trapped, bored, overwhelmed by conflict, or involvement in outside affairs. But extreme closeness is not in itself pathological (Falco, 1991), and it is even possible that what is normative for lesbian couples may be healthy for all couples (Brown, 1989). In my experience, the intense emotional connection experienced by lesbian couples is indeed the most valued aspect of their relationship. When this pattern of intimacy evolves into excessive dependency and loss of self, the couple may seek treatment. One such couple, Arlene and Carol, came into therapy because their initially intense and close relationship had become distant and conflictual. Carol was feeling lonely and rejected, and Arlene was feeling trapped and considering having an affair. Arlene had learned in childhood to keep her feelings to herself, stay in control, and avoid self-pity. Trusting, expressing affection, and becoming vulnerable were unsafe; one could stay safe by withdrawing. Carol described herself as a shy, only child who was lonely, dependent, and terrified of conflict and rejection. Both had distanced themselves from their families of origin and had turned to the other to compensate for earlier losses. As Carol, under extreme stress from employment problems, became increasingly demanding of emotional support from Arlene, she reacted by becoming more distant and withdrawn. Carol was depressed and drinking heavily by the time of their first appointment. They both yearned for their initial intimacy without the anxiety associated with being too close or too distant.

Codependency

Enthusiastic adherents of codependency define it as a primary disease present in every member of an addictive family, involving dependence on approval from others for one's self-worth and identity. Work focusing on codependency often requires clients to view themselves as having a disease stemming from a dysfunctional family of origin, not as members of an oppressed group who have been socialized to be dependent.

In my view, the concept of codependency is not useful in dealing with women with relationship difficulties. Instead of demanding that lesbian couples separate, the challenge is to help them define a separate sense of self within the relationship (Bushway, 1991; Sloven, 1991). Collins (1993) notes that a woman in a relationship with a substance abuser should have her desires for connection and mutuality affirmed. The concept of codependency lacks validity, pathologizes characteristics associated with women, involves generalizations about alcoholic families that focus on pathology, and encourages separation rather than connection with the family of origin (Anderson, 1994).

Treatment Issues

The concept of therapeutic neutrality and the inclusion of families of origin and creation are two treatment issues that are most vulnerable to heterosexist bias.

Neutrality

It is a myth that therapy is or can be completely value-free or neutral (Hare-Mustin & Marecek, 1986). Although it is important to strive for therapeutic neutrality with lesbian couples (for example, avoid colluding with one partner's stories about the other, taking sides, or becoming part of family secrets), it is also important to challenge the status quo of societal oppression. Only a deliberate lesbian affirmative approach recognizes the prejudice faced by lesbian couples and helps them deal with its effects (Fassinger, 1991). In addition, systemic ideas of neutrality stress that partners contribute equally to the etiology and maintenance of problems, ignoring differences in power between partners. Lesbian partners often struggle over power differentials based on education, income, status, or other factors. Finally, neutrality does not allow the therapist to appropriately challenge denial in substance-abusing clients (Pasick & White, 1991).

Including Families of Origin and Creation

The significant others of lesbian couples may include the family of origin, the extended family of lesbian friends, and a committed partner. Lesbian couples are much more likely than heterosexual couples to rate friends rather than family members as providers of social support (Kurdek & Schmitt, 1987). Because many lesbians have not come out to their families and fear their rejection, family members are often avoided by couples. The most comprehensive study of lesbians to date (Bradford, Ryan, & Rothblum, 1994) found that only 27 percent were out to all family members, and 19 percent were out to no family members. Although some families respond to disclosure with anger and rejection, others are affirming of the adult child's identity. In a very small study of lesbian couples who had come out to their parents, Murphy (1989) found that disclosure allowed couples to maintain their sense of integrity and decrease their isolation. Although 70 percent reported parental disapproval of their lesbianism, adverse consequences were overshadowed by benefits to the couple, and there was not one instance of total parental rejection. Of course it is possible that lesbians who choose to come out have more accepting families to begin with. Laird (1993) notes that the biological metaphor has dominated family therapy theory and that we have not fully investigated how created families can fill some of the gaps left by rejecting families of origin.

In my own clinical experience with lesbian couples, I have found that they frequently want and need strong connections with their families of origin and bring unfinished business from those relationships into their current ones. For this reason, I believe that adequate treatment of lesbians who are chemically dependent must take a family perspective that includes both the families of origin and created family systems. Next I will discuss such a model.

A Proposed Model

There are a number of models of couple therapy that can be used when one partner is still drinking, focusing either on active methods of motivating the alcoholic to change or on detachment and self-care of the nonalcoholic partner. I will not address this situation here but will focus instead on cases in which the lesbian couple is voluntarily seeking help for problems related to alcoholism in one or both partners.

Pasick and White (1991) note that few clinicians are trained to reconcile traditional alcohol treatment with family-centered therapy. While addiction treatment typically addresses alcohol abuse before any other problem and focuses on denial in the alcoholic client, family-centered therapists work toward changing the family instead of the identified client and do not impose their opinions on the family. In interpreting these two models, Pasick and White (1991) propose that:

> The goals of treatment are to support the addicted client while challenging the chemical use, and to support the family's recovery while challenging the under-

responsible and overresponsible behavior of its members. The centerpiece is a therapeutic stance founded in part on feminist ideals, one which is collaborative, respectful, non-hierarchical, and appropriately responsible. (p. 89)

Traditional alcohol treatment counselors and family therapists typically disagree about the etiology of alcoholism in women. My own view is that, although alcohol dependency is heavily controlled by genetic vulnerability, internalized homophobia can result in tremendous anxiety and self-hatred that is sometimes assuaged by alcohol. The ultimate etiological model will consider both genetic vulnerability and environmental reactivity.

The specific treatment model proposed in this chapter reflects the integration of my own experience and the adapted models of Wetchler, McCollum, Nelson, Trepper, and Lewis (1993) and Bepko (1989). The model assumes that relationship patterns are repeated multigenerationally and that current relationships play a role in maintaining alcohol abuse. Thus, both historical and present family processes become part of the treatment process (Wetchler et al., 1993).

Stage I: Developing a Collaborative Therapeutic Alliance

The initial interview is framed as a consultation during which I discuss with the couple their concerns, and we make a decision about working together. I assume an active questioning role in this session, taking a thorough drug use history, inquiring about relationship issues, and determining whether alcohol abuse is central to the couple's problems or concurrent with or secondary to an underlying psychiatric disorder. In the latter case, when appropriate, the client is encouraged to obtain an evaluation for psychotropic medication after abstinence is established.

I ask what solutions have been attempted by the couple. In most cases, ongoing drinking has resulted in clear and painful imbalances in underresponsible and overresponsible behavior. There is discussion of how standard responses to drinking, usually controlling or protective behaviors, can contribute to the maintenance of the problem. Feelings of anger, depression, and anxiety are normalized. Education about alcohol abuse and dependency is provided if appropriate. The focus is on coping skills that are working. Severe relationship problems are not addressed until sobriety is well established.

When sufficient trust has been established, typically by the second or third interview, a multigenerational family genogram is completed for each partner. In this process, the clients tell their stories about family emotional relationships, substance abuse, physical and sexual abuse, family rituals, family strengths, family heroines and heroes, and other important relationships and social supports. Clients are routinely asked about other gay or lesbian family members. Although it is typical to focus almost exclusively on alcohol abuse early in treatment, some lesbian clients may need to deal initially with issues around their sexual orientation (Shernoff & Finnegan, 1991). It is critical to explore both internalized heterosexism and sexism and to recognize the multiple sources of stress under which lesbians function. As mentioned, a deliberately lesbian-affirmative approach validates the couple's lifestyle, recognizes the oppression they face, and actively helps them deal with it (Fassinger, 1991).

When clients are alcohol dependent, that is, show tolerance, withdrawal symptoms, or a pattern of compulsive use, abstinence is the most appropriate goal. Although it is optimal that they stop drinking immediately, many alcohol-dependent clients are not capable of this and need ongoing therapeutic support for their attempts to achieve sobriety. I do not refuse to work with couples when one or both are having trouble abstaining, but if a client has numerous relapses without increasing intervals of sobriety between episodes, I encourage her to seriously consider an intensive outpatient or residential treatment program.

In the first phase of treatment, clients are encouraged to avoid situations that trigger drinking and to develop resources and activities that reinforce abstinence and take the place of time spent drinking. Clients are encouraged to create supportive environments by reading material by lesbian authors, meeting more lesbian couples, becoming involved in lesbian groups (Riddle & Sang, 1978), and shopping around for an appropriate self-help group. Involvement in some type of sobriety support group is enormously helpful in achieving and maintaining abstinence. I discuss with all clients the philosophy and format of Alcoholics Anonymous, Rational Recovery, Women for Sobriety, and Secular Organizations for Sobriety. After visiting several groups, most clients are able to find one consistent with their particular needs and values. As they begin this shift to a sober lifestyle, their defenses are supported and redirected instead of interpreted and confronted in order to keep anxiety and the subsequent risk of drinking to a minimum.

Although Bepko (1989) states that in the beginning phase of treatment it may be more effective to work with the alcoholic woman alone, she makes this point while discussing heterosexual couples. My own experience indicates that working with the lesbian couple from the beginning and throughout treatment is the most honoring of their relationship and the most supportive of long-term recovery.

REWRITING AND RECLAIMING HISTORIES OF LOSS: SARAH AND CATE

Sarah, a thirty-six-year-old attorney, and Cate, a thirty-four-year-old medical illustrator, were referred by their internist because of Cate's alcohol problem and couple communication problems, both of which had worsened over the course of their two-year relationship. In the initial interview, I established the norm of having them talk through me to the other, allowing me to hear both of their stories and blocking them from defending their own position. All of my questions were about the self rather than the other or the relationship. A genogram of each woman began the process of understanding how current problems were related to past losses.

Sarah stated that she no longer feels close to Cate, that Cate drinks excessively and is rarely there for her. She periodically tries to control Cate's drinking but typically just withdraws. She described a distant relationship with her older sister and a very uncomfortable, tense relationship with her sixty-eight-year-old mother, whom she described as extremely quiet, never initiating conversations or expressing feelings. She described her father as having been uninvolved with the family. He had died unexpectedly six year earlier, and his death had never been discussed. Sarah stated that she was angry about having always been invisible to both parents and acknowledged that she would like to be closer to her mother. She would like them to be able to talk about her father's death and Sarah's adult relationships. She had come out to her mother ten years earlier, with little response, but had never told her father she was a lesbian. Sarah knew very little about her grandparents and nothing about her great-grandparents.

Cate described a pattern of alcohol use that had become of increasing concern to her over the past ten years. In the past two years she had noticed increased tolerance and mild withdrawal symptoms on Mondays. She had made several unsuccessful attempts to control her drinking, avoided social activities that were alcohol-free, and recognized that her drinking was destroying her relationship with Sarah. Although she was still functioning adequately in her profession, her productivity had declined significantly in the past few years.

Cate viewed her mother as an angry, anxious, cold woman with whom she had never connected, while she described her father as an alcoholic, violent, and physically abusive to her mother. She had a distant relationship with two older brothers, both alcoholic. She had little knowledge of her extended family. Cate had come out to her mother eight years earlier; her mother begged her not to tell her father; she never had.

Cate's alcohol dependence appeared to have connections to both unresolved family of origin issues and internalized homophobia, and perhaps with genetic predisposition. She acknowledged that her drinking increased dramatically when she felt anxiety around contacts with her family or when she was exposed to sexist or homophobic attitudes in the workplace.

At the end of the first interview, I shared with the couple my thinking about Cate's alcohol problem, that is, that she was psychologically and physically dependent and that abstinence was the appropriate goal. She adamantly refused referrals for intensive outpatient treatment and outpatient detoxification but did agree to start shopping around for an appropriate self-help group. I ended the first interview by asking the couple to think about how alcohol was used to "make it safe" in the relationship and what the loss would be to them if the problem did not exist.

The first stage of our work together focused on developing activities that would substitute for the time Cate spent drinking and challenging with respectful questions her denial about the consequences of her drinking. Cate was supported in her attempts to avoid going to bars to drink with friends, do yoga, continue piano lessons she had dropped in college, become active in a political campaign to defeat an antigay ballot measure, and join a lesbian self-help group. She was able to follow through to some extent with all of these activities. The couple was advised to avoid all anxiety-provoking situations. They also were encouraged to discuss their concerns about reactions to their lesbianism. Both talked at length about the hurt they experienced from not having their relationship taken seriously. There was enormous joy and celebration over the siblings' marriages, whereas their commitment to each other was ignored. I asked questions about what these events triggered for each of them and what they did to cope with these injustices.

Stage II: Challenging Behaviors and Expanding Alternatives

This stage usually begins when the alcoholic client has less conscious conflict about abstinence, is taking responsibility for her own drinking behavior, and is beginning to resolve grief around losses due to alcohol and the loss of alcohol itself. Some couples have unrealistic expectations around sobriety and may be destabilized by abstinence. The therapist should always be aware of this possibility, and normalize this phenomenon for the couple.

This phase focuses on the improvement of communication and conflict resolution skills and making explicit the connection between present and past family patterns (Wetchler et al., 1993). Zacks, Green, and Marrow (1988) stress the importance of building on each woman's strengths and viewing high cohesiveness as a positive sign of satisfaction rather than a negative sign of enmeshment or fusion. As mentioned, therapists need to help lesbian clients find a sense of self within healthy connections rather than focusing on autonomy, separation, or codependency (Bushway, 1991). Clients may need to grieve the loss of "heterosexual privilege" in the family of origin and learn ways to challenge parental homophobia (Murphy, 1989).

If couples are struggling with alcohol abuse and lack of differentiation, each can be helped to (1) develop her own differentiated friends and activities, (2) define her own boundaries, set limits, and be assertive, and (3) voice disagreement in nonreactive ways (Zacks et al., 1988). As Bepko (1989) points out, an important goal is to change patterns of underfunctioning and overfunctioning that serve to maintain drinking problems. The therapist needs to assess the adaptive consequences of the alcohol abuse for the relationship, with the objective of attaining relationship goals without the use of alcohol. It is a mistake, however, to assume that shifting the system will eliminate the need for alcohol. As noted by Bepko (1989), "The relationship between the addict and the drug needs to be disrupted as well. Systemic change is a necessary, but not sufficient, response to an addiction" (p. 407). Bepko also notes that AA and Al-Anon tend to reinforce gender stereotypes and do not encourage women to take differentiated positions. Although some lesbian clients find support in lesbian AA groups and alternative twelve-step programs, therapists need to be ready to counteract unhelpful sexist and homophobic messages espoused by some of these groups.

SARAH AND CATE IN PHASE II

As our work continued, it became clearer that Sarah and Cate had similar types of unfinished business with their original families. Both had reactively distanced from their families and looked to the relationship to make up for earlier losses and provide feelings of being safe and special. Although both complained of too much distance in the relationship, their tendency to alternate pursuing and distancing behaviors indicated that they both needed the distance to stay safe. Their anxiety about feeling abandoned by their parents seeped into their relationship, further intensifying each partner's feelings of loss. Cate once stated, "Her coldness makes me so anxious . . . she's like a critical parent . . . I'm so afraid that she'll leave."

In the first few months of treatment, Cate had two brief relapses, which were framed as opportunities to learn more about herself and her grief around the loss of alcohol. As she began to take more responsibility for her drinking behavior, our work began to focus more on the connections between the current relationship, alcohol problems, and families of origin. Both identified multigenerational family themes of loss, lack of safety, and distancing through alcohol abuse and emotional cut-offs. I began to talk about how the distance they felt in their relationship was more about the sadness and anxiety each brought into the relationship than about what the other was doing. As we moved toward exploring the impact of unfinished business on their current needs for distance and on Cate's use of alcohol, I continued to focus my questions on self issues (Freeman, 1992). I asked, for example, What do you want from your partner that you feel you did not get from your original family? What gets stirred up in you (how do you explain it to yourself) when your partner is not there for you? What losses does this remind you of? How do you take care of yourself when you feel you are not good enough? What is different about you when your needs *are* met? How do you teach your partner what you need when you feel sad and alone? What is going on with you when you need your partner to be different? If you changed the way you perceived your partner, how would you have to be different in the relationship?

Stage III: Consolidating Change

In this phase of treatment, clients become more aware of the early warnings of relapse and methods of coping with potential problems (Wetchler et al., 1993). Because the need for abstinence has been internalized, more difficult relationship problems, which often elicit anxiety, may now be addressed. This phase of treatment continues to focus on the needs of women as individuals as well as on the needs of the relationship. I agree with Bepko (1989) that longer term Bowen-based family of origin interventions will maximize sustained change. (See the summary of Bowenian theory concepts in Chapter Eight of this book.)

SARAH AND CATE IN STAGE III

As we moved into our next stage of work, Cate had been abstinent for four months and had a sound understanding of early warning signs of relapse. She had very effective ways of dealing with anxiety and craving and was an active member of her lesbian AA group. In this stage, she spent a great deal of time discussing chronic feelings of self-hatred and shame about being a lesbian. Both she and Sarah had ongoing concerns about being out in the workplace. I continued to validate their lifestyle as well as their legitimate concerns around coming-out issues. As alcohol was removed as a distancing issue, anxiety in the relationship temporarily increased, and both expressed new concerns about the future of their relationship. It was at this point that I began to question and gently challenge their stories about their original families. I asked each what the loss would be to them of changing their story about their mother or father. What would each lose by giving up their old issues with their parents? How would they go about discovering new stories about their families? What would it stir up in them if they were less anxious and reactive when with their families?

Stage IV: Family of Origin Work

Although some couples with alcohol problems choose to terminate therapy at the end of Stage III, most wish to strengthen their relationship by now focusing on unresolved family of origin issues. Lesbians who are alcoholic may have problematic relationships with their families of origin whether or not they have told them about their sexual orientation (Holleran & Novak, 1989). As Freeman (1992) notes, unresolved loss issues with the family of origin often lead to relationship problems, since it is hard to give to your partner what you have not received from your original family. Clients' stories about their unfulfilled needs in their families of origin are replicated in some form in their current relationships. In order to rewrite their own stories, they must hear their parents' stories and observe their parents' anxiety without needing to fix, control, or distance from them. When this is mastered, they will be less anxious and needy in their current relationships and much less likely to relapse into drinking at times of stress.

The difficulty of coming out to parents and siblings is compounded by revealing alcoholism, often resulting in profound feelings of failure in the parents

(Nardi, 1982). Questions about disclosure to parents may permeate all phases of therapy with lesbian couples. For those who have not come out to their family, the last phase of therapy often involves continued discussion of the implications of secrecy and disclosure, the recognition of different timetables for coming out, and preparation for disclosure. The risks involved in coming out should never be underestimated, and the dynamics of the process vary by age, race, ethnicity, social class, and geography. Some well-differentiated clients will choose not to come out to their families, and their wisdom in this decision needs to be respected. Even in these cases, however, the therapist should avoid comments that could serve to solidify distance from family and preclude connections that could be important to long-term recovery. Lesbians, if storied at all, are storied in very negative and oppressive ways. As Laird (1994) notes, clients who are lesbian need to recognize the sources and contexts of their stories, construct new stories, and develop new interpretations of old self and social stories.

When clients are out to their parents and less reactive to them, I prefer to invite parents in for at least one session during the last stage of treatment. The purpose of such sessions is to challenge the family mythology by asking the parents to tell their stories about their lives. As Freeman (1992) notes, these stories inform adult children about how events shaped their parents' responses to them and can be used as positive legacies. The daughter observes but does not participate, and the session is videotaped for future viewing and as a gift to subsequent generations. The rationale for the daughter's silence in the interview is based on Freeman's (1992) observations that adult children often have emotional reactions to their parents' sad stories and the parents worry about these reactions. The therapist is more likely to be able to ask less reactive questions, stay calm, and find aspects of the story that emphasize survival, connections, and competence. In telling their stories, parents are encouraged to talk about their personal losses and loss of expectations for their daughter. In some instances, parents can be helped to revise their self-blaming stories into more empowering ones. Such sessions are usually preceded and followed by Bowen-based visits home by each client to reposition with the family and begin to broaden the story about parents and siblings. Attention is given to the grieving of family of origin losses and finding a way, even if imperfect, to stay connected to family.

SARAH AND CATE IN STAGE IV

The final stage of work with this couple, which began six months after Cate achieved sobriety, focused on active repositioning with the families of origin. I continued to ask questions that introduced doubt into their theories about their parents and wondered how their parents' losses—what *they* didn't get—affected their parenting. As they developed more curiosity about their own histories, we began to discuss the implications of secrecy and Cate's disclosure of her lesbianism to her father and siblings. Each woman decided on different methods of repositioning with her parents. Two examples of their initial efforts will be described.

Sarah's mother was planning a visit from the East Coast and was invited for an interview. Sarah agreed to observe without participating, and the session was videotaped. Her mother's story was one of profound loss and sadness. She was quite young when her family lost everything in the Depression, and her father subsequently developed a serious drinking problem. As an only child, she felt responsible for taking care of her mother's fairly constant sadness. She described herself as a quiet, good child who tried to stay out of the way of her parent's conflicts. She idolized her mother, was very dependent on her, and was devastated by her horrible death from cancer the year before Sarah was born. Her father died six years later. I asked questions about what she had learned from these experiences and what she had learned about survival. I asked what lessons she had learned from her parents and grandparents, who her role models were, and with whom she felt safest. She said that she had only wanted Sarah and her sister to have everything she did not have, like independence and education. She did not want to interfere with their lives or burden them in any way. She viewed her distancing from them as protecting them from her sadness. Sarah commented in the next session that she had reviewed the videotape, and it was a great relief to realize that her mother's parenting of her was about her mother's losses and not about lack of love for her.

Cate chose to initiate repositioning with her father through letters and phone calls. She worked several weeks on a letter in which she came out to him and expressed curiosity about his family. Over the course of several letters, her father acknowledged her lesbianism (although he disapproved), noting that he had known for some time and felt, as always, left out of important information. He thanked her for telling him. For the first time, he began to tell her his own story. He carried a great deal of shame throughout his life for being born out of wedlock to an alcoholic mother in Germany. As a small child, he was abandoned a number of times and abused by his stepfather. He left Nazi Germany and came to New York alone at age twelve, surviving but struggling his whole life with loneliness, depression, and alcoholism. As Cate began to let her father back into her life, she shared with him her memories of how he made her feel special when she was very young, and her sadness about not having a relationship with him for so many years. She also began to make telephone calls to her brothers, came out to them, and had the first visit from her mother without her father. The visit went well, and she began to gradually change her story about her mother as well.

As Sarah and Cate made peace with their original family losses, they were able to change their stories about themselves and each other. They no longer needed to use distance and alcohol to stay safe with each other or to deal with the stresses related to being lesbian in this society.

The Stance of the Therapist

Some therapists continue to maintain that lesbian couples should be treated by "out" lesbian therapists (Gartrell, 1984; McDermott, Tyndall, & Lichtenberg, 1989; Riddle & Sang, 1978). Bradford and colleagues (1994) found that 89 percent of lesbians preferred to see a woman counselor, and 66 percent preferred to see a counselor who was lesbian or gay. A recent analogue study of the effects of sexual orientation similarity and counselor experience level on perceptions by lesbians found that experienced therapists, both lesbian and heterosexual, were rated as more expert (Moran, 1992). It was suggested that sexual orientation of the counselor may be of less concern when the therapeutic issue is not primarily related to sexual orientation. Because of the analogue nature of the study, however, the usual precautions about generalizations to actual therapy sessions must be exercised. Stein (1988) concludes that what the therapist communicates about sexual orientation is more important than actual sexual orientation and that "a therapist's unwillingness to acknowledge a personal sexual orientation may be viewed as a statement that the patient should also continue to keep his or her sexual orientation hidden from others" (p. 86).

As mentioned, a therapeutic stance consistent with feminist ideas, that is, one that is collaborative and democratic, will be most effective. Therapists need to share their opinion about the extent and nature of alcohol use, provide education, and recommend the most appropriate treatment, but not become overresponsible for the client's choices and outcomes. Bepko and Krestan (1985) warn against becoming involved in an "incorrect complementarity" in which there is a one-up, one-down relationship with the client, often replicating the overresponsible-underresponsible dynamic in the lesbian couple. As Pasick and White (1991) point out, denial can be challenged by respectful questions without being controlling and confrontational. You can state your opinions about the role of alcohol in existing problems without insisting that clients agree with you. You can have conversations with clients that include good questions about interpersonal issues as well as the social context. It is critical to discuss with lesbian couples the relationship between oppression and psychosocial functioning. As noted by Saulnier (1991), the disease model of alcoholism pertains to some, but not all, lesbians:

> A focus on the structural etiological factors is as vital to the understanding of lesbian alcoholism as it was to the study of internalized homophobia. It is hoped that lesbian researchers, theorists, and clinicians will design interventions that are appropriate for this population—interventions that address alcohol problems in the context of oppression. The incorporation of sociopolitical and

historical information will probably prove more beneficial to lesbians with alcohol problems. (p. 81)

Conclusion

Competent treatment of lesbian couples with problems resulting from alcoholism in one or both partners requires unbiased attitudes and specialized knowledge. Heterosexist bias is reflected in automatically assuming a client is heterosexual, discounting the client's identification as a lesbian, believing that lesbianism per se is pathological, not addressing or failing to recognize internalized homophobia, or in attempting to change—or automatically attributing problems to—the client's sexual orientation. In addition, heterosexist bias can lead to dealing with the client as a single person when couple therapy is more appropriate and can result in a lack of attention to sociopolitical issues. Problems emanating from heterosexist bias can be compounded by negative attitudes toward alcoholic women.

The lack of heterosexist and negative attitudes does not, however, assure competence in working with lesbian couples with an alcohol problem. Feminist, lesbian-affirming practice is strengths-based, focusing on the clients' development of more empowering stories. The competent therapist understands the nature and diversity of lesbian identity development and relationships, as well as the treatment of substance abuse in women. Clients are seen together to affirm their couple status, and there is appropriate focus on substance abuse as the initial primary issue. Both family of origin and family of creation issues are addressed. Treatment deals with the possible interactions of substance abuse, heterosexist attitudes and oppression, and the particular relationship between the lesbian partners. Much is still to be learned about the dynamics of these variables in lesbian couples from diverse racial, ethnic, and social class backgrounds.

References

Anderson, S. C. (1994). A critical analysis of the concept of codependency. *Social Work, 39,* 677–684.

Anderson, S. C. (in press). Substance abuse and dependency in gay men and lesbians. *Journal of Gay and Lesbian Social Services.*

Anderson, S. C., & Henderson, D. C. (1985). Working with lesbian alcoholics. *Social Work, 30,* 518–525.

Becker, C. S. (1988). *Unbroken ties: Lesbian ex-lovers.* Boston: Allyson.

Benjamin, J. (1988). *The bonds of love: Psychoanalysis, feminism, and the problem of domination.* New York: Pantheon.

Bepko, C. (1989). Disorders of power: Women and addiction in the family. In M. Mc-Goldrick, C. M. Anderson, & F. Walsh (Eds.), *Women in families: A framework for family therapy* (pp. 406–426). New York: Norton.

Bepko, C. S., & Krestan, J. A. (1985). *The responsibility trap: A blueprint for treating the alcoholic family.* New York: Free Press.

Berg-Cross, L. (1988). Lesbians, family process, and individuation. *Journal of College Student Psychotherapy, 3,* 97–112.

Berzoff, J. (1989). Fusion and heterosexual women's friendships: Implications for expanding our adult developmental theories. *Women and Therapy, 8,* 93–107.

Blumstein, P., & Schwartz, P. (1983). *American couples: Money, work, and sex.* New York: Pocket Books.

Bograd, M. (1988). Enmeshment, fusion or relatedness? A conceptual analysis. In L. Braverman (Ed.), *Women, feminism, and family therapy* (pp. 65–80). Binghamton, NY: Haworth Press.

Bowen, M. (1978). *Family therapy in clinical practice.* Northvale, NJ: Aronson.

Bradford, J., Ryan, C., & Rothblum, E. D. (1994). National lesbian health care survey: Implications for mental health care. *Journal of Consulting and Clinical Psychology, 62,* 228–242.

Brown, L. S. (1989). New voices, new visions: Toward a lesbian/gay paradigm for psychology. *Psychology of Women Quarterly, 13,* 445–456.

Buhrke, R. A., & Douce, L. A. (1991). Training issues for counseling psychologists in working with lesbian women and gay men. *Counseling Psychologist, 19,* 216–234.

Burch, B. (1982). Psychological merger in lesbian couples: A joint ego psychological and systems approach. *Family Therapy, 9,* 201–208.

Burch, B. (1986). Psychotherapy and the dynamics of merger in lesbian couples. In T. S. Stein & C. J. Cohen (Eds.), *Contemporary perspectives on psychotherapy with lesbians and gay men* (pp. 57–71). New York: Plenum.

Burch, B. (1987). Barriers to intimacy: Conflicts over power, dependence, and nurturing. In Boston Lesbian Psychologies Collective (Ed.), *Lesbian psychologies: Explorations and challenges* (pp. 126–141). Urbana: University of Illinois Press.

Bushway, D. J. (1991). Chemical dependency treatment for lesbians and their families: The feminist challenge. *Journal of Feminist Family Therapy, 3,* 161–172.

Cabaj, R. P. (1988). Homosexuality and neurosis: Considerations for psychotherapy. *Journal of Homosexuality, 15,* 13–23.

Chodorow, N. (1978). *The reproduction of mothering.* Berkeley: University of California Press.

Clark, W. B. (1981). The contemporary tavern. In Y. Israel, F. B. Glaser, H. Kalant, R. E. Pophem, W. Schmidt, & R. G. Smart (Eds.), *Research advances in alcohol and drug problems* (vol. 6, pp. 425–470). New York: Plenum.

Collins, B. G. (1993). Reconstruing codependency using self-in-relation theory: A feminist perspective. *Social Work, 38,* 470–476.

Corrigan, E. M., & Anderson, S. C. (1985). Graduate social work education in alcoholism. In E. M. Freeman (Ed.), *Social work practice with clients who have alcohol problems* (pp. 335–350). Springfield, IL: Thomas.

Cummerton, J. M. (1982). Homophobia and social work practice with lesbians. In A. Weick & S. T. Vandiver (Eds.), *Women, power, and change* (pp. 104–113). Washington, DC: National Association of Social Workers.

Decker, B. (1984). Counseling gay and lesbian couples. *Journal of Social Work and Human Sexuality, 2,* 39–52.

De Crescenzo, T. A. (1984). Homophobia: A study of the attitudes of mental health professionals toward homosexuality. *Journal of Social Work and Human Sexuality, 2,* 115–136.

Elise, D. (1986). Lesbian couples: The implications of sex differences in separation-individuation. *Psychotherapy, 23,* 305–310.

Falco, K. L. (1991). *Psychotherapy with lesbian clients: Theory into practice.* New York: Brunner/Mazel.

Fassinger, R. E. (1991). The hidden minority: Issues and challenges in working with lesbian women and gay men. *Counseling Psychologist, 19,* 157–176.

Fifield, L. (1975). *On my way to nowhere: Alienated, isolated, and drunk–an analysis of gay alcohol abuse and an evaluation of alcoholism rehabilitation services for the Los Angeles gay community.* Los Angeles: Gay Community Services Center.

Freeman, D. S. (1992). *Family therapy with couples.* Northvale, NJ: Aronson.

Gagnon, J., Keller, S., Lawson, R., Miller, P., Simon, W., & Huber, J. (1982). Report of the American Sociological Association task force group on homosexuality. *American Sociologist, 17,* 164–180.

Garnets, L., Hancock, K. A., Cochran, S. D., Goodchilds, J., & Peplau, L. A. (1991). Issues in psychotherapy with lesbian and gay men: A survey of psychologists. *American Psychologist, 46,* 964–972.

Gartrell, N. (1984). *Issues in psychotherapy with lesbian women.* Work in Progress No. 83–04. Wellesley, MA: Wellesley College, Stone Center for Developmental Services and Studies.

Gilligan, C. (1982). *In a different voice: Psychological theory and women's development.* Cambridge, MA: Harvard University Press.

Goodrich, T. J., Rampage, C., Ellman, B., & Halstead, K. (1988). The lesbian couple. In T. J. Goodrich, C. Rampage, B. Ellman, & K. Halstead (Eds.), *Feminist family therapy: A casebook* (pp. 134–159). New York: Norton.

Green, G. D. (1990). Is separation really so great? *Women and Therapy, 9,* 87–104.

Hare-Mustin, R., & Marecek, J. (1986). Autonomy and gender: Some questions for therapists. *Psychotherapy, 23,* 205–212.

Hellman, R. E., Stanton, M., Lee, J., Tytun, A., & Vachon, R. (1989). Treatment of homosexual alcoholics in government-funded agencies: Provider training and attitudes. *Hospital and Community Psychiatry, 40,* 1163–1168.

Holleran, P. R., & Novak, A. H. (1989). Support choices and abstinence in gay/lesbian and heterosexual alcoholics. *Alcoholism Treatment Quarterly, 6,* 71–83.

Israelstam, S., & Lambert, S. (1989). Homosexuals who indulge in excessive use of alcohol and drugs: Psychosocial factors to be taken into account by community and intervention workers. *Journal of Alcohol and Drug Education, 34,* 54–69.

Kagle, J. D. (1987). Women who drink: Changing images, changing realities. *Journal of Social Work Education, 23*(3), 21–28.

Krestan, J. A., & Bepko, C. S. (1980). The problem of fusion in the lesbian relationship. *Family Process, 19,* 277–289.

Kurdek, L. A., & Schmitt, J. P. (1987). Perceived emotional support from family and friends in members of homosexual, married, and heterosexual cohabiting couples. *Journal of Homosexuality, 14,* 57–68.

Laird, J. (1993). Lesbian and gay families. In F. Walsh (Ed.), *Normal family processes* (2nd ed., pp. 282–328). New York: Guilford Press.

Laird, J. (1994). Lesbian families: A cultural perspective. In M. P. Mirkin (Ed.), *Women in context* (pp. 118–148). New York: Guilford Press.

Lindenbaum, J. P. (1985). The shattering of an illusion: The problem of competition in lesbian relationships. *Feminist Studies, 11,* 85–103.

Lohrenz, L., Connelly, J., Coyne, L., & Spare, K. (1978). Alcohol problems in several Midwestern homosexual communities. *Journal of Studies on Alcohol, 39,* 1959–1963.

McCandlish, B. M. (1982). Therapeutic issues with lesbian couples. *Journal of Homosexuality, 7,* 71–78.

McDermott, D., Tyndall, L., & Lichtenberg, J. W. (1989). Factors relating to counselor preference among gays and lesbians. *Journal of Counseling and Development, 68,* 31–35.

McKenzie, S. (1992). Merger in lesbian relationships. *Women and Therapy, 12,* 151–160.

McKirnan, D. J., & Peterson, P. L. (1989). Alcohol and drug use among homosexual men and women: Epidemiology and population characteristics. *Addictive Behaviors, 14,* 545–553.

Mencher, J. (1990). *Intimacy in lesbian relationships: A critical reexamination of fusion.* Work in Progress No. 42. Wellesley, MA: Wellesley College, Stone Center for Developmental Services and Studies.

Miller, J. B. (1976). *Toward a new psychology of women.* Boston: Beacon Press.

Miller, J. B. (1984). *The development of women's sense of self.* Work in Progress No. 82–06. Wellesley, MA: Wellesley College, Stone Center for Developmental Services and Studies.

Moran, M. R. (1992). Effects of sexual orientation similarity and counselor experience level on gay men's and lesbians' perceptions of counselors. *Journal of Counseling Psychology, 39,* 247–251.

Morin, S. F. (1977). Heterosexual bias in psychological research on lesbianism and male homosexuality. *American Psychologist, 32,* 629–637.

Morin, S. F., & Charles, K. A. (1983). Heterosexual bias in psychotherapy. In J. Murray & P. R. Abramson (Eds.), *Bias in psychotherapy* (pp. 309–338). New York: Praeger.

Murphy, B. C. (1989). Lesbian couples and their parents: The effects of perceived parental attitudes on the couple. *Journal of Counseling and Development, 68,* 46–51.

Nardi, P. M. (1982). Alcohol treatment and the nontraditional "family" structures of gays and lesbians. *Journal of Alcohol and Drug Education, 27,* 83–89.

Nelson, T. S. (1989). Differentiation in clinical and nonclinical women. *Journal of Feminist Family Therapy, 1,* 49–62.

Nicoloff, L. K., & Stiglitz, E. A. (1987). Lesbian alcoholism: Etiology, treatment and recovery. In Boston Lesbian Psychologies Collective (Ed.), *Lesbian psychologies: Explorations and challenges.* Urbana: University of Illinois Press.

Pasick, P., & White, C. (1991). Challenging General Patton: A feminist stance in substance abuse treatment and training. *Journal of Feminist Family Therapy, 3,* 87–102.

Paul, J. P., Stall, R., & Bloomfield, K. A. (1991). Gay and alcoholic: Epidemiologic and clinical issues. *Alcohol Health and Research World, 15,* 151–160.

Pearlman, S. F. (1989). Distancing and connectedness: Impact on couple formation in lesbian relationships. *Women and Therapy, 8,* 77–88.

Peplau, L. A., Cochran, S., Rook, K., & Padesky, C. (1978). Loving women: Attachment and autonomy in lesbian relationships. *Journal of Social Issues, 34,* 7–27.

Rabin, J., Keefe, K., & Burton, M. (1986). Enhancing services for sexual minority clients: A community mental health approach. *Social Work, 31,* 294–298.

Riddle, D. I., & Sang, B. (1978). Psychotherapy with lesbians. *Journal of Social Issues, 34,* 84–100.

Roth, S. (1989). Psychotherapy with lesbian couples: Individual issues, female socialization, and the social context. In. M. McGoldrick, C. M. Anderson, & F. Walsh (Eds.), *Women in families: A framework for family therapy* (pp. 286–307). New York: Norton.

Saghir, M., & Robins, E. (1973). *Male and female homosexuality.* Baltimore: Williams & Wilkins.

Sandmaier, M. (1980). *The invisible alcoholics: Women and alcohol abuse in America.* New York: McGraw-Hill.

Saulnier, C. L. (1991). Lesbian alcoholism: Development of a construct. *Affilia, 6,* 66–84.

Schaefer, S., Evans, S., & Coleman, E. (1987). Sexual orientation concerns among chemically dependent individuals. *Journal of Chemical Dependency Treatment, 1,* 121–140.

Shernoff, M., & Finnegan, D. (1991). Family treatment with chemically dependent gay men and lesbians. *Journal of Chemical Dependency Treatment, 4,* 121–135.

Slater, S., & Mencher, J. (1991). The lesbian family life cycle: A contextual approach. *American Journal of Orthopsychiatry, 61,* 372–382.

Sloven, J. (1991). Codependent or empathically responsive? Two views of Betty. *Journal of Feminist Family Therapy, 3,* 195–210.

Stein, T. S. (1988). Theoretical considerations in psychotherapy with gay men and lesbians. *Journal of Homosexuality, 15,* 75–95.

Stevens, P. E., & Hall, J. M. (1988). Stigma, health beliefs and experiences with health care in lesbian women. *Image: Journal of Nursing Scholarship, 20,* 69–73.

Sussal, C. M. (1993). Object relations couples therapy with lesbians. *Smith College Studies in Social Work, 63,* 301–316.

Tievsky, D. L. (1988). Homosexual clients and homophobic social workers. *Journal of Independent Social Work, 2,* 51–62.

Vargo, S. (1987). The effects of women's socialization on lesbian couples. In Boston Lesbian Psychologies Collective (Ed.), *Lesbian psychologies: Explorations and challenges* (pp. 161–173). Urbana: University of Illinois Press.

Walsh, F., & Scheinkman, M. (1989). (Fe)male: The hidden gender dimension in models of family therapy. In M. McGoldrick, C. M. Anderson, & F. Walsh (Eds.), *Women in families: A framework for family therapy* (pp. 16–41). New York: Norton.

Wetchler, J. L., McCollum, E. E., Nelson, T. S., Trepper, T. C., & Lewis, R. A. (1993). Systemic couples therapy for alcohol-abusing women. In T. J. O'Farrell (Ed.), *Treating alcohol problems* (pp. 236–260). New York: Guilford Press.

Wilke, D. (1994). Women and alcoholism: How a male-as-norm bias affects research, assessment, and treatment. *Health and Social Work, 19,* 29–35.

Wilsnack, S. C. (1991). Barriers to treatment for alcoholic women. *Addiction and Recovery, 11,* 10–12.

Zacks, E., Green, R.-J., & Marrow, J. (1988). Comparing lesbian and heterosexual couples on the circumplex model: An initial investigation. *Family Process, 27,* 471–484.

PART FOUR

LESBIAN AND GAY PARENTS

CHAPTER FOURTEEN

TWO MOMS

Contribution of the Planned Lesbian Family to the Deconstruction of Gendered Parenting

Valory Mitchell

Currently, both popular and scholarly ideas about child development legitimate only one primary caregiver, and parenthood is pervasively gendered. Mothers, always female, are expected to be very different parents than are fathers, who are never female. What then of the planned lesbian family—structured from the outset as a female parenting pair—and their shared children?

Over the past decade, thousands of lesbian couples have decided to "become a family" and have intentionally conceived, birthed, or adopted children. We know very little about these families. In the great preponderance of the psychological literature on lesbian mothers, only women who birthed their children in the context of heterosexual marriages from which they subsequently divorced are considered. Like other families that divorce, these include one mother, one father, and perhaps stepparents (one of whom may be the mother's female couple partner). As such, they are structurally different from the families I will be describing, and they face both similar and quite different issues from the planned lesbian family.

Several clinical and conceptual articles have been written about the planned lesbian family (Ainsley & Feltey, 1991; Crawford, 1987; Laird, 1993; Rohrbaugh, 1992). Two chapters (Patterson, 1994; Steckel, 1987) report research on the

Previously published in the *Journal of Feminist Family Therapy*, Volume 7, #(3/4), pp. 47–63, 1995, and reprinted with the permission of The Haworth Press, Inc., Publisher and the author.

psychological adjustment of the children. However, to my knowledge, the only empirical research on the planned two-mother family and its functioning has been in two unpublished doctoral dissertations (Hand, 1991; Osterweil, 1991).

I believe that the planned two-mother family is a "living laboratory" that embodies feminist critiques of family functioning and gendered parenting. In the first part of this chapter, I will make those critiques explicit by examining some areas in which we have been taught that a two-gender parenting pair is a requisite for the health of the family and its members. Operating from a lesbian-centered perspective, I will question both the sexism and the heterosexism of this (almost always untested) assumption. I will suggest that we work actively in our practice and writings to revise our theory. I will also present some data from a research project that my colleagues and I have begun. These data describe planned two-mother lesbian families and show how lesbian mothers in these families view their parenting roles and family structure.

The Planned Lesbian Family as a Feminist Family Model

Although the lesbian family typically is defined by sexuality, several social scientists (Blumstein & Schwartz, 1983; Kurdek & Schmitt, 1988; Laird, 1993; Luepnitz, 1988) have suggested that gay and lesbian couples and families can help us enlarge our understanding of the impact of gender on relationship quality. There are several ways that the two-mom lesbian family is a model of effective functioning.

The lesbian family is usually headed by a dual-career couple that brings two incomes to the family. Unlike many dual-career couples, however, the quantity of the child's experience with an involved parent is not in jeopardy because both partners are, and expect to be, full partners, sharing parenting tasks and time.

Hochschild (1989), writing of families headed by heterosexual couples, has described what she calls "the second shift" for the woman who comes home from work to another full schedule of housework and child care that depletes her stamina, while the average father spends about three hours per week in direct child care (cited in Ehrensaft, 1987).

A second way that two-mother lesbian families model effective functioning is in their nonhierarchical, flexible process. Since responsibility for housework and child care are equally assumed, lesbian partners do not appear to experience the alienation from one another that often accompanies the skewed role balances of most heterosexual couples as they pass through the transition to parenthood (Cowan & Cowan, 1988). As one lesbian mother put it, the strengths of the planned lesbian family are "two incomes, two parents, and lots of love."

Recently, feminist analysis of the family has helped family therapists to become more aware of the heterosexual couple relationship as a locus of women's oppression (Goldner, 1988; Hare-Mustin, 1987; Johnson, 1988). The third, and perhaps the most important aspect of the lesbian family model is the absence of legitimated oppression of one partner by the other. In their values and ideals, as well as in the actual reported conduct of their daily experience, these adult partners manifest equality. They are both heads of the household. Each is a primary parent; each is the breadwinner.

Theories of Gendered Parenting: Sexist and Anachronistic?

I have argued that planned lesbian families present a viable and valuable model of a functional family in contemporary America. If so, theories of psychological development must be rendered capable of describing and discussing the child's growth in these family environments. What needs to change?

The Primary Caregiver

Much of the literature on infant development includes theories about *the* mother, *the* primary caregiver, or *the* child-caregiver dyad, as if there were only one parent. This language emanates from the post–World War II era in England and in the United States, when the middle-class norm assumed a nuclear family with an at-home female adult doing virtually all of the child care. Winnicott's (1958) work provides a good exemplar.

From a feminist perspective, the construct of the primary caregiver, like so many ideas from developmental psychology (such as those of Sigmund Freud and Erik Erikson), conflates DEscription and PREscription. In cultures, classes, and times when shared parenting, extended families, nannies and wet nurses, and quality day care were rare, it may have been accurate to describe the child's relational life as centering on one (therefore, primary in the numerical as well as evaluative sense) caregiver. In the United States today, however, care of young children is often shared. A singular term no longer provides an accurate description of most contemporary American children's relational environment.

However, it is not just a matter of inaccurate language. Perpetuating the concept of a primary caregiver allows us to diminish the importance of all but one relationship for the very young child. If, instead, following the ideas of Stern (1985) and Kohut (1977), we try to look from the young child's perspective, we rediscover the potentially profound impact of each ongoing caregiving relationship on the development of the self. Each relationship that is characterized by deep and

committed involvement in a young child's nurture and daily care is of developmental importance to that child.

Separation Is to Attachment as Father Is to Mother?

Having linguistically legitimated only one infant-parent relationship, some theories then depict that relationship as a trap that imprisons the growing child. The
jaws of that trap, it is implied, must be wedged apart by an outsider who comes
to represent independence. It will come as no surprise to feminist readers that the
trap is female, the liberator male. In family systems language, the enmeshing
mother is located in gendered complementarity to a disengaged father. From a
more psychoanalytic perspective, even feminist authors (for example, Benjamin,
1991) argue that both male and female children experience mothers as home-
based repositories of regressive symbiotic attachment, while either the father or
some compendium of male cultural icons is seen to personify autonomy.

In a culture and time when most parents—male and female—leave the home
daily to undertake paid work, these images are timeworn and anachronistic adult
projections onto the child. They are also profoundly sexist, denigrating women's
capacity to adapt to their children's changing needs, and framing the caretaking
relationship as impinging on the child's autonomy.

Current research suggests several points of challenge. First, Stern (1985), using
microanalysis of videotapes of infants in interaction with parents, argues strongly
that infants never experience merger or symbiosis. Rather, from their first days when
they learn to gaze at or avert their gaze from the caregiver's face at will, they are experiencing their own separate self in relation to a separate other. From the beginning, the infant's relational life is a dance of separateness in relationship. Second, as
suggested above, this relational dance is engaged with more than one "primary"
caregiver, making dyadic relational exclusivity impossible in the child's experience.

It has been demonstrated, in research specifically addressing issues of individuation, that children of planned two-mother families do not differ from comparison
children on measures of autonomy, separation, or individuation, as assessed by nurs-
ery school teachers, parents, and analyses of children's play (Steckel, 1987). These
findings sharply contradict the predictions of gender-based parenting theories in
which these children would be seen as afflicted by a double dose of mothering.

Chodorow: Once More, with Feeling

Because of its wide currency in feminist psychology circles, I feel it is important
to tread this attachment-separation path one more time, in order to consider
Chodorow's (1978) analysis of the mother-child relationship in heterosexual fam-

ilies. Her analysis is consistent with the stereotype of the overinvolved female parent, but she explains this overinvolvement as a result of the failure of the spousal relationship in satisfying the emotional needs of the woman. According to Chodorow, the woman then turns to her children, particularly her female children, to establish emotionally satisfying relationships. This leads female children to build identities based on connection. When these girls become women, they too, are likely to be dissatisfied with their spousal relationships with men and to turn to their own female children, thus "reproducing motherhood" (or the centrality of the child-rearing task) for women but not for men.

If Chodorow's theory is correct (and this is a big if), Laird (1993) and Rohrbaugh (1992) have suggested that, because the lesbian couple consists of two women, both partners will have more of their emotional needs met in the couple relationship, thus reducing the likelihood of emotional overinvolvement with the children. From this systemic perspective, the essentialist argument that mothers represent symbiosis *because of their gender* becomes untenable.

Whither the Oedipus Complex—or What Do Our Role Models Model?

Although mother is often designated as the pivotal figure in the psychological health of her children, in the theory of the Oedipus complex, the spotlight shines on the father. Awareness of each parent's gender and of the parents' relationship supposedly launches children of heterosexual parents on an intrapsychic journey that culminates in the development of psychological structures, morality, gender-role identification, and the eventual choice of a heterosexual partner in adulthood (Goldner, 1991). By implication, failure to take this journey leaves the growing child confused and vulnerable.

In the Oedipal drama, girls and boys are presumed to become aware of and to desire what their father has (literally the penis, symbolically the phallus). In classical theory, boys retain their penises through giving up their wish to possess the mother and turning to an identification with father; girls symbolically acquire theirs by learning to be like mother in order to eventually be with a man like father and, from him, obtain a baby as a penis substitute. To be sure, the analytic community has debated the accuracy of this conceptualization, particularly as it applies to women. Nonetheless, the centrality of the Oedipus complex for personality development is widely endorsed (Cameron & Rychlak, 1985).

If we apply Oedipal theory to the triadic relations that encompass a female couple and their child, a son presumably will lack the chance to build healthy psychological structures through identification with a same-sex parent, while a daughter will lack the basis for adult motivation and self-regulation. Outside the analytic community, these presumed lacks lead to these questions: Will a boy who has no father (or father figure) feel manly enough? Will a girl with no father (or father figure) know how to relate to men?

For over half a century, critics (Horney, 1939; Johnson, 1988; Thompson, 1964) have argued that what children actually observe, and learn to identify with, in the heterosexual parenting pair of the Oedipus complex, is male supremacy. Father is looked up to, while mother defers. These critics see nothing in the Oedipus complex that is necessary, and show instead that power differences account for gender differences in the rationale for moral decision making. The child's gender identity, gender roles, and sexual orientation have already been engaged or determined for some time, irrespective of the gender distribution of family members (see Johnson, 1988, for a review of developmental studies supporting this argument).

The two-mother family offers children a very different model of triadic relations with which to identify. Privilege and deference do not characterize the parenting couple or the ways the two partners function within the family. In addition, whatever difference or inequality that exists between parents is not tied to gender difference and therefore cannot coalesce with the prevailing stereotypical hierarchical schema in the culture. Feminist family therapists are painfully aware of how rare egalitarian family forms are and how valuable for the achievement of equality in future generations.

In the few studies to date of children emerging from two-mother families (Patterson, 1994; Steckel, 1985), researchers are finding that no problems in adjustment or age-appropriate development distinguish these children from comparison groups raised by heterosexual parents. The few differences they report suggest that children of two mothers are somewhat less aggressive and hostile, more aware of their feelings (both positive and negative), and regard themselves and are regarded by others as a bit more likable. An abundance of mothering, then, appears to foster traits that most mental health professionals would like to see more of in *all* children.

A Descriptive Study of the Planned Two-Mom Family: The Research

In order to find out what planned lesbian families actually look like—their commonalities and variations of structure, functions, strengths, and vulnerabilities across the family life cycle—I have begun collecting data to address a series of research questions. The larger project uses both short-term (and hopefully long-term) as well as cross-sectional data in the form of structured self-report instruments and questionnaires, open-ended queries and comments, and semi-structured interviews and family narratives. By inviting lesbian mothers to participate as members of an ongoing research pool, I hope to accumulate a rich archive of information. Then, as specific questions emerge, the families' responses to these questions can be understood within the context of the informational landscape they have already provided. A first step toward this end, then, has been the gathering of background information. Using measures from studies of heterosexual families, as well as ones designed for this study, I will present some of these research data to sketch the parameters of family function and structure.

Participants

Thirty-two women with a child under ten years of age participated in this study. To be included, all of the women must have been in their current lesbian couple relationship at the time they and their partner birthed or adopted the child. The average age of the women in the sample was thirty-eight years; the range was twenty-eight to fifty-two. The average amount of education was sixteen years (or four years of college), ranging from high school through the doctoral level. Two of the women were full-time homemakers; the remainder held out-of-home jobs. The average age of the oldest child was three; half were girls, half boys. The average length of the couple relationship was 8.57 years. While most of the subjects lived in California, the data also describe families that lived in Illinois, Montana, New Jersey, New Mexico, New York, Oklahoma, Tennessee, Texas, Wisconsin, and Virginia. Ninety-four percent of the sample listed their ethnicity as Caucasian or Jewish.

Measures

I will present data from two standardized parenting measures, as well as some ratings and content analysis of open-ended questions. The two standardized measures are the "Who Does What" and the "Role Pie." Both were designed for the Becoming a Family Project (Cowan & Cowan, 1992)—a longitudinal study of the transition to parenthood in a sample of heterosexual couples drawn from the San Francisco Bay area. Both of these measures also were used in the two dissertations on planned lesbian families, readily permitting comparisons of findings across samples.

The Who Does What measure includes four content areas: thirteen household task items, twelve decision-making items, twenty child-care tasks, and twelve blocks of time (six for weekdays and the same six for weekends) during which child-care responsibility is assessed. Subjects took each measure twice, once to describe how things are now, and a second time to show how they would like things to be.

Each item was rated on a 1–9 scale in which 1 equals "My partner does it all," 5 represents an equal contribution, and 9 means "I do it all."

Ratings and content analysis present the lesbian mothers' views of the two-mother family. These data give the women an opportunity to speak in their own voice and to bring lesbian parenting experiences to life.

Findings

The results underscore the pervasive equality and mutuality that characterizes lesbian couple relationships. For "Who Does What" household tasks, the mean for "now" was 5.12; the "ideal" was 5.0. For decision making, the mean for now was 4.86; the ideal was 4.96. For child care tasks, the mean for now was 5.01; the ideal was 4.86. For child care time, the mean for now was 5.24; the ideal was 5.05. It is clear from the pattern of these data that, whether in reality or in the ideal, the distribution of work, influence, and time was never more than one-quarter of a point from exact equality.

This equality emerges even at the item level. Of the fifty-seven Who Does What items describing how things are done now, the mode is 5 (meaning equally shared) on forty-five items, or 80 percent. Of the same fifty-seven items describing how things would ideally be done, the mode is 5 (meaning equally shared) on fifty-three items, or 93 percent.

To facilitate a comparison, consider the analogous data from heterosexual parents of three-year-old children in the Cowan study described earlier (Cowan, personal communication, 1995). Like lesbian parents, heterosexual parents value and have achieved equal involvement in decision making (means are 4.99 and 5.01). Both husbands and wives saw household tasks as substantially shared; husbands thought they did a little more than their wives (5.08), while wives felt they did more than husbands (5.20)—both hold an ideal of 5.0, or 50–50 sharing of housework. In parenting, however, the traditional division of labor emerges clearly. Looking at child-care tasks, while wives hold a 5.0 ideal, they report now doing considerably more of the tasks (an average of 6.3) than their husbands. Husbands, for their part, see themselves as doing even fewer of the parenting tasks (3.4), and would ideally do more (4.4) but still not share equally.

The Role Pie. The 360-degree circle of the "pie" is intended to be "a picture of you in your life right now." Subjects are asked to slice the pie into roles, "based on how large that part of you feels, not just on how much time you spend being it."

As is shown in Figure 14.1, for this sample, the role of mother clearly embodies the largest share of their subjective sense of self. Of a possible 360 degrees in the "life picture," the role of mother or parent occupied an average of 132 degrees, over one-third of the self. Three subjects assigned less than one-quarter of the pie to mothering. Two subjects assigned more than two-thirds of the pie to it. Interestingly, neither of these were full-time homemakers, although there are two in the sample. The remaining twenty-seven mothers felt that between one-quarter and one-half of their current subjective self-space was invested in the self-as-mother. Three of the subjects were extreme outliers, although their partners were not extreme in the other direction. When the outlier couples are excluded, the average difference between partners in the size of the pie devoted to motherhood is 20 degrees, or 6 percent of the pie.

In comparison, the partner role occupied an average of 88 degrees, or less than one-quarter; the worker role occupied an average of 80 degrees, also less than one-quarter. All other roles *combined*—including individual self, daughter, sister, friend, artist, activist, church-synagogue member, housekeeper-cook-cleaner—accounted, on the average, for 60 degrees, or one- sixth of the "life space."

Although my sample is small, findings from unpublished dissertation studies that used different samples but the same measure (Hand, 1991; Osterweil, 1991) are consistent with these data. The three studies converge to document that, as a group, lesbian parenting couples both expect and attain equally shared involvement in all family tasks and functions on both an objective task-and-time measure and on a subjective measure of self-as-mother.

Again, comparison with a sample of heterosexual parents of three-year-olds (Cowan & Cowan, 1992) makes the contrast more vivid. For women, the parent role occupies an average of 142.6 degrees of the circle. For fathers, however, the parent "slice" takes only 91.7 degrees of the pie, about 40 degrees fewer than the lesbian parents and over 50 degrees smaller than the self-as-parent experienced by their wives.

The traditional complementarity of this division of labor is revealed in the worker role. Men have 136.9 degrees of the pie devoted to the worker role—this is over one-third of the self- space and 45 degrees *larger* than their parent role. Heterosexual women, on the other hand, average 56.7 degrees of their pie devoted to the worker role—this is less than one-sixth of their self-space, and 85 degrees *smaller* than their parent role. The husbands and wives come close together in their views of self-as-partner, however. Men average 72.6 and women average 80.22.

Lesbians Describe the Two-Mom Parenting Pair. Using both rating scales and open-ended questions, mothers were asked to describe their experience of parenting together. They see themselves as a very strong parenting team (a mean of 1.39 on a 5-point scale) yet distinct as parents (a mean of 2.25 on a 4-point scale of similarity). Although there has been considerable speculation in the clinical literature that the two women in the lesbian couple compete for the mother role, these women reported very few feelings of competition about parenting (a mean

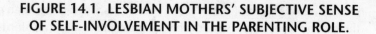

FIGURE 14.1. LESBIAN MOTHERS' SUBJECTIVE SENSE OF SELF-INVOLVEMENT IN THE PARENTING ROLE.

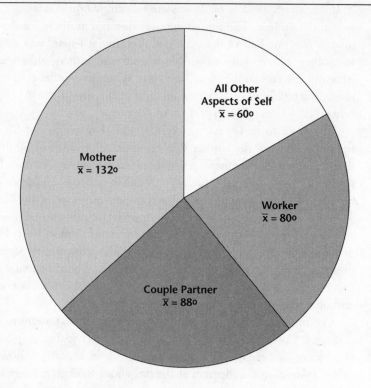

All Other
Aspects of Self
$\bar{x} = 60°$

Mother
$\bar{x} = 132°$

Worker
$\bar{x} = 80°$

Couple Partner
$\bar{x} = 88°$

of 1.41 on a 5-point scale) and are able to talk about almost all aspects of parenting (a partner mean of 4.77 on a 5-point scale).

One mother put it this way: "I feel any child is well served by being in a loving environment, whether that comes from two mothers or any other situation. I don't see my partner and I as having [parenting] 'roles' so much as having [parenting] 'goals.'"

Another wrote, "We each bring to our son our own personalities first. We then take on the role of mother, but our base is in our own selves. We are parenting the whole child, and [believe that] two people can balance the parenting. . . . The quality of our mothering is different, but we are both our son's moms—equal in many respects and complementary in others. . . . I think our son benefits from having 'more of a good thing.'"

Perceived Strengths of the Two-Mother Family. Most of the respondents emphasized the quality of the child's experience as the principal strength of the two-mother family. They felt that the two-mom family provides more of the following: parental involvement, concern, attention, nurturance, physical affection, expression of feelings, talking, sensitivity, love, caring, warmth, or, as one wrote, "Lots of love and twice the mothering." In addition, shared parenting was considered an asset for the child in that it brought freedom from traditional models, a very close relationship with two people, and a first-hand appreciation of differences and diversity that were not tied to gender.

The second common theme was that equally shared parenting was seen as very beneficial for the parents. This way of parenting was said to offer greater support, "help in the hard parts," a balancing of styles, and increased communication.

A few mothers mentioned the absence of men in the home as a positive. One said there was "less to worry about dominant male figures, with whatever repercussions or side-effects that brings." Others suggested that because there were no men in the home, lesbian mothers may make a greater effort to create positive relationships between their children and adult men who are both appropriate models and are interested in children.

One subject reminded us that an important strength of the two-mother family was that every child in that family was a planned and wanted child.

Perceived Problems with the Two-Mother Family. The most commonly perceived problems were located outside of the family: prejudice, ignorance, social pressure, homophobia, attitudes, or simply "how they look at us." Most participants simply designated social attitudes as a problem; others elaborated their concerns, including not being treated like a real family in terms of insurance, wills, and other legal matters, and recognition that the child will have to explain the family structure to others.

Some of the mothers mentioned the lack of male models or a man's perspective as a potential problem for the child in a two-mother family. Of these, it was common to find that they had also planned for a family member or friend to provide this added modeling and perspective.

A third theme focused on pitfalls of collaboration between parents: Disagreement on how to handle problems, duplication of efforts, and leaving gaps with "both thinking the other had taken care of it."

Clinical Implications

Most lesbians seek a therapist who recognizes that being a lesbian is not the problem. Similarly, when lesbian families come for help, it is imperative that we recognize, and affirm for our clients, that the structure of their family is not the problem. This statement, presented so baldly, appears obvious. Translated into greater subtlety and specificity, however, it challenges all of us to scrutinize our presumptions about family life and effective parenting—of girls and of boys, at every phase of childhood.

Two Moms

When family therapists encounter a two-mother lesbian family, if they find themselves wondering which is *the* mother, or the *primary* caregiver, they will likely be thinking in terms that rob legitimacy from the parenting pair and from each of the individual parents. This is problematic for several reasons. It echoes the misunderstandings that are common in the larger culture. Couples often report being asked, "Whose child is it?," or the experience of having one mother presumed to be an aunt or a grandmother because her closeness to the child is apparent. Some families may be particularly vulnerable to this kind of misunderstanding. In communities where either one or both parents is not out as a lesbian or if one is the biological mother of the child, her pregnancy and impending motherhood may receive substantial interpersonal support and celebration. The nonbiological mother, however, may have no way of rendering her motherhood visible and giving it a relational reality outside her immediate lesbian family (Muzio, 1993). Similarly, in most states, only one parent may legally adopt a child, adding to the potential marginalizing of one parent and privileging the other. In all of these circumstances, the therapist's possible alliance with a hostile or ignorant larger culture may enfeeble the therapy.

The therapist's presumption of a primary caregiver is most problematic, however, when one or both mothers feel insecure about their own legitimacy as the child's functional parent. In my nonclinical sample, mothers report that competition between them about parenting is minimal and rare. In clinical settings, however, it is not unknown and may be particularly anguishing (Crawford, 1987). For example, in an instance recounted to me after a family dissolution, one mother recalled forcing herself to walk out of the room where her baby was crying because the other mother wanted to comfort the baby. The infant was well aware of which mother could nurse, and continued to cry and reach toward her as long as she was visible to the child. In this episode, the nonnursing mother's failure to recognize her centrality in other aspects of the baby's life caused her to lose empathy with her child's needs, and the tension between the parents forced the other mother to ignore them. If this kind of tension has drawn a lesbian family into therapy, failure to approach the couple as a shared parenting pair will prevent the possibility of a viable working alliance.

Individuals in Relationships

Because our culture has come to equate maleness with separation, two women parenting together may absorb cultural messages that suggest that, because of their gender, they will be unable to adequately facilitate their children's growth and differentiation. They may avoid books, classes, and other media information about child development and age-appropriate parenting if that advice presents parenting skills as dichotomized by gender. To present a nongendered reformulation is to both include and legitimate the potential of these parents to do their job effectively. If therapists find themselves hypothesizing enmeshment or overly permeable ego boundaries because of the parents' gender, it is incumbent on us to scrutinize our "countertransference" as members of a community in which the discourse has been patriarchal and profoundly sexist.

Modeling Equality and Diversity Independent of Gender

Internalization of the cultural stigma, marginality, and designation of deviance ascribed to homosexuality make developmental concerns about gender role and gendered role models particularly provocative for lesbian parents. Lesbian parents' own unexamined homophobia may stimulate special efforts to cultivate gender-stereotypical interests in their children. I recall a couple telling me joyfully that they were expecting a boy baby. When I asked what pleased them especially about having a boy, they replied that they looked forward to playing sports and building things together with him. Asked if they would not do these things with a daughter, they winced. These same parents contributed regularly to a fund that encouraged girls' athletics—their feminism was (temporarily) eclipsed by a wish to help their child "fit in." For similar reasons, a lesbian mother's attempt to include men in her family may sometimes be done in an odd and disequilibrating way. One mother whom I saw in therapy had invited her startled plumber to Sunday dinners. Her efforts to involve this man in the family confused and distressed both her partner and the children (and the plumber!).

Because cultural stereotypes conflate lesbianism with masculinity, or even with gender confusion, gay parents may feel particular pressure to demonstrate that they are not creating gender nonconformity or confusion in their children. Just as we might question heterosexual parents' failure to expand options for their children, feminist family therapists can powerfully intervene to remind lesbian mothers of their nonsexist child-rearing values and destigmatize lesbian mothers' willingness to allow their children a repertoire that is less constrained by gendered role proscriptions.

Reconstructing Parenting

The desire to do right by one's children is fundamental, as these "families of choice" (Weston, 1991) enact the daily process that creates the relational environment in which they live. If we are to develop appropriate and effective approaches for working with these families, it is important that we deepen our understanding of their lived experience through substantive research in this area. Our current lexicon of family and child development constructs must be deconstructed and reconstructed through the lens of feminist family studies (Luepnitz, 1988; Thorne & Yalom, 1992). For this to occur, we must dust off our consciousness-raising techniques and begin again with ourselves.

There are crucial clinical implications that arise when theory requires change. Currently, mental health professionals are at risk of colluding with traditional expectations about child development and family functioning in ways that can undermine the confidence and legitimacy of the lesbian parenting pair. As feminist therapists, we need to become able to spot the often insidious entry of these expectations into our ways of thinking and working and also to help lesbian parents become conscious of and critical about them.

References

Ainsley, J., & Feltey, K. M. (1991). Definitions and dynamics of motherhood and family in lesbian communities. *Marriage and Family Review, 17,* 63–85.

Benjamin, J. (1991). Father and daughter: Identification with difference—a contribution to gender heterodoxy. *Psychoanalytic Dialogues, 1,* 277–300.

Blumstein, P., & Schwartz, P. (1983). *American couples: Money, work, and sex.* New York: Morrow.

Cameron, N., & Rychlak, J. (1985). *Personality development and psychopathology.* Boston: Houghton-Mifflin.

Chodorow, N. (1978). *The reproduction of mothering.* Berkeley: University of California Press.

Cowan, P., & Cowan, C. (1988). Changes in marriage during the transition to parenthood: Must we blame the baby? In G. Michaels & W. Goldberg (Eds.), *Transition to parenthood: Current theory and research.* Cambridge: Cambridge University Press.

Cowan, C., & Cowan, P. (1992). *When partners become parents.* New York: Basic Books.

Crawford, S. (1987). Lesbian families: Psychosocial stress and the family-building process. In Boston Lesbian Psychologies Collective (Ed.), *Lesbian psychologies: Explorations and challenges* (pp. 195–214). Urbana: University of Illinois Press.

Ehrensaft, D. (1987). *Parenting together: Men and women sharing the care of their children.* New York: Free Press.

Goldner, V. (1988). Generation and gender: Normative and covert hierarchies. *Family Process, 27,* 17–31.

Goldner, V. (1991). Toward a critical relational theory of gender. *Psychoanalytic Dialogues, 1,* 249–272.

Hand, S. (1991). *The lesbian parenting couple.* Unpublished doctoral dissertation, Professional School of Psychology, San Francisco.

Hare-Mustin, R. (1987). The problem of gender in family therapy theory. *Family Process, 26,* 15–33.

Hochschild, A., with Machung, A. (1989). *The second shift: Working parents and the revolution at home.* New York: Viking Penguin.

Horney, K. (1939). *New ways in psychoanalysis.* New York: Norton.

Johnson, M. M. (1988). *Strong mothers, weak wives: The search for gender equality.* Berkeley: University of California Press.

Kohut, H. (1977). *The restoration of the self.* Madison, CT: International Universities Press.

Kurdek, L., & Schmitt, J. P. (1988). Perceived social support in gays and lesbians in cohabiting relationships. *Journal of Personality and Social Psychology, 54,* 504–509.

Laird, J. (1993). Lesbian and gay families. In F. Walsh (Ed.), *Normal family processes* (2nd ed., pp. 282–330). New York: Guilford Press.

Luepnitz, D. (1988). *The family interpreted: Feminist theory in clinical practice.* New York: Basic Books.

Muzio, C. (1993). Lesbian co-parenting: On being/being with the invisible (m)other. *Smith College Studies in Social Work, 63,* 215–229.

Osterweil, D. (1991). *Relationship satisfaction in lesbian first-time parents.* Unpublished doctoral dissertation, California School of Professional Psychology, Alameda.

Patterson, C. (1994). Children of the lesbian baby boom: Behavioral adjustment, self-concepts, and sex role identity. In B. Greene & G. Herek (Eds.), *Lesbian and gay psychology: Theory, research, and clinical applications* (pp. 156–175). Newbury Park, CA: Sage.

Rohrbaugh, J. B. (1992). Lesbian families: Clinical issues and theoretical implications. *Professional Psychology: Research and Practice, 23,* 467–473.

Steckel, A. (1985). *Separation-individuation in children of lesbian and heterosexual couples.* Unpublished doctoral dissertation, Wright Institute, Berkeley, CA.

Steckel, A. (1987). Psychosocial development of children of lesbian mothers. In F. W. Bozett (Ed.), *Gay and lesbian parents* (pp. 75–85). New York: Praeger.

Stern, D. (1985). *The interpersonal world of the infant: A view from psychoanalysis and developmental psychology.* New York: Basic Books.

Thompson, C. (1964). *Interpersonal psychoanalysis.* (M. R. Green, Ed.) New York: Basic Books. (Originally published 1931–1961)

Thorne, B., & Yalom, M. (Eds.) (1992). *Rethinking the family: Some feminist questions.* Boston: Northeastern University Press.

Weston, K. (1991). *Families we choose: Lesbians, gays, and kinship.* New York: Columbia University Press.

Winnicott, D. W. (1958). *Collected papers.* New York: Basic Books.

CHAPTER FIFTEEN

LESBIANS CHOOSING CHILDREN

Creating Families, Creating Narratives

Cheryl Muzio

The concept of narrative as a fluent and dynamic form of self-construction has become a focal point for many contemporary thinkers as they labor to understand and describe the nature of human experience. Indeed, it is with our passage into the linguistic world that we first take up the position of subject (Lorraine, 1990), allowing us to name ourselves and our experiences. It is the language we use to describe our experiences that imparts meaning to them; we construct our lives and relationships in and through narrative forms of communication (White & Epston, 1990).

Not all voices or narratives enjoy equal status or authority, however. The stories that have been privileged within the larger social and academic discourse have, for the most part, been the "his-stories" of White, middle-class, Western European men (Nicholson, 1990; Waldegrave, 1990). Such disparity of representation has more recently been addressed in psychology and family therapy as prominent theorists acknowledge the existence of previously subjugated knowledges and narratives, including those of women (Gergen, 1985, 1991; Gergen & Gergen, 1983; Hare-Mustin, 1987; Laird, 1988, 1989; McGoldrick, 1989;

Previously published in the *Journal of Feminist Family Therapy*, Volume 7, #(3/4), pp. 33–45, 1995 as "Lesbians Choosing Children," and reprinted with the permission of The Haworth Press, Inc., Publisher, and the author.

Tomm, 1989; White & Epston, 1990). The inclusion of previously silenced voices has deepened and complicated our work as clinicians. We have become more aware of the sociocultural contexts in which we practice and consequently have become increasingly more sensitized to the importance of incorporating this knowledge into our work with families (Imber-Black, 1989; Laird, 1989; Mc-Goldrick, 1989; Waldegrave, 1990; White & Epston, 1990).

As women's stories are listened to with increasing attention and respect, notions of what a family is or should be are becoming radically altered. The notion of healthy families existing independent of heterosexual relationships has emerged, and the stories of healthy lesbian families, with or without children, are being told (Crawford, 1987; Muzio, 1993; Slater & Mencher, 1991; Weston, 1991). As these stories provide voice and substance to previously invisible individuals and families, the very personal effects of the dynamics of oppression begin to be revealed.

In this chapter, I will examine the dynamics of oppression as they affect the family-building process of lesbians birthing or adopting children. I will then consider more recent family therapy practices that attempt to address these dynamics (in part) by privileging the narratives of the oppressed. Throughout this inquiry, I will use both clinical and personal examples to provide a clearer sense of the lived life of lesbians and their children within a society that is both misogynist and homophobic.

Lesbians Choosing Children: The Story Imposed

As lesbians begin to widen their narratives to include stories of themselves as mothers, the fact that they are raising children has gradually filtered into the popular culture. With this awareness has come much concern about the fitness of lesbians to be parents as well as the suitability of a lesbian home for a child or children to grow up in. Indeed, even people with relatively liberal attitudes toward homosexuality in general draw the line when it comes to approving gays and lesbians even having contact with children. The reasons for this are as multifaceted and complex as homophobia itself.

The creation and dissemination of a narrative that fosters the subjugation of lesbians and their children is clearly illustrated in a 1993 issue of *Newsweek* magazine (Salholz et al., 1993). The issue in question had a cover story titled "Lesbians—Coming Out Strong: What Are the Limits of Tolerance?" that featured on the cover two traditionally attractive White women, who appeared to be in their thirties, embracing. Some might argue that for lesbians to receive the visibility that such a cover story bestows in and of itself strengthens the public lesbian narrative. However, the subtitle concerning the "limits of tolerance" also clearly signaled two points to its readership: (1) that lesbians can at best be only tolerated in mainstream society and (2) that there are limits even to this tolerance.

When speaking to the aforementioned limits of tolerance, Salholz and colleagues (1993) write:

> For all their new pride, lesbians face a lot of old prejudice. The emergence of openly lesbian couples—publicly affectionate or *with their children*—may test the limits of America's uneasy tolerance of homosexuality. Even many liberals who watched C-SPAN's unexpurgated coverage of the gay-rights march were offended by the spectacle of some women. . . . (p. 56; emphasis added)

As we see here, as lesbians and their children become more visible, they also become the subject (or perhaps, more accurately, the object) of the dominant narrative, a narrative that reflects and re-creates deep-seated doubts about lesbians' efficacy as parents. It is a story that is told to lesbian parents themselves in different ways and in different settings: in schools, in workplaces, in churches and synagogues, in doctors' offices, in major news magazines, and even in the homes of their families of origin. In order to counteract the dominant narrative, lesbian parents must be encouraged to hear clearly the story that is so often imposed on them. They also must be encouraged to tell their own stories of subjugation and, ultimately, of liberation.

Stories of Subjugation

As we have seen, a lesbian who chooses to become a mother either through birth or adoption (or by mothering her partner's children) challenges the dominant story about both mothers and lesbians. A woman who has been lesbian-identified for all or most of her adult life often has never envisioned herself as a mother. To put it another way, motherhood has never been part of the story she heard or told herself about being a lesbian. Indeed, it is only within the very recent past that lesbian mothers have begun to be spoken of at all in the popular culture or that language has even encompassed the idea of lesbian mothers. This is not to suggest that all women should or do want to become mothers. It is to suggest, however, that many lesbians have believed the subjugating narrative that explicitly or implicitly questions their capacity for mothering. Thus lesbians who are considering becoming mothers are opposing a dominant narrative.

As lesbians overcome the internalized obstacles to motherhood, they are invariably confronted with external obstacles in the form of institutionalized homophobia. Whether the lesbian becomes a mother through alternative insemination or adoption, if she wishes to have children, she most likely will have to tell her story to a medical or social service professional, a person who wields considerable power to either facilitate or deny her vision of her own future. Thus a lesbian seeking to become a mother must have a clarity of vision that can withstand and overcome the many subtle and not-so-subtle impediments she will at times encounter.

Forbidden Stories: Adopting as a Lesbian Couple

Although there are rare exceptions, the process of adoption is, for the most part, forbidden to openly lesbian couples. Indeed, even if lesbians have the good fortune of working with a social worker who acknowledges their relationship, agency policy and the law generally allow only one partner to adopt the baby. As a result, lesbian partners attempting to become mothers through adoption are routinely subjected to the need to deny the true nature of their relationship in order for one of them to be deemed a fit parent.

In my practice, I have seen first-hand the relational effects of the stress brought about by the need to be closeted in many (if not all) of the phases of the adoption process. One couple I worked with had saved for years to afford the fees required for adopting a child. Because the adoption agency they used did not approve of lesbian parents, they were closeted throughout the process. Finally, as their dreams began to come to fruition, they appropriately worried about how to hide the true nature of their relationship as they were visited by agency officials conducting the home study.

As the time of the home visit came closer, they worried and fought about each of their appearances, lest one or both of them appear too much "like a lesbian." They rearranged their bedroom, restyled their hair, and purchased new wardrobes to disguise themselves and their relationship. Even more poignantly, they practiced for weeks to eradicate the affectionate words and gestures that had woven themselves into the fabric of their lives over the ten years they had been together.

As they struggled with concealing the nature of their relationship, their fear of losing their opportunity to parent grew stronger. Their anxiety about being judged unfit by virtue of their lesbianism revealed itself in their uncharacteristically harsh judgments of one another. The hostility inherent within the homophobic adoption process was being expressed in very personal and hurtful ways within their relationship, and although this couple had lived within a misogynist and homophobic culture for many years, this was an experience without parallel for them.

This couple, along with many other adoptive couples I have worked with, were grappling with what Bruner (1986) calls "inchoate experience." Inchoate experience encompasses those events we have neither the understanding nor the language to make sense of. A crucial piece of the therapeutic work for this couple consisted of helping them name and understand their experience—to transform inchoate experience into a story that could be told.

Indeed, as they came to understand and tell their story to themselves, to one another, and to others, some of the deeply internalized aspects of their problems were externalized. Externalization is "an approach to therapy that encourages persons to objectify . . . problems that they experience as oppressive" (White & Epston, 1990, p. 38). Some of the benefits gained by externalizing the problem are enumerated by White and Epston: "Through this process of externalization, persons gain a reflexive perspective on their lives, and new options become available to them in challenging the 'truths' that they experience as defining and specifying of them and their relationships" (p. 30). This couple clearly benefited from the reflexive perspective they gained; it helped them to locate the problem outside of themselves and their relationship. They were therefore less likely to blame themselves or one another for their perceived shortcomings and were more likely to work together toward a common goal.

Unfortunately, outside of a very personal realm, our therapeutic work could not provide them with new options for challenging the "truths" of which White and Epston (1990, p. 30) speak. In this case, to publicly define and specify the true nature of their relationship would mean losing the long-fought-for option of having a child. As with many forms of oppression, the power to effect change did not lie with the oppressed, as the consequences of challenging that oppression were simply too great. Therefore, our work together went beyond externalizing the problem in that it provided them with a safe place in which to identify and express the grief and anger they carried as a result of their powerlessness.

What can or should therapists do in response to a client's experience of oppression in working with lesbians choosing children? It is clearly essential for therapists to understand the impact that interfacing with a homophobic system can have on the emotional life of their clients. Sharing this understanding with clients is an important first step in helping them to externalize or gain perspective on their experiences. Dealing with the identification of the psychological effects of oppression in a clinical setting often raises issues concerning therapeutic neutrality. A therapist has an opportunity when dealing with these issues to validate and perhaps share the feelings of powerlessness and anger that often accompany interfacing with a homophobic adoption system. An appropriately emotional response from a therapist can validate and give voice to a client's experience, providing both a model of and a container for the feelings that such situations inevitably provoke.

Therapists also have the option of becoming politically active in response to these issues, working to change local adoption laws, for example, or working to create programs that will educate people about alternative families. These kinds of activities will not, for the most part, have an immediate effect on the laws and attitudes that reflect and maintain the homophobia embedded within our social and cultural institutions. However, they will make a clear statement to both one's clients and one's community, while planting the seeds that may grow into a society more tolerant of diversity.

Lesbian Mothers and their Families of Origin: Changing Stories

As lesbians plan to birth or adopt children, they, like their heterosexual counterparts, are often drawn to their families of origin in looking for information and support (Brazelton & Cramer, 1990). In this way, families of origin traditionally have a central role in the creation and dissemination of the narratives of a newly constituting family (McGoldrick, 1989). Although the birth or adoption of a child requires that any family reconstitute itself, how this happens within lesbian mothers' families is often unpredictable.

I have seen previously loving and supportive families become distant and rejecting when faced with the idea that their lesbian daughter and her partner will become mothers. Alternately, I have worked with individuals and couples whose previously distant families became uncharacteristically accepting and supportive with the announcement of an impending birth or adoption. Whether lesbian mothers' families of origin move closer or further away with the announcement that they will soon become grandparents, the repercussions of such change are keenly felt within the lesbian relationship.

As a couple prepares to have a baby, the work required to renegotiate changing roles within one's family of origin creates added stress. The preadoptive or pregnant couple is already negotiating changing roles within their primary relationship as they work to understand the impact becoming mothers is having on their sense of themselves and their relationship (Muzio, 1993). Renegotiating their relationships with their own mothers or fathers as their own maternal identities are forming complicates an already delicate process. It is an experience that often requires expectant mothers to turn their attention outward toward their family of origin at a time they are needing to turn inward, toward their newly constituting family.

The problem many families have in accepting their lesbian daughter's future offspring, interestingly enough, often organizes itself within a narrative context. That is to say, the families involved often tell their lesbian daughters that they simply do not know what they will tell other people about who the child is to them and who the child's parents are. This is often (but by no means exclusively) true for the families that become grandparents when their daughter's partner is the legal or biological mother of the child in question.

Introducing a child into the larger family often causes long ignored or denied issues of homophobia to emerge. For example, the parents of one of my clients had been apprehensive but supportive as their daughter's partner conceived and birthed a son. They visited their daughter after the birth and were appropriately attentive to their newest grandchild. When the boy was under a year old, my client, her partner, and the child made a trip to her family's home to attend a niece's birthday party. Everything was going quite smoothly until some family friends called to say they would be dropping by. My client's mother became quite panicked at this point and asked my client, along with her partner and their son, to wait in a spare room until these guests had left. Without giving it much thought, they complied.

It was not until after they found themselves hidden away that they began to fully understand the implications of their banishment. When the guests had left, the emotional repercussions were great as the couple worked to address what had happened with the grandparents. As they were forced to confront a previously unrealized level of homophobia within their own family, everyone involved struggled with feelings of hurt, anger, and shame. Subsequent work with this client focused on helping her articulate what she felt she needed from her parents, given their now keenly felt differences. As a result, she was able to continue a dialogue with them that has slowly resulted in greater communication and acceptance between the generations.

As couples negotiate their changing relationships with their families of origin, therapy can help them understand more clearly the nature of their tasks, as well as help externalize the pressures brought to bear (especially) by disapproving parents. Given the extent to which our identities are generationally bound, however, there are clearly limits to the extent to which a problem of this kind can be externalized. This is especially true when lesbian daughters or their children are summarily rejected by their families of origin. In these cases, it is crucial for the therapist, especially at first, to sit with the client's grief or anger and to validate her loss. As the initial shock and crisis of the rejection begin to pass, externalizing interventions can help the client examine and work toward the creation of more legitimizing familial ties, whether or not they include her family of origin. As we will see, the use of narrative to define and support the lesbian family (whether or not it is inclusive of the lesbians' families of origin) can be a powerful antidote to the many homophobic messages lesbian mothers are exposed to on a daily basis.

Creating Families: Creating Narratives

As lesbians decide to pursue motherhood, a network of support groups has emerged within many lesbian communities to help facilitate this process (Pies, 1985; Weston, 1991). These groups, which are not professionally designed or facilitated, become a focal point within an oppressed community by providing information and support. Initial meetings usually focus on resources available, such as sperm banks, adoption agencies, and obstetrics and gynecology (OB-GYN) practices. Stories about particular medical practitioners or adoption agencies emerge as women share their experiences. For example, a story that emerged within one lesbian community told of OB-GYN practitioners who would not inseminate a lesbian without a note from her therapist. One can only guess how many women were able to avoid such demeaning and infantilizing experiences as a result of this shared information.

As groups develop, the information shared often becomes increasingly personal. Successes and setbacks are no longer solely individual triumphs or tragedies but rather, they emerge as part of a larger tapestry woven of their communal experiences. Within these groups, individual experiences are given meaning and context; women are able to externalize their experiences as part of what happens to lesbians choosing children. Consequently, the effects of living in a homophobic culture are less likely to be internalized, and individuals are perhaps less likely to be discouraged by the obstacles they encounter.

Once a child is on the way, these support groups often remain together and evolve into labor or adoption support groups. Eventually, they often take the form of play groups and babysitting cooperatives. In our local community, for example, there is a monthly picnic for lesbians and their children. From the time my family began attending these picnics, and as our daughter has grown, our conversations have moved from diapers to day care to public schools. Over the months, we have formed friendships, and our daughter has had the opportunity to make friends with children from families like hers. It is an event to which we can all look forward. This group, as well as others like it, provides a sense of community for lesbian families, a place where their stories are the norm rather than the exception. This opportunity to hear others and, in turn, to be heard by others helps strengthen and legitimize these families, which often are not acknowledged as families within the dominant narrative.

Certainly, not all lesbians are aware of or have access to such cohesive community resources. Therapists can be instrumental in educating clients about resources that do exist, or they may themselves organize and facilitate short-term groups for lesbians considering parenthood, groups that may subsequently become self-facilitated. In any event, it is incumbent upon therapists to be aware of and educate their clients about the usefulness of creating a supportive community in which to parent.

Life-Cycle Rituals and the Lesbian Family

Within these communities, lesbians are creating rituals that both mark and create significant life transitions. These rituals have been called "the most powerful and meaningful of rituals" (Imber-Black, 1989, p. 459); they are both secular and sacred, providing a platform on which the most crucial of life's dramas can be enacted and acknowledged. Indeed, public acknowledgments and declarations of their family's life cycle are increasingly important to lesbians as they work to solidify their sense of themselves as legitimate and viable family units. As we will see, the rituals give voice to struggles and joys that often are disallowed or discounted by the dominant culture.

The adoptive couple I mentioned earlier had a gathering of their closest people when it became clear that they were going to be able to adopt a child. Although this gathering bore much resemblance to a traditional shower, the importance of telling their story as a healing and confirming ritual of their struggles and joys was clearly of central importance.

In this gathering, they told the story of their journey to parenthood, complete with the fear and frustration they experienced at differing points in the process. Their friends listened, spoke publicly of their joy and confidence in the couple's choices, and presented them with gifts for their future child. They ate together and danced into the early morning hours in celebration of all that had happened and all that was yet to come. The gathering presented an unprecedented opportunity for this couple to publicly acknowledge their bond and the anticipated arrival of the child, as well as to be acknowledged as a legitimate and viable family, despite the obstacles with which they would continue to contend. This gathering helped to define this particular lesbian family unit.

The rituals that are created after the birth or adoption of a child in a lesbian family serve to create and acknowledge a family formed outside of "the usual biogenetically grounded mode of determining what relationships will count as kinship" (Weston, 1991, p. 35). As such, these rituals hold special meaning for the lesbian family as they name and claim their relationships to one another. To illustrate this, I will use an example of another couple with whom I worked.

CASE EXAMPLE: A NAMING CEREMONY

A middle-aged couple had been together for fifteen years when their first child, a daughter, was born. Their need to mark the beginning of a new life for their daughter and themselves led them to plan a naming ceremony for her. It was a small gathering, composed of their closest friends. Their families of origin were notably absent from this gathering, reflecting the fact that they each had lost the parent to whom they felt most bonded. Even before their parents' deaths, they had always considered their friends to be their extended family. They were happy and excited that they had finally created an opportunity to enact and proclaim these strong and loving bonds.

The couple spent much time deciding what their ritual would entail. They chose music that reflected their values and hopes for themselves and their daughter. After playing this music, the nonbiological mother held their daughter in her arms and presented her to those gathered by her full name, which was composed of her given name and both of the partners' surnames. Then, each of them took a turn lighting a candle as they spoke a wish for her. She was wished love, patience, courage, and more, as the room became brighter with the light they created through their wishes. Afterward, they spontaneously spoke of the bond they felt with one another as they changed the usual definition of what family is. It was a ritual that both created and marked an entry into a new life for their family.

The rituals described here helped name and transform the unique challenges of lesbian motherhood into stories and experiences of celebration, of having overcome obstacles and faced adversity successfully. They helped legitimize the bonds so often dismissed in the dominant culture, those of women as life partners and parents, as well as those of friends who are truly considered family.

Conclusion

Because individuals and families often seek therapy when their lived experiences contradict the dominant narrative about them (White & Epston, 1990), it is not unusual for lesbians to seek therapy at some point in their family-building process. As we have seen, the pressures and problems faced by lesbians choosing children begin with the decision to parent. Relationships with family, friends, and professionals as a lesbian becomes pregnant or adopts and ultimately introduces an infant or child into her family often reveal previously concealed homophobic beliefs concerning her suitability to raise children.

The question for therapists working with these families becomes, To what extent is it possible to externalize the problem of homophobia as it affects lesbians choosing children? It is clearly important for couples to understand the nature of their oppression and, in this way, the process of objectifying the problem is a crucial point in helping the lesbian family function more smoothly. On a more symbolic level, therapists who help and encourage their lesbian clients to create their own life-cycle rituals clearly provide them with an invaluable tool that forms and strengthens the very fabric of the lesbian family.

When a couple or individual is directly confronting homophobic beliefs or practices, however, there is an affective experience that must also be addressed. In the case discussed earlier concerning the adoptive parents who were compelled to hide their relationship, externalizing the problem was clearly a significant point in the therapy. However, my acknowledgment and expression of the remarkable sadness I felt for their circumstance not only validated their feelings but created a relationship in which their internalized grief and frustration, that is, those feelings they were left with as an unavoidable by-product of interfacing with a homophobic system, did not need to be hidden but could be seen and held.

By not denying the pain and suffering often felt by lesbians choosing children, therapists acknowledge the full range of lesbians' experience and underscore their remarkable strengths as they overcome the many obstacles they face in creating strong and loving families. Indeed, affirming both the external homophobia and the internal experiences of helplessness and anger allows our clients to externalize what is happening to them without denying them validation for the very real feelings that oppression invariably engenders in the oppressed.

In the case of lesbians choosing children, allowing the expression of a full range of feeling about their experiences provides them with a language for describing those experiences to one another and, when appropriate, to their children. This, in turn, supports the children of lesbians in the telling of their own stories. This kind of support helps families weather difficult times and celebrate joyful ones as they continue to find ways to prosper despite the unique challenges they inevitably face.

References

Brazelton, T., & Cramer, B. (1990). *The earliest relationship.* Reading, MA: Addison-Wesley.

Bruner, E. (1986). Experience and its expressions. In V. Turner & E. Bruner (Eds.), *The anthropology of experience* (pp. 3–30). Urbana: University of Illinois Press.

Crawford, S. (1987). Lesbian families: Psychosocial stress and the family-building process. In Boston Lesbian Psychologies Collective (Ed.), *Lesbian psychologies: Explorations and challenges* (pp. 195–214). Urbana: University of Illinois Press.

Gergen, K. (1985). The social constructionist movement in modern psychology. *American Psychologist, 40*(3), 226–275.

Gergen, K. (1991). *The saturated self: Dilemmas of identity in contemporary life.* New York: Basic Books.

Gergen, K., & Gergen, M. (1983). Narratives of the self. In T. Sarbin & K. Scheibe (Eds.), *Studies in social identity* (pp. 254–273). New York: Praeger.

Hare-Mustin, R. (1987). The problem of gender in family therapy theory. *Family Process, 26*, 15–27.

Imber-Black, E. (1989). Women's relationships with larger systems. In M. McGoldrick, C. M. Anderson, & F. Walsh (Eds.), *Women in families: A framework for family therapy* (pp. 335–356). New York: Norton.

Laird, J. (1988). Women and stories. In E. Imber-Black, J. Roberts, & R. Whiting (Eds.), *Rituals in families and family therapy* (pp. 331–362). New York: Norton.

Laird, J. (1989). Women and stories: Restorying women's self-constructions. In M. McGoldrick, C. M. Anderson, & F. Walsh (Eds.), *Women in families: A framework for family therapy* (pp. 427–450). New York: Norton.

Lorraine, T. E. (1990). *Gender, identity and the production of meaning.* Boulder, CO: Westview Press.

McGoldrick, M. (1989). Women through the family life cycle. In M. McGoldrick, C. M. Anderson, & F. Walsh (Eds.), *Women in families: A framework for family therapy* (pp. 200–226). New York: Norton.

Muzio, C. (1993). Lesbian co-parenting: On being/being with the invisible (m)other. *Smith College Studies in Social Work, 63*(3), 215–229.

Nicholson, L. J. (1990). Introduction. In L. J. Nicholson (Ed.), *Feminism/postmodernism* (pp. 1–16). New York: Routledge, Chapman & Hall.

Pies, C. (1985). *Considering parenthood: A workbook for lesbians.* San Francisco: Spinsters/Aunt Lute.

Salholz, E., Glick, D., Beachy, L., Monserrate, C., King, P., Gordon, J., & Barrett, T. (1993, June 21). The power and the pride. *Newsweek*, pp. 54–60.

Slater, S., & Mencher, J. (1991). The lesbian family life cycle: A contextual approach. *American Journal of Orthopsychiatry, 61*(3), 372–381.

Tomm, K. (1989). Externalizing the problem and internalizing personal agency. *Journal of Strategic and Systemic Therapies, 8*(1), 54–59.

Waldegrave, C. (1990). Social justice and family therapy. *Dulwich Centre Newsletter, 1*, 5–47.

Weston, K. (1991). *Families we choose: Lesbians, gays, and kinship.* New York: Columbia University Press.

White, M., & Epston, D. (1990). *Narrative means to therapeutic ends.* New York: Norton.

CHAPTER SIXTEEN

WORKING WITH GAY FATHERS

Developmental, Postdivorce Parenting, and Therapeutic Issues

Jerry J. Bigner

Over the past several decades, a newly emergent figure has become more visible in homosexual culture—the gay man who is a father. Although there are substantial numbers of such individuals, they constitute a minority within a minority. Researchers estimate that perhaps 20 to 25 percent of self-identified male homosexuals are also fathers (Bell & Weinberg, 1978; Bozett & Sussman, 1989).

Researchers only recently have begun to study gay fathers, their parenting styles, their relationships with their children, and the families they form with a male partner. Although there is not an extensive literature as yet about these individuals, it is clear that gay fathers experience a unique and more complex social-psychological environment than that of most homosexual or heterosexual males. For example, previously married gay fathers are challenged, perhaps more so than childless gay men, to achieve a different personal identity as well as the resolution of more intense and deep feelings of homophobia in order to establish a healthy self-concept.

Developmental Issues of Gay Fathers

How is it that a gay man becomes involved in the typically heterosexual activity and social role of being a father? While there is no single explanation for this phenomenon, a variety of reasons have been suggested (Barret & Robinson, 1990; Bigner & Bozett, 1989; Bigner & Jacobsen, 1989a, 1989b, 1992; Bozett, 1987b).

It appears that the majority of gay men who are fathers remained closeted during their adolescence or early adulthood years. Many of these men entered into heterosexual marriage without full acceptance of their homosexual orientation. Their marriages, however, were not always undertaken as a smoke screen to deflect suspicion about their homosexuality. Most of the men sincerely hoped to have healthy, successful family lives and, at the time of their marriages, did not view themselves as homosexual, although many were aware of attractions to other men (Barret & Robinson, 1990; Bigner & Jacobsen, 1989a, 1989b; Miller, 1979). Reasons for marriage reported in a study of gay fathers who were aware of their orientation prior to becoming married include, in descending order: (1) genuine love for their female spouse; (2) personal and social expectations for family life; and (3) a sincere hope that marriage would eliminate their homosexual desires (Wyers, 1987).

These men may be especially sensitive to the negative social impact of having an openly homosexual lifestyle in our society and thus have extreme difficulty accepting their homosexual attraction to other men. Because of this difficulty, they may have a high level of internalized homophobia that serves as a rationale for continuing to maintain a charade of heterosexuality. At the same time, unable to completely deny their homosexual interests, they may become involved in affairs with other men, participate in anonymous sexual encounters, or use other means for expressing their homosexuality.

Such an arrangement, however, calls for juggling two separate and conflicting personal identities and relying on deception to camouflage their homosexual orientation. As a result of the difficulty in maintaining this dual approach, coupled with the trigger developmental event of midlife transition, divorce from the heterosexual marriage often becomes inevitable when the man discloses his true sexual orientation. The wife usually experiences a number of upsetting, painful feelings in reaction to her husband's disclosure (Barret & Robinson, 1990; Hays & Samuels, 1989), and few marriages remain intact.

For all practical purposes, what has occurred developmentally for the typical prospective gay father is an *identity foreclosure* (Waterman, 1982). This takes place when a person makes a premature commitment to a false sense of self, and in this case, to an ill-fitting lifestyle as a heterosexual. At midlife, many adult males typically address a number of unresolved personal issues and seriously question the meaning and direction of their lives (Gould, 1978; Levinson, 1986). While this is a significant developmental task in itself, the person who is a gay father experiences the additional challenge of addressing personal identity issues that have been postponed. Essentially, a gay father who comes out at or about midlife is developmentally "off-time" in comparison with other gay males who experienced a more developmentally on-time identity development process in adolescence and early adulthood and who also did not react as negatively to pursuing a socially stigmatized, openly gay lifestyle (Troiden, 1979).

Some gay fathers follow a different developmental path toward fatherhood rather than through marriage and may not experience the same developmental challenges. These individuals make an intentional choice to become a parent through a liaison with a single lesbian or a lesbian couple who also wish to become parents. In such instances, it is common for conception to occur via alternative insemination. The lesbian biological mother often retains physical custody of the child or children, while the gay father has joint custody or visitation rights. When this arrangement for assuming parenthood is pursued, carefully researched and negotiated legal arrangements are a priority before initiating a pregnancy. Other gay men enter into a marriage with a heterosexual woman with both partners being aware in advance of the man's sexual orientation. Still other marriages involve a bisexual man with a heterosexual or bisexual woman. Many of these marriages remain intact for many years, during which children are produced and reared.

Explanations for desiring parenthood cited by gay men include having a genuine desire to nurture children via active parenting, the constancy of children in one's life, or simply wanting to reproduce for the same reasons offered by heterosexuals, for example, to achieve some measure of immortality through one's children. When motivations for parenthood have been examined (Bigner & Jacobsen, 1989b), the reasons given by gay fathers for having children are generally similar to those of heterosexual fathers. However, there are also some significant differences. Heterosexual fathers typically desire children for traditional reasons, such as continuing a family name or providing security for parents in their old age. Gay fathers, however, emphasize that the larger culture confers adult status on people who are parents. This reason may be especially important to those gay men who marry women in order to avoid the negative social stigma associated with homosexuality.

The adjustment challenges for men who divorce and undergo delayed personal identity development as a homosexual and father are difficult and problematic. These men enter the gay subculture at some disadvantage because they come out at older ages than other gay men who do not become fathers. They often seek to replicate the kind of committed relationship they experienced or desired in their former heterosexual arrangement. Because they are not typically like other nonparent gay men, gay fathers often experience discrimination and rejection. Many are successful, however, in establishing a partnership with another gay man that is based on long-term commitment, emotional and sexual exclusivity, and economic cooperation. However, very little is known about the nature of these relationships or about a gay stepfamily system, its structure, or its functioning.

There are a number of different ways, then, that a man who is homosexual comes to be a father: through marriage, adoption, foster parenting, donating sperm for alternative insemination with a heterosexual woman or lesbian friend or couple, or forming a stepfamily with another gay man who is the biological father of children. Given that the majority of gay fathers seen by therapists fall into the first category (fatherhood via a past heterosexual marriage), the major focus of this chapter will be on these men and the therapeutic issues usually encountered.

Identity Development of Gay Fathers

A gay man who also is a father is seen as a social enigma in society. To many people, even the label *gay father* represents a contradiction in terms. In societal interpretations, the *gay* label connotes an antifamily stereotype, while the *father* label connotes heterosexuality and a strong interest in sexual reproduction. Thus, gay fathers experience difficulties in reconciling these two divergent and conflicting personal identities into a meaningful whole.

According to several researchers, the dilemma and foremost developmental task of a man who is both gay and a father focuses on the theme of divided personal identity (Barret & Robinson, 1990; Bigner & Bozett, 1989; Bozett, 1981a, 1981b, 1985, 1987b; Bozett & Sussman, 1989; Robinson & Skeen, 1982). More specifically, these men are described as socially marginal, having allegiances to both the gay and heterosexual cultural worlds. In general, the homosexual status involves balancing two lifestyles: functioning in the gay world with its attendant demands while simultaneously functioning in the heterosexual world with its demands. To achieve some level of personal coherence, gays are required to integrate the standards of both worlds into some workable single social status. Often, this is not accomplished successfully, resulting in levels of stress not usually experienced by heterosexuals.

Gays, then, are confronted with the challenge of *status integration* requiring them to reconcile dual standards of social conduct. Theoretically, this places gay men into a low status integration position in general but especially when they have not publicly disclosed their sexual orientation (Jacobsen, Bigner, & Yang, 1994). It is likely that a gay father's public disclosure and his openly gay lifestyle permit a higher level of status integration and lower levels of stress than are experienced by someone who must constantly manage and guard his sexual orientation from the heterosexual world. Low status integration occurs when individuals cannot effectively reconcile the conflicts in having to live with a dual social status, resulting in errors of judgment, absent-minded behavior, accidents, and other self-destructive behaviors such as suicide (Gibbs & Martin, 1964; Lester, 1987; Stack, 1987).

Gay fathers not only must resolve the developmental problem of dual social status but must also reconcile the two polar extremes of what it means to be both a gay man and a father. Since each identity (gay and father) may be unacceptable or inconsistent with the social standards within either subculture, the task for these individuals is to integrate both identities into a new cognitive class called *gay father*. For many gay men, resolution comes from disclosing the gay identity to heterosexuals and the father identity to gays, disclosures that will be met with disapproval and even hostility on the part of some from each group. By a process that has been termed *integrative sanctioning* (Bozett, 1981a, 1981b, 1985, 1987a, 1987b), an individual is encouraged to form close liaisons with those in both homosexual and heterosexual worlds who positively sanction both identities, while simultaneously creating social distance from those who are intolerant.

However, the identity formation process of gay fathers is not resolved so simply. Status integration theory (Gibbs, 1989; Gibbs & Martin, 1964; Jacobsen et al., 1994; Stafford & Gibbs, 1985) predicts that the majority of gay fathers will have additional identity formation challenges because they have had a longer and more intensive grounding in the heterosexual world with its accompanying behavioral demands and standards, and yet they lack equivalent grounding in the homosexual world. This lack of experience may result in behavior that is atypical, inconsistent, and self-destructive.

Bozett (1985) describes the developmental path of gay fathers as characterized by five marker events: dating women, establishing a heterosexual marriage and assuming the husband role, becoming a father, altering the spousal relationship via separation and divorce, and activating a gay lifestyle. Because the majority of gay fathers have had extensive experience participating in the social world of heterosexuality, they need to work on developing a gay identity in a healthy, open manner. However, the gay community may be less accepting of the gay father's history of heterosexual involvement. The gay father represents someone who has had and continues to have long-term emotional and financial responsibilities to others (children), who has time restrictions and loyalties to others, has different living arrangements, and so on. His fathering experiences are likely to have shaped his history as well as his character in ways unlike that of gays who are childless, by promoting an orientation toward "greater responsibility, selflessness, and moderation" (Guttman, 1975); developing a greater appreciation of commitment to others in relationships (Roopnarine & Miller, 1985); and possessing more experience and skill in emotional expressiveness and nurturance (Biller, 1993). These qualities, while likely to promote success in heterosexual relationships, may not be as effective in the gay subculture. Gay subculture typically is singles-oriented. Relationships often are more short-term, in part because society fails to support, encourage, and validate homosexual relationships. This orientation tends to promote less emphasis on intimacy in relationships, few if any financial responsibilities for others, and a heavy focus on personal autonomy. The gay male world also values youthfulness and its attendant emphasis on physical attractiveness. Because gay fathers typically are older upon coming out and because of their unique dual identity, they may experience rejection and discrimination as they try to enter the gay world.

Formation of the gay father identity, then, is facilitated through the process of integrative sanctioning, especially among those who populate the gay side of the gay father's world. Coming out as a gay man and as a father to other gays assists in identity validation by reducing the level of cognitive dissonance. Over time, according to Bozett (1985), there is a melding of the once conflicting identities, the incongruity produced by low status integration disappears, and the level of stress produced by efforts to conceal one's identity is lowered.

Parenting by Gay Fathers

A number of issues are unique to the parenting situations of gay fathers. They include the ability to parent children effectively, the impact of the disclosure of the father's homosexuality on his children, and the dynamics of a homosexual family structure on gay fathers, their partners, and their children.

First, no empirical evidence suggests that the homosexual orientation of a father or other caregiver is detrimental to children's welfare (Patterson, 1992). On the contrary, every study, as well as every review of the literature about the parenting abilities and effectiveness of gay fathers, has failed to demonstrate that children's development or well-being is harmed in any way by being parented by a homosexual father. Studies have repeatedly found that gay fathers are as effective as heterosexual fathers in their ability to parent children and provide for their care properly (Bigner & Jacobsen, 1989a, 1989b, 1992). Gay fathers have been found to be more nurturant than heterosexual fathers and less traditional in perceiving the provider functions as the primary aspect of their fathering role. Relationships with their children are described repeatedly as being warm and positive, and the home life provided for children is repeatedly described as stable and highly structured. As compared with heterosexual fathers, gay fathers are more consistent in setting limits on children's behavior.

Researchers have offered several explanations for these findings. For example, gay fathers may feel more pressure to be as proficient as possible as parents because (1) they may feel guilty about the difficulties that divorce and the disclosure of their homosexual orientation may create for their children; and (2) they may be especially sensitive to the scrutiny of their parenting behavior and home life by the courts, ex-wives, ex-in-laws, the school, and others. They may fear that custody or visitation rights may be challenged at any time solely on the basis of sexual orientation. In addition, gay fathers may be more androgynous than heterosexual fathers in their approach to parenting. Their child-rearing styles appear to incorporate a greater degree of emotional expressiveness and less reliance on traditional sex-role behaviors, which results in more nurturant behaviors with children.

The judicial system, while treating the custodial and visitation arrangements of gay fathers with less prejudice in recent years, nevertheless is vulnerable to the heterosexist and homophobic mythology prevalent in the social environment (Hitchens, 1980). For example, it is not unusual for some courts to assert that children of gay fathers are at risk of becoming homosexual and that they are more likely to experience discrimination if the father's homosexuality is publicly known. Gay fathers are considered by some courts to be unfit role models for children simply by virtue of their homosexual orientation. All of these prejudicial beliefs are founded in heterosexist and homophobic attitudes, as well as hostile feelings about homosexuals as parents, and are not supported by research on gay fathers and their children. For example, the causes and origins of sexual orientation (homosexual as well as heterosexual) remain debatable. Researchers, however, do seem to agree that an individual's sexual orientation is not related to parental modeling or family of origin dynamics. The parents of most homosexuals are heterosexual. If sexual orientation were indeed transmitted by modeling from parent to child, then there would be very few homosexuals. Likewise, courts do not remove children from homes or limit the parenting experiences of racial minority parents on the basis that children will experience discrimination and prejudicial treatment from other children because of their race. Racial minority parents typically teach their children how to cope with prejudicial treatment by others, and gay fathers also teach their children about the irrationality of homophobia and ways to cope with others' prejudice.

Children of Gay Fathers

There are several powerful social myths about homosexuality in general and gay men in particular that continue to have negative and painful ramifications for both gay fathers and their children. In this section, I explore those myths as well as what can be said about the unique issues of children of gay fathers, based on research to date (Barret & Robinson, 1990; Cramer, 1986; Golombok, Spencer, & Rutter, 1983; Gottman, 1989; Lamb, 1982; Mayadas & Duehn, 1976; Patterson, 1992; Robinson & Barret, 1986).

First, if one could cite a theme that consistently runs through the lay public's notions about children of gay fathers, it is that these children are innocent victims by virtue of having a so-called deviant father (Barret & Robinson, 1990). One of the most frequently cited reasons for denying custody or visitation rights to gay fathers is the notion that their same-sex children are likely to be molested sexually not only by the fathers but also by their lovers and gay friends. This is a myth as well as a hostile and veiled homophobic attitude that has little foundation in reality (Barbaree & Marshall, 1989; Cole, 1992). Research into sexual abuse and incest of children reveals that female rather than male children are likely to be targets of perpetrators and that the overwhelming majority, that is, an estimated 99.9 percent, of incest perpetrators are adult heterosexual males who are usually the biological fathers or stepfathers of the abused female children (Langevin & Watson, 1991; Roane, 1992).

Second, there is some concern that the quality of the relationship between gay fathers and their children will be harmed if the father discloses his homosexuality. Researchers find that, rather than producing disruptive effects, disclosure appears to promote healthy relationships between gay fathers and their children (Bozett, 1987a; Dunne, 1987; Miller, 1979). Gay fathers who have disclosed their orientation, in contrast to those who have not, are found to have relatively stable lifestyles that often involve a domestic relationship with another man who is a permanent, committed life partner. These fathers tend to spend greater amounts of time with their children, and this is usually described as quality time. They are described by researchers as dependable sources of caregiving and are seen by children as authentic and genuine. Nondisclosure can have unhealthy effects for both fathers and children, leading to inconsistency of parental behavior and undermining children's trust.

Disclosure to children, however, is a problematic issue for many gay fathers, and many fear losing their children's love (Bigner & Bozett, 1989; Bozett, 1980, 1984; Dunne, 1987). Although disclosure has a significant impact on the spousal relationship, usually resulting in separation and divorce, many gay fathers report that severing the legal tie to their former wives is less disturbing than the potential loss of their parent-child relationships. Although there are exceptions, most children do not reject their father upon disclosure of his sexual orientation (Barret & Robinson, 1990; Bozett, 1980, 1986, 1987a, 1987b; Miller, 1986; Patterson, 1992). Rather than producing alienation and estrangement, disclosure appears to promote a father-child relationship that is emotionally close and based on greater honesty and openness. In addition, disclosure may assist a gay father in positive ways as he develops his identity career. Children typically do not repudiate their father but rather continue to express their love for him. Although not all approve of their father's sexual orientation, they tend to be more accepting following the disclosure than most gay fathers anticipate.

A third commonly held belief is that children of gay fathers will experience serious emotional trauma by being embarrassed and stigmatized by their peers should their father's sexual orientation become public knowledge. There is some truth to this belief in that children who have a gay father can indeed expect to experience bigotry and discrimination when other children become aware of their father's difference. In this respect, the judicial system may be maintaining these unhealthy views of homosexuals and gay fathers by restricting visitation or denying custody to gay fathers. Although children of gay fathers can expect to experience conflicts and harassment at times from other children, this can become a learning experience about human nature and how to deal with irrationality in others. Children of gay fathers can learn the importance of tolerance and the need to recognize individual differences in others (Bigner & Bozett, 1989; Rivera, 1987).

Another fear harbored about children of gay fathers is that their peers will assume that they are gay as well. Research indicates that this fear is unfounded, since children of gay fathers learn how to manage and control how they wish to be perceived by their peers (Bozett, 1987b). This is accomplished through the use of several strategies. First, *boundary controls* may be used by the child in relation to the gay father in several ways: (1) controls exerted on the father's behavior, such as asking the father to conceal his sexual orientation from others; (2) controls exerted on one's own behavior, such as refusing to be seen in public with the father and his lover; or (3) controlling one's behavior with peers, such as refusing to bring friends to the father's home. Second, children of gay fathers may use *nondisclosure* as a means of controlling public knowledge about their father's sexuality. This may be accomplished simply by not sharing this information, especially with their peers. Third, children of gay fathers may use *selective disclosure*. Some peers may be chosen to receive this information about the father's sexual orientation only after a high degree of interpersonal trust has been established. Other children who may be potential discreditors may also be selected to receive this information, since the child may believe that he or she can, in effect, beat them to the punch and turn potential enemies into confidantes.

Certain factors, however, operate to determine the extent to which children of gay fathers rely on these techniques for information and image control. First, children apparently determine the degree to which their father's sexual orientation is *obtrusive* into their personal social life. Second, the degree to which children use controls depends on the level of *mutuality* or connectedness they perceive in their identification with their fathers. When children perceive a high degree of obtrusiveness of their father's sexual orientation into their lives, there often is greater reliance on these controls. However, a high degree of perceived mutuality of identification with the father results in lesser use. Age of children also is a factor—in general, as children grow older, they rely less on using image-management controls.

Gender-Related Issues for Gay Fathers

Homosexual couples as well as the families they form have the advantage of re-defining and reinventing their own meanings for *family* and *parents* because they exist outside of traditionally defined family and parenting roles based on gender (Benkov, 1994; Dickstein, Stein, Pleck, & Myers, 1991; Stein, 1988). Gay fathers, in both challenging and enacting normative gender roles, struggle to integrate the dual aspects of mothers' and fathers' typical roles. This may explain, for exam-ple, why both similarities and differences in the parenting behaviors of gay and heterosexual fathers are found.

It is possible that gay fathers are freed to expand their interpretations of what it means to be a father far beyond the traditional meanings of fatherhood (More-land & Schwebel, 1981). This freedom to explore may allow gay fathers greater opportunities to incorporate the nurturant, expressive functions and behaviors tra-ditionally assigned to mothers. By contrast, heterosexual fathers' tendency to iden-tify with notions of traditional masculinity and gender polarity may constrain their parenting behaviors and styles. It is impossible, however, for gay or lesbian par-ents to completely escape the influence of gendered cultural norms for parenting, and homosexual parents may incorporate more traditional parenting ideas (Han-sen, 1985). For example, in some gay families, both men are defined as father, while in others the biological father is seen as the father and his partner as stepfather. Although there are variations in how homosexual families define themselves and the roles of the participants, it is not uncommon for people outside the family boundaries to ask, "Who's the *real* daddy here?" (Benkov, 1994).

In families formed by gays and lesbians, then, reliance on gender norms to determine who does what and how in child rearing is largely absent, despite the heavy cultural conditioning that shapes our basic ideas of parenting roles. Because there are two same-sex adults in homosexual families, there may be a greater at-tempt to organize androgynous coparenting roles and responsibilities, but such arrangements are accomplished with some difficulty (Benkov, 1994). The diffi-culties may come from the way males are socialized for fatherhood. For exam-ple, in comparison with heterosexual couples, two gay men coparenting children may agree in principle that both should be equally involved with children, shar-ing responsibilities and adjusting schedules and career plans accordingly. Logis-tically, however, it may be difficult to manage this egalitarian structure because males have been socialized to equate personal success in adulthood with success in work roles. For a man to remain home, assume primary parenting responsibil-ities, and not be involved in work outside may be considered suicidal to his career goals. A gay father who assumes primary parenting responsibilities (a role usually assumed by women in heterosexual marriages) may have to compromise his career—a sacrifice for which he has not been socialized and for which he probably has no models or support.

Therapy with Gay Fathers

During the course of one's clinical practice, it is likely that a sizable percentage of gay male clients will be fathers, with children from heterosexual marriage. The present discussion focuses primarily on issues germane to treatment for formerly married gay fathers, their partners, and the family systems they form.

There are no studies describing the therapy experiences of gay fathers, although there are many that address the needs of gay and lesbian clients in general within the mental health system (for example, Beane, 1981; Decker, 1984; Gonsiorek, 1985). In light of the discussion in previous sections of this chapter, clinicians might expect the therapy needs of gay fathers to focus on the following areas: (1) dealing with depressive symptoms; (2) assisting with disclosure to the self, the client's spouse, and children, as well as addressing internalized homophobia; (4) developing a positive identity as a gay father; (5) encouraging opportunities for networking with other gay fathers; (6) addressing couples issues in therapy; and (6) addressing issues of gay stepfamily formation and functioning.

Other therapeutic themes relate to the therapist as a helper for gay fathers. These issues more specifically address the needs of the therapist to (1) confront personal feelings and biases, conscious as well as unconscious, that can influence the conduct of therapy and (2) serve as an advocate for clients who are gay fathers in legal proceedings. While each client comes into therapy with his own history and specific needs, practitioners can expect the course of therapy to follow a general pattern for gay fathers who have had a past heterosexual marriage.

Common Issues in Therapy

A composite case example will help us explore common therapy issues.

CASE EXAMPLE: JOE

Joe is a forty-year-old White middle-class executive who was referred by his family physician to work on better managing the stresses in his life. His presenting problem was that he believed he was bisexual and was increasingly finding it difficult to maintain his marriage relationship of eighteen years. He was the father of three children aged fifteen, thirteen, and ten. During the first appointment, he informed the therapist that he and his wife, Donna, had experienced marital problems over the last three years and that sexual relations with her had been sporadic within the last year. He was becoming increasingly frustrated with his marriage and feeling confused about his sexual orientation. Joe had informed Donna of an affair with his best male friend, Tom, which recently had ended. His guilt about the affair and his sorrow about its ending were complicated by his fears about AIDS and the possibility of having exposed his wife. The stress of maintaining a dual life, of being deceptive and unfaithful to Donna, and of possibly endangering both of their lives was manifested in increased alcohol consumption, sleeping disorders, and panic attacks.

The therapist explored Joe's sexual history in order to determine the extent of his homosexual contacts and to learn whether or not Joe had practiced safer sex in these encounters. Joe informed the therapist that he was well aware of what constituted safer sex practices and that he had consistently followed these in his homosexual encounters. However, he had not done so in his sexual relations with Donna. His homosexual contacts had been relatively few in number within the last five years and limited almost exclusively to mutual masturbation with other men. However, there had been some oral sex experiences with Tom that were unprotected. He stated that he had not used condoms with Donna because he believed that to do so after many years of marriage would arouse her suspicions.

The therapist then inquired as to Joe's HIV status and that of his lover and asked if Donna also had been tested. Joe informed the therapist that he and Tom had recently tested negative. However, he had not told his wife of these results and was certain that she had not been tested. Joe broke into tears in discussing his fears about the possibility that he had exposed his wife to AIDS but was equally fearful of telling her that she ought to be tested. The therapist expressed empathy for Joe's conflict and the anxiety he was experiencing. He reassured Joe that the chance of Donna having been exposed to HIV was most likely minimal but that it was very important for her to be informed of the risk and to be tested. He asked Joe if he needed help informing his wife of this necessity. Joe responded by saying he would somehow find the courage to do so and would offer to accompany his wife to be tested. The therapist also asked a variety of questions to assess Joe's knowledge of AIDS and how the disease is most likely transmitted via sexual contact.[1]

The therapist arranged for Joe to be assessed by the consulting psychiatrist for medication to help manage the anxiety attacks, alcohol abuse, and sleep problems and referred him for training in biofeedback as an adjunct to psychotherapy in learning to manage his stress.

Dealing with Depressive Symptoms. Therapists can expect to observe patterns typical of extreme stress and depression among many gay fathers when they first enter therapy (Miller, 1987). Intrapsychic disturbances often are manifested as anxiety, guilt, anger, irritability, and emotional depression. Physical disturbances ranging from sleep and eating disorders, panic attacks, fatigue, and restlessness to gastrointestinal disorders also follow the usual stress-related patterns. These symptoms usually abate as therapy progresses, although medication sometimes is beneficial in promoting the therapeutic process.

Some gay fathers present suicidal ideation or have attempted suicide after experiencing extreme conflicts about recognizing and confronting their homosexuality at midlife, while feeling trapped within a heterosexual marriage and family life. The depth of personal pain experienced by many of these men is excruciating as they attempt to come to grips with an aspect of themselves they have denied for years. Clinicians need to be sensitive to the possibility of suicidal ideation and attempts as a means of coping with the intense feelings of self-disgust, loneliness, self-degradation, and despair that are experienced by gay fathers in crisis (Bozett, 1985).

Many gay fathers manifest feelings of guilt, anxiety, and anger. For most men, guilt is expressed in the internalized homophobia they experience in reaction to acting upon their sexual attraction to other men. Guilt also may be felt in relation to having lived a life until now that has been marked by deception and lack of authenticity. Their affairs with other men may have been rationalized as a means of alleviating the pain of not being able to be openly gay. Guilt and anxiety may be experienced in relation to anticipated negative consequences of coming out as a gay man not only to themselves but particularly to their wives, children, and family of origin. Furthermore, these feelings may be intensified when considering the options offered by divorce.

Children are as highly valued by gay fathers as heterosexual fathers, and fear of losing children's love is one of the most dreaded possible outcomes of disclosure. Many wives and ex-wives of gay fathers feel betrayed and retain their anger, which aggravates and can intensify the already disruptive effects of separation and divorce (Miller, 1987; Wyers, 1987). These reactions and feelings may be heightened when a gay father's homosexuality is uncovered through scandals, arrest for public sexual activity, blackmail, or when the wife is exposed to a sexually transmitted disease such as herpes or AIDS. More typically, however, a gay father's homosexuality is uncovered by the family's discovery of his romantic involvement with another man. Although many couples attempt to resolve the discovery initially by counseling or realigning the boundaries of the marriage (Matteson, 1987), divorce is the more common outcome eventually for most gay fathers.

The sense of isolation resulting from having been cut off for years from others who are similar to themselves often give rise to the feeling that "I must be the only man in the world who is like me." Many men express deep feelings of resentment about having wasted so many years being in the closet and having lost the opportunities of their youth and early adulthood years in reaching their destiny. As gay fathers are helped by therapists to penetrate the layers of denial about their homosexuality, the clinical focus may shift to helping these men express and discuss their homosexual feelings, perhaps for the first time in many years. Although a variety of techniques may be employed to assist gay fathers with these emotional dynamics, cognitive therapy techniques and role play are useful in helping to alleviate serious symptoms of emotional depression and may be highly effective in promoting a reframing process. For example, many clients respond favorably to writing down a list of their "hot (angry)" thoughts that can be countered by their "cool" thoughts. In many respects, clients' feelings of anger and resentment, once identified, are justifiable. However, techniques that allow countering of angry thoughts may help a client understand that, although anger may be justified, progress can be deterred if these feelings are not redirected into more positive channels. Such a reframing process may help the client take responsibility for perpetuating the anger or the situations that give rise to it rather than attributing such responsibility to others (Burns, 1980).

The man who is coming out or contemplating coming out as a gay father often experiences a profound sense of loss. He may be losing the facade of a supposedly protective heterosexual lifestyle, the familiarity of the marriage relationship, his place of residence, daily contact with his children, and financial resources and be facing disruption of his usual routines and his social network. The compounded nature of these losses and disruptions cannot be ignored, and they sometimes become manifested in self-destructive behaviors such as increased substance abuse.

It is important for therapists to recognize these losses when they occur and to help facilitate the grieving process. Because many gay fathers have become accustomed to using denial as an effective defense mechanism, they will need special help in learning to recognize their own feelings and behavior in relation to these losses. Each client may have his own particular way of grieving the losses he has experienced and will respond differently to therapeutic efforts to facilitate his process. Some clients respond well to cognitive therapy techniques that emphasize the reframing of thoughts and emotions. Others find that bibliotherapy or supportive group work is helpful. The ultimate objective is to help the client come to accept the gravity, extent, and breadth of the changes he has experienced thus far and to help him anticipate and prepare for the additional changes that will be experienced in the future. It is helpful to encourage clients to learn that their attachments to the past have powerful meanings in their lives and that separation from the familiar is painful, distressing, and anxiety provoking. Gay fathers can be helped to learn that the disruptions, disorganization, and sense of loss typically begin to abate as they reach new self-definitions and establish new lifestyles that are congruent with their inner feelings. The length of grieving time varies for each client, but most can expect to experience less pain within one to three years following the initiation of their coming out process, the establishment of a new social network, and redefinition of self and family.

JOE (CONTINUED)

At the next meeting, Joe informed the therapist that although it had been extremely difficult, he had informed his wife, Donna, of her need to be tested for HIV, that she had done so, and that she had tested negative. The therapist praised Joe for his courage and inquired about the emotional effects of this experience for Joe and Donna. Joe replied that it had served to drive a wedge even further between him and Donna, making him even more confused about what course he should take now with his life. The therapist offered to see both Joe and Donna to discuss where things now stood in their relationship, and Joe agreed that this might be helpful.

Throughout a session with the couple, it became apparent that Donna was enraged with Joe and the situation in which they found themselves. She expressed her angry feelings about being deceived by Joe for many years, about how his homosexual experiences might threaten their marriage as well their lives and the well-being of their children, about how her trust in him had been destroyed, and about how she felt stupid for not having guessed the truth about why their marriage was troubled. The therapist suggested that they consider couples therapy with him, or he could refer them to someone else. Donna indicated that she wanted to pursue therapy individually with a female heterosexual therapist. The therapist affirmed this as being appropriate, stating that if she ever changed her mind, he would be glad to discuss options with her. He also offered her a referral to a colleague who worked extensively with spouses and ex-spouses of gay men.

Over the next four weeks, the therapist encouraged Joe to examine his homosexual interests and feelings. At first, Joe was insistent that his orientation was bisexual and that he became involved sexually with men because his wife was frigid and had been generally unresponsive sexually. He rationalized his homosexual interest as encounters in which he "just got off with another guy" to meet his sexual needs. On deeper probing by the therapist, Joe was able to acknowledge that he had always felt attracted to other males and had had occasional mutual masturbation experiences with other teens during his adolescence. He had dated girls in high school and college, but these were superficial relationships that he found unfulfilling.

Joe was especially sensitized to homophobic attitudes as a teenager and young man, since one of his father's brothers was gay, and he was well aware of the family's rejection of his uncle and his lifestyle. At this point, the therapist disclosed his homosexual orientation to Joe and validated Joe's deeply felt homophobic feelings by relating several personal instances in which he had also experienced internalized homophobia. This revelation was reassuring to Joe because Joe was already aware of the therapist's orientation but had no idea how to bring this up in therapy. The increase in Joe's comfort level was apparent as he now began to ask a number of questions about the process of coming out, as well as about gay culture and the gay community. This was one of the turning points in Joe's therapy, as he came to trust the therapist on a deeper level.

Joe had concluded early in his adolescence that he could never reveal his feelings and attractions for other males and be accepted by his family. Survival became a matter of denying his true feelings and desires and learning to cope by seeming to be interested in the usual things that heterosexual adolescent boys and young men like. This arrangement appeared to work well for a number of years, and near the completion of his senior year in college, he met and fell in love unexpectedly with Donna, who seemed to enjoy many of the same people and things he did. Although it was not in his immediate plans for himself, he agreed to marriage, hoping that this would rid him once and for all of the desire for and attraction to men. Within a seven-year period, three children were produced, and Joe became deeply involved in his career and with providing for his family while continuing to experience, but being hesitant to act upon, his homosexual feelings.

Initial Disclosure Issues. One of the most difficult clinical tasks is to assist gay fathers with their disclosure issues, which include coming out to the self and learning to accept in positive ways one's homosexual orientation. This may be followed by helping the client prepare to disclose to his spouse, children, and family of origin members.

Therapists working with gay fathers on coming-out issues should be mindful of the intense difficulty these men have experienced for years in answering the question, Who am I? As mentioned earlier in this chapter, many gay fathers have experienced an identity foreclosure that occurs in adolescence or early adulthood when most individuals typically experiment with answers to this basic question of personal identity (Siegel & Lowe, 1994). Upon reaching early adulthood or at midlife, in particular, many gay fathers first sense the inner rumblings of something missing from their lives, which may have been manifested surreptitiously in homosexual encounters with other men, emerging feelings of emotional attachment or love for a colleague or friend, or the budding acknowledgment that they are indeed gay. For many men, self-recognition is the longest and most difficult phase of coming out (Eichberg, 1990). However, once the inner, subjectively experienced truth is faced, the process begins of constructing a positive self-image as a gay man who also happens to be a father.

The inner truth now may be shared with someone else, and often it is to a therapist that a gay father first shares his awareness of being homosexual. The secret begins to be dismantled and dissipated with less fear of rejection. It is not unusual, however, for gay fathers to express extreme ambivalence about homosexuality early in the coming-out process (Miller, 1987). For some, it is less threatening at the beginning to label homosexual feelings and behavior as an indication of their bisexuality, while others explain their behavior as a compulsion or addiction they cannot control. Clients may discuss homosexuality in highly negative terms at first. There may be intense frustration and anger over their inability to either reject or accept homosexuality. Rationalizations for their feelings are common, such as blaming their desires on being oversexed or being seduced by other homosexual men.

In the beginning of therapy, then, one can expect a gay father who is contemplating cracking open the door to his closet to justify remaining in the closet. Many clients will need help in becoming desensitized about the myths surrounding homosexuality and homosexuals, as well as the negative social consequences of disclosure (Miller, 1987). In this regard, groundwork can be laid by prescribing bibliotherapy using books such as *Loving Someone Gay* (Clark, 1977), *Gay Fathers* (Barret & Robinson, 1990), *On Being Gay* (McNaught, 1988), and *Like Coming Home: Coming Out Letters* (Umans, 1988). The task of therapy at this point is to help the gay father move toward greater self-acceptance by reframing his anger about his homosexuality, about wasting so much time being in the closet, and about his predicament of having been in a heterosexual liaison and becoming a parent (Miller, 1987). The reframing takes the form of helping these men view their circumstances as stemming from their social conditioning and from internalizing society's homophobic attitudes, thereby experiencing a serious form of social injustice as a member of an oppressed minority group in society.

Until this point, some gay fathers may not have disclosed their homosexuality to their wives, and the focus of therapy may involve examining the options available. For other men, the initial thrust of therapy may involve examining the question of whether they truly are homosexual. Still other men seek therapy exclusively to rid themselves of their homosexual feelings so that they can get on with a conventional marriage (Matteson, 1987; Miller, 1987). Finding this impossible, the thrust of therapy may shift to examining whether to disclose to the wife—an excruciating decision for most such clients. Those who decide to disclose to their wives often want assistance from therapists in ending their marriages constructively and learning how to come out of the closet completely.

JOE (CONTINUED)

The gay feelings that Joe had hoped would be buried forever did not disappear with experience in his heterosexual marriage. About five years previously, Joe had felt an incredible restlessness about his life. Around that time, when attending a conference away from home, Joe impulsively entered a gay bar out of curiosity. While there, he was approached by another man whom he found to be attractive, accompanied the man to his home, and allowed himself to have mutual masturbation. In reflecting afterwards, he found the experience to be both exhilarating and frightening. Encounters similar to this took place in the ensuing years, usually when he was away from home on business. These soon ended, however, when Joe could no longer deny to himself that he had fallen in love with Tom, the man whom he considered to be his best friend and hunting buddy. The feelings became manifested during a weeklong camping trip when the men shared a sexual encounter while drinking heavily. The encounters continued for a number of months following the trip, although Joe never truly admitted his feelings for his male lover. The affair terminated shortly before Joe entered therapy when Tom expressed intense feelings of guilt about being involved with another man sexually.

Working with the therapist, Joe eventually acknowledged his feelings of love for his best friend, stating that this must certainly prove that he was gay because he felt alive emotionally for the first time in his life. In the next two months of therapy, the work focused on helping Joe express his feelings of anger, guilt, and regret for the course that his life had taken thus far. The therapist devoted several sessions to helping Joe reframe his feelings as he gradually came out to himself, to the therapist, and to his wife. Joe ultimately concluded that divorce was necessary, as he found his heterosexual lifestyle to be false and very constraining. However, he expressed intense feelings of dismay that he might have to reveal his sexual orientation to his children, and he would not even consider the possibility of disclosure to his family of origin. Although he desired to be in a relationship with his best friend, he believed this or any relationship with another man was a sheer impossibility. He had difficulty visualizing himself as being capable of ever leading an openly gay lifestyle that included a relationship with a man.

The work of dismantling and desensitizing Joe's deeply entrenched homophobia began. The first step was to prescribe his participation in a coming-out group when he felt comfortable enough to do so. The therapist also prescribed bibliotherapy for Joe and referred him to the local gay bookstore owner who helped him select books about gay culture and gay history. Joe's therapist also prescribed participation in a coming-out support group sponsored by the local Gay and Lesbian Community Center and the gay and lesbian parents' support group sponsored by the local chapter of Parents, Families, and Friends of Lesbians and Gays (P-FLAG). These were Joe's first encounters with other people who shared the challenges of coming out and developing a positive, healthy self-image of themselves as homosexuals and as parents.

Developing a Positive Identity as a Gay Father. A major developmental task of gay fathers is positive identity development. Gay fathers accomplish this primarily through the integrative sanctioning process. Disclosures are made and relationships are developed with heterosexuals who validate the gay aspect of the man's identity and with gay men who validate the father aspect of his identity.

Positive identity development also is promoted by encouraging the gay father's socialization experiences as a gay man. This aspect of identity development is facilitated through coming out to other gay men as someone who is both gay and a father. Many gay fathers lack in-depth experiences in the gay world and therefore have a limited, stereotyped, media-based perception of a monolithic "gay lifestyle," which may be unrealistically attractive, repulsive, or both. For some gay fathers, there is an initial tendency to romanticize a world that is largely unknown. Others initially disparage the gay lifestyle, describing themselves as more "responsible," "practical," or even more "sensible" than gay men living an open lifestyle (Miller, 1987). Such stereotypes preserve their denial and ambivalence and stymie their positive identity development as a gay man who also is a father.

As self-disclosure becomes more possible and comfortable, many gay fathers need assistance in working on socialization experiences as a gay man. As closeted gay men attempting to lead a heterosexual lifestyle, most gay fathers have experienced the gay world only in genitally focused activities that occurred clandestinely. This arrangement works efficiently to protect some gay fathers from truly exploring their homosexual emotions while married, but such furtive sexual activity also precludes the development of friendships or deep romantic relationships with other gay men. In addition, these relatively impersonal forays prevent gay fathers from developing positive perceptions of the gay world and of other gay men.

According to Miller (1987), the acculturation process of the newly metamorphic gay father is difficult in four areas: (1) the disadvantages of being a late newcomer to the gay world in which being older is often a liability; (2) the necessity of learning a host of new social skills such as how to approach other gay men in social, nonsexual settings, how to date other men, how to conduct oneself in an intimate, romantic relationship with another man, and so on; (3) the need to reconcile former fantasies about the gay world with reality, which often results in feelings of frustration with the coming-out process; and (4) developing a positive self-identity as a gay father. In this regard, effective therapeutic intervention typically involves taking an educational approach in helping gay fathers debunk their fantasies and stereotypical beliefs about homosexuals and homosexuality, to gain experience in meeting and interacting positively with other gay men, and to gain skills in intimacy, assertiveness, and communication. A particularly effective adjunct to individual therapy at this point may be prescribing group therapy with other gay men or gay fathers or participation in support group functions aimed at men who are involved in working on their coming-out process.

JOE (CONTINUED)

After participating for several months in the support groups, Joe was able to make a few friendships with other men who were just coming out as gay fathers. He found participation in these groups helpful and was fortunate to strike up a friendship with another man who was willing to act as a mentor and coach during Joe's first ventures into the gay world. These experiences were Joe's first nonsexual, socially oriented activities with other gay men, and he found that many of his misgivings and misconceptions about gays and their lifestyles were not supported by what he observed.

He was beginning to be pressured by his ex-wife to disclose his sexual orientation and new lifestyle to his children, since they blamed their mother for alienating their father and being the cause of their divorce. Joe resisted doing so for several months, knowing that he would eventually share this news with his children but feeling afraid of losing their love. He brought up the issue of disclosure with his gay and lesbian parents' support group on several occasions and asked for advice on how to go about it. He also read in several publications about the risks and the advantages of disclosure. He understood that it was important that he share this information with his children before some other source did so. Joe's therapist also offered pointers about how to talk with his children and what he might say. He gave Joe a copy of guidelines suggesting how to disclose to children.

Joe chose a time following a meal he had prepared especially for his children. It was on a weekend when he had them for visitation. He reported having lost sleep the night before and feeling very fretful and distracted during the day prior to the disclosure. Although he had no idea of what to expect, the children sat quietly following the disclosure and looked repeatedly at one another. Finally, the youngest child (age ten) breathed a sign of relief and stated exuberantly, "Thank goodness we can talk about this now. I guess we're just surprised with what you've just told us; we're sorry that we were so hard on Mom." There were some questions posed, but each child, though not enthusiastic about the disclosure, assured Joe of their love as he did for them.

Disclosure to Children. Often, gay fathers want very much to disclose to their children but are not sure of the logistics or timing (Dunne, 1987). Clinical and practical experience in working with many gay fathers suggests that disclosure is accepted more easily by children prior to their attaining puberty. Disclosure to adolescent children may be more problematic because of the sexual identity issues and peer pressures that are occurring developmentally at this time. Similarly, same-sex adolescent children are reported by many gay fathers to experience greater difficulty in handling their father's disclosure than opposite-sex children. This may be due to the fears of same-sex children that they also may be gay and the greater sensitivity to homophobic attitudes of other males their age. There is no research on the effects of coming out to children nor on factors that influence what is said nor in what context. However, based on clinical experience, it is possible to suggest some general guidelines for helping gay fathers talk to their children about their sexual orientation (Bigner & Bozett, 1989).

Guidelines for disclosure of homosexuality to children

1. *Come to terms with your own gayness before disclosing to children.* This is crucial. The father who feels negatively about his homosexuality or is ashamed of it is much more likely to have children who also react negatively. The father must create a setting of acceptance by first being accepting of himself. If he tells his

children when he is ready and comfortable, it is likely to be a positive experience for everyone.

2. *Children are never too young to be told.* They will absorb only as much as they are capable of understanding. Use words appropriate to the age of the child. Details may be added as they grow older.

3. *Discuss it with children before they know or suspect.* When children discover their father's sexual orientation from someone other than the father, they often are upset that their father did not trust them sufficiently to share the information with them. It is exceedingly difficult for children to initiate the subject, and they will not bring it up even though they may want to.

4. *Disclosure should be planned.* Children should not find out about their father's homosexuality by default or discover it accidentally or during an argument between their parents.

5. *Disclose in a quiet setting where interruptions are unlikely to occur.*

6. *Inform; don't confess.* The disclosure should not be heavy or maudlin but positive and sincere. Informing in a simple, natural, and matter-of-fact manner when the father is ready is more likely to foster acceptance by the child. If possible, discuss or rehearse what will be said to children with another gay or lesbian parent who has been through a similar disclosure.

7. *Inform the children that relationships with them will not change as a result of disclosure.* Disclosure will, however, allow the father to be more honest. Children may need reassurance that the father is the same person he was before. Younger children may need reassurance that the father will still be their father.

8. *Be prepared for questions.* Here are some questions and possible answers:
   - *Why are you telling me this?* Because my personal life is important, and I want to share it with you. I am accepting of being gay (homosexual), and you don't need to feel ashamed of me.
   - *What does being gay mean?* It means being attracted to other men so much that I might fall in love with a man and express that love physically and sexually.
   - *What makes a person gay?* No one knows, although there are lots of theories. (This may be a child's way of asking if he or she also will be gay.)
   - *Will I be gay, too?* You won't be gay just because I'm gay. It's not contagious, and it doesn't appear to be hereditary. You will be whatever you're going to be.
   - *Don't you like women?* (The child might be asking, Don't you like Mom? or Do you hate Mom? If this question is asked by a daughter it also may mean, Don't you like me? or Do you hate me?) I do like women, but I'm not physically or romantically attracted to them like I am to men.
   - *What should I tell my friends about it?* A lot of people just don't understand, so it might be best to keep it between us until you feel safe telling others. You

can discuss it with me at any time you want. If you want to tell a close friend, go ahead and try it out. The friend might or might not be accepting, and he or she might tell others. You should be prepared for those possibilities. If you do tell somebody, let me know how it turns out. (Couched in these terms, the father's sexual orientation is not framed as a shameful secret but as a matter of personal privacy for children.)

Developing Intimate Relationships. As a gay father gains in his identity development as a gay man who is also a father, the goal of becoming involved in romantic, intimate relationships with other men eventually takes center stage in his personal life. In this regard, the gay father will need to focus on the different skills for dating men versus women, dealing with the intensity of romantic feelings that may be expressed for the first time in his life, and completing the process of becoming emotionally divorced from his ex-wife.

A common complaint by many gay men who become involved romantically with a gay father is that there is a tendency for the gay father to impose the template of his former heterosexual marriage and manner of relating intimately on what is occurring in the same-sex relationship. Many romantic partners of gay fathers cite this as one reason for not continuing the relationship. They resent the gay father's attempts, or perceived attempts, to treat them as a traditional wife. For example, a gay father may impose expectations on his romantic partner to pick up after him, prepare his meals, coordinate the social calendar, and so on. Negative reactions from his partner can come as a surprise because the gay father often is not aware of his own unconscious expectations or habits in relationships. While the termination of these romances can be painful emotionally, they serve as learning tools about gay relationships and teach the powerful lesson that complete equality and role flexibility of the partners is the foundation of most gay intimate relationships in comparison to traditional heterosexual marital and parental roles.

Newly emergent gay fathers at times are as bewildered as those they are involved with romantically at the intensity and depth of their newly found emotional life. These feelings can be overwhelming for both men. Essentially, gay fathers in this predicament have not had the experiences that help in locating one's emotional brakes, and they can be expected to make some blunders and mistakes in their love lives as a result. For example, they may fall easily and quickly in love with a man before the development of trust and of knowledge that each shares a similar relationship vision (Tennov, 1979).

The therapist can act as a voice of reason and as a mentor for gay fathers who are experiencing identity diffusion which, in many ways, is similar to that of a young adolescent. These men need encouragement to experiment and to grow from the lessons and mistakes they experience in romantic liaisons with other men.

For many gay fathers, this period of their coming-out process allows them to be single men for the first time in years and perhaps for the first time in their lives. As part of the process of completing the emotional divorce from their ex-wives, many gay fathers must learn how to be independent people who are self-sufficient and capable of caring for themselves in every aspect. These issues present another opportunity to encourage the participation of the client in a gay fathers' support group or a coming-out group so that he may benefit by hearing others' experiences.

To develop a complete personal identity as a gay father, the client must complete the emotional divorce from his ex-wife (Bohannan, 1970), perhaps one of the most difficult aspects of attaining such an identity. This does not require, however, that a gay father dissolve his emotional attachment to his ex-wife easily or swiftly. Emotional divorce involves the initiation and resolution of a grieving and mourning process for the loss of a significant aspect of one's life as an adult. Most gay fathers loved their ex-wives, and the loss of both the relationship and the privileges that accompanied a heterosexual lifestyle is like experiencing the death of a significant other. Because there are children involved, the relationship between a gay father and his ex-wife continues, but in a changed manner. The emotional divorce calls for a redefinition of system patterns as new roles, boundaries, and rules that regulate interactions evolve. In order for healthy personal identity and for intimacy with another man to develop, many gay fathers need guidance in healing from the loss of the relationship they had with their ex-wife. While there is no single method or approach that can be prescribed for all gay fathers in this respect, cognitive therapy techniques as well as gestalt methods can be applied with success in helping gay fathers complete this process in individual therapy. For example, use of the empty-chair technique can be helpful in allowing a gay father to express his feelings of anger, guilt, or remorse about himself, his background, his former marriage, his ex-wife, and so on. If the ex-wife is willing to participate, couples sessions may be useful so that both persons can work on grieving, reminiscing, and moving forward in their separate lives as single adults and in their joint tasks as coparents.

JOE (CONTINUED)

Joe continued with therapy on a limited basis for the next three years. During this time, he discovered the gay world and became fully immersed in a gay lifestyle; he gradually emerged from the closet. He had several relationships with other gay men that lasted from as little as three weeks to as long as a year and a half. Although he had never believed it possible, he found that having a committed relationship with another gay man was something he truly desired. Although he had difficulty at times expressing

his feelings of intimacy with a partner, Joe continued to grow in his ability to participate in a solid relationship with a man named Jim, whom he called his "Mr. Right."
However, after moving into a new apartment and establishing a lifestyle as a couple,
Joe and Jim began to experience problems related to Joe's parenting responsibilities
and Jim's desire to be a part of the experience. Essentially, the men were struggling
with issues that are common to all stepfamilies. Because Joe's therapist had worked
with Joe individually over an extended time, he referred Joe and Jim to a colleague
who specialized in working with remarriage and stepfamily problems.

   This therapist helped the gay couple to rework their system boundaries, rules, and
roles. This new therapist also involved Joe's ex-wife in several sessions, as well as the
children in some sessions, and the gay stepfamily system essentially created a new role
for Jim as a gay stepfather. Involving Joe's ex-wife, although increasing everyone's anxiety initially, was crucial in helping reduce the degree of conflict in and between the
binuclear stepfamily households, especially between the former spouses and between
Joe and Jim.

Gay Fathers and Their Life Partners. Many gay fathers eventually establish a committed relationship with another gay man and form a gay stepfamily system. Although only a minority of formerly married gay fathers have physical custody of
their children, most gay fathers exercise their visitation rights with their children
within the context of a committed relationship and stepfamily arrangement.

   Issues presented therapeutically by couples involving gay fathers and their
partners essentially are similar to those of heterosexual couples with one main distinction: gay couples in general may experience more problems relating to boundary issues (Decker, 1984; Ussher, 1991). There is a tendency for gay couples to be
isolated from the gay community, their families of origin, and other social support
networks. Because of this isolation, it is common for a couple to develop unrealistic goals for and expectations of their relationship. Society fails to validate committed homosexual relationships, and thus gay couples experience obstacles not
usually encountered by heterosexual couples. Because the prevailing lifestyle of
the gay community is singles-oriented, many gay couples feel that even their
own community is not especially supportive of their lifestyle and their functioning as a couple.

   Gay couples that include a gay father may share these problems of social isolation along with other problems that are superimposed by the parental status of
the gay father. In some couples, the partner experiences varying degrees of insecurity and even jealousy in the face of the gay father's loyalty to his children. In
this regard, problems may be experienced similar to those found in heterosexual
stepfamilies during their early formative phases (Papernow, 1984). Tensions can
mount in relation to the amount of time given to child-rearing activities, the

amount of money and other resources that are directed to supporting children, and the strength of the alliance between the gay father and his children.

Complicating the situation is the emotional residue of the gay father's divorce or separation from his former female partner. The male partner may not understand easily that a gay father's relationship with his former wife, though modified, often continues as a coparenting arrangement that deeply involves the former spouses. The former wife may harbor resentment toward the gay father and his lover, which makes visitation difficult and renders children's relationships with the father's new partner problematic. In more extreme cases, the former wife may have been successful in legally excluding the father's partner from being present during children's visitations with their father, thus blocking the already difficult gay stepfamily formation process.

Effective work with gay father stepfamilies requires understanding the similarities as well as differences between heterosexual and homosexual couples. Gay couples are distinctive, perhaps, regarding how boundaries outline their relationship (for example, open versus closed), and many heterosexual therapists are baffled by the flexibility and openness of some gay relationships (Markowitz, 1993). Therapy often focuses on how to help couples renegotiate rules and boundaries between the men as well as in relationships with children, ex-spouses, and ex-in-laws.

Gay Stepfamily Parenting Issues. Gay stepfamilies resemble heterosexual stepfamilies in many respects (Baptiste, 1987a, 1987b; Barret & Robinson, 1990). For example, typically, one or both adults have experienced divorce from a previous heterosexual partner. One or both parents may have custody of children. Both gay and heterosexual stepfamilies may experience problems in the affectional relationships between stepparent and stepchildren. Children of gay fathers may have difficulties in accepting their father's partner, just as children in heterosexual stepfamilies do. These problems challenge the functioning of many stepfamily systems regardless of the sexual orientation of the adults.

However, gay and lesbian stepfamily systems experience some unique challenges (Baptiste, 1987a, 1987b; Barret & Robinson, 1990; Shernoff, 1984). First, gay stepfamilies lack legitimacy as a recognized family system by society. The lack of legal and community support can make assimilation of the new adult partner into the stepfamily problematic. Gay stepfamilies usually do not have rituals (such as a legal marriage ceremony) for confirming family membership. Therapy may involve devising ways for legitimizing the new adult's presence, restructuring the interpersonal boundaries between stepparent and stepchildren, or negotiating new rules relating to the discipline of children by the stepparent.

Gay stepfamily functioning may be strained by fears about public exposure regarding the sexual orientation of the adults. This is especially pronounced in those families in which a gay father has custody of children. The perceived need for secrecy often relates to the social stigma attached to homosexuality, which may jeopardize the custody of children, lead to eviction from places of residence, or result in termination of employment if the sexual orientation of the adults becomes known publicly. Such secrecy may create social isolation not only of the gay parents from the community but also of the children from other children. Children sometimes feel more need for secrecy and experience more intense social isolation than do the adults in gay stepfamily systems (Baptiste, 1982).

Gay male stepfamilies may have more difficulty than lesbian stepfamilies in being open about the adults' sexual orientation, since it appears less acceptable in society for two men to raise children than for two women. Also, two adult women living together, as compared with two adult men, generally arouse less suspicion about their sexual orientation. Fears of being open may be most intense in relation to the school system and with immediate neighbors. In spite of the greater acceptance of homosexuality in society, a gay father may be less likely to make his sexual orientation known to his children's teachers, and interactions with this public institution, religious institutions, and other public agencies may be guarded as a means of protecting children and the adults from ostracism and disapproval. Children may not be allowed to, or they may not want to bring friends from school into their homes. If neighbors suspect the sexual orientation of the gay stepfamily parents, they may restrict children from having contact with the gay stepfamily because of irrational fears about children being exposed to the "homosexual lifestyle" or being molested sexually.

Relationships with ex-spouses also are strained in some stepfamilies. Some gay fathers do not disclose to their ex-spouses, even following divorce, for fear of losing child custody and visitation rights. When disclosure has occurred, the acrimony between a gay father and his ex-spouse may be especially difficult to resolve because of the intense anger by the ex-spouse or former in-laws.

When gay stepfamily systems present themselves for therapy, practitioners may wish to begin work first with the relationship between the two adults, as would be the case in working with heterosexual stepfamilies (Martin & Martin, 1992). When the couple relationship can be strengthened, there is strengthening of the entire stepfamily system. Conflicts within the parent-child relationship and the stepparent-stepchild relationship can be due to rejection of the children by the stepparent, competition between the stepparent and stepchildren for the biological parent's time and affections, and uncertainty regarding how the stepparent's role is defined and his permanence (Baptiste, 1987a, 1987b).

Like their heterosexual counterparts, gay stepfamily systems can be helped to form new family rules, boundaries, and rituals that facilitate emotional bonding among the members. Conflicts between stepparents and stepchildren can be reduced by appointing the biological parent as the administrator of discipline. Problems inevitably arise when the stepfather attempts to enforce rules and regulations that may differ from those enforced by the biological father. By initially freeing the stepfather from the role of authority figure and disciplinarian, the relationship between stepfather and stepchildren can proceed first along the lines of friendship development and attachment. The stepparent's authority functions can be added later. Discipline of children by the gay stepfather, however, is necessary sometimes but is done with the understanding that it is situational because of the biological father's temporary absence.

Expressions of intimacy between the adults in the gay stepfamily also may be problematic. Adults may feel the yokes of constraint on their freedom to express intimacy in the presence of children. This can be exacerbated in families in which the adults remain closeted from the children. Being constantly on guard about what is said or about how affection is expressed is a source of high stress in some gay stepfamilies. Even when children are aware of the adults' sexual orientation, they may exert boundary control of adults' behavior, as well as control who knows about the adults' sexual orientation. Children can enforce this strongly when they are in public with both adults (Bozett, 1987a).

Therapists can benefit gay stepfamilies by helping members define their relationships with one another. When children, for example, can be encouraged in family sessions to share their perceptions of the various roles in this new gay stepfamily, especially in relation to how these have changed from what they experienced in their former heterosexual family, all members have an opportunity to understand that stepfamily roles are not parallel to those in traditional family systems (Martin & Martin, 1992). Therapists can assist by helping the adults restructure rules, roles, and boundaries in small ways that support family strengths. Furthermore, unlike working with heterosexual stepfamilies, therapists may be able to assist gay stepfamilies in dismantling secrecy and isolation. Helping gay stepfamilies to network with others who are in a similar situation can be beneficial in this respect.

Despite the added sources of stress for gay father stepfamilies, the process usually proceeds successfully over time unless the courts intervene in destructive, polarizing ways that irrationally restrict children's access to their gay father and his partner.

Therapists Working with Gay Fathers

Although the importance of similarity of sexual orientation between therapist and client is uncertain, initial research suggests that openly gay or lesbian therapists appear to facilitate successful therapy with gay or lesbian clients (Anthony, 1982; Gonsiorek, 1985; Riddle & Sang, 1978; Rochlin, 1982). These findings suggest that it is appropriate and important for gay or lesbian therapists to disclose their orientation to their gay or lesbian clients as part of the therapeutic process. Newly emergent gay fathers may profit considerably from working with a gay therapist who also is a father. In this regard, an openly gay father therapist can act as a knowledgeable and credible role model for the client's coming-out process (Coleman, 1982; Eichberg, 1990) and as someone who may have experienced similar pain, confusion, and turmoil (Malyon, 1982). The therapist can be seen as someone who has acquired the self-acceptance and personal identity of gay fatherhood.

However, such therapist-client similarity is not an absolute prerequisite for effective therapy. Heterosexual therapists can develop informed empathy by seeking gay-oriented and gay-affirmative supervision and training (Clark, 1977, 1987). Regardless of the therapist's sexual orientation, learning occurs through clinical supervision of gay father and lesbian mother cases and participating in the culture of the gay world. Developing personal friendships and joining friendship networks with gay people, especially with gay and lesbian parents and their children, can be helpful. The latter is particularly important for both gay and heterosexual therapists in working with gay fathers, who experience a dramatically different developmental path from that of gay clients who are young, single, never-married, and childless.

Therapists who are unfamiliar or uncomfortable with homosexuality (Nelson, 1982) or with the notion of gays as parents should immediately seek gay-affirmative supervision or refer gay father clients to colleagues more experienced in working with this population. The rationale presented for such a referral can be simply that the new therapist specializes in work with gay fathers and therefore can provide the best therapy in this situation.

Issues Relating to Courtroom Testimony

Therapists working with gay fathers can expect to be asked on occasion to provide expert witness or friend of the court testimony in legal proceedings. For the most part, these requests relate to divorce proceedings of gay fathers and particularly to those legal issues affecting custody of children and visitation rights of gay fathers. Although states differ in their interpretations of privileged communications between client and therapist, one can be asked or subpoenaed to provide testimony. In determining what is in the best interests of the children, courts will want to know the therapist's opinion about a gay father's ability to parent children and the influence of his lifestyle and sexual orientation on the children's welfare.

Therapists may be asked by the court to provide testimony about personal observations and whether the particular father is a fit and proper custodian of children (Larimer, 1992). Depending on state statutes, a therapist may or may not be required to base opinions given in testimony on facts or data that underlie the opinion. The nature of the testimony frequently is discussed with the client's lawyer prior to the court appearance. In these discussions, a lawyer representing the client often is considerably uninformed about gay fathers and the issues that relate to their situation. This provides the therapist with the opportunity to help the client's lawyer formulate questions to be asked during testimony that will allow the court to be well-informed about the client's ability to parent children and the effects of a parent's sexual orientation on children's development. Most judges, as well as lawyers, have not had extensive experience with homosexuals who are parents, and their education is imperative if the client is to be represented well in court.

The following guidelines are based on Larimer's (1992) suggestions regarding giving testimony on behalf of gay fathers who are clients.

Guidelines for giving testimony on behalf of gay fathers

1. Review case notes prior to meetings with lawyers and before court testimony.
2. Bring whatever notes or records that may be helpful in providing testimony to the court appearance.
3. Take time to think before answering any question during direct or cross-examination.
4. Answer only the question that is posed without volunteering any additional information.
5. Your job is to educate the court; however, do not jeopardize the impact of your testimony by lecturing or giving the impression that you hold a superior position because you are more knowledgeable than the court. A "one-down" position, oriented toward serving the court's needs for specific information, is most appropriate.
6. Establish eye contact with the judge or the lawyer asking questions; remain calm and take your time.
7. Avoid the use of jargon in answering questions.
8. Remember that the job of the opposing lawyer is to discredit you and your testimony; do not take this personally; suppress your feelings of pride and ego and answer questions posed in a straightforward manner.
9. Do not be tempted to argue with the opposing lawyer during cross-examination.

As a witness in legal proceedings, a therapist has certain rights that must be respected. First, you have the right to be compensated for your time in preparing for and providing testimony. This should be established early in the process through consultation with the client, the client's lawyer, or both. Some therapists base their compensation on their per hour therapy fee. It is perhaps best to request a retainer fee or a portion of an estimated final fee prior to beginning work for testimony. Compensation is appropriate for providing a deposition before a trial. Most importantly, therapists should seek a protective order from the court that declares what you can and cannot do regarding the confidentiality between yourself and your client in relation to testimony.

Conclusion

Gay fathers present a complex challenge for therapists who try to help them achieve a healthy, positive self-image and lifestyle. Although each client brings a different history and life situation, a general developmental pattern occurs in working with gay fathers that requires resolving a number of common therapeutic issues:

- Addressing the client's depressive symptoms
- Facilitating the coming out process to the self, the client's spouse, and the client's children
- Helping to resolve the client's internalized homophobia and heterosexism, which have contributed substantially to the predicament of being in a heterosexual marriage and becoming a parent
- Promoting the client's development of a positive identity as a gay father
- Encouraging the client to network and form friendships with other gay men and homosexual parents
- Addressing intimate relationship issues as they arise in the course of the client's coming out process
- Assisting clients as they resolve developmental tasks in stepfamily formation and functioning

Homosexual parents are in many respects no different from heterosexual parents, but their uniqueness in society places them at the cutting edge of efforts to reinvent notions of family and functional family structures. Their existence bears witness to the fact that the very idea of "family" must be expanded in American society. In contemporary culture, gay fathers help to create families that transcend traditional limitations as well as rigid sex-role assignments and stereotypes (Bozett, 1987b). Based on research that is scientifically sound, we know that homosexual parents are effective, highly committed, and do not harm the welfare and developmental progress of their children. Gay father families help us broaden our thinking about homosexuality, men's roles in parenting, and the diverse sociocultural contexts of parenting.

The dilemmas experienced by homosexual men who become parents reflect the dilemmas faced by society about homosexuality that are manifested in heterosexist and homophobic attitudes. The majority of gay fathers have internalized these negative stigmas perhaps to a greater degree than other gay men, which has led to denial of their sexual orientation until later in life. Their predicament involves not only themselves but their former spouses, their in-laws, their children, and their families of origin.

Homophobia affects gay fathers by inhibiting them from learning how to function as fully congruent human beings at developmentally appropriate times in their lives (Blumenfeld, 1992). Homophobia later contributes to denial and secrecy during marriage and to a series of extremely painful transitions for everyone in the family. The ability of gay fathers to seek healing and restitution of their integrity by coming out speaks to the courage and determination of all homosexual individuals who strive for self-fulfillment. The continuing compassion and support from their children, ex-wives, male partners, families of origin, and therapists can be profoundly healing for all concerned.

Note

1. Therapists in some states may have a duty to warn sexual partners of clients who are HIV-positive, having unsafe sex, and failing to inform their sexual partners. Because such "duty to warn" laws are evolving rapidly, readers should determine whether or under what conditions duty to warn laws apply to HIV risk situations in their states. In the case of Joe, however, there appears to be no clear basis for a duty to warn because Joe has stated that he is HIV-negative and is practicing safer sex with his male partners. In cases such as Joe's, unless local law would mandate breaking confidentiality to warn spouses or partners, it would seem best to simply encourage the client to inform his sexual partners of possible risks, continually get tested, and follow safe sex guidelines with all sexual partners.

References

Anthony, B. D. (1982). Lesbian client–lesbian therapist: Opportunities and challenges in working together. *Journal of Homosexuality, 7*, 45–58.

Baptiste, D. A., Jr. (1982). Issues and guidelines in the treatment of gay stepfamilies. In A. Gurman (Ed.), *Questions and answers in the practice of family therapy.* (vol. 2, pp. 225–229). New York: Brunner/Mazel.

Baptiste, D. A., Jr. (1987a). The gay and lesbian stepparent family. In F. W. Bozett (Ed.), *Gay and lesbian parents.* New York: Praeger.

Baptiste, D. A., Jr. (1987b). Psychotherapy with gay/lesbian couples and their children in "stepfamilies": A challenge for marriage and family therapists. *Journal of Homosexuality, 14,* 223–238.

Barbaree, H. E., & Marshall, W. L. (1989). Erectile responses among heterosexual child molesters, father-daughter incest offenders and matched non-offenders: Five distinct age preference profiles. *Canadian Journal of Behavioral Science, 21,* 70–76.

Barret, R. L., & Robinson, B. E. (1990). *Gay fathers.* Lexington, MA: Heath.

Beane, J. (1981). "I'd rather be dead than gay": Counseling gay men who are coming out. *Personnel and Guidance Journal, 60,* 222–226.

Bell, A. P., & Weinberg, M. S. (1978). *Homosexualities: A study of diversity among men and women.* New York: Simon & Schuster.

Benkov, L. (1994). *Reinventing the family: The emerging story of lesbian and gay parents.* New York: Crown.

Bigner, J. J., & Bozett, F. W. (1989). Parenting by gay fathers. *Marriage and Family Review, 14,* 155–176.

Bigner, J. J., & Jacobsen, R. B. (1989a). Parenting behaviors of homosexual and heterosexual fathers. *Journal of Homosexuality, 18,* 173–186.

Bigner, J. J., & Jacobsen, R. B. (1989b). The value of children to gay and heterosexual fathers. *Journal of Homosexuality, 18,* 163–172.

Bigner, J. J., & Jacobsen, R. B. (1992). Adult responses to child behavior and attitudes toward fathering: Gay and nongay fathers. *Journal of Homosexuality, 23,* 99–112.

Biller, H. B. (1993). *Fathers and families: Paternal factors in child development.* Westport, CT: Auburn House.

Blumenfeld, W. J. (Ed.). (1992). *Homophobia: How we all pay the price.* Boston: Beacon Press.

Bohannan, P. (1970). The six stations of divorce. In P. Bohannan (Ed.), *Divorce and after.* New York: Doubleday.

Bozett, F. W. (1980). Gay fathers: How and why they disclose their homosexuality to their children. *Family Relations, 29,* 173–179.

Bozett, F. W. (1981a). Gay father: Evolution of the gay father identity. *American Journal of Orthopsychiatry, 51,* 552–559.

Bozett, F. W. (1981b). Gay fathers: Identity conflict resolution through integrative sanctioning. *Alternative Lifestyles, 4,* 90–107.

Bozett, F. W. (1984). Parenting concerns of gay fathers. *Topics in Clinical Nursing, 6,* 60–71.

Bozett, F. W. (1985). Gay men as fathers. In S. Hanson & F. W. Bozett (Eds.), *Dimensions of fatherhood* (pp. 327–335). Newbury Park, CA: Sage.

Bozett, F. W. (1986). *Identity management: Social control of identity by children of gay fathers when they know their father is a homosexual.* Paper presented at the Seventh Biennial Eastern Nursing Research Conference, New Haven, CT.

Bozett, F. W. (1987a). Children of gay fathers. In F. W. Bozett (Ed.), *Gay and lesbian parents* (pp. 39–57). New York: Praeger.

Bozett, F. W. (1987b). Gay fathers. In F. W. Bozett (Ed.), *Gay and lesbian parents* (pp. 3–22). New York: Praeger.

Bozett, F. W., & Sussman, M. B. (1989). Homosexuality and family relations: Views and research issues. In F. W. Bozett & M. B. Sussman (Eds.), *Homosexuality and family relations* (pp. 1–7). Binghamton, NY: Harrington Park Press.

Burns, D. (1980). *Feeling good: The new moral therapy.* New York: Morrow.

Clark, D. (1977). *Loving someone gay.* Millbrae, CA: Celestial Arts.

Clark, D. (1987). *Loving someone gay* (rev. ed.). Berkeley, CA: Celestial Arts.

Cole, W. (1992). Incest perpetrators: Their assessment and treatment. *Psychiatric Clinics of North America, 15,* 689–695.

Coleman, E. (1982). Developmental stages of the coming out process. *Journal of Homosexuality, 7,* 31–44.

Cramer, D. (1986). Gay parents and their children: A review of research and practical implications. *Journal of Counseling and Development, 64,* 504–507.

Decker, B. (1984). Counseling for gay and lesbian couples. *Practice Digest, 7*, 13–15.

Dickstein, L. J., Stein, T. S., Pleck, J. H., & Myers, M. F. (1991). Men's changing social roles in the 1990s: Emerging issues in the psychiatric treatment of men. *Hospital and Community Psychiatry, 42*, 701–705.

Dunne, E. J. (1987). Helping gay fathers come out to their children. *Journal of Homosexuality, 14*, 213–222.

Eichberg, R. (1990). *Coming out: An act of love.* New York: Viking Penguin.

Gibbs, J. P. (1989). *Control: Sociology's central notion.* Urbana: University of Illinois Press.

Gibbs, J. P., & Martin, W. T. (1964). *Status integration and suicide: A sociological study.* Eugene: University of Oregon Press.

Golombok, S., Spencer, A., & Rutter, M. (1983). Children in lesbian and single-parent households: Psychosexual and psychiatric appraisal. *Child Psychology and Psychiatry, 24*, 551–572.

Gonsiorek, J. C. (Ed.). (1985). *A guide to psychotherapy with gay and lesbian clients.* Binghamton, NY: Harrington Park Press.

Gottman, J. S. (1989). Children of gay and lesbian parents. *Marriage and Family Review, 14*, 177–196.

Gould, R. (1978). *Transformations: Growth and change in adult life.* New York: Simon & Schuster.

Guttman, D. (1975). Parenthood: A key to the comparative study of the life cycle. In N. Datan & L. Ginsberg (Eds.), *Lifespan developmental psychology: Normative life crises.* San Diego, CA: Academic Press.

Hansen, S. M. (1985). Fatherhood: Contextual variations. *American Behavioral Scientist, 29*, 55–77.

Hays, D. H., & Samuels, A. (1989). Heterosexual women's perceptions of their marriages to bisexual or homosexual men. *Journal of Homosexuality, 18*, 81–100.

Hitchens, D. (1980). Social attitudes, legal standards, and personal trauma in child custody cases. *Journal of Homosexuality, 5*, 89–95.

Jacobsen, R. B., Bigner, J. J., & Yang, R. K. (1994). *Status integration and homosexuality: A theory of lifestyle duality.* Unpublished manuscript.

Lamb, M. E. (Ed.). (1982). *Nontraditional families: Parenting and child development.* Hillsdale, NJ: Erlbaum.

Langevin, R., & Watson, R. (1991). A comparison of incestuous biological and stepfathers. *Annals of Sex Research, 4*, 141–150.

Larimer, L. V. (1992). *The legal guide for practicing psychotherapy in Colorado.* Colorado Springs, CO: Center for Professional Development.

Lester, D. (1987). Status integration, suicide, and homicide. *Psychological Reports, 61*, 672.

Levinson, D. (1986). A conception of adult development. *American Psychologist, 41*, 3–13.

Malyon, A. K. (1982). Psychotherapeutic implications of internalized homophobia in gay men. *Journal of Homosexuality, 7*, 59–70.

Markowitz, L. M. (1993). Understanding the differences. *Family Therapy Networker, 17*(2), 50–59.

Martin, D., & Martin, M. (1992). *Stepfamilies in therapy: Understanding systems, assessment, and intervention.* San Francisco: Jossey-Bass.

Matteson, D. R. (1987). The heterosexually married gay and lesbian parent. In F. W. Bozett (Ed.), *Gay and lesbian parents* (pp. 138–161). New York: Praeger.

Mayadas, N. S., & Duehn, W. D. (1976). Children in gay families: An investigation of services. *Homosexual Counseling Journal, 3*, 70–83.

McNaught, B. (1988). *On being gay: Thoughts on family, faith, and love.* New York: St. Martin's Press.

Miller, B. (1979). Gay fathers and their children. *Family Coordinator, 28,* 544–552.

Miller, B. (1986). Identity resocialization in moral careers of gay husbands and fathers. In A. Davis (Ed.), *Papers in honor of Gordon Hirabayashi* (pp. 197–216). Edmonton: University of Alberta Press.

Miller, B. (1987). Counseling gay husbands and fathers. In F. W. Bozett (Ed.), *Gay and lesbian parents* (pp. 175–187). New York: Praeger.

Moreland, J., & Schwebel, A. I. (1981). A gender-role-transcendent perspective on fathering. *Counseling Psychologist, 9,* 45–53.

Nelson, J. B. (1982). Religious and moral issues in working with homosexual clients. *Journal of Homosexuality, 7,* 163–176.

Papernow, P. (1984). The stepfamily cycle: An experiential model of stepfamily development. *Family Relations, 33,* 355–363.

Patterson, C. J. (1992). Children of lesbian and gay parents. *Child Development, 63,* 1025–1042.

Riddle, D. I., & Sang, B. (1978). Psychotherapy with lesbians. *Journal of Social Issues, 34,* 84–100.

Rivera, R. R. (1987). Legal issues in gay and lesbian parenting. In F. W. Bozett (Ed.) *Gay and lesbian parenting* (pp. 199–227). New York: Praeger.

Roane, T. H. (1992). Male victims of sexual abuse: A case review within a child protection team. *Child Welfare, 71,* 231–239.

Robinson, B. E., & Barret, R. L. (1986). Gay fathers. In B. E. Robinson & R. L. Barret (Eds.), *The developing father: Emerging roles in contemporary society* (pp. 145–168). New York: Guilford Press.

Robinson, B. E., & Skeen, P. (1982). Sex-role orientation of gay fathers versus gay nonfathers. *Perceptual and Motor Skills, 55,* 1055–1059.

Rochlin, M. (1982). Sexual orientation of the therapist and therapeutic effectiveness with gay clients. *Journal of Homosexuality, 7,* 21–30.

Roopnarine, J. L., & Miller, B. C. (1985). Transitions to fatherhood. In S. Hanson & F. W. Bozett (Eds.), *Dimensions of fatherhood* (pp. 49–63). Newbury Park, CA: Sage.

Shernoff, M. J. (1984). Family therapy for lesbian and gay clients. *Social Work, 29,* 393–396.

Siegel, S., & Lowe, E. (1994). *Uncharted lives: Understanding the life passages of gay men.* New York: Dutton.

Stack, S. (1987). The effect of female participation in the labor force on suicide: A time-series analysis, 1948–1980. *Sociological Forum, 2,* 257–277.

Stafford, M. C., & Gibbs, J. P. (1985). A major problem with the theory of status integration and suicide. *Social Forces, 63,* 643–660.

Stein, T. S. (1988). Homosexuality and new family forms: Issues in psychotherapy. *Psychiatric Annals, 18,* 12–20.

Tennov, D. (1979). *Love and limerance.* New York: Stein & Day.

Troiden, R. R. (1979). Becoming homosexual: A model of gay identity acquisition. *Psychiatry, 42,* 362–373.

Umans, M. (Ed.). (1988). *Like coming home: Coming out letters.* Austin, TX: Banned Books.

Ussher, J. M. (1991). Family and couples therapy with gay and lesbian clients: Acknowledging the forgotten minority. *Journal of Family Therapy, 13,* 131–148.

Waterman, A. S. (1982). Identity development from adolescence to adulthood: An extension of theory and a review of research. *Developmental Psychology, 18,* 341–358.

Wyers, N. L. (1987). Lesbian and gay spouses and parents: Homosexuality in the family. *Social Work, 32,* 143–148.

CHAPTER SEVENTEEN

FAMILIES COPING WITH HIV DISEASE IN GAY FATHERS

Dimensions of Treatment

Stacey Shuster

Very little has been published in the family therapy field about the effects on a family when a family member is HIV-infected or has AIDS. In an analysis of publications in major family therapy journals, Green and Bobele (1994) encountered a nearly total silence regarding HIV, which they thought reflected family therapists' reluctance to address issues of sexuality, a reluctance reinforced by the social stigma against people with AIDS. However, of their sample of clinical members of the American Association for Marriage and Family Therapy, 32 percent had treated a person in therapy whom they knew to have AIDS, and 30 percent were treating such a client currently.

For therapists to focus on families affected by HIV means they must work largely with gay men and their families of choice and of origin, as well as with intravenous drug users and their loved ones—cases that many therapists find daunting and that raise powerful countertransference issues. Only a few authors have addressed the effects of HIV on uninfected family members (Black, 1993; Boyd-Franklin, Steiner, & Boland, 1994; Cates, Graham, Boeglin, & Tielker,

The material presented here is based on my work as Director of Children's Services, AIDS Family Project of Operation Concern, California Pacific Medical Center, and subsequent experiences in private practice. I would like to thank Robert-Jay Green for comments on this chapter and Catherine Cassel and Ken Pinhero for consultation on cases.

1990; Green & Bobele, 1994; Horsley, 1991; Lovejoy, 1990; Maloney, 1988; Walker, 1991).

Similarly, there is a dearth of information on parenting by gay fathers. As of 1990, Bigner and Bozett pointed out that the few articles available focused on case and interview material gleaned from extremely small samples. Often, research on gay parents tends to focus on demonstrating their lack of psychopathology or the prevalence of homosexuality in the offspring of gay parents rather than on understanding more specifically the psychological and sociocultural implications of parenting by gay men.

It has been widely noted that the topics of homosexuality and AIDS carry negative social connotations, reinforced by their relationship to one another (Black, 1993; Green & Bobele, 1994; Maloney, 1988; Nichols, 1986; Walker, 1991). The stigma of illness generated by HIV is made more potent by its association with stigmatized communities and behaviors: homosexuality, minority cultures, (homo)sexual transmission, and intravenous drug use. In a culture that frequently targets homosexuality as a threat to the moral fabric of our society and conceptualizes AIDS as just punishment for homosexual behavior, it is not surprising that gay men with AIDS face multiple levels of discrimination and rejection and wrestle with internalized shame and self-doubt. The families of these men struggle with similar internal and community reactions, as they confront the HIV-positive status of their loved ones.

In this chapter, I address some of the complicated issues that can arise in a family when a man who self-identifies as gay contracts HIV and discloses this information to his children and other family members. I will explore the concerns that may arise in such a family and some of the ways family members attempt to respond. Although the issues of homosexual and intravenous transmission of HIV are by no means mutually exclusive, much of the literature focuses only on gay or on drug-using populations in discussing AIDS. The focus of this chapter is on families of gay men; however, it is noteworthy that one of the cases also involves serious drug use. Case examples describe three such families, all of whom have at least one adolescent child.

Families with adolescents were selected for several reasons. First, adolescence is a time of searching for identity, individuation, and mastery—a transitional time in which parents and other adults are examined and evaluated for appropriateness as role models (Meeks, 1980). Second, it is a period of burgeoning awareness of sexuality and the body and one in which a parent's sexuality may come more sharply into focus. Third, it is an age at which feelings and reactions can be articulated to an extent not possible at earlier ages. By studying the behaviors and symptomatic expressions of adolescent children, we gain clues into the workings of the larger family system.

Coming Out as a Family with AIDS

Men who came out as gay after having entered into heterosexual relationships and fathering children typically have experienced extraordinarily painful self-questioning about their sexual orientation in the process of coming out to themselves and to those around them—particularly to their children and their wives or ex-wives. These issues often arouse feelings of guilt, betrayal, anger, and hurt for all parties. Men who self-identify as gay violate the dominant culture's gender norms; gay men who are fathers face the task of maintaining a relationship with their children in the context of a social role (father) that carries strict gender-based and heterosexist expectations. Thus, gay fathers can find themselves torn between identities and roles that seem incongruent (Bigner & Bozett, 1990).

Men who have contracted HIV from sexual contact with another man (or other men) often face decisions about what to tell loved ones about their health status, symptoms, sexual orientation, relationships, and so on. As stated by Nichols (1986):

> AIDS forces one into a new identity crisis, recapitulating the earlier one [of coming out], and feelings of bewilderment, confusion, and personal and social devaluation may accompany it; patients have referred to this as "coming out as a person with AIDS." . . . In gay men with AIDS there is a resurgence of homophobic feeling . . . as they search to understand what they "did to deserve it." (p. 212)

In turn, their family members face issues that parallel those of the HIV-infected individual. The disclosure of a father's HIV-positive status may trigger a resurgence of homophobic feeling in members of his family, accompanied by feelings of blame, recrimination, and judgment about the father's sexual orientation, behaviors, and lifestyle. Simultaneously, these family members face a series of decisions about the extent to which they are willing to disclose the information to others within and outside the family.

Some of the issues faced by children of gay men echo those faced by their fathers. The children, too, confront feelings of shame and differentness, as well as decisions about to whom and what to disclose in coming out as having gay fathers. Further, a teenager contemplating his or her gay father's sexuality does so with the knowledge that the parent has engaged in sexual behaviors that are scorned by the dominant culture. Adolescents struggling to understand and contain their own sexual impulses might find these challenges overwhelming and confusing.

A father's ability to help his children face these difficult issues will depend partly on his own process of having done so successfully. The more comfortable a gay man feels with his identity, sexuality, and the degree of support he has found (both within the gay community and in the larger culture), the more he will be able to convey a sense of confidence to his children and to empathize with their dilemmas regarding peer conformity, secrecy, and authenticity.

Tasks of the Therapist

An eight-dimension model for assessment and treatment is presented herein for therapists working with families confronting HIV disease in a gay father. My own approach employs techniques from a variety of family therapy models. However, it draws most heavily from intergenerational, structural, and systemic theories of family functioning and from concepts of family development related to chronic and life-threatening illness (Boscolo, Cecchin, Hoffman, & Penn, 1987; Bowen, 1978; Minuchin, 1974; Rolland, 1994). The model is also applicable, with some modification, to families confronting HIV or AIDS in any member.

As in all good therapeutic work, sensitivity to issues of race or ethnicity, social class, and religious background is crucial in assessing family functioning and in tailoring treatment. Issues that may vary from culture to culture include definition of the family unit (for example, extended family members, godparents, close family friends, and so on); degree of comfort with psychotherapy and open discussion of emotions and family dynamics in front of a stranger; and attitudes toward illness and medical care (Rolland, 1994). Additionally, part of any assessment of the role of the therapist includes attention to race, ethnic, class, and cultural differences between the therapist and the clients.

Assessment Tasks

Task 1: *Assessment of family's level of functioning with HIV.* In addition to the usual assessment of functioning of the family system, it is important to evaluate the way HIV has had an impact on the family's functioning to date. In general, the treatment will be tailored to one of three levels of family dysfunction that must be assessed early in treatment:

- Functional families needing support in coping with the immediate stress of severe HIV disease

- Families presenting with recent onset psychological symptoms in one member, whose emerging problems may be related to the father's HIV disease
- Multiproblem families with longstanding dysfunction whose coping responses to the father's HIV are greatly complicated by preexisting and coexisting problems

The therapist must investigate the ways in which HIV plays a role in the family's emotional life. This information may be gleaned from direct reports by clients about such topics as the practical, financial, and emotional consequences of HIV, as well as by identifying dysfunctional symptomatic behaviors related to the unexpressed feelings of one or more family members. The impact of HIV will vary with the stage of the disease, the amount of medical intervention needed, the visibility of HIV-related symptoms, the degree to which the physical and mental health of the infected individual is compromised by the disease, and the psychological functioning of the family.

Task 2: Assessment of family's level of comfort with homosexuality and HIV disease. In working with families in which the father is both gay and HIV-positive, the therapist must also assess the level of comfort each member has with the father's homosexuality and his HIV status. This can be accomplished by direct questioning, as well as by observing the responses of different family members in discussing the topic together and in separate interactions with the therapist.

Treatment Tasks

Task 3: Joining with the family. Because of the extremely volatile nature of the topics involved, it is essential that an atmosphere of safety be created in the therapy room, necessitating a nonjudgmental stance on the therapist's part. Clients often have legitimate concerns about therapists' conscious or unconscious attitudes or judgments regarding homosexuality, sexual behaviors, management of the disease, and so forth, and they may be acutely sensitive to their direct and covert messages. Effective intervention on the part of the therapist calls for a delicate balance of supporting all family members while challenging homophobic or other judgmental attitudes on the part of the uninfected family members and self-destructive behaviors on the part of the individual with HIV.

Task 4: Normalizing (reframing as normal) family members' emotional responses to HIV and AIDS and encouraging them to express these feelings (Walker, 1991). Clients frequently feel that their responses to the appearance of HIV disease in a loved one are shameful, particularly such negative emotions as anger, resentment, or fear

(Gonzalez, Steinglass, & Reiss, 1987). Uninfected family members often resist expressing feelings that they consider selfish or that would appear to the HIV-positive individual to show an unwillingness to care for him. The therapist is often called upon to define these feelings as normal in such a situation and to allow and encourage their expression.

Task 5: *Identifying unexpressed emotional issues.* Often families present with symptomatic behaviors in one or more members that are confusing and frightening to the others. Common examples of this are children's poor school performance, emotional withdrawal, and fighting. In the midst of coping with the crisis of HIV infection, parents frequently feel irritated by and concerned about the acting out behavior of the children or adolescents, and these indirect expressions of stress motivate a family to attend therapy. Therapists have a crucial role to play in articulating the emotions that the identified patient is carrying on behalf of the family in crisis.

Task 6: *Addressing generic issues of chronic illness.* Gonzalez, Steinglass, and Reiss (1987) identify four areas that should be addressed in working with families dealing with chronic illness:

- The normative developmental, practical, and emotional needs of all family members, which may have been neglected by focusing on the illness
- The emotional coalitions and exclusions that have developed in response to, or are exacerbated by, the illness
- The dysfunctional coping strategies employed by the family and maintained for fear that any change will do further damage to persons or relationships
- The social isolation from others maintained by the family in order to cope with the demands of the illness and to preserve a sense of normalcy

These four areas are essential to monitor in working with families coping with AIDS. Because of the stigmatized nature of the disease and the resultant denial and shame that accompany it, these problem areas may manifest themselves more extremely than is commonly seen with other chronic illnesses.

Task 7: *Structuring treatment.* It is often useful to see different configurations of family members in working with families coping with HIV. In addition to observing family members together, the therapist can benefit from hearing what subgroups or individuals say without other members present, and family members often feel less reluctant to bring up sensitive topics in contexts in which the HIV-positive member is not present. Thus, meeting with one or more family subgroups (for example, the HIV-positive individual and his lover; the ex-wife and children; the extended family of friends; the extended family of origin) will enable the therapist to better understand the larger family context.

Similarly, it can be useful to involve extrafamily members such as home-care health providers, physicians, or the infected person's individual therapist in order to ensure that the intervention is received by everyone involved. Should the therapist meet with one or more members separately, it is crucial both to clarify ground rules regarding confidentiality and to avoid triangling.

It is often beneficial to make referrals to adjunctive treatments or community resources when these are available. Support groups are particularly helpful for individuals and families coping with HIV, as they provide a break from the secrecy and social isolation common to these families. It may be helpful to refer a family member or subgroup to another therapist for ongoing work or to utilize bereavement, self-help, and twelve-step groups such as Al-Anon as appropriate.

The length of treatment and frequency of scheduled sessions will vary according to the needs of the family, stage of illness, severity of family dysfunction, and depth of therapeutic intervention.

Task 8: *Therapist countertransference and use of self.* Many therapists are pushed to deal with strong countertransference reactions in working with AIDS. Therapists are not immune to biases found in the larger culture, such as homophobia, irrational concerns about HIV transmission, or judgmental attitudes about unfamiliar sexual practices or variant lifestyle choices.

In addition, working with AIDS usually requires confronting physical and mental deterioration, disability, and death. Profound and overwhelming feelings of grief and loss can affect therapists, especially when a close attachment has been formed with clients. It is sometimes necessary to make home visits when a client is ailing, which alters the usual frame of the therapy. All of these issues make it advisable to seek consultation regularly.

Three Families Confront AIDS

The following case material addresses some of the specific concerns raised by families in therapy attempting to deal with HIV disease in a gay father. Particular attention will be devoted to the adolescents in these families. Each of the three case studies illustrates one of the types of family functioning described above. The first two cases will be summarized briefly and the third in more detail, in order to provide a point-by-point illustration of the model.

CASE 1: A FUNCTIONAL FAMILY CONFRONTS AIDS

The family of Joel (a gay father) came to see me as Joel lay dying of AIDS. The family was White and middle-class, and both parents were college-educated. Although everyone present—including Joel's lover, mother, sister, close friend, and two children—were profoundly affected by Joel's impending death, the family expressed strongest concern about the well-being of David, age eighteen and Julie, age fifteen.

The children's emotional responses to Joel's illness were similar in that they both expressed what seemed to them and to their family members a mysterious numbness when confronted with their father's sickness (and eventually with his death several weeks later). Julie, in particular, provoked concern in the family when she did not cry at the memorial service or for several weeks thereafter.

Both children had been aware for years that their father was gay and that he had HIV. They both spoke poignantly of how difficult, if not impossible, it was for them to tell almost anyone about it. My task with David was to normalize these feelings, as well as to empathize with the difficult dilemmas he faced regarding disclosure to his peers. He seemed hungry for such supportive interventions and was able to thrive at home and at school following his father's death.

Julie's responses to therapy were a bit more complicated. All of her life, she had struggled to be seen as separate from her brother. When she failed to appear for a joint session with David, it became clear that her issues needed to be addressed separately from his. Subsequent sessions alone with Julie and a conjoint session with her and her mother enabled us to identify the connections between the loss of her father, her age-appropriate conflicts regarding alcohol, drugs, and sex, and her feeling excluded from a perceived alliance between her mother and David. She was then able to cry with me and with her mother and to feel closer to her remaining family members.

The most important functions of therapy for this family were to provide support for the anticipatory and actual grieving processes (along with appropriate referrals to bereavement groups), to address the difficulty the children were having in feeling and expressing their grief, to identify the alliance that Julie perceived to be developing between her mother and David, and to facilitate communication between Julie and her other family members before her feelings of exclusion became fixed.

CASE 2: A FAMILY WITH RECENT ONSET SYMPTOMS

This case involves a less obvious and more symptomatic effect of a father's HIV on his adolescent son, although at the time of the initial contacts, there was no mention of HIV infection or illness. This family was also White, middle-class, and well-educated, and the father was a successful small business owner.

I received an initial call from Mark, a gay father who wanted his eighteen-year-old son Jeffrey to have an individual therapist to talk to about the recent changes in his life. After seeing his father on a part-time basis for the many years since his parents' divorce, Jeffrey had now come to live with Mark and his lover, Andy.

In our initial individual sessions, Jeffrey talked about issues important to most eighteen-year-old boys, including school, relationships, and friends. However, as our work progressed, images of death, fears about his health, and vague thoughts of suicide surfaced. He repeatedly experienced flashbacks from a bad LSD trip and was frightened they would recur. He was troubled by obsessive and somewhat paranoid thoughts about his physical and emotional health; for example, he worried that someone might slip LSD into a drink of his.

A referral for psychological testing resulted in information that a thought disorder was not present; therefore, I hypothesized that the source of Jeffrey's worries might be located within the family dynamics. Several weeks into our work together, Jeffrey casually mentioned that his father had told him that he and Andy were both HIV-positive. Little discussion had ensued, and Jeffrey was left feeling confused, upset, and afraid of contagion. Despite receiving reassurance from me about the minimal risks involved in casual contact, Jeffrey increasingly worried about contracting HIV at home or from a cut inflicted while riding his skateboard. I began to view Jeffrey's obsessive worries about his own physical health and safety as related to his father's HIV status and to the lack of continued, open dialogue about it.

At my request, Mark readily agreed to attend sessions with Jeffrey. With my encouragement, Jeffrey told Mark about his confusion concerning his father's health and his worries about his own health. I suggested to both of them that for Jeffrey, focusing on his own physical vulnerabilities might serve to keep him distracted so that he did not have to worry about the very real threat of losing his father and Andy. This led to a crucial discussion of Jeffrey's fears of losing Mark and his catastrophic fears about everyone around him dying. Mark was also able to acknowledge in Jeffrey's presence that he, too, was concerned about his son should he die; at the same time, he reassured him that his health was good for the time being. These discussions were clearly the crux of the therapy for this father-son dyad, and gradually, Jeffrey experienced a lessening of his symptoms of intrusive thoughts of death, contamination, and sickness.

Decreased concern about speaking candidly to his father enabled Jeffrey to realize that he preferred to leave his father's house and return to live near his mother and old friends. Although this cut the therapy short before Andy joined the treatment, it was clear that Jeffrey felt increasingly empowered in his relationship with his father as a result of the work that had been accomplished in therapy. In a follow-up contact with this family several years later, I discovered that Jeffrey had moved across the country to take a job that used his artistic skills and earned him a very good livelihood. He still maintained contact with his father and Andy, and they appeared to be on good terms.

This case presented a challenge for me, because it had not been conceptualized by either Jeffrey or his father as an HIV issue. In fact, HIV was not even mentioned in early contacts with either person. Furthermore, it was Jeffrey, not Mark, who was my primary client. The decisions to encourage Jeffrey to broach the topic of Mark's HIV status with him and to alter the frame of the therapy by inviting Mark into the sessions carried a risk that Mark would experience me as intrusive and judgmental. I chose to do so; I saw the issue of HIV as key to Jeffrey's symptomatic expression. Fortunately, Mark was receptive to the idea of joining in the therapy and quite willing to discuss the impact of his HIV disease on his son, which opened up the therapy and provided considerable relief for all involved.

In a recent follow-up conversation with Mark, he informed me that his lover, Andy, had died several years after this therapy took place. He further told me that Jeffrey had arrived at his father's house twelve hours after Andy's death and had put his arms around his father. Mark felt that Jeffrey's gesture of support had been exactly the right thing to do in their shared moment of grief.

CASE 3: A MULTIPROBLEM FAMILY WITH HIV

Task 1: *Assessment of family's level of functioning with HIV.* This case involves a family that had been in turmoil for many years prior to the father's HIV infection. Therefore, the goals of the treatment were to address problems beyond the HIV infection and, at the same time, to focus on how the family was responding to this major stressor. This family might never have entered therapy if it had not been for the acting-out of the adolescent son, whose behavior was considered problematic by the other family members. The father, Bill, made the initial telephone call to request family therapy. Bill had a history of drug abuse as well as mental and physical illness over the years. Although he was now diagnosed with AIDS-related complex (ARC), his current concern was the behavior of his eighteen-year-old son Nick, who had galvanized the anger of the entire family.

Bill and his ex-wife, Debra, had divorced several years earlier after having been married for over twenty years. During their marriage, Bill had engaged in a number of secret affairs with men, some of whom were also his drug contacts. Despite the divorce, the members of this family continued to be involved with one another. Bill and Debra had remained in frequent communication since splitting up; Nick had lived with each of them in turn; and their older daughter, Karen, remained strongly emotionally involved in the family despite the fact that she attended college out of state.

Race and social class were additional issues that strongly affected this family. Bill was White, from a poor background, and had made a meager living as a visual artist over the years. Debra was Black, the daughter of a successful lawyer, and worked as a mid-level administrator in a nonprofit agency. Money had been a constant source of stress, particularly because Debra's parents had never approved of Bill and had never helped them financially.

In the first session, all members were present, as Karen was visiting for school vacation. Nick had stolen several hundred dollars of Bill's disability money from under his father's mattress. Bill had responded to this act by throwing Nick out of the house. In the past, Nick had been asked to leave Debra's house a number of times and had bounced back and forth between Bill's and Debra's homes. He had dropped out of high school and had a difficult time keeping a job and supporting himself.

Task 2: *Assessment of family's level of comfort with homosexuality and HIV disease.* Although both children had been stunned upon finding out that Bill was gay and learning about his sexual and drug history, the family member who carried the most charge about it was Karen. Being protective of her mother, Karen expressed anger about her father's coming out after so many years of marriage. Bill's declaration that he was gay was associated with his lying and drug use, and the other three had understandable reactions of anger and betrayal at the information. Debra was particularly angry at his having brought drug dealers, who were also his sexual partners, into the house with the children present.

The reaction to AIDS was also particular to this family's history. Because of Bill's repeated hospitalizations for physical ailments and suicide attempts, the others expressed disbelief at his ARC diagnosis. I understood this response to be denial combined with actual disbelief due to Bill's past history of repeated lies. It was only when AIDS-related opportunistic infections set in that the family was able to accept the realities of his diagnosis and mobilize to physically care for him.

Disclosure was a difficult issue for Debra with her family of origin. She kept Bill's illness a secret from her parents and siblings for a long while and experienced shame when she finally told them the truth. The extended family's response was predictably unsupportive and disappointing to Debra and the children and reinforced their feelings of isolation.

Task 3: *Joining with the family.* Bill's history of duplicity and his lack of integrity in dealing with his loved ones made it difficult to empathize with him at times, particularly when he responded defensively to the others' expressions of anger. I had to walk a careful line of supporting Bill's self-identification as gay while empathizing with his ex-wife and children for the adverse effects on them of his process in coming to terms with it. By allowing each individual a voice in stating his or her experience, I worked to create an atmosphere in which all felt safe in discussing this sensitive topic. I supported each of Bill's family members in individually discussing with him the impact of his lying, drug abuse, and surreptitious sexual behavior on the family, and I confronted Bill when he responded defensively or declined to take responsibility for the impact of his behaviors.

Task 4: *Normalizing family members' emotional responses.* All three of Bill's family members were angry at him, yet they felt guilty and reluctant to confront him because of his illness. Debra and Karen both stated that "it might kill him" to hear their feelings. My task was to normalize their emotional responses and encourage them to express them directly to Bill, who repeatedly expressed a willingness to listen.

Task 5: *Identifying unexpressed emotional issues.* Debra mentioned in our first session that she felt that the family had always protected Bill and that currently they were hesitant to confront him due to his AIDS-related health problems. This raised the possibility that Nick's difficulties had distracted the family from focusing on Bill's problems over the years and had held the family together in a joint task since the divorce and Bill's openly self-identifying as gay. Nick's presenting problems seemed to mimic his father's earlier acting-out, that is, lying and drug abuse.

In a solo meeting with me, Nick articulated his anger at his role as the family scapegoat. He recounted the difficulty he had experienced over the years tolerating the fighting between his parents over Bill's drug use and recalled a decision he had made when he was only eleven years old to distract them from their marital difficulties by getting into trouble at school.

It became clear that the family needed assistance in expressing their feelings about losing Bill and about the residue of anger and resentment that had built up over the years, in part to release Nick from his role as the lightning rod of the family's anger. However, when Nick was present at a session with any other member of the family, the focus would inevitably shift to the ways in which Nick had disappointed the family and to issues of limit-setting with him. Although a good deal of this was crucial to address because his acting-out was dramatic and upsetting to the others, it became apparent that I had been drawn into the family's truncating view of the problem to the extent that focus on HIV and on Bill's illness was completely overshadowed by the focus on Nick.

In a crucial session held right before Karen was to return to college, I gently reminded the family of how little time remained for them to spend with Bill. This refocused all of them on the crisis at hand and helped Nick to feel a part of the family again.

In the course of this family's therapy, Nick continued to fulfill his role as scapegoat and to test his parents with his acting-out behavior. However, as Bill got sicker, Nick also took on the job of caring for him. He moved into Bill's apartment and took care of Bill during the nights. It appeared that Nick had found himself a "job" for the time being and would not secure other employment while Bill was alive. Bill's three family members were able to come to grips with the fact that he was dying, and they united to stay by him physically and emotionally through the process.

Task 6: *Addressing generic issues of chronic illness.*

• *Emotional needs of noninfected family members.* Because of Bill's history of repeated illnesses, the emotional needs of other family members had been neglected. Debra, Karen, and Nick had felt unable to directly express their needs over the years out of a desire to protect Bill. The therapeutic tasks were to focus on their feelings of neglect by Bill and to provide them an opportunity to express these feelings to him in a safe atmosphere. In turn, Bill was able to empathize with their perspectives and apologize to them, thereby making amends before he died.

• *Alliances and coalitions.* Nick perceived an alliance between Debra and Karen and felt excluded by them as well as by Debra's family of origin, who disapproved of his underachieving behavior. I hypothesized that Nick may have had a special alliance with Bill to balance the one between the two women and therefore was understandably panicked by the impending loss of his father. Nick's symptomatic behavior of stealing from his father represented both a denial of Bill's fragility due to HIV and a crying out for contact with him. It is not unusual for children to test their sick parents in order to elicit an angry—thus engaged and mobilized—response from them. Therefore, it was important to help Nick reunite with his father before his death and rejoin his mother and his sister as part of the surviving family.

• *Dysfunctional coping strategies.* Nick had employed self-defeating patterns throughout his adolescence. Despite the fact that his behaviors alienated his family members, his role became one of identified patient, which distracted the others from the crisis and brought the family together. Becoming his father's caregiver in the latter part of Bill's illness was a temporary strategy in that it brought Nick no closer to learning to support himself; however, it did provide him with a positive way in which to connect with his father and with the others in a time of crisis.

• *Social isolation.* Each of the members of this family were referred to appropriate adjunctive therapies or support groups during the course of this treatment and as a follow-up to it.

Task 7: Structuring treatment. In order to observe the family's dynamics as well as accomplish the many tasks involved in this therapy, I structured the sessions so as to meet with all of the individuals, each combination of dyads and triads, and the entire family. I also collaborated by telephone with Bill's individual therapist and included the home-care nurse in one family session. Generally, I met with at least one member of the family each week.

Treatment for this family spanned the course of a year. As Bill's health deteriorated, I met with the family at his home, and he participated as much as he was physically and mentally able. After his death, I met with the surviving family members for several months to support them in their grieving process.

Task 8: Therapist countertransference and use of self. Over the course of treatment, I became strongly attached to this family and grew to have great respect for their strength in continuing to stay connected to one another despite the history of hurts and betrayals. As a lesbian, I identified with Bill's coming-out process, despite its clumsiness; I was also able to empathize with the others who had reacted with legitimate indignation to the way he had lied to them over the years.

My most difficult task was to evaluate the meaning and importance of Nick's acting-out behavior. I came to see it as both worthy of direct confrontation and as a distraction from focusing on the time-limited HIV issue. Ongoing consultation enabled me to stay with the AIDS-related focus while continuing to address Nick's symptomatic behaviors.

As Bill's health deteriorated, the need to meet with the family at his home increased. The intimacy of these home visits increased my attachment to the family; thus, Bill's eventual death had a profound and lasting impact on me.

Follow-up contact with this family several years later found Nick living alone in an apartment and holding down a job, and Karen temporarily living with her mother after graduation from college. Each continues to cope with the memory and loss of Bill in his or her own way.

Conclusion

Each case described here is different with respect to the presentation of the problem, the amount of probing needed to identify the impact of HIV on the uninfected family members, and the complications of previous family events, alliances, and coping styles on their functioning. A therapist's treatment plan and ability to intervene successfully with a particular family will vary based on these factors.

In each case, family members felt strongly connected to one another despite feelings engendered by the father's coming out as gay and the parents' divorce. The children experienced a strong loyalty and caring for their fathers, along with feelings of anger, hurt, bewilderment, and sadness. In the two cases in which the fathers were physically well enough to interact with their children, they demonstrated both a capacity and a willingness to listen and to respond to their children's concerns in a nondefensive and empathic manner.

Because AIDS in our culture involves stigma and secrecy, a therapist may or may not choose to encourage family members to disclose information about HIV infection to others in their communities. Full disclosure is not always desirable, as families are often in danger of losing their housing, jobs, insurance, and physical safety or of being socially ostracized when HIV disease is discovered. Therefore, despite the huge emotional cost to clients in the forms of social isolation, reinforcement of shame, and potential betrayal of loved ones, it often is dangerous or inappropriate to counsel families to divulge information regarding a family member's HIV disease to others. Nonetheless, it is important to help clients understand the repercussions of choosing to remain silent and to empathize with the dilemmas involved in making these painful decisions. These issues are poignantly discussed by Black (1993) in his insightful article on AIDS and secrecy.

Walker (1991) points out that despite the very real time pressure of working with a family with a chronic illness, the progress can be painfully slow. In deciding whether and how to broach difficult subjects with families coping with an HIV-related crisis, the therapist must stay cognizant of the sensitive nature of AIDS and the vulnerabilities felt by clients coping with it. At times in the course of the illness, emotional conflicts can be aired freely; at other times, the family has to suppress conflict and offer straightforward caregiving and support.

As the AIDS epidemic continues to grow, more and more therapists will be called upon to work with families confronting HIV disease in a loved one. Essential to psychotherapeutic work with people with AIDS and their loved ones is an empathic, nonjudgmental, and nonhomophobic stance on the part of the therapist, often achieved through rigorous self-examination in consultation with other professionals. For a therapist to maintain this stance, he or she must confront personal issues regarding sexuality and homosexuality, illness and death, and deeply held beliefs about normative family interaction and loyalty. Although this personal confrontation can be painful, the potential benefits are great. The therapist has the privilege of witnessing and participating in the emotional transformation of family members confronting their own or another member's death—profound and moving issues that all of us eventually will experience.

References

Bigner, J. J., & Bozett, F. W. (1990). Parenting by gay fathers. In F. W. Bozett & M. B. Sussman (Eds.), *Homosexuality and family relations* (pp. 155–175). Binghamton, NY: Harrington Park Press.

Black, L. W. (1993). AIDS and secrets. In E. Imber-Black (Ed.), *Secrets in families and family therapy* (pp. 355–369). New York: Norton.

Boscolo, L., Cecchin, G., Hoffman, L., & Penn, P. (1987). *Milan systemic family therapy.* New York: Basic Books.

Bowen, M. (1978). *Family therapy in clinical practice.* Montvale, NJ: Aronson.

Boyd-Franklin, N., Steiner, G. L., & Boland, M. G. (1994). *Children, families, and HIV/AIDS: Psychosocial and therapeutic issues.* New York: Guilford Press.

Cates, J. A., Graham, L. L., Boeglin, D., & Tielker, S. (1990). *Families in Society: The Journal of Contemporary Human Services,* April, 195–201.

Gonzalez, S., Steinglass, P., & Reiss, D. (1987). *Family-centered interventions for people with chronic disabilities.* Washington, DC: George Washington University Medical Center, Rehabilitation Research and Training Center, Department of Psychiatry and Behavioral Sciences.

Green, S. K., & Bobele, M. (1994). Family therapists' response to AIDS: An examination of attitudes, knowledge, and contact. *Journal of Marital and Family Therapy, 20*(4), 349–367.

Horsley, G. C. (1991, April). Restoring family relationships. *Focus,* p. 3.

Lovejoy, N. C. (1990). AIDS: Impact on the gay man's homosexual and heterosexual families. In F. W. Bozett & M. B. Sussman (Eds.), *Homosexuality and family relations* (pp. 285–316). Binghamton, NY: Haworth Press.

Maloney, B. D. (1988). The legacy of AIDS: Challenge for the next century. *Journal of Marital and Family Therapy, 14*(2), 143–150.

Meeks, J. E. (1980). *The fragile alliance* (2nd ed.). Malabar, FL: Krieger.

Minuchin, S. (1974). *Families and family therapy.* Cambridge, MA: Harvard University Press.

Nichols, S. E. (1986). Psychotherapy and AIDS. In T. S. Stein & C. J. Cohen (Eds.), *Contemporary perspectives on psychotherapy with lesbians and gay men* (pp. 209–240). New York: Plenum.

Rolland, J. S. (1994). Mastering family challenges in serious illness and disability. In F. Walsh (Ed.), *Normal family processes* (2nd ed., pp. 444–473). New York: Guilford Press.

Walker, G. (1991). *In the midst of winter: Systemic therapy with families, couples and individuals with AIDS infection.* New York: Norton.

CHAPTER EIGHTEEN

LESBIAN MOTHERS AND THEIR CHILDREN

Findings from the Bay Area Families Study

Charlotte J. Patterson

Although the heterosexual public has, for the most part, been introduced to the notion of lesbian motherhood only recently, lesbian mothers have existed for many years (Golombok, Spencer & Rutter, 1983; Green, 1978; Hoeffer, 1981; Huggins, 1989; Kirkpatrick, Smith, & Roy, 1981; Laird, 1993). Most often, women have borne children in the context of heterosexual relationships and later come out as lesbians, often in the context of a divorce. Although some were denied custody by courts following separation from their male partners, other lesbians retained custody of their children (Falk, 1989; Hitchens, 1979–1980; Ricketts & Achtenberg, 1990). Despite psychological, judicial, and popular prejudices, a substantial body of research now attests to normal adjustment among mothers and normal development among children in these families (Green & Bozett, 1991; Patterson, 1992, 1995b; Tasker & Golombok, 1995).

In contrast to divorced lesbian mothers, those of the so-called lesbian baby boom (Martin, 1993; Patterson, 1992; Riley, 1988; Weston, 1991) came out as les-

I wish to thank the Society for Psychological Study of Social Issues for support of this work. I also give special thanks to Mitch Chyette, Deborah Cohn, Carolyn Cowan, Philip Cowan, Charlene Depner, Ellie Schindelman, and all of the families who participated in the Bay Area Families Study for their valuable support and assistance. Thanks also go to Alicia Eddy, David Koppelman, Meg Michel, and Scott Spence for their efficient work in coding data for this study.

bians first and only later bore or adopted children in the context of their preexisting lesbian identities. Relatively little research has been completed with such families, and there are few data as yet about adjustment among the mothers or development among the children of the lesbian baby boom. Apart from my own work, and in addition to contemporary anthropological research (for example, Lewin, 1993; Weston, 1991), there are only a few studies in the published literature that focus directly on the children of the lesbian baby boom (Flaks, Ficher, Masterpasqua, & Joseph, 1995; McCandlish, 1987; and Steckel, 1985, 1987). For instance, on the basis of extensive family interviews, McCandlish (1987) examined psychosocial development among seven young children born to five lesbian mother families and reported that the children's development appeared normal in all respects.

Steckel (1985, 1987) studied the progress of separation-individuation among three-year-old children born to eleven lesbian and eleven heterosexual couples. Using parent interviews, parent and teacher Q-sorts, and structured doll-play techniques, Steckel compared independence, ego functions, and object relations among children in the two types of families. Like McCandlish, Steckel's principal results documented the striking similarity in development of children in the two groups.

More recently, Flaks and his colleagues (1995) compared social and personal development among fifteen three- to nine-year-old children born to lesbian couples via donor insemination with that among fifteen children from matched, two-parent heterosexual families. Across a wide array of assessments of cognitive and behavioral functioning, there were notable similarities between the children of lesbian and heterosexual parents. The only significant difference between the two groups was in the area of parenting skills and practices; lesbian couples revealed more parenting awareness skills than did heterosexual couples.

In this context, I designed the Bay Area Families Study to contribute to understanding the families of the lesbian baby boom. In this chapter, I describe the study itself and its principal results to date, which fall into four major areas. First, I describe demographic and other characteristics of the participating families. Next, I describe assessments of the adjustment of both mothers and children, relative to normative expectations based on large comparison samples drawn from the population at large. In families that were headed by lesbian couples, the study also examined certain key facets of couple functioning such as relationship satisfaction and division of labor, and I report normative findings in this area. Finally, the study also explored correlates of individual differences in children's adjustment, and I present these also. Although I do not provide statistical details here, all findings described as statistically significant were at the $p < .05$ level. The methods and findings are summarized briefly below, but additional details and commentary are available elsewhere (Patterson, 1994, 1995a, 1995b; Patterson &

Kosmitzki, 1995). In this study, there were no significant results pertaining to comparisons of girls' versus boys' adjustment, so I present results for the child sample as a whole.

Description of Participating Families

Families were eligible to participate in the Bay Area Families Study if they met each of three criteria. First, at least one child between four and nine years of age had to be present in the home. Second, the child had to have been born to or adopted by a lesbian mother or mothers. Third, only families who lived within the greater San Francisco Bay area (for example, San Francisco, Oakland, and San Jose) were considered eligible.

Recruitment began when I contacted friends, acquaintances, and colleagues who might be likely to know eligible lesbian mother families. I described the proposed research and solicited help in locating families. From names gathered in this way, I telephoned each family to describe the study and to ask for their participation. In all, contact was made with thirty-nine eligible families, of whom thirty-seven participated in the study. Thus approximately 95 percent of the families who were contacted did take part. Participation involved a single home visit during which all data reported here were collected.

Twenty-six of the thirty-seven participating families (70 percent) were headed by a lesbian couple. Seven families (19 percent) were headed by a single mother living with her child. In four families (11 percent), the child had been born to a lesbian couple who had since separated, and the child was in de facto joint custody, that is, living part of the time with one mother and part of the time with the other. In the latter group of families, one mother was out of town during the period of testing and did not participate.

Sixty-six lesbian mothers took part in the study. Their ages ranged from twenty-eight to fifty-three years, with a mean age of 39.6. Sixty-one (92 percent) described themselves as White or non-Hispanic Caucasian, two (3 percent) as African American or Black, and three (4 percent) as coming from other racial or ethnic backgrounds. Most were well-educated; 74 percent had received college degrees, and 48 percent had received graduate degrees.

The great majority of mothers (94 percent) were employed on a regular basis outside the home, and about half said that they worked forty hours or more per week. Most (62 percent) of the women were in professional occupations such as law or nursing, but others were in technical or mechanical occupations such as car repair (9 percent), business or sales such as real estate (9 percent), or in other occupations such as artist (14 percent). Only four mothers were not employed outside the home. Thirty-four families reported family incomes above $30,000 per year, and seventeen families reported incomes above $60,000 per year.

In each family, the focal child was between four and nine years of age (average age, six years and two months); there were nineteen girls and eighteen boys. Thirty-four of the children were born to lesbian mothers, and three had been adopted. Thirty of the children were described by their mothers as White or non-Hispanic Caucasian, three as Hispanic, and four as of some other racial or ethnic heritage.

Some additional descriptive information also was collected. Mothers were asked to explain the circumstances surrounding the child's conception, birth, and/or adoption. Mothers also were asked about the child's biological father or sperm donor, the degree to which the mothers had knowledge of or contact with him, and the degree to which the focal child had knowledge of his identity or contact with him. In addition, mothers were asked to give the child's last name and to explain how the child had been given that name.

The mothers' accounts of the conception, birth, and/or adoption of their children made clear that, in general, the focal children were very much wanted. The average amount of time it took for biological mothers to conceive focal children after they began to attempt to become pregnant was ten months. Adoptive mothers reported that, on average, the adoption process took approximately twelve months. In the great majority of cases, then, these lesbian mothers had devoted considerable time and effort to making the birth or adoption of their children possible.

There was tremendous variability in the amount of information that families had about the donor or biological father of the focal child. In seventeen families (46 percent), the child had been conceived via donor insemination (DI) with sperm from an anonymous donor (sperm that had been provided by a sperm bank or clinic). In these cases, families had only limited information (for example, race, height, weight, and hair color) about the donor, and none knew the donor's name. In ten families (27 percent), the child was conceived via DI, with sperm provided by a known donor such as a family friend. In four families (11 percent), children were conceived when the biological mother had intercourse with a man. In three families (8 percent), the child was adopted. In the three remaining families, some other set of circumstances applied or the parents acknowledged that the child had been born to one of the mothers but preferred not to disclose any additional information about their child's conception.

Mothers reported relatively little contact with biological fathers or donors. Twenty-three out of the thirty-seven (62 percent) of the families reported no contact at all with the biological father or donor during the previous year. Only ten families (27 percent) had two or more contacts with the biological father or sperm donor during the previous year.

Given that a majority of families did not know the identity of the child's sperm donor or biological father (46 percent donor insemination and 8 percent adopted) and that most currently had little or no contact with him, it is not surprising that the donor or biological father's role with the child was seen by mothers as being quite limited. In 22 families (60 percent), mothers reported that the donor or biological father had no special role vis à vis the child; this figure includes the families in which the sperm donor had been anonymous. In thirteen families (35 percent), the biological father's identity was known to parents and children, but he took the role of a family friend rather than that of a father. There were only two families in which the biological father was acknowledged as such and in which he was described as assuming a father's role.

In the families of the lesbian baby boom, questions about selection of the child's last name are of particular interest. In this sample, the largest number of children—26 children (70 percent)—bore the last names of their biological or adoptive mothers; this figure includes children in four families in which *all* family members (both mothers and all children) shared the same last name. In seven families, children had been given hyphenated last names, created from the two mothers' last names. Finally, in four families, children had some other last name.

Mental Health of Mothers

The two principal measures of mothers' adjustment were the Rosenberg Self-Esteem Scale (Rosenberg, 1979) and the Derogatis Symptom Checklist (SCL-90-R; Derogatis, 1983). For purposes of presentation, the biological or legal adoptive mother in each family will be referred to as the "biological mother," and the other mother, if any, will be called the "nonbiological mother."

Maternal self-esteem was assessed using the Rosenberg Self-Esteem Scale (Rosenberg, 1979). This scale consists of ten statements, with four response alternatives, indicating the respondent's degree of agreement with each statement. Data analyses showed that the average scores for both biological and nonbiological mothers were almost identical, and both were well within the range of normal functioning. These results indicate that lesbian mothers who took part in this research reported generally positive views about themselves. Their scores were similar to the normative scores of the general population on this questionnaire.

Maternal adjustment was assessed using the Derogatis Symptom Checklist, Revised (SCL-90-R; Derogatis, 1983), which consists of ninety items addressing a variety of psychological and somatic symptoms. Each respondent rated the extent to which she had been distressed by each symptom during the past week (0 = not at all, 4 = extremely). Nine subscales (anger/hostility, anxiety, depression, interpersonal sensitivity, obsessive/compulsiveness, paranoid ideation, phobic anxiety, psychoticism, and somatization) were scored, as well as a Global Severity Index that summarized the respondent's overall level of distress.

Average scores for biological and nonbiological mothers were virtually identical for most subscales as well as for the GSI, and all of these average scores were well within the normative range. None of the average T-scores deviated substantially from the expected mean, indicating that lesbian mothers' reports of symptoms are no greater and no smaller than those expected for other women of the same age. Thus the results for maternal adjustment revealed that lesbian mothers who took part in this study reported few symptoms and good self-esteem.

Mental Health of Children

The three principal assessments of children's adjustment were the Achenbach and Edelbrock Child Behavior Checklist (Achenbach & Edelbrock, 1983), the Eder Children's Self-View Questionnaire (Eder, 1990), and a standard interview relating to sex-role identity (Green, 1978). In what follows, I describe first the assessment procedures and then the results for children's adjustment.

Assessment of Child Adjustment

To assess levels of child social competence and child behavior problems, the Child Behavior Checklist (CBCL) (Achenbach & Edelbrock, 1983) was administered. The CBCL was selected because it discriminates children in the clinical from those in the normative range of functioning for both internalizing (inhibited, overcontrolled behavior) and externalizing (aggressive, antisocial, or undercontrolled behavior) problems, as well as for social competence. It is designed to be completed by parents. In the present study, all participating mothers completed this instrument.

Norms for the CBCL (Achenbach & Edelbrock, 1983) were obtained from heterogeneous normal samples of 200 four- to five-year-olds, and 600 six- to eleven-year-olds, as well as from equivalent numbers of children at each age who were drawn from clinical populations, that is, children receiving services from community mental health centers, private psychological and psychiatric clinics or practices, and so on. For purposes of the present research, mean scores reported by Achenbach and Edelbrock (1983, pp. 210–214) were averaged across four- to five-year and six- to eleven-year age levels to provide estimates of average scores for social competence, internalizing, externalizing, and total behavior problems among normative and clinical populations at the ages studied here. To assess the extent of their resemblance to normal and clinical populations, then, scores for children in the current sample were compared with these figures.

Assessment of children's self-concepts was accomplished using five scales from Eder's Children's Self-View Questionnaire (CSVQ; Eder, 1990). These scales, designed especially to assess psychological concepts of self among children from three to eight years of age, assess five different dimensions of children's views of themselves. The Aggression scale assessed the degree to which children saw themselves as likely to hurt or frighten others. The Social Closeness scale assessed the degree to which children enjoy being with people and prefer to be around others. The Social Potency scale assessed the degree to which children like to stand out or to be the center of attention. The Stress Reaction scale assessed the extent to which children said they often felt scared, upset, or angry. Finally, the Well-Being scale assessed the degree to which children felt joyful, content, and comfortable with themselves. Using hand puppets, the CSVQ was administered individually to participating children, and their answers were tape-recorded for later scoring.

Children's sex-role behavior preferences were assessed in a standard, open-ended interview format, such as that employed in earlier research on children of divorced lesbian mothers (Golombok et al., 1983; Green, 1978; Green, Mandel, Hotvedt, Gray, & Smith, 1986). The interviewer explained to each child that she was interested in learning more about the friends and other children that the child liked to play with and about the child's favorite toys and other things. She then asked each child to name the friends and other children he or she liked to play with. Following this, each child was asked to name favorite toys, favorite games, and favorite characters on television, in movies, or in books. The interviewer wrote down each of the child's responses. Children's responses were also tape-recorded, and the interviewer's notes were later checked for accuracy against the audiotapes.

After testing had been completed, each child's answers for each of four topics (peer friendships, favorite toys, favorite games, and favorite characters) were coded into one of four categories with regard to their sex-role relevant qualities. The four categories were "mainly same-sex" (for example, a boy reports having mostly or entirely male friends), "mixed sexes" (for example, an even or almost-even mix of sexes in the friends mentioned by a child), "opposite sex" (for example, a girl reports having mostly or entirely male friends), and "can't tell" (an answer was unscorable or not clearly sex-typed, for instance, children said that playing Chutes and Ladders was one of their favorite games). Because children's play groups are known to be highly sex-segregated at this age, children were expected to give mainly "same-sex" answers to these questions.

Results for Children's Adjustment

As expected, social competence among children with lesbian mothers was rated as normal. Scores for children of lesbian mothers were significantly higher than those for Achenbach and Edelbrock's (1983) clinical sample but were not different from those for the normal sample. This was true for reports given by both mothers in the lesbian mother families.

Results for behavior problems revealed the same pattern. For internalizing, externalizing, and total behavior problems, scores for children of lesbian mothers were significantly lower than those for children in the clinical sample but did not differ from those in the normal sample. This was true of reports given by both mothers in the lesbian mother families. Overall, then, the behavior problems of lesbian mothers' children were rated as significantly smaller in magnitude than those of children in a clinical sample and as no different from those of children in the normal sample.

On three scales of the Eder Children's Self-View Questionnaire, there were no significant differences between the self-reports of children of lesbian mothers as compared to those of Eder's (1990) heterosexual mothers. Specifically, there were no significant differences between children of lesbian and heterosexual mothers on self-concepts relevant to Aggression, Social Closeness, and Social Potency. Children of lesbian mothers in the present sample did not see themselves as either more or less aggressive, sociable, or likely to enjoy being the center of attention than did children of heterosexual mothers in Eder's sample.

On two scales, however, differences did emerge between children of lesbian and heterosexual mothers. Specifically, children of lesbian mothers reported greater reactions to stress than did children of heterosexual mothers, and they also reported a greater overall sense of well-being than did children of heterosexual mothers. In other words, children of lesbian mothers said they more often felt angry, scared, or upset but also said they more often felt joyful, content, and comfortable with themselves than did children of heterosexual mothers.

The aspect of children's sexual identity studied here was that of preferences for sex-role behavior. As expected, most children reported preferences for sex-role behaviors that are considered to be normative at this age (Green, 1978). For instance, every child reported that his or her group of friends was mainly or entirely made up of same-sex children. The great majority of children also reported favorite toys and favorite characters (from books, movies, or television) that were of the same sex. In the case of favorite games, a number of children mentioned games that were not clearly sex-typed, such as board games like Chutes and Ladders and hence were not categorizable; however, the great majority mentioned games that are generally associated with their own rather than with the opposite sex. In short, preferences for sex-role behavior among the children of lesbian mothers studied here appeared to be quite typical for children of these ages.

Couple Functioning

The principal assessments of couple functioning were accomplished using an adaptation of Cowan and Cowan's (1990) Who Does What? (which assesses division of labor across a number of domains) and an adaptation of Locke and Wallace's (1959) Marital Adjustment Test (which assesses the quality of couple relationships). In this section, the assessment instruments are described first, followed by results for the couples who took part in the study. Although there were thirty-seven families who participated in the study, some were headed by single lesbian mothers. Results are presented here for the twenty-six families that were headed by a lesbian couple.

Assessment of Couple Functioning

To assess division of labor as well as satisfaction with role arrangements in each family, an adapted form of the Who Does What? for parents of five-year-olds (Cowan & Cowan, 1990) was administered to each adult respondent.

The instrument began with thirteen items concerning the division of household labor (for example, planning and preparing meals and cleaning up after meals). Respondents were asked to decide for each item "how it is now" and "how I would like it to be" on a scale of 1 to 9, where 1 meant "she does it all" and 9 meant "I do it all." These are referred to as the "real" and "ideal" divisions of labor, respectively. At the bottom of that page, each respondent was asked to indicate how satisfied overall she was with "the way you and your partner divide the family tasks," and with "the way you and your partner divide the work outside the family"; in each of these two cases, scores ranged from 1 (very dissatisfied) to 5 (very satisfied).

The next page contained twelve items about family decision making, such as making decisions about major expenses and deciding which friends and family to see. Respondents were again asked to indicate the real and ideal division of labor. At the bottom of this second page, each respondent was asked to indicate on a 5-point scale how satisfied overall she was with "the way you and your partner divide family decisions."

The third page contained twenty items about child-care responsibilities (for example, playing with our child, disciplining our child, or picking up after our child). Respondents were again asked to indicate the real and ideal divisions of labor for each item.

The fourth page contained four questions about overall evaluations of child-care responsibilities. Respondents were asked to rate their own and their partner's overall involvement with their child on a scale ranging from "no involvement," to "shared involvement," to "sole responsibility." Respondents also were asked to rate their satisfaction with their own and with their partner's involvement in child-care responsibilities from "very dissatisfied" to "very satisfied."

To assess satisfaction with couple relationships, the Marital Adjustment Test (Locke & Wallace, 1959) was administered to all adult respondents. The Marital Adjustment Test is a sixteen-item instrument designed to record in a standardized format the overall satisfaction of spouses with their heterosexual marriages. A handful of small changes in wording (for example, substituting the word "part-ner" for the word "spouse") made the instrument more suitable for use with les-bian couples. Scoring was accomplished using the methods described by the authors (Locke & Wallace, 1959).

Results for Couple Functioning

The "actual" and "ideal" reported participation of biological and nonbiological mothers in each of three domains of family work were compared. Results showed that biological and nonbiological mothers did not differ in their evaluations of ideal distributions of labor in the three domains; most believed that tasks should be shared relatively evenly in all domains. In terms of the actual division of labor, biological and nonbiological mothers did not differ in their reported participation in household labor or family decision making. In the area of child care, how-ever, biological mothers reported themselves as responsible for more of the work than nonbiological mothers. Thus although lesbian mothers agreed that ideally child care should be evenly shared, they reported that in their families, the bio-logical mother was actually more responsible than the nonbiological mother for child care.

To assess satisfaction with division of labor, comparisons between actual and ideal divisions of labor were made. Results showed that biological mothers re-ported that ideally they would do fewer household tasks and less child care. Non-biological mothers did not report feeling that they should be significantly more involved in household tasks but did agree that an ideal allocation of labor would result in their doing more child care. There were no effects for family decision making. Thus the main result was that both mothers felt that an ideal allocation of labor would involve a more equal sharing of child-care tasks between them.

Each respondent also was asked to provide a global rating of each mother's overall involvement in child-care activities. Biological mothers reported on this measure that they were more involved than nonbiological mothers. Reports of the nonbiological mothers were in the same direction but did not reach statistical significance. Global judgments thus confirmed the more detailed reports described above in showing that, if there is a difference, it is the biological mother who takes more responsibility for child care.

In interviews, parents were asked to give estimates of the average number of hours both biological and nonbiological mothers spent in paid employment each week. Results showed that biological mothers were less likely than nonbiological mothers to be working forty hours per week or more in paid employment. Thus whereas biological mothers reported greater responsibility for child care, nonbiological mothers reported spending more time in paid employment.

There were no differences between relationship satisfaction reported by biological and nonbiological mothers. Consistent with expectations based on earlier findings with lesbian mothers (Koepke, Hare, & Moran, 1992), lesbian mothers reported feeling very satisfied in their couple relationships. Similarly, overall satisfaction with division of family labor was relatively high, and there were no significant differences between biological and nonbiological mothers in this regard.

Parental Division of Labor, Satisfaction, and Children's Adjustment

The study also assessed the strength of overall association between the three measures of child adjustment, on the one hand, and the four measures of parents' division of labor and satisfaction with division of labor, on the other. Results showed a significant association between the two sets of variables. Parents' reports of division of labor, satisfaction with division of labor, and the measures of child adjustment were significantly associated with one another. When biological mothers did less child care and when nonbiological mothers did more and were more satisfied, children's adjustment was rated as being more favorable.

In this study, then, both children and mothers reported more positive adjustment in families in which the nonbiological mother was described as a relatively equal participant in child care and in which the biological mother was not described as bearing an unequal burden of child-care duties. In other words, the most positive outcomes for children occurred in families that reported sharing child-care tasks relatively evenly between parents.

Discussion

The Bay Area Families Study was designed to examine child development and family functioning among families of the lesbian baby boom. Although findings from this study should be regarded as preliminary in a number of respects, three principal results have emerged to date. The first major finding was that, according to the standardized assessment techniques used here, both mothers' and children's adjustment fell clearly within the normative range. Considering that this result is consistent with the findings of other research on lesbian women in general (Gonsiorek, 1991), lesbian mothers in particular (Falk, 1989; Patterson, 1992), children of divorced lesbian and gay parents (Patterson, 1992), and children born to lesbian mothers (Flaks et al., 1995; McCandlish, 1987; Steckel, 1985, 1987), this outcome was not surprising. Particularly in light of judicial and popular prejudices against lesbian and gay families that still exist in many if not most parts of the country, however, the result is worthy of attention. The present data show not only that lesbian mothers' adjustment and self-esteem were within the normative range but also that social and personal development among their children were quite normal as well.

Although psychosocial development among children of lesbian versus heterosexual parents was generally quite similar, there were nevertheless some differences among children in the two groups, most notably in the area of self-concept. Even while their answers were well within the normal range, children of lesbian mothers reported that they experienced more reactions to stress (for example, feeling angry, scared, or upset) and also a greater sense of well-being (for example, feeling joyful, content, and comfortable with themselves) than did the children of heterosexual parents studied by Eder (1990).

The best interpretation of this difference is not yet clear. One possibility is that children of lesbian mothers report greater reactions to stress because they actually experience more stress than do other children. In other words, children of lesbian mothers may actually encounter more stressful events and conditions than do children with heterosexual parents (Lott-Whitehead & Tully, 1993; O'Connell, 1993). If so, then their more frequent reports of emotional responses to stress might simply reflect the more stressful nature of their experience. From this viewpoint, however, it is difficult to account for the greater sense of well-being also reported by children of lesbian mothers.

Another possibility is that, regardless of actual stress levels, children of lesbian mothers may be more conscious of their affective states in general or more willing to report their experiences of negative emotional states. If, as some have suggested (Pollack & Vaughn, 1987; Rafkin, 1990), children raised by two women have more experience with the naming of feelings and with verbal discussion of feelings in general, then they might exhibit increased openness to the expression of negative as well as positive feelings. In this view, the greater tendency of lesbian mothers' children to admit feeling angry, upset, or scared might be attributed not as much to differences in experiences of stress as to a greater awareness and expression of emotional experience of all kinds.

Consistent with this latter interpretation, children of lesbian mothers in the present study reported greater feelings of joy, contentedness, and comfort with themselves than did children of heterosexual mothers in Eder's (1990) sample. Although these findings do not rule out the possibility that children of lesbian women do indeed experience greater stress, they suggest that these children may be more willing than other children to report a variety of intense emotional experiences, whether positive or negative. Because this study was not designed to evaluate alternative interpretations of these differences, however, clarification of these issues must await the results of future research.

A second main finding was that lesbian couples who took part in this study reported that they divide various aspects of the labor involved in household upkeep and child care in a relatively even manner. The fact that lesbian mothers in this sample reported sharing many household and family tasks is consistent with, and expands upon, earlier findings on the division of household labor among lesbian and gay couples. For instance, Kurdek's (1993) study of lesbian, gay, and heterosexual couples without children found that lesbian couples were the most likely to share household responsibilities such as cooking, cleaning, and doing laundry. In the present study, results showed that lesbian couples with children not only reported sharing such household tasks but also reported enjoying equal influence in family decision making. Thus even under pressure of child-rearing responsibilities, lesbian couples seem to maintain egalitarian divisions of household responsibilities (Hand, 1991; Osterweil, 1991). In this way, lesbian couples with children resembled lesbian couples without children.

On the other hand, there were also some indications of specialization in the allocation of labor among lesbian couples who participated in this study. Consistent with patterns of specialization in heterosexual families (Cowan & Cowan, 1992), biological mothers reported greater involvement with child care, and nonbiological mothers reported spending more time in paid employment. In accommodating themselves to the demands of child rearing, it would appear that lesbian couples who took part in this research specialized to some degree with regard to their engagement in child care versus paid work. In this way, lesbian couples with children resembled heterosexual couples with children.

It is important, however, not to overemphasize the similarities in division of labor in lesbian versus heterosexual families. In an unpublished dissertation, Hand (1991) compared division of labor among lesbian and heterosexual couples with children under the age of two years. Consistent with the present findings, she found that household tasks and decision making were shared evenly by both lesbian and heterosexual couples with children and that biological lesbian mothers reported greater involvement in child care than did nonbiological mothers. She also found, however, that both biological and nonbiological lesbian mothers were more involved in child care than were heterosexual fathers. Thus even though differences between biological and nonbiological lesbian mothers were significant, both in the present study and in the study by Hand (1991), they were much less pronounced than the differences between husbands and wives in the matched group of heterosexual families studied by Hand (1991). The imbalance in division of the labor involved in child care was more pronounced between partners in heterosexual than in lesbian couples.

The third major result documented significant associations between division of labor among lesbian couples and psychosocial outcomes for mothers and their children. When lesbian couples shared child care more evenly, mothers were more satisfied and children were more well-adjusted. Thus even within the context of largely egalitarian arrangements, more equal sharing of child care was associated with more positive outcomes among both lesbian mothers and their children.

Mothers' ratings of their children's behavior problems were significantly associated with assessments of equality in the parents' division of labor as well as with the nonbiological mother's satisfaction with the allocation of tasks. Especially striking was the extent to which the nonbiological mother's satisfaction with child-care arrangements was associated with children's self-reports of well-being. Even within this well-adjusted nonclinical sample, children with mothers who shared child-care tasks evenly and who expressed satisfaction with this arrangement appeared to enjoy the most favorable adjustment.

That equal sharing of child care was associated with favorable adjustment among children is a result very much in concert with ideas proposed by Okin and by other scholars working from a feminist perspective (for example, Hochschild, 1989; Okin, 1989). These writers have suggested that models of fairness in division of labor at home are important influences on children's development and that children who observe equal division of responsibilities between their parents may enjoy developmental advantages. Although this is by no means the only possible interpretation of the present findings, these results are certainly consistent with such a view.

One possible pathway through which benefits of equality in parents' division of labor might accrue to children involves parental satisfaction with their couple relationships. Given the egalitarian ideals expressed so clearly by lesbian couples who took part in this research, higher relationship satisfaction was expected among those who succeeded—by equal division of labor—in putting these ideals into action. Contrary to expectations (Belsky, 1984); however, no consistent association emerged among relationship satisfaction and the other study variables. In retrospect, this may have been due to the global nature of the assessments of relationship satisfaction used here. Ruble and her colleagues (1988) have reported that some aspects of marital satisfaction are more tied to division of labor than

others. Future research employing more detailed measures of potential mediators will, it is hoped, explicate more clearly pathways that link parental division
of labor and child adjustment.

Although questions about causal linkages are of great interest, one should
keep in mind that the present data are correlational in nature and cannot support
causal inferences. Are happy, well-adjusted lesbian families more likely to divide
labor evenly? Or does the equal division of labor among lesbian couples with children lead to better adjustment and satisfaction with domestic arrangements? Or
both? The present study was not designed to examine such possibilities, and the
present data do not allow for their evaluation. Future work employing other kinds
of research designs will be needed to disentangle causes and consequences in these
domains.

This research also relied on mothers' and children's reports as sources of data.
The study included no observational assessments, and so the correspondence
between parental reports about division of labor and the actual division of labor
cannot be determined. Likewise, assessments of children's adjustment completed
by independent observers would have been a valuable addition to the study. On
the other hand, the use of well-known and widely used instruments such as the
Locke-Wallace Marital Adjustment Test and the Achenbach and Edelbrock Child
Behavior Checklist enhances the degree to which the present results can be compared with those of other researchers.

Some concerns relevant to sampling issues should also be acknowledged. Most
of the families who took part in the Bay Area Families Study were headed by
lesbian mothers who were White, well-educated, relatively affluent, and living in
the greater San Francisco Bay area. For these reasons, no claims about representativeness of the present sample can be made. The reliability and generalizability
of findings would likely be enhanced by the participation of more diverse samples of lesbian families over longer periods of time.

Conclusion

The Bay Area Families Study was designed to study child development, maternal mental health, and family functioning among the families of the lesbian baby
boom. Results to date suggest that maternal mental health is good and that child
development is proceeding normally. Lesbian couples described equal sharing of
many household and decision-making tasks involved in their lives together, but
they also reported that child care and paid employment were specialized to some
degree. The more evenly they shared child care, the more satisfied mothers reported feeling, and the better adjusted were their children. If confirmed by fu-

ture research, these results will have far-reaching social, psychological, and legal implications.

References

Achenbach, T. M., & Edelbrock, C. (1983). *Manual for the Child Behavior Checklist and Revised Child Behavior Profile.* Burlington: University of Vermont, Department of Psychiatry.

Belsky, J. (1984). The determinants of parenting: A process model. *Child Development, 55,* 83–96.

Cowan, C. P., & Cowan, P. A. (1990). Who does what? In J. Touliatos, B. F. Perlmutter, & M. A. Straus (Eds.), *Handbook of family measurement techniques* (pp. 447–448). Newbury Park, CA: Sage.

Cowan, C. P., & Cowan, P. A. (1992). *When partners become parents: The big life change for couples.* New York: Basic Books.

Derogatis, L. R. (1983). *SCL-90-R administration, scoring, and procedures manual.* Towson, MD: Clinical Psychometric Research.

Eder, R. A. (1990). Uncovering young children's psychological selves: Individual and developmental differences. *Child Development, 61,* 849–863.

Falk, P. J. (1989). Lesbian mothers: Psychosocial assumptions in family law. *American Psychologist, 44,* 941–947.

Flaks, D. (1994). Gay and lesbian families: Judicial assumptions, scientific realities. *William and Mary Bill of Rights Journal, 3,* 345–372.

Flaks, D., Ficher, I., Masterpasqua, F., & Joseph, G. (1995). Lesbians choosing motherhood: A comparative study of lesbian and heterosexual parents and their children. *Developmental Psychology, 31,* 104–114.

Golombok, S., Spencer, A., & Rutter, M. (1983). Children in lesbian and single-parent households: Psychosexual and psychiatric appraisal. *Journal of Child Psychology and Psychiatry, 24,* 551–572.

Gonsiorek, J. C. (1991). The empirical basis for the demise of the illness model of homosexuality. In J. C. Gonsiorek & J. D. Weinrich (Eds.), *Homosexuality: Research implications for public policy* (pp. 115–136). Newbury Park, CA: Sage.

Green, G. D., & Bozett, F. W. (1991). Lesbian mothers and gay fathers. In J. C. Gonsiorek & J. D. Weinrich (Eds.), *Homosexuality: Research implications for public policy* (pp. 197–214). Newbury Park, CA: Sage.

Green, R. (1978). Sexual identity of 37 children raised by homosexual or transsexual parents. *American Journal of Psychiatry, 135,* 692–697.

Green, R., Mandel, J. B., Hotvedt, M. E., Gray, J., & Smith, L. (1986). Lesbian mothers and their children: A comparison with solo-parent heterosexual mothers and their children. *Archives of Sexual Behavior, 7,* 175–181.

Hand, S. I. (1991). *The lesbian parenting couple.* Unpublished doctoral dissertation, Professional School of Psychology, San Francisco.

Hitchens, D. (1979–1980). Social attitudes, legal standards, and personal trauma in child custody cases. *Journal of Homosexuality, 5,* 1–20, 89–95.

Hochschild, A. R. (1989). *The second shift: Working parents and the revolution at home.* New York: Viking Penguin.

Hoeffer, B. (1981). Children's acquisition of sex-role behavior in lesbian-mother families. *American Journal of Orthopsychiatry, 5,* 536–544.

Huggins, S. L. (1989). A comparative study of self-esteem of adolescent children of divorced lesbian mothers and divorced heterosexual mothers. In F. W. Bozett (Ed.), *Homosexuality and the family* (pp. 123–135). Binghamton, NY: Harrington Park Press.

Kirkpatrick, M., Smith, C., & Roy, R. (1981). Lesbian mothers and their children: A comparative survey. *American Journal of Orthopsychiatry, 51,* 545–551.

Koepke, L., Hare, J., & Moran, P. B. (1992). Relationship quality in a sample of lesbian couples with children and child-free lesbian couples. *Family Relations, 41,* 224–229.

Kurdek, L. (1993): The allocation of household labor in homosexual and heterosexual cohabiting couples. *Journal of Social Issues, 49,* 127–139.

Laird, J. (1993). Lesbian and gay families. In F. Walsh (Ed.), *Normal family processes* (2nd ed., pp. 282–328). New York: Guilford Press.

Lewin, E. (1993). *Lesbian mothers: Accounts of gender in American culture.* Ithaca, NY: Cornell University Press.

Locke, H., & Wallace, K. (1959). Short marital adjustment and prediction tests: Their reliability and validity. *Marriage and Family Living, 21,* 251–255.

Lott-Whitehead, L., & Tully, C. T. (1993). The family lives of lesbian mothers. *Smith College Studies in Social Work, 63,* 265–280.

Martin, A. (1993). *The lesbian and gay parenting handbook.* New York: HarperCollins.

McCandlish, B. (1987). Against all odds: Lesbian mother family dynamics. In F. W. Bozett (Ed.), *Gay and lesbian parents* (pp. 23–38). New York: Praeger.

O'Connell, A. (1993). Voices from the heart: The developmental impact of a mother's lesbianism on her adolescent children. *Smith College Studies in Social Work, 63,* 281–299.

Okin, S. M. (1989). *Justice, gender and the family.* New York: Basic Books.

Osterweil, D. A. (1991). *Correlates of relationship satisfaction in lesbian couples who are parenting their first child together.* Unpublished doctoral dissertation, California School of Professional Psychology, Berkeley/Alameda.

Patterson, C. J. (1992). Children of lesbian and gay parents. *Child Development, 63,* 1025–1042.

Patterson, C. J. (1994). Children of the lesbian baby boom: Behavioral adjustment, self-concepts, and sex role identity. In B. Greene & G. M. Herek (Eds.), *Lesbian and gay psychology: Theory, research, and clinical applications* (pp. 156–175). Newbury Park, CA: Sage.

Patterson, C. J. (1995a). Families of the lesbian baby boom: Parents' division of labor and children's adjustment. *Developmental Psychology, 31,* 115–123.

Patterson, C. J. (1995b). Lesbian mothers, gay fathers, and their children. In A. R. D'Augelli & C. J. Patterson (Eds.), *Lesbian, gay and bisexual identities over the lifespan: Psychological perspectives* (pp. 262–290). New York: Oxford University Press.

Patterson, C. J., & Kosmitzki, C. (1995). *Families of the lesbian baby boom: Maternal mental health, household composition, and child adjustment.* Unpublished manuscript, University of Virginia, Department of Psychology.

Pollack, S., & Vaughn, J. (1987). *Politics of the heart: A lesbian parenting anthology.* Ithaca, NY: Firebrand.

Rafkin, L. (1990). *Different mothers: Sons and daughters of lesbians talk about their lives.* Pittsburgh: Cleis.

Ricketts, W., & Achtenberg, R. (1990). Adoption and foster parenting for lesbians and gay men: Creating new traditions in family. In F. W. Bozett & M. B. Sussman (Eds.), *Homosexuality and family relations* (pp. 83–118). Binghamton, NY: Harrington Park Press.

Riley, C. (1988). American kinship: A lesbian account. *Feminist Issues, 8,* 75–94.

Rosenberg, M. (1979). *Conceiving the self.* New York: Basic Books.

Ruble, D. N., Fleming, A. S., Hackel, L. S., & Stangor, C. (1988). Changes in the marital relationship during the transition to first-time motherhood: Effects of violated expectations concerning division of household labor. *Journal of Personality and Social Psychology, 55,* 78–87.

Steckel, A. (1985). *Separation-individuation in children of lesbian and heterosexual couples.* Unpublished doctoral dissertation, Wright Institute, Berkeley, CA.

Steckel, A. (1987). Psychosocial development of children of lesbian mothers. In F. W. Bozett (Ed.), *Gay and lesbian parents* (pp. 75–85). New York: Praeger.

Tasker, F., & Golombok, S. (1995). Adults raised as children in lesbian families. *American Journal of Orthopsychiatry, 65,* 203–215.

Weston, K. (1991). *Families we choose: Lesbians, gays, and kinship.* New York: Columbia University Press.

ABOUT THE AUTHORS

Sandra C. Anderson, Ph.D., is Professor of Social Work in the Graduate School of Social Work at Portland State University. She is a founding faculty member of the Institute for Family Centered Therapy and has a private practice in Portland, Oregon. Her special professional interests include family of origin theory and therapy, lesbian issues, and alcoholism.

Michael Bettinger, Ph.D., is a psychotherapist in private practice in San Francisco, where he specializes in working with gay men and gay male couples. He is also a lecturer at San Francisco State University in the Bisexual, Lesbian, and Gay Studies Program and the Department of Counseling.

Jerry J. Bigner, Ph.D., is Professor of Human Development and Family Studies at Colorado State University. He is the author of *Parent-Child Relations: An Introduction to Parenting* (4th edition) and *Individual and Family Development,* as well as numerous research articles on parenting and clinical issues. He has special research interests and extensive experience in providing expert witness testimony on behalf of gay and lesbian parents. Bigner holds associate membership in the American Association for Marriage and Family Therapy.

Nancy Boyd-Franklin, Ph.D., is Professor of Family Therapy and Clinical Psychology at the Rutgers University Graduate School of Applied and Professional Psychology in Piscataway, New Jersey. Her books include *Black Families in Therapy: A Multisystems Approach* and, with Gloria Steiner and Mary Boland, *Children, Families, and HIV/AIDS: Psychosocial and Therapeutic Issues.* She is widely known for her work on ethnicity and family therapy and the treatment of African American families.

Connie S. Chan, Ph.D., is Associate Professor of Human Services and codirector of the Institute for Asian American Studies at the University of Massachusetts, Boston. Her research and clinical work focus on identity construction for Asian Americans in the context of sexuality, gender, and culture. Her recent publications address sexual identity among Chinese Americans and HIV knowledge and sexual behaviors among Asian American adolescents.

Patricia L. Colucci, M.S.W., is on the faculties of the Family Institute of Westchester and the Urban Institute for Families and Family Therapy Training. She is a member of the Gay and Lesbian Family Project at the Ackerman Institute for Family Therapy and maintains a private practice in Mount Vernon, New York.

Meme English, M.Ed., is a therapist in private practice in Northampton, Massachusetts, a consultant and trainer in refugee mental health in Springfield, Massachusetts, with Vietnamese individuals and families, and a doctoral candidate in counseling psychology at the University of Massachusetts, Amherst. She lives in Amherst with her partner, Peggy Perri. Meme and Peggy are parents to Joni, age twenty-four, who lives in Vermont, and Kate, seventeen, Daniel, sixteen, and Adam, fifteen, who reside with them in Amherst.

Robert-Jay Green, Ph.D., is professor and coordinator of Family-Child Psychology at the California School of Professional Psychology, Berkeley/Alameda. He has published widely on family therapy topics, including two other books—*Family Therapy: Major Contributions* (1981) and *Voices of Women Family Therapists* (in press). Green is on the board of directors of the American Family Therapy Academy, is a Fellow of APA and AAMFT, and serves on the editorial boards of *Family Process,* the *Journal of Marital and Family Therapy, Cultural Diversity and Mental Health,* the *Journal of Feminist Family Therapy,* and the *Family Therapy Networker.*

Beverly Greene, Ph.D., is Professor of Psychology at St. John's University and is a clinical psychologist in private practice in New York City. A Fellow of the American Psychological Association, she is the recipient of the Association for Women in Psychology's 1995 Distinguished Publication Award and the 1995 Women of Color Psychologies Publication Award for her coedited book, *Women of Color: In-*

tegrating Ethnic and Gender Identities in Psychotherapy. She has also received the 1995 Brodsky/Hare-Mustin Psychotherapy with Women Research Award, sponsored by the APA Division of the Psychology of Women, as well as other national awards for her distinguished professional contributions. She is an associate editor of the journal *Violence Against Women;* is co-editor of *Psychological Perspectives on Lesbian and Gay Issues,* a series of annual publications sponsored by the Society for the Psychological Study of Lesbian and Gay Issues of the American Psychological Association; and has contributed numerous other publications to the professional psychological literature.

Ann Hartman, D.S.W., is Professor Emerita of the Smith College School for Social Work, where she served as dean from 1986 to 1994. She has written or edited ten books and monographs and over fifty-five articles in professional books and journals. She served as editor of *Social Work* from 1989 through 1993. Her editorials have recently been published by the National Association of Social Work in *Reflection and Controversy: Essays on Social Work.* On the faculty of the University of Michigan School of Social Work between 1974 and 1986, she was also a cofounder of Ann Arbor Center for the Family and Director of the National Child Welfare Training Center.

Suzanne Iasenza, Ph.D., is an associate professor in the Department of Counseling at the John Jay College of Criminal Justice at the City University of New York. She is a member of the Gay and Lesbian Family Project at the Ackerman Institute for Family Therapy and is in private practice in New York City. She is co-editor, with Judith Glassgold, of the forthcoming book *Lesbians and Psychoanalysis: Revolutions in Theory and Practice,* to be published by the Free Press and is a contributing editor to *In the Family.*

Thomas W. Johnson, M.S.W., Ed.D., is on the faculty of the Family Institute of New Jersey, is clinical coordinator of the Comprehensive Services on Aging program at the University of Medicine and Dentistry of New Jersey's Community Mental Health Center, Piscataway, and is the research co-coordinator of the Gay and Lesbian Family Project at the Ackerman Institute for Family Therapy in New York City.

Michael S. Keren, Psy.D., is a clinical psychologist at the Metuchen Outpatient Team of the University of Medicine and Dentistry of New Jersey's Community Mental Health Center, Piscataway, and a member of the Gay and Lesbian Family Project at the Ackerman Institute for Family Therapy in New York City.

Shoshana D. Kerewsky, M.A., is a doctoral candidate at the Antioch New England Department of Clinical Psychology in Keene, New Hampshire. She is also a crisis intervention specialist for Johnson and Wales University in Rhode Island and is the author of numerous published poems and short stories.

Joan Laird, M.S., is a professor at the Smith College School for Social Work, where she is chair of the Human Behavior in the Social Environment Sequence. A cofounder of the Ann Arbor Center for the Family, where she was involved in clinical practice and training, she has written and presented widely on women's stories, rituals, and secrets and, in recent years, has focused on lesbian families. She is coauthor of *Family-Centered Social Practice* (1983), co-editor of *A Handbook of Child Welfare* (1985), and editor of *Revisioning Social Work Education: A Social Constructionist Approach* (1993). She is currently completing an edited collection titled *Lesbians and Lesbian Families: Multiple Reflections* for Columbia University Press. Professor Laird serves on the editorial boards of several professional journals.

Peter Liu is a doctoral student in the clinical psychology program at the University of Vermont and is a psychology intern at the Center for Children, Youth, and Families in the Child Psychiatry Department of the Fletcher Allen Health Care Hospital in Burlington. He is also a support group facilitator at Outright Vermont, a local organization for lesbian, gay, bisexual, and questioning (LGBQ) youth. Peter's clinical and research interests involve youth and families, particularly LGBQ and Asian American populations, and he is currently researching gender differences among LGBQ youth.

Dusty Miller, Ed.D., is on the core faculty at the Antioch New England Department of Clinical Psychology in Keene, New Hampshire, and is also an adjunct faculty member at the Smith College School for Social Work. She is a licensed clinical psychologist in Vermont and Massachusetts, specializing in consultation and research on women with self-abusive behaviors. Her book, *Women Who Hurt Themselves: A Book of Hope and Understanding,* was published in 1994.

Valory Mitchell, Ph.D., is Associate Professor of Psychology, director of the Institute for the Psychology of Women, and coordinator of Lesbian Family Services at the California School of Professional Psychology in Alameda, California. She also maintains a private practice in Berkeley.

Eduardo Morales, Ph.D., is an associate professor at the California School of Professional Psychology-Alameda and coordinator of the Multicultural and Community Training Program. He is a fellow of the American Psychological

Association and received the 1994 Outstanding Achievement Award from the Committee of Lesbian and Gay Concerns and the Distinguished Contribution Award (1991) in Ethnic Minority Issues from the Society for the Psychological Study of Lesbian and Gay Issues (Division 44) for his significant contributions. He has written several articles and has made numerous presentations on gay, lesbian, and HIV issues and has founded many programs to service those groups.

Cheryl Muzio is a psychotherapist in private practice in Northampton, Massachusetts. She is also an adjunct faculty member of the Smith College School for Social Work, where she teaches a course titled "Gay and Lesbian Identities."

Charlotte J. Patterson, Ph.D., is Associate Professor of Psychology at the University of Virginia. She has published widely in the areas of social and personal development among children and adolescents and has served on the editorial boards of a number of journals. Her Bay Area Families Study, which examined psychosocial development among children born to or adopted by lesbian mothers, has generated several publications. She is co-editor, with Anthony R. D'Augelli, of *Lesbian, Gay and Bisexual Identities over the Lifespan: Psychological Perspectives,* published in 1995 by Oxford University Press.

Barbara Rothberg, D.S.W., is a member of the Gay and Lesbian Family Project at the Ackerman Institute for Family Therapy and maintains a private practice in New York City. She is also an adjunct associate professor at the New York University School of Social Work.

Ritch C. Savin-Williams is Professor of Clinical and Developmental Psychology in the Department of Human Development and Family Studies at Cornell University. He received his Ph.D. from the University of Chicago's Committee on Human Development. His most recent book, with K. M. Cohen, *The Lives of Lesbians, Gays, and Bisexuals: Children to Adults* (1996), follows his earlier *Gay and Lesbian Youth: Expressions of Identity* (1990) and *Adolescence: An Ethological Perspective* (1987). Current research interests include identity development among gay, lesbian, and bisexual youths and the relationships these youths have with family members. He is currently writing a book on the developmental significance of sexual behavior among gay and bisexual youth and is teaching courses on sexual minorities.

Stacey Shuster, Ph.D., is in private practice in San Francisco and is supervisor at the New College of California Community Counseling Center in that city. She was formerly director of children's services in the AIDS Family Project of Operation Concern at the California Pacific Medical Center in San Francisco.

Stanley Siegel, M.S.W., psychotherapist and teacher, is currently director of the New York Center for Lesbian and Gay Psychotherapies and former director of education and senior faculty member of the Ackerman Institute for Family Therapy. He is the author of *The Patient Who Cured His Therapist and Other Tales of Therapy, Uncharted Lives: Understanding the Life Passages of Gay Men,* and *Gay-Centric Therapy: Re-Creating Consciousness and Culture.* Siegel wrote the "Families" column for *New York Newsday* and was the dance editor for *Show Business.*

Gillian Walker, M.S.W., is on the faculty of the Ackerman Institute for Family Therapy. She codirected Ackerman's AIDS and Families Project with John Patten. She is currently codirecting Ackerman's Gender and Violence Project and is the director of Ackerman's Families, Attention Disorders, and Learning Disabilities Project. Her special clinical interests include the integration of neurobiological considerations into systemic therapy, as well as issues of gender and sexual orientation. She is the author of *In the Midst of Winter: Systemic Therapy with Families, Couples, and Individuals with AIDS Infection.*

Ellie Zacks, Ph.D., is a clinical psychologist in private practice in Sacramento, California. A practicing psychotherapist for twenty-two years, she has specialized in work with lesbian couples, adult survivors of abuse, grief work, marriage and family therapy, and long-term psychodynamic psychotherapy. She coauthored one of the first papers on lesbian couples in *Family Process.*

NAME INDEX

A

Achenbach, T. M., 425, 427, 435
Achtenberg, R., 420, 436
Acosta, E., 258, 259, 268
Adams, K., 308, 314
Ainsley, J., 343, 356
Allen, K. R., 2, 11, 96, 120
Almaguer, T., 242, 243, 249
Almeida, R., 242, 249
Amaro, H., 251, 268
Anderson, C. M., 4, 12
Anderson, H., 308, 314
Anderson, S. C., 10, 12, 316–340
Annas, G. J., 81, 84
Anthony, B. D., 397, 400
Antill, J. K., 217, 227
Appathurai, C., 105, 122, 142, 152, 166, 175, 182, 242, 250, 252, 271
Ault-Riche, M., 125, 135

B

Bailey, J. M., 158, 179, 210, 212, 227
Baker, L., 188, 229
Baptiste, D. A., Jr., 394, 395, 400
Barbaree, H. E., 377, 400
Barbaro, F., 77, 84

Barnes, H. L., 193, 194, 225n.6, 229
Barret, R. L., 371, 373, 376, 377, 386, 394, 401, 403
Bartholow, B. N., 284, 296
Bass-Hass, R., 252, 268
Baures, M., 306, 314
Beane, J., 380, 401
Becker, C. S., 321, 336
Bell, A. P., 7, 11, 157, 179, 194, 197, 207, 217, 225n.2, 227, 235, 236, 237, 238, 249, 252, 268, 370, 401
Belsky, J., 433, 435
Bem, S. L., 208, 227
Benjamin, J., 323, 336, 346, 356
Benkov, L., 75, 80, 84, 95, 120, 379, 401
Bepko, C. S., 3, 11, 96, 121, 189, 190–192, 203, 210, 213, 228, 231, 233, 244, 246, 249, 319, 323, 327, 328, 330–331, 332, 335, 337, 338
Berg-Cross, L., 323, 337
Berger, Justice, 78–79
Bernal, G., 274, 296
Bernhardt, S., 94
Bernstein, R., 100, 120
Berzoff, J., 323, 337
Berzon, B., 95, 120

Bettinger, M., 6, 9–10, 185–230
Bigner, J. J., 10, 370–403, 405, 406, 418
Biller, H. B., 374, 401
Biringen, Z. C., 217, 227
Black, L. W., 404, 417, 418
Blasband, D., 215, 227, 238, 239, 249
Bloomfield, K. A., 318, 339
Blumenfeld, W. J., 400, 401
Blumstein, P., 117, 120, 194, 197, 200, 214, 215, 216, 217, 224–225n.2, 227, 236, 238, 239, 249, 319, 337, 344, 356
Bobele, M., 4, 11, 405, 418
Boeglin, D., 404, 418
Bograd, M., 323, 337
Bohannan, P., 392, 401
Boland, M. G., 404, 418
Borhek, M. V., 164, 177, 179
Bork, R., 73
Boscolo, L., 407, 418
Bottoms, S., 78, 97
Bowen, M., 114, 120, 124, 125, 136, 186, 187, 204, 205, 218, 221, 227, 241, 242, 246, 249, 301, 314, 323–324, 337, 407, 418
Boxer, A. M., 155, 157, 160, 161–162, 163, 180

SUBJECT INDEX

A

Abstinence, 328

Acceptance, stages of, 173–174, 175–176

Acculturation: Asian American, 144–146; Latino, 275–276, 290

Activism: of gay couples, 248; of parents of lesbians, gays, and bisexuals, 178–179; of therapists, 248–249, 325, 363

Adolescence, 405–406. *See also* Puberty; Youth

Adoption: by coparents, 80; international market for, 80–81; legal issues of, 80–81; by lesbian couples, 361–363, 423; options for, 80–81; by single parents, 80, 81; states that allow, 80

Adventures of Priscilla, Queen of the Desert, 237

African American gay men, 242–243

African American lesbian couples, 265–268

African American lesbians, 10, 251–268; with children, 266; colloquial names for, 257; in couples, 259–268; ethnosexual stereotypes and, 254–256,

261–262; and family of origin, 258–259, 264–265, 266–267; and heterosexual status, 257; homophobia and, 252–253, 256–258; identity of, 258; in interracial couples, 260–265; invisibility of, 251; and mental health profession, 251–252, 260; psychohistorical context of, 253–259; triple discrimination of, 252–253; versus White lesbians, 252; White partners of, 260–262

Afro-Caribbean religions, 285–286

Afro-Caribbean women, 254, 255, 256–257

Aging, 8

AIDS: and coming out to family of origin, 58, 101; impact of, on gay male couples, 224*n*.1, 237; legal issues and, 75. *See also HIV listings*

Alcoholics Anonymous, 320, 328, 331

Alcoholism: disease model of, 335–336; etiology of, 327, 335–336; lesbians and, 317–318, 335–336; research on, 316; prevalence of, among lesbians, 317–318; therapist stance

on, 335–336; treatment model for, 326, 335; of women versus men, 320. *See also* Chemical dependency; Chemical dependency treatment

Alienation: and feeling different, 66; and secrecy, 39–40

Alternative insemination, 81–82, 365, 423–424

American Association of Marriage and Family Therapy (AAMFT), 3, 4, 404

American Family Therapy Academy (AFTA), 3

Anal penetration: meanings of, to gay men, 42–43; unprotected, in Latino men, 283–284

Androgyny: among gays and lesbians, 210, 212; and gender role nonconformance, 286–287; in indigenous religions, 286

Angels in America, 94

Antigay initiatives, 2, 71–73, 84

Asian Americans, lesbian/gay/bisexual (LGBAAs): acculturation and, 144–146; and attitudes towards sexuality, 137–138, 141; coming out of, to siblings versus parents, 166; coming out experiences of, 147–148; communi-